CLARENCE BYRD
Athabasca University

IDA CHEN
Clarence Byrd Inc.

Byrd & Chen's Canadian Advanced Accounting

International Convergence

Fifth Edition

Toronto

Library and Archives Canada Cataloguing in Publication

Byrd, Clarence E.
Byrd & Chen's Canadian advanced accounting: international convergence.

Once every 2 to 3 years.
5th ed.–
Continues: Advanced financial accounting, ISSN 1487-590X.
ISSN 1914-2668
ISBN 978-0-13-202330-6 (5th edition)

1. Accounting—Canada. I. Chen, Ida II. Title. III. Title: Canadian advanced accounting. IV. Title: Byrd and Chen's Canadian advanced accounting.

HF5636.B95 657'.046 C2007-902928-0

Copyright © 2008, 2003, 1999, 1996, 1994 Clarence Byrd Inc.

Pearson Prentice Hall. All rights reserved. This publication is protected by copyright, and permission should be obtained from the publisher prior to any prohibited reproduction, storage in a retrieval system, or transmission in any form or by any means, electronic, mechanical, photocopying, recording, or likewise. For information regarding permission, write to the Permissions Department.

ISBN-13: 978-0-13-202330-6
ISBN-10: 0-13-202330-X

Editor-in-Chief: Gary Bennett
Executive Editor: Samantha Scully
Executive Marketing Manager: Cas Shields
Developmental Editor: Paul Donnelly
Production Editor: Marisa D'Andrea
Production Coordinator: Deborah Starks
Art Director: Julia Hall
Cover Design: Anthony Leung

2 3 4 5 11 10 09 08

Printed and bound in Canada.

What Is "Advanced" Financial Accounting?

Basic Content

Most Canadian universities and colleges offer either one or two courses in "advanced" financial accounting. Depending on the organization and the province in which it operates, all of Canada's professional accounting organizations require their students to complete one or both of such courses. Clearly there is a need for a text that deals with this subject.

Unfortunately, there is no general agreement as to the content that should be included in such a text. Particularly in the case of universities and colleges that have two semesters of "advanced financial accounting", there is great diversity in the subjects that are covered.

Despite this diversity, there are a number of subjects that appear to be common to all advanced accounting texts and advanced accounting courses. These subjects are:

- Business Combinations
- Investments In Equity Securities
- Preparation Of Consolidated Financial Statements
- Translation Of Foreign Currency Transactions
- Translation Of Foreign Currency Financial Statements

This text provides detailed and comprehensive coverage of all of these subjects. In addition it provides coverage of additional subjects as follows:

- Investments In Joint Ventures
- Accounting For Not-For-Profit Organizations
- Accounting For Partnerships

These other subjects are common to some, but not all advanced financial accounting texts and courses.

Other Subjects

The CD-ROM which accompanies this text contains our ***Guide To Canadian Financial Reporting***. This resource provides coverage of every subject in financial reporting, organized by *CICA Handbook* Section. While it does not contain additional problem material, it has text material which could be used to include additional subjects for coverage in individual advanced accounting courses. This will, of course, be at the option of your instructor.

Using The Book And Its Resources

Web Site

The web site for this book can be found at:

www.pearsoned.ca/byrdchen/caa5e/

Here you will find:

- Updates and corrections to the textbook and Study Guide
- Links to other relevant websites
- A "Guide to Using Your Student CD-ROM"

This web site contains updates and corrections to the text that are available to all users. It also contains an "Instructor's Resource" area that can only be accessed with a user name and password (available from your Pearson Education Canada representative if you are a registered instructor using the book). Please check the web site for additions or corrections to the textbook and Study Guide before using this book.

The Book

Contents And Index

We have made every effort to enhance the usefulness of this book. At the beginning of the book, following this preface, is a detailed table of contents that will direct you to the subject matter in each Chapter. In addition, to facilitate easy access to any subject being researched, there is a comprehensive topical index at the end of the book.

Text

The material in this text is, in general, more detailed and comprehensive than the material that is found in other Canadian advanced accounting texts. Because of this, your instructor may choose not to cover some of the material (e.g., Chapter 7 which deals with advanced topics in preparing consolidated financial statements).

Problems And Solutions

The text contains four types of problems. They can be described as follows:

Exercises These are short problems that are generally focused on a single issue. For your convenience, each Exercise is presented immediately after the text material that is relevant to its solution. We strongly encourage you to attempt these exercises as you work through the text material.

Solutions to the Exercises can be found in the Study Guide which is provided with your text. Note that there are no exercises in Chapters 1 (Introduction), 7 (Advanced Topics In Consolidations), or 11 (Not-For-Profit Accounting).

Self Study Problems These problems are more complex than the Exercises and sometimes deal with more than one subject. These can be attempted as you work through the text material or when you have completed the Chapter. If you wish to attempt them as you work through the material, the Study Guide provides guidance as to when this effort would be appropriate.

As was the case with the Exercises, solutions to the Self Study Problems are included in the Study Guide.

Walk Through Problems At the end of Chapters 4, 5, and 6, you will find what we refer to as a walk through problem. These problems are designed to assist you with your first effort at preparing consolidated financial statements. The assistance takes the form of a "fill-in-the blanks" solution format. This format, along with a complete solution to the problem is included in the Study Guide which accompanies the text.

Assignment Problems These problems are similar to the Self Study Problems in that they often deal with more than one subject. In general, they tend to be somewhat more difficult than the Self Study Problems.

Solutions to these problems are available in a separate Solutions Manual provided only to instructors. We do not make this Solutions Manual available to students.

The Study Guide

Format

The paper version of the Study Guide for this text is provided, at no additional cost, with the text. For your convenience, an electronic copy of this Study Guide is provided in PDF format on the CD-ROM which accompanies the text.

Content

The Study Guide contains a variety of materials to assist you with mastering the content of this text. These materials can be described as follows:

Problem Solutions As we have indicated, solutions to the Exercises, Self Study Problems, and Walk-Through Problems will be found in this Study Guide.

"How To Work Through" Guides Prior to the Exercise and Self Study Problem solutions for each Chapter, you will find detailed guidance on how to work through the material provided for that Chapter. This includes suggestions as to when it would appropriate to attempt each Exercise and Self Study Problem. There is no "How To Work Through" guide for Chapters 1 or 12.

Learning Objectives Following the solutions to the Exercises and Self Study Problems for each Chapter, you will find a list of Learning Objectives for that Chapter. This list includes the text paragraph numbers where the material related to each learning objective is covered. There is no Learning Objectives list for Chapters 1, 7, or 12.

The Accompanying CD-ROM

Study Guide

As we have noted, the CD-ROM which accompanies this text contains a complete copy of the Study Guide in PDF format.

CICA Publications

Through our affiliation with the Canadian Institute Of Chartered Accountants (CICA), we are able to provide you with two major publications from their Virtual Professional Library (the regular price of these products is $230). These are:

Guide To Canadian Financial Reporting This is our comprehensive guide to the content of the *CICA Handbook* in particular, and Canadian financial reporting in general. It contains a detailed Chapter for each accounting *Handbook* Section, including materials on text subjects that we felt were too detailed for the general reader (e.g., summaries of EIC Abstracts on such subjects as foreign currency translation). The version of the Guide that is on your CD-ROM is current through *CICA Handbook* release No. 43 (March, 2007).

Financial Reporting In Canada - 2006 Edition This widely used publication is published each year and contains a survey of the accounting practices of 200 publicly traded companies. In addition to the statistics resulting from the survey, the publication contains examples from annual reports which illustrate the application of each *CICA Handbook* Section on accounting. This publication is a unique resource for reviewing the manner in which Canadian companies actually apply accounting standards.

This advanced text assumes an understanding of the content that is found in standard intermediate accounting courses. If you have not completed these courses recently, you may not recall some of this material or, alternatively, the standards relevant to this material may have changed. In those cases where we believe this may be a problem, we have included what we refer to as **CD-ROM Notes**. These notes refer you to the relevant Chapter in the ***Guide To Canadian Financial Reporting***, permitting you to review the appropriate background material for the issues being covered in this text.

Using Folio Views

The material from the CICA on the CD-ROM is presented in Folio Views. This is an extremely powerful software package that is being used by all Canadian publishers of accounting and tax materials in an electronic format. It provides for sophisticated searching throughout the infobases, with hyperlinks between the various documents contained in the infobases. If you intend to do any work in the accounting area, we strongly recommend that you learn to use this software.

Many of the features of this software are intuitive and can be used with little additional assistance. However, if help is needed, it is available under the Help tab that opens with the infobases included on the CD-ROM.

Note that, while there are hyperlinks in the ***Guide To Canadian Financial Reporting*** to both the *CICA Handbook* and International Financial Reporting Standards, these will only work when you have a subscription to these publications. Subscriptions to these publications are not included on the CD-ROM.

International Convergence

From now until 2011, there will be a gradual convergence of international accounting standards into Canadian GAAP. With various subjects covered in this text, this convergence process will have a varying impact. It is likely to be most dramatic in the areas of business combinations and the preparation of consolidated financial statements.

At this point in time (May, 2007), we would expect international standards for business combinations and consolidated statements to be converged into Canadian GAAP in either 2009 or 2010. However, until that time, the procedures specified in the *CICA Handbook* must still be used for financial statements that reflect Canadian GAAP. Also of importance is that the content of examinations in professional accounting programs will continue to be based on current Canadian standards.

Given this situation, it would be unreasonable to base this text exclusively on international standards. However, it would be equally unreasonable to ignore the changes that will be implemented within two to three years. Our compromise solution is to provide, at the end of each Chapter, a discussion of how the convergence of international standards into Canadian GAAP will affect the content of that Chapter.

In the case of the Chapters dealing with consolidated financial statements, we have included an example which illustrates the application of international standards. This example is supported by both a Self Study Problem and an Assignment Problem which require the application of international standards.

In addition to the material in the text, the accompanying CD-ROM provides comprehensive coverage of the CICA's international convergence plan. Each chapter of the ***Guide To Canadian Financial Reporting*** on the CD-ROM provides a discussion of how international convergence will be implemented for the *CICA Handbook* Section that is under consideration. This includes references to the related international financial reporting standards, as well as the proposed timetable for converging that IFRS into Canadian GAAP.

Abbreviations

To the degree possible, we try to avoid the use of abbreviations in our writings. However, there are a small number of these that are sufficiently common that it would not make sense to completely avoid the use of such short forms. To ensure that this does not create confusion for the users of this text, the following list is provided:

AcG Accounting Guideline
AcSB Accounting Standards Board
CICA Canadian Institute Of Chartered Accountants
EIC Emerging Issues Committee
FASB Financial Accounting Standards Board
GAAP Generally Accepted Accounting Principles
IASB International Accounting Standards Board
IAS International Accounting Standard
IFRSs International Financial Reporting Standards (This term and its abbreviation is commonly used to describe both International Financial Reporting Standards and International Accounting Standards)
SFAS Statement Of Financial Accounting Standards

Acknowledgments

The material in this text has been developed over the course of many years. During this period they have been used by thousands of Canadian accounting students. Many of these students, as well as their instructors, have contributed to the development process by making suggestions for improvements and by helping us find the errors and omissions that are integral to such a process. We would like to thank all of these people for their assistance in improving these materials as well as for their patience in dealing with any problems found in earlier editions.

Also of great importance to us is our long-standing relationship with Pearson Education Canada's acquisitions editor, Samantha Scully. We are notoriously difficult to work with. Fortunately, with Ms. Scully's assistance, we have been able to satisfy our need for editorial independence within the context of publishing books under the banner of one of Canada's largest publishing organizations.

With respect to content, we would like to give special thanks to Professor Steve Fortin, PhD, CA, of McGill University. Professor Fortin, an established authority on accounting for derivatives and hedging, was kind enough to review the material on foreign currency hedging that is found in Chapter 9, as well as the related problem material on this subject. His comments and suggestions were invaluable.

Related Web Sites

Web sites that provide useful resources related to accounting standards are as follows:

Canadian Institute of Chartered Accountants www.cica.ca
Outstanding Exposure Drafts are available on the CICA web site. They can be found under Standards | Documents For Comment.

International Accounting Standards Board www.iasb.org.

Financial Accounting Standards Board (US) www.fasb.org

American Institute of Certified Public Accountants www.aicpa.org

SEDAR www.sedar.com

This last reference is an acronym for "System For Electronic Document Analysis And Retrieval". It is of particular importance in that it contains all of the documents, including annual reports, that are filed with the provincial securities commissions that regulate securities trading in Canada.

Magazine articles that might be of interest can be found in the archives or online issues at the web sites of the following magazines:

CAmagazine archives www.camagazine.com

Journal of Accountancy www.aicpa.org/pubs/jofa/joaiss.htm

Business Week http://search.businessweek.com

A Final Word

As always, we have made every attempt to provide you with material that is free of errors and omissions. However, we are aware that such attempts are never completely successful. We apologize for any inconvenience that these errors and/or omissions may cause for you. Please advise us of any errors or other problems that you encounter. They will be posted on the text web site as soon as we become aware of the problem.

We hope that you find this publication useful and welcome any suggestions for additions or improvements. These can be sent to us at:

Clarence Byrd Inc.
139 Musie Loop Road
Chelsea, Quebec J9B 1Y6
e-mail address: idachen@sympatico.ca

Clarence Byrd — Athabasca University
Ida Chen — Clarence Byrd Inc.

May, 2007

CONTENTS

CHAPTER 1

Introduction

CHAPTER 2

Investments In Equity Securities

(continued)

CHAPTER 2, continued

CHAPTER 3
Business Combinations

CHAPTER 3, continued

CHAPTER 4
Consolidated Balance Sheet At Acquisition

(continued)

CHAPTER 4, continued

CHAPTER 5

Consolidation Subsequent To Acquisition (No Unrealized Intercompany Profits)

(continued)

CHAPTER 5, continued

CHAPTER 6

Consolidation Subsequent To Acquisition (Including Unrealized Intercompany Profits)

CHAPTER 6, continued

CHAPTER 7

Advanced Topics In Consolidations

CHAPTER 8

Interests In Joint Ventures

CHAPTER 9

Translation of Foreign Currency Transactions

CHAPTER 10

Translation Of Foreign Currency Financial Statements

(continued)

CHAPTER 10, continued

CHAPTER 11

Accounting For Not-For-Profit Organizations

CHAPTER 11, continued

CHAPTER 12

Accounting For Partnerships

CHAPTER 12, continued

Introduction

Abbreviations Used In This Text

The abbreviations used in this Chapter and all subsequent chapters are described in the Preface.

International Convergence

The Problem

Canada

1-1. At one point in time, the AcSB focused its efforts almost entirely on the development of effective accounting standards for use in the Canadian reporting environment. The use of these standards was required by all of the bodies responsible for securities regulation in Canada, as well as by the legislation that provided the basis for federally chartered corporations. In fact, many analysts fervently believed that a unique set of Canadian accounting standards was essential to the maintenance of effective financial reporting in the Canadian environment.

1-2. A number of trends have served to alter this situation. We are all aware of the increased importance of international trade. This has resulted in a situation where it is rarely appropriate to view any of our large, publicly traded companies as a "Canadian" company. These companies sell their product and acquire their resources throughout the world, in some cases with only a small proportion of their activity within this country's borders.

1-3. Such multi-national companies operate in a great variety of economic environments. In addition, they are subject to differing legal requirements, including those related to the assessment of taxes. Given this, it is difficult to argue effective reporting by these companies requires a set of accounting standards that is unique to Canada.

1-4. Of even greater importance is the fact that our large, multi-national companies do not restrict their fund raising activities to Canadian capital markets. In actual fact, Canadian capital markets are relatively small, compared to the size of many Canadian companies. This means that these organizations sell their securities in New York, London, and other venues on a regular and ongoing basis. As these alternative venues have differing regulatory bodies, Canadian companies commonly must prepare multiple sets of financial statements in order to comply with the requirements of these foreign capital markets.

Other Countries

1-5. This situation is not unique to Canada. Regardless of their home jurisdiction, multi-national companies are encountering difficulties dealing with the oft-times conflicting requirements of operating and raising capital in multiple jurisdictions. They are having to incur the not insignificant costs of preparing multiple sets of financial statements.

1-6. Further, as differences can be material, the users of financial statements are often confused as to which presentation they should be using to make investment decisions. For example, in 2003, Canadian Pacific Railway reported a Net Income based on Canadian GAAP of $401 million. In the same annual report, they also reported that, under U.S. GAAP, the result would have been a Net Income of $358 million. To further muddy the waters, in the U.S. GAAP results, they reported a Comprehensive Income Figure of $204 million (at this time, there was no Canadian requirement to report Comprehensive Income amounts).

The Canadian Response

1-7. Not surprisingly, the situation described in the preceding paragraphs has led to demands, from both financial statement preparers and financial statement users, for a single set of international accounting standards. At this point in time, these demands are being met in a number of jurisdictions by the adoption of the IFRSs that are produced by the International Accounting Standards Board.

1-8. Canada is one of these jurisdictions. After a lengthy strategic planning process, the AcSB has concluded that it will, at least for publicly accountable enterprises, adopt IFRSs as the primary source of Canadian GAAP. This strategic planning process, as well as the implementation plan for converging with international standards, will be given detailed consideration in the next section of this Chapter.

The Road Ahead: The AcSB's Strategic Plan

Background

1-9. A first draft of the Strategic Plan was published by the AcSB as an invitation to comment in March, 2004. This draft provided an overview of the Canadian standard setting environment and asked readers to comment on whether the Board should continue with the status quo, adopt U.S. standards, or adopt international standards. Comments were also invited on the need to develop alternative standards for different types of entities.

1-10. The AcSB received a wide range of views on the various issues raised in this initial draft of the Strategic Plan. After taking into consideration the feedback that it received on this draft, the Board issued a second invitation to comment in March, 2005.

1-11. The response to this second draft was generally supportive and, as a reflection of this, its content was largely incorporated into the final version which was approved by the AcSB in January, 2006. The Strategic Plan involves a multi-track approach to standard setting, with separate attention being given to the financial reporting needs of:

- publicly accountable enterprises;
- non-publicly accountable enterprises; and
- not-for-profit organizations.

1-12. The term "publicly accountable enterprises" is not directly defined in the *CICA Handbook*. However, its meaning can be determined by referring to Section 1300's definition of "non-publicly accountable enterprises":

> **Paragraph 1300.02(a) Non-publicly accountable enterprises** are enterprises other than public enterprises, co-operative business enterprises, regulated financial institutions and regulated financial institution holding companies, rate-regulated enterprises, government business enterprises and government business-type organizations as defined in the CICA Public Sector Accounting Handbook.

1-13. The Strategic Plan notes that the term "publicly accountable enterprise" is used substantially in accordance with the terminology and definitions in Section 1300. Given this, it encompasses public companies plus some other types of enterprises that have relatively large or diverse classes of financial statement users.

Basis For A Multi-Track Approach

1-14. The Strategic Plan describes the need for a multi-track approach as follows:

> The AcSB will pursue separate strategies for each of the major categories of reporting entities - publicly accountable enterprises, non-publicly accountable enterprises, and not-for-profit organizations. The AcSB recognizes that "one size does not necessarily fit all"; it may not be possible to address the divergent needs of different categories of reporting entities properly within a single strategy. Each category deserves a strategy that specifically addresses the particular needs of the users of financial statements of entities in that category, even though the outcomes of some of the strategies may be the same or similar for all categories.

1-15. This conclusion reflects the fact that the universe of Canadian reporting entities is quite diverse and it is unlikely that a single, monolithic set of standards could meet the needs of all of the members of this universe. As expressed in the comments made, the major concerns with this multi-track approach are:

1. The possibility that identical transactions would be given different treatment in the financial statements of different entities.
2. The possibility that the application of this approach could result in the need to prepare multiple sets of financial statements.
3. Difficulties associated with clarifying which set of standards should be used in particular circumstances.

1-16. The AcSB concluded that these problems were manageable. While the strategies for all three defined categories will be based on the same conceptual framework, they will differ when such differences can be justified by the needs and cost-benefit considerations of the different categories.

1-17. As an additional point here, we would note that it is not uncommon to see the group that the AcSB has referred to as "publicly accountable enterprises" referred to as either public enterprises or public companies. Since the majority of publicly accountable enterprises are, in fact, public companies, this terminology is close to being accurate. However, in this text, we will consistently reflect the intentions of the AcSB by using the correct designation — publicly accountable enterprises.

Implementation Plan

1-18. In June, 2006, the AcSB released *An Implementation Plan For Incorporating IFRSs into Canadian GAAP.* This fairly lengthy document provides a *Handbook* Section by *Handbook* Section analysis of how the AcSB expects IFRSs to be incorporated into Canadian GAAP.

1-19. The Implementation Plan specifies a "changeover date" of January 1, 2011. This is the date that the first year of reporting by publicly accountable enterprises under IFRS-based standards is expected to begin. The changeover will certainly not take place before this date. In fact, most analysts would expect the date to be deferred by at least one year.

1-20. For the *Handbook* material that is covered in this text, we will look at the detailed provisions of this Implementation Plan at the end of the relevant Chapter.

> **CD-ROM Note** If you are interested in additional information on this Implementation Plan, see our *Guide To Canadian Financial Reporting* which can be found on the CD-ROM which accompanies this text. Each Chapter of this *Guide* begins with a discussion of how international convergence will apply to the *Handbook* Section covered in the Chapter.

Strategy For Publicly Accountable Enterprises

A Change In Direction

1-21. In its original deliberations on the approach to be used for dealing with accounting standards for publicly accountable enterprises, the AcSB was faced with a choice between two discrete alternatives:

Harmonization With U.S. GAAP This would require the elimination of significant unjustifiable differences with U.S. standards. While this does not involve copying all elements of U.S. GAAP or even all elements of a particular U.S. standard, it does involve developing standards that do not conflict with U.S. GAAP but may also permit other policies in some cases.

Convergence With International Standards This would require replacing Canadian GAAP with the IFRSs issued by the IASB.

1-22. In its first version of a strategic plan for publicly accountable enterprises, the AcSB focused on harmonization with U.S. GAAP. This approach was based on the fact that the U.S. was Canada's most important trading partner, as well as the fact that most large Canadian companies required access to U.S. capital markets. Further supporting this approach was the acceptance by Canadian securities regulators of financial statements based on U.S. GAAP.

1-23. This changed dramatically with the October, 2002 signing of the Norwalk Agreement between the FASB and the IASB. The basic content of this agreement is as follows:

Norwalk Agreement

At their joint meeting in Norwalk, Connecticut, USA on September 18, 2002, the FASB and the IASB each acknowledged their commitment to the development of high-quality, compatible accounting standards that would be used for both domestic and cross-border financial reporting. At that meeting, both the FASB and the IASB pledged to use their best efforts to:

(a) make their existing financial reporting standards fully compatible as soon as is practicable and
(b) to coordinate their future work programs to ensure that once achieved, compatibility is maintained.

To achieve compatibility, the FASB and IASB (together, the "Boards") agree, as a matter of high priority, to:

(a) undertake a short-term project aimed at removing a variety of individual differences between U.S. GAAP and International Financial Reporting Standards (IFRSs, which include International Accounting Standards, IASs);
(b) remove other differences between IFRSs and U.S. GAAP that will remain at January 1, 2005, through coordination of their future work programs; that is, through the mutual undertaking of discrete, substantial projects which both Boards would address concurrently;
(c) continue progress on the joint projects that they are currently undertaking; and
(d) encourage their respective interpretative bodies to coordinate their activities.

The Boards agree to commit the necessary resources to complete such a major undertaking.

The Boards agree to quickly commence deliberating differences identified for resolution in the short-term project with the objective of achieving compatibility by identifying common, high-quality solutions. Both Boards also agree to use their best efforts to issue an exposure draft of proposed changes to U.S. GAAP or IFRSs that reflect common solutions to some, and perhaps all, of the differences identified for inclusion in the short-term project during 2003.

As part of the process, the IASB will actively consult with, and seek the support of, other national standard setters and will present proposals to standard setters with an official liaison relationship with the IASB, as soon as is practical.

The Boards note that the intended implementation of the IASB's IFRSs in several jurisdictions on or before January 1, 2005, requires that attention be paid to the timing of the effective dates of new or amended reporting requirements. The Boards' proposed strategies will be implemented with that timing in mind.

Note This Norwalk Agreement was reinforced by the two Boards signing a Memorandum Of Understanding (commonly referred to as MOU) in February, 2006.

1-24. This Agreement, along with the supporting Memorandum Of Understanding, constituted a fairly dramatic change in the U.S. approach to globalization of accounting standards. In prior years, there appeared to be a belief in the U.S. that the standards of other countries simply did not measure up to the quality that was inherent in the work of the FASB and should not be given serious consideration. In contrast, this agreement provides a clear indication that U.S. standard setters believe that there is a pressing need to work with other standard setters towards establishing internationally acceptable rules for financial reporting.

1-25. Given this change in the U.S., it no longer made sense for Canada to work towards harmonization with U.S. standards. This was reinforced by the fact that in several jurisdictions, most importantly the European Union and Australia, local standards were being eliminated in favour of the IFRSs. As a consequence of these developments, the AcSB's strategic plan for publicly accountable enterprises is based on convergence with international standards.

The Strategy

1-26. The AcSB's description of its strategy for publicly traded enterprises is as follows:

1. The AcSB will direct its efforts primarily to participating in the movement toward the global convergence of accounting standards. The AcSB has concluded, given the increasing globalization of capital markets and other recent developments, that it is timely for publicly accountable Canadian enterprises to adopt globally accepted high-quality accounting standards by converging Canadian GAAP with International Financial Reporting Standards (IFRSs) over a transitional period. At the end of that period, a separate and distinct Canadian GAAP will cease to exist as a basis of financial reporting for publicly accountable enterprises.

2. The AcSB's general approach to achieving convergence will include:

    (a) Adopting standards newly developed by the International Accounting Standards Board (IASB) that are converged with standards issued by the U.S. Financial Accounting Standards Board (FASB), as these new global standards are issued.
    (b) Replacing other Canadian standards with corresponding IFRSs already issued, in accordance with a separate convergence implementation plan to be developed in consultation with affected stakeholders.
    (c) Working with both the IASB and the FASB to ensure that the Canadian perspective is taken into account in their deliberations.
    (d) Working to promote the further convergence of IASB and FASB standards.

    In taking on a role in the development of global standards, the AcSB will cease to make final decisions on most matters affecting the technical content and timing of implementation of standards applied in Canada.

3. The AcSB's object is to achieve convergence of Canadian GAAP with IFRSs at the changeover date at the end of the transitional period, which is expected to be approximately five years (the currently stated goal is five years). The AcSB believes that by providing reasonable lead time and a clear transition plan, the costs and disruption to affected stakeholders will be minimized.

1-27. There are two other points that should be made with respect to this strategy:

References To Canadian GAAP While a distinct Canadian GAAP will no longer exist as of the changeover date, as a practical matter, IFRSs will be imported into Canadian GAAP and will need to be described as Canadian GAAP for some period of time subsequent to the changeover date. The reflects the fact that, at present, many federal, provincial, and territorial laws, regulatory rules, and other such requirements related to financial reporting, make reference to Canadian GAAP.

AcSB Powers Unchanged In adopting this strategy for publicly accountable enterprises, the AcSB is retaining all of its powers and responsibilities. For example, the AcSB could add disclosure requirements to an IFRS or, in cases where an IFRS provides alternative treatments, specify that only one of these treatments is acceptable in Canada. The resulting financial statements would still meet the convergence goal of compliance with international standards. However, the Strategic Plan indicates that the AcSB's intention is to exercise its powers in such ways only when necessary. In general, it is expected that IFRSs will be adopted without modification.

Strategy For Non-Publicly Accountable Enterprises

Current Situation

1-28. Most analysts believe that, for enterprises that do not have a significant number of external users, the full application of GAAP would not survive any reasonable cost/benefit analysis. As most of you are aware, the current CICA approach to dealing with this problem is to provide differential reporting options for non-publicly accountable enterprises.

1-29. Under this approach, these enterprises can choose not to apply some of the more complex provisions of current Canadian GAAP. For example, a non-publicly accountable enterprise can account for income taxes on a taxes payable basis, rather than becoming involved with the intricacies of Section 3465's tax allocation procedures.

CD-ROM Note If you are interested in a complete discussion of Section 1300's differential reporting provisions, see Chapter 4 of our *Guide To Canadian Financial Reporting* which can be found on the CD-ROM which accompanies this text.

International Convergence

1-30. The Strategic Plan makes clear the AcSB's continuing belief that non-publicly accountable enterprises have different needs. Given this, the AcSB is currently doing research with respect to how these needs can be met in the context of international convergence.

1-31. Current IFRSs make no provision for non-publicly accountable enterprises. If this situation does not change, the AcSB would have three choices:

1. Requiring non-publicly accountable enterprises to use the same IFRSs as publicly accountable enterprises.
2. Continuing with a differential reporting model based on specified exemptions from IFRSs.
3. Developing and maintaining a distinct Canadian GAAP for this sector.

1-32. It appears, however, that the AcSB will not have to choose one of these alternatives. In November, 2006, the IASB issued an Exposure Draft, *International Financial Reporting Standard For Small And Medium-Sized Entities*. The Exposure Draft indicates that "small and medium-sized entities are entities that (1) do not have public accountability, and (2) publish general purpose financial statements for external users. While there are some differences, the IASB term "small and medium-sized entities" would largely include the same group of companies that are covered by the Canadian term "non-publicly accountable enterprises".

1-33. In contrast to the Canadian differential reporting approach, this document proposes a separate set of standards for small and medium-sized enterprises. That is, instead of listing specific exemptions from compliance with individual IFRSs, the Exposure Draft is a 243 page document which includes 28 separate standards covering issues such as "Financial Assets And Liabilities", "Investments In Joint Ventures", and "Impairment Of Non-Financial Assets".

1-34. Given the issuance of this IASB Exposure Draft, it would be our expectation that the differential reporting model will remain in place until the date of the changeover to international standards. At the changeover date, the AcSB will likely adopt whatever final IFRS results from the Exposure Draft on small and medium-sized entities.

Strategy For Not-For-Profit Organizations

Current Situation

1-35. At present, not-for-profit organizations apply many *CICA Handbook* Sections without modification. However, Sections 4400 through 4460 provide guidance in areas where the AcSB has concluded that these organizations have financial reporting needs that are different from those of profit oriented enterprises (e.g., the treatment of pledges).

International Convergence

1-36. At present, IFRSs do not provide any special provisions with respect to not-for-profit organizations. Further, unlike the situation with standards for non-publicly accountable enterprises where there is an Exposure Draft dealing with the needs of these organizations, the IASB's work plan makes no mention of any efforts to provide standards to meet the special needs of not-for-profit organizations. If this situation continues until the January 1, 2011 changeover date, the AcSB will have three choices:

- Require the application of all IFRSs to not-for-profit organizations.
- Allow not-for-profit organizations to use the IFRS that is being developed for non-publicly accountable enterprises.
- Continue the current practice of providing guidance in areas where they believe that these organizations have special needs.

1-37. It would be our guess that the last alternative will be selected. Not-for-profit organizations clearly have unique features. It seems unlikely to us that applying a set of standards developed for application to profit-oriented organizations would provide appropriate financial reporting results.

Writing Textbooks In This Brave New World

The Problem

1-38. There was a time when a financial reporting text could be published with the expectation that its content would be reasonably current for a period of three to five years. In fact, the normal revision cycle for the leading financial accounting texts was three years.

1-39. Even before the AcSB announced its plan to incorporate IFRSs into Canadian GAAP, this situation had changed. For several years, there have been near-monthly revisions to the *CICA Handbook*. Further, some of these revisions have been extremely complex as well as far-reaching in their implications. Examples of this latter problem include the new standards on financial instruments and stock-based compensation.

1-40. The decision to incorporate IFRSs into Canadian GAAP, as well as the AcSB's approach to the convergence process, has exacerbated this situation. In particular, their decision to introduce components of international standards into the *CICA Handbook* on a piecemeal basis over the period leading up to the changeover date means that there will be significant changes in Canadian standards in all of the years leading up to that date.

1-41. We are now living in a world where, given the lead times required between the author's completion of text material and its actual publication, any new financial reporting text will be at least somewhat out-of-date before it is put into the hands of students.

The Advanced Accounting Dilemma

1-42. This is a particularly difficult issue in preparing a text on advanced financial accounting subjects. While the parameters of this area vary considerably, the two subjects that appear to be common to all advanced financial accounting courses are business combinations and the preparation of consolidated financial statements. At least one-half of most advanced courses deal with this complex and extremely technical subject.

1-43. Because of the content of the existing IFRSs and work being done by the FASB and IASB in this area, we are virtually certain that the procedures used to prepare consolidated financial statements are going to change significantly. This change is likely to occur in 2009. Given this, we are faced with two choices:

- We can base our material on existing Canadian standards on business combinations and the preparation of consolidated financial statements. This means that we will be forcing you to learn some very complex procedures which, by the time you will be applying them in practice, will be largely irrelevant in the Canadian environment.
- We can base our material on what we expect to be the content of the IFRSs on business combinations and the preparation of consolidated financial statements. As the IFRSs are currently undergoing revision, there is the possibility that our expectations will not be correct. Further, for those of you writing professional examinations prior to the adoption of the IFRSs, you will not have an understanding of the Canadian statements that are likely to be applicable to these examinations.

Our Compromise Solution

1-44. Neither of the choices described in the preceding paragraph is satisfactory. In fact, no completely satisfactory solution exists. Given this, our compromise approach will be as follows:

- We will include complete coverage of the requirements of the current (1st Quarter, 2007) *CICA Handbook* with respect to the subjects covered in this text.
- In presenting this coverage, we will place extra emphasis on the concepts which underlie the procedures required by the current *CICA Handbook*. This will help you deal with the changes in procedures which we know will be coming in the near future.
- Throughout the text, we will describe the procedures that we expect to be required when IFRSs are converged into the relevant Canadian GAAP. This will include coverage of both current IFRSs, as well as changes that we anticipate as a result of revisions that are currently underway.
- In all chapters where we expect that IFRSs will produce significantly different results than those produced under the current *CICA Handbook* requirements, we will provide detailed examples of the alternative IFRS results.
- As we move closer to the adoption of IFRSs in the relevant subject areas, additional examples of their application will be provided on the web site for this text.

1-45. Also of possible assistance in this area is our *Guide To Canadian Financial Reporting*. This CICA publication provides detailed coverage of the international convergence process for all of the accounting Sections of the *CICA Handbook*.

> **CD-ROM Note** Our *Guide To Canadian Financial Reporting* is available on the CD-ROM which accompanies this text.

1-46. While we would prefer a more satisfactory solution to this problem, we believe that this is the best approach that is currently available.

An Overview Of Investments In Equity Securities And Business Combination Transactions

Our Objective

1-47. Chapters 2 through 7 of this text deal with a group of related subjects which typically constitute the core material of most advanced financial accounting courses. These related subjects are:

- Investments In Equity Securities
- Business Combinations
- Consolidated Financial Statements

1-48. Some business combinations do not involve an investment in equity securities. Correspondingly, some investments in equity securities do not involve a business combination transaction. However, there are business combination transactions in which the combined business is carried on in the form of two separate legal entities, with one of the entities holding a continuing investment in the equity securities of the other entity. In this type of situation, the rules related to the preparation of consolidated financial statements come into play.

1-49. Given this situation, the objective of this section of our introductory Chapter is to provide a description of each of the individual subject areas listed, along with a general explanation of how the subjects are related. While the content of this Chapter is non-technical in nature, a familiarity with the individual subjects, as well as with the basic relationships between them, is essential to an understanding of the more technical material which follows in Chapters 2 through 7.

Investments In Equity Securities

Separate Legal Entities

1-50. A corporation can invest in another corporation either by acquiring assets or, alternatively, by acquiring securities. When the asset approach is used, the assets are recorded on the books of the acquiring company and accounted for as per the other assets of the corporation. While an investment has been made, there would be no separate disclosure of an investment balance.

1-51. Alternatively, when equity securities are acquired, there is a continuing investment relationship between two separate and distinct legal entities. This is depicted in Figure 1-1.

1-52. As can be seen in Figure 1-1, the enterprise that has paid the consideration and acquired the securities will be referred to as the investor company. This enterprise can either acquire the other company's securities directly from the other company or, alternatively, the securities can be acquired in secondary markets from other investors. Regardless of the route chosen, the company whose securities are held will be referred to as the investee company.

Figure 1-1
Separate Legal Entities

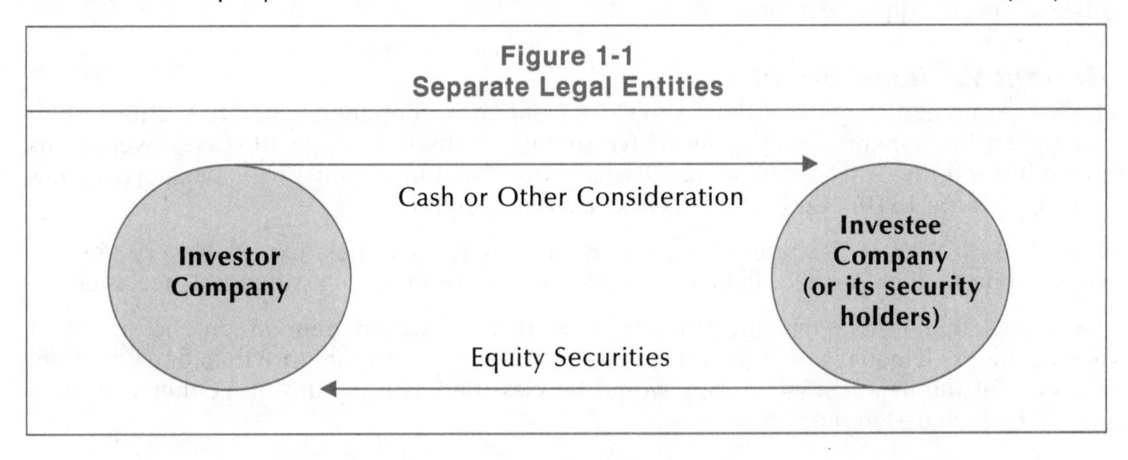

1-53. In the preceding paragraphs, we have referred to the investor "company" and the investee "company". There are, of course, many situations in which the investor, the investee, or both, may be unincorporated business entities. In those cases where such business entities must apply GAAP, the *CICA Handbook* Recommendations are clearly applicable. However, in order to avoid the additional complications associated with other forms of business organizations, we will generally focus on equity investment situations in which both the investor and the investee are incorporated businesses.

Strategic Vs. Non-Strategic Equity Investments

1-54. While this term is not defined in the *CICA Handbook*, we find it useful to classify equity investments into two groups — investments that are a component of the operating strategy of the investor company, and investments that are not part of that operating strategy. We will refer to this latter group as non-strategic investments.

1-55. Within the category of strategic investments, the AcSB and the IASB have found it useful to identify three different ways in which the investor company may relate to the investee company:

Control Some investments in equity securities, generally those involving a majority holding of investee voting shares, give the investor control over the operating and financing decisions of the investee. In such situations, the investor is referred to as the parent, with the investee being referred to as the subsidiary.

Significant Influence Some investments in equity securities, generally those involving a holding of more than 20 percent, but less than 50 percent, of the outstanding voting shares of the investee, give the investor influence but not control over the operating and financing decisions of the investee. In such situations, the investee is referred to as a significantly influenced company.

Joint Control Some investments in equity securities allow the investor to share control of the investee with other investors. The investee in these situations is referred to as a joint venture, with the investors being referred to as joint venturers.

1-56. With respect to non-strategic investments in equity securities, the AcSB and the IASB divide this group into two categories:

Held-For-Trading Investments In general, these investments are held with an objective of generating a profit from short-term fluctuations in price or dealer's margin. However, as will be discussed in more detail in Chapter 2, management has the discretion of classifying any non-strategic investment as held for trading.

Available-For-Sale Investments This category would include any non-strategic investments that are not classified as held for trading.

1-57. Each of these classifications will be given more detailed consideration in Chapter 2, Investments In Equity Securities.

Current Vs. Non-Current

1-58. At an earlier point in time, the *CICA Handbook* contained separate sections titled Temporary Investments and Long-Term Investments. As this is no longer the case, investments in equity securities will have to be classified as current or non-current on the basis of the guidance in Section 1510, "Current Assets And Current Liabilities".

1-59. With respect to strategic investments in equity securities, except in very unusual circumstances, these assets will be classified as non-current in a classified Balance Sheet.

1-60. As to non-strategic investments, classification would depend on the intent of management. If management intends to hold such investments for more than one year from the date of the Balance Sheet, they would be classified as non-current. Otherwise, they would be included in the current assets.

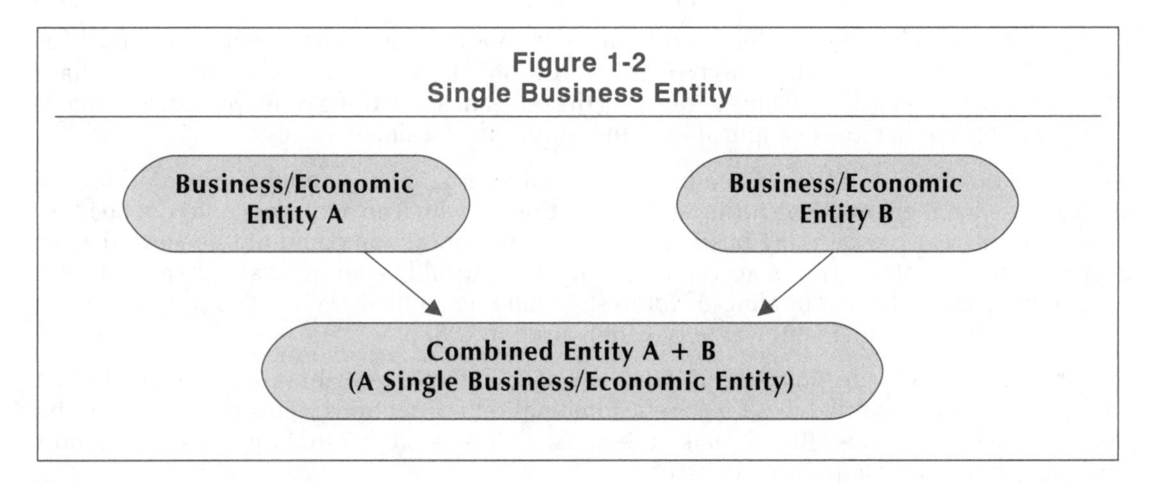

Business Combinations

Defined

1-61. The term "business combination" is defined in Section 1581 of the *CICA Handbook* as follows:

> **Paragraph 1581.06(a)** A business combination occurs when an enterprise acquires net assets that constitute a business, or acquires equity interests of one or more other enterprises and obtains control over that enterprise or enterprises.

1-62. This definition is illustrated graphically in Figure 1-2. In examining this Figure, it is important to understand that there is a difference between the legal and the accounting meanings of the term, business combination. In some situations, the economic unification of two businesses will be accompanied by an actual legal amalgamation of their assets.

1-63. For example, if Entity A pays cash to acquire all of the assets of Entity B, the combined assets of the two entities will wind up on the books of a single legal entity. A similar result would occur if the assets of both Entity A and Entity B were transferred to a new entity established for this purpose. In such situations, the economic and legal entities coincide, and this serves to clearly establish the appropriate accounting entity.

1-64. However, as is indicated in the definition of the term, a business combination may be accomplished through one business entity gaining control over the other through an acquisition of shares. For example, Entity A might acquire 100 percent of the outstanding voting shares of Entity B. In this case, the combining enterprises, Entity A and Entity B, retain their separate identities and, from a legal point of view, no business combination has taken place.

1-65. In substance, however, this situation is no different from the previous one. The assets of both entities are now under common control and, from an economic point of view, a business combination has occurred. In situations such as this, the entity assumption requires that accountants focus on economic substance rather than legal form.

1-66. This means that the accounting procedures will focus on the fact that there has been an economic amalgamation which has resulted in a single economic entity. The resulting financial statements, which ignore the separate legal existence of the two companies, are referred to as consolidated financial statements.

Classification

1-67. In most business combination transactions, one of the combining companies will be clearly identifiable as dominant in the ongoing operations of the combined company. For example, if Company A with 10 million shares outstanding, issues an additional 1 million shares to the shareholders of Company B in return for all of their outstanding voting shares, it seems clear that Company A will be in control of continued operations of the combined company. In the context of business combinations, this dominant company is referred to as the acquirer.

1-68. If an acquirer can be identified, a business combination transaction can be viewed as an acquisition of assets. While this type of acquisition is far more complex than the purchase of a drill press, the basic concepts underlying the relevant accounting principles are not significantly different than those applicable to the purchase of a single asset.

1-69. At one point in time, Canadian, U.S., and international standards provided for the possibility that there might be business combinations in which an acquirer could not be identified. If this was the case, the business combination transaction could not be viewed as an acquisition of assets and other accounting procedures would be appropriate. In particular, a procedure referred to as "pooling-of-interests" could be applied. While this procedure was not widely used in Canada, it was very widely used in U.S. practice.

1-70. At this point in time, the AcSB, the FASB, and the IASB have concluded that an acquirer can be identified in all business combination transactions. This means that in the jurisdictions where these Boards make the rules, all business combination transactions must accounted for as an acquisition of assets.

1-71. The required method of accounting for these transactions is currently referred to as the "purchase method". However, it appears that the FASB and IASB are currently moving toward designating this method the "acquisition method". This will be discussed in more detail in Chapter 3.

The Overlap

1-72. In reading the preceding material, it probably occurred to you that the acquisition of equity shares in another corporation could be a business combination transaction. It is likely that you also noted that, in some business combination transactions, the combining companies may continue as separate investor and investee companies. In an effort to ensure your understanding of this situation, Figure 1-3 (following page) graphically depicts the relationship between business combination transactions and holdings of investments in equity securities.

1-73. As can be seen in Figure 1-3, if Circle A represents the subject matter of investments in equity securities and Circle B represents the subject matter of business combinations, there is an overlap or intersection between the two circles. Including this intersection, three separate areas can be identified. These areas can be described as follows:

Area I This area represents investments in equity securities that have not resulted in an economic unification of the investor and investee companies. Stated alternatively, these are the investment situations where the investor and investee companies have retained both their separate legal identities as well as their separate economic status. In practical terms this includes all non-strategic investments, as well as investments where the investor has significant influence over the investee or shares joint control of that entity. However, situations where the investor company has acquired control (subsidiaries) would be excluded.

Area II This area represents business combinations in which there is no continuing investment relationship between the combining companies. Stated alternatively, these are the business combination transactions where the assets and liabilities of the two companies have been combined into a single legal entity. In general, this would involve situations where one company has acquired the assets of the other company or, alternatively, situations in which the assets of both companies have been transferred to a new company. In either case, all of the assets of the combining companies will be on the books of one legal entity, resulting in a situation in which the legal and economic entities coincide.

Area III (Overlap) In Areas I and II, there is no conflict between the legal and economic entities involved. In Area III, this situation changes. Area III involves situations where the two companies have achieved economic unification by one company acquiring a controlling interest in the shares of the other company. This means that we

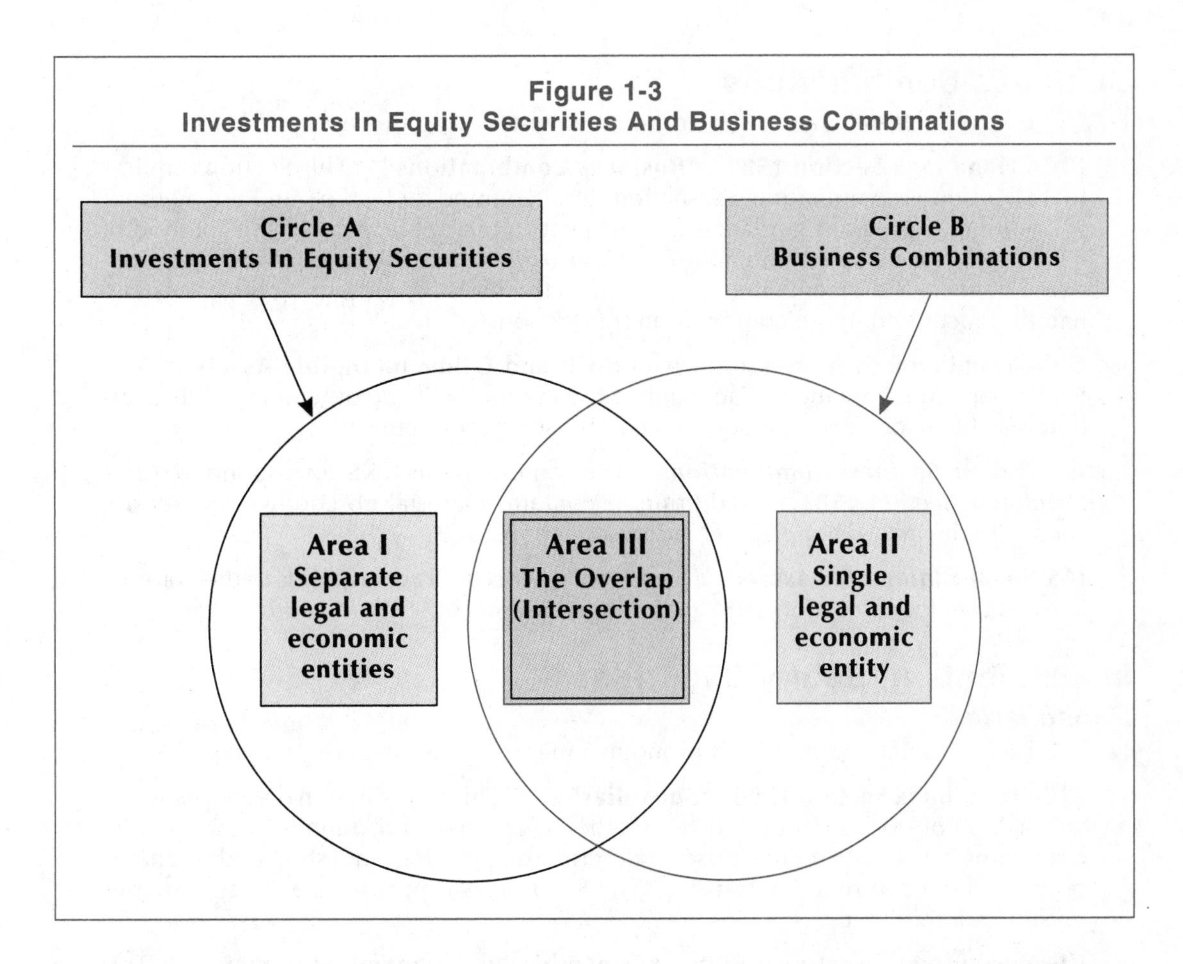

are dealing with two separate legal entities (i.e., a parent and its subsidiary) that are being operated as a single economic unit. When accountants are confronted with a conflict between the economic entity and the legal entity, we have noted previously that the entity assumption requires that attention be directed to the economic entity. The two separate legal entities will have to be accounted for as a single unified business entity, a goal that is achieved through the preparation of consolidated financial statements.

AcSB And IASB Standards

Differences

1-74. This section will provide you with a listing of the various *CICA Handbook* Sections and IFRSs that relate to the subjects of business combinations, investments in equity securities, and the preparation of consolidated financial statements.

1-75. In many cases, there are important differences between the Canadian standard and the corresponding international pronouncement. We do not, however, believe that it would be meaningful to catalogue these differences at this point in the text. Our approach will be to include, at the end of each Chapter of the text, an analysis of how international convergence is likely to change the concepts and procedures discussed in that Chapter. At that point, a discussion of the relevant differences will be far more understandable.

Business Combinations

1-76. The relevant AcSB and IASB pronouncements in this area are as follows:

CICA Handbook Section 1581: "Business Combinations" This Section requires that all business combination transactions be accounted for by the purchase method. In addition, it provides guidance with respect to the application of this method of accounting for business combinations. It is also relevant to the preparation of consolidated financial statements in that it specifies the basis for measuring the assets and liabilities acquired in the combination transaction.

CICA Handbook Section 3062: "Goodwill and Other Intangible Assets" This Section provides guidance on accounting for any goodwill and other intangible assets that may be recognized in a business combination transaction.

IFRS No. 3: *Business Combinations* The content of this IFRS corresponds to *CICA Handbook* Section 1581. In addition, it contains material on goodwill that corresponds to the material in *CICA Handbook* Section 3062.

IAS No. 38: *Intangible Assets* The content of this IFRS corresponds to the material in *CICA Handbook* Section 3062 on intangible assets other than goodwill.

Investments In Equity Securities

Subsidiaries

1-77. The relevant AcSB and IASB pronouncements in this area are as follows:

CICA Handbook Section 1590: "Subsidiaries" This brief Section defines a subsidiary as an enterprise controlled by another enterprise and defines control as the continuing power of an enterprise to determine operating, investing and financing policies of the controlled enterprise. The Section also specifies that all subsidiaries must be consolidated.

CICA Handbook Section 1600: "Consolidated Financial Statements" This Section contains detailed rules for the preparation of consolidated financial statements.

IAS No. 27: *Consolidated And Separate Financial Statements* This IFRS has coverage that corresponds to the combined content of *CICA Handbook* Sections 1590 and 1600.

Significantly Influenced Companies

1-78. The relevant AcSB and IASB pronouncements in this area are as follows:

Section 3051: Investments This Section defines investments in significantly influence companies and requires the use of the equity method to account for these investments.

IAS No. 28: *Investments In Associates* The content of this IFRS corresponds to the content of *CICA Handbook* Section 3051. Note, however, the IASB uses the term "associate" to refer to the companies that Section 3051 refers to as "significantly influenced companies".

Joint Ventures

1-79. The relevant AcSB and IASB pronouncements in this area are as follows:

Section 3055: "Interests In Joint Ventures" This Section defines joint ventures, requires the use of proportionate consolidation to account for joint venture arrangements, and provides specific procedural rules which reflect the unique nature of joint venture arrangements.

IAS No. 31: *Interests In Joint Ventures* The content of this IFRS corresponds to the content of *CICA Handbook* Section 3055. Note, however, it requires the use of the equity method, rather than proportionate consolidation, to account for these investments.

Held-For-Trading And Available-For-Sale Investments

1-80. The relevant AcSB and IASB pronouncements in this area are as follows:

CICA Handbook Section 3855: "Financial Instruments - Recognition And Measurement" This Section defines held-for-trading and available-for-sale investments and, in general, requires that they be recognized and carried at their fair values.

IAS No. 39: *Financial Instruments: Recognition And Measurement* With respect to held-for-trading and available-for-sale investments, the content of this IFRS corresponds to the content of *CICA Handbook* Section 3855.

Summary

1-81. Figure 1-4 summarizes the relevant AcSB and IASB standards for dealing with business combinations and investments in equity securities.

Figure 1-4
AcSB and IASB Standards For Business Combinations And Investments In Equity Securities

Subject	CICA Handbook	IFRS
Business Combinations	Section 1581	IFRS No. 3
	Section 3062	IAS No. 38
Strategic Investments:		
Subsidiaries	Section 1590	
	Section 1600	IAS No. 27
Significantly Influenced Companies	Section 3051	IAS No. 28
Joint Ventures	Section 3055	IAS No. 31
Non-Strategic Investments:		
Held-For-Trading	Section 3855	IAS No. 39
Available-For Sale	Section 3855	IAS No. 39

EIC Abstracts

1-82. In addition to the *CICA Handbook* Sections cited in the preceding material, there are a large number of EIC Abstracts that deal with the subjects of business combinations and investments in equity securities.

1-83. We will be referring to a number of these Abstracts as we move through this material. However, as they often involve issues that are of interest only to those who specialize in this field, we will generally not provide detailed coverage of their content.

CD-ROM Note For anyone with a more detailed interest in this subject, we would refer you to our *Guide to Canadian Financial Reporting* which is included on the CD-ROM which accompanies this text. There is a Chapter in that source for each *CICA Handbook* Section and, at the end of each of these Chapters, there is a comprehensive list of additional readings, including relevant EIC Abstracts. In most cases, the Chapter also includes summaries of the relevant Abstracts.

Investments In Equity Securities and Business Combinations in Canadian Practice

1-84. Both business combinations and investments in equity securities are important areas in Canadian practice. The 2006 edition of *Financial Reporting In Canada* states that, in their 2005 annual reports, all of the companies included in the survey indicated that the statements presented were on a consolidated basis. This, of course, indicates the presence of one or more subsidiaries. Also for 2005, 122 of the 200 companies reported the presence of non-strategic investments, while 80 of the companies reported the presence of joint ventures.

1-85. With respect to business combinations, 69 of the 200 survey companies disclosed that they had implemented one or more business combination transactions during 2005. All of these combination transactions were accounted for using the purchase method.

Approaching The Subject

Canadian Material

1-86. With the completion of this overview of the subject matter of business combinations and investments in equity securities, Chapters 2 through 8 will provide a systematic and detailed presentation of the concepts and procedures associated with these subjects.

1-87. Chapters 2 and 3 will be largely conceptual in their content, dealing with the pronouncements contained in Sections 1581, 1590, and 3051 of the *CICA Handbook*. With these concepts in hand, we will then be in a position to turn our attention to the procedures that are required in the preparation of consolidated financial statements.

1-88. Chapter 4 will introduce this subject by dealing with the preparation of the consolidated Balance Sheet at the date of acquisition of a subsidiary. This will include material on the conceptual alternatives in consolidation, as well as on the allocation of the investment cost to fair value changes and goodwill.

1-89. Chapter 5 extends the analysis to cover consolidation in periods subsequent to the acquisition and covers the preparation of the consolidated Income Statement, the consolidated Statement Of Retained Earnings, and the consolidated Statement of Cash Flows. Procedures dealt with here include write-offs of fair value changes, recognition of goodwill impairment, elimination of intercompany assets and liabilities, elimination of intercompany expenses and revenues and the elimination of intercompany dividends.

1-90. Chapter 6 further expands the coverage of basic consolidation procedures by providing a comprehensive analysis of unrealized intercompany profits. The analysis includes consideration of unrealized profits in opening and closing inventories, unrealized profits on the sale of non-depreciable capital assets, and unrealized profits on the sale of depreciable capital assets. Additional coverage of the equity method of accounting for investments is also included in this Chapter.

1-91. Chapters 4 through 6 provide in depth coverage of basic consolidation procedures, including some material on conceptual alternatives in the preparation of consolidated financial statements. In our view, this coverage is sufficient to meet the needs of most accounting students. However, there are also a number of more advanced topics that related to the preparation of consolidated financial statements that some instructors may wish to cover.

1-92. While it is unlikely that an instructor would choose to cover all of these advanced topics, there does not appear to be a consensus as to which subjects are the most important. In order to deal with this situation, we have relegated coverage of all of these topics to a separate Chapter 7.

1-93. The final Chapter on these subjects is Chapter 8 which deals with the unique features associated with joint venture arrangements. This includes proportionate consolidation procedures, as well as the special treatment of intercompany transactions that is required by Section 3055 of the *CICA Handbook*.

International Convergence

1-94. We have given considerable thought as to the most appropriate manner in which to provide coverage of the IFRSs that relate to the material covered in the text. We considered integrating this material throughout each Chapter and providing coverage of how the international standard differs with respect to each issue covered. However, we concluded that this could lead to confusion with respect to current Canadian requirements.

1-95. Our conclusion was that the best alternative was to provide coverage at the end of each Chapter of how the treatment of the issues covered in that Chapter would be different under the related IFRSs. In the case of the Chapters involving consolidated financial statements, this will include comparative examples of the application of the Canadian and international standards.

Problem Material

1-96. The material in this Chapter has been very general in nature. As a consequence, there is no problem material included for this Chapter.

Investments In Equity Securities

Introduction

Objectives

2-1. This Chapter has three objectives. Stated briefly, these are:

Classification To provide you with an understanding of the classification of various types of investments in equity securities under the recommendations of the *CICA Handbook*. This is of particular importance in that an investment's classification determines the accounting procedures that will be applied.

Accounting Methods To provide you with the ability to apply some of the accounting methods that will be used to account for investments in equity securities.

Matching Of Classifications And Methods To provide you with the ability to select the appropriate accounting method to be applied to each of the identified classifications of investments in equity securities.

2-2. This effort is complicated by the fact that investments in equity securities are dealt with in several different Sections of the *CICA Handbook*. These are:

- Section 1590, "Subsidiaries", provides guidance on the required accounting treatment for subsidiaries.
- Section 1600, "Consolidated Financial Statements", provides guidance on specific consolidation procedures.
- Section 3051, "Investments", provides guidance on the identification of, and the accounting procedures to be used for, significantly influenced investments.
- Section 3055, "Interests In Joint Ventures", provides guidance on the identification of, and the accounting procedures to be used for, joint ventures.
- Section 3855, "Financial Instruments - Recognition And Measurement", provides guidance on the identification of, and the accounting procedures to be used for, held-for-trading and available-for-sale investments.

Classification

2-3. Our introductory Chapter provided a brief discussion of the various types of investments in equity securities that are identified in the *CICA Handbook*. These are:

Non-Strategic Investments
- Held-For-Trading Investments
- Available-For-Sale Investments

Strategic Investments
- Subsidiaries
- Significantly Influenced Companies
- Joint Ventures

2-4. In this Chapter, we will provide a detailed discussion of how each of these classifications is defined, including any conceptual problems that may be associated with the process of identifying investments in each category.

2-5. There is an additional type of investment that we have not included in this list. As some of you may be aware, there are now *CICA Handbook* requirements for the consolidation of what is referred to as a "variable interest entity". Identification of variable interest entities is a very complex process and, in many cases, does not involve holdings of equity securities. For these reasons, we have excluded it from our basic list of investment classifications. However, some discussion of these arrangements will be included with our coverage of subsidiaries.

Accounting Methods

2-6. Depending on the classification of the investment in equity securities, a variety of accounting methods may be used. The ones that are identified in the *CICA Handbook* are as follows:

- cost method
- equity method
- fair value method (with changes in Net Income)
- fair value method (with changes in Comprehensive Income)
- full consolidation
- proportionate consolidation

2-7. This Chapter will provide coverage of all of these methods other than full and proportionate consolidation. Full consolidation procedures are the subject of Chapters 4 through 7 of the text. Proportionate consolidation is dealt with in Chapter 8.

2-8. This Chapter's coverage of the cost method and the two fair value methods will be complete, with no further attention to these methods in subsequent Chapters. With respect to the equity method, basic procedures will be introduced in this Chapter. However, the full application of the equity method requires a complete understanding of the consolidation procedures that will be covered in later Chapters. Given this, we will return to the application of the equity method in both Chapter 5 and Chapter 6.

Organization

2-9. After a section dealing with the conceptual basis for classification of investments in equity securities, the basic material in this Chapter will be organized in terms of investment classifications. A major section will be devoted to each category of investments in equity securities. Each of these sections will include:

- a definition of the investment classification; and
- an indication of the accounting method that must be used for that classification.

2-10. Also included in some of these sections will be detailed coverage of the procedures related to the required accounting method. However, as indicated in Paragraphs 2-7 and 2-8, detailed coverage of full and proportionate consolidation procedures will be presented in later chapters. In addition, coverage of some aspects of the equity method will be deferred to

Chapters 5 and 6.

2-11. At the end of these sections, a summary table of the classifications and their appropriate accounting methods will be presented.

2-12. Additional sections will follow, providing coverage of other issues associated with investments in equity securities. This will include write-downs for impairment, gains and losses on the sale of investments, differential reporting options, disclosure, and the application of international standards to investments in equity securities.

The Conceptual Basis For Classification

2-13. The classification of investments in equity securities is largely related to the ability of the investor company to influence the affairs of the investee. In most cases, that influence is in proportion the percentage of voting shares held. This basic approach to classification is illustrated in Figure 2-1.

Figure 2-1
Spectrum Of Influence Based On Voting Share Ownership

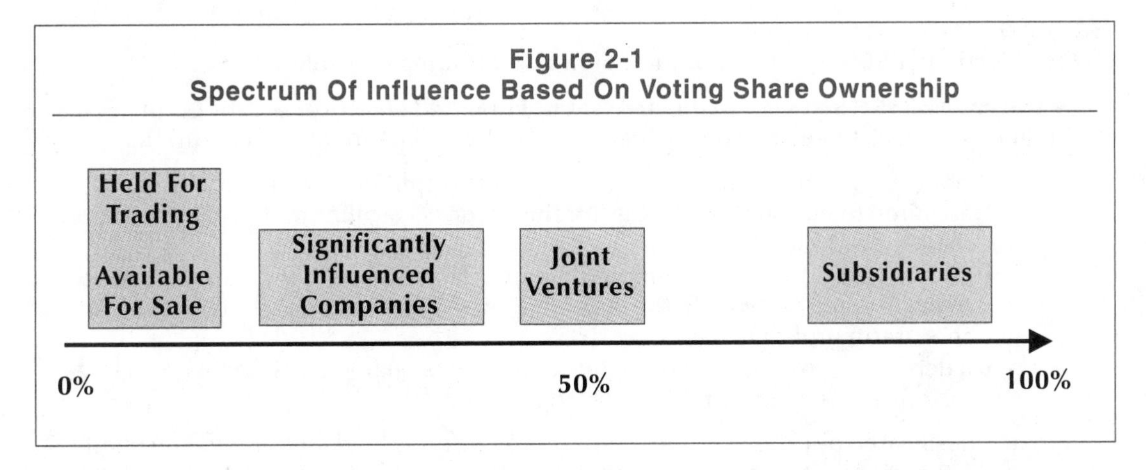

2-14. As shown in Figure 2-1, the investment classification involving the highest degree of influence is subsidiaries. In general, this type of investment involves situations where the investor company owns more than 50 percent of the outstanding voting shares of the investee company. However, as will be discussed in our more detailed discussion of this classification, such majority ownership is not a required part of the definition of a subsidiary.

2-15. At the other extreme we find the investment classifications of held-for-trading and available-for-sale. These are investment situations in which the investor company has little or no influence over the affairs of the investee company and, as can be seen in Figure 2-1, this situation normally involves relatively small holdings of investee voting shares.

2-16. The basic idea with investments in significantly influenced companies is that the investor company has the ability to influence the operating, financing, and investing decisions of the investee, but does not have control over these matters. This would generally require a substantial holding of investee voting shares (the *Handbook* suggests more than 20 percent), but less than the 50 percent plus one share that would give the investor company majority control over the investee.

2-17. Joint ventures involve situations where two or more investors share control of the investee. In Figure 2-1, we have shown this as a 50 percent holding, suggesting that joint control is established through the fact that two investors each own 50 percent of the voting shares of the investee. There are, of course, other possibilities. For example, joint control could be established by an agreement that overrides voting share ownership.

2-18. This overview provides a generalized picture of the investment classifications for equity securities that are found in the recommendations of the *CICA Handbook*. With this in hand, we can now turn to a more detailed consideration of the individual categories.

Held-For-Trading Investments

Definition

Handbook Location

2-19. Investments in equity securities are financial assets and, as such, they are generally subject to the rules in Section 3855 of the *CICA Handbook*, "Financial Instruments - Recognition And Measurement". However, strategic investments in subsidiaries, significantly influenced companies, and joint ventures are excluded from the scope of Section 3855 as they are covered by other specific *Handbook* provisions.

2-20. This is not the case with held-for-trading and available-for-sale investments. These investments are subject to the recognition and measurement rules that are specified in Section 3855. Note, however, the rules for these investments are part of more general recommendations which cover all financial assets and liabilities that are held for trading or available for sale.

General Definition

2-21. Section 3855's general definition of held for trading is as follows:

> **Paragraph 3855.19(f)** A **Financial Asset** or **Financial Liability** held for trading is a financial asset or financial liability that meets either of the following conditions:
>
> (i) it is not a loan or receivable, as defined in paragraph 3855.19(h), and is:
> - acquired or incurred principally for the purpose of selling or repurchasing it in the near term;
> - part of a portfolio of identified financial instruments that are managed together and for which there is evidence of a recent actual pattern of short-term profit taking; or
> - a derivative, except for a derivative that is a designated and effective hedging instrument (see Section 3865, "Hedges"); or
>
> (ii) it is designated by the entity upon initial recognition as held for trading. Any financial instrument within the scope of this Section may be designated when initially recognized as held for trading, except for:
> - financial instruments whose fair value cannot be reliably measured; and
> - financial instruments transferred in a related party transaction that were not classified as held for trading before the transaction.

2-22. It is fairly obvious from a quick reading of this definition, that the term "held for trading" is not appropriate. While the first two bullets under Paragraph 3855.19(f)(i) describe assets that fit the description "held for trading", the remainder of the definition includes two other types of items:

> **Derivatives** Except for derivatives associated with hedging relationships, all derivatives must be classified as held for trading, even in cases where there is no trading activity.
>
> **Designated Items** Paragraph 3855.19(f)(ii) allows any financial asset or financial liability to be designated as held for trading, without regard to an intent to trade or any actual trading activity. Note that, if this designation is made at the initial recognition of the financial asset or financial liability, it cannot be changed at a later date.

Application To Investments In Equity Securities

2-23. Applying this definition to investments in equity securities, we find that two types of items must be classified as held-for-trading investments:

> **Required Items** Equity securities that are held with the objective of generating a profit from short-term fluctuations in price. Management has no discretion in this classification matter.
>
> **Designated Items** Other, non-strategic investments in equity securities that

management has designated as held for trading.

2-24. It is not clear how this designation option will be implemented in practice. Through the use of the designation procedure, a corporation could have all of its non-strategic investments in equity securities classified as held for trading. This would result in a single method of accounting being applied to all of these investments, an advantage that may encourage the use of the designation procedure.

2-25. As we shall see when we look at applicable accounting methods, the disadvantage of designating investments as held for trading is that it will increase the volatility of the Net Income figure. Both held-for-trading and available-for-sale investments must be carried at fair value. The difference is that changes in the fair value of held-for-trading investments must be included in Net Income. On available-for-sale investments, the changes in fair value are included in Comprehensive Income, rather than in Net Income

Required Accounting Procedures

Initial Recognition

2-26. The relevant recommendation here is as follows:

Paragraph 3855.55 *When a financial asset or financial liability is recognized initially, an entity should measure it at its fair value.* (October, 2006)

2-27. Application of this in equity investment situations will be a fairly simple matter. Fair value will simply be the amount paid for the equity securities.

2-28. There is, however, one unusual requirement in Section 3855:

Paragraph 3855.56 *For a financial asset or financial liability classified as held for trading, all transaction costs should be recognized immediately in net income.* (October, 2006).

2-29. This is in contrast to most other asset acquisition procedures where transaction costs are included in the cost of the asset.

Subsequent Measurement

2-30. Paragraph 3855.66 requires that investments that are held for trading continue to be measured at fair value subsequent to their initial recognition. This will require that at each Balance Sheet date, such investments will be written up or written down to reflect their fair value on that date. This raises the question of how to deal with these changes in value in a complete set of financial statements

2-31. With respect to held-for-trading investments, Paragraph 3855.76 requires that changes in fair value be included in Net Income in the period in which they occur. As will be discussed later in this Chapter, this is in contrast to the treatment of available-for-sale investments where the changes in fair value are allocated to Comprehensive Income until such time as there is a disposition of the investment.

Fair Value Method With Changes In Net Income

2-32. There is no short-form name for the accounting method that is used for held-for-trading investments. Given this, we will use the somewhat awkward designation "fair value method with changes in Net Income".

2-33. A simple example will serve to illustrate these procedures:

Example Barkin Ltd. is a Canadian public company with a December 31 year end. On January 1, 2007, the company acquires 2,000 shares of Valor Inc. at a cost of $125 per share. Transaction costs total $2,500. The investment does not give Barkin influence over, or control of, Valor Inc. Barkin classifies these shares as held for trading.

On December 31, 2007, the fair value of the Valor shares has increased to $135 per share. The Valor Inc. shares did not declare or pay any dividends during 2007.

On March 1, 2008, Barkin sells all of the Valor shares for $132 per share. Transaction costs for the disposal are $2,600.

2-34. The journal entries required to record these transactions would be as follows:

January 1, 2007		
Investments [(2,000)($125)]	$250,000	
Miscellaneous Expense	2,500	
Cash [(2,000)($125) + $2,500]		$252,500
December 31, 2007		
Investments [(2,000)($135 - $125)]	$20,000	
Gain (Net Income)		$20,000
March 1, 2008		
Cash [(2,000)($132) - $2,600]	$261,400	
Loss (Net Income) [(2,000)($135 - $132)]	6,000	
Miscellaneous Expense	2,600	
Investments ($250,000 + $20,000)		$270,000

Exercise Two-1

Subject: Held-For-Trading Investments

Porter Inc. is a Canadian public company with a December 31 year end. On January 1, 2007, the company acquires 5,000 shares of Santin Ltd. at a cost of $23 per share. Transaction costs total $1,150. The investment does not give Porter influence over, or control of, Santin. Porter classifies these shares as held for trading.

During the year ending December 31, 2007, Santin Ltd. declares and pays dividends of $0.90 per share. On December 31, 2007, the fair value of the Santin shares has declined to $19 per share.

On March 1, 2008, Porter sells all of the Santin shares for $25 per share. Transaction costs for the disposal are $1,250.

Provide the journal entries to record the preceding information on the books of Porter Inc. and a summary of the effect of the investment in Santin on Porter's Net Income.

End of Exercise. Solution available in Study Guide.

Available-For-Sale Investments

Definition

General Definition

2-35. This category of financial instruments is defined in Section 3855 as follows:

Paragraph 3855.19(i) Available-for-sale financial assets are those non-derivative financial assets that are designated as available for sale, or that are not classified as loans and receivables, held-to-maturity investments, or held for trading.

2-36. This is a default or residual classification for financial assets. It contains those financial instruments that have not been included in one of the other three classifications — loans and receivables, held for trading, or held to maturity. Note that held-to-maturity investments would not be investments in equity securities as equity securities have no maturity date.

Application To Investments In Equity Securities

2-37. Given the scope of Section 3855, the general definition of available-for-sale investments in equity securities is that it includes all holdings of equity securities other than:

- investments in subsidiaries;
- investments in significantly influenced companies;
- investments in joint ventures;
- investments that are, in fact, held for trading; and
- investments that have been designated as held for trading.

2-38. As we have indicated previously, use of the designation procedure may result in an enterprise having no investments that are classified as available for sale.

Required Accounting Procedures

Initial Recognition

2-39. As was the case with held-for-trading investments, Paragraph 3855.55 requires that initial recognition of an investment classified as available for sale should be at fair value. However, in this case the *Handbook* allows management to choose between alternative approaches to recording transaction costs:

> **Paragraph 3855.57** *For a financial asset or financial liability classified other than as held for trading, an entity should adopt an accounting policy of either:*
>
> *(a) recognizing all transaction costs in net income; or*
> *(b) adding transaction costs that are directly attributable to the acquisition or issue of a financial asset or financial liability to the amount determined in accordance with paragraph 3855.55.* [**Byrd/Chen Note** See our Paragraph 2-26.] (October, 2006)

Subsequent Measurement

2-40. The procedures to be used subsequent to acquisition will depend on whether the shares of the investee have a quoted market price in an active market. In those cases where such values are available, the procedures for available-for-sale investments are as follows:

- At each Balance Sheet date after initial recognition, the investment will be revised to reflect its fair value as of that date.
- The periodic changes in fair value will be recognized as items of Other Comprehensive Income and included in the Statement Of Comprehensive Income.
- Dividends and interest on financial investments that have been classified as available for sale must be included in Net Income.
- When there is a disposition of an available-for-sale investment in equity securities, any balance of Accumulated Other Comprehensive Income that is related to that investment will be recognized in Net Income.

CD-ROM Note If you are not familiar with Comprehensive Income, or wish to review the subject, it is covered in Chapter 11 of our *Guide To Canadian Financial Reporting* which is found on the CD-ROM that accompanies your text.

2-41. If the shares of the available-for-sale investee do not have a quoted market price in an active market, Section 3855 indicates that the investment should be accounted for using the cost method.

2-42. Both the fair value method with changes in Comprehensive Income and the cost method will be illustrated in the sections which follow.

Fair Value Method With Changes In Comprehensive Income

2-43. A simple example will serve to illustrate the procedures that will be used for available-for-sale investments in cases where market values are available. With appropriate modifications, we will use the same basic example here that we used to illustrate the procedures used on held-for-trading investments in Paragraph 2-33.

Example Barkin Ltd. is a Canadian public company with a December 31 year end. On January 1, 2007, the company acquires 2,000 shares of Valor Inc. at a cost of $125 per share. Transaction costs total $2,500. The investment does not give Barkin influence over, or control of, Valor Inc. Barkin classifies these shares as available-for-sale and chooses the option of charging the transaction costs to expense.

On December 31, 2007, the fair value of the Valor shares has increased to $135 per share. The Valor Inc. shares did not declare or pay any dividends during 2007.

On March 1, 2008, Barkin sells all of the Valor shares for $132 per share. Transaction costs for the disposal are $2,600.

2-44. The journal entries required to record these transactions would be as follows:

January 1, 2007

Investments [(2,000)($125)]	$250,000	
Miscellaneous Expense	2,500	
Cash [(2,000)($125) + $2,500]		$252,500

December 31, 2007

Investments [(2,000)($135 - $125)]	$20,000	
Other Comprehensive Income - Gain*		$20,000

*After inclusion in the Statement Of Comprehensive Income, this item will be closed to the Balance Sheet account Accumulated Other Comprehensive Income.

March 1, 2008

Other Comprehensive Income - Loss [(2,000)($132 - $135)]	$6,000	
Investments		$6,000
Cash [(2,000)($132) - $2,600]	$261,400	
Miscellaneous Expense	2,600	
Other Comprehensive Income - Reclassification Adjustment	14,000	
Investments ($250,000 + $20,000 - $6,000)		$264,000
Gain (Net Income) [(2,000)($132 - $125)]		14,000

(When the two Other Comprehensive Income items are closed, the balance in Accumulated Other Comprehensive Income will be reduced to nil ($20,000 - $6,000 - $14,000). The sale entry also recognizes the fact that, during the period that it was held, there was a net gain on the investment of $14,000 ($20,000 in 2007 - $6,000 in 2008).)

Exercise Two-2

Subject: Available-For-Sale Investments With Known Market Value

Porter Inc. is a Canadian public company with a December 31 year end. On January 1, 2007, the company acquires 5,000 shares of Santin Ltd. at a cost of $23 per share. Transaction costs total $1,150 and Porter chooses to include them in the cost of the investment. The investment does not give Porter influence over, or control of, Santin. Porter classifies these shares as available for sale.

During the year ending December 31, 2007, Santin Ltd. declares and pays dividends of $0.90 per share. The Santin shares have a quoted market price that is established in an active market. On December 31, 2007, the fair value of the Santin shares has declined to $19 per share.

On March 1, 2008, Porter sells all of the Santin shares for $25 per share. Transaction costs for the disposal are $1,250.

Provide the journal entries to record the preceding information on the books of Porter Inc. and a summary of the effect of the investment in Santin on Porter's Net Income.

End of Exercise. Solution available in Study Guide.

Cost Method

Applicability

2-45. The general rule for available-for-sale investments in equity securities is that they are carried at fair value, with changes in value allocated to Comprehensive Income, rather than to Net Income.

2-46. An exception occurs when the shares of the investee do not have quoted market prices that are established in an active market. In this situation, Paragraph 3855.66(c) indicates that they should be carried at cost.

2-47. While Section 3855 does not use this term, this means that these investments will be accounted for using the cost method. This is the only situation in which this method is applied to investments in equity securities. It can, however, be applied to other types of investments such as real estate and investments in debt securities (for debt securities, the method is referred to as the amortized cost method, reflecting the fact that these securities are often acquired at a premium or a discount).

General Procedures

2-48. The cost method of accounting for investments is a specific application of the general procedures used in accounting for most non-current assets. It is based on the historical cost principle and the fact that an equity investor company's only legal claim to income is based on the amount of dividends declared by the investee company. The *Handbook* defines the method as follows:

> **Paragraph 3051.03(b)** The **cost method** is a basis of accounting for investments whereby the investment is initially recorded at cost; earnings from such investments are recognized only to the extent received or receivable.

2-49. As stated in the preceding Paragraph, the cost method records the investment at its cost and, in most circumstances, the investor company will continue to carry the asset at this value until it is disposed of. In general, the investor will recognize income only when the investee declares dividends ("extent received or receivable"). No recognition is given to changes in the fair value of the investee.

Exercise Two-3

Subject: Available-For-Sale Investments Without Known Market Value

Porter Inc. is a Canadian public company with a December 31 year end. On January 1, 2007, the company acquires 5,000 shares of Santin Ltd. at a cost of $23 per share. Transaction costs total $1,150 and Porter chooses to include them in the cost of the investment. The investment does not give Porter influence over, or control of, Santin. Porter classifies these shares as available for sale.

During the year ending December 31, 2007, Santin Ltd. declares and pays dividends of $0.90 per share.

On March 1, 2008, Porter sells all of the Santin shares for $25 per share. Transaction costs for the disposal are $1,250.

Provide the journal entries to record the preceding information on the books of Porter Inc. and a summary of the effect of the investment in Santin on Porter's Net Income.

End of Exercise. Solution available in Study Guide.

Return Of Capital

2-50. In general, under the cost method, the value recorded for the investment when it is acquired is not altered as long as the investor continues to hold the investment. However, there are situations in which the investee pays dividends in excess of its earnings subsequent to its acquisition by the investor. Such dividends are being paid out of investee Retained Earnings that were present at the time of the investment's acquisition. As the amount paid by the investor reflects this acquisition date balance, such dividends are a return of capital.

2-51. While the *Handbook* no longer discusses this possibility, IAS No. 27, *Consolidated And Separate Financial Statements*, provides a definition of the cost method that requires the recognition of return of capital situations:

> **Paragraph 4** The cost method is a method of accounting for an investment whereby the investment is recognized at cost. The investor recognizes income from the investment only to the extent that the investor receives distributions from accumulated profits of the investee arising after the date of acquisition. Distributions received in excess of such profits are regarded as a recovery of investment and are recognized as a reduction of the cost of the investment.

2-52. As we believe that this is the appropriate conclusion with respect to situations where dividends exceed the investee's post acquisition income, we will provide coverage of the requirements of this definition. A simple example will serve to illustrate this situation:

Example On December 31, 2007, the Fastee Company has the following Shareholders' Equity:

Common Stock - No Par	$3,400,000
Retained Earnings	4,600,000
Total Shareholders' Equity	$8,000,000

On this date, the Fastor Company acquires 10 percent of Fastee's outstanding voting shares at a cost of $800,000. During 2008, Fastee has Net Income of nil and declares dividends of $400,000.

2-53. As Fastee had no Net Income in 2008, the 2008 dividends are being paid out of the December 31, 2007 Retained Earnings balance. From the point of view of Fastee, this is not a liquidating dividend. It is an ordinary dividend being paid on the basis of a Retained Earnings balance that is legally available for this purpose.

2-54. However, from the point of view of Fastor, the $40,000 dividend that they receive from Fastee represents a return of capital. This position is based on the fact that, when they paid $800,000 for their 10 percent share of Fastee, they acquired a 10 percent share of the $4,600,000 Retained Earnings balance that was present in Fastee's December 31, 2007 Balance Sheet. As this balance is being used by Fastee as the basis for the 2008 dividend payment, the $40,000 received by Fastor constitutes a return of part of the original investment and not investment income. Given this, the journal entry to record the receipt of the dividend is as follows:

Cash	$40,000	
Investment In Fastee		$40,000

Exercise Two-4

Subject: Cost Method Return Of Capital

On January 1, 2007, Jondy Ltd. acquires 5 percent of the voting shares of Montag Inc. for $785,000. The investment is classified as available for sale. The Montag shares do not trade in an active market. Jondy Ltd. has a December 31 year end.

During the year ending December 31, 2007, Montag has Net Income of $700,000 and pays dividends of $500,000. During the year ending December 31, 2008, Montag has Net Income of nil but continues to pay dividends of $500,000.

Provide the journal entries to record the preceding information on the books of Jondy Ltd.

End of Exercise. Solution available in Study Guide.

Subsidiaries

Definition

2-55. At one point in time, the *CICA Handbook* defined a subsidiary as an investee for which the investor held a majority of the outstanding voting shares. In general, this was a reasonable definition because majority ownership usually means that an investor company would be able to elect a majority of the investee company's board of directors and, thereby, exercise control over the operating, investing, and financing policies of the investee.

2-56. However, there was a problem in that, under this definition, no recognition was given to situations in which the investor company was able to exercise control without having majority ownership. The failure to recognize this possibility resulted in situations where an investor company which did, in fact, have full control of the investee company would account for its investment using methods that were intended for situations involving only significant influence. In other words, the original *Handbook* recommendation represented an emphasis on legal form, rather than economic substance.

2-57. The current Section 1590 corrects this situation. The definition of a subsidiary found in this Section is as follows:

> **Paragraph 1590.03(a)** A **subsidiary** is an enterprise controlled by another enterprise (the parent) that has the right and ability to obtain future economic benefits from the resources of the enterprise and is exposed to the related risks.

2-58. This represents an improved definition in that it places an emphasis on economic substance (the ability to control the investee) rather than on legal form (ownership of the majority of voting shares).

The Concept Of Control

Handbook Definition

2-59. In conjunction with the definition of a subsidiary, Section 1590 defines control as follows:

> **Paragraph 1590.03(b)** **Control** of an enterprise is the continuing power to determine its strategic operating, investing and financing policies without the co-operation of others.

Varying Interpretations

2-60. While this definition appears to be very straightforward, it is subject to varying interpretations. The most restrictive interpretation of this definition would be that control requires ownership of 100 percent of the outstanding shares of the investee. This is based on the fact that, as long as there are any shareholders in the investee company other than the controlling investor, corporate legislation will prevent the investor company from undertaking transactions that are harmful to the interests of that group.

2-61. For example, if the investor owns 100 percent of the outstanding shares, there is nothing to prevent the investor from selling products to the investee at prices in excess of fair market value. However, if there is a non-controlling (minority) interest present in the investee company, there are provisions in corporate legislation that would constrain the ability of the investor company to undertake such transactions.

2-62. While this very restrictive interpretation of control has some appeal from a legal point of view, it fails to recognize that control over the great majority of operating and financing decisions can be achieved with less than 100 percent ownership. This suggests the use of a less restrictive interpretation of control in practical situations.

2-63. An alternative interpretation of control could be based on the fact that corporate legislation generally requires a two-thirds majority vote for passage of special resolutions. Such transactions as changes in the corporate objectives, amalgamations with other companies, and other changes in the corporate charter would require such a super majority. This means that an interpretation of control based on two-thirds ownership of voting shares would have some appeal from a legal point of view. Again, however, this interpretation is too restrictive in that many of the operating and financing decisions could be controlled with less than two-thirds ownership of the investee company's voting shares.

Practical Interpretation

2-64. A more practical interpretation of control is based on the idea that, in terms of economic substance, the key factor is the ability of the investor company to determine policy for the great majority of operating and financing decisions that are made by the investee company. This ability is generally associated with simple majority ownership of outstanding voting shares. It is this interpretation of control that is contained in the *CICA Handbook* which states:

> **Paragraph 1590.08** The level of equity interest in one enterprise held by another leads to a presumption regarding control. An enterprise is presumed to control another enterprise when it owns, directly or indirectly, an equity interest that carries the right to elect the majority of the members of the other enterprise's board of directors, and is presumed not to control the other enterprise without such ownership. In a particular situation, these presumptions may be overcome by other factors that clearly demonstrate that control exists or does not exist. The greater the difference in an enterprise's voting interest from the 50 percent level, the more persuasive these other factors must be in overcoming the applicable presumption.

2-65. While this statement clearly establishes voting share ownership as the primary measure of control, it leaves open the possibility of other measures being used. Two examples of such other measures are cited:

> **Paragraph 1590.13(a)** Ownership of less than the majority of voting shares combined with an irrevocable agreement with other owners to exercise voting rights may result in majority voting power and may, therefore, confer control.
>
> **Paragraph 1590.13(b)** Control may exist when an enterprise does not own the majority voting interest if it has the continuing ability to elect the majority of the members of the board of directors through ownership of rights, options, warrants, convertible debt, convertible non-voting equity such as preferred shares, or other similar instruments that, if converted or exercised, would give the enterprise the majority voting interest.

2-66. An investor may find situations where its use of the resources of the investee company are subject to certain restrictions. Examples of this would be debt covenants which restrict the investee company's ability to pay dividends, or regulatory restrictions which control the prices that can be charged by the investee company.

2-67. Such normal business restrictions do not preclude control by the investor and the classification of the investee as a subsidiary. However, in some cases the restrictions may involve a transfer of voting rights and this could result in the investor no longer being able to exercise control.

2-68. Section 1590 also notes that a brief interruption of the power to determine strategic policies is not a loss of control. An example of this would be the appointment of a receiver to seize a specific group of assets in order to satisfy a creditor claim.

2-69. Also noted is the fact that the investor company can have control without choosing to exercise it on a day to day basis. In addition, control can be exercised in situations where the investor has obligations related to the investee that exceed the investee's resources. None of these conditions would prevent the investor's holding from being classified as a subsidiary.

2-70. However, there are situations in which the restrictions on the investor company's ability to exercise its ownership rights are so severe that control can no longer be considered present. An example of this would be a foreign investee operating in a country which places severe restrictions on the repatriation of earnings. In such cases, the investment would not be classified as a subsidiary, despite the presence of majority ownership of voting shares.

Indirect Ownership

2-71. The preceding discussion of control dealt only with situations in which the investor company had direct ownership of the investee company's outstanding voting shares. However, an investor company can have indirect control of another company, even in situations where the investor company owns none of the shares of that company. Two examples of such indirect control are provided in Figure 2-2.

2-72. In Example 1, P owns 60 percent of A. This would give P control over A and make this company a subsidiary. In turn, A owns 55 percent of B, giving A control and making B a subsidiary of A. In addition, P's control of A gives P indirect control over B, making B a subsidiary of P as well as a subsidiary of A.

2-73. In Example 2, P controls both X and Y. Between them, these two companies own 70 percent of Z, giving them joint control over this company. Because P controls both X and Y, P has indirect control over Z. This means that Z, as well as X and Y are subsidiaries of P.

2-74. Both of the examples in Figure 2-2 would be referred to as multi-level affiliations. Even more complex relationships can develop if companies acquire shares of other companies that are above them in the chain of control. For example, Z might acquire some of the shares of X or P in Example 2. Shareholdings of this type are referred to as reciprocal shareholdings. The procedures to be used in dealing with both multi-level affiliations and reciprocal shareholdings are dealt with in Chapter 7, Advanced Topics In Consolidations.

2-75. A final point here relates to measurement based on indirect interests. Returning to Example 1, when we measure P's indirect interest in B, the resulting value will be based on the product of the ownership percentages. For example, P's interest in B's earnings is based on 33 percent [(60%)(55%)] of those earnings.

2-76. While such percentages must be used in measurement calculations, they have nothing to do with determining the existence of control. In general, control is based on majority ownership at each stage in the chain of ownership. The fact that an equitable

Figure 2-2
Examples Of Indirect Control

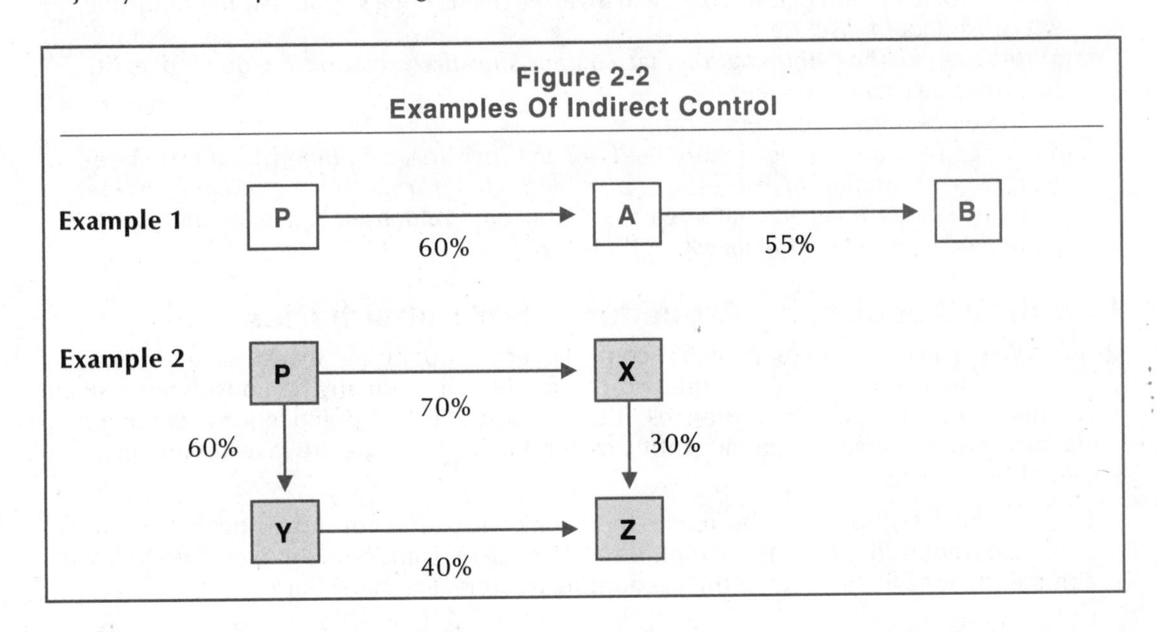

interest, as established by the product of the ownership percentages, is less than 50 percent has nothing to do with whether an indirect interest represents control.

Exercise Two-5

Subject: Indirect Ownership

Morton Ltd. owns 60 percent of the voting shares of Salt Inc. and 40 percent of the voting shares of Backy Inc. In addition, Salt Inc. owns 15 percent of the shares of Backy Inc. Briefly explain how Morton Ltd. should classify and account for its investments in Salt Inc. and Backy Inc.

End of Exercise. Solution available in Study Guide.

Disclosure

2-77. In the usual circumstances, control is identified by the presence of majority ownership of the voting shares of the investee. However, as we have noted in the preceding section, there is the possibility that control can be present without majority ownership, as well as the possibility that majority ownership will not provide control. As both of these situations are exceptions to a general rule, additional disclosure is required.

2-78. When control is present without the investor owning a majority of the investee's voting shares, the disclosure requirement is as follows:

Paragraph 1590.22 *When a reporting enterprise does not own, directly or indirectly through subsidiaries, an equity interest carrying the right to elect the majority of the members of the board of directors of a subsidiary, the reporting enterprise should disclose:*
(a) the basis for the determination that a parent-subsidiary relationship exists;
(b) the name of the subsidiary; and
(c) the percentage ownership (if any). (January, 1992)

2-79. Alternatively, when there is majority ownership and the investee is not classified as a subsidiary, the following disclosure is required.

Paragraph 1590.23 *When a reporting enterprise owns, directly or indirectly through subsidiaries, an equity interest carrying the right to elect the majority of the members of the board of directors of an investee that is not a subsidiary, the reporting enterprise should disclose:*
(a) the basis for the determination that a parent-subsidiary relationship does not exist;
(b) the name of the investee;
(c) the percentage ownership; and
(d) either separate financial statements of the investee, combined financial statements of similar investees or, provided all information significant to the consolidated financial statements is disclosed, condensed financial statements (including notes) of the investee. (January, 1992)

Required Accounting Procedures For Subsidiaries

2-80. When an investor company has control over the operating, investing, and financing activities of an investee company, the two companies can normally be considered a single economic entity. In such circumstances, it is a well established practice for accountants to concentrate on the single economic entity, rather than on the separate investor and investee legal entities.

2-81. As the definition of a subsidiary is based on control, it is not surprising that consolidation is the required accounting method. The *CICA Handbook* makes the following recommendation with respect to the accounting treatment of subsidiaries:

Paragraph 1590.16 *An enterprise should consolidate all of its subsidiaries.* (January, 1992)

2-82. This is a very restrictive rule which provides no flexibility with respect to the consolidation of investments that are classified as subsidiaries. This reflects the fact that, under earlier rules which were less rigid, it appeared that investor companies used the available flexibility to enhance their consolidated statements by excluding certain subsidiaries (e.g., subsidiaries with large debt loads).

Consolidation Described

2-83. Consolidation is an accounting method which accounts for the investor and investee companies as if they were a single entity, adding together all of the assets, liabilities, expenses and revenues of the two companies. However, these procedures always begin with the single entity accounting records of the two companies. Because of this, the procedures required to adjust various asset values and to eliminate the effects of the different intercompany transactions are quite complex. So complex that they are the subject matter of Chapters 4 through 7 of this text. Given this complexity, we will not attempt to illustrate consolidation procedures in this Chapter.

2-84. We would note, however, that when consolidation procedures are applied, the Investment In Subsidiary account on the books of the investor, will always be replaced by the subsidiary's individual assets and liabilities. This means that no Investment In Subsidiary account will be included in the consolidated financial statements presented by the investor company. As a result, investor companies use a variety of different methods to account for the investment account in their single entity records.

2-85. Since the investment account will not be disclosed in the consolidated financial statements, the method by which this balance will be accounted for in the single entity records of the investee company is not subject to GAAP recommendations. This means that the Investment In Subsidiary account can be accounted for by any method that the investor company chooses to use. In order to simplify our presentation, we will generally account for investments in subsidiaries using the cost method.

Variable Interest Entities

The Problem

2-86. While we have only provided you with a superficial description of consolidation procedures, this should be sufficient for you to understand that these procedures will result in any debt that is carried in the financial statements of subsidiaries being included in the Balance Sheet for the consolidated group of companies.

2-87. Because of this debt disclosure problem, there has always been management resistance to consolidating some subsidiaries. In particular, if a parent company had invested in subsidiaries that were highly leveraged, management could present a consolidated Balance Sheet with considerably less debt if these subsidiaries could be accounted for on a cost or equity basis, rather than being incorporated into the consolidated financial statements.

2-88. At one point in time, this was fairly easy to do. The *Handbook* contained a strange little provision which allowed management to exclude a subsidiary from consolidation by simply stating a belief that this was not the most informative disclosure. This provision is no longer available. Under current standards, all subsidiaries must be consolidated. There are no convenient loopholes for excluding a subsidiary for which the parent has voting control.

2-89. Unfortunately, this did not solve the problem. Lawyers and accountants worked diligently to find ways around the consolidation rules and, not surprisingly, they were extremely successful. Methods were developed that allowed companies to achieve effective control over a business entity with little or no holdings of voting shares.

2-90. These arrangements generally involved the use of some type of contractual arrangement that left de facto control of a business in the hands of a corporation that did not have legal control through ownership of voting shares. As these arrangements were not covered by then existing accounting standards, there was no requirement that they be included in the consolidated financial statements.

2-91. This situation formed the basis for a number of widely publicized financial disasters, the most notable of which was the Enron collapse. Enron, as well as a number of other major corporations, was able to make investments that involved responsibility for an enormous amount of debt, without disclosing these liabilities in their consolidated financial statements. As a consequence, the unexpected collapse of these organizations was viewed, at least to some extent, as a failure of accounting standards.

The Solution - Accounting Guideline No. 15

2-92. As an almost direct response to these problems, the FASB issued Interpretation No. 46, *Consolidation Of Variable Interest Entities*. Following the U.S. lead, the AcSB issued Accounting Guideline No. 15 (AcG-15), "Consolidation Of Variable Interest Entities" in June, 2003.

2-93. AcG-15 is an extremely technical document. To cover its content in a meaningful fashion would require adding a full additional Chapter to this text. In our opinion, this would not be appropriate. However, we believe that it is useful for you to be aware of the general issues that are involved.

2-94. The basic idea behind the concept of a variable interest entity is that it is structured in such a manner that its equity interest does not appear to be in a position to exercise control. This would be the case if:

- The total equity interest is not sufficient to permit the entity to finance its activities without additional financial support (the guideline here is 10 percent).
- The equity investors lack any of the usual rights associated with equity interest. These would be the right to make decisions about the entity's activities, the obligation to absorb the expected losses of the entity, and the right to receive the expected residual returns of the entity.

2-95. Once a variable entity has been identified, the next step is to determine its primary beneficiary. This requires a complex analysis of which party to the arrangement has the obligation to absorb expected losses, benefit from residual returns, and make decisions about the activities of the entity.

2-96. Once a primary beneficiary has been identified, this corporation must include the assets, liabilities, expenses, and revenues of the variable interest entity in its consolidated financial statements.

> CD-ROM Note If you have an interest in this subject, we would refer you to our *Guide to Canadian Financial Reporting* which is included on the CD-ROM that accompanies this text. The Appendix to Chapter 14 contains detailed coverage of AcG-15, "Consolidation Of Variable Interest Entities".

Significantly Influenced Companies

Definition

2-97. The major focus of Section 3051, "Investments", is identifying and accounting for investments in significantly influenced companies. Given this, it is somewhat surprising that the Section does not define significant influence. Fortunately, a definition of this concept can be found in IAS No. 28, "Investments In Associates". The definition is as follows:

> **Paragraph 28-2 Significant Influence** is the power to participate in the financial and operating policy decisions of the investee, but is not control or joint control over those policies.

> **Note** In IASB standards, the term associated company has the same meaning as significantly influenced company in AcSB standards.

2-98. In contrast to this definitional approach, Section 3051 leaves the determination of significant influence as a matter of professional judgment. It does, however, indicate some of the factors that should be considered in this determination. These include:

- representation on the board of directors;
- participation in policy-making processes;
- material intercompany transactions;
- interchange of managerial personnel; and
- provision of technical assistance.

2-99. In addition, Section 3051 provides a quantitative guideline for determining significant influence. In Paragraph 3051.05, the AcSB indicates that, if the investor holds less than 20 percent of the voting interest in the investee, it is presumed that the investor does not have the ability to exercise significant influence. Also noted is the idea that holding 20 percent or more of the voting interest in the investee does not, in itself, confirm the ability to exercise significant influence.

2-100. In view of the fact that the existence of significant influence is clearly something that must be determined through the application of judgment on a situation by situation basis, it seems unfortunate that any particular percentage of share ownership was even mentioned. There is no logical reason to believe that 20 percent will be more effective in the determination of significant influence than any other arbitrarily determined percentage of share ownership. Therefore, it is possible to make a case that the exercise of judgment would have received more encouragement had this 20 percent guideline been omitted.

2-101. In applying professional judgment, representation on the board of directors is probably the most reliable indicator of the ability of the investor corporation to exercise significant influence. If the investor company is able to elect one or more members to the investee's board, it would generally be clear that influence is present.

2-102. The ability to get this representation is a function of the percentage of shares owned and the number of positions on the board. It is also dependent on the type of voting that is used by the investee company. For example, assume an investor owns 10 percent of the shares and there are 10 directors on the board. If the investee corporation uses cumulative voting, the investor will be in a position to elect one director. If the investee corporation uses non-cumulative voting, a majority group of shareholders can, in fact, elect the director that will fill each of the ten positions.

Required Accounting Procedures

General Rules

2-103. Under existing Canadian GAAP, most Balance Sheet items are carried at cost. While this traditional approach to asset and liability measurement is still pervasive in the *CICA Handbook*, there is growing use of fair value measurement. This is evident in recent pronouncements on goodwill and other intangible assets, impairment of long-lived assets, and the measurement of financial instruments.

2-104. In choosing an accounting method to apply to significantly influenced companies, the AcSB rejected both cost and fair value as a basis for the measurement of these assets, choosing instead an accounting method that is not in general use for any other type of asset. This choice is reflected in the following recommendation:

> **Paragraph 3051.06** *An investor that is able to exercise significant influence over an investee that is not a subsidiary as defined in Section 1590, "Subsidiaries", a joint venture as defined in Section 3055, "Interests In Joint Ventures", or a variable interest entity consolidated in accordance with AcG-15, "Consolidation of Variable Interest Entities", should account for the investment by the equity method.* (January, 2004)

2-105. Given the pervasive use of either cost or fair value measurement for other asset balances, why did the AcSB choose the equity method? Support for this choice can be found in the *CICA Handbook* as follows:

Paragraph 3051.11 In those situations in which the investor has the ability to exercise significant influence, shareholders would be informed of the results of operations of the investee, and it is appropriate to include in the results of operations of the investor its share of the income or losses of the investee. The equity method of accounting for the investment provides this information.

2-106. The choice of the equity method can also be explained in terms of why it is inappropriate to use either cost or fair value for the measurement of significantly influenced companies:

Rejection Of Cost Method The problem with using the cost method for investments that are subject to significant influence by the investor is that, under this method, investment income is equal to the investor's share of dividends declared by the investee. As dividend policy is one of the factors that could be subject to influence by the investor, this would leave the investor in a position of being able to have some degree of control over the amount of investment income that will be recorded. The fact that this amount could be manipulated by the investor would suggest that use of the cost method in these situations is not appropriate.

Rejection Of Fair Value Measurement The *CICA Handbook* defines fair value as the amount of the consideration that would be agreed upon in an arm's length transaction between knowledgeable, willing parties who are under no compulsion to act. In the case of investments, fair value would often be based on day-to-day market prices for the investor's holdings. As these, in effect, represent liquidation values, they are probably not really representative of the value of the investments to a going concern. This would be particularly true in cases where the investment is part of a strategic plan. Given this consideration, the AcSB rejected the use of fair values for the general measurement of significantly influenced investees.

Equity Method

Defined

2-107. Section 3051 defines the equity method as follows:

Paragraph 3051.03(a) The **equity method** is a basis of accounting for investments whereby the investment is initially recorded at cost and the carrying value, adjusted thereafter to include the investor's pro rata share of post-acquisition earnings of the investee, computed by the consolidation method. The amount of the adjustment is included in the determination of net income by the investor, and the investment account of the investor is also increased or decreased to reflect the investor's share of capital transactions (including amounts recognized in other comprehensive income) and changes in accounting policies and corrections of errors relating to prior period financial statements applicable to post-acquisition periods. Profit distributions received or receivable from an investee reduce the carrying value of the investment.

2-108. Ignoring for the moment special disclosure requirements and the need for consolidation adjustments, we can describe the equity method either in terms of the value of the investment asset, or in terms of the investment income value. These descriptions would be as follows:

Investment (Asset) Value The investment account is initially recorded at cost. In each subsequent accounting period, it is adjusted up or down to reflect the investor company's share of the change in Retained Earnings of the investee company. This adjustment could also be described as a two stage process in which the investment account is increased (decreased) for the investor's share of the investee's Net Income (Net Loss) and reduced for the investor's share of the investee's dividends declared.

Investment Income Investment Income under the equity method is simply the investor company's share of the reported Net Income of the investee company.

Example - Basic Procedures

2-109. The example that follows involves no fair value changes, goodwill, or intercompany transactions. It will serve to illustrate the basic procedures associated with the equity method.

Example On December 31, 2006, the Stor Company purchases 30 percent of the outstanding voting shares of the Stee Company for $6 million in cash. Stor's 30 percent share ownership gives the Company significant influence over the operations of Stee. On this date, the carrying value of the net identifiable assets of the Stee Company total $20 million. All of the Stee Company's assets and liabilities have fair values that are equal to their carrying values. There are no intercompany transactions other than dividend payments during the three years subsequent to December 31, 2006. Dividends are declared on November 1 of each year and paid on December 1 of the same year.

Both companies have a year end of December 31. The Stee Company's Net Income and Dividends Declared and Paid for each of the three years are as follows:

Year	Net Income	Dividends Declared And Paid
2007	$2,000,000	$1,500,000
2008	500,000	1,500,000
2009	3,500,000	1,700,000
Totals	$6,000,000	$4,700,000

The Net Income of the Stee Company does not include any extraordinary items, results of discontinued operations, accounting changes, or capital transactions in any of the years under consideration. In terms of bookkeeping procedures used, Stor records the Stee dividends when received and adjusts accounts for its share of Stee's Net Income at the December 31 year end.

2-110. The journal entries for the Stor Company for the years 2006 through 2009 would be as follows:

December 31, 2006

Investment In Stee	$6,000,000	
Cash		$6,000,000

December 1, 2007

Cash	$450,000	
Investment In Stee		$450,000

(To record the receipt of 30 percent of the Stee Company's $1,500,000 of dividends declared as a reduction in Stor's equity interest in Stee.)

December 31, 2007

Investment In Stee	$600,000	
Investment Income		$600,000

(To record Stor's 30 percent share of Stee's $2,000,000 Net Income as an increase in Stor's equity interest in Stee and as investment income.)

December 1, 2008

Cash	$450,000	
Investment In Stee		$450,000

(To record the receipt of 30 percent of the Stee Company's $1,500,000 of dividends declared as a reduction in Stor's equity interest in Stee.)

December 31, 2008

Investment In Stee	$150,000	
Investment Income		$150,000

(To record Stor's 30 percent share of Stee's $500,000 Net Income as an increase in Stor's equity interest in Stee and as investment income.)

December 1, 2009

Cash	$510,000	
Investment In Stee		$510,000

(To record the receipt of 30 percent of the Stee Company's $1,700,000 of dividends declared as a reduction in Stor's equity interest in Stee.)

December 31, 2009

Investment In Stee	$1,050,000	
Investment Income		$1,050,000

(To record Stor's 30 percent share of Stee's $3,500,000 Net Income as an increase in Stor's equity interest in Stee and as investment income.) Note that the increase in the Investment in Stee account of $390,000 (-$450,000 + $600,000 - $450,000 + $150,000 - $510,000 + $1,050,000) is equal to 30 percent of the $1,300,000 ($6,000,000 - $4,700,000) increase in Stee's Retained Earnings since acquisition.

Exercise Two-6

Subject: Equity Method (See also Exercise Two-10)

On January 1, 2007, Plastor Inc. acquires 20 percent of the outstanding voting shares of Plastee Inc. for $300,000 in cash, a price that was equal to 20 percent of Plastee's net assets. The investment gives Plastor significant influence over Plastee.

During the year ending December 31, 2007, Plastee had Net Income of $150,000 and paid dividends of $100,000. In the year ending December 31, 2008, the Company had a net loss of $40,000 and paid dividends of $50,000. For the year ending December 31, 2009, Plastee's Net Income was $90,000 and it paid dividends of $80,000.

Provide Plastor's journal entries related to its Investment In Plastee for the three years ending December 31, 2007, 2008, and 2009 and calculate the balance in the Investment in Plastee account as at December 31, 2009.

End Of Exercise. Solution available in Study Guide.

Intra Statement Disclosure

2-111. Section 3051 requires that certain types of items that are included in the financial statements of the investee must be given separate disclosure, outside of the Investment Income total, in the financial statements of the investor. This recommendation is as follows:

> **Paragraph 3051.09** *In accounting for an investment by the equity method, the investor's proportionate share of the investee's discontinued operations, extraordinary items, changes in accounting policy, corrections of errors relating to prior period financial statements and capital transactions (including amounts recognized in other comprehensive income) should be presented and disclosed in the investor's financial statements according to their nature.* (April, 1996)

2-112. For certain types of items that may be included in the investee's separate financial statements, this recommendation requires the following special disclosures in the financial statements of the investor:

- Results of discontinued operations and extraordinary items must be shown in the investor's Statement Of Net Income as separate line items after Income Or Loss Before Discontinued Operations And Extraordinary Items.

- Adjustments resulting from investee accounting policy changes or accounting errors must be disclosed in the investor's Statement Of Retained Earnings.
- Investee capital transactions will be part of the investor's disclosure of changes in Shareholder's Equity.
- Items of Comprehensive Income recognized by the investee must be disclosed in the investor's Statement Of Comprehensive Income.

Example - Intra Statement Disclosure

2-113. The following example will illustrate the Paragraph 3051.09 recommendation with respect to the treatment of investee extraordinary items.

Example On December 31, 2007, Nador Ltd. purchases 30 percent of the outstanding voting shares of Nadee Inc. for $6 million in cash. Nador's 30 percent share ownership gives it significant influence over the operations of Nadee. On this date, the carrying value of the net identifiable assets of Nadee Inc. total $20 million. All of Nadee's identifiable assets and liabilities have fair values that are equal to their carrying values.

For the year ending December 31, 2008, the Income Statements of the two Companies were as follows (Nador's Statement does not include Nadee's 2008 results):

	Nador Ltd.	Nadee Inc.
Sales	$3,500,000	$750,000
Expenses	3,000,000	550,000
Income Before Extraordinary Items	$ 500,000	$200,000
Extraordinary Loss	Nil	(80,000)
Net Income	$ 500,000	$120,000

There are no intercompany transactions between Nador Ltd. and Nadee Inc. during 2008.

2-114. Nador Ltd.'s Income Statement for the year ending December 31, 2008, would be as follows:

Nador Ltd.
Income Statement
Year Ending December 31, 2008

Sales	$3,500,000
Ordinary Investment Income [(30%)($200,000)]	60,000
Total Revenues	$3,560,000
Expenses	3,000,000
Income Before Extraordinary Items	$ 560,000
Extraordinary Investment Loss [(30%)($80,000)]	(24,000)
Net Income	$ 536,000

2-115. As can be seen in the preceding Income Statement, the investee's extraordinary item would be disclosed as an extraordinary item in the Income Statement of the investor enterprise. This would be true even if some or all of the items were ordinary transactions from the point of view of the investor company. This is because they remain extraordinary transactions from the point of view of the investee and the related investment income.

Exercise Two-7

Subject: Equity Method Disclosure

On January 1, 2007, Clearly Inc. acquires 25 percent of the outstanding shares of Muddle Ltd. The consideration for the investment was $2 million in cash, plus Clearly Inc. shares with a fair market value of $500,000. At the time of this investment, the net book value of Muddle Ltd. was $10 million and all of the company's assets and liabilities had fair values that were equal to their carrying values. The investment gives Clearly significant influence over Muddle.

Both companies have a December 31 year end. During the year ending December 31, 2007, Muddle Ltd. has Net Income of $20,000 and pays no dividends.

During the year ending December 31, 2008, Muddle Ltd. has Income Before Discontinued Operations of $346,000. However, a loss on discontinued operations reduces Net Income to $46,000. Based on its recent history of profits, Muddle declares and pays dividends which total $103,000 during the year ending December 31, 2008.

Provide the journal entry that would be required on Clearly's books to account for its Investment In Muddle for the year ending December 31, 2008.

End of Exercise. Solution available in Study Guide.

EIC Abstract No. 8 - Losses Exceed Equity Investment Balance

2-116. A problem that can arise in the application of the equity method involves situations where the application of this method results in a credit balance for an investment.

Example On January 1, 2007, Duster Ltd. acquires 35 percent of the outstanding voting shares of Dustee Ltd. for $3,500,000 in cash. At the time of this acquisition, the net book value of Dustee Ltd. was $50 million. Duster Ltd. was able to acquire these shares at this price because it was anticipated that Dustee Ltd. was going to experience severe losses during the next two years. This expectation appears to be correct in that Dustee Ltd.'s loss for the year ending December 31, 2007 is $12 million.

2-117. Under the usual equity method procedures, the journal entry to reflect this result would be as follows:

Investment Loss [(35%)($12,000,000)]	$4,200,000	
Investment In Dustee		$4,200,000

2-118. The problem here is that this entry would create a credit balance of $700,000 ($4,200,000 - $3,500,000) in the Investment In Dustee account and this balance would have to be reported as a liability. Since equity investments in corporations are generally protected by limited liability, the recording of a liability in this situation would not be appropriate in normal circumstances. As a consequence, an investor company would usually stop recording further equity method losses when the related asset balance reaches nil.

2-119. However, the Emerging Issues Committee (EIC) was asked if there were any circumstances in which it would be appropriate to continue recording losses after an equity investment balance reached nil. Their response is reflected in EIC Abstract No. 8, "Recognition Of An Equity Accounted Investee's Losses In Excess Of The Investment", in which they indicate that continuing to record such losses would be appropriate if the investor was likely to share in them. In their view, this would be the case if any of the following conditions are present:

- the investor has guaranteed obligations of the investee; or
- the investor is otherwise committed to provide further financial support for the investee; or
- the investee seems assured of imminently returning to profitability.

2-120. The other issue dealt with in this EIC Abstract was the question of what disclosure should be provided in those cases where the investor does not continue to record equity method losses. In general, the EIC indicated that the information to be disclosed would be a matter of professional judgment, but could include:

- disclosure of unrecognized losses for the period and accumulated to date; and
- the investor's accounting policies with respect to the investment, including the policy to be followed should the investee return to profitability.

2-121. The EIC also indicated that, when losses have not been recorded on an investee that later returns to profitability, the investor should resume recognizing its share of those profits only after its share of the profits equals its share of the losses not recognized.

Exercise Two-8

Subject: EIC Abstract No. 8

On January 1, 2007, Ausser Ltd. acquires 40 percent of the outstanding voting shares of Aussee Inc. for $400,000. Ausser accounts for its Investment In Aussee using the equity method. Ausser has no commitments to provide any type of financial support for Aussee in subsequent fiscal periods.

During the year ending December 31, 2007, Aussee experiences a Net Loss of $1,500,000. During the year ending December 31, 2008, Aussee has Net Income of $800,000. No dividends were paid in either year.

Provide the journal entries to record Ausser's Investment Income (Loss) for the years ending December 31, 2007 and December 31, 2008 and calculate the balance in the Investment in Aussee account as at December 31, 2008.

End of Exercise. Solution available in Study Guide.

Loss Of Significant Influence

2-122. Over time, an investor may lose the ability to exercise significant influence over an investee. This could result from the sale of a portion of the investor's holding of voting shares, from changes in the ownership of other blocks of voting shares, or from changes in the economic relationship between the investor and the investee. Alternatively, an investor could move from having only significant influence to a situation where he has unilateral or joint control. Both of these possibilities are covered in the following recommendation:

Paragraph 3051.07 *When an investor ceases to be able to exercise significant influence over an investee, the investment should be accounted for in accordance with "Financial Instruments — Recognition And Measurement", Section 3855, unless the investor has obtained control or joint control, in which case the investor applies "Subsidiaries", Section 1590, "Interests In Joint Ventures", Section 3055, or AcG-15, "Consolidation of Variable Interest Entities", as appropriate.* (October, 2006)

2-123. In those cases where the investor moves from having significant influence to having control, consolidation will be required.

Example Tazer Ltd. has owned 40 percent of the outstanding voting shares of Tazee Inc. for several years. As Tazer has had significant influence during this period, Tazer has accounted for its investment in Tazee using the equity method. At the beginning of the current year, Tazer Ltd. acquires an additional 20 percent of the voting shares.

Analysis At this point, Tazer Ltd. has gained control over Tazee Inc. As control was acquired through multiple acquisition transactions, this would be a step-by-step purchase. The procedures for preparing consolidated financial statements in this type of situation are found in Section 1600 of the *CICA Handbook*. Our coverage of these rules is found in Chapters 5 and 6.

2-124. The other possibility that is contemplated in Paragraph 3051.07 is that the investor will move from having significant influence to having no influence. If the investment is a financial asset or a non-financial derivative, Section 3855 will apply. Under Section 3855, the accounting procedures to be used will be determined by how the investment is classified (e.g., available for sale vs. held for trading).

2-125. An issue that arises in this situation is what value should be used as the cost of the investment. This issue arises because the investment has been accounted for by the equity method and, given this, it is unlikely that it is being carried at its original cost. One solution to this problem would be a retroactive approach which restores the investment to its original cost.

2-126. However, the AcSB has rejected this approach. Paragraph 3051.16 indicates that, when an investor ceases to be able to exercise significant influence, cost is deemed to be the carrying value of the investment at the time that influence is lost.

Example On January 1, 2005, Zador Ltd. acquires, for $250,000 in cash, 25 percent of the outstanding voting shares of Zadee Inc., an investment that gives Zador significant influence over the affairs of Zadee. At this time, the net assets of Zadee had a carrying value of $1,000,000. All of the individual assets and liabilities had fair values equal to their carrying value.

During the period January 1, 2005 through December 31, 2007, Zadee had total Net Income of $240,000 and paid dividends of $90,000. Other than the dividend payments, there were no transactions between Zador and Zadee during this period.

On January 1, 2008, Zador sells 80 percent of its holding of Zadee shares for $275,000. At this point, Zador is no longer able to influence the affairs of Zadee.

Analysis The January 1, 2008 carrying value of Zador's investment in Zadee is $287,500 [$250,000 + (25%)($240,000 - $90,000)]. The sale of 80 percent of the shares for $275,000 will result in a gain of $45,000 [$275,000 - (80%)($287,500)].

This will leave an investment with a carrying value of $57,500 [(20%)($287,500)]. Under Paragraph 3051.16, this will be deemed to be the cost of the remaining investment.

As equity securities are viewed as financial assets, the remaining investment will fall within the scope of Section 3855. Under the provisions of that Section, the investment will be classified as held for trading or available for sale and accounted for at fair value in subsequent accounting periods.

Different Fiscal Periods

2-127. It would not be uncommon for a significantly influenced investee to have a fiscal period that is different from the fiscal period of the investor. While it would be possible for the investor to make an estimate of the investee's earnings for the period that coincides with their fiscal period, it is not a procedure that is required by the *CICA Handbook*. However, when the investor/investee fiscal periods do not coincide, additional disclosure is required as follows:

Paragraph 3051.10 *When the fiscal periods of an investor and an investee, the investment in which is accounted for by the equity method, are not coterminous, events relating to, or transactions of, the investee that have occurred during the intervening period and significantly affect the financial position or results of operations of the investor should be recorded or disclosed, as appropriate.* (August, 1978)

Consolidation Adjustments

2-128. With respect to the calculation of the investment income resulting from holding an investment in a significantly influenced company, Section 3051 makes the following recommendation:

Paragraph 3051.08 *Investment income as calculated by the equity method should be the amount necessary to increase or decrease the investor's income to that which would have been recognized if the results of the investee's operations had been consolidated with those of the investor.* (August, 1978)

2-129. The preparation of consolidated statements requires a number of adjustments to the single entity statements of the parent and subsidiary before the balances can be combined. In somewhat simplified terms, these are:

1. The elimination of intercompany expenses and revenues (e.g., intercompany sales and purchases).
2. The elimination of intercompany assets and liabilities (e.g., intercompany payables and receivables).
3. Amortization of fair value changes that were recognized when the subsidiary was acquired (the acquisition of a subsidiary is a business combination transaction). In some cases it will also be necessary to adjust for impairment of any goodwill that was recognized at the acquisition date.
4. The elimination of unrealized intercompany profits.

2-130. With respect to the first two items, they will have no influence on the determination of investment income under the equity method. They simply involve eliminating equal amounts of the relevant balances, and do not alter income or net asset values. As the equity method does not include investee expenses, revenues, assets, or liabilities in the financial statements of the investor, changes to these totals do not influence their presentation.

2-131. This is not the case with the last two items. Both the amortization of fair value changes and the elimination of intercompany profits change consolidated Net Income and, as a consequence, will influence the calculation of investment income under the equity method.

2-132. It is our opinion that discussion of these adjustments is not meaningful until you have a more complete understanding of consolidation procedures. As a consequence, we will continue our discussion of the equity method in both Chapter 5 (adjustments for fair value changes and goodwill impairment) and Chapter 6 (adjustments for unrealized intercompany profits).

Disclosure For Significantly Influenced Companies

2-133. Section 3051 contains several recommendations with respect to the disclosure of investments. They are as follows:

Paragraph 3051.25 *The basis of valuation of investments should be disclosed.* (January, 1973)

Paragraph 3051.26 *Investments in companies subject to significant influence, other affiliated companies and other investments should each be shown separately.* (January, 1992)

Paragraph 3051.27 *Income from investments in companies subject to significant influence, other affiliated companies and other investments should each be shown separately. Income calculated by the equity method should be disclosed separately.* (January, 1992)

Paragraph 3051.28 *When investments are accounted for by the equity method, disclosure should be made, in the notes to the financial statements, of the amount of any difference between the cost and the underlying net book value of the investee's assets at the date of purchase, as well as the accounting treatment of the components of such difference.* (January, 1973)

2-134. In addition to these specific requirements, Section 3051 makes several suggestions for additional information:

- When significantly influenced investees are important in the evaluation of enterprise performance, summarized information as to their assets, liabilities, and results of operations may be relevant.
- Disclosure of the investor's proportionate interest in the investees, as well as any contingent issuance of securities by an investee that might affect the investor's share of earnings, may be appropriate.
- Investments reported in the Balance Sheet and investment income reported in the Income Statement should be grouped in the same manner. This will assist users in understanding the relationship between reported income from investments and its source.
- Return on an investment includes both income flows and increases in its value. Given this, information additional to the carrying value of investments, for example, quoted market values, may be useful.

Joint Ventures

Definition

2-135. Section 3055 of the *CICA Handbook* defines a joint venture arrangement as follows:

> **Paragraph 3055.03(c)** A **joint venture** is an economic activity resulting from a contractual arrangement whereby two or more venturers jointly control the economic activity.

2-136. In order to understand this definition, a further definition is required:

> **Paragraph 3055.03(b)** **Joint control** of an economic activity is the contractually agreed sharing of the continuing power to determine its strategic operating, investing and financing policies.

2-137. The basic idea here is that control of the investee is shared by two or more investors. This means that, for an investee to be classified by an investor as a joint venture:

- that investor must participate in control of the investee; and
- no single investor can have unilateral control.

2-138. These concepts will be discussed more fully in Chapter 8 of this text.

Required Accounting Procedures For Joint Ventures

2-139. Section 3055 requires that joint ventures be accounted for using proportionate consolidation. The relevant recommendation is as follows:

> **Paragraph 3055.17** *Interests in joint ventures should be recognized in the financial statements of the venturer using the proportionate consolidation method.* (January, 1995)

2-140. Section 3055 does not contain any exceptions to this rule. We would note, however, that IAS No. 31, *Interests In Joint Ventures*, takes a different approach. This international standard allows enterprises to use either the equity method or proportionate consolidation to account for joint ventures. However, many analysts believe that the IASB will eventually reject the use of proportionate consolidation for this type of investment.

Proportionate Consolidation Described

2-141. Like full consolidation, proportionate consolidation adds together the assets, liabilities, expenses, and revenues of the investor and investee companies. The difference is that in full consolidation, 100 percent of the investee's financial statement items are added to those of the investor company, even in cases where ownership is less than 100 percent.

2-142. In contrast, proportionate consolidation, as its name implies, only adds in the investor's share of the investee assets, liabilities, expenses, and revenues. This reflects the view that, unlike the situation with subsidiaries, the investor company does not have full control over the investee. Control only extends to the investor's proportionate interest in the investee.

2-143. As is the case with full consolidation, the proportionate consolidation method does not lend itself to a brief, overview treatment. This method will, however, be given detailed treatment in Chapter 8 of this text.

Accounting Methods Summarized

2-144. The conclusions reached in Sections 1590, 3051, 3055, and 3855 on the appropriate accounting methods to be used for each classification of investments in equity securities is summarized in Figure 2-3.

Figure 2-3
Summary Of Accounting Methods For Investments In Equity Securities

Investment Classification	Accounting Method
Held For Trading	Fair Value Method - Changes In Net Income
Available For Sale:	
No Quoted Market Price	Cost Method
Quoted Market Price	Fair Value Method - Changes In Comprehensive Income
Significantly Influenced Companies	Equity Method
Joint Ventures	Proportionate Consolidation
Subsidiaries	Full Consolidation

2-145. It is interesting to note that a different method is used for each classification of investments in equity securities. This, of course, creates a fairly complex set of rules for dealing with these investments.

2-146. Given this situation, we would anticipate some simplification as international convergence progresses. Specifically, we are fairly confident that proportionate consolidation will disappear, with the equity method being prescribed for investments in joint ventures. There is also some possibility that enterprises will be given the option of using a fair value approach for significantly influenced companies.

Impairment

Significantly Influenced Companies

General Rules

2-147. Section 3051 recognizes that investments in significantly influenced companies may sometimes experience a loss in value that is unlikely to be reversed. To deal with such situations, it makes the following recommendation:

> **Paragraph 3051.18** *When there has been a loss in value of an investment that is other than a temporary decline, the investment should be written down to recognize the loss. The write-down should be included in the determination of net income and may or may not be an extraordinary item (see Section 3480, "Extraordinary Items").* (January, 1973)

2-148. Given the scope of Section 3051, it would appear that the application of this recommendation is limited to investments in significantly influenced investees and investments in non-financial assets. It would not apply to investments in subsidiaries, joint ventures, or variable interest entities. In addition, it would not be applicable to investments in financial assets that fall within the scope of Section 3855, rather than Section 3051.

2-149. In some cases the application of this recommendation will be fairly easy. If an investee is in bankruptcy, Paragraph 3051.18 is clearly applicable. Similarly, if the investor has agreed to sell its investment at a price that is less than the carrying value of the investment, there would be little question as to the need to reduce the carrying value of the investment.

2-150. However, the application of this provision would not be limited to the obvious applications as described in the preceding paragraph. A write-down could be appropriate if one or more of the following conditions was present:

- There was a prolonged period during which the quoted market value of the investment is less than its carrying value.
- The investee experienced severe losses in the current year or current and prior years.
- The investee experienced continued losses for a period of years.
- There was a suspension of trading in the securities.
- The investee experienced liquidity or going concern problems.
- The current fair value of the investment is less than its carrying value.

2-151. The application of these less objective criteria would, of course, involve the application of professional judgment.

Subsequent Recoveries

2-152. There are situations where an investment is written down to recognize a loss in value and, at a later point in time, the previously recognized loss is reversed. To deal with such cases, Section 3051 makes the following recommendation:

> **Paragraph 3051.19** *A write-down of an investment to reflect a loss in value should not be reversed if there is a subsequent increase in value.* (August, 1978)

2-153. From our point of view, it is difficult to understand why the same kind of evidence that was used to support the write-down of an investment could not be used to support the reversal of such a write-down. However, the approach taken here is consistent with the manner in which write-downs are dealt with for property, plant, and equipment under Section 3063, "Impairment Of Long-Lived Assets", and goodwill and other intangible assets under Section 3062, "Goodwill And Other Intangible Assets".

Other Classifications Of Investments

2-154. With respect to impairment of other classifications of investments in equity securities, our analysis is as follows:

> **Held-For-Trading Investments** These investments are carried at fair value, a measurement that would automatically pick up changes in fair value.
>
> **Available-For-Sale Investments At Fair Value** While these investments are also carried at fair value, the changes are generally included in Comprehensive Income. If impairment of these assets occurs, Paragraph 3855.A73 requires that the cumulative loss that has been recognized in Comprehensive Income be transferred to Net Income.
>
> **Available-For-Sale Investments At Cost** It would appear that these investments are subject to the same rules as significantly influenced companies.
>
> **Subsidiaries And Joint Ventures** There are no specific impairment provisions related to these investments. This likely reflects the fact that the assets and liabilities of the investee would be included in the required consolidated financial statements. Given this, these assets would be subject to the impairment provisions of the *CICA Handbook* related to specific types of assets (e.g., Section 3063 deals with the impairment of property, plant, and equipment).

Gains And Losses On The Sale Of Equity Investments

2-155. An investment in equity securities may consist of a group of identical securities which have been acquired at different points in time and, as a consequence, at different prices. When part of such a group is disposed of, some assumption must be made as to the flow of costs to be allocated to the sale. While there are a number of cost flow assumptions that could be used here, the *CICA Handbook* takes the position that average cost best reflects the gain or loss that would be recognized if the entire investment were disposed of:

> **Paragraph 3051.23** *For the purposes of calculating a gain or loss on the sale of an investment, the cost of the investment sold should be calculated on the basis of the average carrying value.* (January, 1973)

2-156. Note that this recommendation is only applicable to investments in equity securities that are covered by Section 3051, namely investments in significantly influenced companies. These would normally be carried by the equity method. However, as will be noted in the section which follows, there is a differential reporting option that allows such investments to be carried at cost.

2-157. We would also note that this recommendation is consistent with the required income tax treatment of gains and losses on identical properties (See Section 47 of the *Income Tax Act*).

Differential Reporting For Investments In Equity Securities

Qualifying Enterprises

2-158. In January, 2002, Section 1300, "Differential Reporting", was added to the *CICA Handbook*. Section 1300 provides qualifying enterprises with alternative differential reporting options for a group of specified *Handbook* recommendations. A qualifying enterprise is defined as follows:

> **Paragraph 1300.06** *An enterprise is a qualifying enterprise for purposes of the differential reporting options set out in an Accounting Recommendation, Accounting Guideline or Abstract of Issue Discussed by the Emerging Issues Committee when and only when:*
>
> *(a) it is a non-publicly accountable enterprise; and*
> *(b) its owners unanimously consent to the application of differential reporting options in accordance with paragraph 1300.13.* (January, 2002)

Held-For-Trading And Available-For-Sale Investments

2-159. There is no differential reporting option for held-for-trading investments. There is, however, an option for available-for-sale financial assets:

> **Paragraph 3855.86** *After initial recognition, an entity that qualifies under "Differential Reporting", Section 1300, may elect to measure available-for-sale financial assets that would otherwise be measured at fair value in accordance with paragraph 3855.66,* [**Byrd/Chen Note** See our Paragraph 2-30] *other than:*
>
> *(a) financial assets that have a quoted market price in an active market; and*
> *(b) financial assets that are designated and effective hedging instruments (see "Hedges", Section 3865);*
>
> *at cost or amortized cost.* (October, 2006).

2-160. This has no relevance for investments in equity securities because it does not cover available-for-sale investments that have a quoted market value. As we have noted earlier, when available-for-sale investments in equity securities do not have a quoted market value, they can be carried at cost by any enterprise, without regard to whether it qualifies for differential reporting.

Subsidiaries

General Recommendation

2-161. With respect to subsidiaries, Section 1590 includes the following differential reporting option:

> **Paragraph 1590.26** *An enterprise that qualifies under "Differential Reporting", Section 1300, may elect to use either the equity method or the cost method to account for subsidiaries that would otherwise be consolidated in accordance with paragraph 1590.16. All subsidiaries should be accounted for using the same method.* (January, 2002)

Other Requirements

2-162. When qualifying enterprises use this option, several other recommendations are applicable:

> **Paragraph 1590.27** *A loss in value of an investment in a non-consolidated subsidiary that is other than a temporary decline should be accounted for in accordance with the requirements of "Investments", paragraphs 3051.18-.22.* (January, 2002)
>
> **Paragraph 1590.28** *When an enterprise applies one of the alternative methods permitted by paragraph 1590.26, the financial statements should be described as being prepared on a non-consolidated basis and each statement should be labeled accordingly.* (January, 2002)
>
> **Paragraph 1590.29** *Investments in non-consolidated subsidiaries should be presented separately in the balance sheet. Income or loss from those investments should be presented separately in the income statement.* (January, 2002)
>
> **Paragraph 1590.30** *An enterprise that has applied one of the alternative methods permitted by paragraph 1590.26 should disclose:*
>
> *(a) the basis used to account for subsidiaries; and*
> *(b) the particulars of any shares or other securities issued by the enterprise that are owned by non-consolidated subsidiaries.* (January, 2002)

2-163. It is also noted that when subsidiaries are not consolidated, Section 3840, "Related Party Transactions", applies to those intercompany transactions that would have been eliminated on consolidation.

Significantly Influenced Companies

General Recommendation

2-164. Section 3051 contains the following differential reporting option for significantly influenced companies:

> **Paragraph 3051.32** *An enterprise that qualifies under "Differential Reporting", Section 1300, may elect to use the cost method to account for its investments in companies subject to significant influence that would otherwise be accounted for by the equity method in accordance with paragraph 3051.06. All investments in companies subject to significant influence should be accounted for using the same method.* (January, 2002)

Other Requirements

2-165. When this differential reporting option is used, Section 3051 contains two additional disclosure recommendations:

Paragraph 3051.33 *Investments in companies subject to significant influence accounted for using the cost method should be presented separately on the balance sheet. Income from those investments should be presented separately in the income statement.* (January, 2002)

Paragraph 3051.41 *An enterprise that has applied the alternative method permitted by paragraph 3051.32 should disclose the basis of accounting used to account for investments in companies subject to significant influence.* (January, 2002)

Exercise Two-9

Subject: Average Cost

Salson Inc. is a qualifying enterprise as defined in Section 1300 of the *CICA Handbook*, "Differential Reporting". With respect to its investments in equity securities, it has elected to carry its investments in significantly influenced companies using the cost method.

During the year ending December 31, 2007, Salson makes purchases of Tofal Ltd. shares that are sufficient to give Salson significant influence over the affairs of Tofal. These purchases are as follows:

	Number Of Shares	Total Cost
1st Purchase	2,400	$27,600
2nd Purchase	3,450	42,600
3rd Purchase	1,740	22,450
4th Purchase	4,360	72,400

Early in 2008, Salson Inc. sells 5,250 of its Tofal Ltd. shares at a price of $28 per share.

Determine the gain or loss that would be recorded by Salson Inc. on its sale of Tofal Ltd. shares.

Exercise Two-10

Subject: Cost Method Under Differential Reporting (See also Exercise Two-6)

On January 1, 2007, Plastor Inc. acquires 20 percent of the outstanding voting shares of Plastee Inc. for $300,000 in cash, a price that was equal to 20 percent of Plastee's net assets. The investment gives Plastor significant influence over Plastee. Plastor Inc. is a qualifying enterprise as defined in Section 1300 of the *CICA Handbook*, "Differential Reporting". With respect to its investments in equity securities, it has elected to carry its investments in significantly influenced companies using the cost method.

During the year ending December 31, 2007, Plastee had Net Income of $150,000 and paid dividends of $100,000. In the year ending December 31, 2008, Plastee had a net loss of $40,000 and paid dividends of $50,000. For the year ending December 31, 2009, Plastee's Net Income was $90,000 and it paid dividends of $80,000.

Provide Plastor's journal entries related to its Investment In Plastee for the three years ending December 31, 2007, 2008, and 2009 and calculate the balance in the Investment in Plastee account as at December 31, 2009.

End of Exercises. Solutions available in Study Guide.

Joint Ventures

General Recommendation

2-166. A differential reporting option is also provided in Section 3055 with respect to accounting for joint ventures:

> **Paragraph 3055.47** *An enterprise that qualifies under "Differential Reporting", Section 1300, may elect to use either the equity method or the cost method to account for its interests in joint ventures that would otherwise be accounted for using the proportionate consolidation method in accordance with paragraph 3055.17. All interests in joint ventures should be accounted for using the same method.* (January, 2002)

Other Requirements

2-167. Here again, when an alternative method is used, additional disclosure is required as follows:

> **Paragraph 3055.48** A loss in value of an interest in a joint venture not proportionately consolidated that is other than a temporary decline should be accounted for in accordance with the requirements of "Investments", paragraphs 3051.18-.22. (January, 2002)

> **Paragraph 3055.49** *Interests in joint ventures not proportionately consolidated should be presented separately in the balance sheet. Income or loss from those interests should be presented separately in the income statement.* (January, 2002)

> **Paragraph 3055.50** *An enterprise that has applied one of the alternative methods permitted by paragraph 3055.47 should disclose the basis used to account for interests in joint ventures.* (January, 2002)

2-168. Note that these are basically the same recommendations that apply when the differential reporting options are used to exclude subsidiaries from the consolidated financial statements. Also noted here is that the recommendations of Section 3840, "Related Party Transactions" are applicable to the intercompany transactions that would have been eliminated in the preparation of proportionately consolidated financial statements.

International Convergence

Held-For-Trading And Available-For-Sale Investments

Standards

2-169. The Canadian rules for these investments in equity securities are found in Section 3855, "Financial Instruments - Recognition And Measurement". The corresponding international standard is IAS No. 39, *Financial Instruments: Recognition And Measurement*.

Differences

2-170. With respect to investments in equity securities, the differences are as follows:

- IAS No. 39 uses the term "financial asset or financial liability at fair value through profit or loss" instead of "held for trading". While this term is more accurate, it does not exactly roll off the tongue.
- IAS No. 39 only allows investments that are not held for trading to be designated as such only under very limited circumstances. Section 3855 allows such designation without restrictions.
- IAS No. 39 requires available-for-sale investments to be measured at fair value unless that amount is not "readily determinable". Section 3855 allows the cost method when there is no "quoted market value". IAS No. 39 is different in that a fair value may be "readily determinable" when no "quoted market value" exists.

- IAS No. 39 does not provide an optional treatment for transaction costs. If the investment is measured at fair value with changes through income, these costs are charged to income. For other investments, these costs must be added to the amount initially recognized. In the case of available-for-sale assets, Section 3855 allows either treatment.
- IAS No. 39 requires the reversal of impairment costs if there is a recovery in value. This is neither required nor permitted under Section 3855.

Subsidiaries

Standards

2-171. There are three Canadian standards which deal with subsidiaries and consolidated financial statements:

> **Section 1581: Business Combinations** This standard provides guidance on the recognition and measurement of a subsidiary's identifiable assets and goodwill at the time they are acquired.
>
> **Section 1590: Subsidiaries** This standard defines subsidiaries and indicates the required accounting treatment.
>
> **Section 1600: Consolidated Financial Statements** This standard provides the detailed procedures required in the preparation of consolidated financial statements.

2-172. The corresponding international material is found in two IFRSs:

> **IFRS No. 3: Business Combinations** This standard corresponds to Section 1581.
>
> **IAS No. 27: Consolidated And Separate Financial Statements** This standard's content covers the same ground as Section 1590 and Section 1600.

Differences

2-173. The major differences between the Canadian and the international standards are as follows:

Section 1581 The AcSB's Implementation Plan indicates that Section 1581 and IFRS No. 3, *Business Combinations*, are converged except for the following:

- IFRS No. 3 requires that the acquirer to recognize the acquiree's identifiable assets, liabilities, and contingent liabilities at their fair values at the acquisition date, rather than the acquirer's share only. This results in any non-controlling interest in the acquiree being stated at the non-controlling interest's portion of the net fair values of those items.
- IFRS No. 3 requires the acquisition date to be the date on which the acquirer obtains control over the acquired entity or business.
- IFRS No. 3 requires that shares issued as consideration be measured based on their fair value at the date of the exchange transaction.
- IFRS No. 3 does not allow the use of the acquirer's share of the fair value of the net assets or equity instruments acquired if that is more reliably measurable, in determining the cost of a business combination.
- IFRS No. 3 requires that contingent consideration be recognized when it is probable that it will be paid and can be reliably measured.
- IFRS No. 3 requires that any negative goodwill be recognized immediately in profit or loss.

From the point of view of the material in this text, the most important of these differences is the first one. This will require a major change in the way consolidated financial statements are prepared in Canada. The IASB's alternative approach will be illustrated in Chapters 4, 5, and 6.

Section 1590 The AcSB's Implementation Plan indicates that Section 1590 and IAS No. 27, *Consolidated And Separate Financial Statements*, are converged, except that IAS No. 27 assesses control at a point in time, whereas Section 1590 assesses control based on an entity's continuing ability to make strategic policy decisions.

Section 1600 The AcSB's Implementation Plan indicates that Section 1600 is converged with IAS No. 27, *Consolidated And Separate Financial Statements*, and IFRS No. 3, *Business Combinations*, except for the following:

- The IFRSs have less detail on dilution gains and step acquisitions.
- The IFRSs require non-controlling interests to be shown within equity, separately from the parent shareholders' equity. As a consequence, non-controlling interests' shares of Net Income are reported as allocations within equity, rather than as income or expense items in the Income Statement.
- The IFRSs require non-controlling interests to be stated at their proportion of the net fair value of the acquired net assets, rather than at the subsidiary's carrying amount.

Significantly Influenced Companies

Standards

2-174. The Canadian rules for these investments in equity securities are found in Section 3051, "Investments". The corresponding international standard is IAS No. 28, *Investments In Associates*.

Differences

2-175. There is a difference in terminology in that IAS No. 28 refers to "associated companies" while Section 3051 refers to "significantly influenced companies". However, these two terms have the same meaning.

2-176. There is also a difference in the way that Section 3051 and the relevant international standards deal with impairment:

- The IFRSs require an impairment to be recognized when the recoverable amount of an asset is less than the carrying amount, rather than when there is a significant or prolonged decline in value below the carrying amount.
- The IFRSs determine the impairment loss as being the excess of the carrying amount above the recoverable amount (calculated as the higher of fair value reduced by costs to sell and value in use, calculated as the present value of future cash flows from the asset).
- The IFRSs require the reversal of an impairment loss when the recoverable amount increases.

Joint Ventures

Standards

2-177. The Canadian rules for these investments in equity securities are found in Section 3055, "Interests In Joint Ventures". The corresponding international standard is IAS No. 31, *Interests In Joint Ventures*.

Differences

2-178. IAS No. 31 allows the use of either proportionate consolidation or the equity method to account for joint ventures. Section 3055 requires proportionate consolidation and does not allow the use of the equity method.

Investments In Canadian Practice

Statistics From Financial Reporting In Canada

2-179. Our source for statistics on Canadian practice is the 2006 edition of *Financial Reporting In Canada*. This publication surveys the 2005 annual reports of 200 Canadian companies and, as a consequence, it contains no information in Section 3855. In addition, most of the companies surveyed were using the now withdrawn Section 3050, "Long-Term Investments". However, with respect to significantly influenced companies, Section 3050 and Section 3051 have few differences. As a consequence, it is useful to provide you with some information from this publication, despite the fact that it does not reflect current Canadian practices.

2-180. Of the 200 companies surveyed for the 2006 edition of *Financial Reporting in Canada*, 122 disclosed the presence of long-term investments other than joint ventures in their 2005 annual reports. With respect to the valuation of these investments, 68 companies used both cost and equity, 22 used cost only, and 11 used equity only. The remaining 21 companies did not disclose the basis of valuation.

2-181. Of the 122 companies that disclosed the presence of long-term investments other than joint ventures, 78 segregated investment assets by type of investment. Only 52 of the 122 companies disclosing the presence of long-term investments segregated investment income by type.

> **CD-ROM Note** If you are interested in more information on statistics on this subject, the CICA's *Financial Reporting in Canada* is available on the CD-ROM which is included with this text.

Example From Practice

27-182. The following example is from the annual report of Shaw Communications Inc. for the reporting period ending August 31, 2005. This example illustrates detailed disclosure of long-term investments. Included is disclosure of fair market values, company names, dilution gains, and impairment losses. Note that this disclosure is based on the requirements of the now superseded Section 3050, "Long-Term Investments".

Notes To Financial Statements

(all amounts in thousands of Canadian dollars except per share amounts)

Note 1 Significant Accounting Policies (in part)

Investments

Investments in other entities are accounted for using the equity method or cost basis depending upon the level of ownership and/or the Company's ability to exercise significant influence over the operating and financial policies of the investee. Equity method investments include GT Group Telecom Inc. ("GT") until February 4, 2003 (at which time GT was reorganized and resulted in the disposition of the Company's interest in GT), The Biography Channel (Canada) Corp., MSNBC Canada Holdings Corp. and 3773213 Canada Inc. (G4TechTV Canada). Investments of this nature are recorded at original cost and adjusted periodically to recognize the Company's proportionate share of the investees' net income or losses after the date of investment, additional contributions made and dividends received. When net losses from an equity accounted for investment exceed its carrying amount, the investment balance is reduced to zero and additional losses are not provided for unless the Company is committed to provide financial support to the investee. The Company resumes accounting for the investment under the equity method when the entity subsequently reports net income and the Company's share of that net income exceeds the share of net losses not recognized during the period the equity method was suspended. Investments are written down when there is clear evidence that a decline in value that is other than temporary has occurred.

When an equity accounted for investee issues its own shares, the subsequent reduction in the Company's proportionate interest in the investee is reflected in income as a deemed dilution gain or loss on disposition.

Note 5 Investments and Other Assets

	2005 $	2004 $
Investments, at cost net of write-downs:		
Canadian Hydro Developers, Inc. ("Canadian Hydro") (market value $58,920; 2004 – $26,033)	24,432	19,267
Motorola, Inc. ("Motorola") (market value – 2004 – $44,113)	—	8,925
Q9 Networks Inc. ("Q9 Networks") (market value – $2,731; 2004 – $3,710)	1,074	2,500
Investments in private technology companies	2,126	4,063
Investments at equity:		
Investments in specialty channel networks	668	702
Other assets:		
Employee home relocation mortgages and loans [note 18]	6,246	6,899
Other	1,683	1,609
	36,229	43,965

Canadian Hydro

Canadian Hydro, a Canadian public corporation, develops and operates electrical generating plants. A summary of the holdings in Canadian Hydro is as follows:

	2005	2004
	(number of shares/warrants)	
Shares	12,430,364	10,330,364
Warrants – vested – exercise price of $2.35	—	1,100,000
	12,430,364	11,430,364

Motorola

In 2005 the Company settled an equity forward sales contract on the Motorola investment resulting in the realization of a $31,018 pre-tax gain. The Motorola investment had been pledged as collateral for the Zero Coupon Loan (see note 11) and the proceeds of settlement were used to repay the Zero Coupon Loan and accrued interest.

Q9 Networks

During the current year, the Company sold 367,880 shares resulting in a pre-tax gain of $840. In September 2005, the Company sold the remaining 277,281 shares resulting in a pre-tax gain of $1,690.

Write-downs of investments at cost

	2005 $	2004 $	2003 $
Canadian Hydro	—	—	4,925
Other public companies	—	—	27
Specialty channel network	—	401	—
Private companies	1,937	250	10,048
	1,937	651	15,000

Investments at equity

The Company has a one-third interest in three specialty channel networks.

Equity income (loss) on investees consists of the following:

	2005 $	2004 $	2003 $
Specialty channel networks	(346)	(272)	(1,898)
Other	60	22	(23)
	(286)	(250)	(1,921)

Gain on redemption of SHELS

In prior years, the Company issued equity instruments which were collateralized by certain investments. In 2003 the Company settled these equity instruments by delivery of the underlying investments and recorded gains as follows:

Equity instrument	Delivery of underlying security	2005 $	2004 $	2003 $
Series III&IV SHELS	1,452,506 shares of Liberate Technologies	—	—	75,342
Series V SHELS	5,326,827 shares of Terayon Communications Systems	—	—	44,179
		—	—	119,521

Note 19 Financial Instruments (in part)

(ii) Investments and other assets

a) The fair value of publicly traded shares included in this category is determined by the closing market values for those investments. The fair value of investments subject to forward sale agreements, which are pledged as collateral for the Zero Coupon Loan and match the maturity of the loan, are valued at the proceeds received on the loan plus accrued interest thereon.

b) The carrying value of other investments in this category approximates their fair value.

CD-ROM Note If you are interested in more examples of disclosure of investments, the CICA's *Financial Reporting in Canada* is available on the CD-ROM which is included with this text.

Additional Readings

2-183. In writing the material in the text, we have incorporated all of the relevant *CICA Handbook* recommendations, as well as material from other sources that we felt to be of importance. This includes some, but not all, of the EIC Abstracts that relate to investments in equity securities, as well as material from international accounting standards.

2-184. While this approach meets the needs of the great majority of our readers, some of you may wish to pursue this subject in greater depth. To facilitate this, you will find a fairly comprehensive list of additional readings at the end of each relevant Chapter in our *Guide To Canadian Financial Reporting*.

CD-ROM Note Our *Guide To Canadian Financial Reporting* is available on the CD-ROM which is included with this text.

Problems For Self Study

(The solutions for these problems can be found in the separate Study Guide.)

Self Study Problem Two - 1

On June, 30, 2007, Laxator Inc. acquires 2,500 of the outstanding voting shares of Barnes Ltd. at a cost of $55.00 per share. Transaction costs total $500. Laxator classifies the investment in Barnes shares as held for trading.

Laxator has a December 31 year end. On December 31, 2007, the Barnes shares are trading at $61.50 per share. However, by December 31, 2008, their value has declined to $43.20 per share.

On September 5, 2009, Laxator sells the Barnes shares for proceeds of $56.25 per share. Transaction costs total $500.

The Barnes shares do not pay dividends during the period June 30, 2007 through September 5, 2009.

Required: Provide dated journal entries to account for the Barnes shares during the period June 30, 2007 through September 5, 2009. Calculate the effect of the investment in Barnes shares on Laxator's Net Income for the period June 30, 2007 through September 5, 2009.

Self Study Problem Two - 2

On June, 30, 2007, Laxator Inc. acquires 2,500 of the outstanding voting shares of Barnes Ltd. at a cost of $55.00 per share. Transaction costs total $500. Laxator classifies the investment in Barnes shares as available for sale and chooses to expense transaction costs.

Laxator has a December 31 year end. On December 31, 2007, the Barnes shares are trading at $61.50 per share. However, by December 31, 2008, their value has declined to $43.20 per share.

On September 5, 2009, Laxator sells the Barnes shares for proceeds of $56.25 per share. Transaction costs total $500.

The Barnes shares do not pay dividends during the period June 30, 2007 through September 5, 2009.

Required: Provide dated journal entries to account for the Barnes shares during the period June 30, 2007 through September 5, 2009. Calculate the effect of the investment in Barnes shares on Laxator's Net Income for the period June 30, 2007 through September 5, 2009.

Self Study Problem Two - 3

On January 1, the Lestor Company purchased 20 percent of the outstanding voting shares of the Rapone Company. The purchase price, all of which was paid in cash, amounted to $5 million. On the acquisition date, the carrying value and the fair value of the Rapone Company's net assets was $25 million. The Lestor Company's 20 percent shareholding does not result in the ability to exercise significant influence over the operations of the Rapone Company. Lester classifies the investment as available for sale and, because the Rapone shares do not trade in an active market, the investment will be accounted for by the cost method.

During the three years following the acquisition date the Rapone Company had Net Income and dividends declared and paid as follows:

Year	Net Income (Net Loss)	Dividends
1	$1,500,000	$1,000,000
2	(1,000,000)	1,000,000
3	4,000,000	1,000,000

There were no intercompany transactions, other than dividend payments, during any of the years under consideration. Both Companies close their books on December 31.

Required: Provide the Lestor Company's dated journal entries to account for its investment in the Rapone Company for each of the three years. In addition, calculate the balance in the Investment In Rapone account as at December 31 of year 3.

Self Study Problem Two - 4

On January 1, the Lestor Company purchased 20 percent of the outstanding voting shares of the Rapone Company. The purchase price, all of which was paid in cash, amounted to $5 million. On the acquisition date, the carrying value and the fair value of the Rapone Company's net assets was $25 million. The Lestor Company's 20 percent shareholding results in the ability to exercise significant influence over the operations of the Rapone Company.

During the three years following the acquisition date the Rapone Company had Net Income and dividends declared and paid as follows:

Year	Net Income (Net Loss)	Dividends
1	$1,500,000	$1,000,000
2	(1,000,000)	1,000,000
3	4,000,000	1,000,000

There were no intercompany transactions, other than dividend payments, during any of the years under consideration. Both Companies close their books on December 31.

Required: Provide the Lestor Company's dated journal entries to account for its investment in the Rapone Company for each of the three years. In addition, calculate the balance in the Investment In Rapone account as at December 31 of year 3.

Self Study Problem Two - 5

On January 1, 2007, the Buy Company purchased 25 percent of the outstanding voting shares of the Sell Company for cash of $1,500,000. On this date, the Sell Company had net assets of $6,000,000. On the acquisition date, all of the identifiable assets and liabilities of the Sell Company had fair values that were equal to their carrying values.

The Buy Company's 25 percent investment in the shares of the Sell Company gives it significant influence over the Sell Company. As result, the equity method is used to account for its Investment In Sell.

Between January 1, 2007 and December 31, 2009, the Sell Company had a total Net Income of $3,000,000 and paid dividends which totalled $2,000,000. During this period, dividend payments were the only intercompany transactions.

For the year ending December 31, 2010, prior to the Buy Company taking into account any amounts for Investment Income from the Sell Company, the two Companies have the following Income Statements:

Buy And Sell Companies
Income Statements
For the Year Ending December 31, 2010

	Buy	Sell
Revenues Before Investment Income	$5,000,000	$2,000,000
Cost Of Goods Sold	$3,000,000	$1,800,000
Other Expenses	800,000	400,000
Total Expenses	$3,800,000	$2,200,000
Income (Loss) Before Investment Income and Extraordinary Items	$1,200,000	($ 200,000)
Extraordinary Gain	Nil	600,000
Income Before Investment Income	$1,200,000	$ 400,000

On January 1, 2010, the Retained Earnings balance of the Buy Company was $15,000,000. This balance included the Investment Income calculated by the equity method for Buy's Investment In Sell during the period January 1, 2007 through December 31, 2009.

During the year ending December 31, 2010, the Buy Company declares and pays dividends in the amount of $500,000, while the corresponding dividend figure for the Sell Company is $150,000. Also during 2010, the Sell Company discovers a $50,000 expense which was overlooked in 2009.

Required: Prepare the Buy Company's Income Statement and Statement Of Retained Earnings for the year ending December 31, 2010. In addition, calculate the balance in the Investment In Sell account as at December 31, 2010.

Self Study Problem Two - 6

Carson Investments is a manufacturing company with a variety of investments in Canadian companies. These investments can be described as follows:

Best Parts Inc. Carson Investments owns 48 percent of the outstanding common shares of Best Parts Inc. Over 90 percent of this Company's sales are made to Carson Investments. In addition to the holding of common shares, Carson owns 60 percent of the outstanding 7 percent, cumulative preferred shares of Best Parts Inc.

Research Tech Ltd. Carson owns 25 percent of the outstanding common shares of Research Tech Ltd., a company established with three other investors to do research on a new manufacturing process. The other investors each have 25 percent of the outstanding common shares. However, two of these investors do not participate in the management of the Company, leaving all operating decisions in the hands of Carson and one other investor.

Entell Ltd. Carson owns 46 percent of the outstanding voting shares of Entell Ltd. Included in the assets of Entell is an investment in 18 percent of the outstanding common shares of Chelsea Distributors Inc. In recent years, Chelsea has experienced adverse operating results and there is some question as to whether it will be able to continue as a going concern.

Chelsea Distributors Inc. Carson owns, directly, 37 percent of the outstanding common shares of Chelsea Distributors Inc. In addition, Chelsea owns 3 percent of the outstanding voting shares of Carson Investments Ltd.

Required: Describe and justify the recommended accounting treatment for each of the investments, including those made by Carson Investments' investees.

Assignment Problems

(The solutions for these problems are only available in the solutions manual that has been provided to your instructor.)

Assignment Problem Two - 1

On December 31, 2007, Vonex Ltd. acquires 4,200 of the outstanding voting shares of Morex Inc. at a cost of $72.00 per share. Vonex Ltd. pays no transaction costs on its purchase or sale of Morex Inc. shares. Vonex has a December 31 year end.

During the year ending December 31, 2008, Morex Inc. declares and pays dividends of $1.05 per share.

On December 31, 2008, the Morex shares are trading at $78.00 per share.

On May 1, 2009, Vonex sells the 4,200 Morex shares for proceeds of $56.00 per share. Morex did not declare any 2009 dividends prior this disposition.

Required: For the period December 31, 2007 through May 1, 2009, provide the dated journal entries to account for the Morex shares, and calculate the effect of the investment in Morex shares on Venox's Net Income under the following assumptions:

A. Venox classifies the investment in Morex shares as held for trading.

B. Venox classifies the investment in Morex shares as available for sale.

Assignment Problem Two - 2

On December 31, 2007, the Miser Company purchased 25 percent of the outstanding voting shares of the Mercy Company for $4 million in cash. On the acquisition date, all of the net identifiable assets of the Mercy Company had fair values that were equal to their carrying values. The carrying value of Mercy Company's net assets was $16 million.

Mercy's Net Income, dividends declared and paid, and the December 31 fair value of its outstanding shares, for the year of acquisition and the three subsequent years are as follows:

Year	Net Income (Net Loss)	Dividends Declared And Paid	December 31 Fair Value (100 Percent)
2007	$ 600,000	$ 600,000	$16,000,000
2008	(2,000,000)	400,000	17,600,000
2009	1,500,000	500,000	15,500,000
2010	3,000,000	1,000,000	18,200,000

Both Companies close their books on December 31. The 2010 Net Income figure of the Mercy Company includes an Extraordinary Loss of $800,000. There were no intercompany transactions, other than dividend payments, during any of the years under consideration.

Required: Provide the Miser Company's dated journal entries to account for its investment in the Mercy Company for each of the four years and the December 31, 2010 balance in the Investment in Mercy account assuming that:

A. Miser Company's 25 percent holding does not give it significant influence in the operations of Mercy Company. Miser classifies the investment as held for trading.

B. Miser Company's 25 percent holding does not give it significant influence in the operations of Mercy Company. Miser classifies the investment as available for sale.

C. Miser Company's 25 percent holding gives it significant influence in the operations of Mercy Company.

Assignment Problem Two - 3

On January 1, 2007, the Bronson Company purchased 18 percent of the outstanding shares of the Somerset Company. The purchase price, all of which was paid in cash, amounted to $1.8 million. On the acquisition date, the fair value of the Somerset Company's net assets was $10 million and all of the assets and liabilities had fair values that were equal to their carrying values. Both Companies have a fiscal year which ends on December 31.

During the four years following the Bronson Company's acquisition of the Somerset Company's shares, the Somerset Company had income and declared and paid dividends as follows:

Year	Net Income (Net Loss)	Dividends
2007	$ 950,000	$350,000
2008	(1,140,000)	140,000
2009	750,000	160,000
2010	840,000	320,000

Other Information:

1. The Somerset Company's 2009 Net Income includes an Extraordinary Loss of $163,000.

2. During 2010, the Somerset Company changed its accounting policy with respect to the calculation of Depreciation Expense. The change was accounted for retroactively, resulting in an addition to Retained Earnings of $246,000 to reflect the effects of this change on prior periods.

3. There were no intercompany transactions between Bronson and Somerset, other than dividend payments, during any of the years under consideration.

4. Bronson's 18 percent shareholding gives the company significant influence over the operations of Somerset.

Required: Provide the Bronson Company's dated journal entries to account for its Investment In Somerset for the years 2007 through 2010 assuming:

A. that Bronson is a qualifying enterprise for differential reporting purposes and elects to account for its Investment In Bronson using the cost method.

B. that Bronson is a public company and it uses the equity method to account for its Investment In Somerset.

Assignment Problem Two - 4

The Fostor Company purchased 30 percent of the outstanding voting shares of the Festee Company for $1,200,000 in cash on January 1, 2007. On that date, the Festee Company's net assets had a carrying value of $4,000,000. There were no differences between the carrying values and the fair values of any of its identifiable assets or liabilities.

This investment gives the Fostor Company significant influence over the affairs of the Festee Company. The net income and dividends declared and paid by the Festee Company for the two years subsequent to its acquisition were as follows:

	2007	2008
Net Income (Loss)	($100,000)	$160,000
Dividends	40,000	50,000

The Income Statements for the year ending December 31, 2009, prior to the recognition of any Investment Income, for the Fostor and Festee Companies are as follows:

Foster and Festee Companies
Income Statements
Year Ending December 31, 2009

	Fostor	Festee
Sales	$2,000,000	$550,000
Other Revenues	100,000	Nil
Total Revenue	$2,100,000	$550,000
Cost Of Goods Sold	$1,000,000	$300,000
Other Expenses	200,000	50,000
Total Expenses	$1,200,000	$350,000
Income Before Extraordinary Items	$ 900,000	$200,000
Extraordinary Loss	Nil	(30,000)
Net Income	$ 900,000	$170,000

During 2009, the Fostor Company declared and paid dividends of $100,000 while Festee Company declared and paid dividends of $70,000. Other than dividends, there were no transactions between the two companies in any of the years under consideration.

Required: Provide the following:

A. The dated journal entries of the Fostor Company related to its investment in Festee Company for the years ending December 31, 2007, 2008 and 2009.

B. The Income Statement of the Fostor Company, including recognition of any investment income or loss, for the year ending December 31, 2009.

C. The balance in the Investment In Festee account as it would appear on the December 31, 2009 Balance Sheet of the Fostor Company.

Assignment Problem Two - 5

On January 1, 2007, Tribble Company purchased 40 percent of the outstanding voting shares of the Marcus Company for $320,000 in cash. On that date, Marcus had Common Stock - No Par of $500,000, Retained Earnings of $300,000 and all of its identifiable assets and liabilities had fair values that were equal to their carrying values. This investment gives Tribble significant influence over the affairs of Marcus.

Between January 1, 2007 and December 31, 2009, Marcus had Net Income and paid dividends as follows:

	2007	2008	2009
Net Income (Loss)	$300,000	($400,000)	$320,000
Dividends	100,000	50,000	70,000

There were no extraordinary items or prior period adjustments for Marcus in the three years 2007 through 2009. For the year ending December 31, 2010, the Income Statements of the Tribble and Marcus Companies, before recognition of any investment income, were as follows:

Tribble and Marcus Companies
Income Statements
For the Year Ending December 31, 2010

	Tribble	Marcus
Sales	$2,300,000	$850,000
Other Revenues	200,000	Nil
Total Revenues	$2,500,000	$850,000
Cost Of Goods Sold	$1,000,000	$500,000
Other Expenses	500,000	80,000
Total Expenses	$1,500,000	$580,000
Income Before Discontinued Operations	$1,000,000	$270,000
Loss From Discontinued Operations	Nil	(20,000)
Net Income	$1,000,000	$250,000

During 2010, Marcus initiated a change in accounting policy. The change was accounted for retroactively, resulting in a prior period addition to the Company's Retained Earnings balance in the amount of $700,000.

Tribble declared $150,000 in dividends in 2010. Marcus declared and paid dividends of $120,000 in 2010. Assuming the use of the cost method to account for its Investment in Marcus since its acquisition, Tribble has a Retained Earnings balance of $4,600,000 on January 1, 2010.

Required: Prepare the dated journal entries for the Tribble Company related to its investment in the Marcus Company for the years 2007 through 2010, the Income Statement for the Tribble Company for the year ending December 31, 2010, and the Statement of Retained Earnings for the Tribble Company for the year ending December 31, 2010 assuming:

A. that the Tribble Company is a qualifying enterprise and uses the Section 3051 differential reporting option to account for its Investment In Marcus by the cost method.

B. that the Tribble Company is not a qualifying enterprise and, since it was acquired, the Investment In Marcus has been carried by the equity method. (This will require a recalculation of the January 1, 2010 Retained Earnings balance of Tribble.)

Assignment Problem Two - 6

Small World Limited owns a chain of retail stores which sell children's books and toys. The President of Small World, Ted Kidd, hopes that his Company will eventually achieve vertical integration with many of its suppliers. At the moment, Small World owns 52 percent of the outstanding voting shares of Blocks N Things, a toy wholesaler.

Blocks N Things owns 22 percent of the outstanding common shares and 53 percent of the outstanding non-cumulative, non-participating preferred shares of Craftco Limited, a manufacturer of wooden toys. No other Craftco shareholder, or group of related shareholders, holds preferred or common shares to the same extent as Blocks N Things.

Craftco currently owns 13 percent of the outstanding common shares of Delta Inc., a major Canadian pulp and paper company. The market value of Delta's shares has decreased substantially since acquisition.

Small World Limited also owns 40 percent of the outstanding common shares of Delta Inc.

Required: For each of the investments in equity securities that are described, indicate the appropriate classification and accounting treatment. Explain your conclusions.

Business Combinations

Business Combinations Defined

Basic Definition

3-1. The *CICA Handbook* defines a business combination transaction in the following manner:

> **Paragraph 1581.06(a)** A **business combination** occurs when an enterprise acquires net assets that constitute a business, or acquires equity interests of one or more other enterprises and obtains control over that enterprise or enterprises.

3-2. The economic concept that underlies the term "business combination" is that you have two or more independent and viable economic entities that are joined together for future operations as a single economic or business entity. The original economic entities can be corporations, unincorporated entities, or even a separable portion of a larger economic entity. The key factor is that each could be operated as a single, viable, business entity.

3-3. Section 1581 does not define what constitutes a business entity and, as a consequence, this issue had to be considered by the Emerging Issues Committee. EIC Abstract No. 124 provides the following definition of a business:

> **EIC Abstract No. 124** A business is a self-sustaining integrated set of activities and assets conducted and managed for the purpose of providing a return to investors. A business consists of (a) inputs, (b) processes applied to those inputs, and (c) resulting outputs that are used to generate revenues. For a transferred set of activities and assets to be a business, it must contain all of the inputs and processes necessary for it to continue to conduct normal operations after the transferred set is separated from the transferor, which includes the ability to sustain a revenue stream by providing its outputs to customers.

3-4. It was also noted in this Abstract that unless a "business" is acquired in a a transaction, the transaction does not constitute a business combination transaction as contemplated by Section 1581.

Examples

3-5. Examples of business combination transactions include the following:

- A corporation acquires all of the net assets of a second corporation for cash and the activities of the corporation meet the definition of a business.
- A corporation issues shares to the owners of an unincorporated business in return for all of their net assets and these net assets meet the definition of a business.
- A corporation issues new shares as consideration for all of the outstanding shares of a second corporation and the activities of the corporation meet the definition of a business.
- A new corporation is formed and issues shares to the owners of two separate unincorporated businesses in return for all of the net assets of the two enterprises.

3-6. It is also important to delineate what is not included in the definition of a business combination:

- The acquisition of a single asset or a group of assets that do not constitute a business entity.
- A transfer or exchange of assets between a parent and one of its subsidiaries. The parent and subsidiary are already a combined entity from an accounting point of view and any further transactions between them would not change the economic substance of the situation.
- A transfer or exchange of assets or shares between two subsidiaries of the same parent. Similar to the preceding example, the two subsidiaries are already part of a combined entity and any further transactions between them would not change the economic substance of the situation.
- The acquisition of a significantly influenced company.

3-7. The *CICA Handbook* specifically notes that the formation of a joint venture does not constitute a business combination transaction. This, however, does not preclude the possibility that an existing joint venture might participate in a business combination transaction.

Legal Avenues To Combination

The Problem

3-8. In reading the preceding section, it is likely that you recognized that a variety of legal forms can be used to combine the operations of two independent business entities. The choice among these forms involves a great many issues, including tax considerations, the desire to retain the name of one of the enterprises, the ability to access the capital markets in a particular manner, or simply various contractual arrangements that one or both of the enterprises have with suppliers, employees, or customers.

3-9. This is an important issue for accountants as the legal form used can, in some circumstances, obscure the actual economic substance of a transaction. An outstanding example of this type of situation would be transactions that are referred to as reverse takeovers.

> **Example Of Reverse Takeover** Company X, with 100,000 shares outstanding, issues 400,000 shares to acquire all of the shares of Company Y. From a legal perspective, Company X is the parent company and it has acquired Company Y as a subsidiary. However, from an economic point of view, the former shareholders of Company Y now own a controlling interest in Company X. This means that, in actual fact, the subsidiary, Company Y has acquired the parent, Company X.

3-10. As an accountant's mandate is to focus on economic substance, the accountant must be able to look through the complex legal structures that are sometimes used to effect business combinations. This is necessary in order to base accounting procedures on the real events that have occurred. To accomplish this goal, accountants must have some knowledge of the various legal forms that are used. As a result, we will illustrate the basic legal forms that can be used to effect a business combination.

3-11. Note, however, this is an extremely complex area, particularly when consideration is given to tax factors. A full discussion of legal forms for business combinations goes beyond the scope of this text.

Example

3-12. Our discussion of legal form will use a simple example to illustrate the various possible alternatives.

Example Assume that two corporations, the Alpha Company and the Beta Company have, for a variety of reasons, decided to come together in a business combination transaction and continue their operations as a single economic entity. The date of the combination transaction is December 31, 2007 and, on that date the Balance Sheets of the two companies are as follows:

Alpha And Beta Companies
Balance Sheets As At December 31, 2007

	Alpha Company	Beta Company
Current Assets	$153,000	$ 35,000
Non-Current Assets	82,000	85,000
Total Assets	$235,000	$120,000
Liabilities	$ 65,000	$ 42,000
Common Stock:		
(5,000 Shares Issued And Outstanding)	95,000	N/A
(10,000 Shares Issued And Outstanding)	N/A	53,000
Retained Earnings	75,000	25,000
Total Equities	$235,000	$120,000

3-13. In order to simplify the use of this Balance Sheet information in the examples which follow, we will assume that all of the identifiable assets and liabilities of the two Companies have fair values that are equal to their carrying values. In addition, we will assume that the shares of the two Companies are trading at their book values. This would be $34.00 per share for Alpha [($95,000 + $75,000) ÷ 5,000] and $7.80 per share for Beta [($53,000 + $25,000) ÷ 10,000]. This indicates total market values for Alpha Company and Beta Company of $170,000 and $78,000, respectively.

Basic Alternatives

3-14. We will consider four basic alternatives in our discussion of the legal forms for implementing business combination transactions. They can be described as follows:

1. Alpha Company could acquire the net assets of Beta Company through a direct purchase from that Company. The consideration paid to Beta could be cash, other assets, or Alpha Company debt or equity securities.
2. A new organization, Sigma Company, could be formed to directly acquire the net assets of Alpha Company and Beta Company. As the Sigma Company is newly formed, it would not have any assets to use as consideration in this transaction, Alpha and Beta would receive debt or equity securities of Sigma Company. If Sigma shares were used, the proportion of shares issued would likely be based on their respective market values, 68.55% [$170,000 ÷ ($170,000 + $78,000)] for Alpha and the remaining 31.45% for Beta.
3. Alpha could acquire the shares of Beta Company directly from the shareholders of that Company. The consideration paid to the Beta shareholders could be cash, other assets, or Alpha Company debt or equity securities.

4. A new organization, Sigma Company, could be formed. Sigma Company could then issue its debt or equity securities directly to the shareholders of Alpha Company and Beta Company in return for the shares of the two Companies.

3-15. There are other possibilities here. For example, if Alpha had a subsidiary, Alpha could gain control over Beta by having the subsidiary acquire the Beta Company shares from the Beta shareholders. In addition, most corporate legislation provides for what is referred to as a statutory amalgamation. This involves a process whereby two corporations become a single corporation that is, in effect, a continuation of the predecessor corporations. However, an understanding of the four basic approaches we have described is adequate for the purposes of this material. These basic alternatives will be discussed and illustrated in the material which follows.

Acquisition Of Assets By Alpha Company

3-16. Perhaps the most straightforward way in which the Alpha and Beta Companies could be combined would be to have one of the Companies simply acquire the net identifiable assets directly from the other Company. Using our basic example, assume that the Alpha Company gives Beta Company cash of $78,000 (Beta's net book value) to acquire the assets and liabilities of Beta Company. This approach is depicted in Figure 3-1.

Figure 3 - 1
Acquisition Of Assets From Beta Company

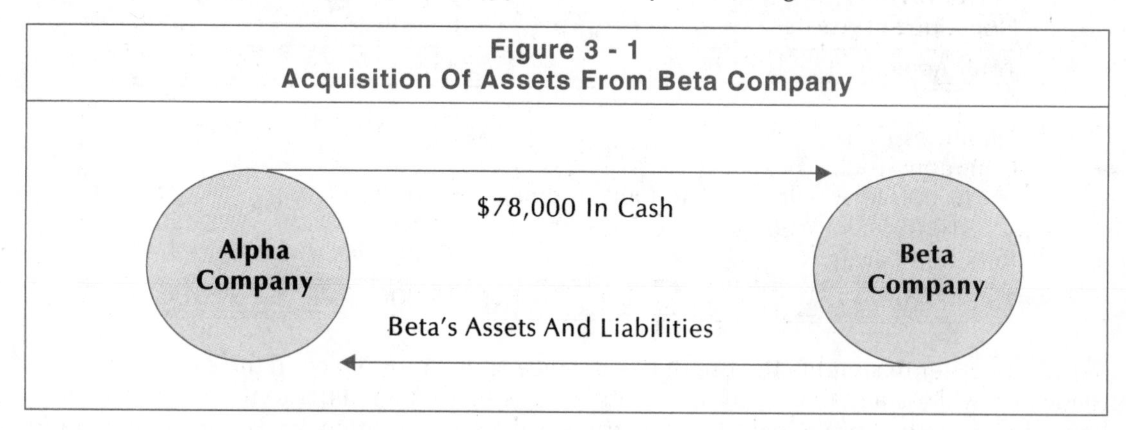

3-17. At this point, it is likely that the Beta Company would go through a windup operation by distributing the cash received from Alpha Company to its shareholders in return for the outstanding Beta Company shares. If this were to happen, the Beta Company shares would be canceled and the Beta Company would cease to exist as a separate legal entity.

3-18. Without regard to the course of action taken by Beta Company after the sale of its net assets, all of the assets and liabilities of the combined Companies will be recorded on Alpha Company's books and the accounting for the combined Companies will take place as a continuation of this Company's records. This means that the business combination transaction has been carried out in such a fashion that both Companies' operations have been transferred to a single continuing legal entity.

3-19. Alpha Company's Balance Sheet subsequent to the business combination transaction would be as follows:

Alpha Company
Balance Sheet As At December 31, 2007
Acquisition Of Beta Assets For Cash

Current Assets ($153,000 - $78,000 + $35,000)	$110,000
Non-Current Assets ($82,000 + $85,000)	167,000
Total Assets	$277,000

Liabilities ($65,000 + $42,000)	$107,000
Common Stock (Alpha's 5,000 Shares)	95,000
Retained Earnings (Alpha's Balance)	75,000
Total Equities	$277,000

3-20. It would not be necessary for Alpha to acquire 100 percent of the net assets of Beta in order to have the transaction qualify as a business combination transaction. If Alpha were to acquire, for example, the manufacturing division of Beta, this transaction would be subject to the accounting rules for business combinations. The key point is that Alpha must acquire a group of assets sufficient to meet the definition of a business entity.

3-21. You should also note that this business combination transaction could have been carried out using Alpha Company shares rather than cash. While the economic outcome would be the same unification of the two Companies, the resulting Alpha Company Balance Sheet would be somewhat different.

3-22. More specifically, the Current Assets would not have been reduced by the $78,000 outflow of cash and there would be an additional $78,000 in Common Stock outstanding. If the new shares were issued at their December 31, 2007 market value of $34.00 per share, this transaction would have required 2,294 new Alpha shares to be issued ($78,000 ÷ $34.00). This alternative Balance Sheet would be as follows:

Alpha Company
Balance Sheet As At December 31, 2007
Acquisition Of Beta Assets For Shares

Current Assets ($153,000 + $35,000)	$188,000
Non-Current Assets ($82,000 + $85,000)	167,000
Total Assets	$355,000
Liabilities ($65,000 + $42,000)	$107,000
Common Stock ($95,000 + $78,000)	173,000
Retained Earnings (Alpha's Balance)	75,000
Total Equities	$355,000

Acquisition Of Assets By Sigma Company

3-23. The acquisition of assets approach could also be implemented through the use of a new corporation. Continuing to use our basic example, assume that a new Company, the Sigma Company, is formed and the new Company decides to issue shares with a fair market value of $10 per share. Based on this value and the respective market values of the two companies, Sigma will issue 17,000 shares to Alpha Company ($170,000 ÷ $10) and 7,800 shares to Beta Company ($78,000 ÷ $10) in return for the assets and liabilities of the two Companies.

3-24. You should note that any value could have been used for the Sigma Company shares as long as the number of shares issued to Alpha and Beta was proportionate to the market values of the two companies. For example, a value of $5 could have been used for the Sigma shares, provided 34,000 shares were issued to Alpha and 15,600 shares to Beta (34,000 shares at $5 equals the $170,000 fair market value for Alpha, while 15,600 shares at $5 equals the $78,000 fair market value for Beta). This approach to bringing the two companies together is depicted in Figure 3-2 (following page).

3-25. Under this approach, Sigma Company acquires the net assets of both Alpha and Beta Companies. As Sigma is a new company, the only consideration that can be used would be newly issued Sigma shares. Sigma Company's Balance Sheet subsequent to the business combination transaction would be as follows:

Figure 3 - 2
New Company Acquisition Of Assets From Beta Company

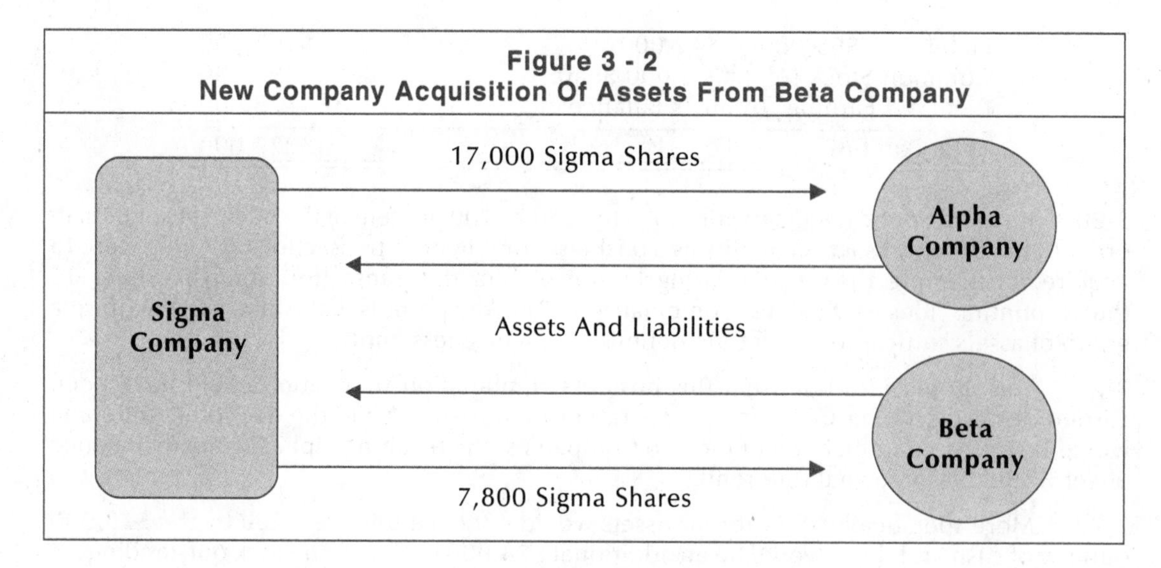

Sigma Company
Balance Sheet As At December 31, 2007

Current Assets ($153,000 + $35,000)	$188,000
Non-Current Assets ($82,000 + $85,000)	167,000
Total Assets	$355,000
Liabilities ($65,000 + $42,000)	$107,000
Common Stock (24,800 Shares Issued And Outstanding)	248,000
Total Equities	$355,000

3-26. As was the case when Alpha acquired the net assets of Beta on a direct basis, the result of the business combination is that both Companies' operations have been transferred to a single continuing legal entity. The only difference here is that the continuing legal entity is a new company rather than one of the combining Companies.

3-27. The resulting Sigma Company Balance Sheet is fundamentally the same as the one that resulted from Alpha Company acquiring the net assets of Beta using Alpha shares as consideration (see Paragraph 3-22). The only difference is that, because Sigma is a new Company, all of the Shareholders' Equity must be allocated to Common Stock, rather than being split between Common Stock and Retained Earnings.

Acquisition Of Shares By Alpha Company

Procedures

3-28. Another legal route to the combination of Alpha and Beta would be to have one of the two Companies acquire a majority of the outstanding voting shares of the other Company. Continuing to use our basic example, the Alpha Company will give $78,000 in cash to the Beta shareholders in return for 100 percent of the outstanding shares of the Beta Company. This approach is depicted in Figure 3-3 (following page).

3-29. While in this example we have assumed that Alpha acquired 100 percent of the shares of Beta, a business combination would have occurred as long as Alpha acquired sufficient shares to achieve control over Beta. In general, this would require acquisition of a majority of Beta's voting shares.

3-30. The acquisition of shares could be carried out in a variety of ways. Alpha could simply acquire the shares in the open market. Alternatively, they could be acquired from a majority shareholder, through a public tender offer to all shareholders, or through some combination of these methods.

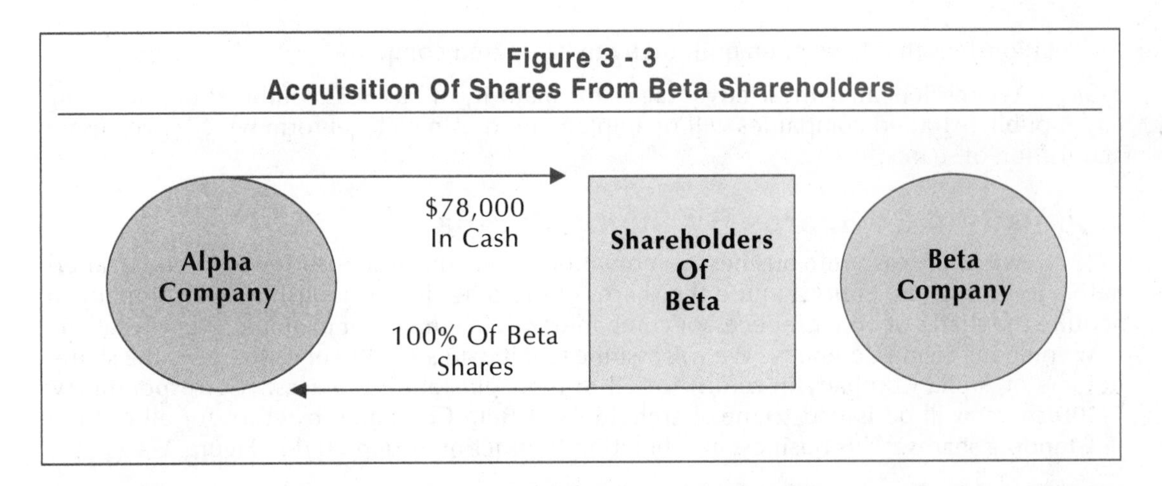

3-31. Regardless of the method used, acquisition of a majority of the outstanding voting shares of Beta Company would mean that Alpha Company is in a position to exercise complete control over the affairs of the Beta Company. As a result of this fact, the two Companies could be viewed as a single economic entity and a business combination could be said to have occurred.

3-32. This would be the case despite the fact that the two Companies have retained their separate legal identities. In this situation, in order to reflect the economic unification of the two Companies, consolidated financial statements would have to be prepared. While we have not yet covered the detailed procedures for preparing consolidated financial statements, the basic idea is that the investee's (subsidiary's) assets and liabilities will be added to those of the investor (parent). The resulting consolidated Balance Sheet would be as follows:

Alpha Company And Subsidiary
Consolidated Balance Sheet As At December 31, 2007

Current Assets ($153,000 - $78,000 + $35,000)	$110,000
Non-Current Assets ($82,000 + $85,000)	167,000
Total Assets	$277,000
Liabilities ($65,000 + $42,000)	$107,000
Common Stock (Alpha's 5,000 Shares)	95,000
Retained Earnings (Alpha's Balance)	75,000
Total Equities	$277,000

Advantages Of Using Shares

3-33. There are a number of advantages that can be associated with acquiring shares rather than assets to effect the business combination transaction:

- The acquisition of shares can be a method of going around a company's management if they are hostile to the idea of being acquired.
- Less financing is needed as only a majority share ownership is required for control over 100 percent of the net assets.
- It may be possible to acquire shares when the stock market is depressed, thereby paying less than the fair values of the identifiable assets of the business.
- Shares, particularly if they are publicly traded, are a much more liquid asset than would be the individual assets of an operating company.
- The acquisition of shares provides for the continuation of the acquired company in unaltered legal form. This means it retains its identity for marketing purposes, the tax basis of all of its assets remain unchanged, and there is no interruption of the business

relationships that have been built up by the acquired company.

3-34. As a result of all of these advantages, the majority of business combinations involving large, publicly traded companies will be implemented using a legal form which involves an acquisition of shares.

Acquisition Of Shares By Sigma Company

3-35. As was the case with business combinations based on an acquisition of assets, an alternative to having one entity acquire the shares of the other is to establish a new company to acquire the shares of both predecessor companies. As in our earlier example, we will call the new company Sigma Company. We will assume that it issues 17,000 of its shares to the shareholders of Alpha Company in return for all of their outstanding shares. Correspondingly, 7,800 shares will be issued to the shareholders of Beta Company in return for all of their outstanding shares. This business combination transaction is depicted in Figure 3-4.

Figure 3 - 4
New Company Acquisition Of Shares From Beta Shareholders

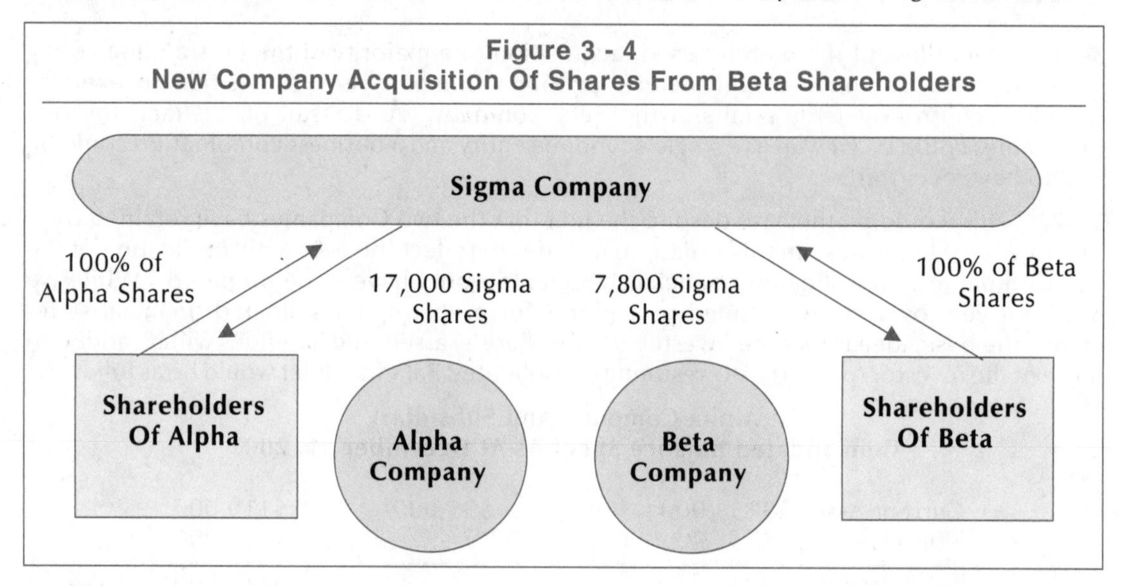

3-36. In this case, there will be three ongoing legal entities. These would be the parent Sigma Company, as well as Alpha Company and Beta Company, which have now become subsidiaries. Once again we are faced with a situation in which, despite the presence of more than one separate legal entity, the underlying economic fact is that we have a single unified economic entity. This requires the information for these three Companies to be presented in a single consolidated Balance Sheet as follows:

Sigma Company And Subsidiaries
Consolidated Balance Sheet As At December 31, 2007

Current Assets ($153,000 + $35,000)	$188,000
Non-Current Assets ($82,000 + $85,000)	167,000
Total Assets	$355,000
Liabilities ($65,000 + $42,000)	$107,000
Common Stock (24,800 Shares Issued And Outstanding)	248,000
Total Equities	$355,000

3-37. You will note that the only differences between this consolidated Balance Sheet and the one that was prepared when Alpha acquired the shares of Beta (see Paragraph 3-32) are:

- Current Assets are $78,000 higher because Alpha used cash as consideration where Sigma issued Common Stock.
- Shareholders' Equity consists only of Common Stock with no Retained Earnings balance because Sigma is a new Company.

Exercise Three-1

Subject Legal Avenues To Combination

Two corporations, Blocker Company and Blockee Company, have decided to combine and continue their operations as a single economic entity. The date of the business combination transaction is December 31, 2007 and, on that date, the Balance Sheets of the two Companies are as follows:

Blocker and Blockee Companies
Balance Sheets As At December 31, 2007

	Blocker Company	Blockee Company
Current Assets	$1,406,000	$ 987,000
Non-Current Assets	2,476,000	1,762,000
Total Assets	$3,882,000	$2,749,000
Liabilities	$ 822,000	$ 454,000
Common Stock:		
(180,000 Shares Outstanding)	1,800,000	N/A
(51,000 Shares)	N/A	1,145,000
Retained Earnings	1,260,000	1,150,000
Total Equities	$3,882,000	$2,749,000

All of the identifiable assets and liabilities of the two Companies have fair values that are equal to their carrying values. The shares of the two Companies are trading at their book values. This would be $17 per share for Blocker [($1,800,000 + $1,260,000) ÷ 180,000] and $45 per share for Blockee [($1,145,000 + $1,150,000) ÷ 51,000]. This indicates total market values for Blocker Company and Blockee Company of $3,060,000 and $2,295,000, respectively.

Prepare the December 31, 2007 Balance Sheet for the economic entity that results from the following business combinations:

A. Blocker acquires 100 percent of the net assets of Blockee in return for $795,000 in cash and debt securities with a maturity value of $1,500,000.

B. Blocker acquires 100 percent of the outstanding shares of Blockee by issuing 135,000 new Blocker shares to the Blockee shareholders.

C. A new company, Blockbuster Inc., is formed. The new company decides to issue shares with a fair market value of $15 per share. The shareholders of Blocker receive 204,000 of the new shares in return for their Blocker shares, while the shareholders of Blockee receive 153,000 of the new shares in return for their Blockee shares.

End of Exercise. Solution available in Study Guide.

Legal Avenues And Tax Considerations

Acquisition Of Assets

Cash Consideration

3-38. While it would not be appropriate in financial reporting material to provide a comprehensive discussion of the tax provisions that are associated with the various legal avenues to combination, these matters are of sufficient importance that a brief description of major tax aspects is required.

3-39. Looking first at combinations involving the acquisition of assets, there is a need to distinguish between situations in which cash and/or other assets are the consideration and those situations in which new shares are issued. If a company acquires the assets of another business through the payment of cash or other assets, the acquired assets will have a completely new tax base, established by the amount of non-share consideration given. There would be no carry over of any of the tax values (i.e., adjusted cost base or undepreciated capital cost) that are associated with the business which gave up the assets.

Share Consideration

3-40. The same analysis could apply to situations in which shares are issued to acquire the assets of another business. However, while the transfer might take place at new tax values, there is also the possibility that different values might be used. As long as the transferor of the assets is a Canadian corporation, the parties to the combination can use the *Income Tax Act* Section 85 rollover provisions. In simplified terms, ITA Section 85 allows assets to be transferred at an elected value that could be anywhere between the fair market value of the assets and their tax values in the hands of the transferor.

Tax Planning

3-41. In general, investors will prefer to acquire assets rather than shares. In most situations, the value of the acquired assets will exceed their carrying values and, if the investor acquires assets, these higher values can be recorded and become the basis for future capital cost allowance (CCA) deductions. In contrast, if the investor acquires shares, the investee company will continue to use the lower carrying values as the basis for CCA, resulting in higher taxable income and taxes payable.

3-42. In addition, if the investor acquires shares, any problems involving the investee's tax returns for earlier years are acquired along with the shares. When the investor company acquires assets, it simply has a group of assets with a new adjusted cost base and any investee tax problems are left with the selling entity.

3-43. From the point of view of a person selling an existing business, they will generally have a preference for selling shares. If shares are sold, any resulting income will be taxed as a capital gain, only one-half of which will be taxable. In the alternative sale of assets, income will include capital gains, but may also include fully taxable recapture of CCA. Further, for the seller to have access to the funds resulting from the sale, it may be necessary to go through a complex windup procedure.

3-44. If the corporation being sold is a qualified small business corporation, there is an additional advantage to selling shares rather than assets. Gains on the sale of shares of this type of corporation may be eligible for the special $500,000 lifetime capital gains deduction.

Acquisition Of Shares

3-45. In looking at situations in which the combination is carried out through an acquisition of shares, the type of consideration used also has some influence. If shares are acquired through the payment of cash or other assets, the shares will have a new tax base equal to their fair market value as evidenced by the amount of consideration given. In addition, any excess of consideration over the adjusted cost base of the shares given up will create an immediate capital gain in the hands of the transferor.

3-46. However, if new shares are issued to acquire the target shares, Section 85.1 of the *Income Tax Act* can be used. This Section provides that in a share for share exchange, any gain on the shares being transferred can effectively be deferred. Under the provisions of this Section, the old shares are deemed to have been transferred at their adjusted cost base and, in turn, the adjusted cost base of the old shares becomes the adjusted cost base of the new shares that have been received.

3-47. While the type of consideration used to effect the business combination can make a significant difference to the transferor of the shares, it does not influence the tax status of the assets that have been indirectly acquired through share ownership. As this legal form of combination results in both parties continuing to operate as separate legal and taxable entities, the assets remain on the books of the separate companies and their tax bases are not affected in any way by the transaction.

3-48. As noted previously, in most cases these tax bases will be lower than the fair market values of the assets and, as a result, lower than the tax bases that would normally arise if the assets were acquired directly. For this reason, the acquiring company will generally prefer to acquire net assets directly, rather than acquiring its right to use the assets through acquisition of a controlling interest in shares.

> **CD-ROM Note** For anyone with a more detailed interest in this subject, we would refer you to our *Guide to Canadian Financial Reporting* which is included on the CD-ROM which accompanies this text. The Chapter on accounting for taxes (Chapter 44) contains a detailed presentation on tax considerations in business combinations. Note, however, knowledge of corporate tax is required to understand this material.

Alternative Accounting Methods

Introduction

3-49. At this time, there is general agreement that only one method should be used to account for business combination transactions. The AcSB, the FASB, and the IASB have adopted standards that require the use of the purchase method. The current *CICA Handbook* requirement is as follows:

> **Paragraph 1509.09** *The purchase method of accounting should be used to account for all business combinations.* (July, 2001)

3-50. The question of methods to be used to account for business combination transactions has been a controversial issue in financial reporting for over 40 years. To knowledgeable individuals, the solution to the controversy has been apparent for most of this period. However, this is an area where the selection of method can have an enormous influence on the reported earnings of the companies that are involved. As a consequence, resolving the business combination problem has proved difficult, particularly in the United States.

3-51. While the purchase method is the only currently applicable method, an understanding of the alternatives that have been used, including one that still has considerable support, will enhance your understanding of the procedures that are required under this method. This section will provide a brief example of three alternative methods that have been considered at various points in time.

Basic Example

3-52. A simple example will serve to illustrate the nature of the problem.

> **Example** On December 31, 2007, Sigma Company has 50,000 common shares outstanding. On this date, Sigma Company acquires all of the outstanding shares of Chi Company by issuing 10,000 Sigma Company shares to the shareholders of Chi Company in return for all of their outstanding shares. At this time, the shares of Sigma are trading at $50 per share, resulting in a total investment cost of $500,000. On this

date, prior to the business combination, the condensed Balance Sheets of the two companies are as follows:

	Sigma Company	Chi Company
Net Assets	$2,500,000	$300,000
Common Shares	$1,500,000	$100,000
Retained Earnings	1,000,000	200,000
Total Equities	$2,500,000	$300,000

On this date, the fair value of the Sigma Company's net identifiable assets is $2,800,000. The corresponding figure for Chi is $350,000.

Investment Analysis Sigma has paid $500,000 for Chi's Shareholders' Equity which has a carrying value of $300,000. The carrying value of the net assets of Chi also total $300,000. The payment can be analyzed as follows:

Investment Cost [(10,000 @ $50)]	$500,000
Chi Shareholders' Equity ($100,000 + $200,000)	(300,000)
Differential (Excess of Cost Over Shareholders' Equity)	$200,000
Fair Value Increase on Identifiable Assets ($350,000 - $300,000)	(50,000)
Goodwill	$150,000

Note The use of this schedule, as well as the nature of goodwill, will be explained in detail when we examine a more complex example later in this Chapter.

The Purchase Method

3-53. Accountants generally attempt to concentrate on the economic substance of transactions rather than their form. This fact is particularly important in accounting for business combinations. As previously described, these combination transactions can assume a great variety of legal forms. However, these forms should not be allowed to obscure the fact that, in the great majority of business combinations, one of the combining business entities will have a dominant or controlling interest in the combined business entity. This certainly appears to be the case in the preceding example. After the issuance of new shares, the original Sigma shareholders will hold 50,000 out of a total of 60,000 shares outstanding.

3-54. Sigma, which is the dominant or controlling company in our example, can be viewed as the acquiring company and, given this analysis, the business combination transaction can then be thought of as an acquisition of assets. The economic substance of this transaction is simply that Sigma (the acquirer) is purchasing the net assets of Chi (the acquiree). It would follow that Sigma should account for this business combination transaction in a manner that is analogous to the treatment which is accorded to other acquisitions of assets.

3-55. The only unique feature involved in a business combination transaction is that it always involves a basket purchase of assets. While Section 3061, Property, Plant, and Equipment, suggests that, in general, the cost of a basket should be prorated on the basis of the relative fair values of the assets acquired, Section 1581 requires somewhat more complex allocation procedures when there is a business combination transaction.

3-56. The purchase method of accounting for business combinations is based on the view that a business combination transaction is simply an acquisition of assets that should be accounted for in a manner similar to any other acquisition of assets. The assets of the acquiring company are not affected by the acquisition and the acquired assets would be recorded at their cost to the acquirer (fair value). Given this, the combined net assets of Sigma and its subsidiary would be as follows:

Net Identifiable Assets ($2,500,000 + $350,000)	$2,850,000
Goodwill	150,000
Combined Net Assets - Sigma And Subsidiary	$3,000,000

The Pooling-Of-Interests Method

3-57. While in our example, the Sigma Company is clearly the acquiring company, the analysis is not always so obvious. If Sigma had issued 50,000 shares to acquire Chi, both shareholder groups would have an equal number of Sigma shares and it would not be clear as to which of the companies was, in fact, the acquirer.

3-58. In these circumstances, it would be possible to argue that the business combination transaction is not an acquisition of assets, but rather a joining together of two enterprises into a combined business enterprise. There are two accounting methods that could be identified with this interpretation:

Pooling-of-Interests Under this approach, the assets of the combining companies are left at their carrying values, with no recognition of either fair value changes or goodwill. In the application of this method a retroactive approach is used, accounting for the combining enterprises as through they had always been combined. Applying this method to our example would result in the following net assets:

Net Assets ($2,500,000 + $300,000)	$2,800,000

New Entity Approach (a.k.a., Fair Value Pooling) Under this approach, the combined company is viewed as a new entity that requires a new basis of accounting for both companies. Carrying values would be replaced by fair values, not just for one of the enterprises, but rather for both of the combining enterprises. Applying this method to our example would result in the following net assets:

Net Assets ($2,800,000 + $350,000)	$3,150,000

3-59. Pooling-of-interests accounting has never been widely used in Canada. However, until 2001, in the United States, this method could be used for almost any business combination. Further, there was tremendous resistance to eliminating this method.

3-60. The basis for this resistance was not difficult to understand. The purchase method requires the recording of the acquiree's fair value changes and goodwill on the books of the combined enterprise. In our example, there would be a 66-2/3 percent increase in the recorded values of Chi's assets, from $300,000 to $500,000 ($350,000 + $150,000). To the extent that this increase involved assets with limited lives, this extra $200,000 would have to be amortized and charged to income.

3-61. In contrast, pooling-of-interests accounting retained the old carrying values for the acquired company, resulting in lower amortization charges and higher net income figures in the years subsequent to the combination transaction. Given the fact that the potential differences resulting from the choice between the two methods were often very significant, it is not surprising that the battle to eliminate this method was fiercely fought.

A Potential Problem

3-62. As we have noted, the purchase method of accounting for business combination transactions is based on the view that such transactions are simply an acquisition of assets. This interpretation requires that one of the combining companies be identified as the acquiring company.

3-63. While this interpretation is appropriate in the great majority of business combination situations, there are also cases where companies of equal economic prowess decide to combine their operations, with neither company clearly identifiable as the acquiring or dominant partner. While the use of the purchase method is not appropriate in these circumstances, international standard setters have apparently concluded that the costs associated with the misuse of the pooling-of-interests method outweigh the benefits of making an exception for the relatively rare situations where it is difficult or impossible to identify an acquirer.

Application of the Purchase Method

Acquisition Date

3-64. Business combinations are usually very complex transactions supported by detailed legal agreements involving the transfer of assets or equity interest to an acquiring business entity. While in some cases a single date may be involved, it is not uncommon for more than one date to be specified for the various components of the transaction.

3-65. Establishing the appropriate acquisition date is an important issue in that this is the date on which the assets of the acquiree will be measured. The choice of date can have a significant influence on these amounts.

3-66. When more than one date is involved, Section 1581 provides the following suggestion:

> **Paragraph 1581.19** The date of acquisition is either:
>
> (a) the date on which the net assets or equity interests are received and the consideration is given; or
>
> (b) the date of a written agreement, or a later date designated therein, which provides that control of the acquired enterprise is effectively transferred to the acquirer on that date, subject only to those conditions required to protect the interests of the parties involved.

3-67. In those cases where the parties to the combination designate an effective date other than the date on which assets are received and consideration given, the cost of the purchase should be reduced by imputed interest at an appropriate current rate for the intervening period. This imputed interest would also reduce the income of the acquirer.

Identification Of An Acquirer

Cash Consideration

3-68. As we have noted, Section 1581 requires the use of the purchase method, even in those situations where the economic substance of the transaction suggests that neither company can be identified as the acquirer. Given this, it is not surprising that Section 1581 provides additional guidance in this area.

3-69. However, before we examine this more detailed guidance, we will look at some situations where the identification process presents no problems. Referring to the various cases that we considered in the discussion of legal forms, assume that Alpha Company gives cash to either Beta Company in order to acquire the net assets of that Company, or to the Beta Company shareholders in order to acquire a controlling interest in its voting shares.

3-70. Where the cash is given to Beta Company to acquire net assets, all of the assets and liabilities of both companies are now on the books of Alpha Company. Since neither Beta Company nor its shareholders have received any of the shares of Alpha Company as part of the combination transaction, they have no continuing participation in the combined company. Clearly Alpha Company is the acquirer.

3-71. If the cash had gone to the Beta Company shareholders, a similar situation would exist. While in this case Beta Company would continue as a legal entity after the combination transaction, its former shareholders would not participate in its ownership. As was the case when the assets were acquired for cash, we would conclude that Alpha Company is the acquirer.

Share Consideration

3-72. The situation becomes more complex when voting shares are used as consideration. This reflects the fact that voting shares allow the pre-combination equity interests in both of the combining companies to have a continuing equity interest in the combined company. This would be the case without regard to whether the shares were issued to acquire assets or, alternatively, to acquire shares.

3-73. Conceptually, the solution to the problem is fairly simple. Assuming that the combining enterprises are both corporations, the acquirer is the company whose shareholders, as a group, wind up with more than 50 percent of the voting shares in the combined company. While the preceding guideline sounds fairly simple, its implementation can be somewhat confusing. Consider, for example, the case depicted in Figure 3-5.

Figure 3 - 5
Identifying An Acquirer

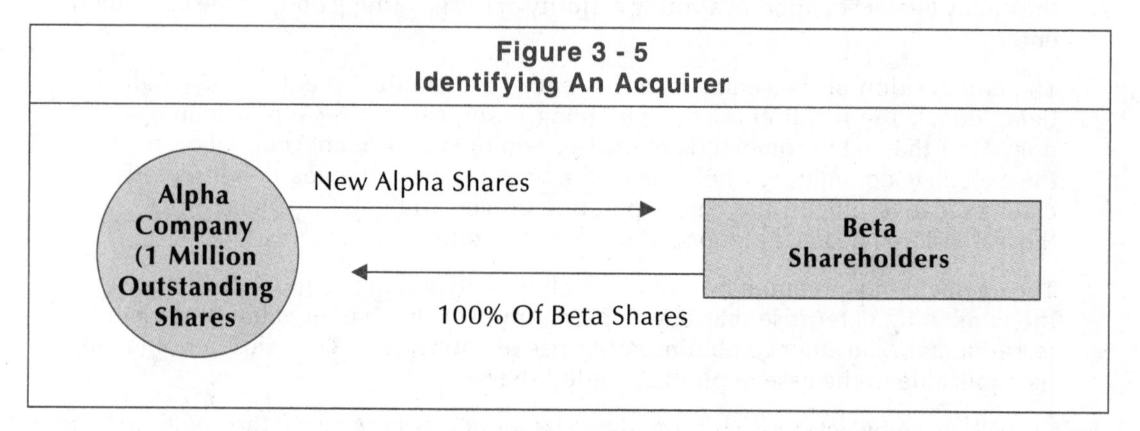

3-74. In this legal form, the combined entity will be the consolidated enterprise consisting of Alpha Company and its subsidiary Beta Company. The Alpha shareholder group will consist of both the original Alpha shareholders and the new Alpha shareholders who were formerly Beta shareholders. In the usual case, fewer than 1 million shares would have been issued to the Beta shareholders and, as a consequence, the original Alpha shareholders will be in a majority position. This means that, generally, Alpha Company will be identified as the acquirer.

3-75. There are, however, other possibilities. If Alpha issued more than 1 million shares to the shareholders of Beta, the Beta shareholders would then own the majority of the voting shares of Alpha and this means that Beta Company would have to be considered the acquirer. This type of situation is referred to as a reverse takeover and will be given more attention later in this section.

Formation Of New Company

3-76. In those combinations where a new company is formed to acquire either the assets or the shares of the two combining companies, the analysis is usually straightforward. The new company will be issuing shares as consideration for the assets or shares of the combining companies. Without regard to whether the new company acquires assets or shares, the acquirer is the predecessor company that receives the majority of shares in the new company.

Additional Handbook Guidance

3-77. Continuing with our example, a further possibility would be that Alpha would issue exactly 1 million shares to the Beta shareholders. In this case, neither shareholder group has a majority of voting shares. This is an example of a type of situation where simply looking at the post-combination holdings of voting shares will not serve to clearly identify an acquirer. Because of the possibility of such complications, Section 1581 provides a list of factors that should be considered in identifying an acquirer. The list includes both voting shares and other factors as follows:

- The relative voting rights in the combined enterprise after the combination — all else being equal, the acquirer is the combining enterprise whose owners as a group retained or received the larger portion of the voting rights in the combined enterprise. In determining which group of owners retained or received the larger portion of the voting rights in the combined enterprise, the existence of any unusual or special voting arrangements, and options, warrants, or convertible securities is considered.

- The existence of a large non-controlling interest in the combined enterprise when no other owner or organized group of owners has a significant interest — all else being equal, the acquirer is the combining enterprise whose single owner or organized group of owners holds the largest non-controlling interest in the combined enterprise.
- The composition of the governing body of the combined enterprise — all else being equal, the acquirer is the combining enterprise whose owners or governing body has the ability to elect or appoint a voting majority of the governing body of the combined enterprise.
- The composition of the senior management of the combined enterprise — all else being equal, the acquirer is the combining enterprise whose senior management dominates that of the combined enterprise. Senior management generally consists of the executive committee, when one exists, or the chair of the board of directors, the chief executive officer, the chief operating officer, the chief financial officer, and those divisional heads that report directly to the officers.
- The payment of a premium over market value — all else being equal, the acquirer is the combining enterprise that pays a premium over the market value of the equity instruments of the other combining enterprise or enterprises. This criteria would only be applicable in the case of publicly traded shares.

3-78. When a new enterprise is formed and issues equity interests to the combining enterprises in order to effect the combination, one of the predecessor enterprises will have to be designated as the acquired. The preceding factors are likely to be useful in this process.

3-79. A further complication arises in situations where the combination involves more than two enterprises. In such situations, it is unlikely that any of the preceding criteria will serve to identify an acquirer. When this happens, the *Handbook* suggests giving consideration to the enterprises that initiated the combination, and to whether the assets or earnings of one of the combining enterprises significantly exceed those of the others. The requirement to identify an acquirer remains in place in such situations, regardless of the difficulty in applying the concept.

Reverse Takeovers

3-80. As we have noted, in some business combination transactions a "reverse takeover" may occur. This involves an acquisition where a company issues so many of its own shares that the acquired company or its shareholders wind up holding a majority of shares in the legal acquirer.

Example Continuing the example from Paragraph 3-73, if Alpha, a company with 1,000,000 shares outstanding, issues 2,000,000 new shares to the Beta shareholders as consideration for their shares, the former Beta shareholders now hold two-thirds (2,000,000/3,000,000) of the outstanding shares of Alpha.

Analysis From a legal point of view, Alpha has acquired control of Beta through ownership of 100 percent of Beta's outstanding voting shares. Stated alternatively, Alpha is the parent company and Beta is its subsidiary. If you were to discuss this situation with a lawyer, there would be no question from a legal viewpoint that Alpha Company is the acquiring company.

However, this is in conflict with the economic picture. As a group, the Beta shareholders own a majority of shares in the combined economic entity and, under the requirements of the *CICA Handbook*, Beta is deemed to be the acquirer. In other words, the economic outcome is the "reverse" of the legal result.

3-81. Reverse takeovers are surprisingly common in practice and are used to accomplish a variety of objectives. One of the more common, however, is to obtain a listing on a public stock exchange. Referring to the example just presented, assume that Alpha is an inactive public company that is listed on a Canadian stock exchange. It is being used purely as a holding company for a group of relatively liquid investments. In contrast, Beta is a very active private company that would like to be listed on a public stock exchange.

3-82. Through the reverse takeover procedure that we have just described, the shareholders of Beta have retained control over Beta. However, the shares that they hold to exercise that control are those of Alpha and these shares can be traded on a public stock exchange. The transaction could be further extended by having Alpha divest itself of its investment holdings and change its name to Beta Company. If this happens, Beta has, in effect, acquired a listing on a public stock exchange through a procedure that may be less costly and time consuming than going through the usual listing procedures. More detailed attention will be given to this subject in Appendix B to Chapter 4.

Exercise Three-2

Subject: Identification Of An Acquirer

For each of the following independent Cases, indicate which of the combining companies should be designated as the acquirer. Explain your conclusion.

A. Delta has 100,000 shares of common stock outstanding. In order to acquire 100 percent of the voting shares of Epsilon, it issues 150,000 new shares of common stock.

B. Delta has 100,000 shares of common stock outstanding. It pays cash of $1,500,000 in order to acquire 48 percent of the voting shares of Epsilon. No other Epsilon shareholder owns more than 5 percent of the voting shares.

C. Delta, Epsilon, Zeta, and Gamma transfer all of their net assets to a new corporation, Alphamega. In return, Gamma receives 40 percent of the shares in Alphamega, while the other three Companies each receive 20 percent of the Alphamega shares.

D. Delta has 100,000 shares of common stock outstanding. Delta issues 105,000 shares to the sole shareholder of Epsilon in return for all of his outstanding shares. As it is the intention of this shareholder to retire from business activities, the management of Delta will be in charge of the operations of the combined company.

End of Exercise. Solution available in Study Guide.

Recognition of Assets and Income

3-83. With respect to the recognition of assets and liabilities acquired in a business combination transaction, Section 1581 contains the following recommendation:

> **Paragraph 1581.11** *The acquirer in a business combination should recognize the assets acquired and liabilities assumed from the date of acquisition, including any assets and liabilities that may not have been recognized on the balance sheet of the acquired enterprise.* (July, 2001)

3-84. The reference to "assets and liabilities that may not have been recognized on the balance sheet of the acquired enterprise" reflects the fact that, prior to the introduction of Section 1581, in many business combination transactions, the acquiree's unrecognized intangible assets were simply included in the goodwill figure. As we shall see later in this Chapter, Section 1581 requires separate recognition of all intangible assets that meet specific recognition criteria. This requirement, in conjunction with the preceding recommendation, should serve to limit this practice.

3-85. The second recognition recommendation in Section 1581 relates to the income of the acquirer:

> **Paragraph 1581.12** *The financial statements of the acquirer for the period in which a business combination occurs should include the earnings and cash flows of the acquired enterprise from the date of acquisition only.* (July, 2001)

3-86. As we have indicated previously, the purchase method treats the business combination transaction as an ordinary acquisition of assets. It is consistent with this view that earnings from the acquired assets would only be included in the income of the combined company from the date on which they are acquired.

Determining the Cost of the Purchase

General Rules

3-87. The basic measurement recommendation in Section 1581 is as follows:

> **Paragraph 1581.21** *Assets acquired and liabilities assumed in a business combination should be measured initially based on the cost of the purchase to the acquirer, determined as of the date of acquisition.* (July, 2001)

3-88. The key factor in implementing this rule is, of course, determining the cost of the purchase. Section 1581's general recommendation on this issue is as follows:

> **Paragraph 1581.22** *The cost of the purchase to the acquirer should be determined by the fair value of the consideration given or the acquirer's share of the fair value of the net assets or equity interests acquired, whichever is more reliably measurable.* (July, 2001)

3-89. The problems involved in implementing this recommendation would vary with the nature of the consideration given. The following guidelines would cover most situations:

- If the acquirer pays cash there is no significant problem.
- If shares with a quoted market price are issued by the acquirer, this market price will normally be used as the primary measure of the purchase price. Section 1581 notes that, if preferred shares are used as consideration, their value might be assessed by reference to debt securities with similar characteristics. It is likely that this guidance only applies when the preferred shares do not have a quoted market price.
- If the acquirer issues shares that do not have a market price or if it is agreed that the market price of the shares issued is not indicative of their fair value, the fair value of the net assets acquired would serve as the purchase price in the application of this method of accounting for business combinations. Section 1581 notes that the values of all of the net assets acquired, including any goodwill, should be assessed in this process.
- In general, no gain or loss would be recognized by the acquirer as part of the business combination transaction. Exceptions to this would be situations where non-cash assets are used as consideration and the fair value differs from their carrying value, or in situations where the fair value of the net assets acquired exceeds the cost of the purchase (see our later discussion of negative goodwill).

3-90. The preceding represents an application of the familiar idea that assets are recorded at the fair value of the consideration given or, if there are significant problems in determining the fair value of that consideration, the fair value of the assets acquired.

Direct Costs Of Combination - General Rules

3-91. Another familiar idea is that all of the direct costs related to the acquisition of a particular asset should be included as a part of the cost of the acquisition. This general rule would apply to the assets acquired in a business combination. This is reflected in the *Handbook* as follows:

Paragraph 1581.27 *The cost of the purchase includes the direct costs of the business combination. Costs of registering and issuing shares issued to effect a business combination should be treated as a capital transaction (see "Capital Transactions", Section 3610). Indirect and general expenses related to business combinations should be recognized as expenses when incurred.* (July, 2001)

3-92. The costs to be capitalized must be incremental and would include finder's fees and other amounts paid to lawyers, accountants, appraisers and other consultants. However, allocations of internal costs, including the costs of maintaining an acquisitions department, are not incremental costs and should be recognized as an expense as incurred.

Contingent Consideration

3-93. It is possible for a business combination agreement to provide for the payment of additional consideration if some specified event or transaction occurs in future accounting periods. The issue that is created by such contingent consideration is whether the consideration should be recorded at the time of the combination transaction or only when the contingency is resolved and the additional amounts are issued or become payable. The *CICA Handbook* contains the following recommendation:

Paragraph 1581.29 *When the amount of any contingent consideration can be reasonably estimated at the date of acquisition and the outcome of the contingency can be determined beyond reasonable doubt, the contingent consideration should be recognized at that date as part of the cost of the purchase. When the amount of contingent consideration cannot be reasonably estimated or the outcome of the contingency cannot be determined without reasonable doubt, details of the contingency should be disclosed. Neither a liability nor outstanding equity instruments are recognized until the contingency is resolved and consideration is issued or becomes issuable.* (July, 2001)

3-94. Additional recommendations provide more detailed guidance for two particular forms of contingency payments. Specific statements are made with respect to contingency payments related to earnings performance of the acquiree and payments related to the future market prices of shares issued to effect a combination transaction.

Payments Contingent On Earnings

3-95. It is not uncommon for the owners of an acquiree to make the argument that the enterprise is really worth more than is being offered by the acquirer and that the earnings of some future period will support this contention. A way of dealing with this possibility is for the acquirer to agree to pay additional consideration should the acquiree's belief about the future earnings prove to be correct. This results in a situation where there is contingent consideration based on the acquiree's future earnings.

3-96. When additional payment is contingent on the future earnings of the acquiree, the *Handbook* states the following:

Paragraph 1581.31 *When additional consideration is contingent on maintaining or achieving specified earnings levels in future periods, the acquirer should recognize the current fair value of the consideration issued or issuable as an additional cost of the purchase when the contingency is resolved and the additional consideration is issued or becomes issuable.* (July, 2001)

3-97. The accounting treatment of contingent consideration based on earnings can be illustrated by the following simple example:

Example On January 1, 2007, the Mor Company issues 3 million of its no par value voting shares in return for all of the outstanding voting shares of the Mee Company. On this date the Mor Company shares have a fair value of $25 per share or $75 million in total. In addition to the current payment, the Mor Company agrees that, if the 2007 earnings per share of the Mee Company is in excess of $3.50, the Mor Company will pay an additional $10 million in cash to the former shareholders of the Mee Company. The appropriate entry on January 1, 2007 would be as follows:

Investment In Mee	$75,000,000	
No Par Common Stock		$75,000,000

If at the end of 2007, the Mee Company's earnings per share has exceeded the contingency level of $3.50, the following entry to record the contingency payment would be required:

Investment In Mee	$10,000,000	
Cash		$10,000,000

Alternatively, if the earnings per share do not exceed $3.50 per share, no additional payment would be made and no journal entry would be required.

Exercise Three-3

Subject: Payments Contingent Of Earnings

On June 30, 2007, Lor Inc. issues 1,250,000 of its no par value voting shares in return for all of the outstanding voting shares of Lee Ltd. At this time, the Lor shares are trading at $11 per share. Negotiators for Lee have argued that this price is too low because it does not reflect the large increase in Earnings Per Share that is expected for their year ending December 31, 2007.

In order to resolve this dispute, Lor agrees to issue an additional 250,000 shares on March 1, 2008, provided Lee's Earnings Per Share for the year ending December 31, 2007 reach or exceed $1.90 per share.

Lee's Earnings Per Share for the year are reported as $2.05 and, on March 1, 2008, Lor issues the required shares. At this time, the Lor shares are trading at $11.50 per share.

Provide the journal entries that would be required to record the issuance of Lor shares on June 30, 2007, and the additional issuance of Lor shares on March 1, 2008.

End of Exercise. Solution available in Study Guide.

Payments Contingent On Share Prices

3-98. When shares are used as consideration in a business combination transaction, the acquirer is likely to be making the argument that the shares being offered are worth more than their current market value and that this view will be supported by some future market price for the stock. In this case, the acquirer may agree to pay additional amounts or issue additional shares if the market value of the shares does not reach a certain price at some future point in time.

3-99. In situations where additional payments are contingent on future price performance of the acquirer's shares, the *Handbook* Recommends the following:

> **Paragraph 1581.32** *Any consideration that will be payable if the market price of the shares issued to effect the combination does not reach at least a specified value by a specified future date should not change the amount recognized as the cost of the purchase. When additional consideration becomes payable, the current fair value of such consideration should be offset by a simultaneous reduction in the value placed on the shares issued at the date of acquisition to their lower current fair value.* (July, 2001)

3-100. The accounting treatment of contingencies based on share prices can be illustrated by extending the previous example used in Paragraph 3-97 to illustrate the accounting treatment of payments contingent on earnings. The revised example is as follows:

Example On January 1, 2007, the Mor Company issues 3 million of its no par value voting shares in return for all of the outstanding voting shares of the Mee Company. On this date the Mor Company shares have a fair value of $25 per share or $75 million in total. In this case we will assume that the Mor Company has agreed to pay an additional $15 million if, on December 31, 2007, the market price of the Mor Company shares is not equal to at least $30 per share.

In this situation, the Mor Company has, in effect, guaranteed the Mee Company shareholders a value of $30 per share for the Mor Company shares. If the market price does not move from its current $25 per share up to at least $30 per share, the Mor Company will provide the difference by paying $15 million (3 million shares at $5 per share). In view of this fact, the purchase price should include this contingency payment and the required journal entry would be as follows:

Investment In Mee [(3,000,000)($30)]	$90,000,000	
No Par Common Stock		$90,000,000

If the Mor Company shares reach $30 by the end of 2007, no further entries will be required and the No Par Common Stock will remain at $90,000,000. On the other hand, if they fail to achieve the specified level and the contingency payment must be made, the No Par Common Stock will be reduced by the following entry:

No Par Common Stock	$15,000,000	
Cash		$15,000,000

Note that the payment of contingent consideration does not affect the cost of the purchase of the Mee Company.

Exercise Three-4

Subject: Payments Contingent On Share Prices

On June 30, 2007, Lor Inc. issues 1,250,000 of its no par value voting shares in return for all of the outstanding voting shares of Lee Ltd. At this time, the Lor shares are trading at $11 per share. Negotiators for Lor have argued that this number of shares is appropriate because current market conditions have kept the share price of Lor below their real value.

In order to resolve this dispute, Lor has agreed to issue an additional 250,000 shares on March 1, 2008 if the market value of its shares is not at least $12.50 per share on December 31, 2007.

On December 31, 2007, the Lor shares are trading at $11.75 per share and, as a consequence, Lor must issue an additional 250,000 shares on March 1, 2008. At this time, the Lor shares are trading at $11.50 per share.

Provide the journal entries that would be required to record the issuance of Lor shares on June 30, 2007, and the additional issuance of Lor shares on March 1, 2008.

End of Exercise. Solution available in Study Guide.

Allocation Of The Purchase Price to Fair Values

General Rules

3-101. It was previously noted that the purchase method of accounting for business combinations is simply a way of treating these transactions in a manner that is analogous to other asset acquisition transactions. The only real complicating factor is the fact that a single purchase price must be allocated over a large group of identifiable assets, identifiable liabilities, and goodwill. The general guidelines for this allocation process are found in the *CICA Handbook* as follows:

Paragraph 1581.40 *The cost of the purchase should be allocated as follows:*

(a) all assets acquired and liabilities assumed in a business combination, whether or not recognized in the financial statements of the acquired enterprise, except goodwill and future income taxes recognized by an acquired enterprise before its acquisition, should be assigned a portion of the total cost of the purchase based on their fair values at the date of acquisition; and

(b) the excess of the cost of the purchase over the net of the amounts assigned to assets acquired and liabilities assumed should be recognized as an asset referred to as goodwill. (July, 2001)

3-102. In somewhat more practical terms, this allocation process can be described as a two-step procedure as follows:

Step A Determine the fair values of the acquiree's identifiable assets and liabilities. This includes both tangible and intangible assets acquired, without regard to whether they were recorded on the books of the acquiree. In practical situations, this is a complex process which will involve considerable effort on the part of both accountants and appraisers. This process is discussed in more detail beginning in Paragraph 3-104.

Step B It is unlikely that the purchase price will be equal to the acquirer's share of the sum of the fair values of the identifiable assets and liabilities of the acquiree. As a consequence, it is necessary to compare the purchase price with the investor's share of the fair values of the identifiable net assets that have been acquired. This comparison can have two possible outcomes:

1. If the purchase price is the larger figure, the excess will be allocated to goodwill. This possibility will be discussed beginning in Paragraph 3-122.
2. If the purchase price is less than the acquirer's share of the fair values, the deficiency is referred to as negative goodwill. The disposition of this balance will be discussed beginning in Paragraph 3-147.

3-103. While the following factors will not be important in this Chapter, these two additional points are essential to the understanding of the material on consolidated financial statements in Chapters 4 through 7:

- When business combinations involve the acquisition of shares, consolidated financial statements will be required. The allocation procedures that we have just described are an integral part of this process.
- When business combinations involve the acquisition of shares, control can be achieved with less than 100 percent ownership. While Paragraph 1581.40 does not emphasize this point, only the investor's share of fair values will be recognized. This point will be clarified when we begin our discussion of consolidated financial statements in Chapter 4.

Determination Of Fair Values - Tangible Assets and Liabilities

3-104. Section 1581 defines fair value as follows:

Paragraph 1581.06(b) **Fair value** is the amount of the consideration that would be agreed upon in an arm's length transaction between knowledgeable, willing parties who are under no compulsion to act.

3-105. Section 1581 makes several general points with respect to the process of determining fair value:

- In determining fair values, independent appraisals and actuarial or other valuations may be used as an aid.
- When the fair value of an asset or liability is based on estimated future cash flows, discounting should be used.

- In those situations where assets, including cash, are subject to particular restrictions, consideration should be given to these restrictions in the valuation process.
- Any goodwill previously recognized by the acquiree should not be recognized in the financial statements of the combined company.

3-106. Paragraph 1581.43 provides general guidance for assigning amounts to particular tangible assets acquired and liabilities assumed. It contains the following:

(a) **Inventories:**
  (i) finished goods and merchandise at estimated selling prices less the sum of:
    - costs of disposal; and
    - a reasonable profit allowance for the selling effort of the acquirer;
  (ii) work in process at estimated selling prices of finished goods less the sum of:
    - costs to complete;
    - costs of disposal; and
    - a reasonable profit allowance for the completing and selling effort of the acquirer based on profit for similar finished goods; and
  (iii) raw materials at current replacement costs.

(b) **Plant and equipment**:
  (i) to be used, at the current replacement cost for similar capacity unless the expected future use of the assets indicates a lower value to the acquirer; and
  (ii) to be sold, at fair value less cost to sell.

  Replacement cost may be determined directly when a used asset market exists. Otherwise, an estimate of depreciated replacement cost is used. The acquirer does not carry forward the accumulated depreciation of the acquired enterprise.

(c) **Intangible assets** that meet the criteria in paragraph 1581.48, at estimated or appraised values.

(d) **Other assets,** including land and natural resources at estimated or appraised values.

(e) Accrued benefit assets or accrued benefit liabilities for **defined benefit plans** for employee future benefits:
  (i) When the plan is to continue in operation, the accrued benefit obligation is calculated using best estimate assumptions, consistent with those that will be used on a going forward basis, in accordance with "Employee Future Benefits", Section 3461. Similarly, plan assets are valued at fair value in accordance with Section 3461. Any previously existing unamortized net actuarial gain (loss), unamortized past service cost, unamortized transitional obligation or unamortized transitional asset is eliminated with the result that the accrued benefit asset or accrued benefit liability is the difference between the accrued benefit obligation and the fair value of plan assets. The carrying amount of an accrued benefit asset in the acquired enterprise's financial statements may need to be reduced when the acquirer expects limitations on its ability to access a plan surplus as a result of existing regulations of the relevant jurisdiction and the plan.
  (ii) When the plan is to be wound up, the accrued benefit asset or accrued benefit liability is valued based on the amount expected to be received or paid on settlement.
  (iii) When the plan of the acquired enterprise is amended as a condition of the business combination (for example, when the change is required by the seller as part of the transaction), the effects of any improvements attributed to services rendered by the employees of the acquired enterprise's plan prior to the date of the business combination are accounted for in valuing the accrued benefit obligation of the acquired enterprise. Otherwise, when improvements to the plan of the acquired enterprise are not a condition of the business combination, credit granted for past service is recognized as a plan amendment by the acquirer. When the acquirer has developed a formal plan

to terminate or curtail the plan, the effects of those actions are considered in measuring the accrued benefit obligation. Otherwise, no future changes to the plan are anticipated.

(f) **Liabilities and accruals**, such as accruals for warranties, vacation pay and deferred compensation — at present values of amounts to be paid determined at appropriate current interest rates.

(g) **Other liabilities and commitments**, such as unfavourable leases, contracts, and commitments and plant closing expense incident to the acquisition — at present values of amounts to be paid determined at appropriate current interest rates.

Determination of Fair Values - Temporary Differences

3-107. If a business combination involves an acquisition of assets, the newly acquired assets will generally have a tax basis equal to their carrying value and no temporary differences will be present. This means that the existing future income asset or liability values (FITAL values) of the acquiree will not be carried forward and no additional FITAL values will be recorded as a result of the business combination transaction.

3-108. However, in many business combination transactions, the fair values of acquired assets will differ from their tax values on the books of the acquired company. This situation can result from two possible causes:

- In situations where assets have been acquired to effect the business combination, the transfer of assets may involve a rollover provision (e.g., ITA 85) under which assets are transferred at elected values without regard to their fair values at the time of the business combination.
- In situations where shares have been acquired to effect the business combination, the acquired subsidiary will continue as a separate legal entity and will retain old tax values for its assets, without regard to their fair values at the time of the business combination.

3-109. In economic terms, temporary differences clearly have an influence on the determination of fair value. An asset that has been fully depreciated for tax purposes has a fair value that is less than the fair value of the same asset when its value is fully deductible. This raises the question of how the presence of temporary differences should be dealt with in the context of business combination transactions. The Section 1581 recommendation is as follows:

Paragraph 1581.46 The values placed by an acquirer on the assets and liabilities of an acquired enterprise are determined based on their fair values, without reference to their values for tax purposes, or tax bases.

3-110. A simple example will serve to clarify this point.

Example Meta Inc. acquires all of the outstanding shares of Acta Ltd. At that time, Acta Ltd. has depreciable assets with an original cost of $540,000, a replacement cost of $500,000, a carrying value on the books of Acta Ltd. of $400,000 and an undepreciated capital cost (UCC) of $200,000. Both companies are subject to a tax rate of 40 percent.

Analysis On the books of Acta Ltd., there would be a Future Income Tax Liability of $80,000 [(40%)($400,000 - $200,000)]. This amount would not be carried forward to the consolidated financial statements.

The depreciable assets would be recorded in the consolidated financial statements at their full replacement cost of $500,000, without regard to the fact that their deductibility is limited to the UCC amount of $200,000. The temporary difference would be reflected in a Future Income Tax Liability of $120,000 [(40%)($500,000 - $200,000)], to be included in the consolidated financial statements.

Exercise Three-5

Subject: Temporary Differences In Business Combination Transactions

Gor Inc. completes a business combination with Gee Ltd. at the end of the current year. At the time of this business combination, Gee Ltd. has property, plant, and equipment with an original cost of $2,432,000, a replacement cost of $1,863,000, and a net book value of $1,578,000. The undepreciated capital cost (UCC) of the various classes to which this equipment has been allocated is $842,000. As Gee Ltd. has been subject to a tax rate of 35 percent, the $736,000 ($1,578,000 - $842,000) temporary difference is reflected in a Future Income Tax Liability of $257,600.

Calculate the Future Income Tax Liability that will be disclosed in the books of the combined company assuming that:

A. Gor acquires the shares of Gee.
B. Gor acquires the assets of Gee.

End of Exercise. Solution available in Study Guide.

Determination of Fair Values - Loss Carry Forwards

3-111. A further tax related consideration involves loss carry forward benefits. Under the provisions of Section 3465, "Income Taxes", the benefit of a loss carry forward can only be recognized as an asset when it is more likely than not that the benefit will be realized. The implementation of this concept involves a number of difficulties in the context of accounting for business combinations.

3-112. The first of these problems is the question of whether the loss carry forward can be transferred to the combined company. If the combination involves an acquisition of assets, it is likely that the loss carry forward will not be available to the combined company. If no rollover provision is used, the benefit of the carry forward will certainly be lost if assets are acquired. However, some rollover provisions (e.g., ITA 87) provide for a transfer of loss carry forward benefits in the context of an acquisition of assets.

3-113. If shares are acquired, the loss carry over will continue on the books of the subsidiary company. However, its availability may be limited by the acquisition of control rules [see ITA 111(4)].

3-114. A full discussion of these issues extends well beyond the scope of this text. What can be said here is this:

- If the loss carry forward benefit is legally available to the combined company; and
- if it is more likely than not that the benefit will be realized by the combined company; then
- its fair value is equal to the amount of the carry forward multiplied by the appropriate tax rate; and
- this amount should be recognized in the financial statements of the combined company, without regard to whether it has been recognized by the acquiree. Note that the combined company may be able to claim that realization is more likely than not, even if the acquiree could not make this claim as a separate company.

Determination of Fair Values - Identifiable Intangible Assets

3-115. Section 1581 defines an intangible asset as follows:

> **Paragraph 1581.06(d)** An intangible asset is an asset, other than a financial asset, that lacks physical substance.

3-116. As such, this term encompasses goodwill, as well as other intangible assets whose source of value can be identified (e.g., a patent). However, a terminology problem arises when one refers to the content of Section 3062, "Goodwill and Other Intangible Assets". In that Section, the term "intangible asset" is used to refer to intangible assets other than goodwill. In order to avoid confusion, as well as the somewhat awkward designation "intangible assets other than goodwill", we will use the term "identifiable intangible assets" to refer to those intangible assets other than goodwill.

3-117. Prior to the issuance of Section 1581, it was believed that, in practice, identifiable intangible assets acquired in business combination transactions were not being recognized, particularly in situations where they had not been recognized on the books of the acquiree. For example, the acquiree might have incurred significant costs in the development of a manufacturing process. As such costs are usually charged to income as they are incurred, this process would not appear as an asset on the books of the acquiree. However, if the company is acquired in a business combination transaction, some portion of the cost of the purchase could represent a payment for this process.

3-118. Given that such intangible assets are not recognized on the books of the acquiree, prior to the issuance of Section 1581 it is likely that the acquirer made little effort to attach a fair value to this process. As a consequence, no separate asset value would be recognized and the value of the process would be included in the total value assigned to goodwill.

3-119. Prior to 2001, when there was a requirement to amortize the resulting goodwill balance, this was not a serious problem. While the cost of the manufacturing process might be amortized over an incorrect useful life, it would, in fact, be amortized and charged to income over some limited period.

3-120. However, the prohibition against amortizing goodwill in Section 3062 created the possibility that, if identifiable intangible assets with limited lives were allocated to goodwill, they would not be subject to any amortization. To deal with this possibility, Section 1581 makes the following recommendation:

> **Paragraph 1581.48** *An intangible asset should be recognized apart from goodwill when:*
>
> *(a) the asset results from contractual or other legal rights (regardless of whether those rights are transferable or separable from the acquired enterprise or from other rights and obligations); or*
>
> *(b) the asset is capable of being separated or divided from the acquired enterprise and sold, transferred, licensed, rented, or exchanged (regardless of whether there is an intent to do so).*
>
> *Otherwise, it should be included in the amount recognized as goodwill.* (July, 2001)

3-121. This recommendation is intended to ensure that an effort is made to record a fair value for all identifiable intangible assets that meet the specified conditions. With respect to the implementation of this provision, several points should be noted:

- Paragraph 1581.48(a) requires an intangible asset acquired in a business combination to be recognized apart from goodwill when it arises from contractual or other legal rights. Intangible assets that meet that criterion are recognized apart from goodwill even when the asset is not transferable or separable from the acquired enterprise or from other rights and obligations. Examples of this type of situation would include:

  (a) An acquired enterprise leases a manufacturing facility under an operating lease that has terms that are favourable relative to market prices. The lease terms explicitly prohibit transfer of the lease (through either sale or sublease). The value arising from that operating lease contract is an intangible asset that meets the criterion for recognition apart from goodwill in Paragraph 1581.48(a), even though the lease contract cannot be sold or otherwise transferred.

  (b) An acquired enterprise owns and operates a nuclear power plant. The license to operate that power plant is an intangible asset that meets the criterion for recognition apart from goodwill in Paragraph 1581.48(a), even when it cannot be sold or transferred separately from the acquired power plant.

  (c) An acquired enterprise owns a technology patent. It has licensed that patent to others for their exclusive use outside Canada in exchange for which the enterprise receives a specified percentage of future non-Canadian revenue. Both the technology patent and the related license agreement meet the criterion for recognition apart from goodwill in Paragraph 1581.48(a) even when it is not practical to sell or exchange the patent and the related license agreement separately from one another.

- When an intangible asset acquired in a business combination does not arise from contractual or other legal rights, Paragraph 1581.48(b) requires that it be recognized apart from goodwill only when it is separable — that is, when it is capable of being separated or divided from the acquired enterprise and sold, transferred, licensed, rented or exchanged. Exchange transactions provide evidence that an intangible asset is separable from the acquired enterprise and might provide information that can be used to estimate its fair value. An acquired intangible asset meets the criterion in Paragraph 1581.48(b) if there is evidence of exchange transactions for that type of asset or for an asset of a similar type. For example, customer and subscriber lists are frequently leased and thus meet the criterion.
- An intangible asset that meets the criterion in Paragraph 1581.48(b) is recognized apart from goodwill even when the acquired enterprise does not intend to sell, lease, or otherwise exchange that asset.
- An intangible asset that is not separable from the enterprise individually still meets the criterion in Paragraph 1581.48(b) when it is separable from the acquired enterprise in combination with a related contract, asset, or liability. Examples of this would include:

  (a) Deposit liabilities and related depositor relationship intangible assets are exchanged in observable exchange transactions. Therefore, the depositor relationship intangible asset is recognized apart from goodwill.

  (b) An acquired enterprise owns a United States registered trademark, a related secret formula, and non-patented technical expertise used to manufacture the trademarked product. To transfer ownership of a trademark in the United States, the owner is also required to transfer everything else necessary for the new owner to produce a product or service indistinguishable from that produced by the former owner. The non-patented technical expertise meets the criterion in Paragraph 1581.48(b) because it must be separated from the enterprise and sold if the related trademark is sold.

CD-ROM Note An Appendix to Section 1581 contains an extensive listing of the types of assets that would meet the Paragraph 1581.48 criteria. If you are interested in this subject, the complete Appendix can be found in Chapter 13 of our *Guide to Canadian Financial Reporting* which is available on the CD-ROM that is included with this text.

Goodwill

The Concept

3-122. In order to record the business combination transaction, the fair values of the identifiable assets and liabilities of the acquiree are determined on an individual basis. When these assets are put together as a business enterprise, it is unlikely that the sum of these fair values will be equal to the value of the business as an operating economic entity.

3-123. If the assets were used in an effective and efficient manner, it is possible for the business to be worth considerably more than the sum of its individual asset values. Alternatively, ineffectual management or other factors can depress the value of a business well below the sum of the fair values of its assets.

3-124. Note that this is not a clear indication that the assets should be liquidated on an individual basis. Fair values are based on the value of an asset to a going concern and, while in some cases they may be equal to liquidation values, this is not likely to be the case for most non-current assets.

3-125. If the business is worth more than the sum of its individual asset values, this will be reflected in the prices paid by an acquirer in a business combination. In this situation, when the acquisition cost exceeds the acquirer's share of the fair values of the acquiree's identifiable net assets, the excess is generally referred to as goodwill. From a conceptual point of view, goodwill is the capitalized expected value of enterprise earning power in excess of a normal rate of return for the particular industry in which it operates. As an example of this concept, consider the following:

Example: Ryerson Ltd. has net identifiable assets with a current fair value of $1 million. Its annual income has been $150,000 for many years and it is anticipated that this level of earnings will continue indefinitely. A normal rate of return in Ryerson's industry is 10 percent as reflected in business values that are typically 10 times reported earnings.

Analysis Given this information, it is clear that Ryerson has goodwill. Normal earnings on Ryerson's $1 million in net assets would be $100,000, well below the Company's $150,000. Based on these earnings and a valuation benchmark of 10 times earnings, the value of Ryerson as a going concern would be $1.5 million. This would suggest the presence of goodwill as follows:

Value Of Ryerson As A Going Concern	$1,500,000
Fair Value Of Ryerson's Net Identifiable Assets	(1,000,000)
Goodwill	$ 500,000

3-126. While it is clear that, in this simplified example, Ryerson has goodwill, it is unlikely that it will be recorded in the Company's Balance Sheet. Even in situations where an enterprise has incurred significant costs for the creation of goodwill (e.g., management training or advertising directed at enhancing the image of the enterprise), GAAP does not permit the recognition of internally generated goodwill. This reflects the belief that there is no reliable procedure for the measurement of such amounts.

3-127. In a more general context, this belief prevents the recognition of most internally generated intangible assets. The only exception to this is the recognition of certain development costs as assets under the provisions of Section 3450 of the *CICA Handbook*, "Research and Development Costs".

Measurement In Practice

3-128. While it is not possible under GAAP to recognize internally generated goodwill, we often find goodwill in corporate balance sheets. In fact, in many cases, it can be a very significant item. However, these amounts almost invariably reflect goodwill that has been recognized as the result of a business combination transaction.

3-129. In practical terms, the only useful definition of goodwill under GAAP is as follows:

Paragraph 3062.05(b) Goodwill is the excess of the cost of an acquired enterprise over the net of the amounts assigned to assets acquired and liabilities assumed. The amount recognized as goodwill includes acquired intangible assets that do not meet the criteria in "Business Combinations", Section 1581, for recognition as an asset apart from goodwill.

3-130. Returning to our example involving Ryerson Ltd., if another enterprise were to purchase either the net assets or the shares of this enterprise for the suggested value of $1,500,000, the acquirer would record the goodwill of $500,000 that was calculated in the example.

3-131. While we will not deal with this issue in detail until we get to Chapter 4, you should note that, when the business combination involves acquisition of less than 100 percent of the acquiree's shares, this definition only provides for recognizing the acquirer's share of goodwill. As will be discussed at the end of this Chapter, international convergence may result in the recognition of 100 percent of goodwill, not just the acquiring company's share.

General Accounting Procedures

3-132. As noted in the previous section, the excess of the cost of an acquisition over the fair values of the identifiable assets acquired is recorded as goodwill. Once goodwill is measured on the basis of this definition, the *CICA Handbook* specifies the following treatment of this amount:

> **Paragraph 3062.22** *Goodwill should be recognized on an enterprise's balance sheet at the amount initially recognized, less any write-down for impairment.* (January, 2002)

3-133. While not explicitly stated, it is clear from the wording of this recommendation that the amount recorded as goodwill will not be subject to amortization. Rather, it will be the subject of a periodic impairment test which may or may not result in a write-down of any amount that is recorded.

3-134. Any goodwill balance that is recognized will generally be tested on an annual basis for impairment. As specified in the following recommendation, the annual test can sometimes be omitted:

> **Paragraph 3062.39** *Goodwill of a reporting unit should be tested for impairment on an annual basis, unless all of the following criteria have been met:*
>
> *(a) The assets and liabilities that make up the reporting unit have not changed significantly since the most recent fair value determination.*
> *(b) The most recent fair value determination resulted in an amount that exceeded the carrying amount of the reporting unit by a substantial margin.*
> *(c) Based on an analysis of events that have occurred and circumstances that have changed since the most recent fair value determination, the likelihood that a current fair value determination would be less than the current carrying amount of the reporting unit is remote.* (January, 2002)

3-135. Alternatively, more frequent testing may be required under some circumstances:

> **Paragraph 3062.42** *Goodwill of a reporting unit should be tested for impairment between annual tests when an event or circumstance occurs that more likely than not reduces the fair value of a reporting unit below its carrying amount.* (January, 2002)

3-136. Examples of such events or circumstances are as follows:

- a significant adverse change in legal factors or in the business climate;
- an adverse action or assessment by a regulator;
- unanticipated competition;
- a loss of key personnel;
- a more-likely-than-not expectation that a significant portion or all of a reporting unit will be sold or otherwise disposed of;
- the testing for write-down or impairment of a significant asset group within a reporting unit; or
- the recognition of a goodwill impairment loss in its separate financial statements by a subsidiary that is a component of the reporting unit.

3-137. Consistent with other *Handbook* Sections which require asset write-downs (e.g., Section 3051, "Investments"), once a goodwill impairment loss is recognized, it cannot be reversed in a subsequent period.

Differential Reporting Option

3-138. As we have noted, there are significant practical difficulties associated with the required periodic testing for goodwill impairment. For non-publicly accountable enterprises, it is unlikely that the costs of such periodic testing can be justified by the benefits received. Because of this, the AcSB has provided a differential reporting option for qualifying enterprises.

3-139. This option, which is found in Paragraph 3062.55, indicates that qualifying enterprises may elect to test goodwill for impairment only when an event or circumstance occurs that indicates that the fair value of a reporting unit may be less than its carrying amount. Examples of such events are listed in Paragraph 3-136.

Goodwill Impairment Losses

3-140. Section 3062 requires that the goodwill impairment losses be measured at the reporting unit level. For this purpose, reporting units are defined as follows:

> A **reporting unit** is the level of reporting at which goodwill is tested for impairment and is either an operating segment (see "Segment Disclosure", Section 1701), or one level below (referred to as a component).

3-141. In practice, this requirement presents significant difficulties. When there is a business combination transaction, any amount recognized as goodwill must be allocated to individual reporting units. In order to accomplish this, all of the other net assets acquired must also be assigned to segments. Further complicating the situation is that, when these new requirements are first adopted, they must be applied retroactively to all previous business combination transactions.

> **CD-ROM Note** For anyone with a more detailed interest in the measurement of goodwill impairment, we would refer you to Chapter 30 of our *Guide to Canadian Financial Reporting* which is included on the CD-ROM that accompanies this text.

Goodwill Presentation and Disclosure

3-142. With respect to presentation of goodwill in the financial statements, the following two recommendations are relevant:

> **Paragraph 3062.48** *The aggregate amount of goodwill should be presented as a separate line item in an enterprise's balance sheet.* (January, 2002)

> **Paragraph 3062.49** *The aggregate amount of goodwill impairment losses should be presented as a separate line item in the income statement before extraordinary items and discontinued operations, unless a goodwill impairment loss is associated with a discontinued operation. A goodwill impairment loss associated with a discontinued operation should be included on a net-of-tax basis within the results of discontinued operations.* (January, 2002)

3-143. With respect to the disclosure of goodwill, the following recommendations are relevant:

> **Paragraph 3062.51** *The financial statements should disclose the following information:*
>
> *(a) The changes in the carrying amount of goodwill during the period including:*
> *(i) the aggregate amount of goodwill acquired;*
> *(ii) the aggregate amount of impairment losses recognized; and*
> *(iii) the amount of goodwill included in the gain or loss on disposal of all or a portion of a reporting unit.*
>
> *Enterprises that report segment information in accordance with "Segment Disclosures", Section 1701, should provide the above information about goodwill in total and for each reportable segment and should disclose any significant changes in the allocation of goodwill by reportable segment. When any portion of goodwill has not yet been allocated to a reporting unit at the date the financial statements are issued, the unallocated amount and the reasons for not allocating that amount should be disclosed.*

(b) and (c) [These additional subparagraphs refer to intangibles other than goodwill.]

Paragraph 3062.53 *For each goodwill impairment loss recognized, the following information should be disclosed in the financial statements that include the period in which the impairment loss is recognized:*

(a) a description of the facts and circumstances leading to the impairment;
(b) the amount of the impairment loss; and
(c) when a recognized impairment loss is an estimate that has not yet been finalized, that fact and the reasons therefor and, in subsequent periods, the nature and amount of any significant adjustments made to the initial estimate of the impairment loss.

When the carrying amount of a reporting unit exceeds its fair value, but the second step of the impairment test is not complete and a reasonable estimate of the goodwill impairment loss cannot be determined (see paragraph 3062.28), that fact and the reasons therefor should be disclosed. (January, 2002)

Evaluation of Goodwill Procedures

3-144. When there is a business combination transaction we have an objective measure of the amount of goodwill that is present at that time. However, we do not attempt to identify the specific reasons that this value exists. Given the lack of any specific explanation for the presence of goodwill, it is extremely difficult to arrive at a rational estimate of its useful life.

3-145. For many years we used an arbitrary solution to the problem — amortization over a period not to exceed 40 years. At one point in time, there appeared to be a belief that this maximum was too long and that goodwill should be written off over a shorter period. In 1993, the IASB recommended that goodwill arising in business combination transactions should be written off over a period not exceeding five years.

3-146. Standard setters in the U.S. and Canada considered similar changes. However, with the possibility of having to use purchase accounting for all business combinations on the horizon, the view that goodwill had an indefinite life moved to the forefront. While it would perhaps be overly cynical to suggest this change was necessary in order to muster the required support for the elimination of the pooling-of-interests method, it certainly facilitated this process. If goodwill had an indefinite life, it would not have to be amortized, thereby eliminating a major depressant of post-combination earnings when the purchase method was applied.

Negative Goodwill

Basic Rules

3-147. Fair values for the identifiable assets of the acquiree are determined on a going concern basis. As these values are, in general, in excess of the liquidation values of the assets, it is possible that an enterprise might be sold for less than the sum of the fair values of its net assets.

Example Loser Inc. has net assets with a carrying value of $650,000 and fair values totaling $900,000. These net assets are acquired in a business combination transaction for $725,000 in cash, resulting in negative goodwill of $175,000. Note that the $900,000 figure reflects fair values and these are not equal to liquidation values. If the sum of the liquidation values of these assets exceeded $725,000, it is likely that Loser Inc. would have been liquidated, rather than sold as a going concern.

3-148. In recording this business combination transaction, the acquired assets will require a debit of $900,000, while the cash payment will be recognized with a credit of $725,000. We are left in need of an additional credit of $175,000, the amount that we have referred to as negative goodwill. There are various possibilities for this credit, depending on how we analyze the reason for its existence. The various possibilities that are considered in the literature on this subject are as follows:

Overstated Fair Values One view would be that an adequate job of determining the fair values of the identifiable assets was not done and, as a result, they are overstated. If this view is adopted, the appropriate credit would be to one or more of the identifiable assets acquired in the business combination transaction. In general, we would assume that the assets to be reduced would be non-financial items.

Bargain Purchase A second view would be that a bargain purchase was involved. The suggestion would be that, perhaps because of poor operating results, the acquiree enterprise is being sold under some form of duress and this has resulted in an artificially low price. Consistent with this view would be a credit to some type of gain on the transaction.

Inadequate Rate of Return A third interpretation is that the discount reflects the fact that the acquired enterprise is not earning a normal rate of return on its assets, resulting in a going concern value that is less than the sum of the fair values of the identifiable net assets. This interpretation would suggest the use of a general valuation account that would be shown as a contra to the total assets balance.

3-149. It is the first of these views that takes precedence in the Section 1581 recommendation on negative goodwill:

Paragraph 1581.50 *When the net of the amounts assigned to assets acquired and liabilities assumed exceeds the cost of the purchase ("excess" — sometimes referred to as negative goodwill):*

(a) that excess should be allocated as a pro rata reduction of the amounts that otherwise would be assigned to all of the acquired assets except:
(i) financial assets other than investments accounted for by the equity method;
(ii) assets to be disposed of by sale;
(iii) future income tax assets;
(iv) prepaid assets relating to employee future benefit plans; and
(v) any other current assets, to the extent the excess is eliminated; and

(b) any remaining excess should be presented as an extraordinary gain. (July, 2001)

3-150. As indicated, this recommendation relies largely on the overstated fair values interpretation of the negative goodwill balance. If the total of the fair values assigned to the various eligible assets was reduced to nil, then any remaining balance would be credited to an extraordinary gain. We would expect this to be a fairly rare situation. Note, however, that when it occurs, the gain is treated as extraordinary, without regard to the general criteria found in Section 3480, "Extraordinary Items" for this classification.

3-151. An additional problem arises when there is negative goodwill in a situation where contingent consideration is involved. In this case, the settlement of the contingency could result in the negative amount being reduced or eliminated. Given this possibility, Section 1581 makes the following recommendation:

Paragraph 1581.52 *When a business combination involves a contingent consideration agreement that might result in recognition of an additional element of cost of the purchase on resolving the contingency, an amount equal to the lesser of the maximum amount of contingent consideration and the excess should be recognized as if it were a liability. When the contingency is resolved and the consideration is issued or becomes issuable, any excess of the fair value of the contingent consideration issued or issuable over the amount initially recognized should be recognized as an additional cost of the purchase. Any excess of the amount initially recognized as if it were a liability over the fair value of the contingent consideration issued or issuable should first be allocated as a pro rata reduction of the amounts assigned to assets acquired in accordance with paragraph 1581.50(a). Any amount that remains should be accounted for in accordance with paragraph 1581.50(b).* (July, 2001)

3-152. In effect, this recommendation provides for deferring the allocation of any negative goodwill until such time as all possible contingent consideration has been issued.

Exercise Three-6

Subject: Negative Goodwill

On December 31, 2007, 100 percent of the shares of Manee Ltd. are acquired by another corporation for $1,850,000 in cash. On this date, the assets and liabilities of Manee Ltd. have the following fair values:

Cash	$ 265,000
Accounts Receivable	340,000
Inventories	855,000
Property, Plant, And Equipment	1,340,000
Liabilities	(425,000)
Net Assets At Fair Values	$2,375,000

Calculate the values that will be recorded in the acquirer's consolidated financial statements to reflect the acquisition of Manee Ltd.

End of Exercise. Solution available in Study Guide.

Treatment Of Shareholders' Equity

3-153. As the purchase method of accounting for business combinations takes the position that the transaction is simply an acquisition of assets, the acquiring company's shareholders' equity would only be changed to the extent that new shares were issued as consideration to the acquired company or its shareholders.

3-154. However, under some of the legal forms of combination this may be in violation of relevant corporate legislation. For example, if the net assets of two existing companies are transferred to a newly established corporation, the *Canada Business Corporations Act* would require that all of the shareholders' equity of the new corporation be classified as contributed capital.

3-155. A further problem would arise if the combination were implemented using a statutory amalgamation provision. In this type of transaction, corporate legislation usually requires that the contributed capital of the amalgamated company be equal to the aggregate of the contributed capital of the amalgamating enterprises.

3-156. This is, of course, in conflict with the purchase accounting requirement that the shareholders' equity of the combined company have the same amounts of contributed capital and retained earnings as the acquiring company. When conflicts of this sort arise, the relevant corporate legislation must be the determining factor in the presentation of the combined company's shareholders' equity. In the case of statutory amalgamations, the *Handbook* suggests that the additional capital be allocated to a contributed surplus account.

Purchase Method Example

Basic Data

3-157. The preceding material has provided a discussion and description of the various procedures that are required in the application of the purchase method of accounting for business combinations. The example which follows will serve to illustrate the application of these procedures. It involves a purchase of net assets, not shares. We will cover in detail business combinations involving share purchases and consolidated financial statements in Chapters 4 to 7. We have ignored tax considerations in this example.

Example On December 31, 2007, the Balance Sheets of the Dor and Dee Companies, prior to any business combination transaction, are as follows:

Balance Sheets
As At December 31, 2007

	Dor Company	Dee Company
Cash	$ 1,200,000	$ 600,000
Accounts Receivable	2,400,000	800,000
Inventories	3,800,000	1,200,000
Plant And Equipment (Net)	4,600,000	2,400,000
Total Assets	$12,000,000	$5,000,000
Liabilities	$ 1,500,000	$ 700,000
Common Stock - No Par*	6,000,000	2,500,000
Retained Earnings	4,500,000	1,800,000
Total Equities	$12,000,000	$5,000,000

*On this date, prior to the transactions described in the following paragraphs, each Company has 450,000 common shares outstanding.

On December 31, 2007, the Dor Company issues 204,000 shares of its No Par Common Stock to the Dee Company in return for 100 percent of its net assets. On this date the shares of the Dor Company are trading at $25 per share. All of the identifiable assets and liabilities of the Dee Company have fair values that are equal to their carrying values except for the Plant And Equipment which has a fair value of $2,700,000 and a remaining useful life of ten years. Both Companies have a December 31 year end and, for the year ending December 31, 2007, Dor reported Net Income of $800,000 and Dee reported Net Income of $250,000.

Identification Of An Acquirer

3-158. Since the Dor Company issued fewer shares (204,000) to the Dee Company than it had outstanding prior to the business combination (450,000), the shareholders of the Dor Company would be the majority shareholders in the combined company and the Dor Company would be identified as the acquirer.

Determination Of Purchase Price

3-159. With a market value of $25 per share, the 204,000 shares issued to effect the business combination would have a total market value in the amount of $5,100,000. This would be the purchase price of the Dee Company.

Investment Analysis

3-160. It is necessary to allocate the cost of the purchase to the fair values of the identifiable assets and liabilities and to establish a value for either a positive or negative goodwill. This requires an analysis of the total cost of the investment.

3-161. In those cases where the legal form of the combination requires the preparation of consolidated financial statements, this investment analysis can be fairly complex. However, in a simple problem such as the one under consideration, there is no need to have a detailed schedule. It is sufficient to simply calculate the total fair value of the Dee Company's net assets and then compare this value with the purchase price to determine the amount of Goodwill.

3-162. The total fair values would be calculated as follows:

Carrying Values - Dee's Net Assets ($5,000,000 - $700,000)	$4,300,000
Fair Value Increase On Plant ($2,700,000 - $2,400,000)	300,000
Fair Values - Dee's Net Assets	$4,600,000

3-163. Given the purchase price and the fair values, the Goodwill that will be recognized from this business combination can be calculated in the following manner:

Investment Cost [(204,000)($25)]	$5,100,000
Fair Values - Dee's Net Assets	(4,600,000)
Goodwill To Be Recognized	$ 500,000

Schedule For Investment Analysis

3-164. As noted previously, we are normally required to prepare consolidated financial statements in more complex situations, usually involving a large number of fair value changes. The calculations are further complicated in that, if the parent does not acquire 100 percent of the subsidiary's shares, only the parent's proportionate interest in the fair value changes will be recognized. This means that a more systematic approach to the investment analysis is required.

3-165. There are many different approaches that can be used to analyze the investment account, all of which will provide a correct solution to the problem. In the case of a purchase of net assets, the investment analysis approach is as follows:

- Subtract the carrying value of the subsidiary's net assets from the cost of the investment. We will refer to the resulting balance as the differential (another term used for this balance is "purchase price discrepancy"). If it is a positive number, it indicates that the investor is paying more than the carrying value of the subsidiary's net assets and that there is a debit amount to be allocated. A negative number reflects a credit balance to be allocated. Note that, as the differential reflects the total of all fair value changes and goodwill to be recognized, a positive balance does not necessarily indicate the presence of goodwill.
- Once the differential has been established, we will then add or subtract the various fair value changes that have been determined for the subsidiary's identifiable assets and liabilities. As a positive differential reflects a debit balance to be allocated, we will subtract any fair value changes which require allocation of debits (increases in assets or decreases in liabilities). Correspondingly, we will add any fair value changes that require credits (decreases in assets or increases in liabilities).
- The resulting balance will be allocated to goodwill if it is positive. If the balance is negative, it will be allocated as per the recommendation in Paragraph 1581.50.

3-166. Applying these rules to Dor Company's purchase of Dee Company's net assets results in the analysis which follows. Note that the Goodwill is equal to that calculated in Paragraph 3-163.

Investment Cost	$5,100,000
Carrying Values - Dee's Net Assets ($5,000,000 - $700,000)	(4,300,000)
Differential	$ 800,000
Fair Value Increase On Plant ($2,700,000 - $2,400,000)	(300,000)
Goodwill	$ 500,000

3-167. In a simple case such as this, the use of this schedule is not particularly helpful. However, in dealing with more complex situations involving the preparation of consolidated financial statements, this approach will provide for an orderly and systematic approach to the allocation of the investment cost.

Journal Entry

3-168. Using the preceding investment analysis, we are now in a position to record the business combination. It would be recorded on the books of the Dor Company as a simple acquisition of net assets. Except for Dee's Plant And Equipment and the Goodwill to be recorded as a result of the business combination, the carrying values from the books of the Dee Company would be used. The entry is as follows:

Cash	$ 600,000	
Accounts Receivable	800,000	
Inventories	1,200,000	
Plant And Equipment (Fair Value)	2,700,000	
Goodwill (Arising From The Acquisition)	500,000	
Liabilities		$ 700,000
Common Stock - No Par (Dor)		5,100,000

Combined Balance Sheet

3-169. The resulting December 31, 2007 Balance Sheet for the Dor Company, which now includes all of the assets and liabilities of the Dee Company, would be as follows:

Dor Company
Balance Sheet
As At December 31, 2007

Cash ($1,200,000 + $600,000)	$ 1,800,000
Accounts Receivable ($2,400,000 + $800,000)	3,200,000
Inventories ($3,800,000 + $1,200,000)	5,000,000
Plant And Equipment ($4,600,000 + $2,700,000)	7,300,000
Goodwill	500,000
Total Assets	$17,800,000
Liabilities ($1,500,000 + $700,000)	$ 2,200,000
Common Stock - No Par ($6,000,000 + $5,100,000)	11,100,000
Retained Earnings (Dor's Only)	4,500,000
Total Equities	$17,800,000

Combined Income and Earnings Per Share

3-170. We noted previously that Paragraph 1581.12 indicates that the income of the acquired company is only included in the combined companies' income from the date of acquisition. As the date of acquisition was December 31, 2007, none of Dee's 2007 Net Income would be included in the Net Income of the combined company. This means that Dor's reported Net Income for the year ending December 31, 2007 will be $800,000.

3-171. With respect to Earnings Per Share, Dor Company would have 654,000 shares outstanding at the end of the year (450,000 original shares, plus the 204,000 shares issued to acquire the net assets of Dee Company). However, the additional 204,000 shares were issued on December 31, 2007 and, in the basic Earnings Per Share calculation, they would have a weight of nil. This means that basic Earnings Per Share for the combined company would be $1.78 ($800,000 ÷ 450,000).

Exercise Three-7

Subject: Application Of The Purchase Method

On December 31, 2007, the Balance Sheets of the Saller and Sallee Companies, prior to any business combination transaction, are as follows:

Balance Sheets
As At December 31, 2007

	Saller Company	Sallee Company
Cash	$ 1,876,000	$ 564,000
Accounts Receivable	3,432,000	1,232,000
Inventories	5,262,000	2,485,000
Property, Plant, And Equipment (Net)	6,485,000	4,672,000
Total Assets	$17,055,000	$8,953,000
Liabilities	$ 4,843,000	$2,237,000
Common Shares Issued And Outstanding:		
Saller (423,000 Shares)	9,306,000	N/A
Sallee (185,000 Shares)	N/A	3,885,000
Retained Earnings	2,906,000	2,831,000
Total Equities	$17,055,000	$8,953,000

On December 31, 2007, the Saller Company issues 135,000 common shares to the Sallee Company in return for 100 percent of its net assets. On this date, the shares of the Saller Company are trading at $52 per share. Sallee's Cash and Accounts Receivable have fair values that are equal to their carrying values. With respect to Sallee's other assets and liabilities, the Inventories have a fair value of $2,732,000, the Property, Plant And Equipment has a fair value of $4,512,000, and the liabilities have a fair value of $2,115,000. Both Companies have a December 31 year end and, for the year ending December 31, 2007, Saller reported Net Income of $1,465,000 and Sallee reported Net Income of $372,000.

Prepare the combined Balance Sheet that would be presented by Saller Company on December 31, 2007. In addition, determine the Net Income and Earnings Per Share of the Saller Company that would be reported for the year ending December 31, 2007.

End of Exercise. Solution available in Study Guide.

Disclosure

General Recommendations

3-172. Section 1581 contains the following disclosure recommendation for business combinations completed during the period:

> **Paragraph 1581.55** *For each material business combination completed during the period, the combined enterprise should disclose the following:*
>
> *(a) the name and a brief description of the acquired enterprise and, when shares are acquired, the percentage of voting shares acquired;*
>
> *(b) the period for which the earnings of the acquired enterprise are included in the income statement of the combined enterprise;*
>
> *(c) the cost of the purchase and, when applicable, the number of equity instruments issued or issuable, the value assigned to those equity instruments, and the basis for determining that value;*
>
> *(d) a condensed balance sheet disclosing the amount assigned to each major class of asset and liability of the acquired enterprise at the date of acquisition;*
>
> *(e) contingent payments, options, or commitments specified in the acquisition agreement and the accounting treatment that will be followed should any such contingency occur (see also Accounting Guideline No. 14, Disclosure of*

Guarantees); and

(f) *for any purchase price allocation that has not been finalized, that fact and the reasons therefor and, in subsequent periods, the nature and amount of any material adjustments made to the initial allocation of the purchase price.* (July, 2001)

3-173. A further disclosure recommendation is applicable when goodwill and other intangible assets acquired are significant:

> **Paragraph 1581.56** *When the amounts assigned to goodwill or other intangible assets acquired are significant in relation to the total cost of the purchase, the combined enterprise should disclose the following:*
>
> (a) *for intangible assets subject to amortization, the total amount assigned and the amount assigned to each major intangible asset class;*
> (b) *for intangible assets not subject to amortization, the total amount assigned and the amount assigned to each major intangible asset class; and*
> (c) *for goodwill:*
> (i) *the total amount of goodwill and the amount that is expected to be deductible for tax purposes; and*
> (ii) *for enterprises that are required to disclose segment information in accordance with "Segment Disclosures", Section 1701, the amount of goodwill by reportable segment.* (July, 2001)

3-174. There is also a disclosure recommendation for situations where a number of immaterial business combinations are, in the aggregate, material:

> **Paragraph 1581.57** *When a series of individually immaterial business combinations are completed during the period that are material in the aggregate, the combined enterprise should disclose the following:*
>
> (a) *the number of enterprises acquired and a brief description of those enterprises;*
> (b) *the aggregate cost of the acquired enterprises, the number of equity instruments issued or issuable, and the value assigned to those equity instruments;*
> (c) *the aggregate amount of any contingent payments, options or commitments and the accounting treatment that will be followed should any such contingency occur (when potentially significant in relation to the aggregate cost of the purchases); and*
> (d) *the information described in paragraph 1581.56, when the aggregate amount assigned to goodwill or to other intangible assets acquired is significant in relation to the aggregate cost of the purchases.* (July, 2001)

Subsequent Events

3-175. Business combinations may occur after the Balance Sheet date but prior to the issuance of financial statements. As such transactions may be very significant with respect to the acquiring enterprise, Section 1581 makes the following recommendation:

> **Paragraph 1581.59** *The information in paragraphs 1581.55-.56 should be disclosed, to the extent practical, for each material business combination completed after the balance sheet date but before the financial statements are completed. (July, 2001)*

Disclosure Examples

Year Of Acquisition

3-176. Appendix B of Section 1581 contains examples of the disclosure that should accompany business combination transactions. The first example illustrates the disclosure of a material business combination in the year of acquisition. It is as follows:

Note C: Acquisitions

On June 30, 20X2, Alpha acquired 100 percent of the outstanding common shares of Beta. The results of Beta's operations have been included in the consolidated financial statements since that date. Beta is a provider of data networking products and services in Canada and Mexico.

The aggregate purchase price was $9,400,000, including $7,000,000 of cash and common stock valued at $2,400,000. The value of the 100,000 common shares issued was determined based on the average market price of Alpha's common shares over the two-day period before and after the terms of the acquisition were agreed to and announced.

The following table summarizes the estimated fair value of the assets acquired and liabilities assumed at the date of acquisition. Alpha is in the process of obtaining third-party valuations of certain intangible assets; thus, the allocation of the purchase price is subject to refinement.

As at June 30, 20X2		
Current assets	$2,400,000	
Property, plant and equipment	1,500,000	
Intangible assets	4,900,000	
Goodwill	2,200,000	
Total assets acquired		$11,000,000
Current liabilities	($ 500,000)	
Long-term debt	(1,100,000)	
Total liabilities assumed		(1,600,000)
Net assets acquired		$ 9,400,000

Of the $4,900,000 of acquired intangible assets, $2,400,000 was assigned to registered trademarks that are not subject to amortization. The remaining intangible assets include computer software of $1,500,000, patents of $800,000, and other assets of $200,000.

The $2,200,000 of goodwill was assigned to the technology and communications segments in the amounts of $1,300,000 and $900,000, respectively. Of that total amount, $250,000 is expected to be deductible for tax purposes.

Individually Immaterial Combinations

3-177. The second example involves the acquisition of several individually immaterial business combinations that are material in the aggregate. It is as follows:

Note C: Acquisitions

In 20X3, Alpha acquired the following four enterprises for a total cost of $1,000,000, which was paid primarily in cash:

- Omega Consulting, based in Zurich, Switzerland, a leading provider of telecommunications consulting services;
- Gamma Systems, based in London, England, a producer of digital networking technology;
- Delta Communications, Inc., based in Portland, USA, a start-up data networking company; and
- Kappa Networks, Inc., based in Atlanta, USA, a designer and manufacturer of wireless communications networks.

Goodwill recognized in those transactions amounted to $300,000, and that amount is expected to be fully deductible for tax purposes. Goodwill was assigned to the communication and technology segments in the amounts of $120,000 and $180,000, respectively.

International Convergence

Business Combinations

Standards

3-178. The Canadian rules for business combinations are found in Section 1581 of the *CICA Handbook*. The corresponding international standard is IFRS No. 3, *Business Combinations*.

Differences

3-179. The AcSB's Implementation Plan indicates that Section 1581 and IFRS No. 3, *Business Combinations*, are converged except for the following:

- IFRS No. 3 requires the acquisition date to be the date on which the acquirer obtains control over the acquired entity or business. Section 1581 indicates that the acquisition date is the later of:
  (a) the date on which the net assets or equity interests are received and the consideration is given; or
  (b) the date of a written agreement, or a later date designated therein, that provides that control of the acquired enterprise is effectively transferred to the acquirer on that date, subject only to those conditions required to protect the interests of the parties involved.
- IFRS No. 3 requires that shares issued as consideration be measured based on their fair value at the date of the exchange transaction. Section 1581 allows measurement over a reasonable period of time.
- IFRS No. 3 does not allow the use of the acquiree's share of the fair value of the net assets or equity instruments acquired, if that is more reliably measurable, in determining the cost of a business combination. Section 1581 allows this alternative.
- IFRS No. 3 requires that contingent consideration be recognized when it is probable that it will be paid and can be reliably measured. Under Section 1581, contingent consideration is only recognized when the amount of any contingent consideration can be reasonably estimated and the outcome of the contingency can be determined beyond reasonable doubt.
- IFRS No. 3 requires that any negative goodwill be recognized immediately in profit or loss. Section 1581 requires that it be allocated on a pro rata basis to non-financial assets.
- IFRS No. 3 requires the acquirer to recognize the acquiree's identifiable assets, liabilities, and contingent liabilities at their fair values at the acquisition date. Section 1581 allows only the acquirer's share of fair value changes to be recognized.

3-180. The last of these differences is the most important in terms of the material that will follow in this text. Adoption of the IFRS No. 3 approach will result in large differences in the amounts to be recognized for the assets acquired in a business combination transaction.

Example Morin Ltd. has Land with a carrying value of $500,000. Its current fair value is $4,500,000. Morin Ltd. is combined with Nareed Inc. through Nareed's acquisition of 60 percent of Morin's outstanding voting shares.

Analysis Under IFRS No. 3, the Land would be recorded on the combined companies books at its fair value of $4,500,000. Under Section 1581, the Land would be recorded at $2,900,000 [(40%)($500,000) + (60%)($4,500,000)], a difference of $1,600,000 ($4,500,000 - $2,900,000).

3-181. This difference not only affects the amount to be recognized at the time of the business combination transaction, it will also influence income in subsequent periods when non-depreciable assets are sold and depreciable assets are amortized. Detailed attention will be given to this issue in Chapters 4 through 7 as we examine the procedures for preparing consolidated financial statements.

Goodwill

Standards

3-182. While Section 1581, "Business Combinations", deals with the initial recognition of goodwill, its subsequent treatment is covered in Section 3062, "Goodwill And Other Intangible Assets". In similar fashion, IFRS No. 3, *Business Combinations*, deals with the initial recognition of goodwill, while its subsequent treatment is found in IAS No. 36, *Impairment Of Assets*, and IAS No. 38, *Intangible Assets*.

Differences

3-183. With respect to the initial recognition of goodwill, Section 1581 and IFRS No. 3 are largely converged. There are, however, some differences between the guidance in Section 3062 and the corresponding provisions of IAS Nos. 36 and 38:

- IAS No. 38 provides more detailed guidance on intangible assets.
- IAS No. 38 permits revaluation to fair value in the case of intangible assets that have an active market.
- IAS No. 36 and IAS No. 38 use a different model for testing impairment. Under these standards, an impairment loss is the excess of the carrying amount of the asset over its recoverable amount. Section 3062 measures this type of loss as the excess of an asset's carrying amount over its fair value.

FASB/IASB Joint Project

3-184. The FASB and IASB are currently (March, 2007) working on a joint project that will result in a converged standard on business combinations. The IASB has indicated that it expects to issue an amended IFRS No. 3 during the third quarter of 2007. There will likely be a simultaneous amendment of SFAS No. 141, *Business Combinations*. The AcSB has indicated that it will incorporate these amended documents into Canadian standards, subsequent to the completion of the FASB and IASB convergence project.

3-185. While there are a number of detailed changes that will result from this project, the most significant change that is contained in the proposals as they stand relates to the measurement of goodwill. Under current FASB, IASB, and AcSB standards, only the acquirer's share of goodwill is recognized at the time of a business combination transaction. Under the proposals that are currently being put forward by the FASB and IASB, any non-controlling share of goodwill would also be recognized.

> **Example** Sardo Inc. has identifiable assets with a fair value of $5 million. Lator Ltd. acquires 60 percent of Sardo's outstanding voting shares by paying $3.6 million in cash.
>
> **Analysis** Under current FASB, IASB, and AcSB standards, Lator would recognized goodwill of $600,000 [$3,600,000 - (60%)($5,000,000)] in this business combination transaction.
>
> In contrast, under the joint FASB/IASB proposals, Lator would recognize the fact that their purchase price of $3.6 million indicates that the total value of Sardo is $6 million ($3,600,000 ÷ .6). This would suggest that Sardo has goodwill of $1 million ($6,000,000 - $5,000,000).

3-186. The FASB and IASB have received a fairly large number of negative comments on this proposal. However, in their most recent statement on the subject, they have indicated that this change will be included in the final version of their new standard on business combinations.

3-187. As was the case with the recognition of 100 percent of the fair values for identifiable assets acquired in a business combination, this proposal will be given more detailed consideration in Chapters 4 through 7 where we deal with the procedures associated with the preparation of consolidated financial statements.

Business Combinations In Canadian Practice

Statistics From Financial Reporting In Canada

3-188. Of the 200 companies surveyed for the 2006 edition of *Financial Reporting in Canada*, 69 companies disclosed one or more business combination transactions in their 2005 annual reports.

13-189. With respect to disclosure, the survey results included the following:

- 69 companies indicated the cost of acquisition.
- 66 companies provided the name of the acquiree.
- 58 companies provided a condensed balance sheet.
- 57 companies provided a description of the business acquired.
- 52 companies indicated the period for which results of operations of the acquired business are included.
- 52 companies indicated the percentage of voting shares acquired.
- 11 companies provided details of contingent consideration.

CD-ROM Note If you are interested in more information on statistics on this subject, the CICA's *Financial Reporting in Canada* is available on the CD-ROM which is included with this text.

Example From Practice

3-190. The following example is from the annual report of Alimentation Couche-Tard Inc. for the reporting period ending April 24, 2005. This example illustrates disclosure of current year business acquisitions as well as changes to the purchase price allocation. Also included are three acquisitions in prior years.

Notes to Consolidated Financial Statements

(in millions of Canadian dollars, except per share amounts)
April 24, 2005, April 25, 2004 and April 27, 2003

Note 5 – Business Acquisitions
The Company has made the following business acquisitions that were accounted for using the purchase method. Earnings from the businesses acquired are included in the consolidated earnings from their respective dates of acquisition.

2005
Changes to the purchase price allocation
During the year, the Company finalized the allocation of the purchase price related to the acquisition of The Circle K Corporation (Circle K) on December 17, 2003. The final allocation resulted in an increase in fixed assets of $21.8 and an increase in asset retirement obligations of $20.1 mainly due to a change in the estimate of the asset retirement obligations and an increase in trademarks and licenses of $17.1 based on an external valuation of trademarks.

In addition, the final allocation resulted in an increase in net working capital of $2.1, an increase in other assets of $1.8, and a decrease in net future income tax assets of $22.7. The preliminary allocation of the purchase price is described below.

Acquisitions
During the year, the Company made the following business acquisitions:

- In April 2005: purchase of nine sites operating under the Thornton and Pit Stop banners in the Midwest region from Thorntons Inc. and Broadus Oil Corporation of Illinois Inc.;

- Effective February 2, 2005: purchase of 19 sites operating under the Pump N Shop banner in the Augusta, Georgia area from QVS Inc. and Brosious & Holt Properties LLC;
- Effective November 3, 2004: purchase of 21 sites in the Phoenix, Arizona area from Shell Oil Products US.

These three acquisitions were settled for a total cash consideration of $85.2 financed from the Company's available cash. The net assets acquired included working capital of $4.0, fixed assets of $78.4 and goodwill of $2.8. Most of the goodwill related to these transactions is deductible for tax purposes.

2004

On December 17, 2003, the Company acquired all of the outstanding shares of Circle K from ConocoPhillips Company. The assets included a chain of 1,663 stores in 16 U.S. states, mainly in the southern United States. Circle K also holds franchise or licensing agreements with another 627 stores in the United States and 4,003 international licenses agreements.

This acquisition was made for a total cash consideration of US$831.8 (CA$1,102.5), including acquisition costs and amounts payable in accordance with a price adjustment clause, based on the working capital acquired. The acquisition was financed by issuing 27,111,076 new Class B subordinate voting shares (see Note 18) and by issuing new debt.

On September 4, 2003, the Company concluded the acquisition of assets of Clark Retail Enterprises Inc. (Clark) including 43 stores in the states of Illinois, Indiana, Iowa, Michigan and Ohio. This acquisition was made for a total cash consideration of $41.0, including acquisition costs. The transaction was financed by using the Company's existing credit facilities. Most of the goodwill related to this transaction is deductible for tax purposes.

The preliminary allocations of the purchase prices of the acquisitions were as follows:

	Circle K	Clark	Total
	$	$	$
Current assets	314.6	4.9	319.5
Fixed assets	778.8	29.9	808.7
Goodwill		7.3	7.3
Trademarks, licenses and other assets	211.0	—	211.0
Future income taxes	37.0	0.1	37.1
	1,341.4	42.2	1,383.6
Current liabilities assumed	218.3	0.6	218.9
Long-term debt assumed	8.9	—	8.9
Deferred credits and other liabilities assumed	11.7	0.6	12.3
	238.9	1.2	240.1
Net assets and total consideration	1,102.5	41.0	1,143.5
Less: Cash from the acquisition	106.8	—	106.8
Net assets excluding cash from the acquisition	995.7	41.0	1,036.7
Less: Balance to be paid to vendors	11.4	—	11.4
Cash consideration	984.3	41.0	1,025.3

Subsequent to the acquisitions of Circle K and Clark, the Company entered into sale and leaseback agreements under which certain fixed assets acquired were sold to financial institutions and re-leased to the Company under long-term leases. Most of these long-term leases are for periods of 15 to 17 years, with the possibility of renewal. These transactions did not result in any gains or losses for the Company. Proceeds related to these transactions amounted to US$267.7, net of related expenses.

2003

On August 20, 2002, the Company acquired certain assets of Dairy Mart Convenience Stores Inc. (Dairy Mart), including a chain of 285 stores in the states of Ohio, Kentucky, Pennsylvania, Michigan and Indiana. This acquisition was for a total cash consideration of $120.1, including acquisition costs. The full amount of the transaction was financed through bank loans.

This transaction included a one-year management agreement for 169 additional stores in this network, some of which could, under certain conditions, be acquired by the Company in the months following the acquisition, sold on behalf of Dairy Mart or closed. Given the temporary nature of the management agreement, the net amount of sales, cost of sales and other operating costs associated with this agreement are shown under Operating, selling, administrative and general expenses. For the year ended April 27, 2003, the management agreement generated sales of $129.3 and operating income of $0.9.

In addition, the Company made four acquisitions of other store networks in Canada and the United States, for a total cash consideration of $36.8 including certain stores managed under the above-mentioned management agreement. These acquisitions are presented as "Other" in the following table.

Most of the goodwill related to these transactions is deductible for tax purposes.

The allocation of the purchase prices of the above-mentioned acquisitions was determined as follows:

	Dairy Mart	Other	Total
	$	$	$
Current assets	18.8	1.6	20.4
Fixed assets	73.2	27.6	100.8
Goodwill	31.3	8.0	39.3
Other assets	—	0.3	0.3
Future income taxes	0.6	—	0.6
	123.9	37.5	161.4
Current liabilities assumed	3.8	0.7	4.5
Net assets	120.1	36.8	156.9
Less: Cash from the acquisition	0.6	0.1	0.7
Cash consideration	119.5	36.7	156.2

CD-ROM Note If you are interested in more examples of business combinations, the CICA's *Financial Reporting in Canada* is available on the CD-ROM which is included with this text.

Additional Readings

3-191. In writing the material in the text, we have incorporated all of the relevant *CICA Handbook* recommendations, as well as material from other sources that we felt to be of importance. This includes some, but not all, of the EIC Abstracts that relate to business combinations, as well as material from international accounting standards.

3-192. While this approach meets the needs of the great majority of our readers, some of you may wish to pursue this subject in greater depth. To facilitate this, you will find a fairly comprehensive list of additional readings at the end of each relevant Chapter in our *Guide To Canadian Financial Reporting*.

CD-ROM Note Our *Guide To Canadian Financial Reporting* is available on the CD-ROM which is included with this text.

Problems For Self Study

(The solutions for these problems can be found in the separate Study Guide.)

Self Study Problem Three - 1

On December 31, 2007, the Balance Sheets of the Graber and the Grabee Companies are as follows:

Graber and Grabee Companies
Balance Sheets
As At December 31, 2007

	Graber	Grabee
Cash	$ 50,000	$ 70,000
Accounts Receivable	250,000	330,000
Inventories	400,000	300,000
Plant and Equipment (Net)	1,200,000	600,000
Land	800,000	400,000
Goodwill	150,000	50,000
Total Assets	$2,850,000	$1,750,000
Current Liabilities	$ 75,000	$ 50,000
Long-Term Liabilities	800,000	400,000
Future Income Tax Liabilities	200,000	100,000
Common Stock (40,000 Shares)	1,200,000	N/A
Common Stock (9,000 Shares)	N/A	900,000
Retained Earnings	575,000	300,000
Total Equities	$2,850,000	$1,750,000

On December 31, 2007, the Graber Company issues 40,000 of its shares to the Grabee Company in return for 100 percent of its net assets. The December 31, 2007 market values for the shares are as follows:

- Graber: $35 Per Share
- Grabee: $250 Per Share

After selling its net assets, the Grabee Company distributes the Graber shares to its shareholders in return for their shares. The Grabee shares are then cancelled and the Company ceases to exist as a separate legal entity. The direct expenses of carrying out this business combination transaction amount to $10,000 and are paid in cash.

Other Information

1. All of the net identifiable assets of the two Companies have fair values that are equal to their carrying values except for the Grabee Company's Goodwill and Future Income Tax Liabilities and the following other accounts:

	Fair Values	
	Graber	Grabee
Plant and Equipment (Net)	$1,800,000	$800,000
Land	1,000,000	300,000
Long-Term Liabilities	750,000	450,000

2. The Net Income of the Graber Company for the year ending December 31, 2007 was $125,000, while that of the Grabee Company amounted to $200,000.

3. The 2007 Net Income of the Graber Company included a $20,000 gain resulting from the sale of land to the Grabee Company on July 8, 2007.

4. The 2007 Net Income of the Grabee Company included a $50,000 gain on sales of merchandise in November to the Graber Company. All of this merchandise remained in the December 31, 2007 Inventories of the Graber Company.

5. Subsequent to the business combination transaction, the combined company will be under the direction of the Graber management team.

Required: Prepare the combined company's Balance Sheet as at December 31, 2007. In addition, calculate the combined company's Net Income and Earnings Per Share for the year ending December 31, 2007.

Self Study Problem Three - 2

On December 31, 2007, the condensed Balance Sheets of the Ero Company and the Tick Company are as follows:

Ero and Tick Company
Condensed Balance Sheets
As At December 31, 2007

	Ero	Tick
Monetary Assets	$ 200,000	$1,000,000
Non-Monetary Assets	3,800,000	4,000,000
Total Assets	$4,000,000	$5,000,000
Monetary Liabilities	$ 100,000	$ 800,000
Common Stock (200,000 Shares Issued)	2,500,000	-0-
Common Stock (100,000 Shares Issued)	-0-	3,000,000
Retained Earnings	1,400,000	1,200,000
Total Equities	$4,000,000	$5,000,000

On December 31, 2007, the Monetary Assets and Liabilities of both Companies have fair values that are equal to their carrying values. The fair values of Ero's Non-Monetary Assets are $400,000 greater than their carrying values, while the fair values of Tick's Non-Monetary Assets are $600,000 less than their carrying values. For both Companies, the Non-Monetary Assets have an estimated remaining useful life of 4 years. Both Companies use the straight line method for all depreciation and amortization calculations. Neither Company owns any intangible assets that result from contractual or other legal rights, or are capable of being separated or divided and sold, transferred, licensed, rented, or exchanged.

The Net Income of the Ero Company for the year ending December 31, 2007 is $400,000 and the Net Income of the Tick Company for the year ending December 31, 2007 is $600,000. If there had been no business combination on December 31, 2007, the 2008 Net Income of Ero would have been $700,000 and that of Tick would have been $800,000. There are no intercompany transactions or dividends declared in 2007 or 2008. Goodwill impairment was determined to be nil for the year ended December 31, 2008.

These two Companies can effect a business combination by different legal avenues. Both of the following independent Cases assume that a business combination takes place on December 31, 2007.

A. Ero issues 100,000 of its shares to Tick in return for 100 percent of Tick's net assets. The shares of Tick are cancelled and Ero is the sole survivor of the combination. Ero shares are trading at $40 per share on this date.

B. A new Company, the Erotick Company, is formed which issues 300,000 no par value common shares. Of these new shares, Tick receives 180,000 in return for 100 percent of its net assets and Ero receives 120,000 shares in return for 100 percent of its net assets. On the date of the combination, Ero shares are trading at $24 per share and Tick shares are trading at $72 per share.

Required: For both of the preceding Cases, prepare the December 31, 2007 Balance Sheet for the combined business entity. In addition, compute Net Income and Basic Earnings Per Share figures for the business entity resulting from the combination for both 2007 and 2008. Prepare the new Company's Shareholders' Equity on the basis of *CICA Handbook* recommendations, without regard to the requirements of corporate legislation.

Self Study Problem Three - 3

On December 31, 2007, the condensed Balance Sheets of the Gold Company and the Medal Company are as follows:

Gold and Medal Companies
Balance Sheets
As At December 31, 2007

	Gold	Medal
Monetary Assets	$ 500,000	$ 300,000
Non-Monetary Assets	5,500,000	3,200,000
Total Assets	$6,000,000	$3,500,000
Monetary Liabilities	$ 300,000	$ 100,000
Shareholders' Equity		
Common Stock (100,000 Shares)	4,200,000	-0-
Common Stock (100,000 Shares)	-0-	2,000,000
Retained Earnings	1,500,000	1,400,000
Total Equities	$6,000,000	$3,500,000

During 2007, the Net Income of the Gold Company was $1 million, while the Net Income of the Medal Company was $200,000. For 2008, if we assume that there is no business combination on December 31, 2007, the corresponding Net Income figures would be $1.5 million and $500,000. No dividends were paid by either Company in 2007 or 2008. No intercompany transactions occurred during 2008. Goodwill impairment was determined to be nil for the year ended December 31, 2008.

The Monetary Assets and Liabilities of both Companies have fair values that are equal to their carrying values. The fair values of the Non-Monetary Assets are $6 million for Gold and $3 million for Medal. The Non-Monetary Assets consist of Plant And Equipment with an estimated useful life of 5 years with no anticipated net salvage value. Both Companies use the straight line method for all depreciation and amortization calculations.

On December 31, 2007, there are several different legal avenues that the two Companies can use to effect a business combination. Three different possibilities are as follows:

A. Medal issues 90,000 of its shares in return for the net assets of Gold. At the date of the combination, the shares of Medal are trading at $65 per share. Gold continues to exist as a separate legal entity.

B. Gold issues 80,000 of its shares in return for the net assets of Medal. The shares of Medal are cancelled and Medal ceases to exist as a legal entity. At the date of the combination, the shares of Gold are trading at $50 per share.

C. A new Company, the Goldmedal Company, is formed and issues 50,000 no par value common shares to Gold in return for all of its net assets and 30,000 shares to Medal in return for all of its net assets. The Gold Company and the Medal Company distribute the Goldmedal shares to their shareholders and cease to exist as separate legal and economic entities. At the date of the combination, the Gold Company shares are trading at $75 and the Medal Company shares are trading at $45 per share.

Required: For each of the preceding independent Cases, prepare the combined Balance Sheet as at December 31, 2007. In addition, compute Net Income and Earnings Per Share figures for the business entity resulting from the combination for both the year ending December 31, 2007 and the year ending December 31, 2008. Your solutions should be prepared based on the *CICA Handbook* Recommendations, without regard to any corporate legislation requirements that may be applicable.

Assignment Problems

(The solutions for these problems are only available in the solutions manual that has been provided to your instructor.)

Assignment Problem Three - 1

On December 31, 2007, the condensed Balance Sheets of the Hyper Company and the Tension Company are as follows:

Hyper and Tension Companies
Condensed Balance Sheets
At December 31, 2007

	Hyper	Tension
Monetary Assets	$1,400,000	$ 800,000
Non-Monetary Assets	4,600,000	2,200,000
Total Assets	$6,000,000	$3,000,000
Monetary Liabilities	$ 500,000	$ 200,000
Common Stock (100,000 Shares)	3,000,000	-0-
Common Stock (10,000 Shares)	-0-	2,000,000
Retained Earnings	2,500,000	800,000
Total Equities	$6,000,000	$3,000,000

The Monetary Assets of both Companies have fair values that are equal to their carrying values. The fair value of the Hyper Company's Non-Monetary Assets is $4 million and the fair value of its Monetary Liabilities is $400,000. The fair value of the Tension Company's Non-Monetary Assets is $2 million and the fair value of its Monetary Liabilities is $250,000. Neither Company owns any intangible assets that result from contractual or other legal rights, or are capable of being separated or divided and sold, transferred, licensed, rented, or exchanged.

These two Companies can effect a business combination by several different legal avenues. Both of the following independent cases assumes that one of these available avenues has been chosen and that a business combination takes place on December 31, 2007.

As the problem is designed to illustrate the concepts involved in the application of purchase accounting, your solutions should be consistent with the concepts associated with these procedures and should ignore any effects that corporate legislation might have on the shareholders' equity of the combined company.

A. The Hyper Company issues 70,000 of its shares in return for the net assets of the Tension Company. The shares of Tension are cancelled and Tension ceases to exist as a separate legal entity. At the date of the combination the shares of the Hyper Company are trading at $45 per share.

B. A new Company, the Hypertension Company, is formed. This new Company issues 15,000 no par value shares to the Hyper Company in return for all of its net assets and 10,000 no par value shares to the Tension Company in return for all of its net assets. Both the Hyper Company and the Tension Company distribute the Hypertension Company shares to their shareholders in return for all of their outstanding shares. The Hyper Company and Tension Company shares are cancelled and the two Companies cease to exist as separate legal entities. At the date of the combination, the Hyper Company shares are trading at $90 per share and the Tension Company shares are trading at $600 per share.

Required: For both of the preceding cases, prepare the appropriate combined Balance Sheet as at December 31, 2007.

Assignment Problem Three - 2

The condensed Balance Sheets of Curly Inc., Larry Ltd., and Moe Inc., on December 31, 2007 are as follows:

Condensed Balance Sheets
December 31, 2007

	Curly	Larry	Moe
Monetary Assets	$ 193,000	$ 154,000	$128,000
Non-Monetary Assets	846,000	862,000	653,000
Total Assets	$1,039,000	$1,016,000	$781,000
Monetary Liabilities	$ 107,000	$ 58,000	$ 47,000
Common Stock (20,000 Shares)	240,000	N/A	N/A
Common Stock (100,000 Shares)	N/A	500,000	N/A
Common Stock (100,000 Shares)	N/A	N/A	150,000
Retained Earnings	692,000	458,000	584,000
Total Equities	$1,039,000	$1,016,000	$781,000

Other information related to the three Companies is as follows:

	Curly	Larry	Moe
Fair Value - Non-Monetary Assets	$723,000	$1,106,000	$685,000
Fair Value - Monetary Liabilities	$107,000	$ 55,000	$ 54,000

On December 31, 2007, there are several different legal avenues that these three Companies can use to effect a business combination. Three different possibilities are as follows:

A. Moe Inc. issues 90,000 shares to Curly Inc. in return for all of the net assets of that Company. Moe also issues 80,000 shares to Larry Ltd. in return for all of the net assets of that Company. Assume that the shares of Moe Inc. are trading at $11 per share at this time.

B. Larry Ltd. issues 85,000 new shares to Curly Inc. in return for all of the net assets of that Company. Larry also issues 75,000 new shares to Moe Inc. in return for all of the net assets of that Company. Assume that the shares of Larry Ltd. are trading at $11.50 per share at this time.

C. A new Company, Stooges Inc., is established. This new Company issues 92,000 of its shares to Curly Inc., 46,000 of its shares to Larry Ltd., and 44,000 of its shares to Moe Inc. In return the new Company acquires all of the net assets of the three Companies. Assume that the shares of Curly, Larry, and Moe are trading at $115 per share, $11.50 per share, and $11.00 per share respectively.

Required: For each of the preceding independent cases, prepare the combined Balance Sheet as at December 31, 2007. Your solutions should be prepared based on the *CICA Handbook* Recommendations, without regard to any corporate legislation requirements that may be applicable.

Assignment Problem Three - 3

On December 31, 2007, the assets and liabilities of the Davis Company and the Jones Company have fair values and book values as follows:

Davis and Jones Companies
Balance Sheets
At December 31, 2007

	Davis		Jones	
	Book Value	**Fair Value**	**Book Value**	**Fair Value**
Cash	$ 450,000	$ 450,000	$ 375,000	$ 375,000
Accounts Receivable	560,000	545,000	420,000	405,000
Inventories	1,200,000	1,150,000	875,000	950,000
Net Plant And Equipment	2,800,000	3,200,000	1,450,000	1,250,000
Goodwill	-0-	-0-	125,000	-0-
Total Assets	$5,010,000	$5,345,000	$3,245,000	$2,980,000
Current Liabilities	$ 325,000	$ 325,000	$ 295,000	$ 295,000
Bonds Payable	1,200,000	1,400,000	870,000	910,000
Future Income Tax Liability	780,000	N/A	430,000	N/A
No Par Common Stock	2,100,000	N/A	1,200,000	N/A
Retained Earnings	605,000	N/A	450,000	N/A
Total Equities	$5,010,000		$3,245,000	

On December 31, 2007, the Davis Company issues 30,000 shares of its No Par Common Stock in return for all of the assets and liabilities of the Jones Company. On this date the Davis Company shares are trading at $65 per share while the Jones Company shares are trading at $32.50 per share.

Other Information:

1. The No Par Common Stock of the Davis Company, prior to the business combination, consists of 42,000 shares issued at an average price of $50 per share. The No Par Common Stock of the Jones Company consists of 60,000 shares issued at an average price of $20 per share.
2. The Jones Company has an unrecognized loss carry forward of $300,000. Both Companies are subject to a combined provincial and federal tax rate of 40 percent. The two Companies feel that there is reasonable assurance that the carry forward benefit will be realized if they are brought together in a business combination transaction.

Required: Prepare the December 31, 2007 Balance Sheet that would be required for the combined company resulting from the business combination transaction.

Assignment Problem Three - 4

On December 31, 2007, Public Ltd. acquires all of the outstanding shares of Private Inc. The consideration consists of 100,000 Public Ltd. shares plus $1,300,000 in cash. At the time of issue, the Public Ltd. shares are trading at $10.50. As part of the acquisition contract, Public Ltd. agrees that, if by the end of 2008 their shares are not trading at a price of $12.00 or more, it will pay an additional $150,000 in cash to the former shareholders of Private Inc.

On December 31, 2007, the pre-business combination Balance Sheets of the two Companies are as follows:

Public Ltd. and Private Inc.
Balance Sheets
As At December 31, 2007

	Public Ltd.	Private Inc.
Cash	$1,892,000	$ 342,000
Accounts Receivable	767,000	Nil
Inventories	1,606,000	641,000
Land	462,000	107,000
Plant And Equipment - Cost	3,272,000	2,727,000
Accumulated Depreciation	(1,203,000)	(776,000)
Patent	-0-	103,000
Goodwill	372,000	-0-
Total Assets	$7,168,000	$3,144,000
Current Liabilities	$ 458,000	Nil
Bonds Payable - Par	1,507,000	$ 800,000
Bond Payable - Premium	48,000	23,000
Public Common Stock - No Par (250,000 Shares)	2,500,000	N/A
Private Common Stock - No Par	N/A	1,200,000
Retained Earnings	2,655,000	1,121,000
Total Equities	$7,168,000	$3,144,000

Other Information:

1. The stock of Public Ltd. is traded on a national stock exchange. As a consequence, they are required to prepare audited financial statements. Private Inc. is a Canadian controlled private corporation and has never needed audited financial statements.

2. As there has been no need for Private Inc. to comply with generally accepted accounting principles (GAAP), the Company records revenues and current expenses on a cash basis. After some investigation, it is determined that on January 1, 2007, Private Inc. had unrecorded Accounts Receivable of $220,000 and unrecorded Accounts Payable of $273,000. The corresponding balances on December 31, 2007 are $326,000 for Accounts Receivable and $473,000 for Accounts Payable.

3. Public Ltd. records Inventories at lower of cost and market. Private Inc.'s Inventories are carried at cost. On December 31, 2007, the net realizable value of Private Inc.'s Inventories was $607,000.

4. On December 31, 2007, the appraised value of Private Inc.'s Land was $93,000.

5. The December 31, 2007 fair value of Private Inc.'s Plant And Equipment is $2,103,000.

6. The Patent on Private Inc.'s books was purchased on January 1, 2002 and is being amortized over what was expected to be its useful life, ten years. However, the process that is covered by the Patent has been replaced by a less costly procedure, and is no longer used by the Company. Private Inc. does not own any other intangible assets.

7. Private Inc.'s Bonds Payable were privately placed with a large insurance company. At current market rates of interest they have a present value of $790,000. However, they can only be retired by paying the insurance company a premium of 10 percent over their par value.

Required: Prepare the December 31, 2007 Balance Sheet for the combined Companies Public Ltd. and its subsidiary, Private Inc.

Assignment Problem Three - 5

As at December 31, 2007, the condensed Balance Sheets of Monson Ltd., Barrister Ltd., and Flex Ltd. are as follows:

Monson Ltd.
Condensed Balance Sheet
At December 31, 2007

	Book Values	**Fair Values**
Current Assets	$ 24,200	$ 25,000
Non-Current Assets	186,500	193,200
Total Assets	$210,700	
Liabilities	$ 78,400	$ 75,600
No Par Common Stock (11,000 Shares)	93,500	
Retained Earnings	38,800	
Total Equities	$210,700	

Barrister Ltd.
Condensed Balance Sheet
At December 31, 2007

	Book Values	**Fair Values**
Current Assets	$ 35,800	$ 34,500
Non-Current Assets	220,600	168,400
Total Assets	$256,400	
Liabilities	$ 56,300	$ 58,200
No Par Common Stock (5,500 Shares)	66,000	
Retained Earnings	134,100	
Total Equities	$256,400	

Flex Ltd.
Condensed Balance Sheet
At December 31, 2007

	Book Values	**Fair Values**
Current Assets	$ 46,300	$ 47,300
Non-Current Assets	152,200	156,600
Total Assets	$198,500	
Liabilities	$ 62,400	$ 59,800
No Par Common Stock (18,000 Shares)	45,000	
Retained Earnings	91,100	
Total Equities	$198,500	

The three Companies intend to combine their activities and are considering a variety of approaches. Three possible approaches are as follows:

> **Approach One** Flex Ltd. would borrow $303,000. Using the loan proceeds, Flex Ltd. would pay cash of $160,000 to Monson Ltd. and cash of $143,000 to Barrister Ltd., in return for all of the assets and liabilities of the two Companies. There will be a wind up of the operations of both Monson Ltd. and Barrister Ltd.
>
> **Approach Two** Barrister Ltd. would borrow $326,000. Using the loan proceeds, Barrister Ltd. would pay cash of $170,000 to the shareholders of Monson Ltd. and cash of $156,000 to the shareholders of Flex Ltd., in return for all of the outstanding shares of these two Companies.
>
> **Approach Three** Monson Ltd. will issue 11,000 new common shares to Barrister Ltd. and 11,000 new common shares to Flex Ltd. In return, Monson Ltd. will receive all of the assets and liabilities of the two Companies. There would be a wind up of the activities of the two Companies. At this time, the common stock of Monson Ltd. is trading at $13.50 per share. Neither Barrister Ltd. nor Flex Ltd. are given representation on the Monson Ltd. board of directors.

Required: Prepare the December 31, 2007 Balance Sheet for the combined company that would result from each of the three approaches described.

Assignment Problem Three - 6

The Haggard Corporation Limited (Haggard, hereafter), a federally chartered Canadian company, has concluded negotiations with the Jones Corporation Limited (Jones, hereafter) for the purchase of all of the latter corporation's assets at fair market value, effective January 1, 2007. Jones Corporation Limited operates a restaurant and a catering business.

An examination at that date by independent experts disclosed that the fair market value of Jones' inventories was $150,000, and of its machinery and equipment was $160,000. The original cost of the machinery and equipment was $140,000. It was determined that accounts receivable were fairly valued at book value.

Jones held 1,000 of the common shares of Haggard and the fair market value of these shares was $62,000. This value corresponds with the value of Haggard's common shares in the open market and would be expected to hold for transactions involving a substantially larger number of shares.

The purchase agreement provides that the total purchase price of all assets will be $490,000, payable as follows:

1. Assumption of the current liabilities of Jones at their book value;
2. Settlement of the Jones debenture debt at its current value in a form acceptable to Jones debenture holders;
3. Haggard shares held by Jones and acquired by Haggard as a result of the transaction would be subsequently returned to Jones at fair market value as part of the consideration;
4. Haggard holds 1,000 shares of Jones and these would be returned to Jones. The value to be ascribed to these shares is 1/10 of the difference between the total purchase price of all assets stated above ($490,000), less the current value of its liabilities.
5. The balance of the purchase consideration was to be entirely in Haggard common shares, except for a possible fractional share element which would be paid in cash.

The Jones debenture holders, who are neither shareholders of Haggard nor Jones, have agreed to accept Haggard bonds in an amount equal to $88,626, the current market value of the bonds. The Haggard bonds carry a 12 percent coupon and trade at par. The face value of each bond is $1,000.

Any amounts assigned to goodwill in this business combination will be deductible for tax purposes as cumulative eligible capital up to a maximum of 75 percent.

Jones, upon conclusion of the agreement, would be wound up. The Balance Sheets of both corporations, as at the date of implementation of the purchase agreement (January 1, 2007), are as follows:

Balance Sheets
As At January 1, 2007

	Haggard	**Jones**
Cash	$ 100,000	Nil
Accounts Receivable	288,000	$112,000
Inventories At Cost	250,000	124,000
Investment In Jones (1,000 Shares)	20,000	N/A
Investment In Haggard (1,000 Shares)	N/A	40,000
Machinery And Equipment - Net	412,000	100,000
Total Assets	$1,070,000	$376,000
Current Liabilities	$ 60,000	$ 35,000
7% Debentures - Due December 31, 2009	N/A	100,000
12% Bonds - Due December 31, 2009	500,000	N/A
Premium On Bonds	20,000	N/A
Common Stock (See Note)	200,000	100,000
Retained Earnings	290,000	141,000
Total Equities	$1,070,000	$376,000

Note Each company has issued 10,000 shares.

Both corporations have fiscal years that are identical to the calendar year.

Required:

A. Prepare Haggard's pro-forma Balance Sheet as at January 1, 2007.

B. Draft a note to the 2007 financial statements disclosing the purchase of Jones' net assets.

C. Indicate how this purchase would be presented in Haggard's 2007 Cash Flow Statement.

D. Assume that Jones had a non-capital loss carry forward for tax purposes of $500,000. Should the form of the purchase of Jones differ? Explain your conclusion.

(CICA Adapted)

Consolidated Balance Sheet At Acquisition

Introduction To Consolidations

The Objective Of Consolidation

4-1. As noted in Chapter 3, in some business combinations, the combining entities maintain their separate legal existence. This means that each of the companies will maintain a separate, single entity, set of books. However, since there has been a business combination, it is necessary to prepare a combined set of financial statements to present to the investors in the acquiring or parent company.

4-2. This follows from the view that when two or more companies are being operated as a single economic entity, the accounting records should reflect that fact. Consolidated financial statements are designed to accomplish that goal. The objective in preparing consolidated financial statements is to account for the parent and its subsidiaries as if they were a single economic entity. This form of accounting will essentially ignore the separate legal existence of these combined companies.

Consolidated Financial Statements And User Needs

4-3. General purpose financial statements find their way into the hands of a wide variety of users. Investors, creditors, government organizations, unions and consumer interest groups would constitute only a partial list of the individuals and organizations that are interested in the external financial reports of Canadian business organizations. Because consolidated financial statements do not reflect the activities of a real legal entity, users of such statements should have a clear understanding of the limits that this situation places on the usefulness of these statements.

4-4. As was implied in the preceding paragraph, consolidated financial statements are prepared primarily to meet the needs of the shareholders of the parent or acquiring company. There are other groups that have some interest in one or more of the combining companies. For the most part, however, these groups will not receive a significant benefit from consolidated financial statements.

4-5. With respect to the legal positions of the various other parties who might have an interest in consolidated financial statements, they can be described as follows:

Creditors Since the consolidated entity has no status as a legal entity, it cannot have creditors. The liabilities that are disclosed in the consolidated Balance Sheet are those of the individual legal entities (parent and subsidiary companies) and creditor claims must be satisfied out of the assets of these legal entities. This conclusion may be modified by the presence of intercompany guarantees on debt obligations.

Taxation Authorities In Canada, there is no legal basis for filing a consolidated tax return. The parent and each of its subsidiaries must file separate tax returns and the consolidated financial statements are essentially ignored by the taxation authorities. This means that the consolidation process will create a significant number of temporary differences, resulting in the need to apply tax allocation procedures.

Non-Controlling Shareholders If there are non-controlling shareholders in one or more of the subsidiary companies, their primary interest will be in the single entity statements of the subsidiary. They have no real way in which to participate in the operating results of the combined company.

Consolidation Policy

4-6. Most published consolidated financial statements provide a note regarding consolidation policy (i.e., which investees are included in the consolidated financial statements). Since the objective of consolidation is to treat a group of legally separate companies that are being operated as a single entity as a single accounting entity, consolidation would be conceptually appropriate for investees where the investor has control, has the right and ability to obtain future economic benefits from the resources of the enterprise, and is exposed to related risks. As noted in Chapter 2, investees that fit this description are called subsidiaries and this means that consolidation is only appropriate for those investees that can be classified as subsidiaries.

4-7. Despite the fact that companies have no real alternatives with respect to the consolidation of subsidiaries, it remains common to have the basis of consolidation discussed in the Statement Of Accounting Policies. In the survey of the 2005 annual reports of 200 companies in the 2006 edition of *Financial Reporting In Canada*, 194 of these companies discussed their basis of consolidation in their Statement of Accounting Policies. This discussion usually includes a listing of the principal subsidiaries, along with the percentage of ownership.

A Note On Terminology

4-8. When a parent company owns less than 100 percent of the outstanding shares of a subsidiary, disclosure will have to be given to the interests of shareholders other than the parent company. At one point in time, subsidiaries were defined in terms of majority ownership and, as a consequence, it was always appropriate to refer to the interests of non-controlling shareholders as a minority interest.

4-9. However, under current GAAP, it is possible for a parent's control to be based on less than a majority of the voting shares of that subsidiary. This means that there can be situations in which the non-controlling interest is not, in fact, a minority interest. Reflecting this possibility, all of the *CICA Handbook* references use the term "Non-Controlling Interest".

4-10. While practice has been slow to change, there is a trend towards increased use of the term Non-Controlling Interest. Referring to statistics on 200 companies collected in the 2006 edition of *Financial Reporting in Canada*, in 2002, 66 companies provided disclosure of this interest in their Income Statement, with 26 using the term Minority Interest and 29 using the term Non-Controlling Interest. In 2005, 86 companies provided disclosure of this interest, with 53 using the term Non-Controlling Interest and 26 using the term Minority Interest.

4-11. In keeping with both the *CICA Handbook* references and the trend in practice, we will use the term Non-Controlling Interest throughout the remainder of this text. Note, however, that in almost all of our examples, the controlling interest is also the majority interest. This means that the term Minority Interest could appropriately be substituted for our use of the term Non-Controlling Interest.

Conceptual Alternatives In Consolidation

Basis For Alternatives

4-12. When consolidated financial statements are being prepared with subsidiaries in which the parent company has 100 percent ownership of the outstanding shares, there is no controversy as to the procedures that are to be used. However, the presence of less than 100 percent ownership introduces non-controlling shareholders into the consolidation process. As there are a variety of views as to the nature of the relationship between the non-controlling shareholders and the consolidated entity, it follows that there are several ways in which this group's interest in the consolidated net income and net assets could be dealt with.

4-13. The literature on consolidations generally makes reference to three different views of the nature of the non-controlling interest and, correspondingly, presents three conceptual alternatives in the preparation of consolidated financial statements. These three approaches are normally referred to as the entity approach, the proprietary approach, and the parent company approach.

4-14. You should note that what is referred to here as the proprietary conceptual approach is, in fact, the basis for proportionate consolidation procedures. As noted previously, proportionate consolidation is the required method in Canada for dealing with joint ventures.

4-15. For a variety of reasons, we believe that you should have some understanding of these three conceptual alternatives. The reasons for this view include:

- An understanding of these conceptual alternatives will enhance your ability to understand the specific procedures that are required in Canada.
- Canadian consolidation requirements do not adopt a consistent conceptual approach. An understanding of the available alternatives will facilitate your understanding of the inconsistencies found in current CICA Recommendations.
- Most importantly, international convergence will, without question, change the conceptual basis that is being used in Canada. As this is likely to happen in either 2009 or 2010, understanding these alternatives will greatly facilitate making the changes that convergence will require in this area.

4-16. This Chapter will provide you with a description of the view of the non-controlling interest that is inherent in each of the three conceptual alternatives. This will be followed by a description of the consolidation procedures that would be consistent with these alternative views. A simple example will be used to illustrate the alternatives as they apply to the valuation of subsidiary assets.

4-17. When the three alternatives have been described, the associated procedures listed, and asset valuation procedures illustrated, there will be an evaluation of the three different concepts. This will be followed by a summary of the procedures that have been adopted:

- under the current provisions of the *CICA Handbook*; and
- under current and proposed IFRSs.

4-18. In reviewing the procedures that are listed under each conceptual alternative, do not be disturbed if you do not fully understand what is being described. They are listed at this point only to give you an overall picture of the relevant conceptual alternatives.

4-19. You may, however, wish to return to these lists periodically as you develop a more complete understanding of specific consolidation procedures. We will return to the list of *CICA Handbook* recommendations at the end of Chapter 6, after we have completed our coverage of basic consolidation procedures. At that point, you should have a full understanding of basic consolidation procedures.

The Entity Concept

Nature Of The Entity Concept

4-20. This conceptual approach to consolidation is based on the view that the non-controlling shareholders are simply part of another class of residual ownership interest and they differ from the controlling shareholders only in the size of their holdings. We have found it helpful to think of the non-controlling interest under the entity concept as being analogous to the position of preferred shareholders in a non-consolidated situation. That is, the non-controlling interest is still clearly part of the residual equity of the business even though its claim may differ somewhat from that of the majority or controlling shareholders.

Associated Procedures

4-21. The following procedures and disclosure would be consistent with the adoption of the entity concept of the nature of the non-controlling interest:

Asset Valuation Both the parent's and the non-controlling interest's share of the fair values, as determined at the acquisition date, of the subsidiary's net identifiable assets would be recorded on the consolidated Balance Sheet. The same would be true for any goodwill that is being recognized as part of the business combination transaction.

Non-Controlling Interest In The Balance Sheet

- **Disclosure** The Non-Controlling Interest would be a component of total shareholders' equity.
- **Calculation** The Non-Controlling Interest in the consolidated Balance Sheet would consist of its proportionate share of the fair values of the subsidiary's net identifiable assets and goodwill, adjusted for all of the same factors that require adjustments to be made to the parent's interest. These factors would include amortization of fair value changes, recognition of goodwill impairment, and the elimination of all of the unrealized intercompany profits of the subsidiary company.

Non-Controlling Interest In The Income Statement

- **Disclosure** Since the non-controlling shareholders are viewed as a residual ownership interest, their proportionate share of subsidiary income would not be deducted in the computation of consolidated net income. Rather, their share would be viewed as a distribution of income in the consolidated Statement Of Retained Earnings. Note the similarity of the treatment given to the non-controlling shareholders to that given to preferred shareholders in non-consolidated situations. The income applicable to both groups would be disclosed as a distribution of income in the Statement Of Retained Earnings, not as a determinant of net income.
- **Calculation** The Non-Controlling Interest in the consolidated Income Statement would consist of its proportionate share of the reported income of the subsidiary, adjusted for all of the same factors that require adjustments to be made to the parent's share. These factors would include the current charge for amortization of fair value changes, recognition of goodwill impairment, the elimination of current subsidiary intercompany profits that are still unrealized from the consolidated point of view, and the addition of subsidiary intercompany profits from previous years that have become realized for consolidation purposes during the current year.

Unrealized Intercompany Profits Of The Subsidiary The entity concept's view that the non-controlling shareholders occupy a residual ownership position would mean that both the parent's and the non-controlling interest's share of unrealized intercompany profits of the subsidiary be treated in a similar fashion. This would require the elimination of all such subsidiary profits with the amounts being charged proportionately to the parent and the non-controlling interest. This approach is sometimes referred to as 100 percent pro rata elimination of unrealized intercompany profits of the subsidiary company.

Asset Valuation Illustrated

4-22. The only consolidation procedure that is relevant to this Chapter's subject of the consolidated Balance Sheet at acquisition is asset valuation. A simple example will be used to illustrate asset valuation procedures under the three conceptual alternatives:

Example Acker Inc. acquires 60 percent of Bloom Ltd. Acker has Land with a carrying value of $2,300,000. At the time of acquisition, Bloom has Land with a carrying value of $400,000 and a fair value of $450,000.

4-23. Under the entity approach, the value for Land that would be included in the consolidated Balance Sheet would be calculated as follows:

Acker Inc. - Carrying Value	$2,300,000
Bloom Ltd. - 100 Percent Of Fair Value	450,000
Consolidated Land	$2,750,000

The Proprietary Concept

Nature Of The Proprietary Concept

4-24. This conceptual approach is based on the view that the non-controlling shareholders are complete outsiders to the consolidated entity. Their interest in the subsidiary's assets, liabilities, expenses, and revenues would be given no consideration in the preparation of consolidated financial statements. Stated alternatively, the proprietary approach is based on the somewhat legalistic view that, with respect to the subsidiary's assets, liabilities, expenses, and revenues, the consolidated entity includes only the parent company's proportionate share of these balances.

Associated Procedures

4-25. The following procedures and disclosure would be consistent with the adoption of the proprietary concept of the nature of the non-controlling interest:

Asset Valuation Only the parent's share of fair values, as determined at the acquisition date, of the subsidiary's net identifiable assets and goodwill would be recorded in the consolidated Balance Sheet.

Non-Controlling Interest In The Balance Sheet Since the proprietary approach excludes the non-controlling interest's share of the subsidiary's net identifiable assets from the consolidated balances, no Non-Controlling Interest would be included in the consolidated Balance Sheet.

Non-Controlling Interest In The Income Statement As this approach excludes the non-controlling interest's share of the subsidiary's expenses and revenues from the consolidated balances, no Non-Controlling Interest would be disclosed in the consolidated Income Statement or Statement Of Retained Earnings.

Unrealized Intercompany Profits Of The Subsidiary As the proprietary approach does not include the non-controlling interest's share of any of the subsidiary balances in the consolidated account balances, it would only be necessary to eliminate the parent's share of the subsidiary's unrealized intercompany profits. This is sometimes referred to as fractional elimination of unrealized intercompany profits of the subsidiary.

Asset Valuation Illustrated

4-26. The same example that was used to illustrate the entity approach to asset valuation will be used here. It is repeated for your convenience:

Example Acker Inc. acquires 60 percent of Bloom Ltd. Acker has Land with a carrying value of $2,300,000. At the time of acquisition, Bloom has Land with a carrying value of $400,000 and a fair value of $450,000.

4-27. Under the proprietary approach, the value for Land that would be included in the consolidated Balance Sheet would be calculated as follows:

Acker Inc. - Carrying Value	$2,300,000
Bloom Ltd. - 60 Percent of $450,000 Fair Value	270,000
Consolidated Land	$2,570,000

The Parent Company Concept

Nature Of The Parent Company Concept

4-28. Like the entity approach, the parent company approach takes the view that the non-controlling interest's share of assets, liabilities, expenses, and revenues are a part of the consolidated economic entity. The difference from the entity approach is that the non-controlling participation is perceived as being a fixed, creditor-like claim.

4-29. This would lead to the conclusion that the non-controlling interest will not be affected by any of the adjustments or eliminations that are required by the parent in the preparation of consolidated financial statements. In other words, the non-controlling shareholders participate in the net assets and results of operations of the consolidated entity, but only to the extent of the book values from the single entity financial statements of the subsidiary.

Associated Procedures

4-30. The following procedures and disclosure would be consistent with the adoption of the parent company concept of the nature of the non-controlling interest:

Asset Valuation The consolidated net identifiable assets would include 100 percent of the subsidiary's carrying values, but only the parent's share of any fair value changes and/or goodwill that was present at the acquisition date.

Non-Controlling Interest In The Balance Sheet

- **Disclosure** As the parent company approach views the Non-Controlling Interest as an outside interest analogous to creditors in non-consolidated statements, it would follow that the Non-Controlling Interest would be grouped with long-term liabilities in the consolidated Balance Sheet.
- **Calculation** The Non-Controlling Interest in the consolidated Balance Sheet would be based on the non-controlling shareholders' proportionate share of the carrying values of the net identifiable assets of the subsidiary company. As this interest is viewed as a fixed or creditor like claim, no adjustments to the single entity records of the subsidiary would be required in the determination of the Non-Controlling Interest that would be disclosed in the consolidated Balance Sheet.

Non-Controlling Interest In The Income Statement

- **Disclosure** As this approach views the non-controlling shareholders as an outside interest similar to creditors, the Non-Controlling Interest would be treated in the same manner as interest charges. That is, it would be deducted in the computation of consolidated Net Income.
- **Calculation** The Non-Controlling Interest in the consolidated Income Statement would be based on the non-controlling shareholders' proportionate share of the reported net income of the subsidiary company. As this interest is viewed as a fixed or creditor like claim, no adjustments to the single entity records of the

subsidiary would be required in the determination of the Non-Controlling Interest in the consolidated Income Statement.

Unrealized Intercompany Profits Of The Subsidiary As the parent company approach views the Non-Controlling Interest as an outside claim that is based on the single entity records of the subsidiary, the non-controlling interest's share of subsidiary unrealized intercompany profits would not be eliminated. In other words, only the parent's share of the subsidiary's unrealized intercompany profits would be eliminated. This is referred to as fractional elimination.

Asset Valuation Illustrated

4-31. The same example that was used to illustrate the entity and proprietary approaches to asset valuation will be used here. The example is repeated for your convenience:

Example Acker Inc. acquires 60 percent of Bloom Ltd. Acker has Land with a carrying value of $2,300,000. At the time of acquisition, Bloom has Land with a carrying value of $400,000 and a fair value of $450,000.

4-32. One way in which the required consolidated Land value could be calculated under the parent company approach is as follows:

Acker Inc. - Carrying Value		$2,300,000
Bloom Ltd.:		
40 Percent Of Carrying Value ($400,000)	$160,000	
60 Percent Of Fair Value ($450,000)	270,000	430,000
Consolidated Land		$2,730,000

4-33. While the preceding calculation reflects the concept underlying the parent company approach (i.e., assets valued at the non-controlling interest's share of carrying value and the parent's share of fair value), an alternative calculation is often more convenient to use. This alternative approach starts with 100 percent of the subsidiary's carrying value. This amount is then increased or decreased for the parent company's share of any fair value change. This alternative calculation is as follows:

Acker Inc. - Carrying Value		$2,300,000
Bloom Ltd.:		
100 Percent Of Carrying Value	$400,000	
[(60%)($450,000 - $400,000)]	30,000	430,000
Consolidated Land		$2,730,000

Exercise Four-1

Subject: Conceptual Alternatives At Acquisition

On December 31, 2007, Placard Ltd. acquires 75 percent of the outstanding voting shares of Sign Inc. At that time, Placard has plant and equipment that cost $2,500,000 and has accumulated amortization of $1,000,000. Sign's plant and equipment cost $700,000, has accumulated amortization of $300,000, and a fair value of $520,000.

Determine the value that would be shown as consolidated plant and equipment (net) for Placard and its subsidiary, Sign, as of December 31, 2007 under:

A. the entity conceptual approach;
B. the proprietary conceptual approach; and
C. the parent company conceptual approach.

End of Exercise. Solution available in Study Guide.

Evaluation Of The Conceptual Alternatives

Proprietary Concept

4-34. The preceding paragraphs have provided you with a general description of the procedures and disclosure that would be required under the three major conceptual alternatives in the preparation of consolidated financial statements. With respect to the proprietary approach, there is little support for this concept as a general solution to the problem of preparing consolidated financial statements.

4-35. It is not difficult to understand the reason for this. The objective that is being satisfied in the preparation of consolidated financial statements is the portrayal of the financial position and the results of operations of the parent and its various subsidiaries as if they were a single economic entity. This is based on the assumption that all of the net assets of the entire group of affiliated companies is under the control of the parent company's management. It is not some legalistically determined fraction of subsidiary net assets that is under common control, it is 100 percent of such assets.

4-36. In view of this fact, the proprietary concept's procedures, which only include the parent company's share of the subsidiary's assets, liabilities, expenses, and revenues in the consolidated financial statements, does not seem to be an appropriate solution. An exception to this would be its application as the proportionate consolidation method used in accounting for joint ventures.

Parent Company Concept

4-37. If the proprietary concept is rejected as a general solution to the problem of preparing consolidated financial statements, one is left with a choice between the parent company concept and the entity concept. Both of these concepts are the same in that they see the non-controlling shareholders as having an interest in the net assets and income of the consolidated entity. The difference is their divergent views on the nature of that interest. As a consequence, the choice between the procedures and disclosures inherent in the two methods should be based on an analysis of the nature of the claims of the non-controlling shareholders.

4-38. The parent company concept views the interest of the non-controlling shareholders as being a creditor like interest. For this to be a reasonable position, the non-controlling shareholders would possess rights similar to those which are associated with other creditor claims. The rights that we normally associate with creditor claims are (1) a contractually specified claim to income, (2) a contractually specified claim to principal and (3) the right to receive this principal sum on a contractually specified future date. It is clear that the relationship of the non-controlling shareholders to the consolidated entity does not have any of these characteristics. Given this fact, it is difficult to support the parent company concept.

Entity Concept

4-39. In our opinion, the non-controlling shareholders have a claim that is best described as a residual equity position. The shares held by this group do not mature, they do not promise any specified return, nor do they purport to return to the investor any specified principal amount under any circumstances that might be encountered by the firm. These characteristics describe an equity relationship and they describe the position of the non-controlling shareholders. This leads us to the conclusion that the entity concept and its associated procedures and disclosures is the most appropriate approach to the preparation of consolidated financial statements.

The Conceptual Approach Of The CICA Handbook

4-40. The preceding paragraph presents a case for the adoption of the entity concept in the preparation of consolidated financial statements. Since we first began writing on this subject, it has been our opinion that the *CICA Handbook* should have adopted this approach in its entirety.

4-41. If it was decided that one of the other concepts was a better alternative, we would have hoped that the recommendations would have applied the concept in a consistent manner. Unfortunately, this did not happen.

4-42. In reviewing the current requirements of the *CICA Handbook*, we find that the AcSB has not applied any of the three basic approaches in a consistent manner. Depending on the issue, we can find instances where the AcSB has required the entity approach, the proprietary approach, and the parent company approach.

4-43. These inconsistencies are one of the major sources of difficulty in the process of learning to prepare consolidated financial statements. As an initial step towards helping you deal with this difficulty, the following paragraph provides a summary list of the approaches that were adopted with respect to each of the major issues in the preparation of consolidated financial statements. In this and subsequent Chapters, we will provide detailed illustrations of all the procedures described in this list.

4-44. The following procedures reflect the recommendations of the *CICA Handbook* with respect to the preparation of consolidated financial statements:

Asset Valuation The recommended approach to asset valuation is the parent company concept. That is, only the parent's share of any fair value changes and goodwill is recognized at the time of acquisition or combination. As a consequence, only the parent's share of the amortization of these values or recognition of their impairment is recorded in subsequent periods.

Non-Controlling Interest In The Balance Sheet

- **Disclosure** Section 1600 is not explicit on this issue. It simply states that the Non-Controlling Interest in the consolidated net assets of the subsidiary companies should be shown separately from shareholders' equity. This eliminates the entity approach and the fact that a non-controlling interest is present eliminates the proprietary approach. This seems to leave the parent company approach. However, in the absence of a clear statement that the Non-Controlling Interest should be disclosed as a part of long-term liabilities, it often ends up presented in a somewhat ambiguous fashion between the long-term liabilities and the consolidated shareholders' equity.

- **Calculation** The inconsistencies of Section 1600 become apparent in the calculation of the Non-Controlling Interest on the Balance Sheet. In general, this computation follows the parent company approach and bases the Non-Controlling Interest on the non-controlling shareholders' proportionate share of the carrying values of the subsidiary. However, because the entity approach is used for the elimination of unrealized subsidiary profits, these transactions must be taken into account in determining the appropriate balance. Stated generally, the Non-Controlling Interest in the consolidated Balance Sheet would be computed by taking the non-controlling shareholders' proportionate interest in the net book value of the subsidiary's assets after they have been adjusted for any unrealized intercompany profits of the subsidiary company.

Non-Controlling Interest In The Income Statement

- **Disclosure** With respect to income before extraordinary items and the results of discontinued operations, Section 1600 requires that Non-Controlling Interest be given disclosure as a separate line item in the consolidated Income Statement. This, of course, reflects an adoption of the parent company approach. For no apparent reason, extraordinary items and the results of discontinued operations are dealt with by a different conceptual alternative. Only the parent company's proportionate interest in these items is disclosed which is an application of the proprietary concept.

- **Calculation** As was the case with the computation of the Non-Controlling Interest for purposes of disclosure in the consolidated Balance Sheet, the computation here is complicated by the presence of inconsistencies in the recommendations of Section 1600. Generally, the Non-Controlling Interest in the consolidated Income Statement is based on the reported income of the subsidiary. Once again, however, adjustments must be made for the adoption of the entity approach in dealing with unrealized subsidiary profits. Stated generally, the Non-Controlling Interest in the consolidated Income Statement is calculated by taking the non-controlling shareholders' proportionate interest in the reported income of the subsidiary with the elimination of current subsidiary intercompany profits that are still unrealized from the consolidated point of view and the addition of subsidiary intercompany profits from previous years that have become realized for consolidation purposes during the year.

Unrealized Intercompany Profits Of The Subsidiary Section 1600 adopts the entity approach here and requires 100 percent pro rata elimination of unrealized intercompany subsidiary profits.

International Convergence And Conceptual Alternatives

Current IFRSs

4-45. We are pleased to see that international convergence will move Canada firmly in the direction of the entity approach. Under the current IFRS No. 3, *Business Combinations*, the acquirer is required to recognize 100 percent of the fair values of a subsidiary's identifiable assets and liabilities. In addition, IAS No. 27, *Consolidated And Separate Financial Statements*, requires the non-controlling interest to be treated as a component of shareholders' equity in the Balance Sheet, with this interest's share of subsidiary income being presented as a distribution of consolidated Net Income. This standard also requires the elimination of 100 percent of subsidiary unrealized intercompany profits.

4-46. The one significant exception to the use of the entity approach in current IFRSs involves the initial recognition of goodwill. Under IFRS No. 3, only the acquirer's share of goodwill is recognized. The non-controlling interest in this important intangible is left unrecognized.

Proposed Changes

4-47. We have noted that the FASB and IASB have a joint project underway that will amend and converge their respective standards for business combinations and the preparation of consolidated financial statements. As these proposals currently stand, they require the recognition of 100 percent of an acquiree's goodwill, even when there is a non-controlling interest.

4-48. Should these proposals be adopted without further modification, international and U.S. standards will require the full application of the entity approach. We would note, however, there is considerable resistance to the treatment of goodwill that is inherent in these proposals.

Conceptual Alternatives In Text Material

Current CICA Handbook

4-49. Our basic material on consolidation procedures is found in Chapters 4 through 6. In these Chapters, the majority of our attention will be given to the current requirements of the *CICA Handbook*. However, in this Chapter 4, as well as in Chapter 5, there will be an overview of how the current Canadian requirements compare to the various conceptual alternatives.

4-50. When we deal with joint ventures in Chapter 8, we will also be concerned with conceptual alternatives. Joint ventures must be accounted for using proportionate consolidation. As we have noted previously, proportionate consolidation reflects the proprietary conceptual approach.

International Convergence

4-51. While the major focus of this text is on current Canadian standards, in the consolidation Chapters 4 through 7, we will be providing detailed comparative examples of how statements prepared under the current and proposed IFRSs would differ from those prepared under current Canadian GAAP. As these international standards are based on the entity approach, we will be, in effect, illustrating this approach in these comparative examples.

A Procedural Approach To Preparing Consolidated Financial Statements

Use Of Worksheets

4-52. With the preceding survey of the conceptual alternatives completed, we can now turn our attention to the development of a procedural approach to the preparation of consolidated financial statements.

4-53. Most advanced accounting texts rely on the use of a worksheet as the basis for the development of consolidation procedures. Under this approach, the various Income Statement and Balance Sheet accounts are listed in the first two columns of the work sheet, followed by columns for adjustments, eliminations, Non-Controlling Interest, consolidated Balance Sheet, and consolidated Income Statement.

4-54. While this approach may be justified by the complex situations encountered in practice, it has very little utility to the student preparing for university or professional examinations. In the context of an examination situation, the mere preparation of the worksheet format would absorb most of the time available for completing a consolidation problem.

4-55. Of even greater importance is the fact that dealing with consolidation problems with the worksheet approach provides no real understanding of the content of these statements. It is very easy to learn the mechanics of filling the appropriate boxes. However, this process provides no insight into the nature of the items that are included in the completed financial statements.

4-56. Because of these factors, this text does not cover the worksheet approach to the preparation of consolidated financial statements.

Direct Definitional Calculations And Journal Entries

An Interim Step

4-57. If you have a thorough understanding of the consolidation process, the most efficient method of preparing consolidated financial statements is to be in a position to make an independent computation of each of the consolidated account balances. However, it would be very difficult to teach this type of approach directly and, as a reflection of this fact, we will develop a set of procedures using journal entries to adjust the existing account balances. These journal entries will be added to or subtracted from the account balances given in the problem in order to arrive at the correct balances for inclusion in the consolidated financial statements.

4-58. Two points should be made with respect to these journal entries. First, we view them largely as an interim teaching device. We encourage you to discontinue using them as soon as you feel that you understand the concepts well enough to make direct computations of the balances that are required for inclusion in the consolidated financial statements.

4-59. This is of particular importance when you are preparing to write examinations on this material. In this context, you will generally not have sufficient time to work through all of the journal entries that are required in a comprehensive, multi-statement consolidation problem. As grading marks are usually allocated to the required financial statements, it is essential that you focus on their preparation, rather than spending valuable time writing out a long series of journal entries.

Working Papers Only

4-60. To the extent that you continue using journal entries, a second point relates to the nature of the journal entries that are being made. They are only working paper entries and are not recorded in the single entity records of either the parent or subsidiary companies (as explained in Appendix A of this Chapter, there would be some exceptions to this if push-down accounting is used).

4-61. It is particularly important to keep this fact in mind when dealing with consolidation subsequent to acquisition. You must recognize that any entries that were made in preparing the 2007 consolidated financial statements were not entered in the accounts and, to the extent they are still applicable, they will have to be repeated in preparing the 2008 statements.

General Approach Outlined

Eliminations And Adjustments

4-62. Consolidation procedures require you to look through the separate financial statements of a parent and its subsidiary and prepare financial statements on the assumption that the two companies are, in fact a single economic entity.

4-63. This will require the elimination of some items. As a simple example, if a parent owes money to a subsidiary, both the the parent's payable and the subsidiary's receivable must be eliminated. This reflects the fact that, if we view these two companies as a single entity, it cannot owe money to itself.

4-64. We will also need to adjust various balances. Fair value changes that are recognized at the time of the business combination (acquisition of the subsidiary) will not be recorded on either company's books. Adjustments will be required each year to reflect these fair value changes and, in the case of amortizable assets, to adjust the related amortization expense.

Procedures

4-65. To deal with these eliminations and adjustments in a systematic manner, we have organized our procedures into three Steps. These will be referred to as Steps A, B, and C, and they can be described as follows:

Step A This Step will involve the elimination of the investment account against the subsidiary common shareholders' equity at the time of acquisition. Also included in this Step will be the establishment of the Non-Controlling Interest for the Balance Sheet at acquisition, as well as the allocation of the excess of the investment cost over the carrying values of the assets acquired, to the various fair value changes and goodwill that have been established by the purchase price. The procedures involved in this Step are given complete coverage in this Chapter.

Step B This Step involves a number of adjustments and eliminations for such things as intercompany assets and liabilities, recognition of goodwill impairment losses, intercompany expenses and revenues, and the elimination of unrealized intercompany profits. As these adjustments and eliminations are only required in periods subsequent to acquisition, they will be dealt with in Chapters 5 and 6.

Step C Step A served to eliminate the subsidiary's Retained Earnings at acquisition. In Step B, the remaining balance will be adjusted for unrealized profits. This final Step C will allocate the remaining balance in the Retained Earnings of the subsidiary between the Non-Controlling Interest in the consolidated Balance Sheet and the consolidated Retained Earnings in the consolidated Balance Sheet. As was the case with the Step B procedures, the Step C procedures are only required in periods subsequent to acquisition. This means that the Step C procedures will also be dealt with in Chapters 5 and 6.

Consolidated Balance Sheet At Acquisition

Consolidations And Business Combinations

4-66. While we have made this point several times before, we would like to remind you again that, in all cases where a parent has acquired control over a subsidiary, a business combination transaction has occurred. As with business combinations that use other legal forms, combinations involving the acquisition of the shares must be accounted for by the purchase method.

4-67. In Chapter 3 we discussed that one of the features of the purchase method is that the acquirer's share of the identifiable assets and liabilities of the acquiree must be recorded at fair values. In the great majority of subsidiary acquisitions, the parent is the acquirer and the subsidiary is the acquiree. As a consequence, the fair values of the identifiable assets and liabilities of the subsidiary must be determined, with the acquirer's share of these values being recorded in the consolidated financial statements.

4-68. In addition, if the investment cost (purchase price) exceeds the parent's share of these fair values, goodwill must also be recorded in the consolidated financial statements.

Examples To Be Used

4-69. The least complex type of consolidation problem involves the preparation of a consolidated Balance Sheet as at the date of acquisition. Our presentation of the procedures required to prepare a consolidated Balance Sheet as at the date of acquisition will use four examples. They can be briefly described as follows:

Example One This very simple example will have the parent company owning 100 percent of the subsidiary company's shares with the investment cost equal to the book value of the subsidiary's Shareholders' Equity and no fair value changes or goodwill present.

Example Two This will also involve 100 percent ownership. However, the investment cost will differ from book value. This differential will be allocated to fair value changes and goodwill.

Example Three We will return to our first assumption of the investment cost being equal to the book value of the subsidiary's Shareholders' Equity with no fair value changes. However, the investor's proportionate share of the subsidiary's shares will be less than 100 percent.

Example Four The final example will involve less than 100 percent ownership of the subsidiary's outstanding shares and will also incorporate fair value changes and goodwill.

Example One - 100 Percent Ownership With No Fair Value Changes

Example

4-70. In this Example, the parent will own 100 percent of the outstanding shares of the subsidiary. There are no fair value changes on any of the subsidiary's identifiable assets or liabilities and the investment cost will be equal to book value.

On December 31, 2007, the Pert Company purchases 100 percent of the outstanding voting shares of the Sert Company for $5 million in cash. On that date, subsequent to the business combination transaction, the Balance Sheets of the two companies are as follows:

Pert and Sert Companies
Balance Sheets
As At December 31, 2007

	Pert	Sert
Cash	$ 800,000	$ 500,000
Accounts Receivable	1,500,000	1,100,000
Inventories	3,400,000	2,500,000
Investment In Sert	5,000,000	N/A
Plant And Equipment (Net)	6,300,000	3,900,000
Total Assets	$17,000,000	$8,000,000
Current Liabilities	$ 800,000	$1,000,000
Long-Term Liabilities	2,200,000	2,000,000
No Par Common Stock	8,000,000	2,000,000
Retained Earnings	6,000,000	3,000,000
Total Equities	$17,000,000	$8,000,000

Other Information:

1. All of the net identifiable assets of the Sert Company have fair values that are equal to the carrying values that are presented in the preceding Balance Sheet.
2. During October, 2007, the Sert Company sold merchandise to the Pert Company for $100,000 and recognized a gross profit on these sales of $40,000. On December 31, 2007, one-half of this merchandise remains in the inventories of the Pert Company.
3. On December 31, 2007, the Pert Company owes the Sert Company $25,000 on open account for merchandise purchased during the year.

Required: Prepare a consolidated Balance Sheet for the Pert Company and its subsidiary, the Sert Company, as at December 31, 2007.

Procedures

4-71. In somewhat simplified terms, preparation of the consolidated Balance Sheet at acquisition involves adding together all of the assets and equities of the parent and subsidiary companies. However, special procedures are required for certain of these balances. Specifically, these procedures relate to the Pert Company's Investment In Sert account and to the Sert Company's shareholders' equity. In addition, in this example it is also necessary to deal with the intercompany receivable.

Investment In Sert

4-72. The Investment In Sert account on the books of the Pert Company reflects the ownership of the net identifiable assets of the Sert Company. Since in preparing consolidated financial statements we are trying to show the two companies as if they were a single economic entity, the net identifiable assets of the Sert Company will be included in the consolidated net identifiable assets.

4-73. If, in addition, we include the Investment In Sert account, we will be counting these net identifiable assets twice. Therefore, it will always be necessary to eliminate 100 percent of the investment account. This will remain the case under our procedures even as the problems become more complex and begin to deal with preparing consolidated financial statements subsequent to acquisition.

Subsidiary Shareholders' Equity

4-74. From the point of view of the consolidated entity, the Sert Company has no shares outstanding. That is, no individual or organization outside of the consolidated entity is holding any of the common shares of the Sert Company. This would mean that in the consolidated financial statements, any contributed capital of Sert that is present at the time of acquisition should be eliminated.

4-75. With respect to Retained Earnings, the purchase method of accounting only includes the income of the acquiree from the date of acquisition forward. As a consequence, none of the Retained Earnings of an acquired company that is present at the time of acquisition would be included in the combined or consolidated company's Retained Earnings. This is reflected in the following *CICA Handbook* Recommendation:

> **Paragraph 1600.22** *The retained earnings or deficit of a subsidiary company at the date(s) of acquisition by the parent should not be included in consolidated retained earnings.* (April, 1975)

4-76. This would necessitate the elimination of any subsidiary Retained Earnings that are present at the time of acquisition. As a general conclusion, it follows that we will always eliminate 100 percent of the subsidiary shareholders' equity at acquisition. Under the procedures that we are developing, this will remain the case even as the problems become more complex and deal with fractional ownership and consolidation subsequent to the date of acquisition.

Investment Elimination Journal Entry

4-77. In the preceding paragraphs, we have developed our first two procedures for preparing consolidated financial statements. As these two procedures are a part of Step A in our general approach to preparing consolidated financial statements, we will designate these procedures as Step A-1 and A-2, respectively.

> **Step A-1 Procedure** Always eliminate 100 percent of the Investment In Subsidiary account.
>
> **Step A-2 Procedure** Always eliminate 100 percent of all the balances in the subsidiary's common shareholders' equity that are present on the acquisition date.

4-78. The journal entry required to carry out these two Steps is as follows:

No Par Common Stock (Sert's)	$2,000,000	
Retained Earnings (Sert's)	3,000,000	
Investment In Sert		$5,000,000

Intercompany Asset And Liability

4-79. In preparing consolidated financial statements, the Pert Company and the Sert Company are viewed as constituting a single economic entity. From this point of view, any intercompany asset and liability balances do not exist and must be eliminated. The following *CICA Handbook* Recommendation is applicable:

> **Paragraph 1600.19** *Intercompany balances should be eliminated upon consolidation.* (April, 1975)

4-80. This provides the basis for a third procedure in preparing consolidated financial statements. However, we will be required to eliminate intercompany asset and liability balances in years subsequent to acquisition as well as at acquisition. As a consequence, it will become part of Step B in our general approach to consolidations. Given this, we will designate this procedure as Step B-1.

Step B-1 Procedure Always eliminate 100 percent of intercompany assets and liabilities.

4-81. In our example, Pert Company owes Sert Company $25,000 on open account. Given this, the entry that is required to implement Step B-1 is as follows:

Current Liabilities	$25,000	
Accounts Receivable		$25,000

Intercompany Gains And Losses

4-82. In contrast to the intercompany asset and liability balances which are still present at the time of the acquisition, Sert's sale of merchandise to Pert took place prior to the business combination transaction. This means that they were transactions between two independent companies dealing at arm's length. Given this, it is not appropriate to eliminate these amounts or to even think of them as intercompany transactions. This is reflected in the following Recommendation:

Paragraph 1600.24 *Where the carrying value of the assets of the parent company or a subsidiary company include gains or losses arising from intercompany transactions which took place prior to the date of acquisition, such gains or losses should not be eliminated unless the transactions were made in contemplation of acquisition.* (April, 1975)

4-83. Since there is no indication in the problem that the 2007 transactions were in contemplation of the business combination, no entry is required for these events.

Consolidated Balance Sheet - Example One

4-84. As indicated in our discussion of the procedural approach to be used, the preparation of the consolidated Balance Sheet involves adding together the asset and equity balances from the individual Balance Sheets of the two companies and then adjusting these amounts for the various journal entries that have been made. In this Example, the resulting consolidated Balance Sheet, with all of the calculations shown parenthetically, is as follows:

Pert Company And Subsidiary
Consolidated Balance Sheet
As At December 31, 2007

Cash ($800,000 + $500,000)	$ 1,300,000
Accounts Receivable ($1,500,000 + $1,100,000 - $25,000)	2,575,000
Inventories ($3,400,000 + $2,500,000)	5,900,000
Investment In Sert ($5,000,000 - $5,000,000)	Nil
Plant And Equipment (Net) ($6,300,000 + $3,900,000)	10,200,000
Total Assets	$19,975,000
Current Liabilities ($800,000 + $1,000,000 - $25,000)	$ 1,775,000
Long-Term Liabilities ($2,200,000 + $2,000,000)	4,200,000
No Par Common Stock (Pert's Only)	8,000,000
Retained Earnings (Pert's Only)	6,000,000
Total Equities	$19,975,000

Notes On Example One Two points are relevant with respect to the procedures and disclosure for Example One:

- In the actual presentation of the consolidated Balance Sheet, the Investment In Sert account would simply not be shown. It is included here to call your attention to the fact that the account was there on the Pert Company's books and has been eliminated.
- Both components of the consolidated shareholders' equity are identical to those of the parent company. This will always be the case in the consolidated Balance Sheet as at the date of acquisition, a result that follows from the rules that are generally applicable in the purchase method of accounting for business combinations. This will not be the case in periods subsequent to the acquisition date unless the parent company carries the investment by the equity method.

Exercise Four-2

Subject: Balance Sheet At Acquisition - 100% Ownership - No FV Changes

On December 31, 2007, Pan Inc. acquires 100 percent of the outstanding voting shares of San Ltd. for $2,630,000 in cash. At that time, all of the identifiable assets and liabilities of San Ltd. have fair values that are equal to their carrying values. The Balance Sheets of the two Companies on this date, subsequent to the business combination, are as follows:

Pan and San Companies
Balance Sheets
As At December 31, 2007

	Pan Inc.	San Ltd.
Cash	$ 426,000	$ 345,000
Accounts Receivable	727,000	623,000
Inventories	1,753,000	1,265,000
Investment In San	2,630,000	N/A
Plant And Equipment (Net)	3,259,000	2,234,000
Total Assets	$8,795,000	$4,467,000
Current Liabilities	$ 398,000	$ 362,000
Long-Term Liabilities	1,272,000	1,475,000
No Par Common Stock	4,450,000	1,250,000
Retained Earnings	2,675,000	1,380,000
Total Equities	$8,795,000	$4,467,000

Prepare a consolidated Balance Sheet for Pan Inc. and its subsidiary, San Ltd., as at December 31, 2007. Include the investment elimination journal entry in your solution.

End of Exercise. Solution available in Study Guide.

Example Two - 100 Percent Ownership With Fair Value Changes And Goodwill

Example

4-85. As was the case in Example One, the parent in this Example will own 100 percent of the outstanding shares of the subsidiary. However, in this Example we have added fair value changes on the subsidiary assets as well as a goodwill balance. As a consequence, we will have to use the procedures introduced in Chapter 3 to analyze the investment cost and allocate the appropriate amounts to fair value changes and goodwill. The basic data for Example Two is as follows:

On December 31, 2007, the Pend Company purchases 100 percent of the outstanding voting shares of the Send Company for $3,500,000 in cash. On that date, subsequent to the business combination transaction, the Balance Sheets of the two companies are as follows:

Pend and Send Companies
Balance Sheets
As At December 31, 2007

	Pend	**Send**
Cash	$ 500,000	$ 300,000
Accounts Receivable	1,200,000	800,000
Inventories	1,800,000	1,200,000
Investment In Send	3,500,000	N/A
Plant And Equipment (Net)	3,000,000	2,700,000
Total Assets	$10,000,000	$5,000,000
Current Liabilities	$ 800,000	$ 500,000
Long-Term Liabilities	1,700,000	1,500,000
No Par Common Stock	4,000,000	1,000,000
Retained Earnings	3,500,000	2,000,000
Total Equities	$10,000,000	$5,000,000

Other Information:

1. All of the net identifiable assets of the Send Company have fair values that are equal to their carrying values except for Plant And Equipment which has a fair value that is $300,000 more than its carrying value and the Long-Term Liabilities which have fair values that are $100,000 less than their carrying values.

2. Prior to the business combination, there were no intercompany transactions between the two companies. On the date of the combination, there are no intercompany asset and liability balances.

Required: Prepare a consolidated Balance Sheet for the Pend Company and its subsidiary, the Send Company, as at December 31, 2007.

Procedures

4-86. As described in Example One, Steps A-1 and A-2 are used to eliminate 100 percent of the Investment In Subsidiary account and 100 percent of the subsidiary's common shareholders' equity at acquisition. Applying these procedures in this Example results in the following journal entry:

No Par Common Stock (Send's)	$1,000,000	
Retained Earnings (Send's)	2,000,000	
Differential	500,000	
Investment In Send		$3,500,000

4-87. The application of Steps A-1 and A-2 in this Example results in a journal entry that does not balance, a situation that we have corrected by adding a $500,000 debit that has been temporarily designated Differential (this amount is also referred to as the Purchase Price Discrepancy, or simply Excess of Cost Over Book Value).

4-88. This is a typical result. In most consolidation problems, there will be a difference between the cost of the investment and the investor's share of the book value of the subsidiary's shareholders' equity that has been acquired. This means that eliminating the investment account against the subsidiary shareholders' equity will result in an imbalance that requires an additional debit or credit.

4-89. If a debit Differential is required, it reflects an excess of investment cost over the investor's share of subsidiary book value. A credit Differential indicates that the investment cost was less than the investor's share of subsidiary book value. Learning to deal with these differentials is the next step in our development of consolidation procedures.

Treatment Of Differentials

4-90. The first thing to understand about such differentials is that they will not disappear. The preceding $500,000 must be included somewhere in the consolidated Balance Sheet. Further, it must be allocated to one or more specific accounts. It cannot simply be included in the consolidated Balance Sheet with the account title Differential or Purchase Price Discrepancy.

4-91. In attempting to allocate such differentials to specific asset and liability accounts, it is essential to understand why they exist. That is, what factors contributed to the Pend Company's decision to pay $500,000 more than the carrying value of the Send Company's net assets in order to acquire 100 percent of its outstanding shares?

4-92. From a conceptual point of view, three possible explanations for this situation can be developed. Note that these explanations are not mutually exclusive and, in fact, would usually occur in various combinations. The three possibilities are as follows:

Specific Identifiable Assets Specific identifiable assets and identifiable liabilities of the Send Company may have fair values that are different from their carrying values. For example, the $500,000 excess of cost over book value in the present example could be explained if the Send Company's Plant And Equipment had a fair value of $3,200,000, $500,000 more than the carrying value of $2,700,000.

Note that this could include intangibles other than goodwill that have not been recognized on the books of the subsidiary. You may recall from Chapter 3 that the Recommendations on purchase accounting require the recognition of any intangible assets of the acquiree that (1) results from contractual or other legal rights , or (2) is capable of being separated or divided from the acquired enterprise and sold, transferred, licensed, rented, or exchanged.

Subsidiary Goodwill A second possible explanation of a difference between investment cost and book value relates to how successfully the enterprise is being operated. As was discussed in Chapter 3, if the enterprise is being operated in an unusually successful manner, it is likely that the enterprise as a going concern will have a fair value that is in excess of the sum of the fair values of its identifiable net assets.

Such an excess would be allocated to goodwill and could be the explanation of the $500,000 excess in the problem that is under consideration. A similar analysis would apply to situations in which the enterprise is being operated at a less than average level of success, resulting in the need to deal with a differential with a credit balance (negative goodwill).

Consolidated Goodwill A final possibility is that extra value is created in the business combination process. There may be so many advantages associated with bringing a particular subsidiary into a combination with a parent company that the parent is prepared to pay more than the net identifiable assets and goodwill of the subsidiary are worth as a single entity. This excess is sometimes referred to as consolidated goodwill and could be the explanation of the $500,000 excess in the problem under consideration.

Note that, unlike the two previous explanations for differentials, the consolidated goodwill argument could not be used to explain a credit differential. It is very difficult to believe that the shareholders of the subsidiary would be willing to sell their shares for less than the value of the enterprise simply because there are so many disadvantages associated with affiliation.

4-93. We would note that while there is clearly a conceptual distinction between subsidiary goodwill and consolidated goodwill, it is of no practical significance. In the application of the purchase method of accounting for business combination transactions, goodwill is currently measured as the excess (deficiency) of the investment cost over the acquirer's share of the fair values of the acquiree's net identifiable assets. No attempt is made to segregate this total goodwill into a component that was present prior to the business combination transaction and a component that results from the business combination transaction.

4-94. Based on the preceding analysis of the possible reasons for the existence of a debit or credit differential, it is clear that the *CICA Handbook* Recommendations on accounting for business combinations require that such balances be allocated to fair value changes on identifiable assets, fair value changes on identifiable liabilities, and to positive or negative goodwill. This provides the basis for an additional procedure in the preparation of consolidated financial statements. As this procedure is part of Step A in our general approach to preparing consolidated financial statements, it will be designated Step A-3.

> **Step A-3 Procedure** The total amount of any debit or credit Differential must be allocated to the parent company's share of fair value changes on identifiable assets, fair value changes on identifiable liabilities, and to positive or negative goodwill. Note that, under current Canadian accounting standards, we will only recognize the parent company's share of any fair value changes or goodwill. This reflects the fact that the *CICA Handbook* requires the use of the parent company approach for the valuation of subsidiary assets.

Investment Analysis Schedule

4-95. As was noted in Chapter 3, in more complex problems it is useful to have a systematic approach to the allocation of fair value changes and goodwill. While it was not really necessary in the relatively simple example that was presented in that Chapter, we introduced such a systematic approach in the form of an investment analysis schedule. The rules that were presented in Chapter 3 related to a purchase of assets. In using the investment analysis schedule for a share purchase, the steps are as follows:

> **Calculating The Differential** Subtract the book value of the subsidiary's common shareholders' equity (or the parent company's proportionate interest therein in cases where the parent company owns less than 100 percent of the subsidiary shares), from the investment cost. This results in a balance that we will refer to as the Differential. If it is a positive number, it indicates that the investor is paying more than his proportionate share of subsidiary book values and that there is a debit amount to be allocated. A negative number reflects a credit balance to be allocated. Note that, as the Differential reflects the total of all fair value changes and goodwill to be recognized, a positive balance does not clearly indicate the presence of goodwill.

> **Allocating The Differential** Once the Differential has been established, we will then add or subtract the various fair value changes that have been determined for the subsidiary's identifiable assets. As a positive differential reflects a debit balance to be allocated, we will subtract any fair value changes which require the allocation of debits (increase in assets or decreases in liabilities). Correspondingly, we will add any fair value changes that require credits (decreases in assets or increases in liabilities). In this example, both the $300,000 fair value increase on Plant And Equipment and the $100,000 fair value decrease on Long-Term Liabilities involve debits and will be subtracted.

> **Dealing With Goodwill** The resulting balance will be allocated to goodwill if it is positive. If the balance is negative or a credit amount, it will first be allocated to a pro rata reduction in the acquired assets (as discussed in Chapter 3, there are certain exceptions such as financial assets and assets that are to be sold). If a credit balance remains after these assets are eliminated, the balance would be treated as an extraordinary gain.

4-96. For this Example, involving the Pend Company and its subsidiary, the Send Company, the investment analysis schedule would be prepared as follows:

Investment Cost	$3,500,000
Send Company - Common Shareholders' Equity ($1,000,000 + $2,000,000)*	(3,000,000)
Differential	$ 500,000
Fair Value Changes:	
Increase On Plant And Equipment	(300,000)
Decrease On Long-Term Liabilities	(100,000)
Goodwill	$ 100,000

*In this example, the subsidiary has only one class of shares outstanding. This means that the common shareholders' equity is equal to the total Shareholders' Equity. Note, however, that if Send had other classes of shares outstanding, for example, preferred shares, their equity would not be included in this calculation. The portion of Shareholders' Equity that belongs to any preferred shares would be allocated to the Non-Controlling Interest unless they were held by the parent company. Any subsidiary preferred shares held by the parent would be eliminated separately against the parent's investment in these shares.

4-97. Goodwill is defined as the excess of the investment cost over the investor's share of the fair values of the net identifiable assets of the investee. Based on this definition, the balance in the preceding schedule can be verified as follows:

Investment Cost		$3,500,000
Less: Fair Value Of Send's Net Identifiable Assets:		
Carrying Value	$3,000,000	
Fair Value Increase On Plant	300,000	
Fair Value Decrease On Liabilities	100,000	3,400,000
Goodwill		$ 100,000

Investment Elimination Journal Entry

4-98. Using the information provided by the preceding investment analysis schedule, we can now complete the journal entry needed for the preparation of the required consolidated Balance Sheet at acquisition. In this entry, we will combine Step A-1 (elimination of the investment account), Step A-2 (elimination of the subsidiary shareholders' equity at acquisition), and Step A-3 (allocation of the Differential to fair value changes and goodwill). The entry is as follows:

No Par Common Stock (Send's)	$1,000,000	
Retained Earnings (Send's)	2,000,000	
Plant And Equipment (Net)	300,000	
Long-Term Liabilities	100,000	
Goodwill	100,000	
Investment In Send		$3,500,000

4-99. Note that this entry still eliminates 100 percent of both the Investment In Send and the shareholders' equity of the Send Company. In addition, the $500,000 balance which we temporarily designated Differential has been allocated to identifiable assets, identifiable liabilities, and goodwill.

Consolidated Balance Sheet - Example Two

4-100. Using the same procedures as in Example One, the Example Two consolidated Balance Sheet can be prepared as follows:

Pend Company And Subsidiary
Consolidated Balance Sheet
As At December 31, 2007

Cash ($500,000 + $300,000)	$ 800,000
Accounts Receivable ($1,200,000 + $800,000)	2,000,000
Inventories ($1,800,000 + $1,200,000)	3,000,000
Investment In Send ($3,500,000 - $3,500,000)	Nil
Plant And Equipment (Net) ($3,000,000 + $2,700,000 + $300,000)	6,000,000
Goodwill	100,000
Total Assets	$11,900,000
Current Liabilities ($800,000 + $500,000)	$ 1,300,000
Long-Term Liabilities ($1,700,000 + $1,500,000 - $100,000)	3,100,000
No Par Common Stock (Pend's Only)	4,000,000
Retained Earnings (Pend's Only)	3,500,000
Total Equities	$11,900,000

4-101. The only difference between the procedures used in preparing this consolidated Balance Sheet and those used in preparing the Example One consolidated Balance Sheet is that allocations are made for the fair value changes and goodwill. Note that the consolidated shareholders' equity is still simply the shareholders' equity of the parent company.

Exercise Four-3

Subject: Balance Sheet At Acquisition - 100% Ownership - FV Changes

On December 31, 2007, Partial Ltd. acquires 100 percent of the outstanding voting shares of Sum Inc. for $2,508,000 in cash. On that date, all of the net identifiable assets of Sum Inc. have fair values that are equal to their carrying values except for Inventories, which have a fair value that is $35,000 less that their carrying value, and Long-Term Liabilities which have fair values that are $57,000 more than their carrying values. The Balance Sheets of the two Companies on this date, subsequent to the business combination, are as follows:

Partial and Sum Companies
Balance Sheets
As At December 31, 2007

	Partial	Sum
Cash	$ 612,000	$ 256,000
Accounts Receivable	1,346,000	632,000
Inventories	2,111,000	943,000
Investment In Sum	2,508,000	N/A
Plant And Equipment (Net)	3,562,000	1,866,000
Total Assets	$10,139,000	$3,697,000
Current Liabilities	$ 726,000	$ 396,000
Long-Term Liabilities	2,212,000	784,000
No Par Common Stock	3,970,000	830,000
Retained Earnings	3,231,000	1,687,000
Total Equities	$10,139,000	$3,697,000

Prepare a consolidated Balance Sheet for Partial Ltd. and its subsidiary, Sum Inc., as at December 31, 2007. Include the investment analysis and the investment elimination journal entry in your solution.

End of Exercise. Solution available in Study Guide.

Example Three - Fractional Ownership With No Fair Value Changes Or Goodwill

Example

4-102. This Example introduces a situation where the parent company owns less than 100 percent of the subsidiary shares (fractional ownership). As a result of this change, we will have to consider the calculation and disclosure of the Non-Controlling Interest in the consolidated Balance Sheet. The basic data for this Example is as follows:

On December 31, 2007, the Pack Company purchases 80 percent of the outstanding voting shares of the Sack Company for $3,200,000 in cash. On that date, subsequent to the business combination transaction, the Balance Sheets of the two Companies are as follows:

Pack and Sack Companies
Balance Sheets
As At December 31, 2007

	Pack	Sack
Cash	$ 600,000	$ 400,000
Accounts Receivable	1,500,000	1,100,000
Inventories	2,100,000	1,400,000
Investment In Sack	3,200,000	-0-
Plant And Equipment (Net)	5,600,000	2,100,000
Total Assets	$13,000,000	$5,000,000
Current Liabilities	$1,200,000	$ 400,000
Long-Term Liabilities	2,800,000	600,000
No Par Common Stock	5,000,000	1,000,000
Retained Earnings	4,000,000	3,000,000
Total Equities	$13,000,000	$5,000,000

Other Information:

1. All of the identifiable assets and liabilities of the Sack Company have fair values that are equal to the carrying values that are presented in the Balance Sheet.
2. Prior to the business combination, there were no intercompany transactions between the two companies. It follows that on the date of the combination there are no intercompany asset or liability balances.

Required: Prepare a consolidated Balance Sheet for the Pack Company and its subsidiary, the Sack Company, as at December 31, 2007.

Procedures

4-103. With no fair value changes, no goodwill, and no intercompany balances, Steps B-1 and A-3 are not relevant in this Example. However, Steps A-1 and A-2 are still required, even with the presence of a non-controlling interest. You will have no difficulty in understanding the continued need for Step A-1, the requirement that we eliminate 100 percent of the Investment In Subsidiary account. However, with some of the subsidiary's shares held by investors outside the consolidated entity, Step A-2's requirement that we eliminate 100 percent of the subsidiary's shareholders' equity does not seem reasonable.

4-104. In this Example Three, 20 percent of Sack Company's shares are in the hands of such outsiders. In the preparation of both the entity and parent company approach consolidated Balance Sheets, the interest of these shareholders in Sack Company's shareholders' equity must be included in the consolidated Balance Sheet.

4-105. The reason for this seemingly unreasonable requirement is a procedural one. It is true that the non-controlling interest's 20 percent share of Sack Company's shareholders' equity will be included in the parent company and entity approach consolidated Balance Sheets. However, this interest will not be disclosed as No Par Common Stock or Retained Earnings. Rather, it will be disclosed as the equity of the Non-Controlling Interest in the consolidated net assets.

4-106. As a result, in our approach to preparing consolidated financial statements, we will continue to eliminate 100 percent of the subsidiary's shareholders' equity at acquisition (Step A-2), but we will add a further procedure. As this new procedure is part of Step A in our general approach to consolidated financial statements, it will be designated Step A-4.

> **Step A-4 Procedure** The non-controlling interest's share of the book value of the subsidiary common Shareholders' Equity at acquisition must be allocated to a Non-Controlling Interest account in the consolidated Balance Sheet.

4-107. The fact that we base the Non-Controlling Interest on the carrying value of the subsidiary's net assets means that we are not recognizing the non-controlling interest's share of either fair value changes or goodwill. This follows from the fact that the *CICA Handbook* requires the use of the parent company approach to asset valuation.

Investment Analysis Schedule

4-108. Given that there are no fair value changes or goodwill in this Example, no investment analysis schedule is required.

Investment Elimination Journal Entry

4-109. As there is no investment analysis required, we can now complete the journal entry needed to prepare the consolidated Balance Sheet. In this entry we will use Step A-1 (elimination of the investment account), Step A-2 (elimination of 100 percent of the subsidiary shareholders' equity at acquisition), and the new Step A-4 (allocation of 20 percent of Sack Company's common shareholders' equity to the Balance Sheet account Non-Controlling Interest).

No Par Common Stock (Sack's)	$1,000,000	
Retained Earnings (Sack's)	3,000,000	
Investment In Sack		$3,200,000
Non-Controlling Interest (20% Of $4,000,000)		800,000

Treatment Of The Non-Controlling Interest

4-110. The preceding journal entry creates an account titled Non-Controlling Interest. This account will have a credit balance and, as a consequence, it will be allocated to the equity side of the consolidated Balance Sheet. Some further discussion, however, is required with respect to both the computation and disclosure of this balance.

> **Computation** With respect to computation, the Non-Controlling Interest in the consolidated Balance Sheet is simply the non-controlling shareholders' proportionate share of the carrying values of the net assets of the subsidiary. This is the approach that is required by the *CICA Handbook*:
>
> > **Paragraph 1600.15** *The non-controlling interest in the subsidiary's assets and liabilities should be reflected in terms of carrying values recorded in the accounting records of the subsidiary company.* (April, 1975)
>
> If the subsidiary has goodwill on its books, Paragraph 1581.40 indicates that none of the cost of the purchase should be allocated to goodwill of the acquiree that is present

at acquisition. This contradicts the requirement of Paragraph 1600.15 that the non-controlling interest in subsidiary assets be based on the carrying values that are recorded in that company's records. In our examples and problems, we follow the Paragraph 1600.15 recommendation which means that the parent's share of the subsidiary's recorded goodwill will be eliminated against the cost of the investment, while the non-controlling interest's share of this balance will be included in the consolidated Balance Sheet.

Disclosure With respect to the disclosure of the Non-Controlling Interest in the consolidated Balance Sheet, the *CICA Handbook* makes the following somewhat ambiguous Recommendation:

> **Paragraph 1600.69** *Non-controlling interest in consolidated subsidiary companies should be shown separately from shareholders' equity.* (April, 1975)

While this Recommendation would allow the Non-Controlling Interest to be shown as part of the long-term liabilities, it is most commonly disclosed in practice as a separate item between the long-term liabilities and shareholders' equity. The 2006 edition of *Financial Reporting in Canada* found that all of the 80 companies that disclosed a non-controlling or minority interest in their Balance Sheets disclosed it as a separate item outside of shareholders' equity.

Other Factors You should understand that, in real world situations, the Non-Controlling Interest in the consolidated Balance Sheet is a highly aggregated piece of information. If the parent company has fractional ownership of a large number of subsidiary enterprises, all of the interests of the various non-controlling shareholder groups would be included in a single Non-Controlling Interest figure.

Further, for those subsidiaries with different classes of non-voting or preferred shares outstanding, these additional equity interests would also become part of the Non-Controlling Interest in the consolidated Balance Sheet. It would be unusual for outstanding subsidiary preferred shares to be disclosed as a separate item in a consolidated Balance Sheet.

Consolidated Balance Sheet - Example Three

4-111. Using the same procedures as in Examples One and Two, the Example Three consolidated Balance Sheet would be prepared as follows:

Pack Company And Subsidiary
Consolidated Balance Sheet
As At December 31, 2007

Cash ($600,000 + $400,000)		$ 1,000,000
Accounts Receivable ($1,500,000 + $1,100,000)		2,600,000
Inventories ($2,100,000 + $1,400,000)		3,500,000
Investment In Sack ($3,200,000 - $3,200,000)		Nil
Plant And Equipment (Net) ($5,600,000 + $2,100,000)		7,700,000
Total Assets		$14,800,000
Current Liabilities ($1,200,000 + $400,000)		$ 1,600,000
Long-Term Liabilities ($2,800,000 + $600,000)		3,400,000
Total Liabilities		$5,000,000
Non-Controlling Interest [(20%)($4,000,000)]		800,000
Shareholders' Equity:		
No Par Common Stock (Pack's Only)	$5,000,000	
Retained Earnings (Pack's Only)	4,000,000	9,000,000
Total Equities		$14,800,000

4-112. Note that we have disclosed the Non-Controlling Interest as a separate item between the Total Liabilities and Shareholders' Equity.

Exercise Four-4

Subject: Balance Sheet At Acquisition - Fractional Ownership - No FV Changes

On December 31, 2007, Pock Inc. acquires 80 percent of the outstanding voting shares of Sock Ltd. for $2,440,000 in cash. On that date, all of the net identifiable assets of Sock Ltd. have fair values that are equal to their carrying values. The Balance Sheets of the two Companies on this date, subsequent to the business combination, are as follows:

Pock and Sock Companies
Balance Sheets
As At December 31, 2007

	Pock	Sock
Cash	$ 943,000	$ 347,000
Accounts Receivable	1,712,000	963,000
Inventories	3,463,000	1,876,000
Investment In Sock	2,440,000	N/A
Plant And Equipment (Net)	4,692,000	1,921,000
Total Assets	$13,250,000	$5,107,000
Current Liabilities	$ 987,000	$ 784,000
Long-Term Liabilities	3,462,000	1,273,000
No Par Common Stock	5,460,000	1,215,000
Retained Earnings	3,341,000	1,835,000
Total Equities	$13,250,000	$5,107,000

Prepare a consolidated Balance Sheet for Pock Inc. and its subsidiary, Sock Ltd., as at December 31, 2007. Include the investment analysis and the investment elimination journal entry in your solution.

End of Exercise. Solution available in Study Guide.

Example Four - Fractional Ownership With Fair Value Changes And Goodwill

Example

4-113. In this final example, we will continue to have fractional ownership. However, we will add fair value changes and goodwill. The basic data for this Example is as follows:

> On December 31, 2007, the Peak Company purchases 90 percent of the outstanding voting shares of the Seek Company for $5,220,000 in cash. On that date, subsequent to the business combination transaction, the Balance Sheets of the two companies are as follows:

Peak and Seek Companies
Balance Sheets
As At December 31, 2007

	Peak	Seek
Cash	$ 1,000,000	$ 700,000
Accounts Receivable	2,100,000	1,200,000
Inventories	3,440,000	2,500,000
Investment In Seek	5,220,000	N/A
Plant And Equipment (Net)	4,240,000	4,600,000
Total Assets	$16,000,000	$9,000,000
Current Liabilities	$ 1,200,000	$1,000,000
Long-Term Liabilities	2,800,000	2,000,000
No Par Common Stock	7,000,000	2,000,000
Retained Earnings	5,000,000	4,000,000
Total Equities	$16,000,000	$9,000,000

Other Information:

1. All of the identifiable assets of the Seek Company have fair values that are equal to their carrying values except for Plant And Equipment which has a fair value that is $600,000 less than its carrying value and Inventories with fair values that are $100,000 more than their carrying values.
2. Prior to the business combination, there were no intercompany transactions between the two companies. It follows that on the date of the combination, there are no intercompany asset or liability balances.

Required: Prepare a consolidated Balance Sheet for the Peak Company and its subsidiary, the Seek Company, as at December 31, 2007.

Procedures

4-114. This fourth Example provides a complete illustration of the procedures that are required in preparing a consolidated Balance Sheet as at the date of acquisition. However, no new procedures are required. As with all of the preceding examples, we will continue to use Step A-1 (eliminate the investment account) and Step A-2 (eliminate 100 percent of the subsidiary's shareholders' equity at acquisition). As in Example Three, we will need Step A-4 to establish a Non-Controlling Interest to be included in the consolidated Balance Sheet. In addition, we will need Step A-3 from Example Two to allocate the Differential to fair value changes and goodwill.

Investment Analysis Schedule

4-115. The investment analysis schedule that will be used in this Example is as follows:

	90 Percent	100 Percent
Investment Cost	$5,220,000	$5,800,000*
Seek - Common Shareholders' Equity	(5,400,000)	(6,000,000)
Differential	($ 180,000)	($ 200,000)
Fair Value Changes:		
Decrease On Plant And Equipment	540,000	600,000
Increase On Inventories	(90,000)	(100,000)
Goodwill	$ 270,000	$ 300,000

*The 100 percent figure for the investment cost is the total value for the business that is implied by the price paid for 90 percent of the business ($5,220,000 equals 90 percent of $5,800,000). It is calculated by dividing the investment cost by the percentage of the common shares acquired.

4-116. In general terms, this schedule operates exactly as it did in the 100 percent ownership case. However, because we are only going to recognize the parent company's share of fair value changes and goodwill, all of the information has to be calculated on a 90 percent basis.

4-117. You will note that, in our schedule, we have retained the 100 percent figures along with the 90 percent figures. As only the fractional calculations are required in preparing a consolidated Balance Sheet at acquisition, it is not really necessary to calculate both the fractional and 100 percent amounts. However, we would urge you to do so, at least in the early stages of your work on consolidations.

4-118. In most consolidation problems, some of the information is given on a fractional basis (investment cost) while other data is given on a 100 percent basis (fair value changes). As a result, one of the most common errors made in solving consolidation problems is to add or subtract a fractional figure to or from a 100 percent figure.

4-119. This two column analysis will virtually eliminate this type of error, particularly if the final goodwill figure is verified using a definitional calculation. In this Example, the investment cost is $5,220,000 and the investor's share of the subsidiary's fair values is $4,950,000 [(90%)($6,000,000 - $600,000 + $100,000)]. This verifies the 90 percent goodwill figure of $270,000 ($5,220,000 - $4,950,000).

Investment Elimination Journal Entry

4-120. The required journal entry would be as follows:

No Par Common Stock (Seek's)	$2,000,000	
Retained Earnings (Seek's)	4,000,000	
Inventories [(90%)($100,000)]	90,000	
Goodwill	270,000	
Plant And Equipment (Net) [(90%)($600,000)]		$ 540,000
Non-Controlling Interest [(10%)($6,000,000)]		600,000
Investment In Seek		5,220,000

4-121. This journal entry uses Step A-1 (elimination of 100 percent of the investment account) and A-2 (elimination of 100 percent of the subsidiary shareholders' equity at acquisition). In addition, under Step A-3, it uses the figure from the 90 percent column in the investment analysis schedule to allocate the investor's proportionate share of fair value changes and goodwill. Finally, under Step A-4, it establishes a Non-Controlling Interest to be included in the consolidated Balance Sheet at acquisition. This Non-Controlling Interest is based on the $6,000,000 ($2,000,000 + $4,000,000) book value of Seek Company's Shareholders' Equity.

Consolidated Balance Sheet - Example Four

4-122. The required consolidated Balance Sheet is as follows:

Peak Company And Subsidiary
Consolidated Balance Sheet
As At December 31, 2007

Cash ($1,000,000 + $700,000)		$ 1,700,000
Accounts Receivable ($2,100,000 + $1,200,000)		3,300,000
Inventories ($3,440,000 + $2,500,000 + $90,000)		6,030,000
Investment In Seek ($5,220,000 - $5,220,000)		Nil
Plant And Equipment (Net) ($4,240,000 + $4,600,000 - $540,000)		8,300,000
Goodwill		270,000
Total Assets		$19,600,000
Current Liabilities ($1,200,000 + $1,000,000)		$ 2,200,000
Long-Term Liabilities ($2,800,000 + $2,000,000)		4,800,000
Total Liabilities		$ 7,000,000
Non-Controlling Interest [(10%)($6,000,000)]		600,000
Shareholders' Equity:		
No Par Common Stock (Peak's Only)	$7,000,000	
Retained Earnings (Peak's Only)	5,000,000	12,000,000
Total Equities		$19,600,000

Note On Asset Valuation The consolidated asset and liability balances that are required under the Recommendations of the *CICA Handbook* can be calculated in two different ways. One approach is to take 100 percent of the parent company's carrying values, the non-controlling interest's 10 percent share of subsidiary carrying values, and the parent company's 90 percent share of subsidiary fair values. Applying this to the Inventories in the preceding example gives $6,030,00 [$3,440,000 + (10%)($2,500,000) + (90%)($2,500,000 + $100,000)].

An alternative approach takes 100 percent of the carrying values of the parent company's individual assets and liabilities, plus 100 percent of the carrying values of the subsidiary's individual assets and liabilities, plus or minus the parent company's 90 percent interest in the fair value changes on the subsidiary's individual assets and liabilities. This would give the same $6,030,000 [$3,440,000 + $2,500,000 + (90%)($2,600,000 - $2,500,000)].

While either of these approaches will produce the required solution, we believe the latter approach is more efficient, as well as less error prone. As a consequence, it will be used throughout the remainder of this text. Given this, we would suggest that you use this approach in solving assignment and self study problems.

Note On Non-Controlling Interest The Non-Controlling Interest has been disclosed as a separate item between the Total Liabilities and Shareholders' Equity.

Exercise Four-5

Subject: Balance Sheet At Acquisition - Fractional Ownership - FV Changes

On December 31, 2007, the Pickle Company purchases 90 percent of the outstanding voting shares of the Sickle Company for $1,480,000 in cash. On that date, most of the net identifiable assets of the Sickle Company have fair values that are equal to their carrying values. However, the Plant And Equipment (Net) has a fair value that is $160,000 less than its carrying value. In addition, Sickle has unrecorded identifiable intangible assets that have a fair value of $230,000. These intangible assets meet the Paragraph 1581.48 criteria for recognition.

On December 31, 2007, subsequent to the business combination transaction, the Balance Sheets of the two Companies are as follows:

Pickle and Sickle Companies
Balance Sheets
As At December 31, 2007

	Pickle	Sickle
Cash	$ 1,365,000	$ 264,000
Accounts Receivable	2,789,000	657,000
Inventories	2,126,000	1,206,000
Investment In Sickle	1,480,000	N/A
Plant And Equipment (Net)	3,972,000	1,249,000
Total Assets	$11,732,000	$3,376,000
Current Liabilities	$ 1,349,000	$ 764,000
Long-Term Liabilities	2,718,000	1,112,000
No Par Common Stock	5,420,000	490,000
Retained Earnings	2,245,000	1,010,000
Total Equities	$11,732,000	$3,376,000

Prepare a consolidated Balance Sheet for the Pickle Company and its subsidiary, Sickle Company, as at December 31, 2007. Include the investment analysis and the investment elimination journal entry in your solution.

End of Exercise. Solution available in Study Guide.

Summary Of Consolidation Procedures

4-123. As described in this Chapter, we are developing a set of consolidation procedures involving three steps. This Chapter has focused on Step A and has introduced all of the procedures required to complete this Step. In addition, one procedure from Step B has been introduced. The procedures introduced in this Chapter are as follows:

Step A-1 Procedure Eliminate 100 percent of the Investment In Subsidiary account.

Step A-2 Procedure Eliminate 100 percent of all the acquisition date balances in the subsidiary's common shareholders' equity (includes both contributed capital and retained earnings).

Step A-3 Procedure Allocate any debit or credit Differential that is present at acquisition to the investor's share of fair value changes on identifiable assets, fair value changes on identifiable liabilities, and positive or negative goodwill.

Step A-4 Procedure Allocate to a Non-Controlling Interest account in the consolidated Balance Sheet, the non-controlling interest's share of the at acquisition book value of the common shareholders' equity of the subsidiary (includes both contributed capital and retained earnings).

Step B-1 Procedure Eliminate 100 percent of all intercompany assets and liabilities.

4-124. The preceding list includes all of the procedures that are required in Step A. These four Procedures will be used in all subsequent consolidation problems. We will also continue to use Step B-1. However, in Chapters 5 and 6, a number of additional procedures will be added to Step B and the Step C procedures will be introduced.

Summary Of Definitional Calculations

4-125. You may recall from our discussion of the procedural approach to be used in preparing consolidated financial statements, that we encouraged you to work towards preparing the required balances in these statements by using direct definitional calculations (see Paragraph 4-57). To assist you in this work, we offer the following definitions that have been developed in this Chapter.

Identifiable Assets And Liabilities The amount to be included in the consolidated Balance Sheet for any identifiable asset or liability is calculated as follows:

- 100 percent of the carrying value of the identifiable asset (liability) on the books of the parent company at the Balance Sheet date; *plus*
- 100 percent of the carrying value of the identifiable asset (liability) on the books of the subsidiary company at the Balance Sheet date; *plus (minus)*
- the parent company's share of the fair value increase (decrease) on the asset (liability) (i.e., the parent company's share of the difference between the fair value of the subsidiary's asset or liability at time of acquisition and the carrying value of that asset or liability at the time of acquisition).

Goodwill The Goodwill to be recorded in the consolidated balance sheet is equal to the excess of the cost of the investment over the parent company's share of the fair values of the subsidiary's net identifiable assets as at the time of acquisition.

Non-Controlling Interest - Balance Sheet The Non-Controlling Interest to be recorded in the consolidated Balance Sheet is an amount equal to the non-controlling interest's ownership percentage of the book value of the subsidiary's common stock equity at the Balance Sheet date. It will also include any preferred stock equity of the subsidiary that is outstanding.

Contributed Capital The Contributed Capital to be recorded in the consolidated Balance Sheet is equal to the contributed capital from the single entity Balance Sheet of the parent company.

Retained Earnings Consolidated Retained Earnings will be equal to the Retained Earnings balance that is included in the Balance Sheet of the parent company.

4-126. We would note that these definitions reflect the current Recommendations of the *CICA Handbook*. As you might expect, some of these definitions will have to be modified as new consolidation procedures are developed in subsequent Chapters.

International Convergence

Standards

4-127. The Canadian rules for preparing a consolidated balance sheet at acquisition are found in Section 1581, "Business Combinations", and Section 1600, "Consolidated Financial

Statements". The international standards which contain the corresponding material are IFRS No. 3, *Business Combinations*, and IAS No. 27, *Consolidated And Separate Financial Statements*.

Differences

4-128. As we have noted, international standards are largely based on the entity approach to preparing consolidated financial statements. Given this, there are two major differences between a consolidated Balance Sheet at acquisition prepared under current Canadian requirements and a consolidated Balance Sheet at acquisition prepared under current international standards:

> **Asset Valuation** IFRS No. 3 requires that 100 percent of fair value changes on identifiable assets be recognized at the time of acquisition. Section 1581 only allows the acquirer's share to be recognized. Note, however, IFRS No. 3 does not allow the recognition of 100 percent of goodwill. Only the acquirer's share of goodwill can be recognized.

> **Non-Controlling Interest** Consistent with the entity approach, IAS No. 27 requires the non-controlling interest to be presented as a component of consolidated Shareholders' Equity. The value to be recognized will include the non-controlling interest's share of fair value changes on identifiable assets and liabilities.

Example

Basic Information

4-129. The following example will be used to illustrate the application of current international standards for preparing a consolidated Balance Sheet at acquisition:

> On December 31, 2007, the Patent Company purchases 80 percent of the outstanding voting shares of the Suede Company for $720,000 in cash. On that date, subsequent to the business combination transaction, the Balance Sheets of the two companies are as follows:

Patent And Suede Companies
Balance Sheets
As At December 31, 2007

	Patent	Suede
Cash And Receivables	$ 365,000	$ 110,000
Inventories	665,000	370,000
Investment In Suede	720,000	N/A
Plant And Equipment - Net	2,850,000	820,000
Total Assets	$4,600,000	$1,300,000
Current Liabilities	$ 115,000	$ 125,000
Long-Term Liabilities	425,000	375,000
No Par Common Stock	1,500,000	450,000
Retained Earnings	2,560,000	350,000
Total Equities	$4,600,000	$1,300,000

Other Information:

1. All of the identifiable assets of the Suede Company have fair values that are equal to their carrying values except for Plant And Equipment which has a fair value that is $50,000 more than its carrying value and Inventories with fair values that are $25,000 less than their carrying values.

2. Prior to the business combination, there were no intercompany transactions between the two companies. On the date of the combination, there are no intercompany asset or liability balances.

Required: Prepare Balance Sheets as at December 31, 2007 for Patent and its subsidiary, Suede, using:

A. current Canadian accounting standards, and
B. current international standards.

Investment Analysis Schedule

4-130. The investment analysis schedule would be the same, regardless of the applicable accounting standards. It would be as follows:

	80 Percent	100 Percent
Investment Cost (Total Fair Value)	$720,000	$900,000
Suede - Common Shareholders' Equity	(640,000)	(800,000)
Differential	$ 80,000	$100,000
Fair Value Changes:		
Increase On Plant And Equipment	($ 40,000)	($ 50,000)
Decrease On Inventories	20,000	25,000
Net Fair Value Change Credit (Debit)	($ 20,000)	($ 25,000)
Goodwill	$ 60,000	$ 75,000

Investment Elimination Journal Entries

4-131. If Canadian standards are used, the required journal entry would be as follows:

No Par Common Stock (Suede's)	$450,000	
Retained Earnings (Suede's)	350,000	
Plant And Equipment - Net	40,000	
Goodwill	60,000	
Inventories		$ 20,000
Investment In Suede		720,000
Non-Controlling Interest [(20%)($800,000)]		160,000

4-132. This entry recognizes only Patent's 80 percent share of the fair value changes and goodwill. Given this, the Non-Controlling Interest is based on the $800,000 ($450,000 + $350,000) book value of Suede's Shareholders' Equity

4-133. The alternative entry under international standards would be as follows:

No Par Common Stock (Suede's)	$450,000	
Retained Earnings (Suede's)	350,000	
Plant And Equipment - Net	50,000	
Goodwill	60,000	
Inventories		$ 25,000
Investment In Suede		720,000
Non-Controlling Interest [(20%)($800,000 + $25,000)]		165,000

4-134. This entry recognizes 100 percent of the fair value changes on Plant And Equipment and Inventories, but only 80 percent of the Goodwill value. Given this, the Non-Controlling Interest is based on 20 percent of the book value of Suede's Shareholders' Equity, adjusted for the net fair value increase on identifiable assets.

Comparative Balance Sheets

4-135. The required Balance Sheets would be as follows:

Patent Company And Suede
Consolidated Balance Sheet
As At December 31, 2007

	Canadian Standards	International Standards
Cash And Receivables ($365,000 + $110,000)	$ 475,000	$ 475,000
Inventories		
($665,000 + $370,000 - $20,000)	1,015,000	
($665,000 + $370,000 - $25,000)		1,010,000
Investment In Suede ($720,000 - $720,000)	Nil	Nil
Plant And Equipment - Net		
($2,850,000 + $820,000 + $40,000)	3,710,000	
($2,850,000 + $820,000 + $50,000)		3,720,000
Goodwill	60,000	60,000
Total Assets	$5,260,000	$5,265,000
Current Liabilities ($115,000 + $125,000)	$ 240,000	$ 240,000
Long-Term Liabilities ($425,000 + $375,000)	800,000	800,000
Total Liabilities	$1,040,000	$1,040,000
Non-Controlling Interest (Canadian Standards)	160,000	N/A
Shareholders' Equity:		
Non-Controlling Interest (International Standards)	N/A	165,000
No Par Common Stock (Patent's Only)	1,500,000	1,500,000
Retained Earnings (Patent's Only)	2,560,000	2,560,000
Total Equities	$5,260,000	$5,265,000

4-136. In addition to the different values for Inventories and Plant And Equipment, note the difference in the presentation of the non-controlling interest. Under Canadian standards, it is perched ambiguously between Total Liabilities and Shareholders' Equity. In contrast, international standards require this balance to be presented as a component of Shareholders' Equity.

Proposed Changes

4-137. The preceding example used current international accounting standards. We have noted previously, however, that there is a joint FASB/IASB project that will amend their existing standards for business combinations. The proposals currently being put forward as part of this project would change the preceding presentation in one respect. Specifically, the proposals would require recognition of 100 percent of any Goodwill.

4-138. In our example, this would increase Goodwill from $60,000 to $75,000, with a corresponding change in the Non-Controlling Interest from $165,000 t0 $180,000. As there is considerable resistance to this change, it is not clear whether this difference will find its way into the final standard that results from this project.

Additional Readings

4-139. In writing the material in the text, we have incorporated all of the relevant *CICA Handbook* recommendations, as well as material from other sources that we felt to be of importance. While this approach meets the needs of the great majority of our readers, some of you may wish to pursue this subject in greater depth. To facilitate this, you will find a fairly comprehensive list of additional readings at the end of each relevant Chapter in our *Guide To Canadian Financial Reporting*.

CD-ROM Note Our *Guide To Canadian Financial Reporting* is available on the CD-ROM which is included with this text.

Appendix A: Push-Down Accounting

General Concepts

4A-1. Throughout the preceding discussion of the consolidated Balance Sheet at the time of acquisition, no adjustments were made to the subsidiary's accounting records as a result of its being acquired. All of the adjustments that were required by the application of purchase accounting were implemented through working paper entries that were not recorded in the single entity financial statements of the subsidiary.

4A-2. Push-down accounting represents an alternative to the procedures that we have described throughout this Chapter, in that it allows fair value changes to be recorded on the books of the subsidiary. In those situations where it is applicable, normally situations involving the ownership of 90 percent or more of the outstanding voting shares of the subsidiary, the use of push-down accounting will significantly simplify the procedures required in the preparation of consolidated financial statements.

4A-3. Section 1625 of the *CICA Handbook*, "Comprehensive Revaluation Of Assets and Liabilities", permits the use of push-down accounting if:

> **Paragraph 1625.04(a)** *All or virtually all of the equity interests in the enterprise have been acquired, in one or more transactions between non-related parties, by an acquirer who controls the enterprise after the transaction or transactions.* (January, 1993)

Example

Basic Data

4A-4. As we noted in the preceding Chapter, an understanding of push-down accounting requires some familiarity with basic consolidation procedures. Now that we have examined consolidation procedures, at least to the extent they apply at the time of acquisition, we can present an example of the push-down accounting procedures.

4A-5. As 90 percent ownership was involved in our Example Four (Paragraph 4-113), we will use the same data to illustrate push-down accounting. This provides an opportunity to compare the procedures that are used when push-down accounting is applied, with those used in situations where push-down accounting is not applied.

4A-6. The Example Four data is repeated here for your convenience:

> **Example** On December 31, 2007, the Peak Company purchases 90 percent of the outstanding voting shares of the Seek Company for $5,220,000 in cash. On that date, subsequent to the business combination transaction, the Balance Sheets of the two Companies are as follows:

Peak and Seek Companies
Balance Sheets As At December 31, 2007

	Peak	Seek
Cash	$ 1,000,000	$ 700,000
Accounts Receivable	2,100,000	1,200,000
Inventories	3,440,000	2,500,000
Investment In Seek	5,220,000	N/A
Plant And Equipment (Net)	4,240,000	4,600,000
Total Assets	$16,000,000	$9,000,000
Current Liabilities	$ 1,200,000	$1,000,000
Long-Term Liabilities	2,800,000	2,000,000
No Par Common Stock	7,000,000	2,000,000
Retained Earnings	5,000,000	4,000,000
Total Equities	$16,000,000	$9,000,000

Other Information:

1. All of the identifiable assets of the Seek Company have fair values that are equal to their carrying values except for Plant And Equipment which has a fair value that is $600,000 less than its carrying value and Inventories with fair values that are $100,000 more than their carrying values.

2. Prior to the business combination there were no intercompany transactions between the two Companies. It follows that on the date of the combination there are no intercompany asset or liability balances.

Required: Prepare a push-down accounting Balance Sheet for the Seek Company as at December 31, 2007. Using this Balance Sheet as a basis for your procedures, prepare a consolidated Balance Sheet for the Peak Company and its subsidiary, the Seek Company, as at December 31, 2007.

CICA Handbook Recommendations

4A-7. In applying push-down accounting to this example, three Recommendations of Section 1625 are relevant. The first is as follows:

> **Paragraph 1625.23** *When a comprehensive revaluation of an enterprise's assets and liabilities is undertaken as a result of a transaction or transactions as described in 1625.04(a), push-down accounting should be applied. The portion of the assets and liabilities related to non-controlling interests should be reflected at the carrying amounts previously recorded by the acquired enterprise.* (January, 1993)

4A-8. This Recommendation reflects the fact that the parent company approach to asset valuation at the time of acquisition is required in the preparation of consolidated financial statements. By indicating that the non-controlling interest must be based on carrying values, it is made clear that asset and liability values can include only the acquiring company's share of fair value changes and goodwill. This means that we can use the 90 percent column of the Example Four investment analysis.

	90 Percent	100 Percent
Investment Cost	$5,220,000	$5,800,000
Seek - Common Shareholders' Equity	(5,400,000)	(6,000,000)
Differential	($ 180,000)	($ 200,000)
Fair Value Changes:		
Decrease On Plant And Equipment	540,000	600,000
Increase On Inventories	(90,000)	(100,000)
Goodwill	$ 270,000	$ 300,000

4A-9. The second relevant Recommendation on the application of push-down accounting is as follows:

> **Paragraph 1625.29** *When a comprehensive revaluation of an enterprise's assets and liabilities is undertaken as a result of a transaction or transactions as described in 1625.04(a), that portion of retained earnings which has not been included in the consolidated retained earnings of the acquirer or is not related to any continuing non-controlling interests in the enterprise should be reclassified to either share capital, contributed surplus, or a separately identified account within shareholders' equity.* (January, 1993)

4A-10. The Paragraph 1625.29 Recommendation requires that, with the exception of two types of items, the Retained Earnings of the subsidiary at acquisition must be reclassified in the application of push-down accounting. The two exceptions are:

- Amounts belonging to a non-controlling interest.
- Amounts that have been included in the calculation of Retained Earnings of the acquirer as the result of an equity interest which existed prior to obtaining control over the subsidiary.

4A-11. The amounts which are reclassified can be allocated to share capital, contributed surplus, or a separately identified account within shareholders' equity. While the Recommendation is flexible in this regard, we would be inclined to allocate the acquirer's share of the subsidiary's retained earnings to a separately identified account within shareholders' equity. This would serve to distinguish this balance from the usual types of shareholders' equity balances.

4A-12. The third relevant *Handbook* Recommendation is as follows:

> **Paragraph 1625.30** *The revaluation adjustment arising from a comprehensive revaluation of an enterprise's assets and liabilities undertaken as a result of a transaction or transactions as described in 1625.04(a) should be accounted for as a capital transaction,* (see "Capital Transactions", Section 3610), *and recorded as either share capital, contributed surplus, or a separately identified account within shareholders' equity.* (January, 1993)

4A-13. With respect to the revaluation adjustment arising from altered asset and liability values, Paragraph 1625.30 also provides for alternative disclosure. Our preference in this case would be to again use a separate account for this amount. An appropriate title would be Capital Arising On Comprehensive Revaluation Of Assets.

Journal Entry - Push-Down Accounting

4A-14. The journal entry required to implement push-down accounting on the books of the Seek Company as at December 31, 2007 would be as follows:

	Debit	Credit
Retained Earnings [(90%)($4,000,000)]	$3,600,000	
Inventories	90,000	
Goodwill	270,000	
Capital Arising On Comprehensive Revaluation Of Assets (Differential)	180,000	
Plant And Equipment (Net)		$ 540,000
Contributed Surplus [(90%)($4,000,000)]		3,600,000

4A-15. This entry reclassifies the parent's share of Retained Earnings as Contributed Surplus, records Peak's proportionate share of the fair value changes on Inventories and Plant And Equipment on Seek's books, records Peak's share of the Goodwill on Seek's books, and establishes a capital revaluation account for the excess of the cost of the investment over Seek's book value. (This is the Differential from the Example Four investment analysis schedule - see Paragraph 4A-8.)

Subsidiary Balance Sheet - Push-Down Accounting

4A-16. Given the preceding journal entry, the push-down accounting Balance Sheet of Seek Company on December 31, 2007 would be prepared as follows:

Seek Company
Push-Down Accounting Balance Sheet
As At December 31, 2007

Cash	$ 700,000
Accounts Receivable	1,200,000
Inventories ($2,500,000 + $90,000)	2,590,000
Plant And Equipment (Net) ($4,600,000 - $540,000)	4,060,000
Goodwill	270,000
Total Assets	$8,820,000
Current Liabilities	$1,000,000
Long-Term Liabilities	2,000,000
No Par Common Stock	2,000,000
Contributed Surplus	3,600,000
Capital Arising On Comprehensive Revaluation Of Assets	(180,000)
Retained Earnings (Non-Controlling Interest)	400,000
Total Equities	$8,820,000

4A-17. Given this push-down accounting Balance Sheet, the procedures for preparing the required consolidated Balance Sheet are simplified. The required journal entry would be as follows:

No Par Common Stock (Seek's)	$2,000,000	
Contributed Surplus (Seek's)	3,600,000	
Retained Earnings (Seek's)	400,000	
Capital Arising On Comprehensive Revaluation Of Assets		$ 180,000
Investment In Seek		5,220,000
Non-Controlling Interest [(10%)($2,000,000) + $400,000]		600,000

4A-18. This entry eliminates all of the subsidiary's Shareholders' Equity balances, eliminates Peak's Investment In Seek, and establishes the Non-Controlling Interest at acquisition. This Non-Controlling Interest balance is equal to their $200,000 [(10%)($2,000,000)] share of No Par Common Stock, plus the $400,000 Retained Earnings Balance.

4A-19. In keeping with the Paragraph 1625.23 requirement that the Non-Controlling Interest must be based on carrying values, the $600,000 can also be calculated by taking 10 percent of the $6,000,000 in Shareholders' Equity from the pre acquisition Balance Sheet of Seek.

4A-20. Given this entry, the required consolidated Balance Sheet is identical to the parent company approach Balance Sheet presented in Example Four (Paragraph 4-122):

Peak Company And Subsidiary
Consolidated Balance Sheet
As At December 31, 2007

Cash ($1,000,000 + $700,000)	$ 1,700,000
Accounts Receivable ($2,100,000 + $1,200,000)	3,300,000
Inventories ($3,440,000 + $2,590,000)	6,030,000
Investment In Seek ($5,220,000 - $5,220,000)	Nil
Plant And Equipment (Net) ($4,240,000 + $4,060,000)	8,300,000
Goodwill	270,000
Total Assets	$19,600,000

Current Liabilities ($1,200,000 + $1,000,000)		$ 2,200,000
Long-Term Liabilities ($2,800,000 + $2,000,000)		4,800,000
Total Liabilities		$ 7,000,000
Non-Controlling Interest [(10%)($6,000,000)]		600,000
Shareholders' Equity:		
No Par Common Stock (Peak's Only)	$7,000,000	
Retained Earnings (Peak's Only)	5,000,000	12,000,000
Total Equities		$19,600,000

Exercise Four-6

Subject: Push-Down Accounting (An Extension Of Exercise Four-5)

On December 31, 2007, the Pickle Company purchases 90 percent of the outstanding voting shares of the Sickle Company for $1,480,000 in cash. On that date, most of the net identifiable assets of the Sickle Company have fair values that are equal to their carrying values. However, the Plant And Equipment (Net) has a fair value that is $160,000 less than its carrying value. In addition, Sickle has unrecorded identifiable intangibles that have a fair value of $230,000. These intangibles meet the Paragraph 1581.48 criteria for recognition.

On December 31, 2007, subsequent to the business combination transaction, the Balance Sheets of the two Companies are as follows:

Pickle and Sickle Companies
Balance Sheets
As At December 31, 2007

	Pickle	Sickle
Cash	$ 1,365,000	$ 264,000
Accounts Receivable	2,789,000	657,000
Inventories	2,126,000	1,206,000
Investment In Sickle	1,480,000	Nil
Plant And Equipment (Net)	3,972,000	1,249,000
Total Assets	$11,732,000	$3,376,000
Current Liabilities	$ 1,349,000	$ 764,000
Long-Term Liabilities	2,718,000	1,112,000
No Par Common Stock	5,420,000	490,000
Retained Earnings	2,245,000	1,010,000
Total Equities	$11,732,000	$3,376,000

Prepare a push-down accounting Balance Sheet for the Sickle Company as at December 31, 2007. Using this Balance Sheet as the basis for your procedures, prepare a consolidated Balance Sheet for the Pickle Company and its subsidiary, the Sickle Company, as at December 31, 2007.

End of Exercise. Solution available in Study Guide.

Disclosure Requirements

4A-21. Before leaving the subject of push-down accounting, we would note that the *CICA Handbook* has several disclosure Recommendations that are applicable when this method is used. These are as follows:

Paragraph 1625.34 *In the period that push-down accounting has been first applied the financial statements should disclose the following:*

(a) the date push-down accounting was applied, and the date or dates of the purchase transaction or transactions that led to the application of push-down accounting;
(b) a description of the situation resulting in the application of push-down accounting; and
(c) the amount of the change in each major class of assets, liabilities and shareholders' equity arising from the application of push-down accounting. (January, 1993)

Paragraph 1625.35 *For a period of at least three years following the application of push-down accounting the financial statements should disclose:*

(a) the date push-down accounting was applied;
(b) the amount of the revaluation adjustment and the shareholders' equity account in which the revaluation adjustment was recorded; and
(c) the amount of retained earnings reclassified and the shareholders' equity account to which it was reclassified. (January, 1993)

International Convergence

4A-22. International standards do not currently provide for the use of push-down accounting. Further, there does not appear to be any intention to put this subject on the agenda of the IASB. Given this, the CICA's IFRS Advisory committee has recommended that Section 1625 be removed from Canadian GAAP at the time of changeover to IFRSs.

Appendix B: Reverse Takeovers

EIC Abstract No. 10 - Reverse Takeover Accounting

4B-1. As discussed in Chapter 3, there are business combination transactions in which the acquiring company, from a legal point of view is, in fact, the acquiree from an economic point of view. This can only happen when the legal acquirer uses its own shares to obtain either the assets or shares of the legal acquiree.

4B-2. If, for example, an acquirer issues such a large block of shares to the shareholders of an acquiree that, subsequent to the business combination transaction, the acquiree shareholders hold a majority of shares in the acquirer, we have a reverse takeover. Although the concept of reverse takeovers was introduced in Chapter 3, detailed consideration of this topic could not be done until the consolidation procedures covered in this Chapter were completed.

4B-3. We noted in the preceding Chapter that the concepts involved in reverse takeover accounting are no different than those involved in other business combinations where an acquirer can be identified. However, there are sufficient complications in the application of these concepts that the Emerging Issues Committee has issued Abstract No. 10, "Reverse Takeover Accounting". In this Abstract, the Committee reaches a consensus on six specific issues related to reverse takeovers. The issues, as well as the consensus reached, are as follows:

> **Issue One** In what circumstances is it appropriate to apply reverse takeover accounting principles?
>
> **Consensus On Issue One** Paragraph 1581.17 identifies the circumstances in which reverse takeover accounting should be applied.. It is as follows:
>
> > **Paragraph 1581.17** Occasionally, an enterprise obtains ownership of the shares of another enterprise but, as part of the transaction, issues enough voting shares as consideration that control of the combined enterprise passes to the shareholders of the acquired enterprise (commonly referred to as a "reverse takeover"). Although legally the enterprise that issues the shares is regarded as the parent or continuing enterprise, the enterprise whose former shareholders now control the combined enterprise is treated as the acquirer. As a result, the issuing enterprise is deemed to be a continuation of the acquirer and the acquirer is deemed to have acquired control of the assets and business of the issuing enterprise in consideration for the issue of capital.
>
> In identifying the acquirer and thereby determining whether a reverse takeover has occurred, the following factors (set out in Paragraphs 1581.14 and .15) would be considered:
>
> - the relative voting rights in the combined enterprise after the combination
> - the existence of a large non-controlling interest in the combined enterprise when no other owner or organized group of owners has a significant interest
> - the composition of the governing body of the combined enterprise
> - the composition of the senior management of the combined enterprise
>
> Reverse takeover accounting should not normally occur unless a business combination transaction takes place. A business combination excludes an exchange of shares between companies under common control and hence the accounting for such exchanges is not dealt with in this discussion.
>
> **Issue Two** How should the consolidated financial statements prepared following a reverse takeover be described and what financial statements should be presented as comparative statements?
>
> **Consensus On Issue Two** The consolidated financial statements (or the financial

statements of the company resulting from a legal amalgamation of the two companies after the exchange of shares) should be issued under the name of the legal parent but described in the notes or elsewhere as a continuation of the financial statements of the legal subsidiary and not of the legal parent. As stated in Paragraph 1581.17 (see Issue One), in a reverse takeover situation, the legal parent is deemed to be a continuation of the acquiring company, i.e., the legal subsidiary. The control of the assets and business of the legal parent is deemed to have been acquired in consideration for the issue of capital by the legal subsidiary. In many cases, a reverse takeover transaction will be accompanied by a name change such that the name of the legal parent becomes similar to the name of the legal subsidiary.

The comparative figures presented in the consolidated financial statements prepared after a reverse takeover should be those of the legal subsidiary. The fact that the capital structure of the consolidated entity, being the capital structure of the legal parent, is different from that appearing in the financial statements of the legal subsidiary in earlier periods due to reverse takeover accounting should be explained in the notes to the consolidated financial statements.

Issue Three How should the cost of the purchase be determined and allocated in a reverse takeover transaction?

Consensus On Issue Three The general principle in Section 1581 is that the cost of the purchase should be determined by the fair value of the consideration given or the acquirer's share of the fair value of the net assets acquired, whichever is more reliably measurable. In a reverse takeover, the consideration is given not by the legal parent but is deemed to be given by the legal subsidiary through the issue of capital.

If the fair value of the shares of the legal subsidiary is used to determine the cost of the purchase, a calculation has to be made to determine the number of shares the legal subsidiary would have had to issue in order to provide the same percentage of ownership of the combined company to the shareholders of the legal parent as they have in the combined company as a result of the reverse takeover transaction. The fair value of the number of shares so calculated would be used as the cost of the purchase.

If the quoted market price (as adjusted, where appropriate) of the shares of the legal subsidiary is not indicative of the fair value of the shares that the legal subsidiary would have had to issue, or the fair value is not otherwise reliably measureable, it would be appropriate to use the total fair value of all the issued shares of the legal parent prior to the exchange of shares as a basis for the determination of the cost of the purchase. It may be appropriate to use the quoted market price of the shares of the legal parent traded in the market, after recognizing the possible effects of the price fluctuations, quantities traded, issue costs and similar items, in order to establish the fair value of such shares.

The cost of the purchase determined on an appropriate basis would be allocated to the assets and liabilities of the legal parent on the basis of their fair value as set out in Section 1581. If the cost of the purchase exceeds the fair values assigned to identifiable assets and liabilities, the excess would be recorded as goodwill in the consolidated financial statements.

The consolidated financial statements following a reverse takeover would reflect the fair values of the assets and liabilities of the legal parent while the assets and liabilities of the legal subsidiary would continue to be carried at their book values..

Issue Four How should the shareholders' equity be determined and presented in the consolidated balance sheet following a reverse takeover transaction?

Consensus On Issue Four Shareholders' equity should be determined and presented on the consolidated balance sheet as if the consolidated financial statements are a continuation of the legal subsidiary. This means that the retained earnings (or deficit) and other surplus accounts in the consolidated financial statements immediately after the reverse takeover would be the same as the accounts of the legal subsidiary at that date. The retained earnings (or deficit) and any other surplus accounts of the legal parent at the date of the legal combination would be eliminated in consolidation.

The amount shown as issued capital in the consolidated balance sheet would be calculated by adding to the issued capital of the legal subsidiary the amount of the cost of the purchase determined as described above, excluding any costs incurred in cash. However, the capital structure, i.e., the number and type of shares issued, appearing in the consolidated balance sheet would reflect that of the legal parent, including the shares issued to effect the reverse takeover.

In many cases, a reverse takeover transaction will be accompanied by a legal amalgamation. Legislation may require that the amount shown as issued share capital of the amalgamated company is to be equal to the aggregate of the issued share capitals of each of the amalgamating companies prior to the amalgamation (as adjusted for any intercompany shareholdings). In such circumstances, any excess of the share capital legally required to be shown in the balance sheet of the amalgamated company over the value attributed to the shares for accounting purposes should be included as a separate debit in shareholders' equity. There should be a description thereof disclosed either in the balance sheet or in the notes to the financial statements.

Issue Five How should the earnings per share be determined for a fiscal year during which a reverse takeover occurs and for the years for which comparative statements are presented?

Consensus On Issue Five For the purpose of computing earnings per share, the number of shares outstanding for the period from the beginning of the fiscal year to the date of the reverse takeover is deemed to be the number of shares issued by the legal parent to the shareholders of the legal subsidiary. For the period from the date of the reverse takeover to the end of the fiscal year, the number of shares to be used in the calculation of the earnings per share would be the actual number of shares of the legal parent outstanding in that period. The weighted average number of shares to be used in computing the earnings per share would be calculated on the basis of the numbers determined for the two periods as described above. The earnings per share to be disclosed for the comparative periods would be computed by dividing the earnings of the legal subsidiary by the number of shares of the legal parent issued in the reverse takeover transaction.

Issue Six When not all the shareholders of the legal subsidiary exchange their shares for shares in the legal parent, how should the interest of such shareholders be accounted for in the consolidated financial statements?

Consensus On Issue Six In such a situation, the shareholders who do not exchange their shares become a minority interest in the legal subsidiary. Although from an accounting viewpoint, the company in which they owned shares acquired another company, i.e., the legal parent, they would be treated as minority shareholders of a subsidiary company in the consolidated financial statements prepared after a reverse takeover transaction. Since the assets and liabilities of the legal subsidiary would be included in the consolidated balance sheet at their book values, the minority interest appearing on the consolidated balance sheet would reflect the minority shareholders' proportionate interest in the book value of the net assets of the legal subsidiary.

Examples

Example With No Non-Controlling Interest

4B-4. EIC Abstract No. 10 includes two examples which illustrate the various conclusions reached on reverse takeover accounting issues. The first example involves a situation in which all of the subsidiary shares are acquired and there is no non-controlling interest:

Alpha Company - Balance Sheets

	December 31 2007	September 30 2008
Current Assets	$ 400	$ 500
Fixed Assets	1,200	1,300
Total Assets	$1,600	$1,800
Current Liabilities	$ 200	$ 300
Long-Term Liabilities	400	300
Redeemable Preferred Shares (100 Shares)	100	100
Common Shares (100 Shares)	300	300
Retained Earnings	600	800
Total Equities	$1,600	$1,800

Beta Company - Balance Sheets

	December 31 2007	September 30 2008
Current Assets	$1,000	$ 700
Fixed Assets	2,000	3,000
Total Assets	$3,000	$3,700
Current Liabilities	$ 500	$ 600
Long-Term Liabilities	900	1,100
Common Shares (60 Shares)	600	600
Retained Earnings	1,000	1,400
Total Equities	$3,000	$3,700

Other Information:

1. For the nine months ended September 30, 2008, Alpha Company had Net Income of $200 while Beta had Net Income of $400. No dividends were declared by either Company during the period. Neither company had any Extraordinary Items or Results Of Discontinued Operations during this period.
2. At September 30, 2008, the fair value of Alpha's common shares was $12 per share while that of Beta's shares was $40 per share.
3. On September 30, 2008, the fair values of Alpha's identifiable assets and liabilities are the same as their carrying values except for fixed assets which have a fair value of $1,500.
4. On September 30, 2008, Alpha issues 150 common shares in exchange for all 60 of the outstanding common shares of Beta.

Investment Analysis

4B-5. As the former Beta shareholders now own 60 percent [150 ÷ (100 + 150)] of the outstanding Alpha shares as compared to 40 percent (100 ÷ 250) for the ongoing Alpha shareholders, we are dealing with a reverse takeover.

4B-6. Had this combination been carried out through an issue of Beta shares, Beta would have had to issue 40 additional shares to Alpha in order to give the Alpha shareholders the same 40 percent interest [40 ÷ (60 + 40)] in the combined company. Using the fair value of Beta shares as the basis for determination, this gives a purchase cost of $1,600 [(40 Shares)($40)] and Goodwill can be calculated as follows:

Purchase Price	$1,600
Alpha - Shareholders' Equity ($300 + $800)	(1,100)
Differential	$ 500
Fair Value Change On Alpha's Fixed Assets ($1,500 - $1,300)	(200)
Goodwill	$ 300

Consolidated Balance Sheet

4B-7. Based on these calculations, the required consolidated Balance Sheet can be prepared as follows:

Alpha Company And Subsidiary
Consolidated Balance
As At September 30, 2008

Current Assets ($700 + $500)		$1,200
Fixed Assets ($3,000 + $1,300 + $200)		4,500
Goodwill (See Preceding Calculation)		300
Total Assets		$6,000
Current Liabilities ($600 + $300)		$ 900
Long-Term Liabilities ($1,100 + $300)		1,400
Shareholders' Equity:		
Redeemable Preferred Shares (100)	$ 100	
Common Shares (Note)	2,200	
Retained Earnings (Beta's)	1,400	3,700
Total Equities		$6,000

Note While the number of shares outstanding is Alpha's 250, the $2,200 is made up of Beta's original contributed capital of $600, plus the $1,600 resulting from the deemed issue of 40 additional shares in the reverse takeover.

Consolidated Net Income

4B-8. In calculating consolidated Net Income for the year ending December 31, 2008, Alpha's income for the nine month period ending September 30, 2008 would be excluded. On this basis, assume that the consolidated Net Income for the combined entity's first full year ending December 31, 2008 is $800. This would be divided by a weighted average of the Alpha Company shares outstanding using 150 shares (the number issued to Beta in the reverse takeover transaction) for the first nine months of 2008 and 250 (the actual number outstanding for this period) for the remaining three months. The weighted average would be calculated as follows:

First Nine Months [(150 Shares)(9/12)]	112.5
Remaining Three Months [(250 Shares)(3/12)]	62.5
Weighted Average Shares Outstanding	175.0

4B-9. Given this weighted average for shares outstanding, the 2008 earnings per share would be calculated as follows:

$$\frac{\text{Consolidated Net Income}}{\text{Weighted Average Shares Outstanding}} = \frac{\$800}{175} = \$4.57$$

4B-10. If we assume that Beta's Net Income for 2007 was $600, the corresponding comparative figure for 2007 would be calculated as follows:

$$\frac{\text{Consolidated Net Income}}{\text{Weighted Average Shares Outstanding}} = \frac{\$600}{150} = \$4.00$$

Example With Non-Controlling Interest

4B-11. The preceding example assumed that all of the Beta shareholders exchanged their shares for those of Alpha. As noted in EIC Abstract No. 10's Issue Six, this may not always be the case and, when it is not, a non-controlling interest is created. Note, however, that this is not the usual non-controlling interest. While it is an interest in the subsidiary, it is not an interest in the acquiree. Rather, it is a minority or non-controlling interest in the acquirer. This means that its presence will not influence the cost of the purchase or the amounts to be allocated to fair value changes or goodwill.

Investment Analysis And Consolidated Balance Sheet

4B-12. To illustrate this possibility, we will modify the original example by assuming that 150 Alpha shares are offered for the full 60 shares of Beta (2.5 Alpha shares for each Beta share). However, in this version of the example only 56 shares of Beta are tendered for exchange, resulting in the issue of only 140 Alpha shares. This means that the former Beta shareholders own 58.3 percent (140 ÷ 240) of the Alpha shares that are outstanding after the reverse takeover.

4B-13. If the combination had been carried out by issuing Beta shares, the issuance of 40 Beta shares would have resulted in the Beta shareholders retaining their 58.3 percent ownership interest [56 ÷ (56 + 40)] in the combined company. This means that the $1,600 purchase price [(40 Shares)($40 Per Share)] would be the same as in the previous example, as would the amount of Goodwill to be recorded in the consolidated Balance Sheet. Given this, the consolidated Balance Sheet would be as follows:

Alpha Company And Subsidiary
Consolidated Balance Sheet
As At December 31, 2008

Current Assets ($700 + $500)		$1,200
Fixed Assets ($3,000 + $1,300 + $200)		4,500
Goodwill		300
Total Assets		$6,000
Current Liabilities ($600 + $300)		$ 900
Long-Term Liabilities ($1,100 + $300)		1,400
Total Liabilities		$2,300
Non-Controlling Interest (Note One)		134
Shareholders' Equity:		
Redeemable Preferred Shares (100)	$ 100	
Common Shares (Note Two)	2,160	
Retained Earnings (Note Three)	1,306	3,566
Total Equities		$6,000

Note One The $134 Non-Controlling Interest is based on 6.7 percent (4 Shares ÷ 60 Shares) of the carrying value of Beta's net assets ($600 + $1,400) prior to the reverse takeover.

Note Two This note would disclose that there are 240 Alpha shares outstanding. The total amount of $2,160 is made up of the $560 associated with 56 of Beta's pre acquisition shares, plus the $1,600 associated with the 40 shares deemed to be issued in the reverse takeover transaction.

Note Three The Retained Earnings reflects the majority's 93.3 percent share (56 Shares ÷ 60 Shares) of the $1,400 in Beta Retained Earnings at the time of the reverse takeover.

Exercise Four-7

Subject: Reverse Takeovers

On December 31, 2007, Revco Inc. issues 115,000 of its common shares to the shareholders of Marco Ltd. in return for all 25,000 of the outstanding Marco Ltd. shares. On this date, prior to the business combination, the condensed Balance Sheets of Revco Inc. and Marco Ltd. are as follows:

Revco and Marco Companies
Condensed Balance Sheets
As At December 31, 2007

	Revco Inc.	**Marco Ltd.**
Net Identifiable Assets	$2,465,000	$3,898,000
No Par Common Stock		
Revco (85,000 Shares Outstanding)	$1,275,000	Nil
Marco (25,000 Shares Outstanding)	Nil	$2,625,000
Retained Earnings	1,190,000	1,273,000
Total Shareholders' Equity	$2,465,000	$3,898,000

Other Information:

1. At this time, all of the identifiable assets of both Companies have fair values that are equal to their carrying values.
2. On December 31, 2007, prior to the business combination transaction, the shares of Marco are trading at $160 per share. The shares of Revco are trading at $34 per share at this time.
3. For the 12 months ending December 31, 2007, Revco Inc. had Net Income of $240,000, while Marco Ltd. had Net Income of $378,000.

Prepare the condensed consolidated Balance Sheet for the combined company as of December 31, 2007. Calculate consolidated Net Income and consolidated Earnings Per Share for the year ending December 31, 2007.

End of Exercise. Solution available in Study Guide.

International Convergence

4B-14. Appendix B of IFRS No. 3, *Business Combinations*, provides guidance that is similar to that found in EIC Abstract No. 10. However, it does not provide detailed examples of the application of this guidance.

Walk Through Problem

Objective Of Walk Through Problems

This is the first example of what we refer to as walk through problems. In these walk through problems you are provided with a fill-in-the-blank solution format to assist you in solving the problem. This solution format is found in the Study Guide which accompanies this text. The Study Guide also contains a complete solution to the problem.

These problems are designed to be an easy way to get started with solving the type of problem illustrated in the Chapter. Having completed this problem, you should proceed to the Self Study Problems which you will have to work without the assistance of a solution format.

Continued In Chapters 5 and 6

Note that this same problem will be continued and extended in Chapters 5 and 6. This is to provide you with a basis for comparison as you move into more difficult procedures that are introduced in these subsequent Chapters.

Basic Data

On December 31, 2007, the Puff Company purchased 60 percent of the outstanding voting shares of the Snuff Company for $720,000 in cash. On that date, subsequent to the completion of the business combination, the Balance Sheets of the Puff and Snuff Companies and the fair values of Snuff's identifiable assets and liabilities were as follows:

	Balance Sheets		Fair Values
	Puff	Snuff	Snuff
Cash And Accounts Receivable	$ 350,000	$ 200,000	$200,000
Inventories	950,000	500,000	450,000
Investment In Snuff	720,000	N/A	N/A
Plant And Equipment (Net)	2,400,000	700,000	800,000
Total Assets	$4,420,000	$1,400,000	
Current Liabilities	$ 400,000	$ 100,000	$100,000
Long-Term Liabilities	1,000,000	400,000	360,000
No Par Common Stock	1,000,000	800,000	N/A
Retained Earnings	2,020,000	100,000	N/A
Total Equities	$4,420,000	$1,400,000	

Required: Using the fill-in-the-blank solution format in the separate Study Guide, prepare a consolidated Balance Sheet for the Puff Company and its subsidiary, the Snuff Company, as at December 31, 2007. Your answer should comply with the Recommendations of the *CICA Handbook*.

Problems For Self Study

(The solutions for these problems can be found in the separate Study Guide.)

Self Study Problem Four - 1

On December 31, 2007, the Shark Company pays cash to acquire 70 percent of the outstanding voting shares of the Peril Company. On that date, subsequent to the acquisition transaction, the Balance Sheets of the two Companies are as follows:

Shark and Peril Companies
Balance Sheets
As At December 31, 2007

	Shark	Peril
Cash	$ 590,000	$ 200,000
Accounts Receivable	2,000,000	300,000
Inventories	2,500,000	500,000
Investment In Peril (At Cost)	910,000	-0-
Plant And Equipment (Net)	4,000,000	1,000,000
Total Assets	$10,000,000	$2,000,000
Liabilities	$ 2,000,000	$ 400,000
Common Stock (No Par)	4,000,000	400,000
Retained Earnings	4,000,000	1,200,000
Total Equities	$10,000,000	$2,000,000

On the acquisition date, the fair values of the Peril Company's identifiable assets and liabilities are as follows:

Cash	$ 200,000
Accounts Receivable	250,000
Inventories	550,000
Plant And Equipment (Net)	700,000
Liabilities	(500,000)
Net Fair Values	$1,200,000

Required: Prepare a consolidated Balance Sheet for the Shark Company and its subsidiary, the Peril Company, as at December 31, 2007. Your solution should comply with the Recommendations of the *CICA Handbook.*

Self Study Problem Four - 2

On December 31, 2007, the Pentogram Company purchased 70 percent of the outstanding voting shares of the Square Company for $875,000 in cash. The Balance Sheets of the Pentogram Company and the Square Company, before the business combination transaction on December 31, 2007, were as follows:

Pentogram and Square Companies
Balance Sheets
As At December 31, 2007

	Pentogram	Square
Cash	$1,200,000	$ 50,000
Accounts Receivable	400,000	250,000
Inventories	2,000,000	500,000
Plant And Equipment	4,000,000	1,400,000
Accumulated Depreciation	(1,000,000)	(300,000)
Total Assets	$6,600,000	$1,900,000
Current Liabilities	$ 200,000	$ 150,000
Long-Term Liabilities	1,000,000	350,000
No Par Common Stock	2,000,000	1,000,000
Retained Earnings	3,400,000	400,000
Total Equities	$6,600,000	$1,900,000

All of the Square Company's identifiable assets and liabilities have carrying values that are equal to their fair values except for Plant And Equipment which has a fair value of $800,000, Inventories which have a fair value of $600,000 and Long-Term Liabilities which have a fair value of $400,000.

Square Company does not own any intangible assets that result from contractual or other legal rights, or are capable of being separated or divided and sold, transferred, licensed, rented, or exchanged.

Required: Prepare a consolidated Balance Sheet for the Pentogram Company and its subsidiary, the Square Company, as at December 31, 2007, subsequent to the business combination. Your answer should comply with all of the requirements of the *CICA Handbook*.

Self Study Problem Four - 3

On December 31, 2007, the Potvin Distributing Company purchased 60 percent of the outstanding voting shares of the Shroder Company. On that date, subsequent to the acquisition transaction, the Balance Sheets of the two Companies were as follows:

Potvin and Shroder Companies
Balance Sheets
As At December 31, 2007

	Potvin	Shroder
Cash	$ 300,000	$ 100,000
Accounts Receivable	2,000,000	200,000
Inventories	3,000,000	400,000
Investment In Shroder (At Cost)	1,200,000	N/A
Plant And Equipment (At Cost)	6,000,000	1,300,000
Accumulated Amortization	(2,000,000)	(500,000)
Total Assets	$10,500,000	$1,500,000
Current Liabilities	$ 1,500,000	$ 200,000
Long-Term Liabilities	2,000,000	300,000
Common Stock (No Par)	3,000,000	1,500,000
Retained Earnings (Deficit)	4,000,000	(500,000)
Total Equities	$10,500,000	$1,500,000

On December 31, 2007, all of the identifiable assets and liabilities of both Companies have carrying values that are equal to their fair values except for the following:

Fair Values	**Potvin**	**Shroder**
Inventories	$2,800,000	$450,000
Plant and Equipment	$4,500,000	$550,000
Long-Term Liabilities	$1,600,000	$400,000

In addition to the preceding information, Shroder holds a copyright which was developed by its employees, but is not recorded on its books. On December 31, 2007, the copyright held by Shroder has a fair value of $200,000 and a remaining useful life of 5 years.

During 2007, the Shroder Company sold merchandise to the Potvin Company for a total amount of $100,000. On December 31, 2007, all of this merchandise has been resold by the Potvin Company, but Potvin still owes Shroder $10,000 on open account for these merchandise purchases.

Required: Prepare a classified Balance Sheet for the Potvin Distributing Company and its subsidiary, the Shroder Company as at December 31, 2007 assuming that the company:

A. is using the recommendations of the *CICA Handbook*.
B. is using the recommendations contained in IFRS No. 3 and IAS No. 27.

Self Study Problem Four - 4

This problem relates to Appendix A of Chapter 4.

On December 31, 2007, the Jarvis Company acquires 95 percent of the outstanding shares of the May Company in return for cash of $1,168,500. The remaining 5 percent of the May Company shares remain in the hands of the public.

Immediately after this acquisition transaction, the Balance Sheets of the two Companies were as follows:

Jarvis And May Companies
Balance Sheets
As At December 31, 2007

	Jarvis	**May**
Cash	$ 200,000	$ 97,000
Accounts Receivable	1,050,000	121,000
Inventories	2,306,500	899,000
Investment In May	1,168,500	N/A
Land	600,000	179,000
Plant And Equipment (Net)	3,000,000	500,000
Total Assets	$8,325,000	$1,796,000
Current Liabilities	$ 500,000	$ 152,000
Long-Term Liabilities	1,525,000	600,000
Common Stock - No Par	3,075,000	390,000
Retained Earnings	3,225,000	654,000
Total Equities	$8,325,000	$1,796,000

At the time of this acquisition, all of the identifiable assets and liabilities of the May Company had fair values that were equal to their carrying values except the Land which had a fair value of $293,000, and the Plant And Equipment which had a fair value of $415,000. Jarvis Company will use push-down accounting, as described in Section 1625 of the *CICA Handbook,* to account for its investment in May.

Required:

A. Prepare the May Company's Balance Sheet that is to be used in preparing the December 31, 2007 consolidated Balance Sheet.

B. Prepare the consolidated Balance Sheet for Jarvis Company and its subsidiary, May, as at December 31, 2007. You answer should comply with all of the recommendations of the *CICA Handbook*.

Self Study Problem Four - 5

This problem relates to Appendix B of Chapter 4.

On December 31, 2007, the Shareholders' Equity section of the Balance Sheets of the Revok Company and the Taken Company are as follows:

	Revok	Taken
Contributed Capital:		
Preferred Shares	$100,000	Nil
Common Shares	450,000	$500,000
Retained Earnings	375,000	340,000
Total Shareholders' Equity	$925,000	$840,000

Other Information:

1. There has been no change in the number of shares outstanding for either Company during the year ending December 31, 2007.

2. Revok has 40,000 Preferred Shares outstanding and 150,000 Common Shares outstanding. On December 31, 2007, the Common Shares are trading at $9 per share.

3. Taken has 200,000 Common Shares outstanding. On December 31, 2007, these shares are trading at $4 per share.

4. Both Companies have a December 31 year end and, during the year ending December 31, 2007, Revok had Net Income of $56,000 and Taken had Net Income of $34,000. Neither Company declared any dividends during the year ending December 31, 2007. Revok's Preferred Shares are non-cumulative.

5. On December 31, 2007, all of the fair values of the net identifiable assets and liabilities of both Companies were equal to their carrying values except:
   - Revok has Land with a carrying value of $50,000 and a fair value of $65,000.
   - Taken has Land with a carrying value of $20,000 and a fair value of $32,000.

6. On December 31, 2007, Taken Company issues 300,000 of its Common Shares to the shareholders of Revok Company, in return for all of their outstanding Common Shares.

Required:

A. Calculate the amount of Goodwill that will be recorded in the December 31, 2007 consolidated Balance Sheet of Taken Company and its subsidiary Revok Company.

B. Prepare the Shareholders' Equity section of the December 31, 2007 consolidated Balance Sheet of Taken Company and its subsidiary Revok Company.

C. Calculate the 2007 consolidated Net Income for Taken Company and its subsidiary Revok Company.

D. Calculate the 2007 Earnings Per Share for Taken Company and its subsidiary Revok Company.

Assignment Problems

(The solutions for these problems are only available in the solutions manual that has been provided to your instructor.)

Assignment Problem Four - 1

On December 31, 2007, before the business combination transaction, the Balance Sheets of the Pike Company and the Stirling Company were as follows:

Pike and Stirling Companies
Balances Sheets
As At December 31, 2007

	Pike	Stirling
Cash	$ 195,000	$ 118,500
Accounts Receivable (Net)	472,500	253,500
Inventories	883,500	596,700
Plant And Equipment (Net)	4,050,000	2,251,500
Goodwill	142,500	45,000
Total Assets	$5,743,500	$3,265,200
Current Liabilities	$ 13,500	$ 45,000
Long-Term Liabilities	1,080,000	1,673,700
Preferred Stock - Par $100	-0-	30,000
Common Stock - No Par	2,550,000	1,500,000
Retained Earnings	2,100,000	16,500
Total Equities	$5,743,500	$3,265,200

On December 31, 2007, Pike Company issues 37,500 of its shares in return for 75 percent of the outstanding shares of Stirling. On this same date, Pike purchased one-half of the issue of Stirling Preferred Stock for $15,000 in cash.

On the combination date, the identifiable assets and liabilities of Stirling Company had fair values that were equal to their carrying values except for the following fair values:

Accounts Receivable	$ 237,000
Inventories	571,500
Long-Term Liabilities	1,823,700

Prior to the business combination transaction, Pike Company had 50,000 No Par Common Shares outstanding with a current market price of $36 per share. The Stirling Company has 20,000 No Par Common Shares outstanding. The Preferred Shares of the Stirling Company are cumulative, non-participating, and have no dividends in arrears. There have been no intercompany transactions prior to December 31, 2007.

Required: Prepare, in accordance with the Recommendations of the *CICA Handbook*, the consolidated Balance Sheet as at December 31, 2007, for Pike Company and its subsidiary, Stirling Company.

Assignment Problem Four - 2

On December 31, 2007, the closed Trial Balances of the Pass Company and the Sass Company, before the business combination transaction, were as follows:

	Pass	Sass
Cash And Receivables	$ 100,000	$ 10,000
Inventories	3,300,000	290,000
Plant And Equipment (At Cost)	9,000,000	3,000,000
Accumulated Amortization	(3,400,000)	(1,200,000)
Total Assets	$9,000,000	$2,100,000
Current Liabilities	$ 300,000	$ 200,000
Long-Term Liabilities	3,500,000	800,000
Mortgage Payable	-0-	300,000
Common Stock - No Par	1,000,000	-0-
Common Stock - Par $50	-0-	900,000
Contributed Surplus	-0-	300,000
Retained Earnings (Deficit)	4,200,000	(400,000)
Total Equities	$9,000,000	$2,100,000

The Pass Company has 25,000 shares outstanding on December 31, 2007 which are trading at $50 per share on this date. On December 31, 2007, the identifiable assets and liabilities of both companies had fair values that were equal to their carrying values except for the following fair values:

Fair Values	Pass	Sass
Plant And Equipment (Net)	$7,000,000	$1,500,000
Long-Term Liabilities	3,000,000	900,000

It was also determined that on December 31, 2007, Sass Company had a registered trademark with a fair value of $120,000 that was not recorded on its books.

Prior to the business combination, in 2007, Pass sold merchandise to Sass for $200,000 and Sass sold Pass merchandise for $100,000. On December 31, 2007, one-half of these intercompany purchases had been resold to parties outside the consolidated entity. These sales provide both Companies with a 20 percent gross margin on sales prices. On December 31, 2007, Sass owed Pass $50,000 on its intercompany merchandise purchases.

On December 31, 2007, Pass issued 15,000 of its shares to acquire 75 percent of the outstanding shares of Sass.

Required: Prepare the combined Companies' Balance Sheet as at December 31, 2007. Your answer should comply with all of the recommendations of the *CICA Handbook*.

Assignment Problem Four - 3

The Excelsior Company purchased 80 percent of the outstanding voting shares of the Excelsiee Company for $120,000 in cash. On the acquisition date, after the business combination transaction, the Balance Sheets of the two Companies and the fair values of the Excelsiee Company's identifiable assets and liabilities were as follows:

Excelsior and Excelsiee Companies
Balance Sheets

	Book Values Excelsior	Book Values Excelsiee	Fair Values Excelsiee
Cash	$ 100,000	$ 120,000	$ 120,000
Accounts Receivable	1,500,000	500,000	490,000
Inventories	2,300,000	400,000	350,000
Investment in Excelsiee (At Cost)	120,000	N/A	N/A
Plant and Equipment (Net)	3,980,000	1,100,000	1,120,000
Total Assets	$8,000,000	$2,120,000	
Accounts Payable	$1,000,000	$ 400,000	$ 400,000
Mortgage Payable	-0-	120,000	120,000
Long-Term Liabilities	2,000,000	1,400,000	1,500,000
Common Stock No Par	2,000,000	150,000	
Retained Earnings	3,000,000	50,000	
Total Equities	$8,000,000	$2,120,000	

Required: Prepare consolidated Balance Sheets for the Excelsior Company and its subsidiary the Excelsiee Company, as at the acquisition date, using the following alternative conceptual approaches:

A. the proprietary concept;

B. the parent company concept; and

C. the entity concept.

Assignment Problem Four - 4

The Peretti Company and the Blakelock Company are two successful Canadian companies operating on Prince Edward Island. On December 31, 2007, the condensed Balance Sheets and the identifiable fair values of the Peretti Company and the Blakelock Company are as follows:

Peretti Company
December 31, 2007

	Balance Sheet	Fair Values
Current Assets	$2,220,000	$2,340,000
Non-Current Assets (Net)	3,600,000	3,900,000
Total Assets	$5,820,000	
Current Liabilities	$ 420,000	$ 420,000
Long-Term Liabilities	1,500,000	1,440,000
Common Stock - No Par	1,800,000	
Retained Earnings	2,100,000	
Total Equities	$5,820,000	

Blakelock Company
December 31, 2007

	Balance Sheet	Fair Values
Current Assets	$1,800,000	$1,980,000
Non-Current Assets (Net)	3,540,000	2,400,000
Total Assets	$5,340,000	
Current Liabilities	$ 720,000	$ 720,000
Long-Term Liabilities	2,400,000	2,520,000
Common Stock - No Par	1,200,000	
Retained Earnings	1,020,000	
Total Equities	$5,340,000	

The Peretti Company has 300,000 common shares outstanding with a market price of $12 per share. The Blakelock Company has 60,000 common shares outstanding with a market price of $23 per share. On December 31, 2007, Peretti owes Blakelock $48,000 for the use of Blakelock's accounting staff during 2007.

On December 31, 2007, subsequent to the preparation of the preceding single entity Balance Sheets, the Peretti Company purchases 60 percent of the outstanding shares of the Blakelock Company for $900,000 in cash.

Required: Prepare a classified Balance Sheet for Peretti and its subsidiary Blakelock, as at December 31, 2007 assuming that the company:

A. is using the recommendations of the *CICA Handbook*.

B. is using the recommendations contained in IFRS No. 3 and IAS No. 27.

Assignment Problem Four - 5

This problem relates to Appendix A of Chapter 4.

On December 31, 2007, the Poplin Company acquires 95 percent of the outstanding shares of Silk Company in return for cash of $1,235,000. The remaining 5 percent of the Silk Company shares remain in the hands of the public.

Immediately after this acquisition transaction, the Balance Sheets of the two Companies were as follows:

Poplin And Silk Companies
Balance Sheets
As At December 31, 2007

	Poplin	**Silk**
Cash	$ 220,000	$ 78,000
Accounts Receivable	1,140,000	125,000
Inventories	2,560,000	972,000
Investment In Silk	1,235,000	Nil
Land	665,000	137,000
Plant And Equipment (Net)	2,750,000	430,000
Total Assets	$8,570,000	$1,742,000
Current Liabilities	$ 560,000	$ 225,000
Long-Term Liabilities	1,340,000	517,000
Common Stock - No Par	2,800,000	450,000
Retained Earnings	3,870,000	550,000
Total Equities	$8,570,000	$1,742,000

At the time of this acquisition, all of the identifiable assets and liabilities of Silk Company had fair values that were equal to their carrying values except the Land which had a fair value of $337,000, and the Plant And Equipment which had a fair value of $380,000. Poplin Company will use push-down accounting, as described in Section 1625 of the *CICA Handbook,* to account for its Investment In Silk.

Required:

A. Prepare the Silk Company's Balance Sheet that is to be used in preparing the December 31, 2007 consolidated Balance Sheet.

B. Prepare the consolidated Balance Sheet for Poplin Company and its subsidiary, Silk, as at December 31, 2007.

Assignment Problem Four - 6

This problem relates to Appendix B of Chapter 4.

The Balance Sheets of the Fortune Company and the Gold Company as at December 31, 2007 and July 1, 2008, prior to any business combination transaction, were as follows:

	Fortune Company		Gold Company	
	1/7/2008	31/12/2007	1/7/2008	31/12/2007
Current Assets	$ 420,000	$ 410,000	$ 620,000	$ 604,000
Fixed Assets (Net)	1,320,000	1,400,000	2,920,000	2,996,000
Total Assets	$1,740,000	$1,810,000	$3,540,000	$3,600,000
Current Liabilities	$ 220,000	$ 230,000	$ 350,000	$ 360,000
Long-Term Liabilities	430,000	680,000	520,000	930,000
Contributed Capital:				
Redeemable Preferred Shares	200,000	200,000	-0-	-0-
Common Shares	500,000	500,000	1,200,000	1,200,000
Retained Earnings	390,000	200,000	1,470,000	1,110,000
Total Equities	$1,740,000	$1,810,000	$3,540,000	$3,600,000

Other Information:

1. For the six month period ending July 1, 2008, the Fortune Company had Net Income of $190,000 and the Gold Company had Net Income of $360,000. These figures did not contain any Extraordinary Items or Results Of Discontinued Operations. Neither Company declared any dividends during this period.

2. On both Balance Sheet dates, the Fortune Company had 20,000 Redeemable Preferred Shares and 50,000 Common Shares outstanding. On July 1, 2008, the Common Shares were trading at $22 per share.

3. On both Balance Sheet dates, the Gold Company had 40,000 Common Shares outstanding. On July 1, 2008, these shares were trading at $75 per share.

4. On July 1, 2008, all of the fair values of Fortune Company's and Gold Company's identifiable assets and liabilities had carrying values that were equal to their fair values, except for Fixed Assets. Fortune's Fixed Assets had a fair value of $1,900,000, while Gold's Fixed Assets had a fair value of $2,800,000.

5. Neither Company owns any intangible assets that result from contractual or other legal rights, or are capable of being separated or divided and sold, transferred, licensed, rented, or exchanged.

Required: For the following two independent cases, use the guidelines provided by the Emerging Issues Committee (EIC) Abstract No. 10 to prepare the July 1, 2008 Consolidated Balance Sheet for Fortune Company and its subsidiary Gold Company. In addition, calculate Consolidated Net Income and Earnings Per Share for the six month period ending July 1, 2008.

A. On July 1, 2008, Fortune Company issues 100,000 additional Common Shares in exchange for all of the outstanding Common Shares of Gold Company.

B. On July 1, 2008, Fortune Company issues 85,000 additional Common Shares in exchange for 36,000 of the outstanding Common Shares of Gold Company.

Consolidation Subsequent To Acquisition (No Unrealized Intercompany Profits)

Procedures Subsequent To Acquisition

5-1. Once we move beyond the date on which the parent acquired its controlling interest in the subsidiary shares, the preparation of consolidated financial statements becomes much more complex. We will have to deal with the concept of consolidated Net Income and the preparation of a consolidated Income Statement. Further, both the Statement Of Retained Earnings and the Cash Flow Statement will have to be prepared on a consolidated basis.

5-2. Even the preparation of a consolidated Balance Sheet in the periods subsequent to the date of acquisition will become more complex as we have to write off fair value changes, recognize any goodwill impairment losses, eliminate intercompany assets and liabilities, and allocate the retained earnings of the subsidiary since acquisition.

5-3. We will begin this Chapter with a simple example of the conceptual alternatives in the presentation of the consolidated Income Statement. While we will find that the *CICA Handbook* requires the use of the parent company approach in preparing a consolidated Income Statement for a parent company and its subsidiaries, this example will also illustrate other alternatives. You should pay particular attention to the entity approach as this is required approach under international accounting standards.

5-4. In addition, you should note that the proprietary approach consolidated Income Statements illustrated do have a practical application. They are identical to the Income Statements that would be prepared when proportionate consolidation is used to account for joint ventures.

Conceptual Alternatives For The Consolidated Income Statement

Example

5-5. In order to provide an illustration of the various possible approaches to the preparation of the consolidated Income Statement, we will use the following example:

The Pick Company owns 60 percent of the outstanding shares of the Stick Company. The purchase was made at a time when all of the identifiable assets and liabilities of the Stick Company had carrying values that were equal to their fair values. The purchase price was equal to 60 percent of the carrying values of the Stick Company's net identifiable assets. In a subsequent year, the condensed Income Statements of the two Companies are as follows:

Pick and Stick Companies
Income Statements

	Pick	Stick
Sales	$4,000,000	$2,000,000
Cost of Goods Sold	$2,500,000	$1,000,000
Other Expenses	700,000	400,000
Total Expenses	$3,200,000	$1,400,000
Net Income	$ 800,000	$ 600,000

Proprietary Concept Solution

5-6. Under this conceptual approach, the expenses and revenues that are disclosed in the consolidated Income Statement consist of 100 percent of the parent company's expenses and revenues plus a share of the subsidiary's expenses and revenues that is based on the parent company's ownership interest (60 percent in this example). The resulting Income Statement is as follows:

Pick Company and Subsidiary
Consolidated Income Statement
Proprietary Approach

Sales [$4,000,000 + (60%)($2,000,000)]	$5,200,000
Cost Of Goods Sold [$2,500,000 + (60%)($1,000,000)]	$3,100,000
Other Expenses [$700,000 + (60%)($400,000)	940,000
Total Expenses	$4,040,000
Consolidated Net Income	$1,160,000

5-7. Since the consolidation procedures remove the non-controlling interest's share of the individual subsidiary expenses and revenues, there is no necessity to disclose a separate Non-Controlling Interest in the consolidated Income Statement. This, of course, is analogous to the procedures that were used in preparing the consolidated Balance Sheet under the proprietary concept.

5-8. You might also note that the consolidated Net Income of $1,160,000 is equal to the sum of the Pick Company's Net Income of $800,000, plus 60 percent of the Stick Company's Net Income of $600,000.

Parent Company Concept Solution

5-9. This conceptual approach views the non-controlling interest as a part of the consolidated entity and, as a consequence, the consolidated Income Statement includes 100 percent of the expenses and revenues of both the parent and the subsidiary company.

5-10. With respect to the nature of the non-controlling interest's participation in the consolidated entity, the parent company approach views these shareholders as having a creditor-like interest. Given this view, the non-controlling interest in the income of the consolidated entity would be viewed as a claim analogous to interest charges on creditor interests. This would require that the Non-Controlling Interest be deducted in the computation of consolidated Net Income.

5-11. The resulting consolidated Income Statement would appear as follows:

Pick Company and Subsidiary
Consolidated Income Statement
Parent Company Approach

Sales ($4,000,000 + $2,000,000)	$6,000,000
Cost Of Goods Sold ($2,500,000 + $1,000,000)	$3,500,000
Other Expenses ($700,000 + $400,000)	1,100,000
Total Expenses	$4,600,000
Combined Income	$1,400,000
Non-Controlling Interest [(40%)($600,000)]	240,000
Consolidated Net Income	$1,160,000

5-12. There are several aspects of this presentation that you should note. First, in our disclosure we have calculated a separate subtotal for Combined Income. This has been done for illustrative purposes only. Normal disclosure would have the Non-Controlling Interest grouped and deducted with the other expenses of the consolidated entity (note that if the subsidiary has a Net Loss, the Non-Controlling Interest will be an addition rather than a deduction).

5-13. Referring to the 2006 edition of *Financial Reporting in Canada*, this publication's survey of 200 Canadian public companies found that, for companies that provided separate disclosure of a non-controlling interest in their 2005 consolidated Income Statements, the location was as follows:

Separate Section After Income Taxes	36
With Income Taxes	31
Other Locations	19
Total Companies Providing Separate Disclosure	86

5-14. As a second point, note that the Non-Controlling Interest is based on the reported income of the subsidiary. Consistent with the view that the non-controlling shareholders have a creditor-like interest, there is no recognition of their share of the adjustments required in the application of consolidation procedures (e.g., fair value changes). As a consequence, the Non-Controlling Interest in the consolidated Income Statement is simply their 40 percent share of Stick Company's reported Net Income of $600,000.

5-15. Finally, note that the consolidated Net Income is the same figure that we arrived at using the proprietary approach. This will always be the case as both the proprietary and the parent company approach ignore the non-controlling interest's share of the various adjustments required in applying consolidation procedures.

5-16. The difference between these two approaches is one of disclosure, with the parent company approach including the Non-Controlling Interest as a separate item in the consolidated Income Statement. In contrast, the proprietary approach deducts the non-controlling interest's share of expenses and revenues on a line-by-line basis, without providing separate disclosure of either the individual amounts deducted or the total amount.

Entity Concept Solution

5-17. As was the case with the parent company approach, the entity approach views the non-controlling interest as being a part of the consolidated entity. This would mean that the consolidated expenses and revenues would again include 100 percent of the reported expenses and revenues of both the parent company and the subsidiary company.

5-18. The difference is that the entity approach views the non-controlling interest as an additional class of owner's equity. Given this, the non-controlling interest in the income of the consolidated entity must be treated in a manner analogous to the treatment of dividends on preferred shares. That is, it will be viewed as a distribution of Net Income rather than as a determinant of Net Income. This means that, instead of being a deduction in the computation of consolidated Net Income, the Non-Controlling Interest under the entity concept would be shown as a distribution of income in the consolidated Statement of Retained Earnings. The entity approach consolidated Income Statement would be as follows:

Pick Company and Subsidiary
Consolidated Income Statement
Entity Approach

Sales ($4,000,000 + $2,000,000)	$6,000,000
Cost Of Goods Sold ($2,500,000 + $1,000,000)	$3,500,000
Other Expenses ($700,000 + $400,000)	1,100,000
Total Expenses	$4,600,000
Consolidated Net Income	$1,400,000

5-19. Note that the figure that was designated Combined Income under the parent company approach has become consolidated Net Income. Further, it is equal to the combined Net Incomes of the individual entities ($800,000 for Pick and $600,000 for Stick).

5-20. In this example, with no fair value changes or goodwill, the Non-Controlling Interest would still be $240,000 or 40 percent of the reported income of the subsidiary. As can be seen in the example, however, it would not be disclosed in the consolidated Income Statement. Rather, it would be shown as a deduction in the consolidated Statement Of Retained Earnings in a manner analogous to the disclosure accorded dividends on preferred stock.

CICA Handbook Requirements

Current Standards

5-21. The position of the *CICA Handbook* on the choice of conceptual approaches to be used in the preparation of the consolidated Income Statement is not internally consistent. With respect to the treatment of the Non-Controlling Interest in Income Before Discontinued Operations And Extraordinary Items, the *Handbook* makes the following Recommendation:

> **Paragraph 1600.67** *The non-controlling interest in the income or loss before discontinued operations and extraordinary items for the period should be disclosed separately in the consolidated income statement. Where there are discontinued operations or extraordinary items, the parent company's portion of such items should be disclosed.* (January, 1990)

5-22. The first part of this recommendation reflects the parent company approach in that it requires a separately disclosed non-controlling interest to be deducted in the determination of income or loss before discontinued operations and extraordinary items.

5-23. However, with respect to the treatment of subsidiary results of discontinued operations and extraordinary items, the recommendation requires disclosing only the parent company's share of these items. This is a reflection of the proprietary conceptual approach to consolidation. No explanation is offered for this apparent inconsistency.

International Convergence

5-24. IAS No. 17, *Consolidated And Separate Financial Statements*, contains the following recommendation:

> **Paragraph 34** The profit or loss is attributed to the parent shareholders and minority interests. Because both are equity, the amount attributed to minority interests is not income or expense.

5-25. As the non-controlling or minority interest is not income or expense, it would be disclosed in the consolidated Statement Of Changes In Shareholders' Equity, not in the consolidated Income Statement. This reflects the entity approach to preparing consolidated financial statements.

Exercise Five-1

Subject: Consolidated Income Statement - Current Canadian Standards

On January 1, 2007, Part Company acquires 65 percent of the outstanding shares of Seam Company. At this time, all of the identifiable assets and liabilities of Seam had fair values that were equal to their carrying values. The cost of the shares was equal to 65 percent of the Shareholders' Equity of Seam. The single entity Income Statements for Part Company and Seam Company, for the year ending December 31, 2007, are as follows:

Part and Seam Companies
Income Statements
Year Ending December 31, 2007

	Part Company	Seam Company
Revenues	$982,000	$463,000
Expenses:		
Cost of Goods Sold	$448,000	$219,000
Other Expenses	374,000	115,000
Total Expenses	$822,000	$334,000
Income Before Results Of Discontinued Operations	$160,000	$129,000
Loss From Discontinued Operations	Nil	(63,000)
Net Income	$160,000	$ 66,000

Prepare the consolidated Income Statement for Part Company and its subsidiary Seam Company, for the year ending December 31, 2007. Your answer should comply with the current recommendations of the *CICA Handbook.*

End of Exercise. Solution available in Study Guide.

General Approach To Problem Solving

The Problem With Consolidation Procedures

5-26. The preparation of consolidated financial statements, to an extent not approached by any other area of financial accounting, has seen a tremendous amount of attention devoted to the development of detailed and extensive technical procedures. In addition to several alternative worksheet approaches, consolidation problems have been solved using a variety of computerized approaches involving spreadsheets and linear programming. Indeed, it seems that anyone who has ever taught this subject has reached the conclusion that they have found a "better way" to deal with such problems.

5-27. In our opinion, there are two basic drawbacks with relying on any set of consolidation procedures, including those that will be used in this text:

1. You can develop great facility with any of the available detailed procedural approaches, without acquiring any real understanding of the content of consolidated financial statements. We have often encountered situations where a student, having developed lightning-like speed in manipulating a work sheet, will

be completely at a loss when asked to do a simple calculation of consolidated Net Income. It appears that focusing on detailed procedures does little to facilitate an understanding of the real content of consolidated financial statements.

2. An equally serious problem with detailed procedural approaches is that they only work when the data for a consolidation problem is presented in the format for which the procedural approach was developed. For example, if you develop a set of procedures that will work when the investment in the subsidiary is carried in the underlying records of the parent company by the cost method, these procedures will not work if the investment is carried by the equity method. Similarly, if procedures are developed for problems which require both a consolidated Income Statement and a consolidated Balance Sheet, they will not work when only a consolidated Balance Sheet is required. If detailed procedures are to be relied on, the only solution to this problem is to develop a full blown set of procedures for every possible problem format.

15-28. As we noted in Chapter 4, it is our belief that if you develop a thorough understanding of the consolidation process, the most efficient method of preparing consolidated financial statements is to be in a position to make an independent computation of each of the consolidated account balances. This approach does not rely on detailed worksheet or journal entry procedures and, as a consequence, there is no need to learn alternative sets of consolidation procedures.

15-29. The problem remains, however, of getting you to the stage where you can efficiently make definitional calculations of the various balances that may be required in a consolidation problem. This requires some type of organized procedural approach and, as we indicated in Chapter 4, we will base our procedures on the use of journal entries applied to the balances that are given in the basic problem data.

15-30. We would stress that we view these procedures as an interim teaching device. We encourage you to discontinue using them as soon as you feel that you understand the concepts well enough to make direct computations of the balances that are required for inclusion in the consolidated financial statements.

Classification Of Problems

Problem Requirements

5-31. As was indicated in the preceding Section, consolidation problems can be presented in a variety of formats. While there is an almost unlimited number of possibilities in this area, we have found it useful to classify problems in terms of:

1. problem requirements and
2. the method of carrying the investment.

5-32. With respect to problem requirements, there are two basic types of problems. We have designated these two types as open trial balance problems and closed trial balance problems. They can be described as follows:

Open Trial Balance Problems This is the designation that we use for any problem that requires the preparation of any consolidated statement or the calculation of any consolidated information, other than all or part of a consolidated Balance Sheet. The use of this designation reflects the fact that such problems are often, but not always, presented as an open trial balance (i.e., a trial balance prepared before expenses and revenues have been closed to retained earnings). A typical problem of this variety would require the preparation of a consolidated Income Statement, a consolidated Statement Of Retained Earnings, and a consolidated Balance Sheet. Procedures are required here to deal with both the beginning of the year balance in subsidiary Retained Earnings, as well as items of expense or revenue that occur during the year.

Closed Trial Balance Problems This is the designation that we use for problems which require only the preparation of all or part of a consolidated Balance Sheet. The use of this designation reflects the fact that such problems are often, but not always, presented as a closed trial balance (i.e., a trial balance prepared after expenses and revenues have been closed to retained earnings.) The procedures developed for this type of problem do not have to deal with either the opening Retained Earnings or expense and revenue items that occur during the year.

Accounting Method

5-33. When consolidated financial statements are prepared, the parent's Investment In Subsidiary account will be eliminated and replaced by the various assets and liabilities of the subsidiary. This means that the parent company can carry this Investment In Subsidiary account by any method they choose. As the account will not be included in the published consolidated financial statements, *CICA Handbook* Recommendations are not applicable.

5-34. While it is not possible to establish this from published financial statements, it is likely that most companies carry their Investment In Subsidiary accounts at cost. It is a less complicated method and, in addition, cost is generally the tax basis for such assets.

5-35. However, it is possible that a problem will be presented with the investment carried at equity. This results in a second approach to the classification of problems — problems in which the Investment In Subsidiary is accounted for by the cost method or problems where the Investment In Subsidiary is carried by the equity method.

Classifications To Be Covered

5-36. Given the two types of problem requirements that we have designated and the two methods by which the investment may be carried, we can identify the following general types of problems:

1. **Open** Trial Balance with the investment at **Cost**
2. **Closed** Trial Balance with the investment at **Cost**
3. **Open** Trial Balance with the investment at **Equity**
4. **Closed** Trial Balance with the investment at **Equity**

5-37. It has been our experience that students have significant difficulties in working with the somewhat awkward consolidation procedures that are required when the investment in the subsidiary is carried by the equity method. Further, it does not appear that working with these procedures either enhances your understanding of consolidated financial statements, or assists you in arriving at the ultimate goal of preparing consolidated financial statements by using direct definitional calculations.

5-38 Given this situation, the comprehensive example that will be used in this Chapter, as well as in Chapter 6, will illustrate only the two types of problems where the Investment In Subsidiary is carried by the cost method. We will not, in either this Chapter or Chapter 6, develop procedures to be used when the investment is carried by the equity method.

5-39. Note, however, we have illustrated the consolidation procedures for investments carried by the equity method in Chapter 7. This Chapter contains coverage of a number of more advanced consolidation topics. These topics may be of interest to you or your instructor.

The Procedures

5-40. As was indicated in Chapter 4, we are going to develop a set of procedures which use the basic data of the problem, adjust and eliminate parts of this basic data using journal entries, and use this information to arrive at final figures to be included in the consolidated financial statements. As outlined in that Chapter, there are three basic Steps involved in these procedures and they can be described as follows:

Step A - Investment Elimination This first Step will eliminate 100 percent of the investment account against the subsidiary shareholders' equity at the time of acquisition. As a part of this Step, entries will also be made to record the investor's share of the acquisition date fair value changes and goodwill of the subsidiary. In addition, a Non-Controlling Interest will be established, representing the non-controlling shareholders' interest in carrying values of the net identifiable assets of the subsidiary as at the date of acquisition.

This Step was dealt with in a comprehensive fashion in Chapter 4 and was codified into a set of four specific procedures to be used. These procedures are repeated here for your convenience:

Step A-1 Procedure Eliminate 100 percent of the Investment In Subsidiary account.

Step A-2 Procedure Eliminate 100 percent of all the balances in the subsidiary's common shareholders' equity that are present on the acquisition date.

Step A-3 Procedure Allocate any debit or credit Differential that is present at acquisition to the investor's share of fair value changes on identifiable assets, fair value changes on identifiable liabilities, and positive or negative goodwill.

Step A-4 Procedure Allocate to a Non-Controlling Interest account in the consolidated Balance Sheet, the non-controlling interest's share of the book value of the total Shareholders' Equity of the subsidiary at acquisition.

Note that these procedures will have to be implemented, even in periods subsequent to the year of acquisition. This reflects the fact that consolidation entries are only working paper entries and are not entered on the books of the individual legal entities. An exception to this would be when push-down accounting is used (see Appendix A of Chapter 4). However, unless push-down accounting is used, the Step A entries required in the year of acquisition will have to be repeated in each subsequent year.

Step B - Adjustments And Eliminations This Step involves making adjustments and eliminations to the various accounts that will be included in the consolidated information. At this stage of the development of our consolidation procedures, we can identify four types of adjustments and eliminations that we must be prepared to deal with. They are as follows:

1. If intercompany asset and liability balances are present, they must be eliminated. This procedure was discussed and illustrated in Chapter 4. It was also stated in terms of a specific procedure as follows:

   Step B-1 Procedure Eliminate 100 percent of all intercompany assets and liabilities.

2. In Step A, the parent company's share of all of the acquisition date fair value changes on the subsidiary's assets and liabilities was recorded. To the extent that these fair value changes were recorded on assets with an unlimited economic life, the recorded fair value changes can be left in place until such time as the assets are sold. If such assets are sold, there will be a need to adjust any resulting gain or loss recorded on the books of the subsidiary to reflect the realization of the fair value change.

   When the fair value changes are recorded on assets or liabilities with a limited life, the subsidiary will record amortization on these assets based on their carrying values. As a consequence, there will be a need to adjust these amortization amounts to reflect the realization of the fair value changes on these assets and liabilities. If such assets are sold prior to the end of their economic life, the resulting gain or loss must be adjusted for the unrealized balance of the fair value change.

   In addition to the preceding adjustments, the consolidation procedures that will be used subsequent to acquisition will require adjustments to recognize any Goodwill Impairment Loss that has occurred in the post acquisition period.

3. If intercompany expenses and revenues are present, they must be eliminated. Note that, in this Chapter, we are dealing only with intercompany expenses and revenues, not unrealized intercompany profits. For example, if there is an intercompany sale of merchandise and the goods have been resold to an arm's length party, the profit on the original sale is realized and the only elimination will be for the intercompany sale and purchase. However, if the goods remain in the inventories of the purchasing company, the profit on the sale is unrealized because the merchandise remains within the consolidated entity. This unrealized intercompany profit must be eliminated. The procedures for dealing with this type of situation will be dealt with in Chapter 6.

4. If intercompany dividends have been declared, they must be removed from the revenues and dividends declared account.

Step C - Distribution Of Subsidiary Retained Earnings Step A eliminated only the at acquisition balance of the subsidiary's retained earnings. In periods subsequent to acquisition, this leaves a balance in the retained earnings of the subsidiary. This balance represents the retained earnings of the subsidiary that have been accumulated since the date of acquisition. If the parent owned 100 percent of the subsidiary and there were no Step B adjustments or eliminations, the subsidiary's retained earnings since acquisition balance would simply become a part of consolidated Retained Earnings.

However, these assumptions are usually not applicable. In most situations there will be less than 100 percent ownership and a portion of the subsidiary retained earnings since acquisition will have to be allocated to the Non-Controlling Interest in the consolidated Balance Sheet. Further, there will almost always be Step B adjustments and eliminations, some of which will alter the subsidiary's retained earnings since acquisition balance. This is further complicated by the fact that some of these Step B changes will apply only to the parent's share of subsidiary retained earnings since acquisition, while others will alter both the parent's and the non-controlling interest's shares of this balance. (This latter situation does not turn up until Chapter 6 when we introduce unrealized intercompany profits.) As a consequence, it is not possible to allocate the parent's and non-controlling interest's shares of the subsidiary's retained earnings since acquisition until we have completed the Step B adjustments and eliminations.

This brings us to Step C. At this point, our one remaining task will be to take the subsidiary's retained earnings since acquisition balance, as adjusted by the Step B adjustments and eliminations, and allocate it between the Non-Controlling Interest in the consolidated Balance Sheet and consolidated Retained Earnings.

5-41. Given this general outline of the procedures to be followed, we can now turn our attention to the application of these three Steps to the open and closed trial balance versions of a comprehensive problem.

Comprehensive Example - Open Trial Balance With Investment At Cost

Basic Data

5-42. Our first example involves a problem in which you are asked to prepare more than just a consolidated Balance Sheet. While a consolidated Cash Flow Statement is not required, a consolidated Income Statement and a consolidated Statement of Retained Earnings are required, in addition to a consolidated Balance Sheet. This means that this problem would be classified as an open trial balance problem. As will always be the case in this Chapter, the Investment In Subsidiary is carried at cost.

On January 1, 2005, the Pleigh Company purchases 80 percent of the outstanding shares of the Sleigh Company for $3,200,000 in cash. On that date, the Sleigh Company had No Par Common Stock of $2,000,000 and Retained Earnings of $1,500,000. On December 31, 2009, the adjusted trial balances of the Pleigh Company and its subsidiary, the Sleigh Company are as follows:

	Pleigh	Sleigh
Cash	$ 500,000	$ 300,000
Current Receivables	800,000	400,000
Inventories	2,500,000	1,700,000
Long-Term Note Receivable	200,000	Nil
Investment In Sleigh - At Cost	3,200,000	N/A
Land	1,500,000	1,000,000
Plant And Equipment (Net)	4,500,000	1,900,000
Cost Of Goods Sold	2,800,000	1,500,000
Amortization Expense	200,000	100,000
Other Expenses	364,000	616,000
Interest Expense	240,000	84,000
Dividends Declared	350,000	100,000
Total Debits	$17,154,000	$7,700,000
Current Liabilities	$ 500,000	$ 200,000
Long-Term Liabilities	2,000,000	700,000
No Par Common Stock	8,000,000	2,000,000
Retained Earnings (January 1)	2,550,000	2,300,000
Sales	4,000,000	2,500,000
Interest Revenue	24,000	Nil
Dividend Revenue	80,000	Nil
Total Credits	$17,154,000	$7,700,000
January 1, 2009 Retained Earnings	$ 2,550,000	$ 2,300,000
2009 Net Income	500,000	200,000
Dividends Declared	(350,000)	(100,000)
December 31, 2009 Retained Earnings	$ 2,700,000	$2,400,000

Other Information:

1. At the date of Pleigh Company's acquisition of the Sleigh Company's shares, all of the identifiable assets and liabilities of the Sleigh Company had fair values that were equal to their carrying values except:
   - Inventories which had fair values that were $100,000 more than their carrying values,
   - Land with a fair value that was $150,000 less than its carrying value, and
   - Plant And Equipment which had a fair value that was $250,000 greater than its carrying value.

   The Plant And Equipment had a remaining useful life on the acquisition date of 20 years while the Inventories that were present on the acquisition date were sold during the year ending December 31, 2005. The Land is still on the books of the Sleigh Company on December 31, 2009. Both companies use the straight line method to calculate amortization.

2. In each of the years since Pleigh acquired control over Sleigh, the goodwill arising on this business combination transaction has been tested for impairment. No impairment was found in any of the years since acquisition.

3. Sleigh Company's Sales during 2009 include sales of $300,000 to Pleigh Company. All of this merchandise has been resold by the Pleigh Company.

4. On December 31, 2009, the Pleigh Company is holding Sleigh Company's long-term note payable in the amount of $200,000. Interest at 12 percent is payable on July 1 of each year. Pleigh Company has been holding this note since July 1, 2007.

Required Prepare a consolidated Income Statement and a consolidated Statement Of Retained Earnings for the year ending December 31, 2009 and a consolidated Balance Sheet as at December 31, 2009 for the Pleigh Company and its subsidiary, the Sleigh Company.

Step A Procedures

Investment Analysis

5-43. As indicated in Chapters 3 and 4, in business combination transactions it is generally useful to prepare an analysis of the investment cost. Using the procedures developed in those Chapters, the analysis of the Pleigh Company's investment in the Sleigh Company is as follows:

	80 Percent	100 Percent
Investment Cost	$3,200,000	$4,000,000
Sleigh Shareholders' Equity At Acquisition	(2,800,000)	(3,500,000)
Differential	$ 400,000	$ 500,000
Fair Value Changes:		
Increase On Inventories	(80,000)	(100,000)
Decrease On Land	120,000	150,000
Increase On Plant And Equipment (Net)	(200,000)	(250,000)
Goodwill	$ 240,000	$ 300,000

5-44. Note that this analysis is based on the values for Sleigh Company's assets at the time of acquisition. This reflects the fact that fair value and goodwill amounts to be recognized are measured at this time.

5-45. At acquisition, the total fair value of the net assets of the Sleigh Company is $3,700,000 ($3,500,000 + $100,000 - $150,000 + $250,000). The Goodwill of $240,000 can be verified by comparing the investment cost of $3,200,000 to $2,960,000, the investor's 80 percent share of the fair values of $3,700,000.

Investment Elimination

5-46. Based on the preceding analysis and using the procedures developed in Chapter 4, the journal entry to eliminate the investment account is as follows:

No Par Common Stock (At Acquisition)	$2,000,000	
Retained Earnings (At Acquisition)	1,500,000	
Plant And Equipment (Net)	200,000	
Inventories	80,000	
Goodwill	240,000	
Land		$ 120,000
Non-Controlling Interest [(20%)($3,500,000)]		700,000
Investment In Sleigh		3,200,000

Step B(1) - Intercompany Assets And Liabilities

Procedure

5-47. The first type of adjustment or elimination that is required in Step B involves the elimination of intercompany assets and liabilities. As was noted in Chapter 4, it is not uncommon for intercompany debts to arise between a parent and a subsidiary. When these two legal entities are viewed as a single economic entity, such intercompany debt has no real economic existence and should be eliminated. The appropriate procedure for this was described in Chapter 4 and codified as Step B-1.

Comprehensive Example

5-48. There are two such items in this problem. The most obvious is the $200,000 long-term note payable from Sleigh to Pleigh. An additional intercompany balance relates to the fact that the last interest payment on this note was July 1, 2009. This would mean that on December 31, 2009, Sleigh would have recorded interest payable and Pleigh would have recorded interest receivable of $12,000 [(6/12)(12%)($200,000)]. The required elimination entries would be as follows:

Long-Term Liabilities	$200,000	
Long-Term Note Receivable		$200,000
Current Liabilities	$ 12,000	
Current Receivables		$ 12,000

5-49. You should note that the purpose of this entry is to avoid the overstatement of the total consolidated assets and equities. The elimination of such intercompany liabilities will never have any influence on the value of the Non-Controlling Interest in the consolidated Balance Sheet or the amount of consolidated Retained Earnings.

Step B(2) - Realization Of Fair Value Changes

General Procedures

5-50. In Step A, we recorded the parent company's share of fair value changes on the subsidiary's identifiable assets and liabilities. In making the Step A entry, you should have noticed that despite the fact that we are several years past acquisition, the amounts that were recorded were the same as those that would have been recorded at the time of acquisition.

5-51. This procedure follows from the fact that we are eliminating an investment that is carried at cost, an amount which reflects the fair values that were present at acquisition. Given that the fair value changes recorded in Step A were those at acquisition, we need a further procedure to recognize the extent to which these fair value changes have been realized in the period subsequent to acquisition.

5-52. Realization of these amounts can take place in one of two ways. In the case of non-current assets with limited lives (Plant And Equipment in our example), realization will occur as the asset is used up. On the books of the subsidiary, the carrying values of the Plant And Equipment would be charged to amortization expense on the basis of their carrying values in the subsidiary's single entity records. For use in the consolidated financial statements, these amortization amounts must be adjusted to reflect the amortization of the related fair value changes. A similar analysis can be made of liabilities with limited lives.

5-53. The alternative way in which a fair value change can be realized is through disposal of the asset by the subsidiary. In the case of current assets (Inventories in our example), this will take place in the normal course of business operations in the one year period following acquisition. On the books of the subsidiary, the sale of the current asset will result in the carrying value of the current asset being charged to expense. In a manner analogous to the adjustment of amortization expense on depreciable assets, the expense to which the current asset was charged must be adjusted for the realization of the fair value change. In the case of Inventories, the adjustment would be to the consolidated Cost Of Goods Sold.

5-54. It is also possible that a non-current asset with a limited life might be sold prior to the end of that life. This would usually result in the recognition of a gain or loss by the subsidiary with the amount being calculated on the basis of the carrying value of the asset. In this situation, the unamortized portion of the fair value change would be considered realized and, in preparing consolidated financial statements, would be treated as an adjustment of the gain or loss recognized by the subsidiary.

5-55. For fair value changes on non-current assets with an unlimited life (Land in our example), it may not be necessary to record any adjustment in Step B. If the asset is still owned by the consolidated entity, the fair value change has become a part of its consolidated carrying value. This adjustment would be recorded as part of Step A. As the asset has an unlimited life, there is generally no need to amortize either the asset or the related fair value change in Step B. However, if the asset is sold in a period subsequent to acquisition, any gain or loss recorded by the subsidiary will have to be adjusted to reflect the fact that all of the fair value change that was recognized in the consolidated financial statements has become realized.

5-56. A further complication in dealing with the adjustments required by the realization of fair value changes is caused by the fact that such realization may occur in either the current period or in an earlier period subsequent to the acquisition date. As all of the subsidiary's expenses and revenues that relate to prior periods would now be accumulated in the subsidiary's Retained Earnings, adjustments for fair value realizations that relate to prior periods will have to be recorded as adjustments of that balance. In contrast, the adjustments for fair value realizations during the current period are made to current expenses or revenues.

5-57. All of the preceding can be stated as Step B-2 as follows:

> **Step B-2 Procedure** Give recognition to the post-acquisition realization of acquisition date fair value changes on assets and liabilities that have been used up or sold during the post-acquisition period. To the extent that this realization occurred in prior periods, this recognition will require an adjustment of the opening Retained Earnings of the subsidiary. Alternatively, if the realization occurred in the current period, the adjustment will be to the subsidiary's current period expenses, revenues, gains, or losses. Note that, in closed trial balance problems, there will be no expenses, revenues, gains, or losses to adjust. This means that, in closed trial balance problems, all of the adjustments will be to the closing Retained Earnings.

5-58. We will now turn our attention to applying this procedure to the fair value changes in our comprehensive example.

Inventories

5-59. With respect to the Inventories that were present at the January 1, 2005 acquisition date, they were sold during 2005. This means that all of Pleigh Company's $80,000 share of the fair value increase on Inventories was realized during that prior year. As the subsidiary would have recorded Cost Of Goods Sold on the basis of the $1,700,000 carrying value of the Inventories, an $80,000 addition to this expense is required. In addition, as the Inventories are no longer the property of the subsidiary, it is necessary to reverse that $80,000 increase in Inventories that was recorded in Step A. The entry required in 2005 is as follows:

Cost Of Goods Sold	$80,000	
Inventories		$80,000

5-60. Since this entry was not recorded on the books of the Sleigh Company, the Retained Earnings of the Sleigh Company will be $80,000 too high in all subsequent years. This would mean that in these subsequent years, including the current 2009 period, the following adjustment will be required in the preparation of consolidated financial statements:

Retained Earnings - Sleigh's Opening	$80,000	
Inventories		$80,000

5-61. While the preceding debit is to the Retained Earnings of Sleigh, you should note that because we are only recognizing the investor's share of the fair value change, this adjustment would only affect the Pleigh Company's share of the Retained Earnings of Sleigh. This would be true of all of the adjustments for the realization of fair value changes that are required in the process of preparing consolidated financial statements.

Plant And Equipment

5-62. When a fair value change has been recorded on an asset or liability that is being allocated to income over several accounting periods, this Step B-2 in the consolidation procedures is somewhat more complex. This is due to the fact that different adjustments are required for each accounting period in which income is influenced by the presence of the asset. In the problem under consideration, we allocated a fair value change of $200,000 [(80%)($250,000)] to Plant And Equipment which had a useful life of 20 years at the time of the acquisition on January 1, 2005. This will require a $10,000 ($200,000 ÷ 20) adjustment to Amortization Expense in each year for the 20 years subsequent to the acquisition date. For example, the required entry for 2005 would be as follows:

Amortization Expense	$10,000	
Plant And Equipment (Net)		$10,000

5-63. This entry serves to increase Amortization Expense by $10,000 and to reverse 1/20 of the fair value change that was recorded in Step A. In each subsequent year, the credit to Plant And Equipment (Net) will increase by $10,000. However, the debit to Amortization Expense will remain at $10,000 and will be accompanied by a debit to Retained Earnings for adjustments to Amortization Expense for prior periods. Note that in this "open trial balance" version of the problem, any adjustments that are made to Sleigh's Retained Earnings are to the opening balance in this account.

5-64. Based on this analysis, the entries that would have been required in 2006, 2007, and 2008 are as follows:

2006		
Retained Earnings - Sleigh's Opening (1 year)	$10,000	
Amortization Expense	10,000	
Plant And Equipment (Net) (2 years)		$20,000
2007		
Retained Earnings - Sleigh's Opening (2 years)	$20,000	
Amortization Expense	10,000	
Plant And Equipment (Net) (3 years)		$30,000
2008		
Retained Earnings - Sleigh's Opening (3 years)	$30,000	
Amortization Expense	10,000	
Plant And Equipment (Net) (4 years)		$40,000

5-65. The entry specifically required in this problem would adjust Sleigh's opening Retained Earnings for the four years 2005 through 2008 and the Amortization Expense for the current year. This entry would be as follows:

Required Entry		
Retained Earnings - Sleigh's Opening (4 years)	$40,000	
Amortization Expense	10,000	
Plant And Equipment (Net) (5 years)		$50,000

5-66. Here again, the adjustment to the Retained Earnings of the Sleigh Company will only affect the parent company's share of this balance, a reflection of the parent company conceptual approach to the asset valuation problem in the preparation of consolidated financial statements.

5-67. You should also note that an adjusting entry will still be required, even after the Plant And Equipment is fully amortized. With the Investment In Sleigh being carried at cost, our Step A procedures will continue to allocate a part of this cost to the acquisition date fair value change of $200,000. After the asset is fully amortized, this total amount will be reversed, accompanied by charge to Retained Earnings to adjust the Amortization Expense of all prior periods.

Land

5-68. This problem also involves a fair value change on a piece of land which was owned by the Sleigh Company on the acquisition date. This fair value change was recorded in Step A and, since land is not normally subject to amortization, no further entry is required here as long as the Sleigh Company still owns the land. Since the problem indicates that Sleigh is still holding the land on December 31, 2009, no Step B entry is required for the land.

Summary

5-69. The preceding illustrates the procedures required by the three different types of fair value changes that you might encounter. These are fair value changes on current assets, fair value changes on assets with unlimited lives and fair value changes on long-term assets and liabilities with limited lives. We remind you that under the parent company approach to asset valuation, these adjustments have no effect on the interest of the non-controlling shareholders, either in the consolidated Balance Sheet or in the consolidated Income Statement.

Step B(3) - Goodwill Impairment

5-70. In Step A, we recognized Goodwill in the amount of $240,000. Prior to 2002, the *CICA Handbook* required that this balance be amortized over a period not exceeding 40 years. Under these rules, the Step B treatment of Goodwill was analogous to the treatment given to fair value changes on depreciable assets. That is, in each period subsequent to acquisition, an adjustment would be required to reflect the amortization of this balance. Under the old rules, goodwill could be dealt with under Step B(2), with no need for specifying a separate procedure.

5-71. This is no longer the case. Under the provisions of Section 3062, "Goodwill And Other Intangible Assets", the amortization of goodwill is not permitted. In many cases this will mean that we can treat goodwill like we treat fair value changes on non-depreciable assets such as land. That is, the appropriate amount of goodwill will be recorded in Step A, with no Step B adjustment required in subsequent years.

5-72. This, however, will not always be the case. As you will recall from our discussion of goodwill in Chapter 3, Section 3062 requires that the goodwill balance be tested each year to determine if it has been impaired. If it is determined that impairment has occurred, the balance must be written down and the amount of impairment charged to income as an impairment loss. This will require a consolidation adjustment to recognize a loss in any year in which it is determined that impairment has occurred. This entry will require a debit to Goodwill Impairment Loss and a credit to the Goodwill balance that was recorded in Step A.

5-73. As is the case with other types of fair value write-offs, the Goodwill Impairment Loss that is recorded in the consolidated financial statements will not be recorded in the records of the subsidiary. This means that, from the point of view of the consolidated financial statements, the subsidiary's Retained Earnings will be overstated at the end of the write-off period and in all subsequent years. As a consequence, in all of the years subsequent to the recognition of the first consolidated Goodwill Impairment Loss, there will have to be an adjustment to Retained Earnings to reduce this balance for the cumulative Goodwill Impairment Losses of previous years.

5-74. Stated as a procedure, the required adjustment is as follows:

> **Step B-3 Procedure** Recognize current and cumulative goodwill impairment losses that have been measured since the acquisition of the subsidiary and the initial recognition of the goodwill balance. To the extent that the impairment took place during the current period, the measured amount will be charged to Goodwill Impairment Loss. To the extent that it occurred in prior periods, it will be charged to Retained Earnings. Note that, in closed trial balance problems, you will not be recording a Goodwill Impairment Loss. This means that, in this type of problem, both the current amount of Goodwill Impairment Loss and the amount recognized in all previous periods subsequent to the acquisition, will be charged to the closing Retained Earnings.

5-75. The Other Information in our comprehensive problem notes that, while goodwill has been tested for impairment in each year since the acquisition of Sleigh Company, no impairment has been found. As a consequence, no Step B-3 entry is required in this problem.

Step B(4) - Intercompany Expenses And Revenues

General Procedure

5-76. The fourth type of adjustment or elimination that is required in Step B involves the elimination of intercompany expenses and revenues. The principles that are involved here are identical to those involved in intercompany asset-liability situations. If we view a parent company and its subsidiaries as a single accounting entity, intercompany expenses and revenues reflect transactions which have no real economic existence. Stated as a procedure, the required elimination is as follows:

Step B-4 Procedure Eliminate 100 percent of all intercompany expenses and revenues.

5-77. Note that in both Step B-1 which deals with the elimination of intercompany assets and liabilities and with this new Step B-4, we eliminate 100 percent of the relevant items, without regard to the percentage of subsidiary shares that are owned by the parent company.

5-78. You should also note that the elimination of intercompany expenses and revenues does not have any effect on either the minority or majority share of income. The purpose of this entry is simply to avoid overstating expenses and revenues and, in the absence of unrealized profits related to the items eliminated, the calculation of total income will not be altered.

Intercompany Sales

5-79. In this problem, Sleigh Company sells merchandise to the Pleigh Company for $300,000. Assume (this information is not part of the basic problem) that Sleigh purchased this merchandise for $180,000 and Pleigh resold it for $350,000. If we simply added together the single entity results for this transaction, the result would be as follows:

Sales ($300,000 + $350,000)	$650,000
Cost Of Goods Sold ($180,000 + $300,000)	(480,000)
Gross Margin	$170,000

5-80. From the perspective of the two companies as a single consolidated entity, the correct figures would be a revenue from sales outside the consolidated entity of $350,000 and an expense resulting from purchases outside the consolidated entity of $180,000. To achieve this result we must eliminate both the intercompany expense and intercompany revenue. The required entry is as follows:

Sales	$300,000	
Cost Of Goods Sold		$300,000

5-81. The effect of this entry is to reduce total expenses and total revenues. It has no influence on gross margin which will remain at $170,000 ($350,000 - $180,000). Further, it will not influence either the non-controlling interest's share or the parent's portion of that income.

5-82. You should also note that this entry is based on the fact that all of the merchandise that Pleigh has acquired from Sleigh has been resold. If this were not the case, any profit resulting from the sale would be viewed as unrealized and the procedures here would have to be altered. We will deal with this issue in Chapter 6.

Intercompany Interest Expense And Revenue

5-83. There is a second item in this problem to which this general procedure applies. This is the interest of $24,000 [(12%)($200,000)] on the intercompany note payable. The entry to eliminate this item is as follows:

Interest Revenue	$24,000	
Interest Expense		$24,000

5-84. As was the case with the intercompany sales entry, the purpose of the preceding entry is to reduce total revenues and expenses. Neither the non-controlling interest's nor the parent's share of Net Income is influenced by this elimination.

Step B(5) - Intercompany Dividends

5-85. The final Step B elimination in this problem involves the intercompany dividends. The Sleigh Company declared and paid $100,000 in dividends during 2009 and the Pleigh Company recorded the $80,000 of these which it received as a dividend revenue. Obviously, some type of elimination is required.

5-86. To understand this elimination, recall that under the requirements of the *CICA Handbook*, consolidated Net Income is defined using the parent company concept. This means that non-controlling shareholders' share of subsidiary Net Income is subtracted in the determination of consolidated Net Income. As a consequence, in the consolidated Statement Of Retained Earnings, when we show distributions of consolidated Net Income, a figure which does not include the non-controlling shareholders' interest, the dividends to be disclosed will be those of the parent company only.

5-87. Since the consolidated Statement Of Retained Earnings discloses only the parent company's dividends, we will have to eliminate 100 percent of the Dividends Declared of the subsidiary. Of this total, the parent company's 80 percent share will be eliminated from the Dividend Revenues of the parent company while the remaining 20 percent will be treated as a direct reduction of the Non-Controlling Interest in the Balance Sheet. This analysis can be expressed in the form of Step B-5 as follows:

> **Step B-5 Procedure** Eliminate 100 percent of subsidiary dividends declared. The controlling share of this amount will be deducted from the revenues of the parent company and the non-controlling share of this amount will be deducted from the Non-Controlling Interest in the consolidated Balance Sheet.

5-88. Using this procedure, the required entry is as follows:

Dividend Revenue	$80,000	
Non-Controlling Interest (Balance Sheet)	20,000	
Dividends Declared		$100,000

5-89. With the $20,000 in dividends to the non-controlling shareholders being charged directly to the Non-Controlling Interest account on the consolidated Balance Sheet, the only separate disclosure of this $20,000 item will be in the consolidated Cash Flow Statement.

5-90. As a final point, you should note that there is no need to make any adjustments for dividends paid by the subsidiary in earlier periods. In periods after the dividends are declared, the $80,000 parent's share will be included in the Retained Earnings of the parent company and will become a component of consolidated Retained Earnings. This is appropriate in that these resources are still within the consolidated entity.

Summary Of Step B Adjustments And Eliminations

5-91. The preceding paragraphs have demonstrated and explained the five basic adjustments that are required in Step B for this problem. An additional adjustment will be introduced in Chapter 6 which deals with unrealized intercompany profits. All of these adjustments are common to the great majority of consolidation problems that you will encounter and are, as a consequence, of considerable significance. We will now turn our attention to the final Step of our consolidation procedures, Step C.

Step C - Distribution Of The Subsidiary Retained Earnings

The Problem

5-92. At this point, our one remaining task is to determine the appropriate distribution of the balance that is left in the Retained Earnings account of the Sleigh Company. In the original trial balance, the January 1, 2009 balance in this account was $2,300,000. The remaining balance in this account can be calculated as follows:

Sleigh's January 1, 2009 Balance	$2,300,000
Step A Elimination (Retained Earnings At Acquisition)	(1,500,000)
Balance Since Acquisition	$ 800,000
Step B Adjustments:	
Fair Value Increase On Inventories	(80,000)
Amortization Of Fair Value Increase On Plant And Equipment (4 Years At $10,000)	(40,000)
Balance To Be Distributed	$ 680,000

5-93. As this remaining balance represents Sleigh earnings that have accrued subsequent to the business combination transaction in which Pleigh acquired Sleigh, a portion of this will be included in the Retained Earnings of the consolidated entity. However, we must also allocate an appropriate portion of this amount to the Non-Controlling Interest in the consolidated Balance Sheet.

5-94. As more factors enter into our consolidation problems, the computation involved in this distribution becomes fairly complex. A good deal of this complexity results from the fact that the *CICA Handbook* is not consistent with respect to the conceptual approach that is required in the preparation of consolidated financial statements. However, in this Section the only adjustments that have an effect on this distribution are related to fair value changes and goodwill and, as we have previously noted, these adjustments follow the approach that is used for the valuation of consolidated net assets. This is the parent company approach.

5-95. It follows that none of the Step B adjustments affect the non-controlling interest's share of these Retained Earnings. This means that the non-controlling interest's share of the subsidiary's Retained Earnings since acquisition can simply be based on the carrying value of the subsidiary's Retained Earnings since acquisition.

5-96. Despite this simplicity, we will introduce an approach to this computation that can be applied without regard to how complex the problem becomes. While this approach and schedule are not really essential at this stage, it will serve us well when we introduce unrealized intercompany profits in Chapter 6.

Retained Earnings Distribution Schedule

5-97. This schedule begins with the opening Retained Earnings balance of the subsidiary and immediately removes the portion of this balance that was present at the time of acquisition. In more complex situations, the next step would be to adjust the remaining amount for unrealized upstream profits, the only adjustment which has an effect on the non-controlling interest in subsidiary Retained Earnings. Since there are no unrealized intercompany profits in this problem, we can proceed immediately to the computation and deduction of the non-controlling interest in the Retained Earnings of the subsidiary since acquisition.

5-98. All other Step B adjustments are then accounted for to arrive at the amount which represents the parent company's share of the adjusted Retained Earnings of the subsidiary since acquisition. This amount, sometimes referred to as an equity pickup, will then be allocated to consolidated Retained Earnings. Stated as a procedure, this allocation can be described as follows:

> **Step C-1 Procedure** Determine the appropriate allocation of the subsidiary's adjusted Retained Earnings since acquisition. The non-controlling interest's share will be based on book value. In contrast, the allocation to consolidated Retained

Earnings will be the parent company's share of book values, adjusted for the realization of fair value changes and any goodwill impairment losses that have occurred since acquisition.

5-99. Based on this Step, the required schedule can be completed as follows:

Retained Earnings Distribution Schedule

January 1, 2009 Balance As Per Trial Balance	$2,300,000
January 1, 2005 Balance At Acquisition	(1,500,000)
Balance Since Acquisition	$ 800,000
Non-Controlling Interest [(20%)($800,000)]	(160,000)
Available To The Controlling Interest	$ 640,000
Step B Adjustments:	
Fair Value Increase On Inventories	(80,000)
Amortization Of Fair Value Increase On Plant And Equipment (4 Years At $10,000)	(40,000)
To Consolidated Retained Earnings	$ 520,000

5-100. Note that the Step B adjustments in this schedule reflect the journal entries that were made in the Step B procedures.

5-101. With the information from this schedule, we can now make the Step C distribution entry to distribute the subsidiary's retained earnings since acquisition balance.

Retained Earnings Distribution Entry

5-102. The final procedure can be stated as follows:

Step C-2 Procedure Eliminate the subsidiary's adjusted Retained Earnings since acquisition. This amount will be allocated to the Non-Controlling Interest in the consolidated Balance Sheet and to consolidated Retained Earnings as determined in Step C-1.

5-103. The entry required to distribute the Sleigh Company's retained earnings since acquisition is as follows:

Retained Earnings - Sleigh	$680,000	
Non-Controlling Interest (Balance Sheet)		$160,000
Consolidated Retained Earnings		520,000

5-104. This journal entry reduces the Sleigh Company's Retained Earnings balance to zero, distributing the remaining balance to the parent and non-controlling interest. With this entry completed we have established the opening balance for consolidated Retained Earnings. It is simply the Pleigh Company's January 1, 2009 balance of $2,550,000 plus the $520,000 allocation resulting from the preceding journal entry, for a total of $3,070,000.

Preparation Of Consolidated Financial Statements

5-105. With the addition of the Step C distribution entry, we have completed all of the procedures necessary for the preparation of consolidated financial statements. We will now take the individual account balances from the original trial balance, add and subtract the adjustments that have been made in Steps A, B, and C of our procedures, thereby arriving at the figures to be included in the consolidated financial statements.

5-106. These computations will be disclosed parenthetically, a method of disclosure that we would recommend for use on examinations. We remind you again that, if your grasp of the procedures which we are using is sufficiently solid, the most efficient approach to the preparation of consolidated financial statements is the direct computation of the individual statement items without taking the time to prepare the preceding working paper journal entries.

Consolidated Income Statement

Statement Disclosure

5-107. The consolidated Income Statement of the Pleigh Company and its subsidiary for 2009 would be prepared as follows:

Pleigh Company And Subsidiary
Consolidated Income Statement
Year Ending December 31, 2009

Sales ($4,000,000 + $2,500,000 - $300,000)	$6,200,000
Interest Revenue ($24,000 - $24,000)	Nil
Dividend Revenue ($80,000 - $80,000)	Nil
Total Revenues	$6,200,000
Cost Of Goods Sold ($2,800,000 + $1,500,000 - $300,000)	$4,000,000
Amortization Expense ($200,000 + $100,000 + $10,000)	310,000
Interest Expense ($240,000 + $84,000 - $24,000)	300,000
Other Expenses ($364,000 + $616,000)	980,000
Total Expenses	$5,590,000
Combined Income	$ 610,000
Non-Controlling Interest [(20 Percent)($200,000)]	40,000
Consolidated Net Income	$ 570,000

5-108. We note again that the subtotal for Combined Income is not normal disclosure. It has been included for computational purposes only. Normal disclosure under the required parent company approach would have the Non-Controlling Interest included among the other deductions from revenue. Similarly, there would not be disclosure of the nil balances in Interest Revenue and Dividend Revenue in an actual consolidated Income Statement. We have included these items here to emphasize that specific procedures were required to reduce these balances to nil.

Definitional Calculation

5-109. In addition to being able to prepare a consolidated Income Statement in the manner illustrated, it is useful to know how to prepare an independent calculation of the final consolidated Net Income figure. Being able to do this will enhance your understanding of the content of this important figure. In addition, this calculation can be used to verify the consolidated Net Income figure which results from the preparation of a consolidated Income Statement. You will also find that some problems require you to determine this figure without providing you with the detailed expense and revenue information that is needed to prepare a complete Income Statement.

5-110. There are a variety of ways in which this calculation can be made. However, we have found that the approach which is sometimes referred to as the definitional calculation seems to be the easiest to understand. This calculation is as follows:

Pleigh Company's Net Income	$500,000
Intercompany Dividend Revenues [(80%)($100,000)]	(80,000)
Pleigh's Net Income Less Dividends	$420,000
Pleigh's Equity In The Net Income Of Sleigh [(80%)($200,000)]	160,000
Income Before Adjustments	$580,000
Adjustment For Fair Value Amortization	(10,000)
Consolidated Net Income	$570,000

Consolidated Statement Of Retained Earnings

Statement Disclosure

5-111. Using the preceding Net Income data, we can now prepare the consolidated Statement Of Retained Earnings for 2009 of the Pleigh Company and its subsidiary. It would be as follows:

Pleigh Company And Subsidiary
Consolidated Statement Of Retained Earnings
Year Ending December 31, 2009

Balance - January 1, 2009 ($2,550,000 + $520,000)	$3,070,000
2009 Consolidated Net Income	570,000
2009 Dividends (Pleigh's Only)	(350,000)
Balance - December 31, 2009	$3,290,000

Definitional Calculation

5-112. As was the case with consolidated Net Income, you will frequently find it useful to be able to make an independent computation of the end of the year balance in the Retained Earnings account. Here again, this independent computation can be used to verify the figure that was arrived at in the preparation of the consolidated Statement Of Retained Earnings or as a more efficient method of determining this balance when the complete Statement Of Retained Earnings is not required. The definitional approach to the computation of this amount is as follows:

Pleigh's December 31, 2009 Balance	$2,700,000
Pleigh's Share Of Sleigh's Retained Earnings Since Acquisition [(80%)($2,400,000 - $1,500,000)]	720,000
Step B Adjustments:	
Fair Value Increase On Inventories	(80,000)
Amortization Of Fair Value Increase On Plant And Equipment (5 Years At $10,000)	(50,000)
December 31, 2009 Consolidated Retained Earnings	$3,290,000

5-113. Note that, in this calculation, the calculation of Pleigh's share of Sleigh's Retained Earnings since acquisition is based on that company's book figures ($2,400,000 - $1,500,000 + $900,000) with no adjustments. This reflects the fact that, to this point, all of our consolidation procedures are based on the parent company approach, with all of the adjustments being charged against the parent's share of Retained Earnings. This will change when we introduce unrealized intercompany profits in Chapter 6.

5-114. Also note that, because we are dealing with end of the period Retained Earnings, the fair value adjustments are for five years. This is in contrast to our earlier adjustments to the opening Retained Earnings which were for only four years.

5-115. If you are required to prepare a consolidated Statement of Retained Earnings, you have the option of calculating the opening balance first or, alternatively, the closing balance first and working backwards to the opening balance. If the consolidated Statement of Retained Earnings is not required, there may be no need to calculate the opening balance except for verification purposes.

5-116. The procedures we are using in this problem calculate the opening balance first. If this is done correctly and you have the appropriate figures for both Net Income and Dividends Declared, then the statement itself will calculate the correct closing balance. However, an error in the opening balance calculation, in Net Income or in Dividends Declared will produce an incorrect closing balance. We would suggest that you make an independent verification of the closing balance whenever time.

Consolidated Balance Sheet

Non-Controlling Interest

5-117. While it is not the most efficient way to solve this problem, we can use the procedures that we have just developed to calculate the Non-Controlling Interest on the Balance Sheet. Using this approach, the calculation would be as follows:

Step A Allocation (Balance At Acquisition)	$700,000
Step B Adjustment For Dividends	(20,000)
Step C Allocation (Retained Earnings Since Acquisition)	160,000
Non-Controlling Interest In Income (From Income Statement)	40,000
Non-Controlling Interest (Balance Sheet)	$880,000

5-118. A more conceptual approach would be based on the fact that the December 31, 2009 Sleigh Company's Shareholders' Equity consists of $2,000,000 in No Par Common Stock and $2,400,000 in Retained Earnings. This means that the subsidiary's net assets total $4,400,000 and since, in this problem, none of the adjustments or eliminations have any influence on the Non-Controlling Interest, this interest can be calculated by simply taking the non-controlling interest's share of these net assets. That is, 20 percent of $4,400,000 is the required $880,000.

Statement Disclosure

5-119. With the Non-Controlling Interest established, the consolidated Balance Sheet as at December 31, 2009 of the Pleigh Company and its subsidiary would be prepared as follows:

Pleigh Company And Subsidiary
Consolidated Balance Sheet
As At December 31, 2009

Cash ($500,000 + $300,000)	$ 800,000
Current Receivables ($800,000 + $400,000 - $12,000)	1,188,000
Inventories ($2,500,000 + $1,700,000 + $80,000 - $80,000)	4,200,000
Long-Term Note Receivable ($200,000 - $200,000)	Nil
Investment In Sleigh ($3,200,000 - $3,200,000)	Nil
Land ($1,500,000 + $1,000,000 - $120,000)	2,380,000
Plant And Equipment (Net)	
($4,500,000 + $1,900,000 + $200,000 - $50,000)	6,550,000
Goodwill	240,000
Total Assets	$15,358,000
Current Liabilities ($500,000 + $200,000 - $12,000)	$ 688,000
Long-Term Liabilities ($2,000,000 + $700,000 - $200,000)	2,500,000
Non-Controlling Interest (Paragraph 5-117)	880,000
No Par Common Stock (Pleigh's Balance)	8,000,000
Retained Earnings ((Paragraph 5-111)	3,290,000
Total Equities	$15,358,000

5-120. Most of the preceding computations follow directly from the trial balance data adjusted by the various journal entries that we have made. The exceptions to this are the Retained Earnings balance and the Non-Controlling Interest which were computed in the preceding sections. Note that the Investment In Sleigh and Long-Term Note Receivable accounts would not be disclosed in actual consolidated financial statements. They have been included in this presentation simply to show the disposition of all of the balances included in the problem data.

Exercise Five-2

Subject: Open Trial Balance Problem

On January 1, 2005, the Parker Company purchases 65 percent of the outstanding shares of the Schaffer Company for $1,350,000 in cash. On that date, the Schaffer Company had No Par Common Stock of $700,000 and Retained Earnings of $1,000,000. On December 31, 2009, the adjusted trial balances of the Parker Company and its subsidiary, the Schaffer Company are as follows:

	Parker	Schaffer
Monetary Assets	$ 2,850,000	$ 725,000
Investment In Schaffer - At Cost	1,350,000	N/A
Non-Monetary Assets	6,475,000	2,045,000
Total Expenses	2,940,000	530,000
Dividends Declared	250,000	50,000
Total Debits	$13,865,000	$3,350,000
Liabilities	$ 1,712,500	$ 425,000
No Par Common Stock	3,000,000	700,000
Retained Earnings (January 1)	5,895,000	1,550,000
Sales	3,225,000	675,000
Dividend Revenue	32,500	Nil
Total Credits	$13,865,000	$3,350,000
2009 Net Income	$ 317,500	$ 145,000
December 31, 2009 Retained Earnings	$ 5,962,500	$1,645,000

Other Information:

1. At the date of Parker Company's acquisition of the Schaffer Company's shares, all of the identifiable assets and liabilities of the Schaffer Company had fair values that were equal to their carrying values except for a group of non-monetary assets that had a fair value that was $150,000 greater than its carrying value. These non-monetary assets had a remaining useful life of 15 years. Both companies use the straight-line method for all amortization calculations.

2. In each of the years since Parker acquired control over Schaffer, the goodwill arising on this business combination transaction has been tested for impairment. In 2007, a Goodwill Impairment Loss of $35,000 was recognized. In addition, the impairment test for 2009 found a further impairment of $25,000.

3. Schaffer Company's Sales during 2009 include sales of $85,000 to Parker Company. All of this merchandise has been resold by the Parker Company. However, as a result of these sales, on December 31, 2009, Parker still owes Schaffer $15,000 on open account.

Prepare a consolidated Income Statement and a consolidated Statement Of Retained Earnings for the year ending December 31, 2009 and a consolidated Balance Sheet as at December 31, 2009 for the Parker Company and its subsidiary, the Schaffer Company.

End of Exercise. Solution available in Study Guide.

Comprehensive Example - Closed Trial Balance With Investment At Cost

Basic Data

5-121. In this second version of the comprehensive example, the only requirement is the preparation of a consolidated Balance Sheet. As a consequence, the data is presented in the form of a closed trial balance.

On January 1, 2005, the Pleigh Company purchases 80 percent of the outstanding voting shares of the Sleigh Company for $3,200,000 in cash. On that date the Sleigh Company had No Par Common Stock of $2,000,000 and Retained Earnings of $1,500,000. On December 31, 2009, the adjusted trial balances of the Pleigh Company and its subsidiary, the Sleigh Company are as follows:

	Pleigh	Sleigh
Cash	$ 500,000	$ 300,000
Current Receivables	800,000	400,000
Inventories	2,500,000	1,700,000
Long-Term Note Receivable	200,000	Nil
Investment In Sleigh - At Cost	3,200,000	N/A
Land	1,500,000	1,000,000
Plant And Equipment (Net)	4,500,000	1,900,000
Total Debits	$13,200,000	$5,300,000
Current Liabilities	$ 500,000	$ 200,000
Long-Term Liabilities	2,000,000	700,000
No Par Common Stock	8,000,000	2,000,000
Retained Earnings	2,700,000	2,400,000
Total Credits	$13,200,000	$5,300,000

Other Information:

1. At the date of Pleigh Company's acquisition of the Sleigh Company's shares, all of the identifiable assets and liabilities of the Sleigh Company had fair values that were equal to their carrying values except:
   - Inventories which had fair values that were $100,000 more than their carrying values,
   - Land with a fair value that was $150,000 less than its carrying value, and
   - Plant And Equipment which had a fair value that was $250,000 greater than its carrying value.

   The Plant And Equipment had a remaining useful life on the acquisition date of 20 years while the Inventories that were present on the acquisition date were sold during the year ending December 31, 2005. The Land is still on the books of the Sleigh Company on December 31, 2009. Both companies use the straight line method to calculate amortization.

2. In each of the years since Pleigh acquired control over Sleigh, the goodwill arising on this business combination transaction has been tested for impairment. No impairment was found in any of the years since acquisition.

3. Sleigh Company's Sales during 2009 include sales of $300,000 to Pleigh Company. All of this merchandise has been resold by the Pleigh Company.

4. On December 31, 2009, the Pleigh Company is holding Sleigh Company's long-term note payable in the amount of $200,000. Interest at 12 percent is payable on July 1 of each year. Pleigh Company has been holding this note since July 1, 2007.

Required: Prepare a consolidated Balance Sheet as at December 31, 2009 for the Pleigh Company and its subsidiary, the Sleigh Company.

Procedural Approach

5-122. The procedural approach here is similar to that used in our first version of this problem. The basic differences can be described as follows:

- All of the Step B fair value write-off entries will now be made to Sleigh's December 31, 2009 Retained Earnings balance, rather than to the January 1, 2009 balance.
- The Step C entry will involve distributing the December 31, 2009 retained earnings, rather than the January 1, 2009 balance.
- As no consolidated Income Statement is being prepared, there is no need to adjust or eliminate any expense or revenue items.
- As all dividends received have been closed to Retained Earnings, there is no need to eliminate intercompany dividends declared.

Step A Procedures

Investment Analysis

5-123. The analysis of the investment in Sleigh is identical to the one used in the "open trial balance" version of this problem (Paragraph 5-43). It is as follows:

	80 Percent	100 Percent
Investment Cost	$3,200,000	$4,000,000
Sleigh Shareholders' Equity At Acquisition	(2,800,000)	(3,500,000)
Differential	$ 400,000	$ 500,000
Fair Value Changes:		
Increase On Inventories	(80,000)	(100,000)
Decrease On Land	120,000	150,000
Increase On Plant And Equipment (Net)	(200,000)	(250,000)
Goodwill	$ 240,000	$ 300,000

Investment Elimination

5-124. As was the case with the investment analysis, the journal entry here will be the same as in the "open trial balance" version of the problem. It is as follows:

No Par Common Stock (At Acquisition)	$2,000,000	
Retained Earnings (At Acquisition)	1,500,000	
Plant And Equipment (Net)	200,000	
Inventories	80,000	
Goodwill	240,000	
Land		$ 120,000
Non-Controlling Interest [(20%)($3,500,000)]		700,000
Investment In Sleigh		3,200,000

Step B(1) - Intercompany Assets And Liabilities

5-125. The elimination of intercompany asset and liability balances is also the same as in the "open trial balance" version of this problem. The required entries are:

Long-Term Liabilities	$200,000	
Long-Term Note Receivable		$200,000
Current Liabilities	$ 12,000	
Current Receivables		$ 12,000

Step B(2) - Realization Of Fair Value Changes

General Procedures

5-126. With the investment at cost, recognition will have to be given to realization of fair value changes for the entire period since acquisition. This means that the entries in this version of the problem will have the same effect on the asset and liability accounts as did the entries which were made in the first version of this comprehensive problem.

5-127. The only difference in the entries is that, since we are working with a closed trial balance, it is no longer possible to adjust expense and revenue accounts. These accounts have been closed into Sleigh's ending Retained Earnings balance and, as a consequence, the portion of the adjustments that were allocated to expenses and revenues in the open trial balance versions of this problem will now go to Retained Earnings.

Inventories

5-128. Since the fair value change on Inventories had no effect on the 2009 expenses or revenues, the entry here will be the same as it was in the open trial balance version of this problem (Paragraph 5-60). It is as follows:

Retained Earnings - Sleigh's Closing	$80,000	
Inventories		$80,000

Plant And Equipment

5-129. As was the case in the previous version of this problem, we will credit the Plant And Equipment account for 5 years (January 1, 2005 through December 31, 2009) of additional amortization expense on the fair value change. However, instead of splitting the debits between Retained Earnings and the current Amortization Expense (Paragraph 5-65), the entire amount will go to Retained Earnings. The entry would be as follows:

Retained Earnings - Sleigh's Closing	$50,000	
Plant And Equipment (Net)		$50,000

Land

5-130. As the Land is still on the books of the Sleigh Company, no entry is required to adjust the fair value change on this account.

Step B(3) - Goodwill Impairment

5-131. As there has been no impairment of goodwill in any of the years since Pleigh acquired Sleigh, no entry is required for this step in our procedures.

Step B(4) - Intercompany Expenses And Revenues

5-132. In the "open trial balance" version of this problem, we made an entry here to eliminate intercompany expenses and revenues. We noted that this entry was simply to avoid overstating expenses and revenues. Since all of the expenses and revenues are now closed to retained earnings, no entry is required in this closed trial balance version of the problem.

Step B(5) - Intercompany Dividends

5-133. In the "open trial balance" version of this problem, we made an entry here to eliminate intercompany dividend payments. The entry involved reducing Dividend Revenue or Investment Income and Dividends Declared (Paragraph 5-87). Since all of these accounts have been closed to Retained Earnings, no entry is required for intercompany dividends in this closed trial balance version of the problem.

5-134. The Non-Controlling Interest in consolidated net assets in the previous version of this problem was reduced to the extent of dividend payments to non-controlling shareholders. This effect will be automatically picked up in Step C when we base the allocation to the Non-Controlling Interest on the end of the year Retained Earnings balance of the Sleigh

Company. This end of year balance has had all of the Sleigh Company's 2009 dividends deducted as part of the closing entries.

Step C - Distribution Of The Subsidiary Retained Earnings

Retained Earnings Balance

5-135. Our one remaining task at this point is to determine the appropriate distribution of the balance that is left in the Retained Earnings account of the Sleigh Company. Note that, in this closed trial balance version of our comprehensive problem, we are concerned with the December 31, 2009 balance of Sleigh's Retained Earnings. The balance that is left in this account can be calculated as follows:

Balance - December 31, 2009	$2,400,000
Step A Elimination (Balance At Acquisition)	(1,500,000)
Balance Since Acquisition	$ 900,000
Step B Adjustments:	
Fair Value Increase On Inventories	(80,000)
Amortization Of Fair Value Increase On Plant And Equipment (5 Years At $10,000)	(50,000)
Balance To Be Distributed	$ 770,000

5-136. Since we are dealing with Sleigh's closing Retained Earnings balance, all of the Step B adjustments are for five years, rather than for four years as was the case in the open trial balance version of this comprehensive problem (Paragraph 5-92).

Retained Earnings Distribution Schedule

5-137. As indicated in the preceding calculation, $770,000 remains in the December 31, 2009 Retained Earnings account of the Sleigh Company. We will use the same type of schedule that was introduced in the "open trial balance" version of this problem to analyze the distribution of this amount. It is as follows:

December 31, 2009 Balance As Per Trial Balance	$2,400,000
January 1, 2005 Balance At Acquisition	(1,500,000)
Balance Since Acquisition	$ 900,000
Non-Controlling Interest [(20%)($900,000)]	(180,000)
Available To The Controlling Interest	$ 720,000
Step B Adjustments:	
Fair Value Increase On Inventories	(80,000)
Amortization Of Fair Value Increase On Plant And Equipment (5 Years At $10,000)	(50,000)
To Consolidated Retained Earnings	$ 590,000

Retained Earnings Distribution Entry

5-138. Using this schedule, we can now make the required Step C distribution entry. The journal entry required to distribute the Sleigh Company's Retained Earnings since acquisition is as follows:

Retained Earnings - Sleigh	$770,000	
Non-Controlling Interest (Balance Sheet)		$180,000
Consolidated Retained Earnings		590,000

5-139. When the $590,000 from the preceding entry is added to the balance of $2,700,000 that is in the Pleigh Company's Retained Earnings account, we have the December 31, 2009 consolidated Retained Earnings figure of $3,290,000.

Consolidated Balance Sheet

Non-Controlling Interest

5-140. The calculation of the Non-Controlling Interest using the procedures would start with the Step A allocation of $700,000, and add the Step C allocation of $180,000. Alternatively, an easier way to compute the Non-Controlling Interest is to take 20 percent of the end of the year Shareholders' Equity of the Sleigh Company. This calculation would be as follows:

December 31, 2009 - No Par Common Stock	$2,000,000
December 31, 2009 - Retained Earnings	2,400,000
Sleigh's Shareholder's Equity	$4,400,000
Non-Controlling Percent	20%
December 31, 2009 Non-Controlling Interest	$ 880,000

Statement Disclosure

5-141. We are now in a position to complete the required consolidated Balance Sheet as at December 31, 2009 of the Pleigh Company and its subsidiary. It is identical to the open trial balance version (Paragraph 5-119). It would be prepared as follows:

Pleigh Company And Subsidiary
Consolidated Balance Sheet
As At December 31, 2009

Cash ($500,000 + $300,000)	$ 800,000
Current Receivables ($800,000 + $400,000 - $12,000)	1,188,000
Inventories ($2,500,000 + $1,700,000 + $80,000 - $80,000)	4,200,000
Long-Term Note Receivable ($200,000 - $200,000)	Nil
Investment In Sleigh ($3,200,000 - $3,200,000)	Nil
Land ($1,500,000 + $1,000,000 - $120,000)	2,380,000
Plant And Equipment (Net) ($4,500,000 + $1,900,000 + $200,000 - $50,000)	6,550,000
Goodwill	240,000
Total Assets	$15,358,000
Current Liabilities ($500,000 + $200,000 - $12,000)	$ 688,000
Long-Term Liabilities ($2,000,000 + $700,000 - $200,000)	2,500,000
Non-Controlling Interest (Paragraph 5-140)	880,000
No Par Common Stock (Pleigh's Balance)	8,000,000
Retained Earnings (Paragraph 5-139)	3,290,000
Total Equities	$15,358,000

Exercise Five-3

Subject: Closed Trial Balance Problem

Note: This is a closed trial balance version of Exercise Five-2.

On January 1, 2005, the Parker Company purchases 65 percent of the outstanding shares of the Schaffer Company for $1,350,000 in cash. On that date, the Schaffer Company had No Par Common Stock of $700,000 and Retained Earnings of $1,000,000. On December 31, 2009, the adjusted trial balances of the Parker Company and its subsidiary, the Schaffer Company are as follows:

	Parker	Schaffer
Monetary Assets	$ 2,850,000	$ 725,000
Investment In Schaffer - At Cost	1,350,000	N/A
Non-Monetary Assets	6,475,000	2,045,000
Total Debits	$10,675,000	$2,770,000
Liabilities	$ 1,712,500	$ 425,000
No Par Common Stock	3,000,000	700,000
Retained Earnings	5,962,500	1,645,000
Total Credits	$10,675,000	$2,770,000

Other Information:

1. At the date of Parker Company's acquisition of the Schaffer Company's shares, all of the identifiable assets and liabilities of the Schaffer Company had fair values that were equal to their carrying values except for a group of non-monetary assets that had a fair value that was $150,000 greater than its carrying value. These non-monetary assets had a remaining useful life of 15 years. Both companies use the straight-line method for all amortization calculations.

2. In each of the years since Parker acquired control over Schaffer, the goodwill arising on this business combination transaction has been tested for impairment. In 2007, a Goodwill Impairment Loss of $35,000 was recognized. In addition, the impairment test for 2009 found a further impairment of $25,000.

3. Schaffer Company's Sales during 2009 include sales of $85,000 to Parker Company. All of this merchandise has been resold by the Parker Company. However, as a result of these sales, on December 31, 2009, Parker still owes Schaffer $15,000 on open account.

Prepare a consolidated Balance Sheet as at December 31, 2009 for the Parker Company and its subsidiary, the Schaffer Company.

End of Exercise. Solution available in Study Guide.

Application Of The Equity Method

Basic Concepts

5-142. In Chapter 2, we indicated that the Net Income of an investor using the equity method for an investee had to be equal to the consolidated Net Income that would result from the consolidation of that investee. This requirement is based on the following recommendation:

> **Paragraph 3051.08** *Investment income as calculated by the equity method should be the amount necessary to increase or decrease the investor's income to that which would have been recognized if the results of the investee's operations had been consolidated with those of the investor.* (August, 1978)

5-143. With respect to this Chapter, this means that all of the adjustments for fair value changes and goodwill impairment that would be required in the consolidation process, are also required in the application of the equity method. There is, however, a major difference in the disclosure of these adjustments. In consolidation, the various adjustments are included in specific consolidated account balances. For example, if a fair value change on a depreciable asset is recorded in the consolidated Balance Sheet, the related write-off will be disclosed as an addition to Amortization Expense in the consolidated Income Statement.

5-144. In contrast, the equity method deals with all of these adjustments as modifications of the Investment Asset and Investment Income accounts. This means that an investor using the equity method would not record the fair value change in its single entity Balance Sheet, nor would such an investor record the related write-off as an addition to Amortization Expense. Rather, the fair value amortization amount would be calculated and deducted from Investment Income and from the equity pickup which is added to the Investment Asset account. This is why the application of the equity method is sometimes referred to as a "one line consolidation".

Comprehensive Example

Income Statement

5-145. To illustrate the basic procedures under the equity method, we will use the same comprehensive example that we have been working with throughout this Chapter. The basic data for this problem is presented in Paragraph 5-42 and will not be repeated here. The only change is that we will assume that Pleigh Company's majority ownership does not give it control over the Sleigh Company and, as a consequence, the investment cannot be consolidated and must be accounted for by the equity method.

5-146. From our previous experience with the Pleigh Company problem, we know that consolidated Net Income for 2009 amounts to $570,000. We also know that Pleigh's Net Income from its operations equals $420,000 (the cost method $500,000, less the $80,000 in dividends received from Sleigh). Given these figure, the only Investment Income amount that would satisfy the requirement stated in Paragraph 3051.08 is $150,000 ($570,000 - $420,000).

5-147. Using this Investment Income amount, the Income Statement of the Pleigh Company with the Investment In Sleigh carried by the equity method would be as follows:

Pleigh Company
Income Statement
Year Ending December 31, 2009

Sales	$4,000,000
Interest Revenue	24,000
Investment Income	150,000
Total Revenues	$4,174,000
Cost Of Goods Sold	$2,800,000
Amortization Expense	200,000
Interest Expense	240,000
Other Expenses	364,000
Total Expenses	$3,604,000
Net Income	$ 570,000

5-148. Under this approach, we have determined Investment Income as a "plug" figure which serves as an amount that will result in Pleigh Company's Net Income satisfying the condition that it must be equal to the amount that would result from the application of consolidation procedures. Note, however, that this amount can be calculated directly as follows:

Pleigh's Interest In Sleigh's Income [(80%)($200,000)]	$160,000
Fair Value Amortization Of Plant And Equipment	(10,000)
Pleigh's Equity Method Investment Income	$150,000

Balance Sheet

5-149. If Pleigh was not consolidating its investment in Sleigh, and used the equity method in its single entity statements, the Balance Sheet account Investment In Sleigh would have to be increased to reflect Pleigh's equity in this investee. As is the case with Investment Income under the equity method, this Balance Sheet account would be subject to the same types of adjustments that would be required in the preparation of consolidated financial statements. The required balance would be calculated as follows:

Investment In Sleigh At Cost		$3,200,000
Equity Pickup:		
Sleigh's December 31, 2009 Retained Earnings	$2,400,000	
Balance At January 1, 2005 Acquisition	(1,500,000)	
Balance Since Acquisition	$ 900,000	
Ownership Percentage	80%	
Pleigh's Share	$ 720,000	
Fair Value Adjustments:		
Fair Value Increase On Inventories	(80,000)	
Amortization Of Fair Value Increase On Plant And Equipment (5 Years At $10,000)	(50,000)	590,000
Investment In Sleigh At Equity		$3,790,000

5-150. If this amount is used on the asset side of Pleigh's single entity Balance Sheet, there will have to be a corresponding $590,000 ($3,790,000 - $3,200,000) adjustment to Retained Earnings on the equity side of the single entity Balance Sheet resulting in Retained Earnings of $3,290,000 ($2,700,000 + $590,000). On a comparative basis, Pleigh's equity method Balance Sheet, along with the consolidated Balance Sheet that was prepared in earlier versions of this problem, would be as follows:

Pleigh Company
Comparison Of Single Entity and Consolidated Balance Sheet
As At December 31, 2009

	Equity Method	Consolidated
Cash	$ 500,000	$ 800,000
Current Receivables	800,000	1,188,000
Inventories	2,500,000	4,200,000
Long-Term Note Receivable	200,000	Nil
Investment In Sleigh (At Equity)	3,790,000	N/A
Land	1,500,000	2,380,000
Plant And Equipment (Net)	4,500,000	6,550,000
Goodwill	Nil	240,000
Total Assets	$13,790,000	$15,358,000
Current Liabilities	$ 500,000	$ 688,000
Long-Term Liabilities	2,000,000	2,500,000
Non-Controlling Interest	Nil	880,000
No Par Common Stock	8,000,000	8,000,000
Retained Earnings	3,290,000	3,290,000
Total Equities	$13,790,000	$15,358,000

5-151. Note that, when the equity method is used, the resulting Retained Earnings figure in Pleigh's single entity Balance Sheet is equal to the consolidated Retained Earnings figure resulting from the application of consolidation procedures. This result follows from the Paragraph 3051.08 requirement that investment income as calculated by the equity method must be the amount necessary to increase or decrease the investor's income to that which would have been recognized if the results of the investee's operations had been consolidated with those of the investor.

Exercise Five-4

Subject: Application Of The Equity Method

Note: This is an equity method version of Exercise Five-2.

On January 1, 2005, the Parker Company purchases 65 percent of the outstanding shares of the Schaffer Company for $1,350,000 in cash. On that date, the Schaffer Company had No Par Common Stock of $700,000 and Retained Earnings of $1,000,000. On December 31, 2009, the adjusted trial balances of the Parker Company and its subsidiary, the Schaffer Company are as follows:

	Parker	Schaffer
Monetary Assets	$ 2,850,000	$ 725,000
Investment In Schaffer - At Cost	1,350,000	N/A
Non-Monetary Assets	6,475,000	2,045,000
Total Expenses	2,940,000	530,000
Dividends Declared	250,000	50,000
Total Debits	$13,865,000	$3,350,000
Liabilities	$ 1,712,500	$ 425,000
No Par Common Stock	3,000,000	700,000
Retained Earnings (January 1)	5,895,000	1,550,000
Sales	3,225,000	675,000
Dividend Revenue	32,500	Nil
Total Credits	$13,865,000	$3,350,000
2009 Net Income	$ 317,500	$ 145,000
December 31, 2009 Retained Earnings	$ 5,962,500	$1,645,000

Other Information:

1. At the date of Parker Company's acquisition of the Schaffer Company's shares, all of the identifiable assets and liabilities of the Schaffer Company had fair values that were equal to their carrying values except for a group of non-monetary assets that had a fair value that was $150,000 greater than its carrying value. These non-monetary assets had a remaining useful life of 15 years. Both companies use the straight-line method for all amortization calculations.
2. In each of the years since Parker acquired control over Schaffer, the goodwill arising on this business combination transaction has been tested for impairment. In 2007, a Goodwill Impairment Loss of $35,000 was recognized. In addition, the impairment test for 2009 found a further impairment of $25,000.
3. Schaffer Company's Sales during 2009 include sales of $85,000 to Parker Company. All of this merchandise has been resold by the Parker Company. However, as a result of these sales, on December 31, 2009, Parker still owes Schaffer $15,000 on open account.
4. The Parker Company's majority ownership of Schaffer shares has never provided control over that Company and, as a consequence, the Investment in Schaffer has been accounted for by the equity method since its acquisition.

Provide the Parker Company's single entity Income Statement for the year ending December 31, 2009, and its single entity Balance Sheet as at December 31, 2009. Note that the Parker Company's trial balance given in the problem accounts for the Investment In Schaffer using the cost method.

End of Exercise. Solution available in Study Guide.

Consolidated Cash Flow Statement

Differences In Procedures

5-152. In general, the procedures for preparing a consolidated Cash Flow Statement are very similar to those required for a single entity Cash Flow Statement (specific differences are described in the paragraphs which follow).

5-153. In most circumstances, it is not necessary to prepare a complete set of consolidated financial statements in order to complete a consolidated Cash Flow Statement. However, as a minimum, the data for consolidated Net Income, the change in consolidated cash, and the change in other working capital items is needed. In addition, some of the consolidated expenses and revenues will have to be determined in order to provide an appropriate conversion of consolidated Net Income into consolidated Cash Flows From Operating Activities.

5-154. As was indicated, most of the procedures are the same, without regard to whether a consolidated or a single entity Cash Flow Statement is being prepared. As the procedures for preparing single entity Cash Flow Statements are usually covered in introductory and intermediate accounting texts, we will not present them in this material.

> **CD-ROM Note** If you are not reasonably comfortable preparing single entity Cash Flow Statements, you may wish to review Chapter 12, "Cash Flow Statements", of our *Guide To Canadian Financial Reporting* which is found on the CD-ROM that accompanies your text. This Chapter provides detailed coverage of the procedures required in preparing single entity Cash Flow Statements.

5-155. There are, however, some procedures that are unique to preparing consolidated Cash Flow Statements. They can be described as follows:

- Consolidated Net Income is defined in Section 1600 as being after the deduction of the Non-Controlling Interest. Since this deduction does not involve an outflow of consolidated cash, it will be treated in a manner similar to amortization and other expenses which do not involve cash outflows. That is, it will be added back to consolidated Net Income in order to arrive at consolidated Cash Flows From Operating Activities.
- In a single entity Cash Flow Statement, the dividends shown will be the same amount as shown in the Statement Of Retained Earnings. This will not be the case here. The consolidated Cash Flow Statement would disclose all dividends which involve an outflow of consolidated cash. This would include both the dividends declared by the parent company and the dividends declared by the subsidiary and payable to the non-controlling shareholders. You will recall that in the consolidated Statement Of Retained Earnings, we deducted only the dividends declared by the parent company.
- Also unique to the consolidation situation is the possibility that the parent may acquire additional subsidiary shares. Two possible situations can be identified here:

  1. If the shares are acquired for cash directly from the subsidiary, it is an intercompany transaction that would be eliminated and would not appear in the consolidated Cash Flow Statement.
  2. If the shares are acquired for cash from the non-controlling shareholders, the transaction would be disclosed as an outflow of consolidated cash.

  A similar analysis can be made when a part of the subsidiary shares are sold.

Section 1540 On Business Combinations

5-156. In addition to providing general guidelines for the preparation of the Cash Flow Statement, Section 1540, "Cash Flow Statements", also provides specific guidance in the area of business combinations. With respect to acquisitions and disposals of business units, the following recommendations are provided:

Paragraph 1540.42 *The aggregate cash flows arising from each of business combinations accounted for using the purchase method and disposals of business units should be presented separately and classified as cash flows from investing activities.* (August, 1998)

Paragraph 1540.43 *An enterprise should disclose, in aggregate, in respect of both business combinations accounted for using the purchase method and disposals of business units during the period each of the following:*

(a) the total purchase or disposal consideration;
(b) the portion of the purchase or disposal consideration composed of cash and cash equivalents;
(c) the amount of cash and cash equivalents acquired or disposed of; and
(d) the total assets, other than cash or cash equivalents, and total liabilities acquired or disposed of. (August, 1998)

Example - Consolidated Cash Flow Statement

Basic Data

5-157. In order to illustrate the procedures and concepts related to business combinations, a simple example of a consolidated Cash Flow Statement will be presented. The basic data is as follows:

On December 31, 2005, the Pam Company acquired 80 percent of the outstanding shares of the Sam Company for $3,600,000 in cash. On this date, all of the Sam Company's identifiable assets and liabilities had carrying values that were equal to their fair values. The carrying values of the Sam Company's net identifiable assets amounted to $4,000,000.

On December 31, 2008, the Pam Company acquired 100 percent of the outstanding shares of the Tam Company for cash in the amount of $2,200,000. On that date, the Tam Company had cash of $100,000, net non-cash current assets of $400,000, identifiable non-current assets of $2,000,000 and liabilities of $500,000. All of the Tam Company's identifiable assets and liabilities had carrying values that were equal to their fair values.

The comparative condensed Balance Sheets of the Pam Company and its subsidiary, the Sam Company, on December 31, 2007 and December 31, 2008 are as follows:

Pam And Sam Companies
Balance Sheets
As At December 31, 2007

	Pam	Sam
Cash	$ 400,000	$ 300,000
Net Non-Cash Current Assets	5,600,000	1,700,000
Investment In Sam (At Cost)	3,600,000	N/A
Plant And Equipment	12,000,000	8,000,000
Accumulated Amortization	(5,600,000)	(2,000,000)
Total Assets	$16,000,000	$8,000,000
Long-Term Liabilities	$ 3,000,000	$2,000,000
No Par Common Stock	5,000,000	2,000,000
Retained Earnings	8,000,000	4,000,000
Total Equities	$16,000,000	$8,000,000

Pam And Sam Companies
Balance Sheets
As At December 31, 2008

	Pam	Sam
Cash	$ 800,000	$ 600,000
Net Non-Cash Current Assets	4,800,000	2,200,000
Investment In Sam (Cost)	3,600,000	N/A
Investment In Tam (Cost)	2,200,000	N/A
Plant And Equipment	13,000,000	8,400,000
Accumulated Amortization	(6,400,000)	(2,200,000)
Total Assets	$18,000,000	$9,000,000
Long-Term Liabilities	$ 3,000,000	$2,500,000
No Par Common Stock	6,000,000	2,000,000
Retained Earnings	9,000,000	4,500,000
Total Equities	$18,000,000	$9,000,000

Other Information:

1. During 2008, the Sam Company issued $500,000 in Long-Term Liabilities for cash.

2. During 2008, the Sam Company purchased Plant And Equipment for $800,000 in cash and sold Plant And Equipment with a cost of $400,000 and a net book value of $200,000 for cash of $60,000.

3. During 2008, Pam issues common shares for $1 million in cash. The proceeds are immediately invested in new Plant And Equipment.

4. The 2008 Net Income and Dividends Paid for the three Companies are as follows:

	Pam	Sam	Tam
Net Income	$2,000,000	$1,000,000	$300,000
Dividends Paid	1,000,000	500,000	100,000

5. It was determined that there was a goodwill impairment loss for 2008 of $40,000 related to Pam Company's purchase of Sam Company shares.

Required: For the year ending December 31, 2008, prepare a consolidated Cash Flow Statement for the Pam Company and its subsidiaries, the Sam Company and the Tam Company.

Preliminary Computations

5-158. Before proceeding directly to the preparation of the consolidated Cash Flow Statement, it will be useful to provide computations for consolidated Net Income and the change in the consolidated working capital and cash position. These calculations are contained in the material which follows.

5-159. We will calculate the consolidated Net Income using the definitional approach. You should note that the Tam Company's Net Income does not have a place in this calculation. This reflects the fact that its acquisition date was December 31, 2008 and the Tam Company's income would only accrue to the consolidated entity subsequent to the acquisition date. Given this, the calculation of the 2008 consolidated Net Income is as follows:

Pam Company's Net Income	$2,000,000
Intercompany Dividends - Sam To Pam [(80%)($500,000)]	(400,000)
Pam's Net Income Exclusive Of Subsidiary Dividends	$1,600,000
Equity Pickup - 80 Percent Of Sam's Net Income	800,000
Income Before Adjustments	$2,400,000
Goodwill Impairment Loss	(40,000)
Consolidated Net Income	$2,360,000

5-160. The increase in cash for the year ending December 31, 2008 can be calculated as follows:

December 31, 2008 Balance:		
Pam	$800,000	
Sam	600,000	
Tam*	100,000	$1,500,000
December, 31, 2007 Balance:		
Pam	($400,000)	
Sam	(300,000)	(700,000)
2008 Increase In Cash		$ 800,000

* While Tam's cash is included in the December 31, 2008 balance, it is not included in the December 31, 2007 balance as Tam was not part of the consolidated entity at this time.

5-161. A similar calculation provides the change in net non-cash current assets for the year ending December 31, 2008:

December 31, 2008 Balance:		
Pam	$4,800,000	
Sam	2,200,000	
Tam	400,000	$7,400,000
December, 31, 2007 Balance:		
Pam	($5,600,000)	
Sam	(1,700,000)	(7,300,000)
2008 Increase In Cash		$ 100,000

Consolidated Cash Flow Statement

5-162. As this example was designed to illustrate the acquisition of a subsidiary, it does not contain all of the information needed to provide the disclosure required by Section 1540 (e.g., cash paid for income taxes).

5-163. In most Cash Flow Statements, the most difficult figure to compute is Cash Flows From Operating Activities. It can be calculated by the direct approach, starting at zero, adding operating revenues that generate cash, and deducting operating expenses that involve outflows of cash. However, in this example, we have used the indirect approach, starting with Net Income and adjusting this figure for non-cash expense and revenue items.

Consolidated Net Income	$2,360,000
Amortization Expense (Note One)	1,200,000
Non-Controlling Interest [(20%)($1,000,000)]	200,000
Loss On Sale Of Equipment ($400,000 - $200,000 - $60,000)	140,000
Goodwill Impairment Loss	40,000
Consolidated Working Capital From Operating Activities	$3,940,000
Decrease In Consolidated Net Non-Cash Current Assets (Note Two)	300,000
Consolidated Cash Flows From Operating Activities	$4,240,000

Note One The Amortization Expense is equal to the increase in Pam's Accumulated Amortization of $800,000 ($6,400,000 - $5,600,000), the increase in Sam's Accumulated Amortization of $200,000 ($2,200,000 - $2,000,000), plus the accumulated amortization of $200,000 on the Plant And Equipment which was retired.

Note Two Note that, while there was an overall increase in Net Non-Cash Current Assets of $100,000, this was net of the $400,000 increase which resulted from the acquisition of the Tam Company. As this increase did not relate to operating activities of the consolidated group, it would be removed from the adjustment required to arrive at Cash Flows From Operating Activities, leaving a decrease of $300,000 (an increase of $100,000, less the $400,000 from the Tam Company acquisition).

5-164. The consolidated Cash Flow Statement for the year ending December 31, 2008 would be prepared as follows:

Pam Company And Subsidiaries
Consolidated Cash Flow Statement
Year Ending December 31, 2008

Cash Flows From (Used In):		
Operating Activities		
Cash Flows From Operating Activities (Paragraph 5-163)		$4,240,000
Financing Activities		
Issuance Of Long-Term Debt For Cash	$ 500,000	
Issuance Of Common Stock For Cash	1,000,000	
Dividends Paid By Pam	(1,000,000)	
Dividends Paid By Subsidiaries To Non-Controlling Interests (20% of $500,000)	(100,000)	400,000
Investing Activities		
Acquisition Of Subsidiary (Note One)	($2,100,000)	
Proceeds From The Sale Of Plant	60,000	
Acquisition Of Plant For Cash ($1,000,000 + $800,000)	(1,800,000)	(3,840,000)
Increase In Cash		$ 800,000
Cash At Beginning Of Year (Excluding Tam)		700,000
Cash At End Of Year (Including Tam)		$1,500,000

Note One There are a variety of ways in which the acquisition of the Tam Company could be disclosed in a note to the Cash Flow Statement. One way of accomplishing this is as follows:

Tam Company's Cash Acquired	$ 100,000
Tam's Net Non-Cash Current Assets Acquired	400,000
Tam's Identifiable Non-Current Assets Acquired	2,000,000
Tam's Liabilities Assumed	(500,000)
Tam's Goodwill Acquired (Balancing Figure)	200,000
Cash Paid For Tam Company Shares	$2,200,000

Exercise Five-5

Subject: Consolidated Statement Of Cash Flows

On January 1, 2003, the Parco Company acquires 80 percent of the outstanding voting shares of the Subco Company for $1,000,000 in cash. At this time the Subco Company has No Par Common Stock of $1,000,000 and Retained Earnings of $200,000. Also on this acquisition date, all of the identifiable assets and liabilities of Subco Company had fair values that were equal to their carrying values except for Inventories which had a fair value that was $400,000 less than its carrying value and Equipment which had a fair value that was $300,000 more than its carrying value. The Inventories were sold during 2003, while the Equipment had a remaining useful life on January 1, 2003 of ten years with no anticipated salvage value. Both the Parco Company and the Subco Company use the straight line method for all amortization calculations.

Comparative Balance Sheets for the two companies as at December 31, 2007 and December 31, 2008 are as follows:

Parco (000's)

	2008	2007
Cash	$ 800	$ 400
Accounts Receivable	1,500	1,800
Inventories	2,000	2,600
Investment In Subco (At Cost)	1,000	1,000
Land	1,000	800
Plant And Equipment (Net)	4,800	6,400
Total Assets	$11,100	$13,000
Accounts Payable	$ 400	$ 1,000
Bonds Payable - Par	3,000	4,000
Common Stock - No Par	4,000	4,000
Retained Earnings	3,700	4,000
Total Equities	$11,100	$13,000

Subco (000's)

	2008	2007
Cash	$ 365	$ 270
Accounts Receivable	900	650
Inventories	800	500
Land	450	850
Plant And Equipment (Net)	600	800
Total Assets	$3,115	$3,070
Accounts Payable	$ 700	$ 750
Bonds Payable - Par	800	800
Bonds Payable - Premium	15	20
Common Stock - No Par	1,000	1,000
Retained Earnings	600	500
Total Equities	$3,115	$3,070

Other Information:

1. During 2008, the Parco Company retires outstanding debt with a par value of $1,000,000 for $1,000,000 in cash.
2. During 2008, the Parco Company experiences a Net Loss of $300,000 and does not declare any dividends. This Net Loss includes an $800,000 write-down of Plant And Equipment to reflect the fact that its net carrying amount exceeded its net recoverable amount.
3. During 2008, the Subco Company earns Net Income of $500,000 and declares dividends of $400,000. All of the dividends declared are paid prior to December 31, 2008.
4. The goodwill measured at the time Parco acquired Subco has been tested for impairment in each subsequent year. No impairment has been found.
5. The changes in the Land accounts reflect purchases of land for cash and sales of land for cash. The proceeds from the land sales were equal to the carrying value of the land sold. There were no purchases or sales of Plant and Equipment.

Calculate consolidated Net Income for the Parco Company and its subsidiary, the Subco Company, for the year ending December 31, 2008.

Prepare a consolidated Cash Flow Statement for the Parco Company and its subsidiary, the Subco Company, for the year ending December 31, 2008. Your solution should comply with all of the requirements of the *CICA Handbook*.

End of Exercise. Solution available in Study Guide.

Step-By-Step Acquisitions

Definition And Accounting Recommendations

5-165. A step-by-step acquisition involves a situation in which an investor acquires control of an investee in a sequence of two or more purchases. Several purchases and a considerable period of time might elapse before a particular investee becomes a subsidiary. However, when control is achieved, the accounting procedures are not conceptually different than those used in dealing with a single step acquisition of a subsidiary. This is reflected in the following *CICA Handbook* Recommendation:

> **Paragraph 1600.13** *Where an investment in a subsidiary is acquired through two or more purchases, the parent company's interest in the subsidiary's identifiable assets and liabilities should be determined as follows:*
>
> (a) *the assignable costs of the subsidiary's identifiable assets and liabilities should be determined as at each date on which an investment was required;*
>
> (b) *the parent company's interest in the subsidiary's identifiable assets and liabilities acquired at each step in the purchase should be based on the assignable costs of all such assets and liabilities at that date.* (April, 1975)

5-166. The meaning of assignable costs in the preceding recommendation is fair values adjusted, if applicable, for any excess of such values assigned over the cost of the purchase. This means that this recommendation calls for the establishment and allocation of fair values at each purchase date. While these are the same procedures that would be used in the case of a single step acquisition, implementation difficulties may arise as a result of the step-by-step acquisition process.

Implementation Problems

5-167. As indicated in the previous paragraph, the appropriate solution to accounting for this type of situation would require the determination and allocation of fair value changes and goodwill at each step of an acquisition. However, there are situations in which, at the time of one or more of the early share acquisitions, there is no intent to acquire controlling ownership.

5-168. If these initial investments involve significant influence, the equity method will be used and this will require the appropriate determination of fair values for the investee's assets. However, if the investor does not acquire significant influence, these initial investments will be classified as held for trading or available for sale. In this case, there will be no need to determine the fair values of the investee's assets. If no effort is made to make these determinations, the information will not be available when control is acquired and consolidated procedures are applied.

5-169. In view of this problem, the *CICA Handbook* makes the following suggestion:

> **Paragraph 1600.11** Where the investment position has been reached as the result of two or more purchases, the assigned costs of the subsidiary's identifiable assets and liabilities should reflect this fact. For practical purposes, assignable costs will normally be determined as at the time the first use of equity accounting becomes appropriate (or as at the time the first use of consolidation becomes appropriate, if equity accounting has not previously been appropriate) and at each further major purchase...

5-170. For those purchases where fair value data is not available, there will still be a differential between investment cost and the investor's proportionate share of carrying values. This differential, if a debit amount, will have to be allocated to goodwill. If a credit is involved, it will be deducted from identifiable non-monetary assets.

5-171. An additional modification of general procedures is also suggested. This involves situations in which there are a large number of small purchases. It is stated as follows:

> **Paragraph 1600.11** ...Where there are numerous small purchases, it is appropriate to group a series of such purchases into one step, in order to treat the series in the same way as a major purchase.

Example - Step-By-Step Acquisition

Basic Data

5-172. While the concepts involved in step-by-step acquisitions are identical to those used in single step acquisitions, the procedures involved are sufficiently different to warrant the presentation of a simple illustration of this situation. The basic data for this example is as follows:

> **Example** On December 31, 2007, the Alpha Company purchases 30 percent of the outstanding shares of the Morgan Company for $2,250,000. On this date, the book value of the Morgan Company's Shareholders' Equity is $5,000,000, made up of $2,000,000 in No Par Common Stock and $3,000,000 in Retained Earnings. All of the fair values of the individual identifiable assets and liabilities of the Morgan Company have carrying values that are equal to their fair values except for a piece of Equipment. The equipment has a remaining useful life of six years and a fair value that exceeds its carrying value by $1,000,000. Both companies use the straight line method to calculate amortization.
>
> On December 31, 2008, the Alpha Company purchases an additional 40 percent of the outstanding shares of the Morgan Company for $3,500,000. On this date, the book value of the Morgan Company's Shareholders' Equity is $6,000,000, made up of $2,000,000 in No Par Common Stock and $4,000,000 in Retained Earnings. All of the fair values of the identifiable assets and liabilities of the Morgan Company have carrying values that are equal to their fair values except for the piece of Equipment on

which there was a fair value change on December 31, 2007. However, the fair value change has increased to a total of $1,500,000 on December 31, 2008. The remaining useful life of this asset is now five years.

The Goodwill measured in the purchase transactions has been tested for impairment in each subsequent year. These tests have found no impairment in either 2008 or 2009.

During the years 2007, 2008, and 2009 there are no intercompany transactions between the Alpha Company and its subsidiary the Morgan Company. The Alpha Company carries its investments in the Morgan Company using the cost method.

On December 31, 2009, the condensed Balance Sheets of the Alpha Company and its subsidiary the Morgan Company are as follows:

Alpha and Morgan Companies
Condensed Balance Sheets
As At December 31, 2009

	Alpha	**Morgan**
Investment In Morgan Company	$5,750,000	N/A
Other Net Identifiable Assets	4,150,000	$6,500,000
Total Assets	$9,900,000	$6,500,000
No Par Common Stock	$5,000,000	$2,000,000
Retained Earnings	4,900,000	4,500,000
Total Equities	$9,900,000	$6,500,000

Required: Prepare a consolidated Balance Sheet for the Alpha Company and its subsidiary, the Morgan Company, as at December 31, 2009.

Procedures

5-173. In a problem such as this, the easiest solution usually involves direct computations of the balances to be included in the consolidated Balance Sheet. While the journal entries used in our general procedures can be used in step-by-step acquisitions, we have found this approach to be very awkward. As a consequence, we would encourage you to solve step-by-step problems by using direct calculations of the required items, an approach that will be illustrated with this example.

Analysis Of Investments

5-174. Before proceeding to the direct computation of the various accounts for inclusion in the consolidated Balance Sheet, it is useful to analyze the two investment transactions through which the Alpha Company acquired control of the Morgan Company. The analysis of the first transaction is as follows:

	30 Percent	**100 Percent**
Investment Cost	$2,250,000	$7,500,000
Morgan Shareholders' Equity	(1,500,000)	(5,000,000)
Differential	$ 750,000	$2,500,000
Fair Value Increase On Equipment	(300,000)	(1,000,000)
Goodwill	$ 450,000	$1,500,000

5-175. In similar fashion, the analysis of the second investment transaction would appear as follows:

	40 Percent	100 Percent
Investment Cost	$3,500,000	$8,750,000
Morgan Shareholders' Equity	(2,400,000)	(6,000,000)
Differential	$1,100,000	$2,750,000
Fair Value Increase On Equipment	(600,000)	(1,500,000)
Goodwill	$ 500,000	$1,250,000

Consolidated Net Identifiable Assets

5-176. At the end of Chapter 4 we provided the following definitional calculation for identifiable assets and liabilities:

Identifiable Assets And Liabilities The consolidated balance for any identifiable asset or liability is calculated as follows:

- 100 percent of the carrying value o f the identifiable asset or liability on the books of the parent company; *plus*
- 100 percent of the carrying value of the identifiable asset or liability on the books of the subsidiary company; *plus (minus)*
- the parent company's share of the increase (decrease) in the fair value of the subsidiary's asset (liability) balance.

5-177. As we are now in a period subsequent to acquisition, a further component must be added to this definition to recognize that parts of the fair value changes have been realized and must be charged to income. This further component could be stated as follows:

- *minus (plus)* the portion of the fair value increase (decrease) that has become realized since acquisition through usage of the asset, or through its disposal.

5-178. This definition can be used in dealing with this step-by-step acquisition. The only difference here is that there are two acquisition dates and fair values must be picked up with respect to both of them. The calculation, including accumulated amortization on the fair value changes to December 31, 2009, would be as follows:

December 31, 2009 Carrying Values:		
Alpha Company's		$ 4,150,000
Morgan Company's		6,500,000
Total Book Values - December 31, 2009		$10,650,000
Fair Value Changes:		
December 31, 2007 Purchase (30%)	$300,000	
Amortization [(2)($300,000 ÷ 6)]	(100,000)	200,000
December 31, 2008 Purchase (40%)	$600,000	
Amortization [(1)($600,000 ÷ 5)]	(120,000)	480,000
Consolidated Net Identifiable Assets		$11,330,000

5-179. Note carefully that fair value changes are only included to the extent that they are purchased. Changes in fair values that occur subsequent to a particular purchase are not retroactively picked up. As an example, in this situation you would not record the first purchase's 30 percent share of the increase in the fair value change on the piece of equipment from $1,000,000 on December 31, 2007 to $1,500,000 on December 31, 2008. This is, of course, consistent with the general approach under the parent company concept in that only the investor's purchased share of fair value changes and goodwill is recognized.

Goodwill

5-180. As the problem indicates that there has been no impairment of Goodwill in either 2008 or 2009, the consolidated goodwill will simply be $950,000 ($450,000 + $500,000), the sum of the values measured at the two purchase dates.

Consolidated Retained Earnings

5-181. A definitional calculation can be made here of the required balance for the consolidated Retained Earnings as at December 31, 2009. The only difference that is created by the multiple steps in the acquisition is that multiple equity pickups will be recorded. The calculation is as follows:

Alpha Company's Retained Earnings		$4,900,000
Equity Pickups:		
First Purchase [(30%)($4,500,000 - $3,000,000)]	$450,000	
Second Purchase [(40%)($4,500,000 - $4,000,000)]	200,000	650,000
Amortization Of Fair Value Change		
($100,000 + $120,000)		(220,000)
Consolidated Retained Earnings		$5,330,000

5-182. There is an alternative approach to the calculation of the total equity pickup of $650,000. It is as follows:

First Purchase [(30%)($4,000,000 - $3,000,000)]	$300,000
Second Purchase [(70%)($4,500,000 - $4,000,000)]	350,000
Total Equity Pickup	$650,000

5-183. While either approach will provide a consistently correct answer, we would suggest you try to use one or the other on a consistent basis.

Consolidated Balance Sheet

5-184. Using the preceding information, the consolidated Balance Sheet would be prepared as follows:

Alpha Company And Subsidiary
Consolidated Balance Sheet
As At December 31, 2009

Net Identifiable Assets (Paragraph 5-178)	$11,330,000
Goodwill ($450,000 + $500,000)	950,000
Total Assets	$12,280,000
Non-Controlling Interest [(30%)($6,500,000)]	$ 1,950,000
No Par Common Stock (Alpha Company's Balance)	5,000,000
Retained Earnings (Paragraph 5-181)	5,330,000
Total Equities	$12,280,000

Exercise Five-6

Subject: Step-By-Step Acquisition

On December 31, 2007, the Best Company purchases 40 percent of the outstanding shares of the Worst Company for $1,875,000. On this date, the book value of the Worst Company's Shareholders' Equity is $3,250,000 (Common Stock of $2,000,000, plus Retained Earnings of $1,250,000). All of the fair values of the individual identifiable assets and liabilities of the Worst Company have carrying values that are equal to their fair values except for Plant And Equipment. Plant And Equipment has a carrying value of $2,000,000 and a fair value of $2,725,000. On this date, these assets have a remaining useful life of four years.

On December 31, 2008, the Best Company purchases an additional 15 percent of the outstanding shares of the Worst Company for $820,000. On this date, the book value of the Worst Company's Shareholders' Equity is $4,250,000 (Common Stock of $2,000,000, plus Retained Earnings of $2,250,000). All of the fair values of the identifiable assets and liabilities of the Worst Company have carrying values that are equal to their fair values except for Plant And Equipment. Plant And Equipment has a carrying value of $1,600,000, and a fair value of $2,300,00. On this date, these assets have a remaining useful life of three years.

There has been no impairment of goodwill in either 2008 or 2009.

On December 31, 2009, the carrying values for Best's and Worst's Plant And Equipment are $3,520,000 and $1,600,000, respectively. The Retained Earnings balance of Best on December 31, 2009 is $4,275,000 while Worst's Retained Earnings balance is $2,450,000.

Calculate the amount that would be shown on the December 31, 2009 consolidated Balance Sheet for Goodwill, Plant And Equipment and Retained Earnings.

End of Exercise. Solution available in Study Guide.

Summary Of Consolidation Procedures

5-185. In Chapter 4, we began the development of a set of procedures that could be used in the preparation of a consolidated Balance Sheet at the date of the subsidiary's acquisition. As this Chapter begins to deal with the preparation of a complete set of consolidated financial statements for periods subsequent to acquisition, it contains a significant expansion of these procedures.

5-186. In addition, some modifications of the procedures developed in Chapter 4 were required in order to deal with periods subsequent to acquisition and the need to prepare additional types of consolidated statements. Specifically we have added Steps B-2 to C-2 to deal with procedures required subsequent to the acquisition of the subsidiary. At this point, we will provide you with a complete summary of the procedures developed in Chapters 4 and 5. This summary is as follows:

Step A-1 Procedure Eliminate 100 percent of the Investment In Subsidiary account.

Step A-2 Procedure Eliminate 100 percent of all the acquisition date balances in the subsidiary's shareholders' equity (includes both contributed capital and retained earnings).

Step A-3 Procedure Allocate any debit or credit Differential that is present at acquisition to the investor's share of fair value changes on identifiable assets, fair value changes on identifiable liabilities, and positive or negative goodwill.

Step A-4 Procedure Allocate to a Non-Controlling Interest account in the consolidated Balance Sheet, the non-controlling interest's share of the at acquisition book value of the common shareholders' equity of the subsidiary (includes both contributed capital and retained earnings).

Step B-1 Procedure Eliminate 100 percent of all intercompany assets and liabilities.

Step B-2 Procedure Give recognition to the post-acquisition realization of acquisition date fair value changes on assets and liabilities that have been used up or sold during the post-acquisition period. To the extent that this realization occurred in prior periods, recognition will require an adjustment of the opening retained earnings of the subsidiary. Alternatively, if the realization occurred in the current period, the adjustment will be to the subsidiary's current period expenses, revenues, gains, or losses.

Step B-3 Procedure Recognize current and cumulative goodwill impairment losses that have been measured since the acquisition of the subsidiary and the initial recognition of the goodwill balance. To the extent that the impairment took place during the current period, the measured amount will be charged to Goodwill Impairment Loss. To the extent that it occurred in prior periods, it will be charged to retained earnings.

Step B-4 Procedure Eliminate 100 percent of all intercompany expenses and revenues.

Step B-5 Procedure Eliminate 100 percent of subsidiary dividends declared. The parent's share of this amount will be deducted from the revenues of the parent company and the non-controlling interest's share of this amount will be deducted from the Non-Controlling Interest in the Balance Sheet.

Step C-1 Procedure Determine the appropriate allocation of the subsidiary's adjusted retained earnings since acquisition. The Non-Controlling Interest's share will be based on book value. After the Non-Controlling Interest's share is subtracted, the resulting balance will be adjusted for the fair value write-offs called for in Step B(2), as well as any goodwill impairment as described in Step B(3). The balance remaining after these adjustments will be allocated to consolidated Retained Earnings.

Step C-2 Procedure Eliminate the subsidiary's adjusted Retained Earnings since acquisition. This amount will be allocated to the Non-Controlling Interest in the consolidated Balance Sheet and to consolidated Retained Earnings as determined in Step C-1.

5-187. The preceding represents a complete set of consolidation procedures for dealing with problems that do not have unrealized intercompany profits. The development of the procedures for dealing with unrealized intercompany profits will be found in Chapter 6.

5-188. We would call your attention to the fact that, as stated, the listed procedures apply to open trial balance problems in which the investment is carried at cost. In other types of problems, modifications will be required. For example, in applying Step B-2 in a closed trial balance problem, there will be no adjustments to current expenses, revenues, gains, or losses as these amounts have been closed to the subsidiary's Retained Earnings account. Such required modifications were illustrated in the closed trial balance version of our comprehensive example (Paragraph 5-122).

Summary Of Definitional Calculations

5-189. We continue to encourage you to work towards preparing the required balances in consolidated financial statements by using direct definitional calculations. To assist you in this work, we offer the following definitions that have been developed in the course of Chapters 4 and 5.

Identifiable Assets And Liabilities The amount to be included in the consolidated Balance Sheet for any identifiable asset or liability is calculated as follows:

- 100 percent of the carrying value of the identifiable asset (liability) on the books of the parent company at the Balance Sheet date; *plus*
- 100 percent of the carrying value of the identifiable asset (liability) on the books of the subsidiary company at the Balance Sheet date; *plus (minus)*
- the parent company's share of the fair value increase (decrease) on the asset (liability) (i.e., the parent company's share of the difference between the fair value of the subsidiary's asset or liability at time of acquisition and the carrying value of that asset or liability at the time of acquisition); *minus (plus)*
- amortization of the parent company's share of the fair value increase (decrease) on the asset (liability) for the period since acquisition to the current Balance Sheet date.

Goodwill The Goodwill to be recorded in the consolidated Balance Sheet is equal to:

- the excess of the cost of the investment over the parent company's share of the fair values of the subsidiary's net assets at the time of acquisition; *minus*
- the amount of any goodwill impairment that has been recognized in the period since the acquisition to the current Balance Sheet date.

Non-Controlling Interest - Balance Sheet The Non-Controlling Interest to be recorded in the consolidated Balance Sheet is an amount equal to the non-controlling interest's ownership percentage of the book value of the subsidiary's common stock equity at the Balance Sheet date.

Contributed Capital The Contributed Capital to be recorded in the consolidated Balance Sheet is equal to the contributed capital from the single entity Balance Sheet of the parent company.

Retained Earnings The Retained Earnings amount to be included in the consolidated Balance Sheet is calculated as follows:

- 100 percent of the Retained Earnings of the parent company; *plus (minus)*
- the parent company's share of the subsidiary's Retained Earnings (Deficit) since acquisition; *plus (minus)*
- 100 percent of the adjustments to consolidated expenses, revenues, gains, and losses for realized fair value changes during the period since acquisition to the current Balance Sheet date; *minus*
- 100 percent of any goodwill impairment that has been recognized since the acquisition to the current Balance Sheet date.

Revenue The amount of any revenue to be included in the consolidated Income Statement is calculated as follows:

- 100 percent of the amount reported in the parent company's financial statements; *plus*
- 100 percent of the amount reported in the subsidiary's financial statements; *minus*
- 100 percent of any intercompany amounts included in the parent or subsidiary figures; *plus (minus)*
- the parent's share of any fair value changes realized during the period through usage or sale of subsidiary assets (fair value amortization and amounts realized through the sale of subsidiary assets prior to the end of their economic life). It would be unusual for fair value realizations to be related to revenues. However, it could happen. For example, amortization of a fair value change on a long-term receivable would be treated as an adjustment of interest revenue.

Expense The amount of any expense to be included in the consolidated Income Statement is calculated as follows:

- 100 percent of the amount reported in the parent company's financial statements; *plus*
- 100 percent of the amount reported in the subsidiary's financial statements;
- *minus*
- 100 percent of any intercompany amounts included in the parent or subsidiary figures; *plus (minus)*
- the parent's share of any fair value changes realized during the period through usage or sale of subsidiary assets (fair value amortization and amounts realized through the sale of subsidiary assets prior to the end of their economic life).

Goodwill Impairment Loss If the required annual test of goodwill for impairment determines that any impairment has occurred during the current period, this amount will be recorded as a Goodwill Impairment Loss.

Non-Controlling Interest - Income Statement The non-controlling interest in the consolidated Income Statement is an amount equal to the non-controlling interest's ownership percentage of the reported Net Income. Note that, if the subsidiary has extraordinary items or results from discontinued operations, this Non-Controlling Interest will be based on the subsidiary's Income Before Extraordinary Items And Discontinued Operations. Also note that, in situations where there are preferred shares with a prior claim on the income of the subsidiary, the Non-Controlling Interest to be disclosed in the consolidated Income Statement will include such claims.

Consolidated Net Income Consolidated Net Income can be calculated as follows:

- 100 percent of the parent company's Net Income, excluding dividends received from the subsidiary; *plus (minus)*
- the parent's share of the subsidiary's reported Net Income (Net Loss); *plus (minus)*
- the parent's share of any fair value changes realized during the period through usage or sale of subsidiary assets (fair value amortization and amounts realized through the sale of subsidiary assets prior to the end of their economic life); *minus*
- any Goodwill Impairment Loss that is recognized during the period.

5-190. These definitions are applicable to problems which do not involve the presence of unrealized intercompany profits. When we introduce unrealized intercompany profits in the next Chapter, these definitions will require significant modification.

International Convergence

Standards

5-191. The Canadian rules for preparing consolidated financial statements are found in Section 1581, "Business Combinations", which provides recommendations for all business combinations, and Section 1600, "Consolidated Financial Statements", which provides additional recommendations for those business combinations which involve an acquisition of shares.

5-192. The international standards which contain the corresponding material are IFRS No. 3, *Business Combinations*, and IAS No. 27, *Consolidated And Separate Financial Statements*.

Differences In Standards

Current IFRSs

5-193. As we have noted, current international standards for preparing consolidated financial statements are largely based on the entity approach. As the current Canadian approach is largely based on the parent company approach, international convergence will introduce significant changes in Canadian GAAP.

5-194. In general terms, the major differences between Canadian standards and current international standards can be described as follows:

> **Asset Valuation** IFRS No. 3 requires that 100 percent of fair value changes on identifiable assets be recognized at the time of acquisition. Section 1581 only allows the acquirer's share to be recognized. Note, however, IFRS No. 3 does not allow the recognition of 100 percent of goodwill. Only the acquirer's share of this asset can be recognized.
>
> **Non-Controlling Interest** Consistent with the entity approach, IAS No. 27 requires the non-controlling interest to be presented as a component of consolidated Shareholders' Equity. The value to be recognized will include the non-controlling interest's share of fair value changes on identifiable assets.
>
> **Terminology** IAS No. 27 continues to use the term Minority Interest, rather than the more accurate Non-Controlling Interest. However, this is certain to be changed by the amendments resulting from the FASB/IASB project. Given this, we will ignore this difference in presenting examples based on current IFRSs.

Proposed Changes

5-195. The amendments resulting from the FASB/IASB project on business combinations will result in a variety of changes. From the perspective of the issues dealt with in this Chapter, the most important change that is being proposed is the recognition of 100 percent of the goodwill that is recognized in a business combination transaction. As we have noted, IFRS No. 3 defines goodwill as the excess of the cost of the acquisition over the acquirer's share of the fair value of the acquiree's identifiable assets and liabilities.

5-196. While there is considerable resistance to this proposed change, the most recent news releases from the two Boards indicate that it will be approved. However, it appears that exemptions may be provided.

Example: Open Trial Balance Problem

Basic Data

5-197. In order to illustrate the application of international standards to an open trial balance problem, we will use the same example that was originally presented in Paragraph 5-42. It is repeated here for your convenience.

On January 1, 2005, the Pleigh Company purchases 80 percent of the outstanding shares of the Sleigh Company for $3,200,000 in cash. On that date, the Sleigh Company had No Par Common Stock of $2,000,000 and Retained Earnings of $1,500,000. On December 31, 2009, the adjusted trial balances of the Pleigh Company and its subsidiary, the Sleigh Company are as follows:

	Pleigh	Sleigh
Cash	$ 500,000	$ 300,000
Current Receivables	800,000	400,000
Inventories	2,500,000	1,700,000
Long-Term Note Receivable	200,000	Nil
Investment In Sleigh - At Cost	3,200,000	N/A
Land	1,500,000	1,000,000
Plant And Equipment (Net)	4,500,000	1,900,000
Cost Of Goods Sold	2,800,000	1,500,000
Amortization Expense	200,000	100,000
Other Expenses	364,000	616,000
Interest Expense	240,000	84,000
Dividends Declared	350,000	100,000
Total Debits	$17,154,000	$7,700,000
Current Liabilities	$ 500,000	$ 200,000
Long-Term Liabilities	2,000,000	700,000
No Par Common Stock	8,000,000	2,000,000
Retained Earnings (January 1)	2,550,000	2,300,000
Sales	4,000,000	2,500,000
Interest Revenue	24,000	Nil
Dividend Revenue	80,000	Nil
Total Credits	$17,154,000	$7,700,000
January 1, 2009 Retained Earnings	$ 2,550,000	$ 2,300,000
2009 Net Income	500,000	200,000
Dividends Declared	(350,000)	(100,000)
December 31, 2009 Retained Earnings	$ 2,700,000	$2,400,000

Other Information:

1. At the date of Pleigh Company's acquisition of the Sleigh Company's shares, all of the identifiable assets and liabilities of the Sleigh Company had fair values that were equal to their carrying values except:
   - Inventories which had fair values that were $100,000 more than their carrying values,
   - Land with a fair value that was $150,000 less than its carrying value, and
   - Plant And Equipment which had a fair value that was $250,000 greater than its carrying value.

   The Plant And Equipment had a remaining useful life on the acquisition date of 20 years while the Inventories that were present on the acquisition date were sold during the year ending December 31, 2005. The Land is still on the books of the Sleigh Company on December 31, 2009. Both companies use the straight line method to calculate amortization.

2. In each of the years since Pleigh acquired control over Sleigh, the goodwill arising on this business combination transaction has been tested for impairment. No impairment was found in any of the years since acquisition.

3. Sleigh Company's Sales during 2009 include sales of $300,000 to Pleigh Company. All of this merchandise has been resold by the Pleigh Company.
4. On December 31, 2009, the Pleigh Company is holding Sleigh Company's long-term note payable in the amount of $200,000. Interest at 12 percent is payable on July 1 of each year. Pleigh Company has been holding this note since July 1, 2007.

Required Using current international financial reporting standards, prepare a consolidated Income Statement and a consolidated Statement Of Retained Earnings for the year ending December 31, 2009 and a consolidated Balance Sheet as at December 31, 2009 for the Pleigh Company and its subsidiary, the Sleigh Company.

Step A Procedures

5-198. The investment analysis that was used in preparing consolidated financial statements under Canadian standards, can also be used when international standards are applied. This analysis is as follows:

	80 Percent	100 Percent
Investment Cost (Total Fair Value)	$3,200,000	$4,000,000
Sleigh Shareholders' Equity At Acquisition	(2,800,000)	(3,500,000)
Differential	$ 400,000	$ 500,000
Fair Value Changes:		
Increase On Inventories	($ 80,000)	($ 100,000)
Decrease On Land	120,000	150,000
Increase On Plant And Equipment (Net)	(200,000)	(250,000)
Total Fair Value Change Credit (Debit)	($ 160,000)	($ 200,000)
Goodwill	$ 240,000	$ 300,000

5-199. The investment elimination entry would be different under international standards in that 100 percent of the fair value changes on identifiable assets would be recognized. This would require a corresponding change to the Non-Controlling Interest credit in order to record their share of these fair value changes.

No Par Common Stock (At Acquisition)	$2,000,000	
Retained Earnings (At Acquisition)	1,500,000	
Plant And Equipment (100%))	250,000	
Inventories (100%)	100,000	
Goodwill (80%)	240,000	
Land (100%)		$ 150,000
Non-Controlling Interest [(20%)($3,500,000 + $200,000)]		740,000
Investment In Sleigh		3,200,000

Step B(1) - Intercompany Assets And Liabilities

5-200. These entries are unchanged by the application of international standards.

Long-Term Liabilities	$200,000	
Long-Term Note Receivable		$200,000

Current Liabilities	$ 12,000	
Current Receivables		$ 12,000

Step B(2) - Realization Of Fair Value Changes

5-201. The entries required to write off recognized fair value changes would be different under international standards in that they would be based on 100 percent of the fair value changes, rather than Pleigh's 80 percent share of these values. The 2009 entries for Inventories and Plant And Equipment would be as follows:

Retained Earnings - Sleigh's Opening	$100,000	
Inventories		$100,000
Retained Earnings - Sleigh's Opening	$50,000	
Amortization Expense ($250,000 ÷ 25)	12,500	
Plant And Equipment (Net)		$62,500

(The $50,000 debit to Sleigh's opening Retained Earnings is for the four years 2005 through 2008. The credit to Plant And Equipment is for the five years 2005 through 2009.

Step B(3) - Goodwill Impairment

5-202. The Other Information in this problem indicates that there has been no goodwill impairment in any of the years under consideration. Given this, no entry is required under either Canadian or international standards. However, if an entry had been required, it would not be altered by the application of current international standards. This reflects the fact that IFRS No. 3 allows recognition of only the acquirer's share of any goodwill that is measured at the date of the business combination.

Step B(4) - Intercompany Expenses And Revenues

5-203. The entries for eliminating the intercompany Sales and intercompany Interest Expense would not be altered by the application of international standards. These entries are as follows:

Sales	$300,000	
Cost Of Goods Sold		$300,000
Interest Revenue	$24,000	
Interest Expense		$24,000

Step B(5) - Intercompany Dividends

5-204. The entry to eliminate intercompany dividends would not be altered by the application of international standards. The entry is as follows:

Dividend Revenue	$80,000	
Non-Controlling Interest (Balance Sheet)	20,000	
Dividends Declared		$100,000

Step C - Distribution Of The Subsidiary Retained Earnings

5-205. The difference here is that the fair value write-offs affect both the controlling and non-controlling interests. This reflects the fact that they are based on 100 percent of the fair value changes, rather than just the acquirer's share of these changes. The required schedule would be as follows:

Retained Earnings Distribution Schedule

January 1, 2009 Balance As Per The Trial Balance	$2,300,000
Balance At Acquisition	(1,500,000)
Balance Since Acquisition	$ 800,000
Fair Value Realizations:	
100% Fair Value Increase On Inventories	(100,000)
Amortization Of 100% Fair Value Increase On Plant And Equipment (4 Years At $12,500)	(50,000)
Adjusted Balance Since Acquisition	$ 650,000
Non-Controlling Interest [(20%)($650,000)]	(130,000)
To Consolidated Retained Earnings	$ 520,000

5-206. Based on this schedule, the required distribution entry would be as follows:

Retained Earnings - Sleigh	$650,000	
Non-Controlling Interest (Balance Sheet)		$130,000
Consolidated Retained Earnings		520,000

5-207. Note that the amount distributed to consolidated Retained Earnings has not been changed by the application of international standards (Paragraph 5-99).

Consolidated Income Statement

5-208. Applying international standards, the 2009 consolidated Income Statement of the Pleigh Company and its subsidiary would be prepared as follows:

Pleigh Company And Subsidiary
Consolidated Income Statement (International Standards)
Year Ending December 31, 2009

Sales ($4,000,000 + $2,500,000 - $300,000)	$6,200,000
Interest Revenue ($24,000 - $24,000)	Nil
Dividend Revenue ($80,000 - $80,000)	Nil
Total Revenues	$6,200,000
Cost Of Goods Sold ($2,800,000 + $1,500,000 - $300,000)	$4,000,000
Amortization Expense ($200,000 + $100,000 + $12,500)	312,500
Interest Expense ($240,000 + $84,000 - $24,000)	300,000
Other Expenses ($364,000 + $616,000)	980,000
Total Expenses	$5,592,500
Consolidated Net Income	$ 607,500

5-209. You will note that the application of international standards results in an Income Statement that is very similar to that produced under Canadian standards (Paragraph 5-107). The differences that you should note are as follows:

- Amortization has been increased by $2,500 to reflect the fact that 100 percent of the fair value change on Plant And Equipment has been recognized and is subject to amortization.
- The final consolidated Net Income figure is before any recognition of the non-controlling interest's share of this income. As this interest is viewed as a distribution of consolidated Net Income, it will be disclosed in the consolidated Statement Of Retained Earnings.

Definitional Calculation Of Consolidated Net Income

5-210. When international standards are applied, a definitional calculation of consolidated Net Income would be prepared as follows:

Pleigh Company's Net Income		$500,000
Intercompany Dividend Revenues		(80,000)
Pleigh's Net Income Less Dividends		$420,000
Sleigh's Net Income	$200,000	
Fair Value Adjustment Of Amortization Expense	(12,500)	187,500
Consolidated Net Income		$607,500

Consolidated Statement Of Retained Earnings

5-211. Applying international standards, the 2009 consolidated Statement Of Retained Earnings for the Pleigh Company and its subsidiary would be prepared as follows:

Pleigh Company And Subsidiary
Consolidated Statement Of Retained Earnings (International Standards)
Year Ending December 31, 2009

Balance - January 1, 2009 ($2,550,000 + $520,000)	$3,070,000
2009 Consolidated Net Income	607,500
Available For Distribution	$3,677,500
Non-Controlling Interest In 2009 Subsidiary Income [(20%)($187,500) From Paragraph 5-210]	(37,500)
2009 Dividends (Pleigh's Only)	(350,000)
Balance - December 31, 2009	$3,290,000

5-212. As was the case with the Income Statement, the application of international standards results in a Statement of Retained Earnings that is very similar to that produced under Canadian standards. In fact, the opening and closing balances are unchanged from the Canadian standards version (Paragraph 5-111). The differences that should be noted are as follows:

- The consolidated Net Income figure is before any deduction for the non-controlling interest's share of Sleigh's Net Income.
- As it was not included in the determination of consolidated Net Income, the Non-Controlling Interest is shown in this Statement Of Retained Earnings as a distribution of consolidated Net Income.

Definitional Calculation Of Consolidated Retained Earnings

5-213. A definitional calculation could be used to verify the closing balance that has been determined in the preceding Statement Of Retained Earnings:

Pleigh's Closing Balance		$2,700,000
Sleigh's Balance - December 31, 2009	$2,400,000	
Balance At Acquisition	(1,500,000)	
Balance Since Acquisition	$ 900,000	
Fair Value Realizations:		
100% Fair Value Increase On Inventories	(100,000)	
Amortization Of 100% Fair Value Increase On Plant And Equipment (5 Years At $12,500)	(62,500)	
Adjusted Balance Since Acquisition	$ 737,500	
Pleigh's Interest	80%	590,000
Consolidated Retained Earnings As At December 31, 2009		$3,290,000

Consolidated Balance Sheet

5-214. The most complex item in the consolidated Balance Sheet is usually the non-controlling interest. As we noted in the Canadian standards version of this example, we can use the procedures that we have just developed to calculate this figure. Using this approach, the calculation would be as follows:

Step A Allocation (Balance At Acquisition)	$740,000
Step B Adjustment For Dividends	(20,000)
Step C Allocation (Retained Earnings Since Acquisition)	130,000
Non-Controlling Interest In Income (Paragraph 5-211)	37,500
Non-Controlling Interest (Balance Sheet)	$887,500

5-215. This figure can also be calculated directly from the Balance Sheet items:

Sleigh's Common Stock	$2,000,000
Sleigh's December 31, 2009 Retained Earnings	2,400,000
Unrealized Fair Value Changes:	
Increase On Inventories ($100,000 - $100,000)	Nil
Decrease On Land	(150,000)
Increase On Plant ($250,000 - $62,500)	187,500
Adjusted Balance	$4,437,500
Non-Controlling Interest Share	20%
Non-Controlling Interest	$ 887,500

5-216. Using these figures, the consolidated Balance Sheet can be prepared as follows:

Pleigh Company And Subsidiary
Consolidated Balance Sheet (International Standards)
As At December 31, 2009

Cash ($500,000 + $300,000)	$ 800,000
Current Receivables ($800,000 + $400,000 - $12,000)	1,188,000
Inventories ($2,500,000 + $1,700,000 + $100,000 - $100,000)	4,200,000
Long-Term Note Receivable ($200,000 - $200,000)	Nil
Investment In Sleigh ($3,200,000 - $3,200,000)	Nil
Land ($1,500,000 + $1,000,000 - $150,000)	2,350,000
Plant And Equipment (Net) ($4,500,000 + $1,900,000 + $250,000 - $62,500)	6,587,500
Goodwill	240,000
Total Assets	$15,365,500
Current Liabilities ($500,000 + $200,000 - $12,000)	$ 688,000
Long-Term Liabilities ($2,000,000 + $700,000 - $200,000)	2,500,000
Non-Controlling Interest (Paragraph 5-214)	887,500
No Par Common Stock (Pleigh's Balance)	8,000,000
Retained Earnings (Paragraph 5-211)	3,290,000
Total Equities	$15,365,500

5-217. Here again, the financial statement that results from the application of international standards is similar to the one we prepared under Canadian standards (Paragraph 5-119). The differences that should be noted are as follows:

- The figures for Land and Plant And Equipment are different in that they include 100 percent of the fair value changes on these assets, not just Pleigh's share of these changes.
- The value for the Non-Controlling Interest is changed to reflect their share of the fair value changes that are included in the Balance Sheet.
- While this point is not made clear in this unclassified Balance Sheet, the Non-Controlling Interest would be presented as a component of the consolidated Shareholders' Equity, not as a separate item outside of Shareholders' Equity.

Example: Step-By-Step Acquisitions

Basic Data

5-218. While the concepts involved in step-by-step acquisitions are not different than those involved with single step purchases of an acquiree, implementation procedures are somewhat more complex. In order to illustrate the application of international accounting standards in these situations, we will return to the same example that was presented in Paragraph 5-172. It is repeated here for your convenience.

Example On December 31, 2007, the Alpha Company purchases 30 percent of the outstanding shares of the Morgan Company for $2,250,000. On this date, the book value of the Morgan Company's Shareholders' Equity is $5,000,000, made up of $2,000,000 in No Par Common Stock and $3,000,000 in Retained Earnings. All of the fair values of the individual identifiable assets and liabilities of the Morgan Company have carrying values that are equal to their fair values except for a piece of Equipment. The equipment has a remaining useful life of six years and a fair value that exceeds its carrying value by $1,000,000. Both companies use the straight line method to calculate amortization.

On December 31, 2008, the Alpha Company purchases an additional 40 percent of the outstanding shares of the Morgan Company for $3,500,000. On this date, the book value of the Morgan Company's Shareholders' Equity is $6,000,000, made up of $2,000,000 in No Par Common Stock and $4,000,000 in Retained Earnings. All of the fair values of the identifiable assets and liabilities of the Morgan Company have carrying values that are equal to their fair values except for the piece of Equipment on which there was a fair value change on December 31, 2007. However, the fair value change has increased to a total of $1,500,000 on December 31, 2008. The remaining useful life of this asset is now five years.

The Goodwill measured in the purchase transactions has been tested for impairment in each subsequent year. These tests have found no impairment in either 2008 or 2009.

During the years 2007, 2008, and 2009 there are no intercompany transactions between the Alpha Company and its subsidiary the Morgan Company. The Alpha Company carries its investments in the Morgan Company using the cost method.

On December 31, 2009, the condensed Balance Sheets of the Alpha Company and its subsidiary the Morgan Company are as follows:

Alpha and Morgan Companies
Condensed Balance Sheets
As At December 31, 2009

	Alpha	Morgan
Investment In Morgan Company	$5,750,000	N/A
Other Net Identifiable Assets	4,150,000	$6,500,000
Total Assets	$9,900,000	$6,500,000
No Par Common Stock	$5,000,000	$2,000,000
Retained Earnings	4,900,000	4,500,000
Total Equities	$9,900,000	$6,500,000

Required: Using current international financial reporting standards, prepare a consolidated Balance Sheet for the Alpha Company and its subsidiary, the Morgan Company, as at December 31, 2009.

Analysis Of Investments

5-219. The investment analyses that were prepared in our Canadian standards version of this problem can be used in preparing the international standards version. The analysis of the first investment is as follows:

	30 Percent	100 Percent
Investment Cost	$2,250,000	$7,500,000
Morgan Shareholders' Equity	(1,500,000)	(5,000,000)
Differential	$ 750,000	$2,500,000
Fair Value Increase On Equipment	(300,000)	(1,000,000)
Goodwill	$ 450,000	$1,500,000

5-220. In similar fashion, the analysis of the second investment transaction would appear as follows:

	40 Percent	100 Percent
Investment Cost	$3,500,000	$8,750,000
Morgan Shareholders' Equity	(2,400,000)	(6,000,000)
Differential	$1,100,000	$2,750,000
Fair Value Increase On Equipment	(600,000)	(1,500,000)
Goodwill	$ 500,000	$1,250,000

Consolidated Net Identifiable Assets

5-221. International standards would require inclusion of 100 percent of the fair value changes that are measured at the date the business combination occurs (i.e., the step at which the acquirer gains control). Based on this concept, the consolidated Net Identifiable Assets would be calculated as follows:

December 31, 2009 Book Values:		
Alpha Company's		$ 4,150,000
Morgan Company's		6,500,000
Total Book Values - December 31, 2009		$10,650,000
Fair Value Increase On December 31, 2008 (100%)	$1,500,000	
2009 Amortization ($1,500,000 ÷ 5)	(300,000)	1,200,000
Consolidated Net Identifiable Assets		$11,850,000

5-222. This differs significantly from the Canadian standards solution to this problem in that we do not have to give separate recognition to the fair value changes present at each purchase date (Paragraph 5-178). We simply pick up 100 percent of the fair value changes that are present on December 31, 2008, the date on which Alpha acquired a controlling interest in Morgan (i.e., the date of the business combination transaction).

Goodwill

5-223. Unlike the situation with identifiable assets, current international standards only give recognition to the acquirer's share of goodwill. This means the Goodwill figure will be measured at each step of the acquisition, with the total being the same $950,000 ($450,000 + $500,000 that was recognized under the Canadian standards version of this problem.

Consolidated Retained Earnings

5-224. The application of international accounting standards would have an influence on the calculation of consolidated Retained Earnings. This is because the amortization of fair value changes would be altered by the recognition of 100 percent of the fair value changes that are present at the step where control is acquired. The required calculation would be as follows:

Alpha Company's Retained Earnings		$4,900,000
Equity Pickups:		
First Purchase [(30%)($4,500,000 - $3,000,000)]	$450,000	
Second Purchase[(40%)($4,500,000 - $4,000,000 - $150,000))]	140,000	590,000
Consolidated Retained Earnings		$5,490,000

Consolidated Balance Sheet

5-225. The Non-Controlling Interest can be calculated from the Balance Sheet Items as follows:

Morgan's Common Stock	$2,000,000
Morgan's Retained Earnings - December 31, 2009	4,500,000
Fair Value Increase At December 31, 2008 Acquisition	1,500,000
Amortization Of Fair Value Change (1 year)	(300,000)
Adjusted Balance	$7,700,000
Non-Controlling Share	30%
Non-Controlling Interest	$2,310,000

5-226. Using the preceding information, the consolidated Balance Sheet would be prepared as follows:

Alpha Company And Subsidiary
Consolidated Balance Sheet (International Standards)
As At December 31, 2009

Net Identifiable Assets (Paragraph 5-221)	$11,850,000
Goodwill ($450,000 + $500,000)	950,000
Total Assets	$12,800,000
Non-Controlling Interest (Paragraph 5-225)	$ 2,310,000
No Par Common Stock (Alpha Company's Balance)	5,000,000
Retained Earnings (Paragraph 5-224)	5,490,000
Total Equities	$12,800,000

Walk Through Problem

Note

This problem is an extension of the Walk Through Problem that was presented at the end of Chapter 4. As was explained in that Chapter, these problems provide you with a fill-in-the-blank solution format to assist you in solving the problem. These problems are designed to be an easy introduction to solving the type of problem illustrated in the Chapter.

Basic Data

On December 31, 2007, the Puff Company purchased 60 percent of the outstanding voting shares of the Snuff Company for $720,000 in cash. On that date, subsequent to the completion of the business combination, the Balance Sheets of the Puff and Snuff Companies and the fair values of Snuff's identifiable assets and liabilities were as follows:

	Balance Sheets		Fair Values
	Puff	Snuff	Snuff
Cash And Accounts Receivable	$ 350,000	$ 200,000	$200,000
Inventories	950,000	500,000	450,000
Investment In Snuff	720,000	N/A	N/A
Plant And Equipment (Net)	2,400,000	700,000	800,000
Total Assets	$4,420,000	$1,400,000	
Current Liabilities	$ 400,000	$ 100,000	$100,000
Long-Term Liabilities	1,000,000	400,000	360,000
No Par Common Stock	1,000,000	800,000	N/A
Retained Earnings	2,020,000	100,000	N/A
Total Equities	$4,420,000	$1,400,000	

The December 31, 2007 Inventories of Snuff are sold during 2008. The Plant And Equipment of Snuff on December 31, 2007 has an estimated useful life of 10 years while the Long-Term Liabilities that were present on that date mature on December 31, 2010. Both Companies use the straight line method of amortization. Puff carries its Investment In Snuff by the cost method.

The Income Statements for the year ending December 31, 2009 and the Balance Sheets as at December 31, 2009 of the Puff and Snuff Companies are as follows:

Puff and Snuff Companies
Income Statements
For The Year Ending December 31, 2009

	Puff Company	Snuff Company
Sales	$2,500,000	$1,300,000
Other Revenues	100,000	30,000
Total Revenues	$2,600,000	$1,330,000
Cost Of Goods Sold	$1,200,000	$ 750,000
Amortization Expense	400,000	250,000
Other Expenses	800,000	180,000
Total Expenses	$2,400,000	$1,180,000
Net Income	$ 200,000	$ 150,000

Balance Sheets
As At December 31, 2009

	Puff Company	Snuff Company
Cash	$ 100,000	$ 70,000
Accounts Receivable	430,000	180,000
Inventories	1,150,000	400,000
Investment In Snuff	720,000	N/A
Plant And Equipment (Net)	2,150,000	850,000
Total Assets	$4,550,000	$1,500,000
Current Liabilities	$ 300,000	$ 40,000
Long-Term Liabilities	1,000,000	400,000
No Par Common Stock	1,000,000	800,000
Retained Earnings	2,250,000	260,000
Total Equities	$4,550,000	$1,500,000

Other Information:

1. During 2009, the Puff Company declared and paid $100,000 in dividends while the Snuff Company declared and paid $40,000.

2. Included in the 2009 Sales of the Snuff Company are sales of $200,000 to the Puff Company. The Puff Company has resold all of this merchandise to purchasers outside of the consolidated entity. Puff owes Snuff $100,000 on December 31, 2009 for the merchandise purchases.

3. On December 31, 2009, Snuff still owes Puff for management fees earned during 2009. Fees of $25,000 have been charged by Puff and none of this amount has been paid by Snuff in 2009.

4. Goodwill has been tested for impairment in both 2008 and 2009. The test procedures found impairment of $16,000 in 2008, an amount that was recognized as a Goodwill Impairment Loss in that year. A further impairment of $20,000 was found in 2009.

Required: For the Puff Company and its subsidiary the Snuff Company, prepare, using the fill-in-the-blank solution format in the separate Study Guide:

A. A consolidated Income Statement for the year ending December 31, 2009.

B. A consolidated Statement Of Retained Earnings for the year ending December 31, 2009.

C. A consolidated Balance Sheet as at December 31, 2009.

In addition, provide calculations which verify:

- Consolidated Net Income for the year ending December 31, 2009,
- the December 31, 2009 consolidated Retained Earnings, and
- the December 31, 2009 Non-Controlling Interest that would be disclosed on the consolidated Balance Sheet.

Problems For Self Study

(The solutions for these problems can be found in the separate Study Guide.)

Self Study Problem Five - 1

Note This problem uses the same data that is found in Self Study Problem Five-6. However, in that problem, the solution should comply with international financial reporting standards.

On December 31, 2004, the Pastel Company purchased 90 percent of the outstanding voting shares of the Shade Company for $5,175,000 in cash. On that date, the Shade Company had No Par Common Stock of $2,000,000 and Retained Earnings of $4,000,000. All of the Shade Company's identifiable assets and liabilities had carrying values that were equal to their fair values except for:

1. Accounts Receivable with fair values that were $50,000 less than their carrying values.
2. Land which had a fair value that was $100,000 greater than its carrying value.
3. Equipment which had fair values that were $1,000,000 less than their carrying values and a remaining useful life of 10 years.
4. Long-Term Liabilities which had fair values that were $200,000 less than their carrying values and mature on December 31, 2009.

The Balance Sheets of the Pastel Company and the Shade Company as at December 31, 2009 were as follows:

Pastel and Shade Companies
Balance Sheets
As At December 31, 2009

	Pastel	Shade
Cash And Current Receivables	$ 2,625,000	$ 800,000
Inventories	8,000,000	2,000,000
Equipment (Net)	24,000,000	4,000,000
Buildings (Net)	10,000,000	2,000,000
Investment In Shade (Cost)	5,175,000	N/A
Land	2,000,000	1,200,000
Total Assets	$51,800,000	$10,000,000
Dividends Payable	Nil	$ 100,000
Current Liabilities	$ 1,800,000	900,000
Long-Term Liabilities	10,000,000	1,000,000
No Par Common Stock	20,000,000	2,000,000
Retained Earnings	20,000,000	6,000,000
Total Equities	$51,800,000	$10,000,000

The Income Statements of the Pastel and Shade Companies for the year ending December 31, 2009 were as follows:

Pastel And Shade Companies
Income Statements
For The Year Ending December 31, 2009

	Pastel	Shade
Sales	$8,000,000	$2,000,000
Gain On Sale Of Land	500,000	Nil
Other Revenues	800,000	100,000
Total Revenues	$9,300,000	$2,100,000
Cost Of Goods Sold	$3,800,000	$ 800,000
Amortization Expense	1,400,000	300,000
Other Expenses	2,000,000	400,000
Total Expenses	$7,200,000	$1,500,000
Net Income	$2,100,000	$ 600,000

Other Information:

1. In each of the years since Pastel acquired control over Shade, the Goodwill arising on this business combination transaction has been tested for impairment. After completing the annual impairment test, it was determined that the Goodwill Impairment Loss for 2009 was $15,000. No impairment was found in any of the other years since acquisition.
2. Both Companies use the straight line method to calculate all amortization charges and the First-In, First-Out inventory flow assumption.
3. Pastel uses the cost method to carry its Investment In Shade.
4. The Sales account in the Pastel Company's Income Statement includes only sales of merchandise. All other income is accounted for in Other Revenues or a separate Gain account.
5. During 2009, Pastel charged Shade $100,000 for management fees. None of this amount has been paid during 2009.
6. During 2009, dividends of $200,000 were declared and paid by Pastel and dividends of $100,000 were declared by Shade. On December 31, 2009, the dividends that were declared by the Shade Company during 2009 had not yet been paid.
7. During 2009, Shade sold to Pastel $500,000 worth of merchandise, all of which was resold by Pastel in 2009. Pastel owes Shade $75,000 on December 31, 2009 due to these purchases.
8. During 2009, Pastel sold merchandise to Shade for $150,000. All of this merchandise was resold in 2009. Shade has not paid for these purchases as at December 31, 2009.

Required: Prepare, for the Pastel Company and its subsidiary, the Shade Company:

A. The consolidated Income Statement for the year ending December 31, 2009.
B. The consolidated Statement Of Retained Earnings for the year ending December 31, 2009.
C. The consolidated Balance Sheet as at December 31, 2009.

Self Study Problem Five - 2

On January 1, 2002, the Puberty Company acquired 80 percent of the outstanding voting shares of the Senile Company for $4,000,000 in cash. On that date, the Senile Company had no par value common shares of $1 million outstanding and Retained Earnings of $2 million.

At the acquisition date, all identifiable assets and liabilities of the Senile Company had fair values equal to their carrying values except for a building with a remaining useful life of 25 years which had a fair value that was $4,000,000 greater than its carrying value, and an issue of 20 year bonds that had a fair value that was $2,000,000 greater than the value at which they were carried on Senile's books. The bonds were issued on January 1, 1998. In addition, on January 1, 2002, Senile had Goodwill of $1,000,000 on its books.

On December 31, 2008, the adjusted trial balances of the Puberty Company and its subsidiary, the Senile Company are as follows:

	Puberty	Senile
Cash and Current Receivables	$ 1,100,000	$ 400,000
Long-Term Receivables	1,000,000	200,000
Inventories	4,000,000	1,300,000
Plant and Equipment (Net)	6,000,000	4,000,000
Goodwill	Nil	1,000,000
Investment in Senile (Cost)	4,000,000	N/A
Cost of Goods Sold	5,000,000	1,500,000
Other Expenses	3,000,000	1,800,000
Dividends Declared	400,000	300,000
Total Debits	$24,500,000	$10,500,000
Current Liabilities	$ 300,000	$ 400,000
Notes Payable	200,000	600,000
Long-Term Liabilities	2,000,000	2,500,000
Common Stock - No Par Value	4,000,000	1,000,000
Retained Earnings	8,000,000	3,200,000
Sales	9,000,000	2,500,000
Other Revenues	1,000,000	300,000
Total Credits	$24,500,000	$10,500,000

Other Information:

1. Puberty carries its investment in Senile by the cost method. In each of the years since Puberty acquired control over Senile, the goodwill arising on this business combination transaction has been tested for impairment. After completing the annual impairment test, it was determined that the goodwill impairment loss for 2008 was $140,000 due to the current year's loss. No impairment was found in any of the other years since acquisition. The goodwill on Senile's books has suffered no impairment in any year.
2. Both Companies use the straight line method to calculate all amortization charges.
3. Puberty's 2008 Sales include $1,000,000 in sales to Senile which were priced to provide Puberty with a gross profit of 30 percent of the sales price. This merchandise has been resold by Senile in 2008.
4. Puberty holds a 12 percent, $500,000 Note which is payable by Senile in 2012. Interest is payable April 1 and October 1 on the principal. Puberty has been holding this Note since July 1, 2008.
5. Puberty's Other Revenues include any Investment Income received, as well as $100,000 in management fees which are payable by Senile in 2009.

Required: Prepare, for the Puberty Company and its subsidiary, the Senile Company:

A. the consolidated Income Statement for the year ending December 31, 2008;

B. the consolidated Statement of Retained Earnings for the year ending December 31, 2008; and

C. the consolidated Balance Sheet as at December 31, 2008.

Self Study Problem Five - 3

On January 1, 2002 the Prude Company purchased 60 percent of the outstanding voting shares of the Sybarite Company for $750,000 in cash. On that date, the Balance Sheet of the Sybarite Company and the fair values of its identifiable assets and liabilities were as follows:

Sybarite Company
Balance Sheet
As At January 1, 2002

	Carrying Values	Fair Values
Cash	$ 10,000	$ 10,000
Current Receivables	200,000	150,000
Inventories	1,090,000	640,000
Plant and Equipment	1,000,000	1,050,000
Accumulated Amortization	(300,000)	N/A
Total Assets	$2,000,000	
Current Liabilities	$ 200,000	$ 200,000
Long-Term Liabilities	500,000	600,000
No Par Common Stock	1,000,000	N/A
Retained Earnings	300,000	N/A
Total Equities	$2,000,000	

The difference between the carrying value and fair value of the Plant and Equipment relates to a building with a remaining useful life of 14 years. The Long-Term Liabilities all mature on January 1, 2007.

On December 31, 2008, the Balance Sheets of the Prude Company and its subsidiary, the Sybarite Company are as follows:

Prude and Sybarite Companies
Balance Sheets
As At December 31, 2008

	Prude	Sybarite
Cash	$ 50,000	$ 300,000
Current Receivables	300,000	400,000
Inventories	700,000	1,750,000
Investment in Sybarite (Cost)	750,000	N/A
Plant and Equipment	9,000,000	1,000,000
Accumulated Amortization	(3,000,000)	(650,000)
Total Assets	$7,800,000	$2,800,000
Current Liabilities	$ 300,000	$ 100,000
Long-Term Liabilities	1,000,000	300,000
No Par Common Stock	4,000,000	1,000,000
Retained Earnings	2,500,000	1,400,000
Total Equities	$7,800,000	$2,800,000

Other Information:

1. Both Companies use the straight line method for the calculation of amortization.
2. The Prude Company's Sales include sales of $50,000 to the Sybarite Company. Although

this merchandise has been sold by Sybarite, it has not paid Prude for any of this merchandise during the year. Prude has levied an interest charge of $5,000 on this unpaid amount which is also outstanding on December 31, 2008.

3. There have been no additions or disposals of Plant and Equipment by Sybarite since January 1, 2002.
4. During 2008, Prude had Net Income of $1,000,000 and declared dividends of $200,000, while Sybarite had Net Income of $600,000 and declared and paid dividends of $100,000.
5. In each of the years since Prude acquired control over Sybarite, the goodwill arising on this business combination transaction has been tested for impairment. In 2005, a Goodwill Impairment Loss of $42,000 was recognized. No impairment was found in any of the other years since acquisition.

Required: Prepare a consolidated Balance Sheet as at December 31, 2008 for the Prude Company and its subsidiary, the Sybarite Company.

Self Study Problem Five - 4

For the year ending December 31, 2007, the comparative Balance Sheets for the Primate Company and its subsidiary the Savage Company are as follows:

Primate and Savage Companies
Comparative Balance Sheets

	December 31, 2007		December 31, 2006	
	Primate	**Savage**	**Primate**	**Savage**
Cash	$ 660,000	$ 400,000	$1,000,000	$ 200,000
Accounts Receivable	700,000	250,000	500,000	200,000
Inventories	900,000	500,000	1,000,000	400,000
Investments:				
Savage (At Cost)	900,000	N/A	900,000	N/A
Mastodon (At Equity)	250,000	Nil	235,000	Nil
Saber T. (At Cost)	1,500,000	Nil	Nil	Nil
Plant & Equipment (Net)	1,590,000	750,000	1,490,000	700,000
Land	1,000,000	400,000	875,000	500,000
Total Assets	$7,500,000	$2,300,000	$6,000,000	$2,000,000
Current Liabilities	$1,300,000	$ 600,000	$1,000,000	$ 500,000
Long-Term Liabilities	Nil	100,000	Nil	Nil
Common Stock - No Par	3,000,000	500,000	2,000,000	500,000
Retained Earnings	3,200,000	1,100,000	3,000,000	1,000,000
Total Equities	$7,500,000	$2,300,000	$6,000,000	$2,000,000

Other Information:

1. The Primate Company purchased 80 percent of the outstanding voting shares of the Savage Company on January 1, 2002 for $800,000 in cash. On that date, Savage had Retained Earnings of $500,000 and Common Stock - No Par of $500,000. The fair values of the identifiable assets and liabilities of Savage were equal to their carrying values.
2. The Investment in Mastodon was made in 2001 and constitutes a holding of 30 percent of the outstanding voting shares of the Mastodon Company. The Investment was acquired at

book value and there have been no intercompany transactions, other than dividend payments between Primate and Mastodon. Since Primate exercises significant influence over the affairs of Mastodon, it is carried at equity. During 2007, Mastodon had net income of $100,000 and paid dividends of $50,000.

3. On December 31, 2007, Primate acquired 100 percent of the outstanding voting shares of the Saber T. Company. The consideration consisted of $500,000 in cash and Primate Company shares with a fair value of $1,000,000. At the date of the acquisition, the Plant and Equipment of the Saber T. Company had a fair value that was $200,000 in excess of its carrying value. The Plant and Equipment had a remaining useful life of 10 years on this date. On the acquisition date, the Saber T. Company's Balance Sheet was as follows:

Saber T Company
Balance Sheet
As At December 31, 2007

Cash	$ 200,000
Accounts Receivable	200,000
Inventories	400,000
Plant and Equipment (Net)	500,000
Total Assets	$1,300,000
Current Liabilities	$ 100,000
Common Stock - No Par	500,000
Retained Earnings	700,000
Total Equities	$1,300,000

4. During 2007, information on Net Income and dividends paid for the Primate Company and its subsidiaries is as follows:

	Primate	Savage	Saber T.
Net Income	$400,000	$200,000	$225,000
Dividends	200,000	100,000	150,000

5. During 2007, Savage issued long-term bonds with a fair value of $100,000 in return for Plant and Equipment. Savage had no other acquisitions or retirements of Plant and Equipment during 2007.

6. During 2007, Primate acquired Plant and Equipment for cash of $400,000. Plant and Equipment with an original cost of $300,000 and Accumulated Amortization of $200,000 was sold for $200,000.

7. During 2007, Savage sold Land for cash in an arm's length transaction for its carrying value of $100,000. Also during 2007, Primate acquired Land for cash of $125,000.

8. During 2007, $200,000 of the Primate Company's sales were made to the Savage Company. None of this merchandise remains in the December 31, 2007 Inventories of Savage Company. There were no other intercompany inventory sales in 2006 or 2007.

Required:

A. Compute consolidated Net Income for the year ending December 31, 2007 and prepare the consolidated Statement of Retained Earnings for the year ending December 31, 2007 for the Primate Company and its subsidiaries.

B. Prepare the consolidated Cash Flow Statement for the year ending December 31, 2007 for the Primate Company and its subsidiaries.

Self Study Problem Five - 5

On December 31, 2007, the Port Company acquired 30 percent of the outstanding voting shares of the Ship Company for $3,000,000. On December 31, 2008, the Port Company acquired an additional 30 percent of the Ship Company's outstanding voting shares for $3,600,000. The Ship Company's Balance Sheets as at December 31, 2007 and December 31, 2008 were as follows:

Ship Company
Balance Sheets
As At December 31

	2007	2008
Net Monetary Assets	$2,000,000	$3,500,000
Plant And Equipment (Net)	5,000,000	4,500,000
Total Assets	$7,000,000	$8,000,000
Common Stock - No Par	$4,000,000	$4,000,000
Retained Earnings	3,000,000	4,000,000
Total Equities	$7,000,000	$8,000,000

All of the Ship Company's identifiable assets and liabilities had carrying values that were equal to their fair values at both acquisition dates except for a building included in Plant And Equipment. On December 31, 2007, the fair value of the Ship Company's Building was $2,000,000 greater than its carrying value and its remaining useful life on that date was 10 years. At the time of the second purchase, the fair value of the Ship Company's Building was $3,000,000 greater than its carrying value. There had been no additions to the account during the year.

All amortization charges are calculated on a straight line basis for both Companies.

In each of the years since Port acquired shares of the Ship Company, the Goodwill arising from the share purchases has been tested for impairment. No impairment was found in any of the years.

On December 31, 2009, the Balance Sheets of the two Companies were as follows:

Port And Ship Companies
Balance Sheets
As At December 31, 2009

	Port	Ship
Net Monetary Assets	$ 3,400,000	$4,500,000
Investment In Ship (Cost)	6,600,000	N/A
Plant And Equipment (Net)	10,000,000	4,000,000
Total Assets	$20,000,000	$8,500,000
Common Stock - No Par	$10,000,000	$4,000,000
Retained Earnings	10,000,000	4,500,000
Total Equities	$20,000,000	$8,500,000

Required: Prepare, for the Port Company and its subsidiary the Ship Company, a consolidated Balance Sheet as at December 31, 2009.

Self Study Problem Five - 6

Note This problem uses the same data that is found in Self Study Problem Five-1. However, in this case the solution should comply with international financial reporting standards. The data is repeated here for your convenience.

On December 31, 2004, the Pastel Company purchased 90 percent of the outstanding voting shares of the Shade Company for $5,175,000 in cash. On that date, the Shade Company had No Par Common Stock of $2,000,000 and Retained Earnings of $4,000,000. All of the Shade Company's identifiable assets and liabilities had carrying values that were equal to their fair values except for:

1. Accounts Receivable with fair values that were $50,000 less than their carrying values.
2. Land which had a fair value that was $100,000 greater than its carrying value.
3. Equipment which had fair values that were $1,000,000 less than their carrying values and a remaining useful life of 10 years.
4. Long-Term Liabilities which had fair values that were $200,000 less than their carrying values and mature on December 31, 2009.

The Balance Sheets of the Pastel Company and the Shade Company as at December 31, 2009 were as follows:

Pastel and Shade Companies
Balance Sheets
As At December 31, 2009

	Pastel	Shade
Cash And Current Receivables	$ 2,625,000	$ 800,000
Inventories	8,000,000	2,000,000
Equipment (Net)	24,000,000	4,000,000
Buildings (Net)	10,000,000	2,000,000
Investment In Shade (Cost)	5,175,000	N/A
Land	2,000,000	1,200,000
Total Assets	$51,800,000	$10,000,000
Dividends Payable	Nil	$ 100,000
Current Liabilities	$ 1,800,000	900,000
Long-Term Liabilities	10,000,000	1,000,000
No Par Common Stock	20,000,000	2,000,000
Retained Earnings	20,000,000	6,000,000
Total Equities	$51,800,000	$10,000,000

The Income Statements of the Pastel and Shade Companies for the year ending December 31, 2009 were as follows:

Pastel And Shade Companies
Income Statements
For The Year Ending December 31, 2009

	Pastel	Shade
Sales	$8,000,000	$2,000,000
Gain On Sale Of Land	500,000	Nil
Other Revenues	800,000	100,000
Total Revenues	$9,300,000	$2,100,000
Cost Of Goods Sold	$3,800,000	$ 800,000
Amortization Expense	1,400,000	300,000
Other Expenses	2,000,000	400,000
Total Expenses	$7,200,000	$1,500,000
Net Income	$2,100,000	$ 600,000

Other Information:

1. In each of the years since Pastel acquired control over Shade, the Goodwill arising on this business combination transaction has been tested for impairment. After completing the annual impairment test, it was determined that the Goodwill Impairment Loss for 2009 was $15,000. No impairment was found in any of the other years since acquisition.

2. Both Companies use the straight line method to calculate all amortization charges and the First-In, First-Out inventory flow assumption.

3. Pastel uses the cost method to carry its Investment In Shade.

4. The Sales account in the Pastel Company's Income Statement includes only sales of merchandise. All other income is accounted for in Other Revenues or a separate Gain account.

5. During 2009, Pastel charged Shade $100,000 for management fees. None of this amount has been paid during 2009.

6. During 2009, dividends of $200,000 were declared and paid by Pastel and dividends of $100,000 were declared by Shade. On December 31, 2009, the dividends that were declared by the Shade Company during 2009 had not yet been paid.

7. During 2009, Shade sold to Pastel $500,000 worth of merchandise, all of which was resold by Pastel in 2009. Pastel owes Shade $75,000 on December 31, 2009 due to these purchases.

8. During 2009, Pastel sold merchandise to Shade for $150,000. All of this merchandise was resold in 2009. Shade has not paid for these purchases as at December 31, 2009.

Required: Using the recommendations of IFRS No. 3, *Business Combinations*, and IAS No. 27, *Consolidated And Separate Financial Statements*, prepare, for the Pastel Company and its subsidiary, the Shade Company, the following:

A. The consolidated Income Statement for the year ending December 31, 2009.

B. The consolidated Statement Of Retained Earnings for the year ending December 31, 2009.

C. The consolidated Balance Sheet as at December 31, 2009.

Assignment Problems

(The solutions for these problems are only available in the solutions manual that has been provided to your instructor.)

Assignment Problem Five - 1

Note This problem uses the same data that is found in Assignment Problem Five-7. However, in that problem, the solution should comply with international financial reporting standards.

On December 31, 2004, the Percy Company purchased 75 percent of the outstanding voting shares of the Stern Company for $3,000,000 in cash. On that date, Stern had No Par Common Stock of $2,000,000 and Retained Earnings of $1,000,000.

On December 31, 2004 all of the identifiable assets and liabilities of Stern had fair values that were equal to their carrying values with the following exceptions:

1. Inventories with fair values that were $400,000 less than their carrying values.
2. Land with a fair value that was $800,000 greater than its carrying value.
3. Long-Term Liabilities, maturing on January 1, 2010, with fair values that were $200,000 less than their carrying values.

Both Companies use the straight line method to calculate amortization. In its single entity records, Percy carries its investment in Stern at cost.

The Land which was on the books of the Stern Company on December 31, 2004 has not been sold as at December 31, 2009.

Financial statements for Percy and Stern for the year ending December 31, 2009 are as follows:

Income Statements
For The Year Ending December 31, 2009

	Percy	Stern
Merchandise Sales	$5,000,000	$2,000,000
Other Revenues	1,000,000	500,000
Total Revenues	$6,000,000	$2,500,000
Cost Of Goods Sold	$2,000,000	$1,000,000
Amortization Expense	400,000	300,000
Other Expenses	600,000	400,000
Total Expenses	$3,000,000	$1,700,000
Net Income	$3,000,000	$ 800,000

Statements Of Retained Earnings
For The Year Ending December 31, 2009

	Percy	Stern
Opening Balance	$10,000,000	$1,600,000
Net Income	3,000,000	800,000
Balance Available	$13,000,000	$2,400,000
Dividends Declared	(1,000,000)	(400,000)
Closing Balance	$12,000,000	$2,000,000

Balance Sheets
As At December 31, 2009

	Percy	Stern
Cash And Current Receivables	$ 1,500,000	$1,200,000
Note Receivable	1,000,000	Nil
Inventories	4,500,000	1,000,000
Investment In Stern (At Cost)	3,000,000	N/A
Plant And Equipment (Net)	9,000,000	3,000,000
Land	2,000,000	800,000
Total Assets	$21,000,000	$6,000,000
Current Liabilities	$ 500,000	$ 200,000
Long-Term Liabilities	3,500,000	1,800,000
Common Stock - No Par	5,000,000	2,000,000
Retained Earnings	12,000,000	2,000,000
Total Equities	$21,000,000	$6,000,000

Other Information:

1. The Long-Term Liabilities of the Stern Company include a $1,000,000 note that is payable to the Percy Company. During 2009, interest expense on this note was $110,000 and on December 31, 2009, $100,000 of this interest had not been paid by Stern. The note is to be paid on December 31, 2012.
2. In each of the years since Percy acquired control over Stern, the Goodwill arising on this business combination transaction has been tested for impairment. In 2006, a Goodwill Impairment Loss of $50,000 was recognized. No impairment was found in any of the other years since acquisition.
3. During 2009, Stern had sales of $1,500,000 to Percy, while Percy had $500,000 in sales to Stern. All of the merchandise which was transferred in these intercompany sales has been resold during 2009 to companies outside of the consolidated entity.

Required: Prepare, for the Percy Company and its subsidiary, the Stern Company, the following:

A. The consolidated Income Statement for the year ending December 31, 2009.

B. The consolidated Statement Of Retained Earnings for the year ending December 31, 2009.

C. The consolidated Balance Sheet as at December 31, 2009.

Assignment Problem Five - 2

On January 1, 2007, the Perry Company purchased 72 percent of the outstanding voting shares of the Styan Company for $3,975,000 in cash. On that date, the Styan Company had No Par Common Stock of $1,680,000 and Retained Earnings of $3,570,000. All of the Styan Company's identifiable assets and liabilities had carrying values that were equal to their fair values except for:

1. Inventories which had fair values of $1,806,000 and carrying values of $2,037,000.
2. Buildings which had fair values that were $175,000 more than their carrying values and a remaining useful life of 20 years.
3. Land which had a fair value of $1,596,000 and a carrying value of $1,400,000.

4. A Patent with a nil carrying value and a fair value of $154,000. The patent has a remaining life of two years.
5. Long-Term Liabilities which had fair values that were $210,000 more than their carrying values and mature on December 31, 2016.

The Balance Sheets of the Perry Company and the Styan Company as at December 31, 2009 were as follows:

Perry and Styan Companies
Balance Sheets
As At December 31, 2009

	Perry	Styan
Cash	$ 175,000	$ 17,500
Current Receivables	910,000	140,000
Inventories	1,709,750	1,050,000
Equipment (Net)	3,584,000	2,248,750
Buildings (Net)	3,727,500	2,187,500
Investment in Styan (Cost)	3,975,000	N/A
Land	1,406,250	1,400,000
Total Assets	$15,487,500	$7,043,750
Dividends Payable	Nil	$ 70,000
Current Liabilities	$ 840,000	350,000
Long-Term Liabilities	3,587,500	3,064,000
Preferred Stock	280,000	Nil
No Par Common Stock	9,100,000	1,680,000
Retained Earnings	1,680,000	1,879,750
Total Equities	$15,487,500	$7,043,750

The Income Statements of the Perry and Styan Companies for the year ending December 31, 2009 were as follows:

Perry and Styan Companies
Income Statements
For The Year Ending December 31, 2009

	Perry	Styan
Sales	$3,800,000	$1,120,000
Other Revenues	62,400	200,000
Total Revenues	$3,862,400	$1,320,000
Cost of Goods Sold	$1,412,000	$ 623,000
Amortization Expense	525,000	175,000
Other Expenses	1,567,000	235,000
Total Expenses	$3,504,000	$1,033,000
Income Before Extraordinary Items	$ 358,400	$ 287,000
Extraordinary Loss (Net of Taxes of $1,300,000)	Nil	(2,052,500)
Net Income (Loss)	$ 358,400	($1,765,500)

Other Information:

1. In both of the years since Perry acquired control over Styan, the goodwill arising on this business combination transaction has been tested for impairment. No impairment was

found in either 2007 or 2008. However, due to the large loss for 2009, the goodwill related to the purchase of Styan shares has a nil fair value on December 31, 2009.

2. Both Companies use the straight line method to calculate amortization charges and the First-In, First-Out inventory flow assumption.

3. In its single entity records, Perry uses the cost method to carry its Investment In Styan.

4. The Sales account in both Companies' Income Statements include only sales of merchandise. All other income is accounted for in Other Revenues.

5. The Styan Company has sold no Land since January 1, 2007.

6. During 2009, dividends of $175,000 were declared and paid by Perry and dividends of $70,000 were declared by Styan.

7. During 2009, Perry sold to Styan merchandise worth $217,000 which was resold by Styan for a gross profit of $162,000 outside of the consolidated entity in 2009. Styan owes Perry $84,000 on December 31, 2009 due to these purchases.

8. During October, 2009, Styan charged the Perry Company $70,000 for the services of a team of computer programmers. The wages paid to the programmers for this work totalled $58,500. Perry still has a balance of $3,500 outstanding for this charge on December 31, 2009.

Required:

A. Prepare the consolidated Income Statement for the year ending December 31, 2009 of the Perry Company and its subsidiary, the Styan Company.

B. Prepare the consolidated Statement Of Retained Earnings for the year ending December 31, 2009 of the Perry Company and its subsidiary, the Styan Company.

C. Prepare the consolidated Balance Sheet as at December 31, 2009 of the Perry Company and its subsidiary, the Styan Company.

D. Assume that the Perry Company, despite its majority ownership, does not have control over Styan and carries its Investment In Styan using the equity method. Calculate and disclose the amount(s) of investment income that would be shown in the Perry Company's Income Statement under this assumption. (An Income Statement is not required.)

E. Discuss the factors that should be considered when reviewing the issue of whether the Investment in Styan account should be written down on the single entity financial statements of Perry Company.

Assignment Problem Five - 3

On January 1, 2004, the Prospect Company purchases 80 percent of the outstanding voting shares of the Suspect Company for $1,760,000 in cash. On that date, the Shareholders' Equity of the Suspect Company is as follows:

Common Stock - No Par	$1,050,000
Retained Earnings - Unrestricted	560,000
Reserve For Contingencies	140,000
Total	$1,750,000

On the acquisition date, all of the identifiable assets and liabilities of the Suspect Company have fair values that are equal to their carrying values except for a patent. The patent is carried on Suspect's books at $500,000. Its fair value on the acquisition date is $1,100,000 and its remaining useful life on that date is 10 years.

Between January 1, 2004 and December 31, 2009, the Suspect Company earns $980,000 and pays dividends of $280,000. The Company's Reserve For Contingencies is unchanged during this period.

During the year ending December 31, 2009 the Prospect Company has Net Income of $300,000 and Suspect has Net Income of $100,000. Prospect pays no dividends during 2009 while Suspect pays $50,000. On December 31, 2009, the Prospect Company has Retained Earnings of $2,000,000.

Prospect carries its Investment In Suspect at cost and its Net Income includes Investment Income calculated by this method. Both Companies calculate amortization charges using the straight line method and, during the year ending December 31, 2009, there are no intercompany transactions other than dividend payments.

Both companies have a December 31 year end.

Required:

A. Calculate consolidated Net Income for the year ending December 31, 2009 for the Prospect Company and its subsidiary the Suspect Company.

B. Calculate the amounts that would be shown on the consolidated Balance Sheet of the Prospect Company and its subsidiary the Suspect Company, as at December 31, 2009 for the following accounts:

i. Goodwill,
ii. Patent,
iii. Non-Controlling Interest, and
iv. Retained Earnings balance.

Assignment Problem Five - 4

On April 1, 2007, the Perle Company acquired 70 percent of the outstanding voting shares of the Thane Company for $1,785,000 in cash. On this date the book value of the Thane Company's Shareholders' Equity was $2,600,000 and all of the Thane Company's identifiable assets and liabilities had fair values that were equal to their carrying values except for the following:

	Carrying Value	Fair Value
Marketable Securities	$ 28,000	$ 35,000
Fleet of Trucks	324,000	365,000
Division F - Building and Equipment (Net)	631,000	453,000
Land	96,000	118,000
Long-Term Liabilities - Par $2,000,000	1,983,000	2,010,000

The Marketable Securities were sold on March 17, 2008 for $33,000. The fleet of trucks have an estimated remaining useful life of four years on April 1, 2007 and no anticipated salvage value. The Division F Building and Equipment was purchased on April 1, 1995 and had an estimated useful life of 20 years on that date. When purchased they had an anticipated salvage value of $80,000 and there is no change in the estimates of salvage value or total useful life on April 1, 2007. The parcel of Land is being held in anticipation of expansion in 2013. The Long-Term Liabilities are scheduled to mature on April 1, 2013.

Both Companies use the straight line method for amortization calculations and the Perle Company carries its investment in Thane Company using the cost method. The Perle Company's investment income consists of $5,000 in interest revenue and its income from the Thane Company. During the period April 1, 2007 until December 31, 2009, neither the Perle Company nor the Thane Company issue or retire shares of common stock.

For the year ending December 31, 2009, the Income Statements for the Perle Company and the Thane Company are as follows:

Perle and Thane Companies
Income Statements
For The Year Ending December 31, 2009

	Perle	Thane
Sales Revenue	$4,887,000	$1,450,000
Investment Income	29,500	12,000
Total Revenues	$4,916,500	$1,462,000
Cost Of Goods Sold	$2,117,000	$ 829,000
Amortization Expense	935,000	135,000
Other Expenses and Losses	1,284,000	246,000
Total Expenses	$4,336,000	$1,210,000
Net Income	$ 580,500	$ 252,000

Other Information:

1. On January 1, 2009, the Retained Earnings balance of the Perle Company was $8,463,000. During 2009, the Perle Company paid dividends totalling $115,000.
2. Between April 1, 2007 and December 31, 2008, Thane earned Net Income of $192,000 and declared dividends totalling $46,000.
3. In each of the years since Perle acquired control over Thane, the goodwill arising on this business combination transaction has been tested for impairment. No impairment was found in any of the years since acquisition.
4. During 2009, the Thane Company used the services of several of the Perle Company's accountants and agreed to pay a fee of $5,600 for these services. On December 31, 2009, this fee remains unpaid. This amount is included in the Sales Revenues of the Perle Company and in the Other Expenses of the Thane Company. The salaries paid to the accountants by the Perle Company for the work done on the Thane Company amount to $4,200 and are included in the Other Expenses of the Perle Company.
5. On January 1, 2009, the Perle Company rented a building from the Thane Company for a monthly rent of $2,000. On December 31, 2009, the Perle Company owed three months rent. The rent is included in the Sales Revenues of the Thane Company and in the Other Expenses of the Perle Company.

Required:

A. For the year ending December 31, 2009, prepare the consolidated Income Statement and the consolidated Statement Of Retained Earnings of the Perle Company and its subsidiary, the Thane Company.

B. Calculate the Non-Controlling Interest that would be shown in the December 31, 2009 consolidated Balance Sheet of the Perle Company and its subsidiary, the Thane Company.

C. Assume that on December 31, 2009, the Thane Company sold the Division F assets to someone outside the consolidated entity for $380,000, creating a loss of $61,594 on Thane Company's books. The sale consisted of the Building and Equipment which had the fair value change on April 1, 2007. Provide the journal entries to record the effect of the loss on the consolidated Income Statement of the Perle Company and its subsidiary, the Thane Company for the year ending December 31, 2009 assuming:

   i. The loss is included in the Other Expenses and Losses of Thane.

   ii. The loss is classified as a Loss From Discontinued Operations on the Income Statement of Thane.

Assignment Problem Five - 5

The ledger account balances for the Pump Company and the Slump Company on December 31, 2008 and 2009 are as follows:

	December 31, 2009		December 31, 2008	
	Pump	**Slump**	**Pump**	**Slump**
Cash	$ 42,200	$ 69,400	$ 113,400	$ 19,600
Accounts Receivable	99,400	128,400	108,400	63,000
Other Current Receivables	82,600	44,800	64,600	49,000
Inventories	93,200	128,800	99,600	96,800
Investment in Slump (Cost)	356,800	N/A	356,800	N/A
Other Investments (Cost)	21,600	66,800	185,600	66,800
Land	36,400	30,000	57,400	30,000
Buildings	271,600	174,000	213,400	130,000
Equipment	122,000	90,000	96,000	90,000
Dividends Declared	48,000	28,000	Nil	Nil
Total Debits	$1,173,800	$760,200	$1,295,200	$545,200
Bad Debt Allowance	$ 9,000	$ 7,800	$ 8,200	$ 7,400
Accumulated Amortization	139,000	101,200	82,600	62,400
Accounts Payable	45,800	91,800	62,400	73,600
Notes Payable	82,000	50,000	176,800	Nil
Dividends Payable	Nil	28,000	Nil	Nil
Other Accruals	11,800	41,600	25,400	25,200
Taxes Payable	39,200	38,800	73,000	24,600
Bonds Payable	Nil	Nil	60,000	Nil
Common Stock - No Par	584,000	226,400	584,000	226,400
Opening Retained Earnings	222,800	125,600	124,600	77,400
Net Income	40,200	49,000	98,200	48,200
Total Credits	$1,173,800	$760,200	$1,295,200	$545,200

Other Information:

1. On January 2, 2008, the Pump Company acquired from the shareholders of the Slump Company, 90 percent of the Slump Company's outstanding voting shares for the following consideration:

500 Shares of Pump Common Stock - No Par	$200,000
Note Payable - Due June 30, 2011	156,800
Total Consideration	$356,800

   On that date, the Slump Company's identifiable assets and liabilities had carrying values that were equal to their fair values. The excess of the purchase price over Pump's share of these values has been allocated to Goodwill. There was no impairment of this Goodwill in either 2008 or 2009.

   The Note Payable was unexpectedly paid in advance on June 30, 2009. All other Notes Payable present on both December 31, 2008 and 2009 are current.

2. On January 1, 2009, Pump sold Other Investments for proceeds of $202,600. These investments had been carried at a cost of $170,800. Pump also sold Land which had cost $21,000, for proceeds of $37,600.

3. On June 30, 2009, Pump demolished an unneeded Building which had cost $37,800 and had a net book value of $10,800.

4. During 2009, Pump declared and paid cash dividends of $48,000. On December 1, 2009, Slump declared a $28,000 cash dividend. This dividend was payable on January 15, 2010, to holders of record on December 20, 2009. Pump has recorded the dividends in Other Current Receivables. Slump declared no other dividends during 2009.

5. The Pump Company's Bonds Payable were retired in 2009. Cash of $65,000 was paid which included $60,000 in par value, $1,200 in accrued interest and a $3,800 penalty for early retirement.

6. On December 31, 2009, Pump Company's Other Current Receivables include a $50,000 non-interest bearing Note Payable by Slump. Slump Company's December 31, 2009 Accounts Receivable includes $37,000 due from Pump for merchandise purchases. Slump had sold the merchandise to Pump for an amount equal to the cost of the merchandise to Slump. There are no intercompany receivables or payables on December 31, 2008.

Required: Prepare a consolidated Cash Flow Statement for the Pump Company and its subsidiary, the Slump Company for the year ending December 31, 2009.

Assignment Problem Five - 6

The carrying value and fair value of the net identifiable assets of the Slice Company are as follows:

	Carrying Value	Fair Value
December 31, 2007	$4,265,000	$4,365,000
December 31, 2008	$4,865,000	$5,065,000

On December 31, 2007, the Piece Company acquires 20 percent of the outstanding voting shares of the Slice Company for cash of $904,000. The remaining useful life of the Slice Company assets on which the fair value changes exist is 10 years and no salvage value is anticipated.

On December 31, 2008, the Piece Company acquires an additional 50 percent of the outstanding voting shares of the Slice Company for cash of $2,873,000. The remaining life of the Slice Company assets on which the fair value changes exist is 9 years.

On December 31, 2009, the book values of the net identifiable assets of the Piece Company and the Slice Company are as follows:

	Piece	Slice
Total Net Identifiable Assets	$8,973,000	$5,653,000

On December 31, 2009, the Retained Earnings balance of the Piece Company is $4,235,000.

Other Information:

1. Both Companies amortize all assets and liabilities using the straight line method.
2. In both 2008 and 2009, the goodwill arising on the Slice share purchases has been tested for impairment. In 2009, a Goodwill Impairment Loss of $40,250 was recognized. No impairment of the Goodwill was found in 2008.
3. During the period January 1, 2007 through December 31, 2009, neither the Piece Company nor the Slice Company issues or retires any of their shares of common stock.
4. During the period January 1, 2007 through December 31, 2009, the only intercompany transactions were dividends declared and paid to the Piece Company by the Slice Company.

5. The Piece Company carries its Investment In Slice Company using the cost method.

6. There is no Goodwill on the single entity books of either the Piece Company or the Slice Company.

Required: Calculate the amounts that would be shown on the consolidated Balance Sheet of the Piece Company and its subsidiary the Slice Company as at December 31, 2009 for the following accounts:

A. Net Identifiable Assets,

B. Goodwill,

C. Non-Controlling Interest, and

D. Retained Earnings.

Assignment Problem Five - 7

Note This problem uses the same data that is found in Assignment Problem Five-1. However, in this case the solution should comply with international financial reporting standards. The data is repeated here for your convenience.

On December 31, 2004, the Percy Company purchased 75 percent of the outstanding voting shares of the Stern Company for $3,000,000 in cash. On that date, Stern had No Par Common Stock of $2,000,000 and Retained Earnings of $1,000,000.

On December 31, 2004 all of the identifiable assets and liabilities of Stern had fair values that were equal to their carrying values with the following exceptions:

1. Inventories with fair values that were $400,000 less than their carrying values.
2. Land with a fair value that was $800,000 greater than its carrying value.
3. Long-Term Liabilities, maturing on January 1, 2010, with fair values that were $200,000 less than their carrying values.

Both Companies use the straight line method to calculate amortization. In its single entity records, Percy carries its investment in Stern at cost.

The Land which was on the books of the Stern Company on December 31, 2004 has not been sold as at December 31, 2009.

Financial statements for Percy and Stern for the year ending December 31, 2009 are as follows:

Income Statements
For The Year Ending December 31, 2009

	Percy	Stern
Merchandise Sales	$5,000,000	$2,000,000
Other Revenues	1,000,000	500,000
Total Revenues	$6,000,000	$2,500,000
Cost Of Goods Sold	$2,000,000	$1,000,000
Amortization Expense	400,000	300,000
Other Expenses	600,000	400,000
Total Expenses	$3,000,000	$1,700,000
Net Income	$3,000,000	$ 800,000

Statements Of Retained Earnings
For The Year Ending December 31, 2009

	Percy	Stern
Opening Balance	$10,000,000	$1,600,000
Net Income	3,000,000	800,000
Balance Available	$13,000,000	$2,400,000
Dividends Declared	(1,000,000)	(400,000)
Closing Balance	$12,000,000	$2,000,000

Balance Sheets
As At December 31, 2009

	Percy	Stern
Current Assets:		
Cash And Current Receivables	$ 1,500,000	$1,200,000
Non-Current Assets:		
Note Receivable	1,000,000	Nil
Inventories	4,500,000	1,000,000
Investment In Stern (At Cost)	3,000,000	N/A
Plant And Equipment (Net)	9,000,000	3,000,000
Land	2,000,000	800,000
Total Assets	$21,000,000	$6,000,000
Current Liabilities	$ 500,000	$ 200,000
Long-Term Liabilities	3,500,000	1,800,000
Shareholders' Equity:		
Common Stock - No Par	5,000,000	2,000,000
Retained Earnings	12,000,000	2,000,000
Total Equities	$21,000,000	$6,000,000

Other Information:

1. The Long-Term Liabilities of the Stern Company include a $1,000,000 note that is payable to the Percy Company. During 2009, interest expense on this note was $110,000 and on December 31, 2009, $100,000 of this interest had not been paid by Stern. The note is to be paid on December 31, 2012.
2. In each of the years since Percy acquired control over Stern, the Goodwill arising on this business combination transaction has been tested for impairment. In 2006, a Goodwill Impairment Loss of $50,000 was recognized. No impairment was found in any of the other years since acquisition.
3. During 2009, Stern had sales of $1,500,000 to Percy, while Percy had $500,000 in sales to Stern. All of the merchandise which was transferred in these intercompany sales has been resold during 2009 to companies outside of the consolidated entity.

Required: Using the recommendations of IFRS No. 3, *Business Combinations*, and IAS No. 27, *Consolidated And Separate Financial Statements*, prepare, for the Percy Company and its subsidiary, the Stern Company, the following:

A. The consolidated Income Statement for the year ending December 31, 2009.

B. The consolidated Statement Of Retained Earnings for the year ending December 31, 2009.

C. The consolidated Balance Sheet as at December 31, 2009.

Consolidation Subsequent To Acquisition (Including Unrealized Intercompany Profits)

Unrealized Intercompany Profits

Basic Concepts

6-1. From the point of view of the consolidated entity, profits on intercompany transactions are said to be unrealized until verified by an arm's-length transaction with an individual or organization that is outside or independent of the consolidated entity.

6-2. For example, if a subsidiary sells merchandise to a parent company and recognizes a profit on the transaction, the profit of the subsidiary is said to be unrealized until such time as the parent resells the merchandise outside of the consolidated entity.

6-3. Correspondingly, if there is an intercompany sale of a capital asset, any gain or loss recognized by the vendor is unrealized until such time as the purchaser either sells the asset or uses it up.

6-4. To say that these profits are unrealized from the point of view of the consolidated entity is the equivalent of saying that they do not exist from the consolidated point of view. This problem is the major focus of Chapter 6. We will be concerned with introducing procedures for the elimination of these unrealized intercompany profits in the preparation of consolidated financial statements.

6-5. We would also note the possibility of unrealized intercompany losses. Similar procedures will be required when such losses arise. In either case, the required procedures will involve adjustments to both expenses and revenues in the consolidated Income Statement, as well as to assets and liabilities in the consolidated Balance Sheet.

6-6. The problem of unrealized intercompany profits should not be confused with the problem of intercompany expenses and revenues. While they are often related, they should be dealt with as two separate and distinct issues. For example, if there is an intercompany payment of interest on a note that is carried on both companies' books at face value, there is an intercompany expense and revenue but no unrealized intercompany profit or loss.

6-7. In other situations, an unrealized profit may arise at the time of an intercompany expense and revenue. This would be the case, for example, if there was an intercompany sale of merchandise. Note, however, if the purchasing company has resold the merchandise to parties outside the consolidated entity, there will still be an intercompany expense and revenue to be eliminated. However, there will not be an intercompany unrealized profit.

6-8. A final point here is that a profit that is unrealized in one accounting period may become realized in a subsequent period. If, for example, the closing inventories of a subsidiary contained goods purchased from the parent, any profit recorded by the parent on the sale of these goods is unrealized and must not be included in the consolidated figures. However, the closing inventories that contained the unrealized profit are likely to be sold during the following accounting period. If the goods are sold to a party outside of the consolidated entity, the parent company's profit becomes realized at that point and should be included in the consolidated income figures.

6-9. The point being made here is that the procedures that will be developed in this Chapter must deal with both the removal of unrealized intercompany profits, and with adding them back when they become realized in some future period or periods.

Types Of Unrealized Intercompany Profits

6-10. From a conceptual point of view, all types of unrealized intercompany profits are the same. However, in terms of the procedures to be used in preparing consolidated financial statements, we will find it useful to classify such profits into three categories. These categories are based on the type of asset being sold and can be described as follows:

1. **Capital Assets With Unlimited Lives.** The primary example of this situation would be intercompany sales of land.
2. **Capital Assets With Limited Lives.** These assets are subject to amortization and would include plant and equipment, intangible assets with limited lives and natural resources.
3. **Current Assets.** The most common example of this situation would be intercompany sales of merchandise or manufactured items that are being held for resale.

6-11. In this Chapter's comprehensive example we will find that the procedures are somewhat different for each of these categories.

Conceptual Alternatives In The Consolidated Income Statement

Downstream Unrealized Profits

6-12. With respect to downstream profits (unrealized profits resulting from the parent recording a profit on a sale to a subsidiary are commonly referred to as downstream profits), there are no conceptual alternatives. Since the profit is that of the parent company, no non-controlling interest is present. As a consequence, all such profits will be subject to 100 percent elimination. The elimination will, of course, be charged against consolidated Net Income and consolidated Retained Earnings.

Upstream Unrealized Profits

6-13. With upstream profits (unrealized profits resulting from the subsidiary recording a profit on a sale to the parent are commonly referred to as upstream profits), there is the possibility of a non-controlling interest being present. Such a non-controlling interest would have a claim on the profits of the subsidiary and, as was the case with other consolidation procedures, this would raise the question of how this non-controlling interest should be dealt with in the consolidated financial statements. A simple example will be used to illustrate these conceptual alternatives. The basic data for this example is as follows:

Example The Play Company owns 70 percent of the outstanding voting shares of the Stay Company. The purchase was made at a time when all of the identifiable assets and liabilities of the Stay Company had carrying values that were equal to their fair values. The purchase price was equal to 70 percent of the carrying value of the Stay Company's Shareholders' Equity. In a subsequent year, the Income Statements of the two Companies are as follows:

Play And Stay Companies
Condensed Income Statements

	Play	Stay
Sales Revenue	$7,500,000	$2,200,000
Gain On Sale Of Land To Play Company	Nil	400,000
Total Revenues	$7,500,000	$2,600,000
Expenses	5,600,000	1,900,000
Net Income	$1,900,000	$ 700,000

Proprietary Concept Solution

6-14. You will recall that under the proprietary conceptual approach, the expenses and revenues that are disclosed in the consolidated Income Statement consist of 100 percent of the parent company's expenses and revenues plus a share of the subsidiary's expenses and revenues that is based on the parent company's ownership interest (70 percent in this example). This requires the elimination of the non-controlling interest's $120,000 share of the gain.

6-15. In addition, because the Gain On Sale Of Land is an unrealized intercompany profit, the parent's $280,000 share of this item would also be removed. The resulting consolidated Income Statement would appear as follows:

Play Company And Subsidiary
Consolidated Income Statement
(Proprietary Approach)

Sales Revenue [$7,500,000 + (70%)($2,200,000)]	$9,040,000
Gain On Sale Of Land To Play Company [(70%)($400,000) - $280,000]	Nil
Total Revenues	$9,040,000
Expenses [$5,600,000 + (70%)($1,900,000)]	6,930,000
Consolidated Net Income	$2,110,000

6-16. As was the case when this concept was illustrated in Chapter 5, the removal of the non-controlling interest's share of the individual expenses and revenues eliminates the need to disclose a Non-Controlling Interest in the consolidated Income Statement. With respect to the treatment of the unrealized intercompany profit, we eliminated the non-controlling interest's share as part of the general application of the proprietary concept. The balance, or the parent company's share, was removed because it was unrealized.

6-17. The consolidated Net Income of $2,110,000 can be verified by taking Play Company's Net Income of $1,900,000 plus $210,000 or 70 percent of Stay Company's realized income of $300,000 ($700,000 - $400,000).

Parent Company Concept Solution

6-18. This conceptual approach views the non-controlling interest as a part of the consolidated entity and, as a consequence, the consolidated Income Statement would include 100 percent of the expenses and revenues of both the parent and the subsidiary company. With respect to the nature of the non-controlling interest's participation in the consolidated entity, it is viewed as being a creditor-like interest, somewhat akin to an issue of long-term debt.

6-19. Given this view, the Non-Controlling Interest would not be adjusted for its share of unrealized intercompany profits. Further, the non-controlling interest in the income of the consolidated entity would be viewed as a claim analogous to interest charges on creditor interests and would be deducted in the computation of consolidated Net Income. Based on this approach, the consolidated Income Statement would appear as follows:

Play Company And Subsidiary
Consolidated Income Statement
(Parent Company Approach)

Sales Revenue ($7,500,000 + $2,200,000)	$9,700,000
Gain On Sale Of Land To Play Company ($400,000 - $280,000)	120,000
Total Revenues	$9,820,000
Total Expenses ($5,600,000 + $1,900,000)	7,500,000
Combined Income	$2,320,000
Non-Controlling Interest [(30%)($700,000)]	210,000
Consolidated Net Income	$2,110,000

6-20. Note that this is the same consolidated Net Income that we arrived at under the proprietary approach, indicating that in some respects, the parent company approach is simply a modified version of the proprietary approach.

6-21. Also note that the Non-Controlling Interest continues to be based on the reported income of the subsidiary. This result, which is inherent in the application of the parent company approach, could only be achieved in this situation by leaving the non-controlling interest's share of the unrealized intercompany profit in the consolidated revenues.

Entity Concept Solution

6-22. You will recall that under the entity approach, the non-controlling interest is viewed as a part of the consolidated entity. However, in contrast to the parent company approach, the non-controlling interest here is viewed as an additional class of owner's equity. It would follow that the non-controlling interest should be dealt with in a manner that is equivalent to the treatment accorded the controlling interest.

6-23. With respect to unrealized intercompany profits of the subsidiary company, this view would require the elimination of both the non-controlling and the controlling interests' shares of such profits with the reduction in income being charged in a proportionate manner to the two respective interests. This approach is normally referred to as 100 percent pro rata elimination of subsidiary unrealized profits. It is illustrated in the following consolidated Income Statement:

Play Company And Subsidiary
Consolidated Income Statement
(Entity Approach)

Sales Revenue ($7,500,000 + $2,200,000)	$9,700,000
Gain On Sale Of Land To Play Company ($400,000 - $400,000)	Nil
Total Revenues	$9,700,000
Expenses ($5,600,000 + $1,900,000)	7,500,000
Consolidated Net Income	$2,200,000

6-24. Note that the consolidated Net Income is equal to the sum of the two Companies' Net Incomes ($1,900,000 + $700,000), less the $400,000 unrealized intercompany profit. No Non-Controlling Interest is shown in the preceding Income Statement. Rather, it would be shown in the consolidated Statement Of Retained Earnings as a distribution of consolidated Net Income.

6-25. Note that this treatment is analogous to the treatment that would be given to dividends on preferred shares and that this is consistent with the entity concept view that the non-controlling interest is an equity interest.

6-26. Because we have eliminated 100 percent of the unrealized intercompany profit, the non-controlling interest in the consolidated Statement Of Retained Earnings would be $90,000. This is 30 percent of $300,000 (the reported income of the Stay Company of $700,000, less the unrealized intercompany profit of $400,000).

CICA Handbook Requirements

6-27. The Canadian requirements for dealing with unrealized intercompany profits in consolidated financial statements can be found in two Paragraphs of the *CICA Handbook*. The first is as follows:

> **Paragraph 1600.30** *Unrealized intercompany gains or losses arising subsequent to the date of an acquisition on assets remaining within the consolidated group should be eliminated. The amount of elimination from assets should not be affected by the existence of a non-controlling interest.* (April, 1975)

6-28. This calls for 100 percent elimination of all unrealized intercompany profits but does not indicate specifically whose interest should be charged with the elimination. This latter question is clarified as follows:

> **Paragraph 1600.32** *Where there is an unrealized intercompany gain or loss recognized by a subsidiary company in which there is a non-controlling interest, such gain or loss should be eliminated proportionately between the parent and non-controlling interest in that company's income.* (April, 1975)

6-29. Taken together, these two Paragraphs call for 100 percent, pro rata elimination of unrealized intercompany profits. This, of course, is an adoption of the entity approach for dealing with this issue. It is somewhat difficult to understand this Recommendation as, in dealing with most of the other issues in consolidation, the *CICA Handbook* has taken the view that the parent company approach is the most appropriate conceptual alternative.

6-30. While we have already noted our disagreement with the parent company view of the nature of the non-controlling interest, we would have found its adoption considerably more acceptable had it been applied in a consistent manner. However, this is not the case and this inconsistency in dealing with unrealized intercompany profits is one of the major sources of confusion and difficulty in the preparation of consolidated financial statements.

6-31. Using the data for the example in Paragraph 6-13, the consolidated Income Statement of the Play Company and its subsidiary which would comply with the requirements of the *CICA Handbook* would be as follows:

Play Company And Subsidiary
Consolidated Income Statement

Sales Revenue ($7,500,000 + $2,200,000)	$9,700,000
Gain On The Sale Of Land To Play Company ($400,000 - $400,000)	Nil
Total Revenues	$ 9,700,000
Expenses ($5,600,000 + $1,900,000)	7,500,000
Combined Income	$2,200,000
Non-Controlling Interest [(30%)($700,000 - $400,000)]	90,000
Consolidated Net Income	$2,110,000

6-32. This is the same consolidated Net Income that was computed under the parent company approach. However, the non-controlling share of the unrealized profit has been removed from both Total Revenues and the Non-Controlling Interest.

Exercise Six-1

Subject: Consolidated Income Statement - Current Canadian Standards

Note This Exercise is identical to Exercise Five-1 except for the unrealized profits.

On January 1, 2007, Part Company acquires 65 percent of the outstanding shares of Seam Company. At this time, all of the identifiable assets and liabilities of Seam had fair values that were equal to the carrying values. The cost of the shares was equal to 65 percent of the Shareholders' Equity of Seam. The single entity Income Statements for Part Company and Seam Company, for the year ending December 31, 2007, are as follows:

Part and Seam Companies
Income Statements
Year Ending December 31, 2007

	Part Company	Seam Company
Revenues	$982,000	$463,000
Expenses:		
Cost Of Goods Sold	$448,000	$219,000
Other Expenses	374,000	115,000
Total Expenses	$822,000	$334,000
Income Before Results Of Discontinued Operations	$160,000	$129,000
Loss From Discontinued Operations	Nil	(63,000)
Net Income	$160,000	$ 66,000

The 2007 Revenues of Seam Company include a $75,000 gain resulting from the sale of land to Part Company. Also included in Seam's Revenues are $82,000 in merchandise sales to Part Company. The goods are priced to provide a gross margin of 40 percent on sales prices and have all been resold by Part Company during 2007.

Prepare the consolidated Income Statement for Part Company and its subsidiary Seam Company, for the year ending December 31, 2007. Your answer should comply with the current recommendations of the *CICA Handbook*.

End of Exercise. Solution available in Study Guide.

Comprehensive Example - Open Trial Balance With Investment At Cost

Basic Data

6-33. We will now turn our attention to a comprehensive example that will illustrate in greater detail the treatment of unrealized intercompany profits. We will use the same basic problem that was used in the comprehensive example in Chapter 5. However, in this Chapter, unrealized intercompany profits have been added. Also, as was the case in Chapter 5, we will deal with two versions of this problem, both with the investment in the subsidiary being carried by the cost method on the books of the parent company.

6-34. The basic data for this open trial balance version of our comprehensive problem is as follows:

On January 1, 2005, the Pleigh Company purchases 80 percent of the outstanding shares of the Sleigh Company for $3,200,000 in cash. On that date, the Sleigh Company had No Par Common Stock of $2,000,000 and Retained Earnings of $1,500,000. On December 31, 2009, the adjusted trial balances of the Pleigh Company and its subsidiary, the Sleigh Company are as follows:

	Pleigh	Sleigh
Cash	$ 500,000	$ 300,000
Current Receivables	800,000	400,000
Inventories	2,500,000	1,700,000
Long-Term Note Receivable	200,000	Nil
Investment In Sleigh - At Cost	3,200,000	N/A
Land	1,500,000	1,000,000
Plant And Equipment (Net)	4,500,000	1,900,000
Cost Of Goods Sold	2,800,000	1,500,000
Amortization Expense	200,000	100,000
Other Expenses	364,000	616,000
Interest Expense	240,000	84,000
Dividends Declared	350,000	100,000
Total Debits	$17,154,000	$7,700,000
Current Liabilities	$ 500,000	$ 200,000
Long-Term Liabilities	2,000,000	700,000
No Par Common Stock	8,000,000	2,000,000
Retained Earnings (January 1)	2,550,000	2,300,000
Sales	4,000,000	2,500,000
Interest Revenue	24,000	Nil
Dividend Revenue	80,000	Nil
Total Credits	$17,154,000	$7,700,000

	Pleigh	Sleigh
January 1, 2009 Retained Earnings	$ 2,550,000	$ 2,300,000
2009 Net Income	500,000	200,000
Dividends Declared	(350,000)	(100,000)
December 31, 2009 Retained Earnings	$ 2,700,000	$2,400,000

Other Information:

1. At the date of Pleigh Company's acquisition of the Sleigh Company's shares, all of the identifiable assets and liabilities of the Sleigh Company had fair valJues that were equal to their carrying values except:

- Inventories which had fair values that were $100,000 more than their carrying values,
- Land with a fair value that was $150,000 less than its carrying value, and
- Plant And Equipment which had a fair value that was $250,000 greater than its carrying value.

The Plant And Equipment had a remaining useful life on the acquisition date of 20 years while the Inventories that were present on the acquisition date were sold during the year ending December 31, 2005. The Land is still on the books of the Sleigh Company on December 31, 2009. Both companies use the straight line method to calculate amortization.

2. In each of the years since Pleigh acquired control over Sleigh, the goodwill arising on this business combination transaction has been tested for impairment. No impairment was found in any of the years since acquisition.

3. Sleigh Company's Sales during 2009 include sales of $300,000 to Pleigh Company. The December 31, 2009 Inventories of the Pleigh Company contain $100,000 of this merchandise purchased from Sleigh Company during 2009. In addition, the January 1, 2009 Inventories of the Pleigh Company contained $70,000 in merchandise purchased from Sleigh Company during 2008. All intercompany sales are priced to provide the selling company a gross margin on sales price of 40 percent.

4. On December 31, 2009, the Pleigh Company is holding Sleigh Company's long-term note payable in the amount of $200,000. Interest at 12 percent is payable on July 1 of each year. Pleigh Company has been holding this note since July 1, 2007.

5. During 2007, the Pleigh Company sold Land to the Sleigh Company for $100,000 in cash. The Land had a carrying value on the books of the Pleigh Company of $75,000.

6. During 2008, the Sleigh Company sold Land to the Pleigh Company for $150,000. This Land had a carrying value on the books of the Sleigh Company of $110,000.

7. On December 31, 2007, the Sleigh Company sold Equipment to the Pleigh Company for $600,000. The Equipment had originally cost the Sleigh Company $800,000 and, at the time of the intercompany sale, had accumulated amortization of $350,000. On this date, it was estimated that the remaining useful life of the Equipment was three years with no net salvage value.

Required: Prepare a consolidated Income Statement and a consolidated Statement Of Retained Earnings for the year ending December 31, 2009 and a consolidated Balance Sheet as at December 31, 2009 for the Pleigh Company and its subsidiary, the Sleigh Company.

Procedural Approach

6-35. The same basic approach that was used in solving the comprehensive problem in Chapter 5 will be used here. Some modifications will be generated by the presence of unrealized intercompany profits. These modifications will be mentioned briefly here and described in detail in the solution which follows:

Step A This step will not be changed by the inclusion of unrealized intercompany profits.

Step B The adjustments and eliminations that were introduced in this Step in Chapter 5 will remain the same. However, the presence of unrealized intercompany profits will require that additional eliminations be made.

Step C From a conceptual point of view, this Step is unchanged from Chapter 5. However, the fact that the *CICA Handbook* requires the use of the entity approach for the elimination of unrealized intercompany profits creates significant complications in determining the appropriate distribution of the subsidiary's retained earnings since acquisition.

Step A Procedures

Investment Analysis

6-36. The following investment analysis is unchanged from its presentation of this comprehensive problem in Chapter 5:

	80 Percent	100 Percent
Investment Cost	$3,200,000	$4,000,000
Sleigh Shareholders' Equity At Acquisition	(2,800,000)	(3,500,000)
Differential	$ 400,000	$ 500,000
Fair Value Changes:		
Increase On Inventories	(80,000)	(100,000)
Decrease On Land	120,000	150,000
Increase On Plant And Equipment	(200,000)	(250,000)
Goodwill	$ 240,000	$ 300,000

Investment Elimination

6-37. The investment elimination entry would also be unchanged. It is as follows:

No Par Common Stock	$2,000,000	
Retained Earnings	1,500,000	
Plant And Equipment (Net)	200,000	
Inventories	80,000	
Goodwill	240,000	
Land		$ 120,000
Non-Controlling Interest		700,000
Investment In Sleigh		3,200,000

Step B(1) - Intercompany Assets And Liabilities

6-38. The entries for the elimination of intercompany assets and liabilities are unchanged from Chapter 5. They are as follows:

Long-Term Liabilities	$200,000	
Long-Term Note Receivable		$200,000
Current Liabilities	$12,000	
Current Receivables		$12,000

Step B(2) - Realization Of Fair Value Changes

6-39. The entries required for the realization or amortization of fair value changes are unchanged from the Chapter 5 version of this comprehensive problem. As the Land is still on the books of Sleigh, no entry is required to adjust the fair value change on this account. The entries are as follows:

Retained Earnings - Sleigh's Opening	$80,000	
Inventories		$80,000
Retained Earnings - Sleigh's Opening	$40,000	
Amortization Expense	10,000	
Plant And Equipment (Net)		$50,000

Step B(3) - Goodwill Impairment

6-40. The Other Information in our comprehensive problem notes that, while goodwill has been tested for impairment in each year since the acquisition of Sleigh Company occurred, no impairment has been found. As a consequence, no Step B(3) entry is required in this problem.

Step B(4) - Intercompany Expenses And Revenues

6-41. The entries for the elimination of intercompany expenses and revenues are unchanged from Chapter 5. They are as follows:

Sales	$300,000	
Cost Of Goods Sold		$300,000
Interest Revenue	$ 24,000	
Interest Expense		$ 24,000

6-42. Note that under our procedures, the entry for eliminating the intercompany expense and revenue related to the sale of merchandise has not been affected by the fact that a part of the goods remain in the inventories of the purchasing company. That is, we continue to eliminate 100 percent of the intercompany amount. While there are other approaches to dealing with intercompany merchandise sales, we believe that it is best to leave the intercompany expense and revenue procedure unchanged by the presence of an intercompany inventory profit.

6-43. Using this approach, an additional entry will be required to remove the unrealized profit from the closing inventories of the Pleigh Company. This, however, will not alter the fact that we always eliminate 100 percent of intercompany expenses and revenues. This procedure will be discussed more fully when we deal with the unrealized profits in the opening and closing Inventories.

Step B(5) - Intercompany Dividends

6-44. The entry to eliminate the effects of intercompany dividends is unchanged from the Chapter 5 example. It is as follows:

Dividend Revenue	$80,000	
Non-Controlling Interest (Balance Sheet)	20,000	
Dividends Declared		$100,000

Step B(6) - Unrealized Intercompany Profits

Elimination Of Unrealized Profits

6-45. The only new material in this problem is the addition of unrealized intercompany profits. Four such items have been added:

- There is a downstream unrealized profit resulting from Pleigh Company's 2007 sale of Land to Sleigh Company.
- There is an upstream unrealized profit resulting from Sleigh Company's 2008 sale of Land to Pleigh Company.
- There are unrealized upstream profits in both the opening and closing inventories of Pleigh, resulting from Sleigh's sales of merchandise to that company in 2008 and 2009. Recognition will also have to be given to the fact that the opening inventory profit that was unrealized at the beginning of 2009 has become realized during 2009.
- There is an upstream unrealized profit resulting from Sleigh Company's 2007 sale of Plant And Equipment to Pleigh Company. Recognition will also have to be given to the fact that a portion of this profit has become realized in each year subsequent to the year of the sale.

6-46. The presence of these unrealized intercompany profits creates the need to introduce the final procedures that are required in the preparation of basic consolidated financial statements. The first of these procedures involves the elimination of any unrealized profits that are present at the end of the current period and can be stated as follows:

Step B-6(a) Procedure Eliminate 100 percent of all unrealized intercompany profits (losses) that are present in the single entity financial statements. There are three groups of such profits to consider:

1. Profits that were recognized in the single entity statements of the parent or subsidiary in a previous period, remain unrealized at the beginning of the current period, and are realized during the current period (for example, unrealized profits in beginning of the period inventories that are sold during the current period). Such profits will be deducted from the opening retained earnings of the company that recognized them in their single entity financial statements. Subsequently, they will be added back to income through an adjustment of current expenses or revenues.

2. Profits that were recognized in the single entity statement of the parent or subsidiary in the current period and remain unrealized at the end of the current period (for example, unrealized profits on current period inventory sales). These profits will be removed from current income through an adjustment of the current expenses or revenues. Note that 100 percent of the profit will be removed, without regard to whether it is an upstream profit or a downstream profit. If it is an upstream profit, its removal will reduce both consolidated Net Income and the Non-Controlling Interest that is included in the consolidated Income Statement.

3. Profits that were recognized in the single entity statement of the parent or subsidiary in the current or a previous period, and remain unrealized at the end of the current period (for example, an unrealized profit in the previous year on the sale of a machine with a four year life). These profits will be removed from both the opening and the closing retained earnings of the company that recognized them in their single entity financial statements. If some part of the profit is realized during the current period, this will be recognized through an adjustment of current expenses or revenues. In such cases, the adjustment to the opening retained earnings will differ from the adjustment to the closing retained earnings.

6-47. While all of the references in the preceding paragraphs are to unrealized profits, there is also the possibility of unrealized losses resulting from intercompany transactions. While the concepts involved with losses are the same as with unrealized profits, the applicable signs will be reversed (e.g., unrealized losses will be added back to income, rather than deducted as is the case with unrealized profits).

Realization Of Previously Unrealized Profits

6-48. We have noted previously that profits that are unrealized from a consolidated point of view in one period, may become realized in subsequent periods. If a parent sells merchandise to a subsidiary during 2007 and that merchandise remains in the December 31, 2007 Inventories of the subsidiary, the profit is unrealized and must be eliminated in the preparation of the 2007 consolidated financial statements.

6-49. However, in most situations, the subsidiary will sell this merchandise during 2008, thereby realizing the profit from the point of view of the consolidated entity. As the profit will not be included in the 2008 single entity income records of the parent company, it must be added back in the preparation of consolidated financial statements. In other words, unrealized intercompany profits and losses must be eliminated in the preparation of the 2007 consolidated financial statements, with these amounts normally being added back in the preparation of the 2008 consolidated financial statements. While Step B-5(a) can be used to eliminate the 2007 profit, we need an additional procedure to record the 2008 realization of this profit. This procedure can be described as follows:

> **Step B-6(b) Procedure** Recognize the amount of previously unrealized intercompany profits or losses that have become realized during the period, either through the sale of the related asset or through usage of that asset. The amount that was previously unrealized from the consolidated point of view would be a deduction from the opening single entity retained earnings of the parent or subsidiary company. To the extent the profit has become realized during the period, it will be included in

the current consolidated Net Income through an adjustment of an expense or revenue. Any amount of the profit that remains unrealized at the end of the period will be deducted from the closing retained earnings of the relevant parent or subsidiary. As was the case with Step B-6(a), 100 percent of the previously unrealized profit will be recognized, without regard to whether it is upstream or downstream. If it is an upstream profit, the addition will increase both consolidated Net Income and the Non-Controlling Interest in the Income Statement.

6-50. In the case of intercompany profits on inventories or non-depreciable assets, the realization will take place through a sale transaction that occurs in a single accounting period. This means that Step B-6(a) will be first implemented in the period in which the parent or subsidiary records the unrealized profit and will continue to be applied until the relevant asset is sold. In the period of sale, Step B-6(b) will be used to recognize the realization of the profit in the consolidated financial statements. In other words, for these types of unrealized intercompany profits, Steps B-6(a) and B-6(b) will be applied separately.

6-51. In contrast, when the unrealized profit is related to the sale of a depreciable asset, the profit becomes realized through usage of the asset. Perhaps the best way to understand this is to think of a depreciable asset as a bundle of economic services. In effect, these services are being sold on a piecemeal basis as the asset is used. This means that the intercompany profit will become realized as the asset is being amortized.

6-52. Because this realization process is carried out over several accounting periods, we have generally found it easier to net Steps B-6(a) and B-6(b). That is, when dealing with unrealized profits resulting from the intercompany sale of depreciable assets, we will not use separate entries to record the unrealized amount and the amount realized during subsequent periods. Rather, we will use a single net entry that reflects the unrealized amount at the beginning of the period (a Retained Earnings adjustment), the amount realized during the current period (an adjustment of a current expense or revenue), and the remaining unrealized amount at the end of the current period (an adjustment of the relevant asset balance).

Presentation Of Material

6-53. In presenting this material on unrealized intercompany profits, we will often provide you with the entries that were recorded in the single entity records of the parent or subsidiary companies. Such entries are certainly not a required part of the consolidation procedures. However, we believe that the best way to understand this difficult material is to compare the values that are contained in the underlying records of the individual companies with the amounts that are required for consolidation purposes. Once these amounts are carefully established, the appropriate adjustment or elimination becomes a relatively simple bookkeeping problem.

6-54. We will also consider the consolidation entries that were required in the year in which the intercompany transaction took place, even when this is not the current year. While these entries are not required in solving the problem under consideration, they do serve to enhance your understanding of the procedures required in dealing with unrealized intercompany profits.

Step B(6) - Downstream Profit On Land

Year Of Sale Procedures

6-55. In 2007, Pleigh Company sold Land with a carrying value of $75,000 to Sleigh Company for $100,000. To record this transaction, the following entry was made in Pleigh's single entity records:

Cash	$100,000	
Land		$75,000
Gain On Sale Of Land		25,000

6-56. At the same time, the Sleigh Company would have recorded the purchase of Land in its single entity records as follows:

Land	$100,000	
Cash		$100,000

6-57. From the point of view of the consolidated entity, this transaction did not occur. This would mean that the Land should still be in the consolidated statements at the old value of $75,000 and that no Gain On Sale should be included in consolidated Net Income. The Step B-6(a) elimination entry which would have accomplished this result in 2007 would be as follows:

Gain On Sale Of Land	$25,000	
Land		$25,000

6-58. This restores the Land value to $75,000 and removes the gain from the records of the Pleigh Company. While this entry would have been made in the process of preparing consolidated financial statements in 2007, it was a working paper entry and the unadjusted values would still remain in the records of the two Companies. That is, the Land would still be on the Sleigh Company's books at $100,000 and the $25,000 Gain would be included in the Retained Earnings of the Pleigh Company. Consequently, until the land is resold to an arm's length entity, in every year subsequent to 2007 (including the current year), the following elimination entry would be required:

Retained Earnings - Pleigh's Opening	$25,000	
Land		$25,000

6-59. You should note that since this is a downstream profit, this elimination will have no effect on the Non-Controlling Interest in either the consolidated Income Statement or the consolidated Balance Sheet.

Sale In Future Period

6-60. As noted, the gain on the Land would remain unrealized until such time as the asset is sold outside the consolidated entity. In the year in which such a sale takes place, separate entries would be required for Steps B-6(a) and B-6(b). They would be as follows:

Retained Earnings - Pleigh's Opening	$25,000	
Land		$25,000
Land	$25,000	
Gain On Sale Of Land		$25,000

6-61. This Gain would be added to any additional gain recorded on the sale by Sleigh in its single entity records and the total would be disclosed in the consolidated Income Statement. If, for example, Sleigh had sold the Land for $130,000, they would have recorded a gain of $30,000 ($130,000 - $100,000) in their records. This adjustment would result in a total gain of $55,000 ($30,000 + $25,000) being shown in the consolidated Income Statement.

6-62. Subsequent to a sale of the Land, no further entries would be required and the Gain would become a legitimate part of the consolidated Retained Earnings.

Step B(6) - Upstream Profit On Land

Year Of Sale Procedures

6-63. With respect to the 2008 transaction in which Sleigh sold Land with a carrying value of $110,000 to Pleigh for $150,000, the procedures are basically the same as those required on the downstream sale. In the underlying records of the two Companies, Sleigh would have recorded the sale of Land and Pleigh would have recorded the purchase as follows:

Cash	$150,000	
Land		$110,000
Gain On Sale Of Land		40,000
Land	$150,000	
Cash		$150,000

6-64. The 2008 Step B-6(a) entry to eliminate this Gain and reduce the Land value to the appropriate $110,000, is as follows:

Gain On Sale Of Land	$40,000	
Land		$40,000

6-65. In contrast to the previous case, this elimination is charged on a pro rata basis to the non-controlling and controlling interests in income. More specifically, the 2008 Non-Controlling Interest in the consolidated Income Statement is reduced by $8,000 [(20%)($40,000)] and consolidated Net Income is reduced by $32,000 [(80%)($40,000)]. This allocation is required because the unrealized intercompany profit is an upstream one and relates to the income of the subsidiary.

6-66. As we have noted previously, the fact that the elimination of this profit is split on a pro rata basis does not alter the fact that 100 percent of the profit must be removed from the consolidated revenues. The consolidated expenses and revenues include 100 percent of the parent and subsidiary expenses and revenues and, under the *CICA Handbook* requirements, 100 percent of both upstream and downstream profits must be removed from these figures.

6-67. When a non-controlling interest is involved, the effect of this elimination must be split between that interest and the parent. However, this does not take place in the calculation or disclosure of consolidated expenses and revenues. This pro rata split takes place only in the calculation of the Non-Controlling Interest and consolidated Net Income.

Future Periods

6-68. Because the 2008 entry was only recorded in the consolidation working papers, it will be necessary to reduce the Land account and remove the profit from the Retained Earnings of the subsidiary in 2009 and all subsequent years the Land is on the consolidated books. The entry to accomplish this is as follows:

Retained Earnings - Sleigh's Opening	$40,000	
Land		$40,000

6-69. Here again, the effect of this entry will be split between the non-controlling and controlling interests in the consolidated entity. The Non-Controlling Interest in the consolidated Balance Sheet will be reduced $8,000 [(20%)(40,000)] while consolidated Retained Earnings will be reduced by $32,000 [(80%)(40,000)].

Step B(6) - Upstream Inventory Profits

Determining The Amount

6-70. Most problems you encounter will give you the amount of sales that remain in the inventories of the purchasing company. For example, in this problem we know that the Sleigh Company sold $300,000 in merchandise to the Pleigh Company and that $100,000 of this merchandise is still in the closing inventories of the parent company.

6-71. However, the amount to be eliminated is not the sales price of the merchandise that is still in the inventories of the purchasing company. Rather, it is the amount of gross profit that was recognized by the selling company when these goods were sold. The amount of this gross profit can be communicated by the problem in a variety of ways. The more common ones are as follows:

- The most straightforward situation is when the amount of the profit is simply stated. For example, this problem could have indicated that the amount of gross profit on the goods that were sold to Pleigh Company and remain in its inventories was $40,000.
- A common approach is the one used in this comprehensive problem. That is, to provide you with a gross margin percentage based on sales prices. This problem states that intercompany transfers are priced to provide the selling company with a gross margin of 40 percent. We then multiply this 40 percent times the $100,000 in merchandise that is still on hand at the end of 2009 to arrive at the unrealized

intercompany profit in the closing inventories of $40,000.

- Some problems will state a gross margin percentage that is based on cost rather than selling prices. For example, our problem could have stated that intercompany transfers are priced to provide the selling company with a gross margin equal to two-thirds of cost. We would then have to solve the following simple equation:

[(Cost)(166-2/3%)]	= $100,000
Cost	= ($100,000 ÷ 166-2/3%)
Cost	= $60,000

  Subtracting this cost from the sales price of $100,000 would give us the same $40,000 gross profit to be eliminated.

- While we avoid using this approach, we have seen problems where nothing is explicitly stated with respect to profit amounts or percentages. In these cases, a gross margin percentage must be extracted from the income statement data. The Sleigh Company had Sales Revenue of $2,500,000 and a Cost Of Goods Sold of $1,500,000. Its gross margin of $1,000,000 is equal to 40 percent of Sales Revenue. Applying this 40 percent to the merchandise in the inventories of the Pleigh Company gives an unrealized profit in the closing inventories of $40,000. The application of the same percentage to the Sleigh Company sales in the opening inventories of the Pleigh Company gives $28,000 [(40%)($70,000)]. We would note that this approach relies on the somewhat unreasonable assumption that the gross margin percentage on intercompany sales is the same as the gross margin percentage on all other sales.

6-72. Part 3 of the Other Information in our comprehensive example (Paragraph 6-34) stated that the January 1, 2009 Inventories of Pleigh contained merchandise purchases from Sleigh in the amount of $70,000, with the corresponding figure for the December 31, 2009 Inventories at $100,000. This means that the upstream profits to be eliminated from the opening inventories is $28,000 [(40%)($70,000)], while the corresponding figure for the closing inventories is $40,000 [(40%)($100,000)].

Procedures - Closing Inventory Profits

6-73. In Step B-4 we noted that we would continue to eliminate 100 percent of intercompany sales, even in those cases where some of the transferred merchandise remained in the closing inventories of the purchasing company. This point requires some additional explanation.

6-74. During 2009, Sleigh sold merchandise to Pleigh for $300,000. Based on a 40 percent gross margin, the cost of this merchandise to Sleigh and the real cost of the merchandise to the consolidated entity is $180,000. If Pleigh had resold all of this merchandise, the $300,000 transfer price would have been included in that Company's Cost Of Goods Sold and the elimination of $300,000 of both Sales and Cost Of Goods Sold is an obvious requirement. This leaves the consolidated Cost Of Goods Sold equal to the appropriate $180,000 as recorded in Sleigh's single entity statements.

6-75. In the actual data of the problem, $100,000 of this merchandise remains in Pleigh's Inventories and only $200,000 has been included in Pleigh's Costs Of Goods Sold. This would suggest that only $200,000 of Pleigh's Cost Of Goods Sold should be eliminated.

6-76. Further, the $40,000 profit that was recorded on this intercompany transfer would have to be removed from Pleigh's Inventories and, since from the point of view of the consolidated entity this merchandise has not been sold, its original $60,000 cost would have to be removed from Sleigh's Cost Of Goods Sold. This would suggest the use of the following elimination entry:

Sales	$300,000	
Cost Of Goods Sold (Pleigh's)		$200,000
Cost Of Goods Sold (Sleigh's)		60,000
Inventories (Pleigh's)		40,000

6-77. This approach has logical appeal and will, of course, provide you with a correct solution. However, we have found it preferable to keep separate the individual consolidation procedures and will use an alternative, but equivalent approach. This alternative approach uses the basic Cost Of Goods Sold equation which is as follows:

Cost Of Goods Sold = Opening Inventories + Purchases - Closing Inventories

6-78. Under our alternative procedure, separate entries are made to reflect the need for adjustments to Purchases and to Closing Inventories. Continuing with the data from the comprehensive problem, the full $300,000 of intercompany sales would be included in the Purchases component of the equation and this means we will eliminate 100 percent of this amount. This is consistent with the entry that we made in Step B-4 which is repeated here for your convenience:

Sales	$300,000	
Cost Of Goods Sold		$300,000

6-79. A second entry will then be used to reflect the fact that the Closing Inventories contained a $40,000 unrealized profit. Removing this from the Closing Inventories figure in the preceding equation requires an increase in Cost Of Goods Sold. The entry to accomplish this, and to remove the profit from the Inventories figure in the consolidated Balance Sheet, is as follows:

Cost Of Goods Sold	$40,000	
Inventories		$40,000

6-80. As you can see, the net effect of these two entries is identical to that of the single entry used in the alternative analysis. This latter approach has the advantage of clearly separating Step B-4 from Step B-6 and we have found it to be somewhat easier to understand. As a consequence, this two entry approach will be used in all of the problem solutions that follow.

6-81. Note that since the increase in the Cost Of Goods Sold is related to the elimination of an unrealized upstream profit, the effect will be shared pro rata by the controlling and the non-controlling interests. The Non-Controlling Interest in the consolidated Income Statement will be reduced by $8,000, while consolidated Net Income will be reduced by the balancing $32,000.

Procedures - Opening Inventories

6-82. The profits that were unrealized in the opening inventories were included in the income of the selling company in the previous year and are included in the opening balance of that company's Retained Earnings for the current year. This means that our elimination would have to take these profits out of the opening Retained Earnings of the selling company.

6-83. In addition, the selling company calculated the current year's Cost Of Goods Sold using the overstated opening inventory figure and this results in a Cost Of Goods Sold figure that is overstated in a corresponding manner. Consequently, our elimination entry would have to reduce the current year's Cost Of Goods Sold. The resulting increase in income reflects the fact that any unrealized inventory profits that were present at the beginning of the current year would normally be realized by the end of the year. This means that we need to apply Step B-6(b) using the following journal entry:

Retained Earnings - Sleigh's Opening	$28,000	
Cost Of Goods Sold		$28,000

6-84. Since we are again dealing with an upstream profit, the effect of the $28,000 reduction in the Cost Of Goods Sold would be split between the parent and the non-controlling interest. That is, the Non-Controlling Interest in the consolidated Income Statement would increase by $5,600 [(20%)($28,000)] and consolidated Net Income would increase by $22,400 [(80%)($28,000)].

Step B(6) - Upstream Profit On Depreciable Assets

Basic Concepts

6-85. Within the context of preparing consolidated financial statements, we have defined realization in terms of transactions with individuals or enterprises that are outside the consolidated entity. That is, an intercompany profit is said to be unrealized until such time as it is verified by a transaction with some entity that is independent of the consolidated group.

6-86. This idea is very easy to grasp in the case of intercompany profits on the sale of land or inventories. As we have seen, these profits are treated as unrealized until such time as the land or inventories are resold outside of the consolidated entity. The same general principles apply in the case of assets with limited lives of more than one accounting period. In fact, if such assets were resold to an outsider subsequent to an intercompany sale, any unrealized profit that is present at the time of the sale would be considered to be realized at that point in time.

6-87. However, depreciable assets are normally used in the business rather than sold. Further, any unrealized profits resulting from intercompany sales of these assets will become realized through the use of such assets. As we noted earlier, the best way to visualize this process is to think of a depreciable asset as a bundle of economic services that is being sold on a piecemeal basis as the asset is used over its economic life.

6-88. While alternative approaches could be justified, the normal procedure is to recognize the realization of the unrealized intercompany profit on depreciable assets using the same allocation pattern that is being used to depreciate the asset. As a consequence, this recognition will take the form of an adjustment of consolidated Amortization Expense.

6-89. Consider the intercompany sale in our comprehensive example (Paragraph 6-34 - Other Information item 7). In this example, Sleigh sold an item of Plant And Equipment with a carrying value of $450,000 ($800,000 - $350,000) to Pleigh for $600,000. As a result of this transaction, Sleigh recorded a gain of $150,000 and Pleigh recorded the Plant And Equipment at a value of $600,000.

6-90. Using the straight line method, Pleigh will record amortization on this asset at a rate of $200,000 per year. From the point of view of the consolidated entity, the correct amortization base is $450,000 (Sleigh's old carrying value) and this amount would be amortized over the three year remaining life at a rate of $150,000 per year.

6-91. The required $50,000 per year reduction of consolidated Amortization Expense ($200,000 - $150,000) would increase combined income by $50,000. This, in effect, would represent the realization of one-third of the $150,000 intercompany profit that the Sleigh Company recorded on this sale. Over the three year life of the asset, the $50,000 per year reduction in Amortization Expense would reflect realization of the entire intercompany profit on this transaction.

Presentation

6-92. As we noted earlier, in dealing with depreciable assets, the fact that realization of the intercompany profit takes place over a number of accounting periods means that it is generally easier to combine Steps B-6(a) and B-6(b) into a single net entry for each year. We will follow that approach in the presentation which follows.

6-93. We also believe that it is useful to discuss all of the annual entries that would have been made since the time of the intercompany asset sale. As a consequence, the following presentation includes entries for 2007, 2008, 2009, and 2010. We remind you that the 2007, 2008, and 2010 entries are for discussion purposes only and are not required to complete the solution. Only the entry for 2009 is needed to prepare the consolidated financial statements for that year.

Profit On Depreciable Asset - Required Entry For 2007 (Year Of Sale)

6-94. When the intercompany sale took place on December 31, 2007, the Sleigh Company would have made the following entry on its books:

Cash	$600,000	
Plant And Equipment (Net)		$450,000
Gain On Sale		150,000

6-95. At the same time, the Pleigh Company would have recorded the acquisition of the asset as follows:

Plant And Equipment (Net)	$600,000	
Cash		$600,000

6-96. As this sale is not a real transaction from the point of view of the combined business entity, the Plant And Equipment is $150,000 too high for inclusion in the consolidated Balance Sheet and the Sleigh Company has recorded a $150,000 Gain On Sale which should not be included in consolidated Net Income. To remedy this situation, the following elimination entry is required:

Gain On Sale	$150,000	
Plant And Equipment (Net)		$150,000

6-97. This entry leaves Plant And Equipment at the correct figure of $450,000 and eliminates the unrealized intercompany Gain On Sale. You should note that none of the intercompany profit becomes realized during 2007 as there would have been no usage of the asset subsequent to the December 31 transfer date. As a consequence, there is no adjustment of the 2007 Amortization Expense.

Profit On Depreciable Asset - Required Entry For 2008

6-98. The entry for 2008 would be more complex in that additional accounts would require adjustment. On the books of the Pleigh Company, the Plant And Equipment is written down to $400,000 ($600,000 - $200,000). As the appropriate figure for consolidation purposes is $300,000 ($450,000 - $150,000), this balance will require adjustment.

6-99. In addition, the current year's Amortization Expense will have to be adjusted downward by $50,000 ($200,000 - $150,000). The resulting increase in income reflects the current year's realization of the intercompany gain.

6-100. Finally, the entire 2007 unrealized profit of $150,000 has been recorded in the Retained Earnings of the Sleigh Company. Since on January 1, 2008, none of this profit had been realized through reduced Amortization Expense, the full $150,000 must be removed from Sleigh's opening Retained Earnings.

6-101. The entry to accomplish all of the preceding adjustments would be as follows:

Retained Earnings - Sleigh's Opening	$150,000	
Amortization Expense (2008)		$ 50,000
Plant And Equipment (Net)		100,000

6-102. Since we are dealing with an upstream profit, all of the effects of this entry will be reflected in pro rata adjustments of the parent's and the non-controlling interest's share of income and net assets. That is, the $150,000 debit to Retained Earnings will reduce the beginning of the year Non-Controlling Interest in net assets (Balance Sheet) by $30,000 [(20%)($150,000)] and the opening consolidated Retained Earnings by $120,000 [(80%)($150,000)].

6-103. The $50,000 reduction in Amortization Expense will increase the Non-Controlling Interest in the 2008 consolidated Income Statement by $10,000 [(20%)($50,000)] and consolidated Net Income by $40,000 [(80%)($50,000)].

6-104. Note that, at the end of the year, the net adjustment would be $100,000, the original unrealized amount of $150,000, less the $50,000 realization which took place during 2008.

If end of the period figures were being calculated, the elimination of this $100,000 would reduce the Non-Controlling Interest in the consolidated Balance Sheet by $20,000 [(20%)($100,000)] and consolidated Retained Earnings by $80,000 [(80%)($100,000)].

Profit On Depreciable Asset - Required Entry For 2009

6-105. For the problem under consideration, the relevant entry is the one for 2009. This entry would be as follows:

Retained Earnings - Sleigh's Opening	$100,000	
Amortization Expense (2009)		$50,000
Plant And Equipment (Net)		50,000

6-106. On the books of the Pleigh Company, the Plant And Equipment has been written down to a value of $200,000 ($600,000 - $400,000) while the correct figure for consolidation purposes is $150,000 ($450,000 - $300,000). The $50,000 credit to Plant And Equipment provides the adjustment for this difference.

6-107. As at January 1, 2009, the Retained Earnings balance of the Sleigh Company contains the full $150,000 of intercompany profit that was recognized on the sale of the depreciable asset. Since $50,000 of this was realized through reduced Amortization Expense in 2008, the remaining unrealized balance on January 1, 2009 is $100,000. It is this amount that the preceding journal entry removes from the Retained Earnings of the Sleigh Company.

6-108. The credit to Amortization Expense serves to reduce the 2009 Amortization Expense from the $200,000 that is on the books of the Pleigh Company to the appropriate $150,000 for consolidation purposes.

6-109. As was explained in conjunction with the 2008 entry, both the reduction in the Retained Earnings of the Sleigh Company and the increase in current income resulting from the reduced Amortization Expense will be reflected on a pro rata basis in both the parent's and the non-controlling interest's share of net assets and income.

Profit On Depreciable Asset - Required Entry For 2010

6-110. As was the case with the 2007 and 2008 entries, the 2010 entry is not a necessary part of the solution. However, it will be presented in order to provide a complete illustration of the treatment of a profit on the intercompany sale of a depreciable asset. The entry is as follows:

Retained Earnings - Sleigh's Opening	$50,000	
Amortization Expense		$50,000

6-111. The debit to the Retained Earnings of the Sleigh Company reflects the fact that of the original unrealized profit of $150,000, $100,000 was realized through reduced amortization expense in 2008 and 2009, leaving an unrealized balance of $50,000. The $50,000 credit to Amortization Expense is the usual reduction in this expense from $200,000 to $150,000. Note that the credit to Plant And Equipment is no longer present since the asset would now be fully depreciated. It would have a net book value of zero in the records of the Pleigh Company and this is the appropriate figure for consolidation purposes.

6-112. As in the entries for the previous two years, the effects of the reduced Retained Earnings and Amortization Expense would be allocated on a pro rata basis to the parent and the non-controlling interest.

6-113. One additional point needs to be made in this final year of the asset's life. In 2007, the year of the intercompany sale, we removed the $150,000 Gain On Sale from income in the process of preparing consolidated financial statements. In the subsequent three years, we reversed this elimination by increasing income at a rate of $50,000 per year. As at December 31, 2010, these two effects will have netted out and no further adjustments or eliminations will be required in subsequent years.

6-114. Note that this is contrast to the situation with fair value changes. When the cost method is used to carry the investment, the fair value changes will always be recorded as part of the investment elimination and, to the extent that they have been realized through amortization or sale, adjusted for presentation in the Balance Sheet of the current year. Based on the procedures that we are using, these adjustments will continue to be necessary, even if the relevant asset is no longer included in the consolidated Balance Sheet.

Step C - Distribution Of The Subsidiary Retained Earnings

The Problem

6-115. At this point, the remaining task is to determine the appropriate distribution of the balance that is left in the Retained Earnings account of the Sleigh Company. The amount of this balance, as adjusted by the Step A and Step B procedures, can be determined as follows:

Sleigh's January 1, 2009 Balance	$2,300,000
Step A Elimination (Retained Earnings At Acquisition)	(1,500,000)
Balance Since Acquisition	$ 800,000
Step B Adjustments:	
Fair Value Increase On Inventories	(80,000)
Amortization Of Fair Value Increase On Plant And Equipment (4 Years At $10,000)	(40,000)
Unrealized Upstream Profit On Land Sale	(40,000)
Unrealized Upstream Profit In Opening Inventories	(28,000)
Unrealized Upstream Profit On Equipment	(100,000)
Balance After Adjustments	$ 512,000

6-116. As this schedule indicates, we are left with $512,000 as the January 1, 2009 adjusted balance of the Sleigh Company's Retained Earnings since acquisition. We must now determine the appropriate distribution between the Non-Controlling Interest in consolidated net assets and consolidated Retained Earnings. We will find that the presence of unrealized upstream profits will significantly complicate this process.

6-117. If we were consistently using the entity conceptual approach, all of the Step B adjustments would be reflected proportionately in both the non-controlling interest and the controlling interest. The distribution of the remaining balance would be a simple matter of allocating it in proportion to the two respective ownership interests. That is, we could split the remaining $512,000 on a 20 percent, 80 percent basis.

6-118. Correspondingly, if we were applying the parent company concept in a consistent manner, none of the Step B adjustments would have any influence on the amount of the non-controlling interest in net assets. We could calculate the non-controlling interest in Retained Earnings since acquisition by multiplying the non-controlling percent times the unadjusted Retained Earnings of the subsidiary since acquisition. Then all of the Step B adjustments and eliminations would be charged against the parent company's share of the subsidiary's Retained Earnings since acquisition.

6-119. In this example, the non-controlling interest in Sleigh's Retained Earnings since acquisition would be $160,000 [(20%)($800,000)], and all of the Step B adjustments for the realization of fair value changes and unrealized intercompany profits would be deducted from the controlling interest.

6-120. Unfortunately, the *CICA Handbook* did not adopt a consistent conceptual approach to the preparation of consolidated financial statements. While most of the Recommendations are based on the parent company concept, there is one important exception. This is the fact that the entity approach is used in the elimination of unrealized intercompany profits. This means that, unlike the adjustments for the realization of fair value changes, the adjustments for unrealized upstream profits will influence the calculation of the non-controlling interest. As a consequence, we will need a two stage distribution schedule in which unrealized upstream profits are dealt with separately from the other Step B adjustments related to the realization of fair value changes and any goodwill impairment losses.

Retained Earnings Distribution Schedule

6-121. As was the case in Chapter 5, this schedule begins with the Retained Earnings balance of the subsidiary and, using Step A procedures, removes the portion of this balance that was present at the time of acquisition. As indicated in the preceding section, the presence of unrealized upstream profits means that we cannot calculate the non-controlling interest as a percentage of total retained earnings since acquisition. We must first modify this total for all of the Step B adjustments and eliminations that involve upstream profits which are unrealized at the beginning of the year.

6-122. Note that we are concerned here with the January 1, 2009 unrealized profits. This reflects the fact that, in this open trial balance problem, we are distributing the beginning of the year Retained Earnings since acquisition balance.

6-123. After the removal of the non-controlling interest from the modified balance, all other Step B adjustments and eliminations are added or subtracted to arrive at the appropriate allocation to consolidated Retained Earnings. This two stage schedule reflects a combination of entity and parent company procedures and would appear as follows:

January 1, 2009 Balance From Trial Balance	$2,300,000
Balance At Acquisition	(1,500,000)
Balance Since Acquisition	$ 800,000
Unrealized Upstream Profits On January 1, 2009:	
Land	(40,000)
Opening Inventories	(28,000)
Equipment ($150,000 - $50,000)	(100,000)
Adjusted Balance Since Acquisition	$ 632,000
Non-Controlling Interest [(20%)($632,000)]	(126,400)
Available To The Controlling Interest	$ 505,600
Other Step B Adjustments:	
Fair Value Increase On Inventories	(80,000)
Amortization Of Fair Value Increase On Plant And Equipment (4 Years At $10,000)	(40,000)
To Consolidated Retained Earnings	$ 385,600

Retained Earnings Distribution Entry

6-124. Using the information from the preceding schedule, the journal entry to distribute Sleigh's Retained Earnings since acquisition is as follows:

Retained Earnings - Sleigh's Opening	$512,000	
Non-Controlling Interest (Balance Sheet)		$126,400
Consolidated Retained Earnings		385,600

6-125. This entry reduces the Sleigh Company's Retained Earnings balance to zero and distributes the total to the controlling and non-controlling interests. With this entry completed we have established the opening balance for consolidated Retained Earnings. It is simply the Pleigh Company's January 1, 2009 balance of $2,550,000, less the $25,000 downstream profit on land, plus the $385,600 allocation resulting from the preceding journal entry, for a total of $2,910,600.

Consolidated Income Statement

Non-Controlling Interest Computation

6-126. With the addition of the Step C distribution entry, we have completed all of the procedures necessary for the preparation of consolidated financial statements. As was the case in Chapter 5 we will begin with the consolidated Income Statement.

60-127. In Chapter 5, the calculation of the Non-Controlling Interest in the consolidated Income Statement was simply a matter of multiplying the reported income of the subsidiary by the non-controlling ownership percentage. With the introduction of upstream unrealized profits, the calculation becomes more complex.

6-128. The reason for this is, of course, the fact that the elimination of these profits is being dealt with using entity concept procedures. This means that we must adjust the reported income of the subsidiary for included profits that have not been realized during the year (e.g., closing inventory profits), as well as for previously unrealized profits that have become realized during the year (e.g., opening inventory profits). Only then can we calculate the appropriate Non-Controlling Interest for inclusion in the consolidated Income Statement. The required calculation would be as follows:

Sleigh Company's Reported Income	$200,000
Realization Of Opening Inventory Profits	28,000
Unrealized Closing Inventory Profits	(40,000)
Realization Of Equipment Profit	50,000
Sleigh's Adjusted Income	$238,000
Non-Controlling Percent	20%
Non-Controlling Interest In Consolidated Net Income	$ 47,600

6-129. In presenting this calculation, we stress the fact that upstream unrealized profits are the only adjustments or eliminations that have any influence on the amount of the Non-Controlling Interest. This statement is always true and would apply to both the Non-Controlling Interest in the consolidated Income Statement and the Non-Controlling Interest in the consolidated Balance Sheet.

Statement Disclosure

6-130. The consolidated Income Statement would be prepared as follows:

Pleigh Company And Subsidiary
Consolidated Income Statement
Year Ending December 31, 2009

Sales ($4,000,000 + $2,500,000 - $300,000)	$6,200,000
Interest Revenue ($24,000 - $24,000)	Nil
Dividend Revenue ($80,000 - $80,000)	Nil
Total Revenues	$6,200,000
Cost Of Goods Sold	
($2,800,000 + $1,500,000 - $300,000 + $40,000 - $28,000)	$4,012,000
Amortization Expense ($200,000 + $100,000 + $10,000 - $50,000)	260,000
Interest Expense ($240,000 + $84,000 - $24,000)	300,000
Other Expenses ($364,000 + $616,000)	980,000
Total Expenses	$5,552,000
Combined Income	$ 648,000
Non-Controlling Interest (Paragraph 6-128)	(47,600)
Consolidated Net Income	$ 600,400

6-131. Note again that the subtotal for Combined Income is not normal disclosure. Rather, it has been included for computational purposes. Normal disclosure would have the Non-Controlling Interest included as part of the total expenses.

Verification Of Consolidated Net Income

6-132. As was explained in Chapter 5, it is often useful to be able to make a definitional calculation of consolidated Net Income. In this version of the comprehensive problem, the definitional calculation of consolidated Net Income is as follows:

Pleigh Company's Net Income	$500,000
Intercompany Dividend Revenues [(80%)($100,000)]	(80,000)
Pleigh's Net Income Less Dividends	$420,000
Pleigh's Equity In Sleigh's Adjusted Net Income [(80%)($238,000)]	190,400
Income Before Adjustments	$610,400
Adjustment For Fair Value Amortization	(10,000)
Consolidated Net Income	$600,400

6-133. Note that Pleigh's interest in the income of the Sleigh Company is not based on the reported income of the Sleigh Company. Rather, it is based on the same $238,000 adjusted subsidiary income figure that was used in the computation of the Non-Controlling Interest in consolidated Net Income (see Paragraph 6-128).

Consolidated Statement Of Retained Earnings

Statement Disclosure

6-134. Using the Net Income data, we can now prepare a consolidated Statement Of Retained Earnings. It would be as follows:

Pleigh Company And Subsidiary
Consolidated Statement Of Retained Earnings
Year Ending December 31, 2009

Balance - January 1, 2009 (Paragraph 6-125)	$2,910,600
2009 Net Income ((Paragraph 6-130))	600,400
2009 Dividends Declared (Pleigh's Only)	(350,000)
Balance - December 31, 2009	$3,161,000

Verification Of Consolidated Retained Earnings

6-135. As was the case with consolidated Net Income, you will often find it useful to be able to make an independent computation of the end of the year balance in the consolidated Retained Earnings account. In picking up Pleigh's share of the Retained Earnings of the Sleigh Company since acquisition, we must remove the effects of unrealized intercompany profits. The equity pickup included in the verification of consolidated Retained Earnings would be calculated as follows:

Sleigh's December 31, 2009 Retained Earnings		$2,400,000
Balance At Acquisition		(1,500,000)
Balance Since Acquisition		$ 900,000
Unrealized Upstream Profits:		
Land	($40,000)	
Closing Inventories	(40,000)	
Equipment ($150,000 - $100,000)	(50,000)	(130,000)
Adjusted Balance		$ 770,000
Controlling Percent		80%
Equity Pickup		$ 616,000

6-136. The definitional approach to the computation of the year end consolidated Retained Earnings is as follows:

Pleigh's December 31, 2009 Balance	$2,700,000
Pleigh's Share Of Sleigh's Retained Earnings Since Acquisition (Equity Pickup From Paragraph 6-135)	616,000
Step B Adjustments:	
Fair Value Increase On Inventories	(80,000)
Amortization Of Fair Value Increase On Plant And Equipment (5 Years At $10,000)	(50,000)
Downstream Profit On Land	(25,000)
December 31, 2009 Consolidated Retained Earnings	$3,161,000

Consolidated Balance Sheet

Non-Controlling Interest

6-137. There are two basic ways to determine the Non-Controlling Interest that is shown on the Balance Sheet. One approach would be to use the Sleigh Company's book values adjusted for upstream unrealized profits. This calculation would be as follows:

December 31, 2009 - No Par Common Stock		$2,000,000
December 31, 2009 - Retained Earnings		2,400,000
Unrealized Upstream Profits (Same As Paragraph 6-135):		
Land	($40,000)	
Closing Inventories	(40,000)	
Equipment	(50,000)	(130,000)
Sleigh's Adjusted Book Values		$4,270,000
Non-Controlling Percent		20%
December 31, 2009 Non-Controlling Interest		$ 854,000

6-138. An alternative calculation of the Non-Controlling Interest would start with the Step A allocation of $700,000, deduct the $20,000 Step B adjustment for dividends to non-controlling shareholders and add the Step C allocation of $126,400 and the Non-Controlling Interest of $47,600 from the consolidated Income Statement.

Statement Disclosure

6-139. The consolidated Balance Sheet of the Pleigh Company and its subsidiary would be prepared as follows:

Pleigh Company And Subsidiary
Consolidated Balance Sheet
As At December 31, 2009

Cash ($500,000 + $300,000)	$ 800,000
Current Receivables ($800,000 + $400,000 - $12,000)	1,188,000
Inventories ($2,500,000 + $1,700,000 + $80,000 - $80,000 - $40,000)	4,160,000
Long-Term Note Receivable ($200,000 - $200,000)	Nil
Investment In Sleigh ($3,200,000 - $3,200,000)	Nil
Land ($1,500,000 + $1,000,000 - $120,000 - $40,000 - $25,000)	2,315,000
Plant And Equipment ($4,500,000 + $1,900,000+ $200,000 - $50,000 - $50,000)	6,500,000
Goodwill	240,000
Total Assets	$15,203,000

Current Liabilities ($500,000 + $200,000 - $12,000)	$ 688,000
Long-Term Liabilities ($2,000,000 + $700,000 - $200,000)	2,500,000
Non-Controlling Interest (Paragraph 6-137)	854,000
No Par Common Stock (Pleigh's Balance)	8,000,000
Retained Earnings (Paragraph 6-134)	3,161,000
Total Equities	$15,203,000

6-140. Most of the preceding computations follow directly from the trial balance data adjusted by the various journal entries that we have made. The exceptions to this are the Retained Earnings balance (which was computed in the consolidated Statement Of Retained Earnings), and the Non-Controlling Interest.

Exercise Six-2

Subject: Open Trial Balance Problem

Note This Exercise is identical to Exercise Five-2 except for Parts 3 and 4.

On January 1, 2005, the Parker Company purchases 65 percent of the outstanding shares of the Schaffer Company for $1,350,000 in cash. On that date, the Schaffer Company had No Par Common Stock of $700,000 and Retained Earnings of $1,000,000. On December 31, 2009, the adjusted trial balances of the Parker Company and its subsidiary, the Schaffer Company are as follows:

	Parker	Schaffer
Monetary Assets	$ 2,850,000	$ 725,000
Investment In Schaffer - At Cost	1,350,000	N/A
Non-Monetary Assets	6,475,000	2,045,000
Total Expenses	2,940,000	530,000
Dividends Declared	250,000	50,000
Total Debits	$13,865,000	$3,350,000
Liabilities	$ 1,712,500	$ 425,000
No Par Common Stock	3,000,000	700,000
Retained Earnings (January 1)	5,895,000	1,550,000
Sales	3,225,000	675,000
Dividend Revenue	32,500	Nil
Total Credits	$13,865,000	$3,350,000
January 2009 Retained Earnings	$5,895,000	$1,550,000
2009 Net Income	317,500	145,000
2009 Dividends Declared	(250,000)	(50,000)
December 31, 2009 Retained Earnings	$ 5,962,500	$1,645,000

Other Information:

1. At the date of Parker Company's acquisition of the Schaffer Company's shares, all of the identifiable assets and liabilities of the Schaffer Company had fair values that were equal to their carrying values except for a group of non-monetary assets that had a fair value that was $150,000 greater than its carrying value. These non-monetary assets had a remaining useful life of 15 years. Both Companies use the straight-line method for all amortization calculations.

2. In each of the years since Parker acquired control over Schaffer, the goodwill arising on this business combination transaction has been tested for impairment.

In 2007, a Goodwill Impairment Loss of $35,000 was recognized. In addition, the impairment test for 2009 found a further impairment of $25,000.

3. Schaffer Company's Sales during 2009 include sales of $85,000 to Parker Company. One-half of the merchandise remains in the December 31, 2009 inventories of Parker Company. The pricing on these sales provided Schaffer with a 30 percent gross margin based on sales price. In addition, as a result of these sales, on December 31, 2009, Parker still owes Schaffer $15,000 on open account. There were no intercompany sales in 2008.

4. On January 1, 2008, Schaffer sells a piece of equipment to Parker for $120,000 in cash. At this time, the carrying value of the machine on Schaffer's books is $100,000 and it has a remaining useful life of four years.

Prepare a consolidated Income Statement and a consolidated Statement Of Retained Earnings for the year ending December 31, 2009 and a consolidated Balance Sheet as at December 31, 2009 for the Parker Company and its subsidiary, the Schaffer Company.

End of Exercise. Solution available in Study Guide.

Comprehensive Example - Closed Trial Balance With Investment At Cost

Basic Data

6-141. In this version of the problem, Investment In Sleigh will continue to be carried at cost. However, the data will be presented in the form of a closed trial balance and only a consolidated Balance Sheet will be required. The data is as follows:

On January 1, 2005, the Pleigh Company purchases 80 percent of the outstanding voting shares of the Sleigh Company for $3,200,000 in cash. On that date the Sleigh Company had No Par Common Stock of $2,000,000 and Retained Earnings of $1,500,000. On December 31, 2009, the adjusted trial balances of the Pleigh Company and its subsidiary, the Sleigh Company are as follows:

	Pleigh	Sleigh
Cash	$ 500,000	$ 300,000
Current Receivables	800,000	400,000
Inventories	2,500,000	1,700,000
Long-Term Note Receivable	200,000	Nil
Investment In Sleigh - At Cost	3,200,000	N/A
Land	1,500,000	1,000,000
Plant And Equipment (Net)	4,500,000	1,900,000
Total Debits	$13,200,000	$5,300,000
Current Liabilities	$ 500,000	$ 200,000
Long-Term Liabilities	2,000,000	700,000
No Par Common Stock	8,000,000	2,000,000
Retained Earnings	2,700,000	2,400,000
Total Credits	$13,200,000	$5,300,000

Other Information:

1. At the date of Pleigh Company's acquisition of the Sleigh Company's shares, all of the identifiable assets and liabilities of the Sleigh Company had fair values that were equal to their carrying values except:

   - Inventories which had fair values that were $100,000 more than their carrying values,
   - Land with a fair value that was $150,000 less than its carrying value, and
   - Plant And Equipment which had a fair value that was $250,000 greater than its carrying value.

   The Plant And Equipment had a remaining useful life on the acquisition date of 20 years while the Inventories that were present on the acquisition date were sold during the year ending December 31, 2005. The Land is still on the books of the Sleigh Company on December 31, 2009. Both companies use the straight line method to calculate amortization.

2. In each of the years since Pleigh acquired control over Sleigh, the goodwill arising on this business combination transaction has been tested for impairment. No impairment was found in any of the years since acquisition.

3. Sleigh Company's Sales include sales of $300,000 to Pleigh Company. The December 31, 2009 Inventories of the Pleigh Company contain $100,000 of this merchandise purchased from Sleigh Company during 2009. In addition, the January 1, 2009 Inventories of the Pleigh Company contained $70,000 in merchandise purchased from Sleigh Company during 2008. All intercompany sales are priced to provide the selling company a gross margin on sales price of 40 percent.

4. On December 31, 2009, the Pleigh Company is holding Sleigh Company's long-term note payable in the amount of $200,000. Interest at 12 percent is payable on July 1 of each year. Pleigh Company has been holding this note since July 1, 2007.

5. During 2007, the Pleigh Company sold Land to the Sleigh Company for $100,000 in cash. The Land had a carrying value on the books of the Pleigh Company of $75,000.

6. During 2008, the Sleigh Company sold Land to the Pleigh Company for $150,000. This Land had a carrying value on the books of the Sleigh Company of $110,000.

7. On December 31, 2007, the Sleigh Company sold Equipment to the Pleigh Company for $600,000. The Equipment had originally cost the Sleigh Company $800,000 and, at the time of the intercompany sale, had accumulated amortization of $350,000. On this date, it was estimated that the remaining useful life of the Equipment was three years with no net salvage value.

Required: Prepare a consolidated Balance Sheet as at December 31, 2009 for the Pleigh Company and its subsidiary, the Sleigh Company.

Procedural Approach

6-142. The procedural approach here is similar to that used in the open trial balance, cost method version of this problem. The basic difference is that all of the Step B adjustments to expenses and revenues will now be made to Sleigh's Retained Earnings account and the Step C entry will involve distributing the December 31, 2009 Retained Earnings, rather than the January 1, 2009 balance.

Step A Procedures

Investment Analysis

6-143. The analysis of the investment will be identical to the one used in the open trial balance, cost method version of this problem. It is as follows:

	80 Percent	100 Percent
Investment Cost	$3,200,000	$4,000,000
Sleigh Shareholders' Equity At Acquisition	(2,800,000)	(3,500,000)
Differential	$ 400,000	$ 500,000
Fair Value Changes:		
Increase On Inventories	(80,000)	(100,000)
Decrease On Land	120,000	150,000
Increase On Plant And Equipment (Net)	(200,000)	(250,000)
Goodwill	$ 240,000	$ 300,000

Investment Elimination

6-144. Based on the preceding analysis, the journal entry to eliminate the Investment In Sleigh account is as follows:

No Par Common Stock	$2,000,000	
Retained Earnings	1,500,000	
Plant And Equipment (Net)	200,000	
Inventories	80,000	
Goodwill	240,000	
Land		$ 120,000
Non-Controlling Interest [(20%)($3,500,000)]		700,000
Investment In Sleigh		3,200,000

Step B(1) - Intercompany Assets And Liabilities

6-145. The elimination of intercompany asset and liability balances is the same in both open trial balance and closed trial balance versions of this problem. The entries are:

Long-Term Liabilities	$200,000	
Long-Term Note Receivable		$200,000
Current Liabilities	$ 12,000	
Current Receivables		$ 12,000

Step B(2) - Realization Of Fair Value Changes

6-146. The entries in this version of the problem will have the same effect on the asset and liability accounts as did the entries in the first version of this problem. The only difference is that since we are working with a closed trial balance it is no longer possible to adjust expense and revenue accounts. As these accounts have been closed into the ending retained earnings balances, adjustments will now go to the Retained Earnings account of the Sleigh Company.

6-147. Since the fair value change on Inventories had no effect on the 2009 expenses or revenues, the entry here will be the same as it was in the first version of this problem. It is as follows:

Retained Earnings - Sleigh's Closing	$80,000	
Inventories		$80,000

6-148. As was the case in the first version of this problem, we will credit Plant And Equipment for 5 years (January 1, 2005 through December 31, 2009) of additional amortization expense on the fair value change. However, instead of splitting the debits between Retained Earnings and the current Amortization Expense, the entire amount will go to Retained Earnings. The entry is as follows:

Retained Earnings - Sleigh's Closing	$50,000	
Plant And Equipment (Net)		$50,000

6-149. As the Land is still on the books of Sleigh, no entry is required to adjust the fair value change on this account.

Step B(3) - Goodwill Impairment

6-150. The Other Information in our comprehensive problem notes that, while goodwill has been tested for impairment in each year since the acquisition of Pleigh Company occurred, no impairment has been found. As a consequence, no Step B(3) entry is required in this problem.

Step B(4) - Intercompany Expenses And Revenues

6-151. In the open trial balance versions of this problem, we made an entry here to eliminate intercompany expenses and revenues. We noted that this entry was simply to avoid overstating expenses and revenues. Since all of the expenses and revenues are now closed to retained earnings, no entry is required in this closed trial balance version of the problem.

Step B(5) - Intercompany Dividends

6-152. In the open trial balance version of this problem we made an entry here to eliminate dividend payments. The entry involved reducing Pleigh's revenues, Dividends Declared and the Non-Controlling Interest in the consolidated Balance Sheet. As Pleigh's revenues and the Dividends Declared accounts have been closed to retained earnings, no entry is required for these adjustments.

6-153. With respect to the reduction of the Non-Controlling Interest in the consolidated Balance Sheet, this effect will be automatically picked up in Step C when we base our allocation to this account on the end of the year Retained Earnings balance of the Sleigh Company. This end of year balance has, of course, had all of the Sleigh Company's 2009 dividends taken out as part of the closing entries.

Step B(6) - Unrealized Intercompany Profits

Procedures

6-154. In the open trial balance version of this problem, our adjustments and eliminations for unrealized intercompany profits had to take into consideration such profits in the opening consolidated Retained Earnings balance, the current period's consolidated expenses and revenues, and the closing balances for inclusion in the consolidated Balance Sheet.

6-155. In this closed trial balance version of the problem, we are only concerned with unrealized intercompany profits to the extent that they have an effect on the accounts to be included in the December 31, 2009 consolidated Balance Sheet. We will find that this will simplify and, in the case of profits in the opening inventories, eliminate the entries that are required in dealing with unrealized intercompany profits.

Downstream And Upstream Profits On Land

6-156. This problem contains a 2007 intercompany profit of $25,000 on the sale of Land from Pleigh Company to Sleigh and a similar 2008 profit of $40,000 on the sale of Land from Sleigh to Pleigh. The amounts of these profits are unchanged from the beginning of the current accounting period and, as a consequence, the appropriate elimination entries to be used here are the same as those that were required in the open trial balance version of this problem. The entry for the downstream profit is as follows:

Retained Earnings - Pleigh's Closing	$25,000	
Land		$25,000

6-157. For the upstream profit, the entry is:

Retained Earnings - Sleigh's Closing	$40,000	
Land		$40,000

Upstream Inventory Profits

6-158. In this problem there are Sleigh Company profits in the opening Inventories of the Pleigh Company in the amount of $28,000 and a similar balance in the closing Inventories of the Pleigh Company of $40,000.

6-159. With respect to the $28,000 opening inventory profit, in the open trial balance version of this problem we found it necessary to reduce the January 1, 2009 Retained Earnings of the Sleigh Company and increase the 2009 income figures by reducing the 2009 consolidated Cost Of Goods Sold. The combined effect of these two adjustments on the December 31, 2009 Retained Earnings of Sleigh would be nil as the reduction in the January 1, 2009 Retained Earnings would be offset by the increase in 2009 income created by the decrease in Cost Of Goods Sold.

6-160. As a reflection of this situation, no entry is required for opening inventory profits in closed trial balance problems. An additional way of looking at this situation would be to note that the Inventories that Pleigh was holding at the beginning of 2009 have been sold and the Sleigh Company's unrealized opening inventory profit has now been realized. Therefore, no elimination entry is required.

6-161. The unrealized profit in the closing Inventories of the Pleigh Company does, however, require an adjustment. The consolidated Inventories must be reduced as was the case in the open trial balance version of the problem. However, the accompanying debit can no longer go to the Cost Of Goods Sold account. Since this account has been closed into the ending Retained Earnings, the adjustment must be to Retained Earnings and would appear as follows:

Retained Earnings - Sleigh's Closing	$40,000	
Inventories		$40,000

Upstream Profit On Equipment

6-162. On December 31, 2007, there was a profit of $150,000 recognized by the Sleigh Company on the sale of a depreciable asset with a three year life to the Pleigh Company. During 2008, $50,000 of this profit was realized through a reduction in consolidated Amortization Expense. This left $100,000 to be removed from the January 1, 2009 Retained Earnings of the Sleigh Company in the open trial balance version of this problem. Now that we are dealing with a closed trial balance, we must account for the fact that an additional profit realization of $50,000 occurred during 2009. This means that at the end of 2009, the only adjustment will be for the remaining $50,000 which is still unrealized on this date. The entry would be as follows:

Retained Earnings - Sleigh's Closing	$50,000	
Plant And Equipment (Net)		$50,000

6-163. Note that, as with the other intercompany profit eliminations, there is no adjustment of the current year's expenses or revenues as they have been closed to Retained Earnings in this closed trial balance problem.

Step C - Distribution Of The Subsidiary Retained Earnings

Retained Earnings Balance

6-164. The Retained Earnings account of the Sleigh Company in the trial balance for this problem was $2,400,000. In Step A we removed $1,500,000 of this amount, leaving a balance in the amount of $900,000 which had accrued between the acquisition date of January 1, 2005 and the current date of December 31, 2009. Our one remaining task in this problem is to determine how much of this balance is left after the Step B adjustments and to distribute this balance to the parent and non-controlling interest. The remaining balance can be determined as follows:

Balance Since Acquisition ($2,400,000 - $1,500,000)	$ 900,000
Step B Adjustments:	
Fair Value Increase On Inventories	(80,000)
Amortization Of Fair Value Increase On Plant And Equipment (5 Years At $10,000)	(50,000)
Unrealized Upstream Profit On Land Sale	(40,000)
Unrealized Upstream Profit In Closing Inventories	(40,000)
Unrealized Upstream Profit On Equipment Sale ($150,000 - $100,000)	(50,000)
Balance After Adjustments	$ 640,000

Retained Earnings Distribution Schedule

6-165. The schedule for allocating the balance from the preceding Paragraph would be as follows:

December 31, 2009 Balance As Per Trial Balance	$2,400,000
January 1, 2005 Balance At Acquisition	(1,500,000)
Balance Since Acquisition	$ 900,000
Unrealized Upstream Profits:	
Land	(40,000)
Closing Inventories	(40,000)
Equipment Sale ($150,000 - $100,000)	(50,000)
Adjusted Balance Since Acquisition	$ 770,000
Non-Controlling Interest [(20%)($770,000)]	(154,000)
Available To The Controlling Interest	$ 616,000
Other Step B Adjustments:	
Fair Value Increase On Inventories	(80,000)
Amortization Of Fair Value Increase On Plant And Equipment (5 Years At $10,000)	(50,000)
To Consolidated Retained Earnings	$ 486,000

6-166. With the information from this schedule, we can now make the required Step C distribution entry.

Retained Earnings Distribution Entry

6-167. Using the information from the preceding schedule, the journal entry to distribute Sleigh's Retained Earnings since acquisition is as follows:

Retained Earnings - Sleigh	$640,000	
Non-Controlling Interest (Balance Sheet)		$154,000
Consolidated Retained Earnings		486,000

6-168. This entry reduces the Sleigh Company's Retained Earnings balance to nil and distributes the total to the parent and non-controlling interest. When the credit of $154,000 to the Non-Controlling Interest is added to the Step A credit to this account of $700,000, we have established the appropriate balance of $854,000 for inclusion in the consolidated Balance Sheet as at December 31, 2009.

6-169. Further, if we take the Pleigh Company's Retained Earnings balance of $2,700,000 from the trial balance, subtract the downstream profit on the intercompany sale of land of $25,000 and add the allocation from Paragraph 6-167 of $486,000, we arrive at a figure of $3,161,000. This figure is the correct figure for consolidated Retained Earnings to be included in the December 31, 2009 Balance Sheet.

Consolidated Balance Sheet

6-170. With the addition of the Step C distribution entry, we have completed all of the procedures necessary for the preparation of the consolidated Balance Sheet. As expected, this closed trial balance version of the problem produces a Balance Sheet that is identical to the one in the open trial balance version. All of the balances flow directly from the preceding journal entries, resulting in the consolidated Balance Sheet that is presented as follows:

Pleigh Company And Subsidiary
Consolidated Balance Sheet
As At December 31, 2009

Cash ($500,000 + $300,000)	$ 800,000
Current Receivables ($800,000 + $400,000 - $12,000)	1,188,000
Inventories	
($2,500,000 + $1,700,000 + $80,000 - $80,000 - $40,000)	4,160,000
Long-Term Note Receivable ($200,000 - $200,000)	Nil
Investment In Sleigh ($3,200,000 - $3,200,000)	Nil
Land ($1,500,000 + $1,000,000 - $120,000 - $40,000 - $25,000)	2,315,000
Plant And Equipment	
($4,500,000 + $1,900,000 + $200,0000 - $50,000 - $50,000)	6,500,000
Goodwill	240,000
Total Assets	$15,083,000
Current Liabilities ($500,000 + $200,000 - $12,000)	$ 688,000
Long-Term Liabilities ($2,000,000 + $700,000 - $200,000)	2,500,000
Non-Controlling Interest (Paragraph 6-168)	854,000
No Par Common Stock	8,000,000
Retained Earnings (Paragraph 6-169)	3,161,000
Total Equities	$15,083,000

Exercise Six-3

Subject: Closed Trial Balance Problem

Note This is a closed trial balance version of Exercise Six-2.

On January 1, 2005, the Parker Company purchases 65 percent of the outstanding shares of the Schaffer Company for $1,350,000 in cash. On that date, the Schaffer Company had No Par Common Stock of $700,000 and Retained Earnings of $1,000,000. On December 31, 2009, the adjusted trial balances of the Parker Company and its subsidiary, the Schaffer Company are as follows:

	Parker	Schaffer
Monetary Assets	$ 2,850,000	$ 725,000
Investment In Schaffer - At Cost	1,350,000	N/A
Non-Monetary Assets	6,475,000	2,045,000
Total Debits	$10,675,000	$2,770,000
Liabilities	$ 1,712,500	$ 425,000
No Par Common Stock	3,000,000	700,000
Retained Earnings	5,962,500	1,645,000
Total Credits	$10,675,000	$2,770,000

Other Information:

1. At the date of Parker Company's acquisition of the Schaffer Company's shares, all of the identifiable assets and liabilities of the Schaffer Company had fair values that were equal to their carrying values except for a group of non-monetary assets that had a fair value that was $150,000 greater than its carrying value. These non-monetary assets had a remaining useful life of 15 years. Both companies use the straight-line method for all amortization calculations.

2. In each of the years since Parker acquired control over Schaffer, the goodwill arising on this business combination transaction has been tested for impairment. In 2007, a Goodwill Impairment Loss of $35,000 was recognized. In addition, the impairment test for 2009 found a further impairment of $25,000.

3. Schaffer Company's Sales during 2009 include sales of $85,000 to Parker Company. One-half of the merchandise remains in the December 31, 2009 inventories of Parker Company. The pricing on these sales provided Schaffer with a 30 percent gross margin based on sales price. In addition, as a result of these sales, on December 31, 2009, Parker still owes Schaffer $15,000 on open account. There were no intercompany sales in 2008.

4. On January 1, 2008, Schaffer sells a piece of equipment to Parker for $120,000 in cash. At this time, the carrying value of the machine on Schaffer's books is $100,000 and it has a remaining useful life of four years.

Prepare a consolidated Balance Sheet as at December 31, 2009 for the Parker Company and its subsidiary, the Schaffer Company.

End of Exercise. Solution available in Study Guide.

Review Of The Conceptual Alternatives Adopted By Section 1600

6-171. Now that you have an understanding of all of the basic consolidation procedures, including unrealized intercompany profits, the summary of the conceptual alternatives that was originally presented in Chapter 4 is repeated here for your convenience. The following procedures reflect the recommendations of the *CICA Handbook* with respect to the preparation of consolidated financial statements:

Asset Valuation The recommended approach to asset valuation is the parent company concept. That is, only the parent's share of any fair value changes and goodwill is recognized at the time of acquisition or combination. As a consequence, only the parent's share of the amortization of these values or recognition of their impairment is recorded in subsequent periods.

Non-Controlling Interest In The Balance Sheet

- **Disclosure** Section 1600 is not explicit on this issue. It simply states that the Non-Controlling Interest in the consolidated net assets of the subsidiary companies should be shown separately from shareholders' equity. This eliminates the entity approach and the fact that a non-controlling interest is present eliminates the proprietary approach. This seems to leave the parent company approach. However, in the absence of a clear statement that the Non-Controlling Interest should be disclosed as a part of long-term liabilities, it often ends up presented in a somewhat ambiguous fashion between the long-term liabilities and the consolidated shareholders' equity.

- **Calculation** The inconsistencies of Section 1600 become apparent in the calculation of the Non-Controlling Interest on the Balance Sheet. In general, this computation follows the parent company approach and bases the Non-Controlling

Interest on the non-controlling shareholders' proportionate share of the carrying values of the subsidiary. However, because the entity approach is used for the elimination of unrealized subsidiary profits, these transactions must be taken into account in determining the appropriate balance. Stated generally, the Non-Controlling Interest in the consolidated Balance Sheet would be computed by taking the non-controlling shareholders' proportionate interest in the book value of the subsidiary's Shareholders' Equity after this total has been adjusted for any unrealized intercompany profits of the subsidiary company.

Non-Controlling Interest In The Income Statement

- **Disclosure** With respect to income before extraordinary items and the results of discontinued operations, Section 1600 requires that the Non-Controlling Interest be given disclosure as a separate line item in the consolidated Income Statement. This, of course, reflects an adoption of the parent company approach. For no apparent reason, extraordinary items and the results of discontinued operations are dealt with by a different conceptual alternative. Only the parent company's proportionate interest in these items is disclosed which is an application of the proprietary concept.

- **Calculation** As was the case with the computation of the Non-Controlling Interest for purposes of disclosure in the consolidated Balance Sheet, the computation here is complicated by the presence of inconsistencies in the Recommendations of Section 1600. Generally, the Non-Controlling Interest in the consolidated Income Statement is based on the reported income of the subsidiary. Once again, however, adjustments must be made for the adoption of the entity approach in dealing with unrealized subsidiary profits. Stated generally, the Non-Controlling Interest in the consolidated Income Statement is calculated by taking the non-controlling shareholders' proportionate interest in the reported income of the subsidiary with the elimination of current subsidiary intercompany profits that are still unrealized from the consolidated point of view and the addition of subsidiary intercompany profits from previous years that have become realized for consolidation purposes during the year.

Unrealized Intercompany Profits Of The Subsidiary As already noted, Section 1600 adopts the entity approach here and requires 100 percent pro rata elimination of unrealized intercompany subsidiary profits.

Application Of The Equity Method

Basic Concepts

6-172. In Chapter 5, we indicated that the Net Income of an investor using the equity method for an investee had to be equal to the consolidated Net Income that would result from the consolidation of that investee. This requirement was based on the following Recommendation:

> **Paragraph 3051.08** *Investment income as calculated by the equity method should be the amount necessary to increase or decrease the investor's income to that which would have been recognized if the results of the investee's operations had been consolidated with those of the investor.* (August, 1978)

6-173. In Chapter 5 this meant that all of the adjustments for fair value write-offs and any goodwill impairment losses that would be required in the consolidation process, are also required in the application of the equity method. As you would expect, similar adjustments are required for the unrealized intercompany profits that were introduced in this Chapter.

6-174. As was noted in Chapter 5, however, there is a major difference in the disclosure of these adjustments when the equity method is applied. In consolidation, the various adjustments are included in specific consolidated account balances. In contrast, the equity method deals with all of these adjustments as modifications of the Investment Asset and Investment Income accounts. This is why equity method results are sometimes referred to as "one line consolidations".

Comprehensive Example

Income Statement

6-175. As we did in Chapter 5, we will use the comprehensive example that we have been working with throughout this Chapter to illustrate the application of the equity method. The basic data for this problem was presented in Paragraph 6-34 and will not be repeated here. The only change is that we will assume that Pleigh Company's majority ownership does not give it control over the Sleigh Company and, as a consequence, the investment cannot be consolidated.

6-176. From our previous experience with the Pleigh Company problem, we know that consolidated Net Income for 2009 amounts to $600,400 (Paragraph 6-130). Since the Pleigh Company's net income without the inclusion of any revenues from its Investment In Sleigh amounts to $420,000 ($500,000 cost method income less $80,000 dividend revenue), the only Investment Income that would satisfy the requirement stated in Paragraph 3051.08 is $180,400 ($600,400 - $420,000). This figure can be verified as follows:

Pleigh's Interest In Sleigh's Income:		
Sleigh's Reported Net Income	$200,000	
Realization Of Opening Inventory Profits	28,000	
Unrealized Closing Inventory Profits	(40,000)	
Realization Of Equipment Profit	50,000	
Sleigh's Adjusted Income	$238,000	
Pleigh's Proportionate Interest	80%	$190,400
Adjustment For Fair Value Amortization		(10,000)
Pleigh's Equity Method Investment Income		$180,400

6-177. Sleigh's Adjusted Income of $238,000 is also used to calculate the Non-Controlling Interest disclosed on the consolidated Income Statement (see Paragraph 6-130). Using the equity method Investment Income, the Income Statement of the Pleigh Company with the Investment In Sleigh carried by the equity method would be as follows:

Pleigh Company
Income Statement
Year Ending December 31, 2009

Sales	$4,000,000
Interest Revenue	24,000
Investment Income (Paragraph 6-176)	180,400
Total Revenues	$4,204,400
Cost Of Goods Sold	$2,800,000
Amortization Expense	200,000
Interest Expense	240,000
Other Expenses	364,000
Total Expenses	$3,604,000
Net Income	$ 600,400

Balance Sheet

6-178. If Pleigh was not consolidating its investment in Sleigh, and used the equity method in its single entity statements, the Balance Sheet account Investment In Sleigh would have to be increased to reflect Pleigh's equity in this investee. As is the case with Investment Income under the equity method, this Balance Sheet account would be subject to the same types of adjustments that would be required in the preparation of consolidated financial statements. The following equity pickup uses the same $770,000 Adjusted (Retained Earnings) Balance Since Acquisition as was used in the Retained Earnings distribution schedule in Paragraph 6-165. The required balance would be calculated as follows:

Investment In Sleigh At Cost		$3,200,000
Equity Pickup:		
Sleigh's December 31 2009 Retained Earnings	$2,400,000	
Balance At January 1, 2005 Acquisition	(1,500,000)	
Balance Since Acquisition	$ 900,000	
Unrealized Upstream Profits:		
Land	(40,000)	
Closing Inventories	(40,000)	
Equipment	(50,000)	
Adjusted Balance Since Acquisition	$ 770,000	
Ownership Percentage	80%	
Pleigh's Share	$ 616,000	
Adjustments:		
Fair Value Increase On Inventories	(80,000)	
Amortization Of Fair Value Increase On Plant And Equipment (5 Years At $10,000)	(50,000)	
Downstream Profit On Land	(25,000)	461,000
Investment In Sleigh At Equity		$3,661,000

6-179. If this amount is used on the asset side of Pleigh's single entity Balance Sheet, there will have to be a corresponding $461,000 ($3,661,000 - $3,200,000) adjustment to Retained Earnings on the equity side of the single entity Balance Sheet. This will leave Pleigh with the following single entity Balance Sheet under the equity method:

Pleigh Company
Single Entity Balance Sheet
As At December 31, 2009

Cash	$ 500,000
Current Receivables	800,000
Inventories	2,500,000
Long-Term Note Receivable	200,000
Investment In Sleigh (At Equity)	3,661,000
Land	1,500,000
Plant And Equipment (Net)	4,500,000
Total Assets	$13,661,000
Current Liabilities	$ 500,000
Long-Term Liabilities	2,000,000
No Par Common Stock	8,000,000
Retained Earnings ($2,700,000 + $461,000)	3,161,000
Total Equities	$13,661,000

6-180. Note that, when the equity method is used, the resulting Retained Earnings figure in Pleigh's single entity Balance Sheet is equal to the consolidated Retained Earnings figure resulting from the application of consolidation procedures (see Paragraph 6-170). This result follows from the Paragraph 3051.08 requirement that investment income as calculated by the equity method must be the amount necessary to increase or decrease the investor's income to that which would have been recognized if the results of the investee's operations had been consolidated with those of the investor.

Alternative Disclosure

6-181. In the example we have just considered, there were no downstream intercompany profits in the 2009 Net Income of the Pleigh Company. If such profits had been present, it would have been acceptable under the requirements of the *CICA Handbook* to simply deduct them from the Investment Income total. In view of the fact that such downstream profits are not included in the reported income of the Sleigh Company, this does not seem to be a particularly desirable form of disclosure. This inappropriateness is recognized in the *CICA Handbook* which provides for alternative disclosure of unrealized downstream profits. The relevant provision is as follows:

> **Paragraph 3051.15** The elimination of an unrealized intercompany gain or loss has the same effect on net income whether the consolidation or equity method is used. However, in consolidated financial statements, the elimination of a gain or loss may affect sales and cost of sales otherwise to be reported. In the application of the equity method, the gain or loss is eliminated by adjustment of investment income from the investee or by separate provision in the investor's financial statements, as is appropriate in the circumstances.

6-182. This Paragraph permits the disclosure of unrealized downstream profits as a separate item in the Income Statement of the investor company which is applying the equity method. It would be our view that such disclosure would be preferable to the deduction of such profits from the Investment Income account.

Exercise Six-4

Subject: Application Of The Equity Method

Note This is an equity method version of Exercise Six-2.

On January 1, 2005, the Parker Company purchases 65 percent of the outstanding shares of the Schaffer Company for $1,350,000 in cash. On that date, the Schaffer Company had No Par Common Stock of $700,000 and Retained Earnings of $1,000,000. On December 31, 2009, the adjusted trial balances of the Parker Company and its subsidiary, the Schaffer Company are as follows:

	Parker	Schaffer
Monetary Assets	$ 2,850,000	$ 725,000
Investment In Schaffer - At Cost	1,350,000	N/A
Non-Monetary Assets	6,475,000	2,045,000
Total Expenses	2,940,000	530,000
Dividends Declared	250,000	50,000
Total Debits	$13,865,000	$3,350,000
Liabilities	$ 1,712,500	$ 425,000
No Par Common Stock	3,000,000	700,000
Retained Earnings (January 1)	5,895,000	1,550,000
Sales	3,225,000	675,000
Dividend Revenue	32,500	Nil
Total Credits	$13,865,000	$3,350,000
January 2009 Retained Earnings	$5,895,000	$1,550,000
2009 Net Income	317,500	145,000
2009 Dividends Declared	(250,000)	(50,000)
December 31, 2009 Retained Earnings	$ 5,962,500	$1,645,000

Other Information:

1. At the date of Parker Company's acquisition of the Schaffer Company's shares, all of the identifiable assets and liabilities of the Schaffer Company had fair values that were equal to their carrying values except for a group of non-monetary assets

that had a fair value that was $150,000 greater than its carrying value. These non-monetary assets had a remaining useful life of 15 years. Both Companies use the straight-line method for all amortization calculations.

2. In each of the years since Parker acquired control over Schaffer, the goodwill arising on this business combination transaction has been tested for impairment. In 2007, a Goodwill Impairment Loss of $35,000 was recognized. In addition, the impairment test for 2009 found a further impairment of $25,000.

3. Schaffer Company's Sales during 2009 include sales of $85,000 to Parker Company. One-half of the merchandise remains in the December 31, 2009 inventories of Parker Company. The pricing on these sales provided Schaffer with a 30 percent gross margin based on sales price. In addition, as a result of these sales, on December 31, 2009, Parker still owes Schaffer $15,000 on open account. There were no intercompany sales in 2008.

4. On January 1, 2008, Schaffer sells a piece of equipment to Parker for $120,000 in cash. At this time, the carrying value of the machine on Schaffer's books is $100,000 and it has a remaining useful life of four years.

Assume that the Parker Company's majority ownership of Schaffer shares has never provided control over that Company and, as a consequence, consolidated financial statements cannot be prepared. Provide the Parker Company's single entity Income Statement for the year ending December 31, 2009, and its single entity Balance Sheet as at December 31, 2009, assuming the Investment In Schaffer is accounted for by the equity method since its acquisition. Note that the Parker Company's trial balance given in the problem accounts for the Investment In Schaffer using the cost method.

End of Exercise. Solution available in Study Guide.

Consolidated Cash Flow Statement

6-183. The preparation of a consolidated Cash Flow Statement was covered in Chapter 5. While this Chapter has added coverage of unrealized intercompany profits, this new material does not alter the procedures used to prepare the consolidated Cash Flow Statement. This means that there is no requirement for further discussion of this important financial statement in this Chapter. However, to facilitate your understanding of the procedures involved with the preparation of consolidated Cash Flow Statements, we are including an Exercise which illustrates this process.

Exercise Six-5

Subject: Consolidated Statement Of Cash Flows

Note This Exercise is identical to Exercise Five-5, except for Parts 5 and 6.

On January 1, 2003, the Parco Company acquires 80 percent of the outstanding voting shares of the Subco Company for $1,000,000 in cash. At this time the Subco Company has No Par Common Stock of $1,000,000 and Retained Earnings of $200,000. Also on this acquisition date, all of the identifiable assets and liabilities of Subco Company had fair values that were equal to their carrying values except for Inventories which had a fair value that was $400,000 less than its carrying value and Equipment which had a fair value that was $300,000 more than its carrying value. The Inventories were sold during 2003, while the Equipment had a remaining useful life on January 1, 2003 of ten years with no anticipated salvage value. Both the Parco Company and the Subco Company use the straight line method for all amortization calculations.

Comparative Balance Sheets for the two companies as at December 31, 2007 and December 31, 2008 are as follows:

Parco (000's)

	2008	2007
Cash	$ 800	$ 400
Accounts Receivable	1,500	1,800
Inventories	2,000	2,600
Investment In Subco (At Cost)	1,000	1,000
Land	1,000	800
Plant And Equipment (Net)	4,800	6,400
Total Assets	$11,100	$13,000
Accounts Payable	$ 400	$ 1,000
Bonds Payable - Par	3,000	4,000
Common Stock - No Par	4,000	4,000
Retained Earnings	3,700	4,000
Total Equities	$11,100	$13,000

Subco (000's)

	2008	2007
Cash	$ 365	$ 270
Accounts Receivable	900	650
Inventories	800	500
Land	450	850
Plant And Equipment (Net)	600	800
Total Assets	$3,115	$3,070
Accounts Payable	$ 700	$ 750
Bonds Payable - Par	800	800
Bonds Payable - Premium	15	20
Common Stock - No Par	1,000	1,000
Retained Earnings	600	500
Total Equities	$3,115	$3,070

Other Information:

1. During 2008, the Parco Company retires outstanding debt with a par value of $1,000,000 for $1,000,000 in cash.
2. During 2008, the Parco Company experiences a Net Loss of $300,000 and does not declare any dividends. This Net Loss includes an $800,000 write-down of Plant And Equipment to reflect the fact that its net carrying amount exceeded its net recoverable amount.
3. During 2008, the Subco Company earns Net Income of $500,000 and declares dividends of $400,000. All of the dividends declared are paid prior to December 31, 2008.
4. The goodwill measured at the time Parco acquired Subco has been tested for impairment in each subsequent year. No impairment has been found.
5. During 2008, the Subco Company sells Land to the Parco Company for cash of $200,000. The carrying value of this Land on the books of the Subco Company was $400,000. There were no purchases or sales of Plant And Equipment.

6. During 2008, the Subco Company sells merchandise to the Parco Company at a sales price of $400,000. On December 31, 2008, $100,000 of this merchandise is in the Inventories of the Parco Company and this merchandise contains a gross profit in the amount of $40,000. In addition, at this year end date, Parco Company still owes Subco Company $100,000 on open account. During 2007, there were no intercompany sales of merchandise.

Calculate consolidated Net Income for the Parco Company and its subsidiary, the Subco Company, for the year ending December 31, 2008. In addition, prepare a consolidated Cash Flow Statement for the Parco Company and its subsidiary, the Subco Company, for the year ending December 31, 2008.

End of Exercise. Solution available in Study Guide.

Step-By-Step Acquisitions

6-184. As was the case with the consolidated Cash Flow Statement, basic procedures for step-by-step acquisitions were covered in Chapter 5. While there is no need for further discussion of this type of acquisition in this Chapter, we believe that it is useful to include an Exercise to illustrate the required procedures when unrealized intercompany profits are included. As with the other Exercises in this Chapter, Exercise Six-6 is an extension of the similar Exercise in Chapter 5.

Exercise Six-6

Subject Step-By-Step Acquisition

Note This Exercise is identical to Exercise Five-6 except for the addition of unrealized intercompany profits.

On December 31, 2007, the Best Company purchases 40 percent of the outstanding shares of the Worst Company for $1,875,000. On this date, the carrying values of the Worst Company's net identifiable assets amount to $3,250,000 (Common Stock of $2,000,000, plus Retained Earnings of $1,250,000). All of the fair values of the individual identifiable assets and liabilities of the Worst Company have carrying values that are equal to their fair values except for Plant And Equipment. Specialized machinery with a remaining useful life of four years has a carrying value of $2,000,000 and a fair value of $2,725,000.

On December 31, 2008, the Best Company purchases an additional 15 percent of the outstanding shares of the Worst Company for $820,000. On this date, the carrying values of the Worst Company's net identifiable assets total $4,250,000 (Common Stock of $2,000,000, plus Retained Earnings of $2,250,000). All of the fair values of the identifiable assets and liabilities of the Worst Company have carrying values that are equal to their fair values except for Plant And Equipment. The specialized machinery now has a useful life of three years, a carrying value of $1,600,000, and a fair value of $2,300,000.

There has been no impairment of goodwill in either 2008 or 2009.

During 2008, Worst sold Land to Best for $250,000. The carrying value of the Land on Worst's books was $200,000.

During 2009, Worst sold merchandise to Best for $450,000. The sales were priced to provide Worst with a gross margin of 25 percent on the sales price. One-third of this merchandise remains in the December 31, 2009 inventories of Best.

On December 31, 2009, the carrying values for Best's and Worst's Plant And Equipment are $3,520,000 and $1,600,000, respectively. The Retained Earnings balance of Best on December 31, 2009 is $4,275,000, while Worst's Retained Earnings balance is $2,450,000.

Calculate the amount that would be shown on the December 31, 2009 consolidated Balance Sheet for Goodwill, Plant And Equipment and Retained Earnings.

End of Exercise. Solution available in Study Guide.

Summary Of Consolidation Procedures

6-185. In Chapter 4, we began the development of a set of procedures that could be used in the preparation of a consolidated Balance Sheet at the date of the subsidiary's acquisition. In Chapter 5 we made substantial additions to this list involving intercompany expenses and revenues, fair value amortization, and the distribution of subsidiary retained earnings since acquisition. In this Chapter, in addition to modifying some of the Chapter 5 procedures to reflect the presence of unrealized intercompany profits, we added new Step B procedures for eliminating and restoring such items. Specifically we have added Step B-6 and modified Step C-1 to deal with unrealized intercompany profits. We are now in a position to provide a complete summary of basic consolidation procedures as developed in this text. This summary is as follows:

Step A-1 Procedure Eliminate 100 percent of the Investment In Subsidiary account.

Step A-2 Procedure Eliminate 100 percent of all the acquisition date balances in the subsidiary's shareholders' equity (includes both contributed capital and retained earnings).

Step A-3 Procedure Allocate any debit or credit Differential that is present at acquisition to the investor's share of fair value changes on identifiable assets, fair value changes on identifiable liabilities, and positive or negative goodwill.

Step A-4 Procedure Allocate to a Non-Controlling Interest account in the consolidated Balance Sheet, the non-controlling interest's share of the at acquisition book value of the common shareholders' equity of the subsidiary (includes both contributed capital and retained earnings).

Step B-1 Procedure Eliminate 100 percent of all intercompany assets and liabilities.

Step B-2 Procedure Give recognition to the post-acquisition realization of acquisition date fair value changes on assets and liabilities that have been used up or sold during the post-acquisition period. To the extent that this realization occurred in prior periods, recognition will require an adjustment of the opening retained earnings of the subsidiary. Alternatively, if the realization occurred in the current period, the adjustment will be to the subsidiary's current period expenses, revenues, gains, or losses.

Step B-3 Procedure Recognize current and cumulative goodwill impairment losses that have been measured since the acquisition of the subsidiary and the initial recognition of the goodwill balance. To the extent that the impairment took place during the current period, the measured amount will be charged to Goodwill Impairment Loss. To the extent that it occurred in prior periods, it will be charged to retained earnings.

Step B-4 Procedure Eliminate 100 percent of all intercompany expenses and revenues.

Step B-5 Procedure Eliminate 100 percent of subsidiary dividends declared. The parent's share of this amount will be deducted from the revenues of the parent company and the non-controlling interest's share of this amount will be deducted from the Non-Controlling Interest in the Balance Sheet.

Step B-6(a) Procedure Eliminate 100 percent of all unrealized intercompany profits (losses) that are present in the single entity financial statements. There are three groups of such profits to consider:

1. Profits that were recognized in the single entity statements of the parent or subsidiary in a previous period, remain unrealized at the beginning of the current period, and are realized during the current period (for example, unrealized profits in beginning of the period inventories that are sold during the current period). Such profits will be deducted from the opening retained earnings of the company that recognized them in their single entity financial statements. Subsequently, they will be added back to income through an adjustment of current expenses or revenues.
2. Profits that were recognized in the single entity statement of the parent or subsidiary in the current period and remain unrealized at the end of the current period (for example, unrealized profits on current period inventory sales). These profits will be removed from current income through an adjustment of the current expenses or revenues. Note that 100 percent of the profit will be removed, without regard to whether it is an upstream profit or a downstream profit. If it is an upstream profit, its removal will reduce both consolidated Net Income and the Non-Controlling Interest that is included in the consolidated Income Statement.
3. Profits that were recognized in the single entity statement of the parent or subsidiary in the current or a previous period, and remain unrealized at the end of the current period (for example, an unrealized profit in the previous year on the sale of a machine with a four year life). These profits will be removed from both the opening and the closing retained earnings of the company that recognized them in their single entity financial statements. If some part of the profit is realized during the current period, this will be recognized through an adjustment of current expenses or revenues. In such cases, the adjustment to the opening retained earnings will differ from the adjustment to the closing retained earnings.

While all of the references in the preceding paragraphs are to unrealized profits, there is also the possibility of unrealized losses resulting from intercompany transactions. While the concepts involved with losses are the same as with unrealized profits, the applicable signs will be reversed (e.g., unrealized losses will be added back to income, rather than deducted as is the case with unrealized profits).

Step B-6(b) Procedure Recognize the amount of previously unrealized intercompany profits or losses that have become realized during the period, either through the sale of the related asset or through usage of that asset. The amount that was previously unrealized from the consolidated point of view would be a deduction from the opening single entity retained earnings of the parent or subsidiary company. To the extent the profit has become realized during the period, it will be included in the current consolidated Net Income through an adjustment of an expense or revenue. Any amount of the profit that remains unrealized at the end of the period will be deducted from the closing retained earnings of the relevant parent or subsidiary. As was the case with Step B-6(a), 100 percent of the previously unrealized profit will be recognized, without regard to whether it is upstream or downstream. If it is an upstream profit, the addition will increase both consolidated Net Income and the Non-Controlling Interest in the Income Statement.

Step C-1 Procedure Determine the appropriate allocation of the subsidiary's adjusted retained earnings since acquisition. The book value of the subsidiary retained earnings since acquisition will first be adjusted for upstream profits that are unrealized as of the date applicable to the retained earnings balance (opening retained earnings in open trial balance problems). This adjusted balance will be multiplied by the ownership percentage of the non-controlling interest, with the product being allocated to the non-controlling interest. After the non-controlling interest is subtracted, the resulting balance will be adjusted for the fair value write-offs called for in Step B-2, as well as any goodwill impairment as described in Step B-3. The balance remaining after these adjustments will be allocated to consolidated retained earnings.

Step C-2 Procedure Eliminate the subsidiary's adjusted retained earnings since acquisition. This amount will be allocated to the Non-Controlling Interest in the consolidated Balance Sheet and to consolidated retained earnings as determined in Step C-1.

6-186. As we did in Chapter 5, we would remind you that, as stated, the listed procedures apply to open trial balance problems with the investment in the subsidiary carried by the cost method. In dealing with closed trial balance problems these procedures will need to be modified. Such required modifications were illustrated in the closed trial balance version of our comprehensive example.

Summary Of Definitional Calculations

6-187. With this Chapter's coverage of the procedures required to deal with unrealized intercompany profits, we can now provide you with a comprehensive list of the definitions to be used in preparing consolidated financial statements. We continue to encourage you to work towards preparing the required balances in consolidated financial statements by using these direct definitional calculations. The list is as follows:

Identifiable Assets And Liabilities The amount to be included in the consolidated Balance Sheet for any identifiable asset or liability is calculated as follows:

- 100 percent of the carrying value of the identifiable asset (liability) on the books of the parent company at the Balance Sheet date; *plus*
- 100 percent of the carrying value of the identifiable asset (liability) on the books of the subsidiary company at the Balance Sheet date; *plus (minus)*
- the parent company's share of the fair value increase (decrease) on the asset (liability) (i.e., the parent company's share of the difference between the fair value of the subsidiary's asset or liability at time of acquisition and the carrying value of that asset or liability at the time of acquisition); *minus (plus)*
- amortization of the parent company's share of the fair value increase (decrease) on the asset (liability) for the period since acquisition to the current Balance Sheet date; *minus (plus)*
- upstream and downstream intercompany profits (losses) that are unrealized as of the Balance Sheet date.

Goodwill The Goodwill to be recorded in the consolidated Balance Sheet is equal to:

- the excess of the cost of the investment over the parent company's share of the fair values of the subsidiary's net assets at the time of acquisition; *minus*
- the amount of any goodwill impairment that has been recognized in the period since the acquisition to the current Balance Sheet date.

Non-Controlling Interest - Balance Sheet The Non-Controlling Interest to be recorded in the consolidated Balance Sheet is an amount equal to the non-controlling interest's ownership percentage multiplied by:

- the book value of the subsidiary's common stock equity at the Balance Sheet date; *minus (plus)*

- upstream intercompany profits (losses) that are unrealized as of the Balance Sheet date.

Contributed Capital The Contributed Capital to be recorded in the consolidated Balance Sheet is equal to the contributed capital from the single entity Balance Sheet of the parent company.

Retained Earnings The Retained Earnings amount to be included in the consolidated Balance Sheet is calculated as follows:

- 100 percent of the Retained Earnings of the parent company; *plus (minus)*
- the parent company's share of the subsidiary's Retained Earnings (Deficit) since acquisition, adjusted for upstream intercompany profits (losses) that are unrealized as of the Balance Sheet date; *plus (minus)*
- 100 percent of the adjustments to consolidated expenses, revenues, gains, and losses for realized fair value changes during the period since acquisition to the current Balance Sheet date; *minus*
- 100 percent of any goodwill impairment that has been recognized since the acquisition to the current Balance Sheet date; *minus (plus)*
- any downstream intercompany profits (losses) that are unrealized as of the Balance Sheet date.

Revenue The amount of any revenue to be included in the consolidated Income Statement is calculated as follows:

- 100 percent of the amount reported in the parent company's financial statements; *plus*
- 100 percent of the amount reported in the subsidiary's financial statements; *minus*
- 100 percent of any intercompany amounts included in the parent or subsidiary figures; *plus (minus)*
- the parent's share of any fair value changes realized during the period through usage or sale of subsidiary assets (fair value amortization and amounts realized through the sale of subsidiary assets prior to the end of their economic life). It would be unusual for fair value realizations to be related to revenues. However, it could happen. For example, amortization of a fair value change on a long-term receivable would be treated as an adjustment of interest revenue. An additional example could result from the sale of an asset on which a fair value change has been recorded in the consolidated financial statements. If there was a gain (revenue) on the transaction, it would have to be adjusted for the realized fair value change; *minus (plus)*
- 100 percent of any upstream or downstream unrealized intercompany profits (losses) that are included in the parent or subsidiary company revenues (e.g., gain on an intercompany sale of land during the current year); *plus (minus)*
- 100 percent of any upstream or downstream unrealized intercompany profits (losses) that were unrealized in a previous period, but have become realized during the current period (e.g., gain on an intercompany sale of land in a previous year, with the land being resold outside the consolidated entity during the current year).

Expense The amount of any expense to be included in the consolidated Income Statement is calculated as follows:

- 100 percent of the amount reported in the parent company's financial statements; *plus*
- 100 percent of the amount reported in the subsidiary's financial statements; *minus*
- 100 percent of any intercompany amounts included in the parent or subsidiary figures; *plus (minus)*
- the parent's share of any fair value changes realized during the period through usage or sale of subsidiary assets (fair value amortization and amounts realized through the sale of subsidiary assets prior to the end of their economic life); *plus (minus)*
- 100 percent of any upstream or downstream unrealized profits (losses) that are included in the parent or subsidiary company expenses (e.g., unrealized intercompany profits in the closing inventories would be added to the consolidated Cost Of Goods Sold); *minus (plus)*
- 100 percent of any upstream or downstream unrealized profits (losses) that were eliminated in a previous period because they were unrealized, but that have become realized during the current period (e.g., unrealized intercompany profits in the opening inventories would be subtracted from the consolidated Cost Of Goods Sold).

Goodwill Impairment Loss If the required annual test of goodwill for impairment determines that any impairment has occurred during the current period, this amount will be recorded as a Goodwill Impairment Loss.

Non-Controlling Interest - Income Statement The Non-Controlling Interest in the consolidated Income Statement is an amount equal to the non-controlling interest's ownership percentage multiplied by:

- the reported Net Income of the subsidiary; *minus (plus)*
- 100 percent of upstream unrealized intercompany profits (losses) that are included in the Net Income of the subsidiary (e.g., upstream unrealized profits in the closing inventories); *plus (minus)*
- 100 percent of upstream profits that were eliminated in a previous period because they were unrealized, but that have become realized during the current period (e.g., upstream unrealized profits in the opening inventories).

Note that, if the subsidiary has extraordinary items or results from discontinued operations, this Non-Controlling Interest will be based on the subsidiary's Income Before Extraordinary Items And Discontinued Operations. Also note that, in situations where there are preferred shares with a prior claim on the income of the subsidiary, the Non-Controlling Interest to be disclosed in the consolidated Income Statement will include such claims.

Consolidated Net Income Consolidated Net Income can be calculated as follows:

- 100 percent of the parent company's Net Income, excluding dividends received from the subsidiary; *plus (minus)*
- the parent's share of the sum of:
    - the subsidiary's reported Net Income (Net Loss); *minus (plus)*
    - upstream unrealized intercompany profits (losses) that are included in the Net Income of the subsidiary (e.g., upstream unrealized profits in the closing inventories); *plus (minus)*

- upstream profits that were eliminated in a previous period because they were unrealized, but that have become realized during the current period (e.g., upstream unrealized profits in the opening inventories).

minus (plus)

- the parent's share of any fair value changes realized during the period through usage or sale of subsidiary assets (fair value amortization and amounts realized through the sale of subsidiary assets prior to the end of their economic life); *minus*
- any Goodwill Impairment Loss that is recognized during the period; *minus (plus)*
- 100 percent of downstream profits (losses) that are included in the Net Income of the parent (e.g., downstream unrealized profits in the closing inventories); *plus (minus)*
- 100 percent of downstream profits that were eliminated in a previous period because they were unrealized, but that have become realized during the current period (e.g., downstream unrealized profits in the opening inventories).

6-188. This comprehensive list of definitions can be used to solve any basic consolidation problem in which the investment in the subsidiary is carried by the cost method. We would encourage the use of them in solving the problems which accompany this Chapter.

International Convergence

Differences In Standards

No Intercompany Profits

6-189. As was noted in Chapter 5, the relevant international standards are IFRS No. 3, *Business Combinations*, and IAS No. 27, *Consolidated And Separate Financial Statements*. Also as noted in that Chapter, there are several differences between the recommendations of these IFRSs and the corresponding Canadian standards:

> **Asset Valuation** IFRS No. 3 requires that 100 percent of fair value changes on identifiable assets be recognized at the time of acquisition. Section 1581 only allows the acquirer's share to be recognized. Note, however, IFRS No. 3 does not allow the recognition of 100 percent of goodwill. Only the acquirer's share of this asset can be recognized.
>
> **Non-Controlling Interest** Consistent with the entity approach, IAS No. 27 requires the non-controlling interest to be presented as a component of consolidated Shareholders' Equity. The value to be recognized will include the non-controlling interest's share of fair value changes on identifiable assets.
>
> **Terminology** IAS No. 27 continues to use the term Minority Interest, rather than the more accurate Non-Controlling Interest. However, this is certain to be changed by the amendments resulting from the FASB/IASB project. Given this, we will ignore this difference in presenting examples based on current IFRSs.

Intercompany Profits

6-190. As discussed in this Chapter 6, Section 1600 requires 100 percent elimination of all unrealized intercompany profits. In addition, the Section specifically indicates that, in the case of upstream profits, the elimination should be allocated proportionately between controlling and non-controlling interests.

6-191. The relevant international recommendation on unrealized intercompany profits is found in IAS No. 27 as follows:

> **Paragraph 25** Intragroup balances and transactions, including income, expenses and dividends, are eliminated in full. Profits and losses resulting from intragroup transactions that are recognised in assets, such as inventory and fixed assets, are eliminated in full. Intragroup losses may indicate an impairment that requires recognition

in the consolidated financial statements. IAS 12, *Income Taxes,* applies to temporary differences that arise from the elimination of profits and losses resulting from intragroup transactions.

6-192. This recommendation is consistent with Canadian standards in that it requires 100 percent elimination of the unrealized amounts. While IAS No. 27 is not specific as to how the elimination of upstream unrealized amounts would be allocated, it would clearly allow the Canadian approach of pro rata allocation to the controlling and non-controlling interests.

6-193. While this Chapter dealing with unrealized intercompany profits has not introduced additional differences between Canadian and international standards, we believe that it is useful to present our basic example in its open trial balance version as it would appear when international standards are applied.

Example: Open Trial Balance Problem

Basic Data

6-194. In order to illustrate the application of international standards to an open trial balance problem, we will use the same example that was originally presented in Paragraph 6-34. It is repeated here for your convenience.

On January 1, 2005, the Pleigh Company purchases 80 percent of the outstanding shares of the Sleigh Company for $3,200,000 in cash. On that date, the Sleigh Company had No Par Common Stock of $2,000,000 and Retained Earnings of $1,500,000. On December 31, 2009, the adjusted trial balances of the Pleigh Company and its subsidiary, the Sleigh Company are as follows:

	Pleigh	Sleigh
Cash	$ 500,000	$ 300,000
Current Receivables	800,000	400,000
Inventories	2,500,000	1,700,000
Long-Term Note Receivable	200,000	Nil
Investment In Sleigh - At Cost	3,200,000	N/A
Land	1,500,000	1,000,000
Plant And Equipment (Net)	4,500,000	1,900,000
Cost Of Goods Sold	2,800,000	1,500,000
Amortization Expense	200,000	100,000
Other Expenses	364,000	616,000
Interest Expense	240,000	84,000
Dividends Declared	350,000	100,000
Total Debits	$17,154,000	$7,700,000
Current Liabilities	$ 500,000	$ 200,000
Long-Term Liabilities	2,000,000	700,000
No Par Common Stock	8,000,000	2,000,000
Retained Earnings (January 1)	2,550,000	2,300,000
Sales	4,000,000	2,500,000
Interest Revenue	24,000	Nil
Dividend Revenue	80,000	Nil
Total Credits	$17,154,000	$7,700,000
January 1, 2009 Retained Earnings	$ 2,550,000	$ 2,300,000
2009 Net Income	500,000	200,000
Dividends Declared	(350,000)	(100,000)
December 31, 2009 Retained Earnings	$ 2,700,000	$2,400,000

Other Information:

1. At the date of Pleigh Company's acquisition of the Sleigh Company's shares, all of the identifiable assets and liabilities of the Sleigh Company had fair val]ues that were equal to their carrying values except:

   - Inventories which had fair values that were $100,000 more than their carrying values,
   - Land with a fair value that was $150,000 less than its carrying value, and
   - Plant And Equipment which had a fair value that was $250,000 greater than its carrying value.

   The Plant And Equipment had a remaining useful life on the acquisition date of 20 years while the Inventories that were present on the acquisition date were sold during the year ending December 31, 2005. The Land is still on the books of the Sleigh Company on December 31, 2009. Both companies use the straight line method to calculate amortization.

2. In each of the years since Pleigh acquired control over Sleigh, the goodwill arising on this business combination transaction has been tested for impairment. No impairment was found in any of the years since acquisition.

3. Sleigh Company's Sales during 2009 include sales of $300,000 to Pleigh Company. The December 31, 2009 Inventories of the Pleigh Company contain $100,000 of this merchandise purchased from Sleigh Company during 2009. In addition, the January 1, 2009 Inventories of the Pleigh Company contained $70,000 in merchandise purchased from Sleigh Company during 2008. All intercompany sales are priced to provide the selling company a gross margin on sales price of 40 percent.

4. On December 31, 2009, the Pleigh Company is holding Sleigh Company's long-term note payable in the amount of $200,000. Interest at 12 percent is payable on July 1 of each year. Pleigh Company has been holding this note since July 1, 2007.

5. During 2007, the Pleigh Company sold Land to the Sleigh Company for $100,000 in cash. The Land had a carrying value on the books of the Pleigh Company of $75,000.

6. During 2008, the Sleigh Company sold Land to the Pleigh Company for $150,000. This Land had a carrying value on the books of the Sleigh Company of $110,000.

7. On December 31, 2007, the Sleigh Company sold Equipment to the Pleigh Company for $600,000. The Equipment had originally cost the Sleigh Company $800,000 and, at the time of the intercompany sale, had accumulated amortization of $350,000. On this date, it was estimated that the remaining useful life of the Equipment was three years with no net salvage value.

Required: Using current international financial reporting standards, prepare a consolidated Income Statement and a consolidated Statement Of Retained Earnings for the year ending December 31, 2009 and a consolidated Balance Sheet as at December 31, 2009 for the Pleigh Company and its subsidiary, the Sleigh Company.

Step A Procedures

6-195. The investment analysis that was used in preparing consolidated financial statements under Canadian standards, can also be used when international standards are applied. This analysis is as follows:

	80 Percent	100 Percent
Investment Cost (Total Fair Value)	$3,200,000	$4,000,000
Sleigh Shareholders' Equity At Acquisition	(2,800,000)	(3,500,000)
Differential	$ 400,000	$ 500,000
Fair Value Changes:		
Increase On Inventories	($ 80,000)	($ 100,000)
Decrease On Land	120,000	150,000
Increase On Plant And Equipment (Net)	(200,000)	(250,000)
Total Fair Value Change Credit (Debit)	($ 160,000)	($ 200,000)
Goodwill	$ 240,000	$ 300,000

6-196. The investment elimination entry would be different under international standards in that 100 percent of the fair value changes on identifiable assets would be recognized. This would require a corresponding change to the Non-Controlling Interest credit in order to record their share of these fair value changes.

No Par Common Stock (At Acquisition)	$2,000,000	
Retained Earnings (At Acquisition)	1,500,000	
Plant And Equipment (100%))	250,000	
Inventories (100%)	100,000	
Goodwill (80%)	240,000	
Land (100%)		$ 150,000
Non-Controlling Interest [(20%)($3,500,000 + $200,000)]		740,000
Investment In Sleigh		3,200,000

Step B(1) - Intercompany Assets And Liabilities

6-197. These entries are unchanged by the application of international standards.

Long-Term Liabilities	$200,000	
Long-Term Note Receivable		$200,000
Current Liabilities	$ 12,000	
Current Receivables		$ 12,000

Step B(2) - Realization Of Fair Value Changes

6-198. The entries required to write off recognized fair value changes would be different under international standards in that they would be based on 100 percent of the fair value changes, rather than Pleigh's 80 percent share of these values. The 2009 entries for Inventories and Plant And Equipment would be as follows:

Retained Earnings - Sleigh's Opening	$100,000	
Inventories		$100,000
Retained Earnings - Sleigh's Opening	$50,000	
Amortization Expense ($250,000 ÷ 25)	12,500	
Plant And Equipment (Net)		$62,500

(The $50,000 debit to Sleigh's opening Retained Earnings is for the four years 2005 through 2008. The credit to Plant And Equipment is for the five years 2005 through 2009.

Step B(3) - Goodwill Impairment

6-199. The Other Information in this problem indicates that there has been no goodwill impairment in any of the years under consideration. Given this, no entry is required under either Canadian or international standards. However, if an entry had been required, it would not be altered by the application of current international standards. This reflects the fact that IFRS No. 3 allows recognition of only the acquirer's share of any goodwill that is measured at the date of the business combination.

Step B(4) - Intercompany Expenses And Revenues

6-200. The entries for eliminating the intercompany Sales and intercompany Interest Expense would not be altered by the application of international standards. These entries are as follows:

Sales	$300,000	
Cost Of Goods Sold		$300,000
Interest Revenue	$24,000	
Interest Expense		$24,000

Step B(5) - Intercompany Dividends

6-201. The entry to eliminate intercompany dividends would not be altered by the application of international standards. The entry is as follows:

Dividend Revenue	$80,000	
Non-Controlling Interest (Balance Sheet)	20,000	
Dividends Declared		$100,000

Step B(6) - Downstream Profit On Land

6-202. The entry to eliminate the unrealized profit on the 2007 downstream sale of land would not be altered by the application of international standards. The 2009 entry is as follows:

Retained Earnings - Pleigh's Opening	$25,000	
Land		$25,000

Step B(6) - Upstream Profit On Land

6-203. The entry to eliminate the unrealized profit on the 2008 upstream sale of land would not be altered by the application of international standards. The 2009 entry is as follows:

Retained Earnings - Sleigh's Opening	$40,000	
Land		$40,000

Step B(6) - Upstream Closing Inventory Profits

6-204. The entry to eliminate the unrealized upstream profits in the December 31, 2009 inventories of Pleigh would not be altered by the application of international standards. The entry is as follows:

Cost Of Goods Sold	$40,000	
Inventories		$40,000

Step B(6) - Upstream Opening Inventory Profits

6-205. The entry to eliminate the unrealized upstream profits in the January 1, 2009 inventories of Pleigh would not be altered by the application of international standards. The entry is as follows:

Retained Earnings - Sleigh's Opening	$28,000	
Cost Of Goods Sold		$28,000

Step B(6) - Upstream Profit On Equipment

6-206. The entry to eliminate the unrealized upstream profits from the 2007 intercompany sale of equipment would not be altered by the application of international standards. It would be as follows:

Retained Earnings - Sleigh's Opening	$100,000	
Amortization Expense (2009)		$50,000
Plant And Equipment (Net)		50,000

Step C - Distribution Of The Subsidiary Retained Earnings

6-207. The difference here is that the fair value write-offs affect both the controlling and non-controlling interests. This reflects the fact that they are based on 100 percent of the fair value changes, rather than just the acquirer's share of these changes. However, the treatment of unrealized profits is not altered by the application of international standards. The required schedule would be as follows:

Retained Earnings Distribution Schedule

January 1, 2009 Balance As Per The Trial Balance	$2,300,000
Balance At Acquisition	(1,500,000)
Balance Since Acquisition	$ 800,000
Unrealized Upstream Profits On January 1, 2009:	
Land	(40,000)
Opening Inventories	(28,000)
Equipment Sale ($150,000 - $50,000)	(100,000)
Fair Value Realizations:	
100% Fair Value Increase On Inventories	(100,000)
Amortization Of 100% Fair Value Increase On Plant And Equipment (4 Years At $12,500)	(50,000)
Adjusted Balance Since Acquisition	$ 482,000
Non-Controlling Interest [(20%)($482,000)]	(96,400)
To Consolidated Retained Earnings	$ 385,600

6-208. Based on this schedule, the required distribution entry would be as follows:

Retained Earnings - Sleigh	$482,000	
Non-Controlling Interest (Balance Sheet)		$ 96,400
Consolidated Retained Earnings		385,600

6-209. The opening balance for consolidated Retained Earnings is simply the Pleigh Company's January 1, 2009 balance of $2,550,000, less the $25,000 downstream profit on land, plus the $385,600 allocation resulting from the preceding journal entry, for a total of $2,910,600. Note that the amount distributed to consolidated Retained Earnings has not been changed by the application of international standards (Paragraph 6-123).

Consolidated Income Statement

6-210. Applying international standards, the 2009 consolidated Income Statement of the Pleigh Company and its subsidiary would be prepared as follows:

Pleigh Company And Subsidiary
Consolidated Income Statement (International Standards)
Year Ending December 31, 2009

Sales ($4,000,000 + $2,500,000 - $300,000)	$6,200,000
Interest Revenue ($24,000 - $24,000)	Nil
Dividend Revenue ($80,000 - $80,000)	Nil
Total Revenues	$6,200,000
Cost Of Goods Sold ($2,800,000 + $1,500,000 - $300,000 + $40,000 - $28,000)	$4,012,000
Amortization Expense ($200,000 + $100,000 + $12,500 - $50,000)	262,500
Interest Expense ($240,000 + $84,000 - $24,000)	300,000
Other Expenses ($364,000 + $616,000)	980,000
Total Expenses	$5,554,500
Consolidated Net Income	$ 645,500

6-211. You will note that the application of international standards results in an Income Statement that is very similar to that produced under Canadian standards (Paragraph 6-130). The differences that you should note are as follows:

- Amortization has been increased by $2,500 to reflect the fact that 100 percent of the fair value change on Plant And Equipment has been recognized and is subject to amortization.
- The final consolidated Net Income figure is before any recognition of the non-controlling interest's share of this income. As this interest is viewed as a distribution of consolidated Net Income, it will be disclosed in the consolidated Statement Of Retained Earnings.

Definitional Calculation Of Consolidated Net Income

6-212. When international standards are applied, a definitional calculation of consolidated Net Income would be prepared as follows:

Pleigh Company's Net Income		$500,000
Intercompany Dividend Revenues		(80,000)
Pleigh's Net Income Less Dividends		$420,000
Sleigh's Net Income	$200,000	
Fair Value Adjustment Of Amortization Expense	(12,500)	
Realization Of Opening Inventory Profits	28,000	
Unrealized Closing Inventory Profits	(40,000)	
Realization Of Equipment Profit	50,000	225,500
Consolidated Net Income		$645,500

Consolidated Statement Of Retained Earnings

6-213. Applying international standards, the 2009 consolidated Statement Of Retained Earnings for the Pleigh Company and its subsidiary would be prepared as follows:

Pleigh Company And Subsidiary
Consolidated Statement Of Retained Earnings (International Standards)
Year Ending December 31, 2009

Balance - January 1, 2009 (Paragraph 6-209)	$2,910,600
2009 Consolidated Net Income	645,500
Available For Distribution	$3,556,100
Non-Controlling Interest In 2009 Subsidiary Income [(20%)($225,500) From Paragraph 6-212]	(45,100)
2009 Dividends (Pleigh's Only)	(350,000)
Balance - December 31, 2009	$3,161,000

6-214. As was the case with the Income Statement, the application of international standards results in a Statement of Retained Earnings that is very similar to that produced under Canadian standards. In fact, the opening and closing balances are unchanged from the Canadian standards version (Paragraph 6-134). The differences that should be noted are as follows:

- The consolidated Net Income figure is before any deduction for the non-controlling interest's share of Sleigh's Net Income.
- As it was not included in the determination of consolidated Net Income, the Non-Controlling Interest is shown in this Statement Of Retained Earnings as a distribution of consolidated Net Income.

Definitional Calculation Of Consolidated Retained Earnings

6-215. A definitional calculation could be used to verify the closing balance that has been determined in the preceding Statement Of Retained Earnings:

Pleigh's Closing Balance		$2,700,000
Sleigh's Balance - December 31, 2009	$2,400,000	
Balance At Acquisition	(1,500,000)	
Balance Since Acquisition	$ 900,000	
Unrealized Upstream Profits:		
Land	(40,000)	
Closing Inventories	(40,000)	
Equipment Sale	(50,000)	
Fair Value Realizations:		
100% Fair Value Increase On Inventories	(100,000)	
Amortization Of 100% Fair Value Increase On Plant And Equipment (5 Years At $12,500)	(62,500)	
Adjusted Balance Since Acquisition	$ 607,500	
Pleigh's Interest	80%	486,000
Downstream Profit On Land		(25,000)
Consolidated Retained Earnings As At December 31, 2009		$3,161,000

Consolidated Balance Sheet

6-216. The most complex item in the consolidated Balance Sheet is usually the non-controlling interest. As we noted in the Canadian standards version of this example, we can use the procedures that we have developed to calculate this figure. Using this approach, the calculation would be as follows:

Step A Allocation (Balance At Acquisition)	$740,000
Step B Adjustment For Dividends	(20,000)
Step C Allocation (Retained Earnings Since Acquisition)	96,400
Non-Controlling Interest In Income (Paragraph 6-213)	45,100
Non-Controlling Interest (Balance Sheet)	$861,500

6-217. This figure can also be calculated directly from the Balance Sheet items:

Sleigh's Common Stock	$2,000,000
Sleigh's December 31, 2009 Retained Earnings	2,400,000
Unrealized Upstream Profits:	
Land	(40,000)
Closing Inventories	(40,000)
Equipment Sale	(50,000)
Unrealized Fair Value Changes:	
Increase On Inventories ($100,000 - $100,000)	Nil
Decrease On Land	(150,000)
Increase On Plant ($250,000 - $62,500)	187,500
Adjusted Balance	$4,307,500
Non-Controlling Interest Share	20%
Non-Controlling Interest	$ 861,500

6-218. Using these figures, the consolidated Balance Sheet can be prepared as follows:

Pleigh Company And Subsidiary
Consolidated Balance Sheet (International Standards)
As At December 31, 2009

Cash ($500,000 + $300,000)	$ 800,000
Current Receivables ($800,000 + $400,000 - $12,000)	1,188,000
Inventories ($2,500,000 + $1,700,000 + $100,000 - $100,000 - $40,000)	4,160,000
Long-Term Note Receivable ($200,000 - $200,000)	Nil
Investment In Sleigh ($3,200,000 - $3,200,000)	Nil
Land ($1,500,000 + $1,000,000 - $150,000 - $40,000 - $25,000)	2,285,000
Plant And Equipment (Net) ($4,500,000 + $1,900,000 + $250,000 - $62,500 - $50,000)	6,537,500
Goodwill	240,000
Total Assets	$15,210,500
Current Liabilities ($500,000 + $200,000 - $12,000)	$ 688,000
Long-Term Liabilities ($2,000,000 + $700,000 - $200,000)	2,500,000
Non-Controlling Interest (Paragraph 6-216)	861,500
No Par Common Stock (Pleigh's Balance)	8,000,000
Retained Earnings (Paragraph 6-213)	3,161,000
Total Equities	$15,210,500

6-219. Here again, the financial statement that results from the application of international standards is similar to the one we prepared under Canadian standards (Paragraph 6-139). The differences that should be noted are as follows:

- The figures for Land and Plant And Equipment are different in that they include 100 percent of the fair value changes on these assets, not just Pleigh's share of these changes.
- The value for the Non-Controlling Interest is changed to reflect their share of the fair value changes that are included in the Balance Sheet.
- While this point is not made clear in this unclassified Balance Sheet, the Non-Controlling Interest would be presented as a component of the consolidated Shareholders' Equity, not as a separate item outside of Shareholders' Equity.

Additional Readings

6-220. In writing the material in the text, we have incorporated all of the relevant *CICA Handbook* recommendations, as well as material from other sources that we felt to be of importance. This includes some material from international accounting standards.

6-221. While this approach meets the needs of the great majority of our readers, some of you may wish to pursue this subject in greater depth. To facilitate this, you will find a fairly comprehensive list of additional readings at the end of each relevant Chapter in our *Guide To Canadian Financial Reporting*.

CD-ROM Note Our *Guide To Canadian Financial Reporting* is available on the CD-ROM which is included with this text.

Walk Through Problem

Note

This problem is an extension of the Walk Through Problem that was presented at the end of Chapters Four and Five. As previously explained, these problems provide you with a fill-in-the-blank solution format to assist you in solving the problem. These problems are designed to be an easy introduction to solving the type of problem illustrated in the Chapter.

Basic Data

On December 31, 2007, the Puff Company purchased 60 percent of the outstanding voting shares of the Snuff Company for $720,000 in cash. On that date, subsequent to the completion of the business combination, the Balance Sheets of the Puff and Snuff Companies and the fair values of Snuff's identifiable assets and liabilities were as follows:

	Balance Sheets		Fair Values
	Puff	Snuff	Snuff
Cash And Accounts Receivable	$ 350,000	$ 200,000	$200,000
Inventories	950,000	500,000	450,000
Investment In Snuff	720,000	N/A	N/A
Plant And Equipment (Net)	2,400,000	700,000	800,000
Total Assets	$4,420,000	$1,400,000	
Current Liabilities	$ 400,000	$ 100,000	$100,000
Long-Term Liabilities	1,000,000	400,000	360,000
No Par Common Stock	1,000,000	800,000	N/A
Retained Earnings	2,020,000	100,000	N/A
Total Equities	$4,420,000	$1,400,000	

The December 31, 2007 Inventories of Snuff are sold during 2008. The Plant And Equipment of Snuff on December 31, 2007 has an estimated useful life of 10 years while the Long-Term Liabilities that were present on that date mature on December 31, 2010. Both Companies use the straight line method of amortization. Puff carries its Investment In Snuff by the cost method.

The Income Statements for the year ending December 31, 2011 and the Balance Sheets as at December 31, 2011 of the Puff and Snuff Companies are as follows:

Income Statements
For The Year Ending December 31, 2011

	Puff Company	Snuff Company
Sales	$3,700,000	$2,000,000
Other Revenues	200,000	50,000
Total Revenues	$3,900,000	$2,050,000
Cost Of Goods Sold	$2,000,000	$1,100,000
Amortization Expense	600,000	400,000
Other Expenses	900,000	350,000
Total Expenses	$3,500,000	$1,850,000
Net Income	$ 400,000	$ 200,000

Balance Sheets
As At December 31, 2011

	Puff Company	Snuff Company
Cash	$ 80,000	$ 75,000
Accounts Receivable	500,000	325,000
Inventories	1,375,000	750,000
Investment In Snuff	720,000	N/A
Plant And Equipment (Net)	2,325,000	1,100,000
Total Assets	$5,000,000	$2,250,000
Current Liabilities	$ 400,000	$ 220,000
Long Term Liabilities	1,000,000	750,000
No Par Common Stock	1,000,000	800,000
Retained Earnings	2,600,000	480,000
Total Equities	$5,000,000	$2,250,000

Other Information:

1. During 2011, Puff declared and paid $150,000 in dividends while Snuff declared and paid $75,000 in dividends.

2. Included in the 2011 Sales of Snuff are sales of $300,000 to Puff on which Snuff earned a gross profit of $125,000. Of these sales, $60,000 remain in the December 31, 2011 inventories of Puff. The January 1, 2011 inventories of Puff contained merchandise purchased from Snuff for $75,000 on which Snuff had earned a gross profit of $35,000. Puff owes Snuff $45,000 on December 31, 2011 for the merchandise purchases.

3. During 2011, Puff had sales of $175,000 to Snuff. Of these sales, $80,000 are on hand in the December 31, 2011 inventories of Snuff. Of the $250,000 of sales from Puff to Snuff in 2010, $110,000 were not resold in 2010. Puff's intercompany sales are priced to provide a gross margin of 40 percent of sales price.

4. Goodwill has been tested for impairment in the years 2008 through 2011. The test procedures found impairment or $16,000 in 2008, an amount that was recognized as a Goodwill Impairment Loss in that year. A further impairment loss of $20,000 was found and recognized in 2009. No impairment was found in 2010 or 2011.

5. On January 1, 2008, the Snuff Company sold the Puff Company a machine for $250,000. The machine had been purchased by Snuff on January 1, 2007 for $360,000 and had an estimated useful life on that date of six years with no salvage value expected. On December 31, 2007, the date of the business combination, this machine had a fair value that was equal to its carrying value.

5. On December 12, 2011, the Snuff Company sold a piece of land that it had purchased for $15,000 on July 21, 2007 to Puff for $33,000. This price is to be paid on February 24, 2012.

Required: For the Puff Company and its subsidiary the Snuff Company, prepare, using the fill-in-the-blank solution format in the separate Study Guide:

A. A consolidated Income Statement for the year ending December 31, 2011.

B. A consolidated Statement Of Retained Earnings for the year ending December 31, 2011.

C. A consolidated Balance Sheet as at December 31, 2011.

In addition, provide calculations which verify:

- Consolidated Net Income for the year ending December 31, 2011,
- the December 31, 2011 consolidated Retained Earnings, and
- the December 31, 2011 Non-Controlling Interest that would be disclosed on the consolidated Balance Sheet.

Problems For Self Study

(The solutions for these problems can be found in the separate Study Guide.)

Self Study Problem Six - 1

Note This problem is an expanded version of Self Study Problem Five-1. It is also used as Self Study Problem Six-7 to illustrate the application of international accounting standards.

On December 31, 2004, the Pastel Company purchased 90 percent of the outstanding voting shares of the Shade Company for $5,175,000 in cash. On that date, the Shade Company had No Par Common Stock of $2,000,000 and Retained Earnings of $4,000,000. All of the Shade Company's identifiable assets and liabilities had carrying values that were equal to their fair values except for:

1. Accounts Receivable with fair values that were $50,000 less than their carrying values.
2. Land which had a fair value that was $100,000 greater than its carrying value.
3. Equipment which had fair values that were $1,000,000 less than their carrying values and a remaining useful life of 10 years.
4. Long-Term Liabilities which had fair values that were $200,000 less than their carrying values and mature on December 31, 2009.

The Balance Sheets of the Pastel Company and the Shade Company as at December 31, 2009 were as follows:

Pastel and Shade Companies
Balance Sheets
As At December 31, 2009

	Pastel	Shade
Cash And Current Receivables	$ 2,625,000	$ 800,000
Inventories	8,000,000	2,000,000
Equipment (Net)	24,000,000	4,000,000
Buildings (Net)	10,000,000	2,000,000
Investment In Shade (Cost)	5,175,000	N/A
Land	2,000,000	1,200,000
Total Assets	$51,800,000	$10,000,000
Dividends Payable	Nil	$ 100,000
Current Liabilities	$ 1,800,000	900,000
Long-Term Liabilities	10,000,000	1,000,000
No Par Common Stock	20,000,000	2,000,000
Retained Earnings	20,000,000	6,000,000
Total Equities	$51,800,000	$10,000,000

The Income Statements of the Pastel and Shade Companies for the year ending December 31, 2009 were as follows:

Pastel And Shade Companies
Income Statements
For The Year Ending December 31, 2009

	Pastel	Shade
Sales	$8,000,000	$2,000,000
Gain On Sale Of Land	500,000	Nil
Other Revenues	800,000	100,000
Total Revenues	$9,300,000	$2,100,000
Cost Of Goods Sold	$3,800,000	$ 800,000
Amortization Expense	1,400,000	300,000
Other Expenses	2,000,000	400,000
Total Expenses	$7,200,000	$1,500,000
Net Income	$2,100,000	$ 600,000

Other Information:

1. In each of the years since Pastel acquired control over Shade, the Goodwill arising on this business combination transaction has been tested for impairment. After completing the annual impairment test, it was determined that the Goodwill Impairment Loss for 2009 was $15,000. No impairment was found in any of the other years since acquisition.
2. Both Companies use the straight line method to calculate all amortization charges and the First-In, First-Out inventory flow assumption.
3. Pastel uses the cost method to carry its Investment In Shade.
4. The Sales account in the Pastel Company's Income Statement includes only sales of merchandise. All other income is accounted for in Other Revenues or a separate Gain account.
5. During 2009, Pastel charged Shade $100,000 for management fees. None of this amount has been paid during 2009.
6. During 2009, dividends of $200,000 were declared and paid by Pastel and dividends of $100,000 were declared by Shade. On December 31, 2009, the dividends that were declared by the Shade Company during 2009 had not yet been paid.
7. During 2009, Shade sold to Pastel $500,000 worth of merchandise, of which 75 percent had been resold by Pastel in 2009. Pastel owes Shade $75,000 on December 31, 2009 due to these purchases. The December 31, 2008 Inventories of Pastel contained $300,000 of merchandise purchased from Shade in 2008. The Shade Company's sales are priced to provide it with a 60 percent gross margin on its sales price.
8. During 2008, Pastel sold $300,000 of merchandise to the Shade Company and earned a total gross profit of $120,000 on these sales. On December 31, 2008, $150,000 of this merchandise is still in the inventories of Shade. During 2009, Pastel sold merchandise which had cost it $60,000 to Shade for $150,000. None of this merchandise was resold in 2009. Shade has not paid for these 2009 purchases as at December 31, 2009.
9. On January 1, 2006, Shade sold a piece of Equipment that it had purchased on January 1, 2003 for $180,000 to Pastel for $120,000. On January 1, 2003, the Equipment had an estimated useful life of 18 years with no net salvage value and there is no change in these estimates at the time of the sale to Pastel.
10. On December 30, 2009, Pastel sold to Shade for cash of $1,500,000, a Building with a net book value of $800,000 and the Land it was situated on which had originally cost $200,000. Shade allocated $1,100,000 of the purchase price to the Building and the remainder to the Land. The Building has an estimated remaining useful life of 25 years on

this date. The gain on this sale is disclosed separately for reporting purposes on Pastel's books.

Required: Prepare, for the Pastel Company and its subsidiary, the Shade Company:

A. The consolidated Income Statement for the year ending December 31, 2009.

B. The consolidated Statement Of Retained Earnings for the year ending December 31, 2009.

C. The consolidated Balance Sheet as at December 31, 2009.

Self Study Problem Six - 2

On December 31, 2004, the Plate Company purchased 80 percent of the outstanding shares of the Stone Company for $7,800,000 in cash. On this date, the identifiable assets and liabilities of the Stone Company had carrying values and fair values as follows:

	Carrying Values	Fair Values
Cash	$ 500,000	$ 500,000
Accounts Receivable	1,500,000	1,500,000
Inventories	3,000,000	4,000,000
Land	1,500,000	1,000,000
Plant And Equipment	9,000,000	8,000,000
Accumulated Amortization	(3,000,000)	Nil
Software Programs	Nil	500,000
Total Assets	$12,500,000	
Current Liabilities	$ 1,000,000	$ 1,000,000
Long-Term Liabilities	4,500,000	6,000,000
Common Stock - No Par	3,000,000	
Reserve For Contingencies	1,000,000	
Unrestricted Retained Earnings	3,000,000	
Total Equities	$12,500,000	

On December 31, 2004, the Plant And Equipment of the Stone Company had a remaining useful life of 20 years. The December 31, 2004 Inventories of Stone were sold in 2005. On December 31, 2004, the Stone Company had internally developed software that was patent protected. The asset was written off by Stone in 2006 when technological advances made the software obsolete.

On December 31, 2009, the adjusted trial balances for the Plate Company and the Stone Company are as follows:

	Plate	Stone
Cash	$ 3,000,000	$ 700,000
Accounts Receivable	7,500,000	2,100,000
Inventories	14,300,000	5,600,000
Land	9,000,000	2,500,000
Plant And Equipment	26,400,000	12,000,000
Patents	1,400,000	Nil
Investment In Stone (At Cost)	7,800,000	N/A
Cost Of Goods Sold	6,400,000	3,400,000
Other Expenses	3,800,000	1,600,000
Dividends Declared	2,000,000	1,000,000
Total Debits	$81,600,000	$28,900,000

	Plate	Stone
Accumulated Amortization	$10,600,000	$ 6,500,000
Current Liabilities	8,500,000	1,200,000
Long-Term Liabilities	15,000,000	4,500,000
Common Stock - No Par	20,000,000	3,000,000
Reserve For Contingencies	Nil	500,000
Unrestricted Retained Earnings	11,000,000	6,200,000
Total Revenues	16,500,000	7,000,000
Total Credits	$81,600,000	$28,900,000

	Plate	Stone
January 1, 2009 Retained Earnings	$11,000,000	$6,700,000
2009 Net Income	6,300,000	2,000,000
2009 Dividends Declared	(2,000,000)	(1,000,000)
December 31, 2009 Retained Earnings	$15,300,000	$7,700,000

Other Information:

1. There have been no additions or disposals of Plant And Equipment by the Stone Company between December 31, 2004 and December 31, 2009. The Land on the books of the Stone Company on December 31, 2004 has not been sold.

2. In each of the years since Plate acquired control over Stone, the goodwill arising on this business combination transaction has been tested for impairment. No impairment was found in any of the years since acquisition.

3. All of the Long-Term Liabilities of the Stone Company mature on December 31, 2014.

4. On January 1, 2006, the Stone Company purchased a Patent for $1,100,000. On that date, the remaining legal life of the Patent was 11 years. On January 1, 2007, the Patent had a carrying value on the Stone Company's books of $1,000,000. At this time, the Patent was sold to the Plate Company for $2,000,000.

5. During 2009, the Plate Company sold Land to the Stone Company for $1,000,000. The carrying value of the Land on the books of the Plate Company was $500,000.

6. During 2009, $2,000,000 of the Stone Company's sales were made to the Plate Company. A total of $500,000 of this merchandise remains in the December 31, 2009 Inventories of the Plate Company. The December 31, 2008 Inventories of the Plate Company contained merchandise purchased from the Stone Company for $800,000. All intercompany sales are priced to provide the selling company with a gross profit margin on sales price of 30 percent.

7. Both Companies use the straight line method to calculate all amortization.

Required:

A. Prepare a consolidated Income Statement for the Plate Company and its subsidiary, the Stone Company, for the year ending December 31, 2009.

B. Prepare a consolidated Statement Of Retained Earnings for the Plate Company and its subsidiary, the Stone Company, for the year ending December 31, 2009.

C. Prepare a consolidated Balance Sheet for the Plate Company and its subsidiary, the Stone Company, as at December 31, 2009.

Self Study Problem Six - 3

On January 1, 2007, the Prime Company acquired 60 percent of the outstanding voting shares of the Sublime Company for $3,000,000 in cash. On this date, the Sublime Company had No Par Common Stock of $3,000,000 and Retained Earnings of $2,000,000.

All of Sublime's identifiable assets and liabilities had fair values that were equal to their carrying values except for:

- the Accounts Receivable, which had a total net realizable value that was $100,000 less than its stated value; and
- equipment with a fair value that was $400,000 less than its carrying value (remaining useful life is 3 years).

Both Companies use the straight line method to calculate amortization expenses. Prime carries its Investment In Sublime by the cost method.

On December 31, 2009, the Balance Sheets of the Prime Company and its subsidiary, the Sublime Company, are as follows:

Balance Sheets
As At December 31, 2009

	Prime	Sublime
Cash And Current Receivables	$ 1,600,000	$ 1,000,000
Inventories	2,400,000	1,500,000
Investment In Sublime (At Cost)	3,000,000	N/A
Long-Term Receivables	1,500,000	Nil
Plant and Equipment (Net)	14,000,000	8,500,000
Land	5,000,000	2,000,000
Total Assets	$27,500,000	$13,000,000
Current Liabilities	$ 4,500,000	$ 2,000,000
Long-Term Liabilities	5,000,000	3,000,000
No Par Common Stock	6,000,000	3,000,000
Retained Earnings	12,000,000	5,000,000
Total Equities	$27,500,000	$13,000,000

Other Information:

1. The Prime Company sold merchandise to the Sublime Company in 2008, of which $300,000 remained in the December 31, 2008 Inventories of Sublime. This merchandise was sold in 2009 and Prime made no further sales of inventories to Sublime in 2009. Prime's sales are priced to provide it with a 40 percent gross margin on cost.

2. Sublime's Sales in 2009 included $500,000 in sales to Prime. Of these sales, $200,000 remain in the December 31, 2009 Inventories of Prime. Prime's January 1, 2009 inventories contained $400,000 of merchandise purchased from Sublime, of which $300,000 was purchased in 2008 and sold in 2009. The remaining $100,000 was specialized merchandise purchased in 2006, prior to the business combination and $50,000 of this specialized merchandise remains in Prime's December 31, 2009 Inventories. Sublime's sales are priced to provide it with a 25 percent gross margin on cost.

3. On July 1, 2009, the Sublime Company sold a machine it had built for a cost of $200,000 to the Prime Company for $150,000. The machine had an estimated useful life on July 1, 2009 of 5 years. On December 31, 2009, the Prime Company has a liability outstanding of 80 percent of the purchase price and this will be paid in 2010.

4. The Sublime Company purchased Land for $2,000,000 from Prime on November 1, 2008. The Land was originally purchased by Prime for $1,000,000. The purchase price is to be paid in 5 equal installments of $400,000 on January 1 of each year subsequent to the sale.

5. During 2009, Prime earned Net Income of $2,000,000 and paid dividends of $400,000, and Sublime earned Net Income of $500,000 and paid dividends of $100,000.

6. In each of the years since Prime acquired control over Sublime, the Goodwill arising on this business combination transaction has been tested for impairment. No impairment was found in any of the years since acquisition.

Required: Prepare a consolidated Balance Sheet for the Prime Company and its subsidiary, the Sublime Company, as at December 31, 2009.

Self Study Problem Six - 4

On January 1, 2006, the Pork Company purchased 80 percent of the outstanding voting shares of the Salt Company for $1,000,000 in cash. At the acquisition date, the carrying value of the net assets of Salt was equal to $1,000,000 and all of its identifiable assets and liabilities had fair values that were equal to their carrying values, except for an issue of 10 percent coupon Bonds Payable which had a fair value which was $100,000 less than its carrying value. The bonds mature on January 1, 2016.

The condensed Income Statements for the two Companies for the year ending December 31, 2009 are as follows:

Pork And Salt Companies
Income Statements
For The Year Ending December 31, 2009

	Pork	Salt
Sales	$600,000	$400,000
Cost Of Goods Sold	$250,000	$300,000
Other Expenses	300,000	150,000
Total Expenses	$550,000	$450,000
Income (Loss) Before Extraordinary Items	$ 50,000	($ 50,000)
Extraordinary Gain (Loss)	100,000	(200,000)
Net Income (Loss)	$150,000	($250,000)

Other Information

1. In each of the years since Pork acquired the shares of Salt, the Goodwill arising on this business combination transaction has been tested for impairment. In 2009, a Goodwill Impairment Loss of $40,000 was recognized. No impairment was found in any of the other years since the shares were acquired.

2. On January 1, 2008, the Salt Company sold a building to the Pork Company for $4,500,000. When Salt purchased the building on January 1, 2003 for $5,500,000, it had an estimated useful life of 20 years.

3. During 2009, Pork paid $100,000 in dividends and no dividends were paid by Salt.

4. Both Companies use the straight line method to calculate amortization.

Required:

A. Prepare a consolidated Income Statement for the Pork Company and its subsidiary, the Salt Company, for the year ending December 31, 2009.

B. Assume that the Pork Company does not classify the Salt Company as a subsidiary. Prepare an Income Statement for the Pork Company for the year ending December 31, 2009 assuming it uses the equity method to account for its investment in the Salt Company.

Self Study Problem Six - 5

On July 1, 2009, the Patco Company paid $720,000 in cash to acquire 80 percent of the outstanding voting shares of the Stand Company. At this date, the fair values of all of Stand Company's identifiable assets and liabilities had fair values that were equal to their carrying values except for a group of fixed assets and a copyright. The fixed assets had a carrying value that exceeded their fair value by $120,000. These assets have a remaining useful life on July 1, 2009 of four years. The copyright is the only intangible asset owned by Stand and it has a fair value of $90,000 on July 1, 2009.

The following condensed financial statements for the two Companies have been provided by the chief accountant for Patco:

2009 Balance Sheets

	January 1 Patco	July 1 Stand	December 31 Patco	December 31 Stand
Cash	$ 25,000	$ 10,000	$ 12,000	$ 6,000
Non-Cash Current Assets	1,000,000	140,000	663,000	84,000
Investment In Stand	Nil	N/A	720,000	N/A
Fixed Assets (Net)	1,500,000	900,000	1,680,000	1,050,000
Intangible Assets	700,000	60,000	525,000	54,000
Total Assets	$3,225,000	$1,110,000	$3,600,000	$1,194,000
Current Liabilities	$ 450,000	$ 60,000	$ 450,000	$ 75,000
Long-Term Liabilities	600,000	300,000	675,000	300,000
Common Stock	1,500,000	225,000	1,500,000	225,000
Retained Earnings	675,000	525,000	975,000	594,000
Total Equities	$3,225,000	$1,110,000	$3,600,000	$1,194,000

2009 Income Statements

	Patco Year Ended December 31	Stand Six Months Ended December 31
Sales	$4,600,000	$600,000
Cost Of Goods Sold	$2,700,000	$375,000
Amortization Of Fixed Assets	525,000	120,000
Amortization Of Intangibles	175,000	6,000
Other Expenses	900,000	30,000
Total Expenses	$4,300,000	$531,000
Net Income	$ 300,000	$ 69,000

In addition to the preceding single entity financial statements, Patco's accountant also provides the following consolidated Balance Sheet for Patco Company and its subsidiary, Stand Company:

Consolidated Balance Sheet
As At December 31, 2009

Cash	$ 18,000
Non-Cash Current Assets	730,000
Fixed Assets	2,659,650
Intangible Assets	792,600
Total Assets	$4,200,250
Current Liabilities	$ 525,000
Long-Term Liabilities	975,000
Non-Controlling Interest	163,130
Common Stock	1,500,000
Retained Earnings	1,037,120
Total Equities	$4,200,250

Other Information:

1. The Patco Company carries its Investment In Stand by the cost method. Both Companies use the straight line method for amortization calculations.

2. During the period July 1, 2009 through December 31, 2009, Stand sells merchandise to Patco in the total amount of $170,000. One-half of this merchandise is in the closing inventories of Patco. The intercompany sales are priced to provide a markup of 25 percent on its invoice cost.

3. On October 1, 2009, Stand sold equipment to Patco for $98,000. The equipment had a carrying value on the books of Stand of $112,000 and, at the time of the sale, its remaining useful life was estimated to be 10 years. On July 1, 2009, the carrying value of this equipment was equal to its fair value.

4. On March 1, 2009, Patco purchased a building for $218,000. The vendor accepted a $75,000, 5 year mortgage from Patco and the remainder of the purchase price was paid in cash.

5. All intangible assets are tested annually for impairment by both Companies. No impairment was found in any year.

Required:

A. Calculate consolidated Net Income for Patco Company and its subsidiary, Stand Company, for the year ending December 31, 2009.

B. Verify the calculations used by the Patco Company accountant in establishing the consolidated Balance Sheet values for:
   1. Intangible Assets.
   2. Non-Controlling Interest.
   3. Retained Earnings.

C. Prepare a consolidated Cash Flow Statement for the Patco Company and its subsidiary, Stand Company, for the year ending December 31, 2009.

Self Study Problem Six - 6

On December 31, 2002, the Rosebud Company purchased 20 percent of the outstanding voting shares of the Ginko Company for $600,000 in cash. On that date, the Ginko Company's Balance Sheet and the fair values of its identifiable assets and liabilities were as follows:

	Carrying Values	Fair Values
Cash And Current Receivables	$ 300,000	$ 300,000
Inventories	1,000,000	800,000
Plant And Equipment (Net)	2,000,000	2,400,000
Total Assets	$3,300,000	
Current Liabilities	$ 200,000	$ 200,000
Long-Term Liabilities	600,000	600,000
Common Stock - No Par	1,000,000	
Retained Earnings	1,500,000	
Total Equities	$3,300,000	

On this date, the remaining useful life of the Ginko Company's Plant And Equipment is estimated to be 10 years.

On December 31, 2005, the Rosebud Company purchased an additional 55 percent of the outstanding voting shares of the Ginko Company for $1,705,000 in cash. This increases its total percentage of ownership to 75 percent. On that date, the Ginko Company's Balance Sheet and the fair values of its identifiable assets and liabilities were as follows:

	Carrying Values	Fair Values
Cash And Current Receivables	$ 500,000	$ 500,000
Inventories	1,375,000	1,375,000
Land	425,000	475,000
Plant And Equipment (Net)	1,400,000	1,600,000
Total Assets	$3,700,000	
Current Liabilities	$ 300,000	$ 300,000
Long-Term Liabilities	600,000	700,000
Common Stock - No Par	1,000,000	
Retained Earnings	1,800,000	
Total Equities	$3,700,000	

There has been no purchase or sale of Plant And Equipment by the Ginko Company during the years 2003 through 2005. The Long-Term Liabilities mature on December 31, 2025. The Rosebud Company accounts for its Investment In Ginko by the cost method.

The Income Statements and Statements Of Retained Earnings of the Rosebud and Ginko Companies for the year ending December 31, 2010, and their Balance Sheets as at December 31, 2010 are as follows:

Balance Sheets
As At December 31, 2010

	Rosebud	Ginko
Cash And Current Receivables	$ 500,000	$ 600,000
Inventories	600,000	1,200,000
Investment In Ginko	2,305,000	Nil
Land	795,000	500,000
Plant And Equipment (Net)	2,900,000	2,200,000
Total Assets	$7,100,000	$4,500,000
Current Liabilities	$ 500,000	$ 400,000
Long-Term Liabilities	1,000,000	600,000
Common Stock - No Par	2,000,000	1,000,000
Retained Earnings	3,600,000	2,500,000
Total Equities	$7,100,000	$4,500,000

Income Statements
For The Year Ending December 31, 2010

	Rosebud	Ginko
Sales Of Merchandise	$5,000,000	$2,000,000
Other Revenues	200,000	100,000
Total Revenues	$5,200,000	$2,100,000
Cost Of Goods Sold	$2,500,000	$ 800,000
Other Expenses And Losses	1,000,000	900,000
Total Expenses And Losses	$3,500,000	$1,700,000
Net Income	$1,700,000	$ 400,000

Statements Of Retained Earnings
For The Year Ending December 31, 2010

	Rosebud	Ginko
Opening Balance	$2,500,000	$2,200,000
Net Income	1,700,000	400,000
Balance Available	$4,200,000	$2,600,000
Dividends Declared	(600,000)	(100,000)
Closing Balance	$3,600,000	$2,500,000

Other Information:

1. In each of the years since Rosebud acquired control over Ginko, the goodwill arising on this business combination transaction has been tested for impairment. No impairment was found in any of the years since acquisition.

2. There has been no sale of Plant And Equipment or Land by the Ginko Company during the years under consideration except for a piece of equipment which was purchased on January 1, 2006 for $300,000. On that date, it had an expected useful life of 6 years. The piece of equipment was sold to Rosebud for $100,000 on January 1, 2008.

3. During 2009, Rosebud had sales of $400,000 to Ginko of which $150,000 were not resold by Ginko until 2010. In 2010, of the $550,000 in total sales from Rosebud to Ginko, $220,000 remained in the December 31, 2010 inventories of Ginko. On December 31, 2010, Ginko still owes Rosebud $175,000 for 2010 merchandise purchases. All of Rosebud's sales to Ginko are priced to provide a gross margin on sales prices of 50 percent.

4. In 2009, Ginko had sales of $160,000 to Rosebud of which all but $20,000 was resold by Rosebud during 2009. During 2010, Rosebud purchased $190,000 of merchandise from Ginko of which $45,000 remained in the December 31, 2010 inventories of Rosebud. All of Ginko's sales to Rosebud are priced to provide a gross margin on sales prices of 60 percent.

5. The Rosebud Company and the Ginko Company account for inventories on a first-in, first-out basis. Both Companies use the straight line method to calculate all amortization charges.

6. On December 15, 2010, the Rosebud Company sold a parcel of land to the Ginko Company for $75,000, payable in two equal installments on December 15, 2010 and January 15, 2011. The Rosebud Company had purchased this parcel of land for $118,000 in 2004.

Required: Prepare a consolidated Income Statement and Statement Of Retained Earnings for the year ending December 31, 2010, and a consolidated Balance Sheet as at December 31, 2010 for the Rosebud Company and its subsidiary, the Ginko Company.

Self Study Problem Six - 7

Note This problem uses the same data that is found in Self Study Problem Six-1. However, in this case the solution should comply with international financial reporting standards. The data is repeated here for your convenience.

On December 31, 2004, the Pastel Company purchased 90 percent of the outstanding voting shares of the Shade Company for $5,175,000 in cash. On that date, the Shade Company had No Par Common Stock of $2,000,000 and Retained Earnings of $4,000,000. All of the Shade Company's identifiable assets and liabilities had carrying values that were equal to their fair values except for:

1. Accounts Receivable with fair values that were $50,000 less than their carrying values.
2. Land which had a fair value that was $100,000 greater than its carrying value.
3. Equipment which had fair values that were $1,000,000 less than their carrying values and a remaining useful life of 10 years.
4. Long-Term Liabilities which had fair values that were $200,000 less than their carrying values and mature on December 31, 2009.

The Balance Sheets of the Pastel Company and the Shade Company as at December 31, 2009 were as follows:

Pastel and Shade Companies
Balance Sheets
As At December 31, 2009

	Pastel	Shade
Cash And Current Receivables	$ 2,625,000	$ 800,000
Inventories	8,000,000	2,000,000
Equipment (Net)	24,000,000	4,000,000
Buildings (Net)	10,000,000	2,000,000
Investment In Shade (Cost)	5,175,000	N/A
Land	2,000,000	1,200,000
Total Assets	$51,800,000	$10,000,000
Dividends Payable	Nil	$ 100,000
Current Liabilities	$ 1,800,000	900,000
Long-Term Liabilities	10,000,000	1,000,000
No Par Common Stock	20,000,000	2,000,000
Retained Earnings	20,000,000	6,000,000
Total Equities	$51,800,000	$10,000,000

The Income Statements of the Pastel and Shade Companies for the year ending December 31, 2009 were as follows:

Pastel And Shade Companies
Income Statements
For The Year Ending December 31, 2009

	Pastel	Shade
Sales	$8,000,000	$2,000,000
Gain On Sale Of Land	500,000	Nil
Other Revenues	800,000	100,000
Total Revenues	$9,300,000	$2,100,000
Cost Of Goods Sold	$3,800,000	$ 800,000
Amortization Expense	1,400,000	300,000
Other Expenses	2,000,000	400,000
Total Expenses	$7,200,000	$1,500,000
Net Income	$2,100,000	$ 600,000

Other Information:

1. In each of the years since Pastel acquired control over Shade, the Goodwill arising on this business combination transaction has been tested for impairment. After completing the annual impairment test, it was determined that the Goodwill Impairment Loss for 2009 was $15,000. No impairment was found in any of the other years since acquisition.

2. Both Companies use the straight line method to calculate all amortization charges and the First-In, First-Out inventory flow assumption.

3. Pastel uses the cost method to carry its Investment In Shade.

4. The Sales account in the Pastel Company's Income Statement includes only sales of merchandise. All other income is accounted for in Other Revenues or a separate Gain account.

5. During 2009, Pastel charged Shade $100,000 for management fees. None of this amount has been paid during 2009.

6. During 2009, dividends of $200,000 were declared and paid by Pastel and dividends of $100,000 were declared by Shade. On December 31, 2009, the dividends that were declared by the Shade Company during 2009 had not yet been paid.

7. During 2009, Shade sold to Pastel $500,000 worth of merchandise, of which 75 percent had been resold by Pastel in 2009. Pastel owes Shade $75,000 on December 31, 2009 due to these purchases. The December 31, 2008 Inventories of Pastel contained $300,000 of merchandise purchased from Shade in 2008. The Shade Company's sales are priced to provide it with a 60 percent gross margin on its sales price.

8. During 2008, Pastel sold $300,000 of merchandise to the Shade Company and earned a total gross profit of $120,000 on these sales. On December 31, 2008, $150,000 of this merchandise is still in the inventories of Shade. During 2009, Pastel sold merchandise which had cost it $60,000 to Shade for $150,000. None of this merchandise was resold in 2009. Shade has not paid for these 2009 purchases as at December 31, 2009.

9. On January 1, 2006, Shade sold a piece of Equipment that it had purchased on January 1, 2003 for $180,000 to Pastel for $120,000. On January 1, 2003, the Equipment had an estimated useful life of 18 years with no net salvage value and there is no change in these estimates at the time of the sale to Pastel.

10. On December 30, 2009, Pastel sold to Shade for cash of $1,500,000, a Building with a net book value of $800,000 and the Land it was situated on which had originally cost $200,000. Shade allocated $1,100,000 of the purchase price to the Building and the remainder to the Land. The Building has an estimated remaining useful life of 25 years on this date. The gain on this sale is disclosed separately for reporting purposes on Pastel's books.

Required: Using the recommendations of IFRS No. 3, *Business Combinations*, and IAS No. 27, *Consolidated And Separate Financial Statements*, prepare, for the Pastel Company and its subsidiary, the Shade Company, the following:

A. The consolidated Income Statement for the year ending December 31, 2009.

B. The consolidated Statement Of Retained Earnings for the year ending December 31, 2009.

C. The consolidated Balance Sheet as at December 31, 2009.

Assignment Problems

(The solutions for these problems are only available in the solutions manual that has been provided to your instructor.)

Assignment Problem Six - 1

Note This problem is an expanded version of Assignment Problem Five-1. It is also used as Assignment Problem Six-8 to illustrate the application of international accounting standards.

On December 31, 2004, the Percy Company purchased 75 percent of the outstanding voting shares of the Stern Company for $3,000,000 in cash. On that date, Stern had No Par Common Stock of $2,000,000 and Retained Earnings of $1,000,000.

On December 31, 2004 all of the identifiable assets and liabilities of Stern had fair values that were equal to their carrying values with the following exceptions:

1. Inventories with fair values that were $400,000 less than their carrying values.
2. Land with a fair value that was $800,000 greater than its carrying value.
3. Long-Term Liabilities, maturing on January 1, 2010, with fair values that were $200,000 less than their carrying values.

Both Companies use the straight line method to calculate amortization. In its single entity records, Percy carries its investment in Stern at cost.

The Land which was on the books of the Stern Company on December 31, 2004 has not been sold as at December 31, 2009.

Financial statements for Percy and Stern for the year ending December 31, 2009 are as follows:

Income Statements
For The Year Ending December 31, 2009

	Percy	Stern
Merchandise Sales	$5,000,000	$2,000,000
Other Revenues	1,000,000	500,000
Total Revenues	$6,000,000	$2,500,000
Cost Of Goods Sold	$2,000,000	$1,000,000
Amortization Expense	400,000	300,000
Other Expenses	600,000	400,000
Total Expenses	$3,000,000	$1,700,000
Net Income	$3,000,000	$ 800,000

Statements Of Retained Earnings
For The Year Ending December 31, 2009

	Percy	Stern
Opening Balance	$10,000,000	$1,600,000
Net Income	3,000,000	800,000
Balance Available	$13,000,000	$2,400,000
Dividends Declared	(1,000,000)	(400,000)
Closing Balance	$12,000,000	$2,000,000

Balance Sheets
As At December 31, 2009

	Percy	Stern
Cash And Current Receivables	$ 1,500,000	$1,200,000
Note Receivable	1,000,000	Nil
Inventories	4,500,000	1,000,000
Investment In Stern (At Cost)	3,000,000	N/A
Plant And Equipment (Net)	9,000,000	3,000,000
Land	2,000,000	800,000
Total Assets	$21,000,000	$6,000,000
Current Liabilities	$ 500,000	$ 200,000
Long-Term Liabilities	3,500,000	1,800,000
Common Stock - No Par	5,000,000	2,000,000
Retained Earnings	12,000,000	2,000,000
Total Equities	$21,000,000	$6,000,000

Other Information:

1. The Long-Term Liabilities of the Stern Company include a $1,000,000 note that is payable to the Percy Company. During 2009, interest expense on this note was $110,000 and on December 31, 2009, $100,000 of this interest had not been paid by Stern. The note is to be paid on December 31, 2012.

2. In each of the years since Percy acquired control over Stern, the Goodwill arising on this business combination transaction has been tested for impairment. In 2006, a Goodwill Impairment Loss of $50,000 was recognized. No impairment was found in any of the other years since acquisition.

3. Stern had sales of $1,500,000 to Percy during 2009, of which $400,000 remained in the December 31, 2009 Inventories of Percy. The 2008 sales of $2,000,000 from Stern to Percy left $800,000 of merchandise in the December 31, 2008 Inventories of Percy. All intercompany sales and purchases are priced to provide the selling company with a gross margin of 50 percent of the sales price.

4. Stern's purchases for 2009 included $500,000 of merchandise from Percy. Of these purchases, 60 percent remained in the December 31, 2009 Inventories of Stern. There had been no purchases from Percy remaining in the December 31, 2008 Inventories of Stern.

5. On January 1, 2007, Stern sold a machine with a net book value of $250,000 to Percy for $350,000. At that time, the machine had a remaining useful life of 5 years.

6. On September 1, 2009, Percy sold a parcel of Land, which was purchased in 2005 for $100,000, to Stern for $350,000. The gain on this sale is included in Other Revenues.

Required: Prepare, for the Percy Company and its subsidiary, the Stern Company, the following:

A. The consolidated Income Statement for the year ending December 31, 2009.

B. The consolidated Statement Of Retained Earnings for the year ending December 31, 2009.

C. The consolidated Balance Sheet as at December 31, 2009.

Assignment Problem Six - 2

On December 31, 2005, the Pumpkin Company purchased 75 percent of the outstanding voting shares of the Squash Company for $4,200,000 in cash. On that date, the Squash Company had No Par Common Stock of $3,900,000 and Retained Earnings of $600,000. All of the Squash Company's identifiable assets and liabilities had carrying values that were equal to their fair values except for:

1. Inventories with fair values that were $60,000 more than their carrying values.
2. Land which had a fair value that was $300,000 greater than its carrying value.
3. Equipment which had a fair value of $270,000 more that its carrying value. Its remaining useful life is 15 years with no expected salvage value.
4. Long-Term Liabilities which had fair values that were $90,000 more than their carrying values and mature on December 31, 2011.

The Balance Sheets of the Pumpkin Company and the Squash Company as at December 31, 2009 were as follows:

Pumpkin and Squash Companies
Balance Sheets
As At December 31, 2009

	Pumpkin	Squash
Cash and Current Receivables	$ 1,620,000	$ 930,000
Inventories	1,800,000	660,000
Long-Term Receivables	840,000	300,000
Plant and Equipment (Net)	4,500,000	2,700,000
Investment in Squash (Cost)	4,200,000	N/A
Land	2,400,000	1,200,000
Total Assets	$15,360,000	$5,790,000
Current Liabilities	$ 480,000	$ 240,000
Long-Term Liabilities	660,000	390,000
No Par Common Stock	10,200,000	3,900,000
Retained Earnings	4,020,000	1,260,000
Total Equities	$15,360,000	$5,790,000

The Income Statements of the Pumpkin and Squash Companies for the year ending December 31, 2009 were as follows:

Pumpkin and Squash Companies
Income Statements
For The Year Ending December 31, 2009

	Pumpkin	Squash
Sales	$5,610,000	$1,770,000
Interest Revenue	84,000	30,000
Other Revenues	90,000	-0-
Total Revenues	$5,784,000	$1,800,000
Cost of Goods Sold	$3,900,000	$1,260,000
Interest Expense	66,000	45,000
Other Expenses	690,000	240,000
Total Expenses	$4,656,000	$1,545,000
Net Income	$1,128,000	$ 255,000

Other Information:

1. In each of the years since Pumpkin acquired control over Squash, the goodwill arising on this business combination transaction has been tested for impairment. In 2007, a Goodwill Impairment Loss of $84,000 was recognized. No impairment was found in any of the other years since acquisition.

2. Both Companies use the straight line method to calculate amortization charges and the First-In, First-Out inventory flow assumption.

3. Pumpkin uses the cost method to carry its Investment in Squash.

4. During 2009, dividends of $360,000 were declared and paid by Pumpkin and dividends of $120,000 were declared and paid by Squash.

5. The Pumpkin Company manufactures machines with a five year life. Its Sales total in the Income Statement includes only sales of these machines. Intercompany sales of these machines are priced to provide Pumpkin with a 20 percent gross profit on sales prices in all the years under consideration. On December 31, 2007, Pumpkin sold machines it had manufactured to Squash for $150,000. Squash uses the machines in its production process. On January 1, 2009, Pumpkin sold an additional $300,000 of these machines to the Squash Company. There were no other intercompany sales of these machines in any of the years under consideration.

6. The Squash Company manufactures paper products used in offices. During 2008, Squash sold to Pumpkin $18,000 worth of office supplies of which all but $3,000 were used by Pumpkin in 2008. During 2009, Pumpkin purchased $15,000 worth of merchandise from Squash. During 2009, the Pumpkin Company used $9,000 worth of the paper products purchased from Squash. Squash's intercompany sales are priced to provide it with a 50 percent gross margin on its sales price.

7. On January 1, 2007, Squash sold a piece of equipment to Pumpkin for 20 percent more than its carrying value of $300,000. At this time, the equipment has an estimated remaining useful life of eight years, with no anticipated salvage value.

8. During 2008, Squash sold land that had a carrying value of $240,000 to Pumpkin for a profit of $30,000. One-half of the proceeds was paid at that date and the remainder is due on July 1, 2010. The Land that had the fair value increase of $300,000 on December 31, 2005 is still on the books of Squash.

9. On December 31, 2009, Squash had current receivables of $6,000 from Pumpkin and Pumpkin is owed $18,000 by Squash. Intercompany interest which was paid during 2009 on outstanding intercompany payables totalled $1,000 for Squash and $1,400 for Pumpkin.

Required:

A. Prepare the consolidated Income Statement for the year ending December 31, 2009 of the Pumpkin Company and its subsidiary, the Squash Company.

B. Prepare the consolidated Statement of Retained Earnings for the year ending December 31, 2009, of the Pumpkin Company and its subsidiary, the Squash Company.

C. Prepare the consolidated Balance Sheet as at December 31, 2009 of the Pumpkin Company and its subsidiary, the Squash Company.

Assignment Problem Six - 3

On January 1, 2004, the Paul Company acquired 75 percent of the outstanding voting shares of the Saul Company for $6,000,000 in cash. On this date the Saul Company had No Par Common Stock of $6,200,000 and Retained Earnings of $2,800,000.

At this acquisition date, the Saul Company had Plant And Equipment that had a fair value that was $600,000 less than its carrying value, Long-Term Liabilities that had a fair value that was $200,000 more than their carrying values and Inventories with a fair value that was less than their carrying values in the amount of $800,000.

All of the other identifiable assets and liabilities of the Saul Company had fair values that were equal to their carrying values on the date of acquisition. The remaining useful life of the Plant And Equipment was 12 years with no anticipated salvage value. The Long-Term Liabilities were issued at par of $4,000,000 and mature on January 1, 2014.

On January 1, 2007, the Saul Company sells a broadcast licence to the Paul Company for $900,000. On this date the carrying value of this broadcast licence on the books of the Saul Company was $1,000,000 and the remaining useful life was five years. Amortization is calculated on a straight line basis by both companies.

Between January 1, 2004 and January 1, 2009, the Saul Company had Net Income of $2,200,000 and paid dividends of $800,000. On January 1, 2009, the Retained Earnings of the Paul Company were $30,000,000.

During 2009, the Paul Company declared and paid dividends of $200,000 and the Saul Company declared and paid dividends of $100,000. The Paul Company carries its Investment in Saul by the cost method.

The condensed Income Statements of the two Companies for the year ending December 31, 2009 are as follows:

Paul and Saul Companies
Income Statements
For The Year Ending December 31, 2009

	Paul	Saul
Total Revenues	$5,000,000	$2,000,000
Cost Of Goods Sold	$3,000,000	$1,200,000
Other Expenses	1,500,000	600,000
Total Expenses	$4,500,000	$1,800,000
Net Income	$ 500,000	$ 200,000

During 2009, 40 percent of the Saul Company's Revenues resulted from sales to the Paul Company. Half of this merchandise remains in the ending inventories of the Paul Company and has not yet been paid for. The December 31, 2009 inventory balances for the Paul and Saul Companies are $950,000 and $380,000 respectively.

On January 1, 2009, the inventories of the Paul Company contained purchases from the Saul Company of $500,000. All intercompany merchandise transactions are priced to provide Saul with a gross margin on sales prices of 40 percent.

The Saul Company has not issued any additional Common Stock or Long-Term Liabilities since the date of its acquisition by the Paul Company. On December 31, 2009, the Paul Company had $15,000,000 in Long-Term Liabilities.

In each of the years since Paul purchased the shares of Saul, the goodwill arising from this share purchase has been tested for impairment. No impairment was found in any of the years since acquisition.

Required:

A. Prepare the consolidated Income Statement for the year ending December 31, 2009 for the Paul Company and its subsidiary, the Saul Company, in compliance with the Recommendations of the *CICA Handbook.*

B. Calculate the amounts, showing all computations, that would be included in the consolidated Balance Sheet as at December 31, 2009 of the Paul Company and its subsidiary, the Saul Company for the following accounts:

1. Retained Earnings
2. Non-Controlling Interest
3. Inventories
4. Broadcast Licence
5. Long-Term Liabilities

Assignment Problem Six - 4

On January 1, 2005, the Plantor Company purchased 75 percent of the outstanding voting shares of the Plantee Company for $850,000 in cash. This amount was $100,000 greater than the Plantor Company's share of the carrying values of the Plantee Company's net identifiable assets. The entire $100,000 is allocated to a building and will be charged to income over a 20 year period.

No dividends were paid by either Company in 2009. Plantor Company carries its investment in the Plantee Company using the cost method. The Income Statements of the two Companies for the year ending December 31, 2009 are as follows:

Income Statements
For The Year Ending December 31, 2009

	Plantor	Plantee
Sales	$500,000	$200,000
Cost of Goods Sold	$300,000	$100,000
Other Expenses	140,000	76,000
Total Expenses	$440,000	$176,000
Income Before Extraordinary Items	$ 60,000	$ 24,000
Extraordinary Gain	Nil	6,000
Net Income	$ 60,000	$ 30,000

Other Information:

1. During 2009, the Plantor Company sold $100,000 in merchandise to the Plantee Company. Of these sales, $15,000 remains in the December 31, 2009 inventories of the Plantee Company. These intercompany sales are priced to provide Plantor with a 40 percent gross margin on sales price.

2. During 2009, the Plantee Company sold $50,000 in merchandise to the Plantor Company. Of these sales, $20,000 remains in the December 31, 2009 inventories of the Plantor Company. These intercompany sales are priced to provide Plantee with a 50 percent gross profit on sales price.

3. There were no intercompany inventory sales prior to 2009.

4. On January 2, 2007, the Plantee Company sold equipment to the Plantor Company for $100,000. On that date, the equipment was carried on the Plantee Company's books at $135,000 and had a remaining useful life of 5 years.

5. Both Companies use the straight line method to calculate amortization.

Required:

A. Prepare a consolidated Income Statement for the Plantor Company and its subsidiary, the Plantee Company, for the year ending December 31, 2009.

B. Assume that the Plantor Company cannot classify the Plantee Company as a subsidiary. Prepare the Plantor Company's Income Statement for the year ending December 31, 2009 assuming it uses the equity method to account for its investment in the Plantee Company.

Assignment Problem Six - 5

The Norwood Company purchased 75 percent of the outstanding voting shares of the Sollip Company on January 1, 2006 for $2,000,000 in cash. On the acquisition date, Sollip had Retained Earnings of $1,400,000 and Common Stock of $600,000.

At this time, the Sollip Company's identifiable assets and liabilities had fair values that were equal to their carrying values except for:

- Plant And Equipment, which had a fair value that was $40,000 more than carrying value. This Plant And Equipment had a remaining life of 10 years with no anticipated salvage value.
- Long-Term Liabilities with a fair value that was $80,000 less than carrying value. These Long-Term Liabilities mature on January 1, 2016.

The Norwood Company carries its Investment In Sollip by the cost method. Both Companies use the straight line method to calculate amortization.

The comparative Balance Sheets and the condensed Statement of Income And Change In Retained Earnings for the year ending December 31, 2009 of the Norwood Company and its subsidiary, the Sollip Company are as follows:

Balance Sheets
As At December 31

	Norwood		Sollip	
	2009	**2008**	**2009**	**2008**
Cash	$1,009,988	$ 360,000	$1,200,000	$ 600,000
Accounts Receivable	1,394,000	64,000	780,000	200,000
Inventories	310,000	170,000	480,000	320,000
Investment In Sollip (At Cost)	2,000,000	2,000,000	N/A	N/A
Plant And Equipment	6,240,000	6,000,000	4,000,000	4,000,000
Accumulated Amortization	(3,045,667)	(2,800,000)	(1,988,000)	(1,600,000)
Land	120,000	120,000	60,000	Nil
Total Assets	$8,028,321	$5,914,000	$4,532,000	$3,520,000
Current Liabilities	$2,468,321	$ 714,000	$1,452,000	$ 760,000
Long-Term Liabilities	900,000	800,000	560,000	360,000
Common Stock - No Par	2,020,000	2,000,000	600,000	600,000
Retained Earnings	2,640,000	2,400,000	1,920,000	1,800,000
Total Equities	$8,028,321	$5,914,000	$4,532,000	$3,520,000

Statements Of Income And Retained Earnings
Year Ending December 31, 2009

	Norwood	Sollip
Total Revenues	$2,760,000	$2,000,000
Cost Of Goods Sold	$1,200,000	$ 790,000
Amortization Expense	410,667	548,000
Other Expenses And Losses	849,333	342,000
Total Expenses And Losses	$2,460,000	$1,680,000
Net Income	$ 300,000	$ 320,000
Retained Earnings, January 1	2,400,000	1,800,000
Balance Available	$2,700,000	$2,120,000
Dividends	(60,000)	(200,000)
Balance, December 31	$2,640,000	$1,920,000

Other Information:

1. On January 1, 2007, the Sollip Company sold furniture to the Norwood Company for $31,000. The furniture had a net book value of $85,000 and an estimated useful life on this date of four years with no anticipated salvage value.

2. On December 31, 2008, the Norwood Company had in its Inventories $35,000 of merchandise that it had purchased from Sollip during 2008. During 2009, Norwood purchased $200,000 of merchandise from Sollip, of which $75,000 remain in the December 31, 2009 Inventories of Norwood. The Norwood Company sold $120,000 of merchandise to Sollip during 2009, which was resold during the year for $165,000. Intercompany inventory sales are priced to provide the selling company with a 30 percent gross profit on sales price.

3. On December 31, 2009, due to the intercompany inventory sales, the Norwood Company owed the Sollip Company $60,000 and the Sollip Company owed the Norwood Company $80,000. There were no intercompany accounts payable balances on December 31, 2008.

4. On January 1, 2009, to raise cash, the Norwood Company took out a $100,000 second mortgage on its assets. In addition, it sold office equipment that had cost $195,000 and had accumulated amortization of $165,000 for $20,000.

5. On December 31, 2009, the Sollip Company sold a machine to the Norwood Company for $55,000. The machine had been purchased on January 1, 2006 for $200,000 and had an expected life at that date of 5 years with no anticipated salvage value. The Sollip Company had taken amortization for 2009 on the machine before the sale. The only Plant And Equipment acquisition of the Sollip Company was a $200,000 machine to replace the one sold to Norwood.

6. On June 30, 2009, the Norwood Company also purchased other Equipment for a combination of $360,000 in cash and 4,000 No Par Common Shares. The stock was trading at $5 per share on this date.

7. On April 1, 2009, the Sollip Company issued 20 year, 14 percent bonds for $200,000 and used part of the proceeds to purchase a parcel of land.

8. In the year of acquisition of Sollip, a Goodwill Impairment Loss of $200,000 was recognized due to an unfavourable ruling in a court case. No impairment was found in any of the other years since acquisition.

Required: (Note that in Parts A, B and C, financial statements are not required.)

A. Compute consolidated Net Income for the year ending December 31, 2009 for the Norwood Company and its subsidiary, the Sollip Company.

B. Calculate consolidated Retained Earnings as at December 31, 2009 for the Norwood Company and its subsidiary, the Sollip Company.

C. Compute the Non-Controlling Interest that would be disclosed on the consolidated Balance Sheet of the Norwood Company and its subsidiary, the Sollip Company as at December 31, 2009.

D. Prepare the consolidated Cash Flow Statement for the year ending December 31, 2009 for the Norwood Company and its subsidiary, the Sollip Company.

Assignment Problem Six - 6

On December 31, 2006, the Plain Company acquired 25 percent of the outstanding voting shares of the Steppe Company for $1,250,000. On December 31, 2008, the Plain Company acquired an additional 40 percent of the outstanding voting shares of the Steppe Company for $1,680,000.

At this time, the fair values of the identifiable assets and liabilities of the Steppe Company were equal to their carrying values except for Current Assets and Long-Term Liabilities.

The condensed Balance Sheets and the fair values of the Steppe Company on the acquisition dates were as follows:

Balance Sheets
As At December 31

	2008	2006
Current Assets	$ 800,000	$1,200,000
Plant And Equipment (Net)	5,400,000	5,300,000
Total Assets	$6,200,000	$6,500,000
Current Liabilities	$ 300,000	$ 500,000
Long-Term Liabilities	2,000,000	2,000,000
Common Stock - No Par	3,000,000	3,000,000
Retained Earnings	900,000	1,000,000
Total Equities	$6,200,000	$6,500,000

Fair Values

	2008	2006
Current Assets	$ 600,000	$ 800,000
Long-Term Liabilities	$1,700,000	$1,800,000

The Long-Term Liabilities were issued on December 31, 1996 and mature on December 31, 2016. The Plain Company carries its investment in the Steppe Company by the cost method. Both Companies use the straight line method to calculate amortization.

The condensed Balance Sheets of the Plain Company and the Steppe Company as at December 31, 2009 are as follows:

Balance Sheets
As At December 31, 2009

	Plain	Steppe
Current Assets	2,070,000	$1,400,000
Investment In Steppe	2,930,000	N/A
Plant And Equipment (Net)	9,000,000	6,200,000
Total Assets	$14,000,000	$7,600,000
Current Liabilities	$ 1,000,000	$ 600,000
Long-Term Liabilities	5,000,000	2,000,000
Common Stock - No Par	3,000,000	3,000,000
Retained Earnings	5,000,000	2,000,000
Total Equities	$14,000,000	$7,600,000

In each of the years since Plain acquired shares of the Steppe Company, the Goodwill arising from the share purchases has been tested for impairment. No impairment was found in any of the years.

During 2009, the Steppe Company declared and paid $100,000 in dividends and the Plain Company declared $150,000 in dividends which were not paid until January, 2010.

The Steppe Company sold $300,000 of merchandise to the Plain Company during 2009. Of these sales, merchandise which contained a $50,000 gross profit for the Steppe Company remained in the December 31, 2009 inventories of the Plain Company. Merchandise containing a gross profit of $75,000 for the Steppe Company had been included in the December 31, 2008 inventories of the Plain Company.

Required: Prepare a consolidated Balance Sheet for the Plain Company and its subsidiary, the Steppe Company as at December 31, 2009.

Assignment Problem Six - 7

The single entity and consolidated Balance Sheets and Income Statements for the Pomp Company and its subsidiary, the Sircumstance Company, for the year ending December 31, 2009, are as follows:

Balance Sheets
As At December 31, 2009

	Pomp	Sircumstance	Consolidated
Cash	$ 20,000	$ 15,000	$ 35,000
Accounts Receivable	400,000	250,000	520,000
Inventories	380,000	335,000	635,000
Investment In Sircumstance	1,500,000	N/A	Nil
Land	800,000	1,200,000	2,100,000
Plant And Equipment (Net)	3,000,000	2,300,000	5,500,000
Goodwill	Nil	Nil	190,000
Total Assets	$6,100,000	$4,100,000	$8,980,000
Current Liabilities	$ 200,000	$ 100,000	$ 190,000
Dividends Payable	50,000	25,000	55,000
Bonds Payable	2,000,000	1,475,000	3,475,000
Non-Controlling Interest	Nil	Nil	524,000
Common Stock (No Par)	3,000,000	1,000,000	3,000,000
Retained Earnings	850,000	1,500,000	1,736,000
Total Equities	$6,100,000	$4,100,000	$8,980,000

Income Statements
For The Year Ending December 31, 2009

	Pomp	Sircumstance	Consolidated
Sales	$3,200,000	$2,500,000	$5,400,000
Cost Of Goods Sold	(2,000,000)	(1,000,000)	(2,720,000)
Other Expenses	(800,000)	(1,400,000)	(2,300,000)
Goodwill Impairment Loss	Nil	Nil	(10,000)
Investment Income	40,000	Nil	Nil
Non-Controlling Interest	Nil	Nil	4,000
Net Income	$ 440,000	$ 100,000	$ 374,000
Dividends Declared	(200,000)	(50,000)	(200,000)
Increase In Retained Earnings	$ 240,000	$ 50,000	$ 174,000

Other Information:

1. Pomp Company acquired its investment in the Common Stock of the Sircumstance Company on January 1, 2005. At that time, all of the identifiable assets and liabilities of the Sircumstance Company had fair values that were equal to their carrying values except for Land which had a fair value that was $125,000 in excess of its carrying value. The Land is still on the books of the Sircumstance Company on December 31, 2009.
2. In each of the years since Pomp acquired control over Sircumstance, the goodwill arising on this business combination transaction has been tested for impairment. No impairment was found in any year prior to 2009.
3. Both Companies calculate amortization using the straight line method.
4. The Sircumstance Company regularly sells merchandise to the Pomp Company and, after further processing, the merchandise is resold by the Pomp Company.
5. On January 1, 2007, the Sircumstance Company sold equipment to the Pomp Company at a loss. At the time, the remaining useful life of this equipment was five years.
6. Since the Pomp Company acquired its investment in the Sircumstance Company, there has been no change in the number of Sircumstance Company common shares outstanding.

Required: On the basis of the information you can develop from an analysis of the preceding individual and consolidated financial statements, provide answers to the following questions.

A. What percentage of the outstanding common shares of the Sircumstance Company were purchased by the Pomp Company on January 1, 2005?

B. Does the Pomp Company carry its investment in the Common Stock of the Sircumstance Company by the cost method or the equity method? Explain the basis for your conclusion.

C. Assume that $1,500,000 was the cost of the Pomp Company's investment in the Common Stock of the Sircumstance Company. What was the balance in the Retained Earnings account of the Sircumstance Company on January 1, 2005?

D. What is the amount of intercompany inventory sales that the Sircumstance Company made to the Pomp Company during 2009?

E. What is the explanation for the difference between the consolidated Cost Of Goods Sold and the combined Cost Of Goods Sold of the two affiliated Companies? Your answer should include the computation of any intercompany profit in the opening inventories of the Pomp Company and the computation of any intercompany profit in the closing inventories of the Pomp Company. The amount of intercompany sales previously calculated should also be used in this computation.

F. On January 1, 2007, what was the amount of unrealized loss on the intercompany sale of Plant And Equipment by Sircumstance Company to the Pomp Company?

G. Prepare a schedule of intercompany debts and, if possible, indicate which Company is the creditor and which is the debtor.

H. Verify the Non-Controlling Interest in consolidated Net Income for the year ending December 31, 2009.

I. Using the information given and your answers calculated in the preceding parts of this question, verify the consolidated Net Income for the year ending December 31, 2009.

J. Verify the Non-Controlling Interest in the consolidated Balance Sheet as at December 31, 2009.

K. Using the information given and your answers calculated in the preceding parts of this question, verify the consolidated Retained Earnings figure as at December 31, 2009.

Assignment Problem Six - 8

Note This problem uses the same data that is found in Assignment Problem Six-1. However, in this case the solution should comply with international financial reporting standards. The data is repeated here for your convenience.

On December 31, 2004, the Percy Company purchased 75 percent of the outstanding voting shares of the Stern Company for $3,000,000 in cash. On that date, Stern had No Par Common Stock of $2,000,000 and Retained Earnings of $1,000,000.

On December 31, 2004 all of the identifiable assets and liabilities of Stern had fair values that were equal to their carrying values with the following exceptions:

1. Inventories with fair values that were $400,000 less than their carrying values.
2. Land with a fair value that was $800,000 greater than its carrying value.
3. Long-Term Liabilities, maturing on January 1, 2010, with fair values that were $200,000 less than their carrying values.

Both Companies use the straight line method to calculate amortization. In its single entity records, Percy carries its investment in Stern at cost.

The Land which was on the books of the Stern Company on December 31, 2004 has not been sold as at December 31, 2009.

Financial statements for Percy and Stern for the year ending December 31, 2009 are as follows:

Income Statements
For The Year Ending December 31, 2009

	Percy	Stern
Merchandise Sales	$5,000,000	$2,000,000
Other Revenues	1,000,000	500,000
Total Revenues	$6,000,000	$2,500,000
Cost Of Goods Sold	$2,000,000	$1,000,000
Amortization Expense	400,000	300,000
Other Expenses	600,000	400,000
Total Expenses	$3,000,000	$1,700,000
Net Income	$3,000,000	$ 800,000

Statements Of Retained Earnings
For The Year Ending December 31, 2009

	Percy	Stern
Opening Balance	$10,000,000	$1,600,000
Net Income	3,000,000	800,000
Balance Available	$13,000,000	$2,400,000
Dividends Declared	(1,000,000)	(400,000)
Closing Balance	$12,000,000	$2,000,000

Balance Sheets
As At December 31, 2009

	Percy	Stern
Cash And Current Receivables	$ 1,500,000	$1,200,000
Note Receivable	1,000,000	Nil
Inventories	4,500,000	1,000,000
Investment In Stern (At Cost)	3,000,000	N/A
Plant And Equipment (Net)	9,000,000	3,000,000
Land	2,000,000	800,000
Total Assets	$21,000,000	$6,000,000
Current Liabilities	$ 500,000	$ 200,000
Long-Term Liabilities	3,500,000	1,800,000
Common Stock - No Par	5,000,000	2,000,000
Retained Earnings	12,000,000	2,000,000
Total Equities	$21,000,000	$6,000,000

Other Information:

1. The Long-Term Liabilities of the Stern Company include a $1,000,000 note that is payable to the Percy Company. During 2009, interest expense on this note was $110,000 and on December 31, 2009, $100,000 of this interest had not been paid by Stern. The note is to be paid on December 31, 2012.

2. In each of the years since Percy acquired control over Stern, the Goodwill arising on this business combination transaction has been tested for impairment. In 2006, a Goodwill Impairment Loss of $50,000 was recognized. No impairment was found in any of the other years since acquisition.

3. Stern had sales of $1,500,000 to Percy during 2009, of which $400,000 remained in the December 31, 2009 Inventories of Percy. The 2008 sales of $2,000,000 from Stern to Percy left $800,000 of merchandise in the December 31, 2008 Inventories of Percy. All intercompany sales and purchases are priced to provide the selling company with a gross margin of 50 percent of the sales price.

4. Stern's purchases for 2009 included $500,000 of merchandise from Percy. Of these purchases, 60 percent remained in the December 31, 2009 Inventories of Stern. There had been no purchases from Percy remaining in the December 31, 2008 Inventories of Stern.

5. On January 1, 2007, Stern sold a machine with a net book value of $250,000 to Percy for $350,000. At that time, the machine had a remaining useful life of 5 years.

6. On September 1, 2009, Percy sold a parcel of Land, which was purchased in 2005 for $100,000, to Stern for $350,000. The gain on this sale is included in Other Revenues.

Required: Using the recommendations of IFRS No. 3, *Business Combinations*, and IAS No. 27, *Consolidated And Separate Financial Statements*, prepare, for the Percy Company and its subsidiary, the Stern Company, the following:

A. The consolidated Income Statement for the year ending December 31, 2009.

B. The consolidated Statement Of Retained Earnings for the year ending December 31, 2009.

C. The consolidated Balance Sheet as at December 31, 2009.

Advanced Topics In Consolidations

Introduction To Advanced Topics

7-1. A full treatment of the subject of preparing consolidated statements could easily require a full one semester course to cover the many procedures that are inherent in this complex process. Most of the users of this book do not believe that such extensive coverage is appropriate in a standard course in advanced accounting.

7-2. The material in Chapters 4 through 6 provide a coverage of consolidated financial statements that we believe is appropriate for such courses. However, this text is also used by professional accountants whose needs extend beyond this coverage. In addition, the material in Chapters 4 through 6 is based on our opinion of what constitutes appropriate coverage of this subject. It is certain that other instructors will have different views on the subjects that should be included.

7-3. To accommodate both of these groups, we have included this additional Chapter which deals with most of the remaining issues that arise in the preparation of consolidated financial statements. The subjects covered here are as follows:

- Multi-Level Affiliations
- Reciprocal Shareholdings
- Intercompany Bondholdings
- Subsidiary Preferred Stock
- Transactions Involving Subsidiary Shares
- Consolidation With Investment At Equity

7-4. With these additional subjects included, this text now provides the most extensive coverage of Canadian consolidation procedures that is currently available from any source.

7-5. Because we anticipate that use of this material will be more limited than is the case with other Chapters in this text, we have not provided Exercises or problems which illustrate international convergence. However, we have provided a Self Study Problem and an Assignment Problem for each of the subjects covered.

Multiple Investment Situations

Introduction

7-6. It is possible to classify three types of situations in which more than one investment holding is included in a single consolidated entity. In two of these situations, multi-company and multi-level relationships, two or more subsidiaries are engendered by the multiple investments. In the third situation (reciprocal holdings) only one subsidiary is required as the investment moves both upstream and downstream. A brief description, including some indication of the nature of the accounting problems that will be encountered, is provided for each of these situations.

Multi-Company Affiliation

7-7. The term "multi-company affiliation" is used to describe situations in which a single parent company has acquired, by direct investment in each investee, two or more subsidiaries. This type of arrangement is shown in Figure 7-1. There are no particular complications in this situation. It is simply a matter of dealing with each subsidiary as though it were the only investee of this type and then summing the resulting financial data.

Figure 7 - 1
Multi-Company Affiliation

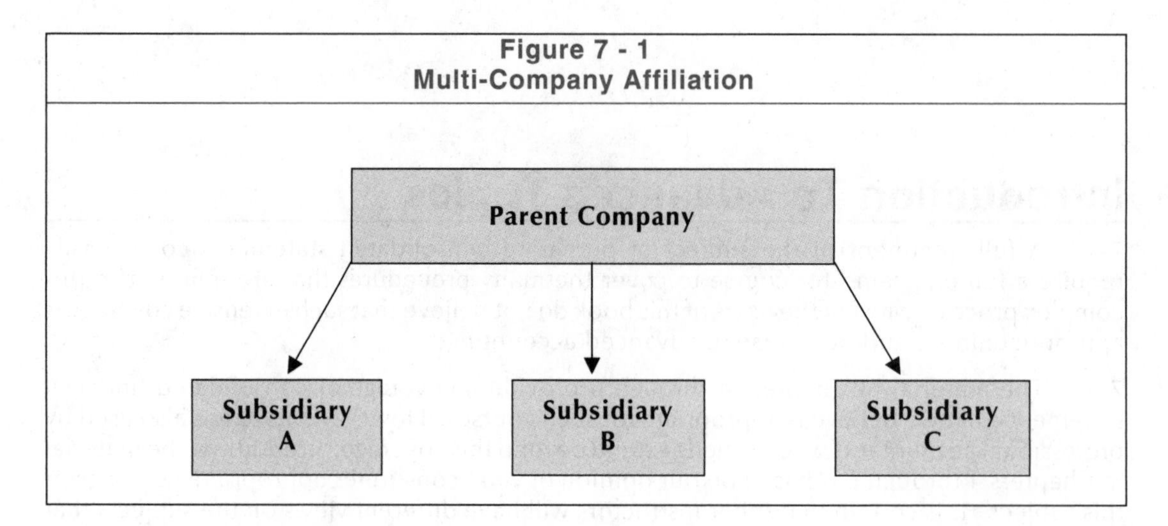

Multi-Level Affiliation

7-8. The distinguishing feature of multi-level affiliations is the presence of indirect ownership. That is, control is achieved, not through the more usual channel of holding the investee's voting shares, but through holding voting shares of a company which in turn owns a controlling interest in an additional investee's shares.

7-9. This type of arrangement is shown in Figure 7-2. The term "multi-level affiliation" also encompasses situations in which control is accomplished via a combination of direct and indirect ownership. However, to remain in this category, all of the investment must be in one

Figure 7 - 2
Multi-Level Affiliation

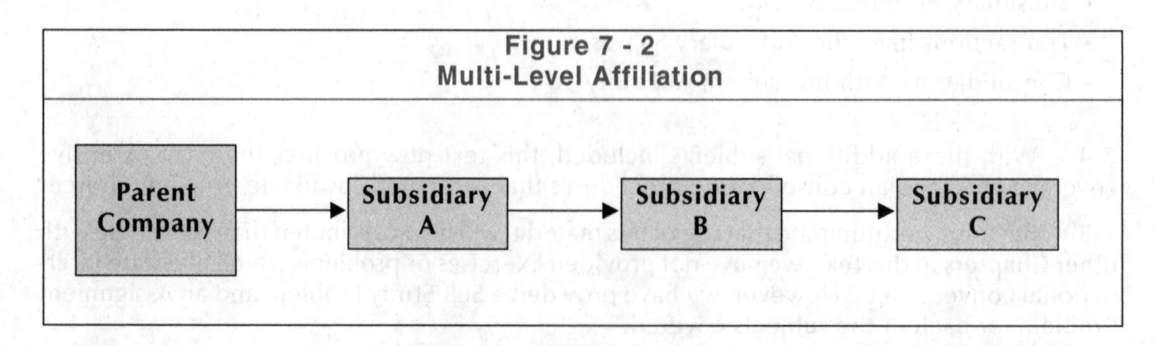

direction. While multi-level affiliations do not involve any real conceptual differences from those present in single investment situations, the application of these procedures is somewhat more complex. As a consequence, we will provide two examples in this Chapter of multi-level affiliations.

Reciprocal Holdings

7-10. The distinguishing feature of reciprocal holdings is the presence of both upstream and downstream investments. That is, we find situations in which a parent has invested in a subsidiary and the subsidiary, in turn, has acquired shares of the parent. This latter investment creates the reciprocal holdings situation. This type of situation is shown in Figure 7-3.

Figure 7 - 3
Reciprocal Holdings

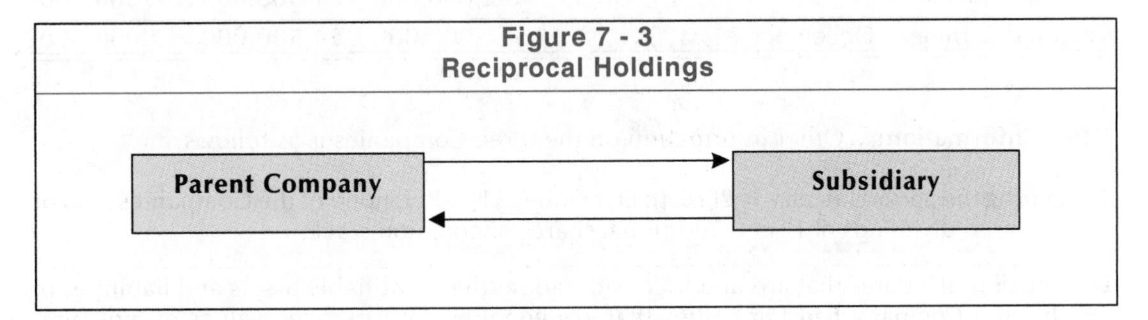

7-11. Reciprocal holdings add considerable complexity to problems. The basic reason for this is that in order to determine the parent's share of the retained earnings of the subsidiary since acquisition, you must determine the subsidiary's share of the retained earnings of the parent subsequent to the date of the investment. Since this latter figure involves the former, simultaneous equations are necessary to arrive at a solution to this problem. We will provide three examples in this Chapter which illustrate the procedures required to deal with reciprocal investment relationships.

Multi-Level Affiliations

Approach

7-12. We will examine two different cases involving multi-level relationships. In order to reduce the amount of facts that you will be required to deal with, the same basic data will be used in both of these illustrations. The investment patterns will be varied in the two cases in order to demonstrate the two types of situations that can arise in this area.

- **Case One** The parent will acquire a subsidiary and this subsidiary will subsequently acquire a second subsidiary.

- **Case Two** The parent company will acquire a subsidiary that already has a subsidiary.

Basic Data

7-13. The basic data involves three companies which we will designate the Run Company, the Sun Company, and the Tun Company. Data on the No Par Common Stock, Retained Earnings and Net Income of the three Companies is as follows:

	Run	Sun	Tun
No Par Common Stock	$ 5,000,000	$1,000,000	$3,500,000
Retained Earnings - January 1, 2007	$ 5,000,000	$1,000,000	$ 500,000
2007 Net Income	1,500,000	1,000,000	500,000
Retained Earnings - December 31, 2007	$ 6,500,000	$2,000,000	$1,000,000
2008 Net Income	2,500,000	1,000,000	500,000
Retained Earnings - December 31, 2008	$ 9,000,000	$3,000,000	$1,500,000
2009 Net Income	2,000,000	1,500,000	500,000
Retained Earnings - December 31, 2009	$11,000,000	$4,500,000	$2,000,000

Other Information: Other information on the three Companies is as follows:

1. During the period January 1, 2007 to December 31, 2009, none of the Companies paid or declared dividends or issued additional shares of common stock.

2. On all of the dates that are under consideration, the identifiable assets and liabilities of the Sun Company had fair values that are equal to their carrying values except for a building. On January 1, 2007, the fair value of this building exceeds its carrying value by $2,500,000. On December 31, 2007, this fair value increment has increased to $3,000,000 and it remains at that level until December 31, 2009. It is anticipated that this building will be used until December 31, 2016 and it is not expected to have any net salvage value. It is being amortized by the straight line method.

3. On all of the dates that are under consideration, the identifiable assets and liabilities of the Tun Company have fair values that are equal to their carrying values.

4. All investments that arise in either version of this problem are carried by the cost method.

5. During 2009, the Tun Company sells merchandise to the Sun Company for $2,000,000 and to the Run Company for $2,800,000. Of these sales, $500,000 made to the Sun Company and $250,000 made to the Run Company remain in the December 31, 2009 inventories of the purchasing Company. The Tun Company's sales are priced to provide it with a gross margin of 20 percent on sales prices. There have been no intercompany sales prior to 2009.

Case One

Description Of Affiliation

7-14. In this first situation, assume that on January 1, 2007, the Run Company acquires 80 percent of the outstanding voting shares of the Sun Company for $5,000,000 in cash. One year later, on December 31, 2007, the Sun Company acquires 75 percent of the outstanding voting shares of the Tun Company for $3,375,000 in cash. On that same date, the Run Company purchases 10 percent of the outstanding voting shares of the Tun Company for $450,000 in cash.

7-15. It was determined that there was a goodwill impairment loss of $35,000 for 2009 related to Run Company's investment in Sun Company.

> **Required For Case One:** Compute consolidated Net Income for the year ending December 31, 2009 and the Non-Controlling Interest that would be shown in the December 31, 2009 consolidated Balance Sheet. In addition, prepare a consolidated Statement Of Retained Earnings for the year ending December 31, 2009.

Investment Analysis - Run In Sun

7-16. The analysis of the Run Company's investment in the Sun Company is as follows:

	80 Percent	100 Percent
Investment Cost	$5,000,000	$6,250,000
Sun Shareholders' Equity ($1,000,000 + $1,000,000)	(1,600,000)	(2,000,000)
Differential	$3,400,000	$4,250,000
Fair Value Increase On Building	(2,000,000)	(2,500,000)
Goodwill	$1,400,000	$1,750,000

7-17. The fair value increase on the Building would be amortized over 10 years at the rate of $200,000 per year.

Investment Analysis - Run In Sun In Tun

7-18. On December 31, 2007, the Shareholders' Equity of the Tun Company amounts to $4,500,000 ($3,500,000 + $1,000,000). When, on this date, the Run Company purchases 10 percent of Tun for $450,000 and the Sun Company buys 75 percent of Tun for $3,375,000, the investments are made at a price that is equal to the investor's proportionate share of the book value of Tun Company. Since the basic data for the problem states that all of the Tun Company's net identifiable assets have fair values that are equal to their carrying values, it will not be necessary to make any adjustments for amortization of fair value changes. There is also no goodwill to be recognized in the this business combination transaction.

Procedures

7-19. While it would be possible to apply our general consolidation procedures involving the use of journal entries to this problem, it is much more convenient to provide the information required using definitional calculations. This approach will be used here and in the Case Two version of this problem.

Consolidated Net Income

7-20. Tun Company's Net Income must be adjusted for the $150,000 [(20%)($500,000 + $250,000)] unrealized intercompany inventory profit. The consolidated Net Income for the year ending December 31, 2009 can be calculated as follows:

Run Company's Net Income	$2,000,000
Run Company's Share Of Net Income Of Sun Company [(80%)($1,500,000)]	1,200,000
Run Company's Share Of Adjusted Net Income Of Tun Company:	
Direct [(10%)($500,000 - $150,000)]	35,000
Indirect [(80%)(75%)($500,000 - $150,000)]	210,000
Amortization Of Fair Value Increase On Building	(200,000)
Goodwill Impairment Loss On Sun Investment	(35,000)
2009 Consolidated Net Income	$3,210,000

Consolidated Statement Of Retained Earnings

7-21. In preparing this consolidated financial statement, we will begin with the following calculation of the opening balance in consolidated Retained Earnings:

Run Company's January 1, 2009 Balance		$ 9,000,000
Equity Pickup In Sun:		
Sun's January 1, 2009 Balance	$3,000,000	
Balance At Acquisition	(1,000,000)	
Balance Since Acquisition	$2,000,000	
Run's Proportionate Interest	80%	1,600,000
Equity Pickup In Tun:		
Tun's January 1, 2009 Balance	$1,500,000	
Balance At Acquisition	(1,000,000)	
Balance Since Acquisition	$ 500,000	
Run's Proportionate Interest [(80%)(75%) + 10%]	70%	350,000
Balance Before Fair Value Adjustments		$10,950,000
Amortization Of Fair Value Increase On Building (2 Years At $200,000)		(400,000)
Consolidated January 1, 2009 Balance		$10,550,000

7-22. Given this calculation, the consolidated Statement Of Retained Earnings would be prepared as follows:

Run Company And Subsidiaries
Consolidated Statement Of Retained Earnings
For The Year Ending December 31, 2009

Balance - January 1, 2009	$10,550,000
Consolidated Net Income	3,210,000
Balance - December 31, 2009	$13,760,000

7-23. The closing balance of $13,760,000 can be verified by the following calculation:

Run Company's December 31, 2009 Balance		$11,000,000
Equity Pickup In Sun:		
Balance Since Acquisition ($4,500,000 - $1,000,000)	$3,500,000	
Run's Proportionate Interest	80%	2,800,000
Equity Pickup In Tun:		
Balance Since Acquisition ($2,000,000 - $1,000,000)	$1,000,000	
Unrealized Inventory Profits	(150,000)	
Adjusted Balance	$ 850,000	
Run's Proportionate Interest [(80%)(75%) + 10%]	70%	595,000
Balance Before Adjustments		$14,395,000
Goodwill Impairment Loss		(35,000)
Amortization Of Fair Value Increase On Building (3 Years At $200,000)		(600,000)
December 31, 2009 Consolidated Balance		$13,760,000

7-24. The preceding calculation serves to verify the balance that was computed in the consolidated Statement Of Retained Earnings by adding consolidated Net Income to the opening balance of consolidated Retained Earnings.

Non-Controlling Interest

7-25. The remaining requirement of this Case One is to compute the Non-Controlling Interest that would be shown in the consolidated Balance Sheet as at December 31, 2009.

This non-controlling Interest is made up of the interests of two groups of shareholders. These are the non-controlling shareholders in the Sun Company and the non-controlling shareholders in the Tun Company. Note, however, that there are three components to the non-controlling interest. They can be described as follows:

Sun In Sun The 20 percent non-controlling shareholder group in Sun Company have a direct interest in all of the net assets of that Company. This interest will be based on the book value of Sun's Shareholder's Equity. It does not include any unrealized intercompany profits.

Tun In Tun The 15 percent non-controlling shareholder group in Tun Company have a direct interest in all of the net assets of that Company. This interest will be based on the book value of Tun's Shareholders' Equity, less the $150,000 unrealized intercompany profit.

Sun In Tun The non-controlling shareholders in Sun Company have an indirect interest in the realized Retained Earnings of the Tun Company that have accrued since it was acquired by the Sun Company. If Sun carried its Investment In Tun by the equity method, this interest would be reflected in the net assets of the Sun Company and would be picked up in the calculation of the direct interest of the non-controlling shareholders of Sun. However, as Sun carries its Investment In Tun by the cost method, a separate calculation of this indirect non-controlling interest is required. Note that the Tun Retained Earnings will have to be adjusted for the $150,000 unrealized intercompany profit.

7-26. The relevant calculations are as follows:

Sun Shareholders' Direct Interest In Sun:		
Common Stock [(20%)($1,000,000)]		$ 200,000
Retained Earnings [(20%)($4,500,000)]		900,000
Sun Shareholders' Indirect Interest In Tun:		
Retained Earnings Balance	$2,000,000	
Balance At Acquisition	(1,000,000)	
Balance Since Acquisition	$1,000,000	
Unrealized Inventory Profits	(150,000)	
Adjusted Balance	$ 850,000	
Proportionate Interest [(20%)(75%)]	15%	127,500
Tun Shareholders' Direct Interest In Tun:		
Common Stock [(15%)($3,500,000)]		525,000
Realized Retained Earnings [(15%)($1,850,000)]		277,500
Total Non-Controlling Interest		$2,030,000

Case Two

7-27. In this situation, we will assume that on December 31, 2007, the Sun Company acquires 75 percent of the outstanding voting shares of the Tun Company for $3,375,000 in cash. One year later, on December 31, 2008, the Run Company acquires 80 percent of the outstanding voting shares of the Sun Company for $7,500,000 in cash.

7-28. It was determined that there was a goodwill impairment loss for 2009 of $40,000 related to the Run Company's investment in Sun Company.

Required For Case Two: Compute consolidated Net Income for the year ending December 31, 2009 and the Non-Controlling Interest that would be shown in the December 31, 2009 consolidated Balance Sheet. In addition, prepare a consolidated Statement Of Retained Earnings for the year ending December 31, 2009.

Investment Analysis - Sun in Tun

7-29. On December 31, 2007, the Shareholders' Equity of the Tun Company amounts to $4,500,000. When on this date, the Sun Company buys 75 percent of Tun for $3,375,000, the investment is made at a price that is equal to the investor's proportionate share of this value. Since the basic data for the problem states that all of the Tun Company's net identifiable assets have fair values that are equal to their carrying values, it will not be necessary to make any adjustment for amortization of fair value changes. There is also no goodwill in this investment analysis.

Investment Analysis - Run In Sun

7-30. The analysis of the Run Company's investment in the Sun Company is as follows:

	80 Percent	100 Percent
Investment Cost	$7,500,000	$9,375,000
Sun Shareholders' Equity (See Note)	(3,500,000)	(4,375,000)
Differential	$4,000,000	$5,000,000
Fair Value Increase on Building	(2,400,000)	(3,000,000)
Goodwill	$1,600,000	$2,000,000

Note On Sun Shareholders' Equity At the time the Run Company acquired its interest in the Sun Company, the Sun Company had been holding a controlling interest in the Tun Company for a period of one year. During this period, the Tun Company earned and retained income of $500,000 (the Tun Company's 2008 Net Income). Since the Sun Company is carrying its investment in Tun by the cost method, Sun's equity in Tun's income since acquisition is not reflected on the books of the Sun Company. However, it should be included as part of the book value that is being purchased by the Run Company. Therefore, the book value for the Sun Company that is included in the investment analysis schedule is computed as follows:

Sun's Common Stock	$1,000,000
Sun's Retained Earnings	3,000,000
Sun's Equity Pickup In Tun's Earnings [(75%)($500,000)]	375,000
Total	$4,375,000

7-31. With respect to the treatment of the fair value change in subsequent accounting periods, the fair value increase on the building would be amortized over 8 years at a rate of $300,000 ($2,400,000 ÷ 8) per year.

Procedures

7-32. Here again, we will not become involved with a complete application of the consolidation procedures. Rather, we will use direct calculations of the various balances that are required in completing the problem.

Consolidated Net Income

7-33. The first computation that is required in this Case Two is consolidated Net Income for the year ending December 31, 2009. This figure is calculated as follows:

Run Company's Net Income	$2,000,000
Run Company's Share Of:	
Net Income Of Sun Company [(80%)($1,500,000)]	1,200,000
Adjusted Net Income Of Tun Company [(80%)(75%)($500,000 - $150,000)]	210,000
Amortization Of Fair Value increase On Building	(300,000)
Goodwill Impairment Loss	(40,000)
Consolidated Net Income	$3,070,000

Consolidated Statement Of Retained Earnings

7-34. Since the Run Company acquired the combined Sun and Tun Companies on December 31, 2008, the consolidated Retained Earnings balance on that date would simply be that of the Run Company or a balance of $9,000,000. Given this fact, the consolidated Statement Of Retained Earnings would be prepared as follows:

Run Company And Subsidiaries
Consolidated Statement Of Retained Earnings
For The Year Ending December 31, 2009

Balance - January 1, 2009	$ 9,000,000
Consolidated Net Income	3,070,000
Balance - December 31, 2009	$12,070,000

7-35. As usual, we would recommend that you verify the final balance in this consolidated financial statement using a definitional calculation. This calculation would be as follows:

Run Company's December 31, 2009 Balance		$11,000,000
Equity Pickup In Sun:		
Sun's December 31, 2009 Balance	$4,500,000	
Balance At Acquisition	(3,000,000)	
Balance Since Acquisition	$1,500,000	
Run's Proportionate Interest	80%	1,200,000
Equity Pickup In Tun:		
Tun's December 31, 2009 Balance	$2,000,000	
Balance At Acquisition	(1,500,000)	
Balance Since Acquisition	$ 500,000	
Unrealized Inventory Profits	(150,000)	
Tun's Adjusted Balance	$ 350,000	
Run's Proportionate Interest [(80%)(75%)]	60%	210,000
Balance Before Adjustments		$12,410,000
Goodwill Impairment Loss		(40,000)
Fair Value Change - Building (1 Year)		(300,000)
Consolidated December 31, 2009 Balance		$12,070,000

7-36. This serves to verify the balance that was computed in the consolidated Statement Of Retained Earnings by adding consolidated Net Income to the opening balance of consolidated Retained Earnings.

Non-Controlling Interest

7-37. The non-controlling Interest as at December 31, 2009, is again made up of the interest of two groups of non-controlling shareholders. These are the non-controlling shareholders of the Sun Company and the non-controlling shareholders of the Tun Company. Further, the non-controlling shareholders of the Sun Company have an interest in the net assets of both the Sun Company and the Tun Company. As the Sun Company is once again carrying its investment in the Tun Company by the cost method, a separate computation will have to be made in order to pick up the Sun Company's non-controlling shareholders' interest in the Retained Earnings of the Tun Company since its acquisition by the Sun Company. The complete calculation is as follows:

Sun Shareholders' Interest In Sun:		
Common Stock [(20%)($1,000,000)]		$ 200,000
Retained Earnings [(20%)($4,500,000)]		900,000
Sun Shareholders' Interest In Tun:		
Retained Earnings Balance	$2,000,000	
Balance At Acquisition	(1,000,000)	
Balance Since Acquisition	$1,000,000	
Unrealized Intercompany Profit	(150,000)	
Adjusted Balance	$ 850,000	
Sun Shareholders' Interest [(20%)(75%)]	15%	127,500
Tun Shareholders' Interest In Tun:		
Common Stock [(25%)($3,500,000)]		875,000
Realized Retained Earnings [(25%)($2,000,000 - $150,000)]		462,500
Total Non-Controlling Interest		$2,565,000

7-38. This schedule completes the requirements of Case Two and the presentation of the problems associated with preparing consolidated financial statements in multi-level affiliations.

Reciprocal Shareholdings

The Basic Problem

(If you did not do so, we suggest that you read the overview of multiple investment situations in Paragraphs 7-6 to 7-11.)

7-39. The term reciprocal holdings refers to situations in which one or more subsidiaries has turned upstream and invested either in a subsidiary at a higher level in the ownership hierarchy or in the parent company itself.

7-40. The basic problem that arises in situations where, for example, a parent owns the majority of the outstanding voting shares of a subsidiary and the subsidiary owns some portion of the outstanding shares of the parent, relates to the computation of the proportionate equities in the income and Retained Earnings of the two companies.

7-41. In order to determine the parent's share of the income of the subsidiary one must first determine the income of the subsidiary and, this in turn, will require the determination of the subsidiary's share of the income of the parent. The solution to this obviously circular process requires the application of simultaneous equations. While this is a basic algebraic technique for solving a group of equations which have a number of variables that is equal to or less than the number of equations, it is not commonly used by accountants and, as a consequence, can generate a certain amount of difficulty in solving problems involving reciprocal holdings. Other than this problem, you will find that reciprocal shareholdings do not involve any new concepts or procedures.

Case One

Basic Data

7-42. The first example will involve a very simple situation.

Company Aye acquires 70 percent of the voting shares of Company Bye on January 1, 2003 and, also on this date, Company Bye acquires 10 percent of the voting shares of Company Aye. As both companies were newly incorporated on this date, there are no fair value changes, Goodwill or Retained Earnings at acquisition to be dealt with in this problem. On December 31, 2007, the Balance Sheets of the two Companies appeared as follows:

Balance Sheets
As At December 31, 2007

	Aye	Bye
Investment In Bye (At Cost)	$ 140,000	N/A
Investment In Aye (At Cost)	N/A	$ 50,000
Other Net Assets	1,060,000	450,000
Total Assets	$1,200,000	$500,000
Common Stock - No Par	$ 500,000	$200,000
Retained Earnings	700,000	300,000
Total Equities	$1,200,000	$500,000

There were no additions or deletions to either Company's Common Stock - No Par accounts during the period January 1, 2003 to December 31, 2007. In addition, there were no intercompany transactions during this period.

Required: Prepare a consolidated Balance Sheet for the Aye Company and its subsidiary, the Bye Company, as at December 31, 2007.

Retained Earnings Allocation

7-43. The only real difficulty in this problem is the allocation of the $1,000,000 in Retained Earnings to the respective shares of the non-controlling and controlling interests. This is where the application of simultaneous equations plays a role. The following two equations can be used to express the respective interest of the two Companies in the balances of the Retained Earnings accounts:

Aye = $700,000 + (70 Percent Of Bye)
Bye = $300,000 + (10 Percent Of Aye)

7-44. Solving these two equations gives the following values:

Aye = $978,494
Bye = $397,849

7-45. As would be expected, the sum of these two figures is in excess of the amount to be allocated. This reflects the fact that each amount contains a proportionate share of the other balance. This duplication will not, of course, find its way into the completed financial statements.

Non-Controlling Interest

7-46. The Aye balance of $978,494 contains a 10 percent non-controlling interest of $97,849 that is included in the Bye interest and must be removed in order to arrive at the appropriate consolidated Retained Earnings figure of $880,645.

7-47. The Bye balance of $397,849 contains a controlling interest that is reflected in the preceding consolidated Retained Earnings balance. To arrive at the non-controlling interest in Retained Earnings since acquisition, this 70 percent controlling interest of $278,494 must be removed. This will leave $119,355 as the non-controlling interest in Retained Earnings since acquisition. If we add the $60,000 non-controlling interest in the Common Stock of Bye to this amount, we are left with a total non-controlling Interest to be presented in the consolidated Balance Sheet of $179,355.

Case One Consolidated Balance Sheet

7-48. The Balance Sheet that is required in this example can be completed as follows:

Aye Company And Subsidiary
Consolidated Balance Sheet
As At December 31, 2007

Other Net Assets ($1,060,000 + $450,000)		$1,510,000
Non-Controlling Interest		$ 179,355
Shareholders' Equity		
Common Stock - No Par	$500,000	
Retained Earnings	880,645	
Shares In Aye Held By Subsidiary	(50,000)	1,330,645
Total Equities		$1,510,000

7-49. Note that the Bye Company's investment in the shares of the Aye Company has been shown as a deduction from the total consolidated Shareholders' Equity. This reflects the Recommendation of Paragraph 1600.71 of the *CICA Handbook*. This Recommendation is as follows:

> **Paragraph 1600.71** *Where a subsidiary company holds shares of the parent company, the issued share capital of the parent should be set out in full, with the cost of the shares held by the subsidiary shown as a deduction from shareholders' equity.* (See "Share Capital," Section 3240) (April, 1975)

Case Two

Basic Data

7-50. This example of reciprocal shareholding procedures involves three companies.

On January 1, 2002, the Ex Company buys 70 percent of the voting shares of the Why Company and 80 percent of the voting shares of the Zee Company. Also on this date, Why purchases 10 percent of the voting shares of the Zee Company and Zee purchases 20 percent of the voting shares of the Why Company. As in the previous example, all of the Companies are newly incorporated on this date and, as a result, there are no problems associated with fair value changes, Goodwill, or Retained Earnings at acquisition. On December 31, 2007, the Balance Sheets of the three Companies are as follows:

Balance Sheets
As At December 31, 2007

	Ex	Why	Zee
Investment In Why	$ 350,000	N/A	$100,000
Investment In Zee	320,000	$ 40,000	N/A
Other Net Assets	930,000	710,000	400,000
Total Net Assets	$1,600,000	$750,000	$500,000
Common Stock - No Par	$1,000,000	$500,000	$400,000
Retained Earnings	600,000	250,000	100,000
Total Equities	$1,600,000	$750,000	$500,000

There are no additions or deletions to any Company's Common Stock account during the period January 1, 2002 through December 31, 2007. In addition, there were no intercompany transactions during this period. All investment accounts are carried by the cost method.

Required: Prepare a consolidated Balance Sheet for the Ex Company and its subsidiaries, the Why and Zee Companies, as at December 31, 2007.

Retained Earnings Allocation

7-51. Here again, our basic problem is the allocation of the Retained Earnings balances to the respective controlling and non-controlling interests. The equations on which this allocation is to be based are as follows:

Ex = \$600,000 + (70 Percent Of Why) + (80 Percent Of Zee)
Why = \$250,000 + (10 Percent Of Zee)
Zee = \$100,000 + (20 Percent Of Why)

7-52. Solving these three equations gives the following values:

Ex = \$908,163
Why = \$265,306
Zee = \$153,061

7-53. As in this case, neither subsidiary has any interest in the earnings of the parent company, the consolidated Retained Earnings balance is simply the \$908,163 calculated above for the Ex Company. This also means that there will be no deduction in the consolidated shareholders' equity for subsidiary holdings of parent company shares.

Non-Controlling Interest

7-54. The total Non-Controlling Interest can be calculated as follows:

Common Stock - Why (10 Percent Of \$500,000)	\$ 50,000
Common Stock - Zee (10 Percent Of \$400,000)	40,000
Retained Earnings - Why (10 Percent Of \$265,306)	26,531
Retained Earnings - Zee (10 Percent Of \$153,061)	15,306
Total Non-Controlling Interest	\$131,837

Case Two Consolidated Balance Sheet

7-55. The Balance Sheet that is required in this example can be completed as follows:

Ex Company And Subsidiaries
Consolidated Balance Sheet
As At December 31, 2007

Other Net Assets (\$930,000 + \$710,000 + \$400,000)	\$2,040,000
Non-Controlling Interest (Paragraph 7-54)	\$ 131,837
Common Stock - No Par (Ex's Only)	1,000,000
Retained Earnings (Paragraph 7-53)	908,163
Total Equities	\$2,040,000

Case Three

Basic Data

7-56. As should be fairly obvious to you, the preceding examples are very elementary. There have been no fair value changes or goodwill, no unrealized intercompany profits and, in general, a lack of the types of complicating factors that are often found in consolidation problems. As such, they are consistent with the examples contained in the Illustrative Examples at the end of Section 1600 of the *CICA Handbook*.

7-57. This final Case is intended to provide a more complex illustration involving both differential allocations and intercompany profits. In putting this example together, we would note that there are alternative procedures that can be used for dealing with these new issues. Further, it is not completely clear from reading Section 1600 which alternatives are to be used.

7-58. As noted previously, Paragraph 1600.71 of the *CICA Handbook* requires that the cost of the subsidiary's holdings in the parent be deducted from consolidated shareholders' equity. Further, if the subsidiary has acquired the parent company's shares at a price which is different from the proportionate share of the parent's book value, the non-controlling interest in this differential must be recognized. This is reflected in the following Recommendation:

> **Paragraph 1600.52** *A difference arising from the elimination of reciprocal shareholdings among companies in the consolidated group should be allocated to parent and non-controlling interests on the basis of their proportionate shareholdings.* (April, 1975)

7-59. Taken together, these two Paragraphs would indicate that any difference between the cost of the subsidiary's investment in the parent and its proportionate share of the related book values would not be allocated to assets at the time of acquisition or written off against income in subsequent accounting periods.

7-60. When we turn to dealing with any differential that might arise on the parent's investment in the subsidiary and to the treatment of upstream and downstream unrealized profits, Section 1600 does not contain any Recommendations specific to reciprocal holdings situations. However, the general rules would appear to be applicable here and will be used in the example which follows.

Example On December 31, 2004, the single entity Balance Sheets of the Noar and Soar Companies are as follows:

Condensed Balance Sheets
As At December 31, 2004

	Noar	Soar
Net Assets	$8,000,000	$4,000,000
No Par Common Stock	$5,000,000	$3,000,000
Retained Earnings	3,000,000	1,000,000
Total Shareholders' Equity	$8,000,000	$4,000,000

On this date, the Noar Company purchases 85 percent of the outstanding voting shares of the Soar Company for $3,800,000 in cash, while the Soar Company purchases 10 percent of the outstanding voting shares of the Noar Company for $900,000 in cash. On the acquisition date, all of the identifiable assets and liabilities of both Companies have fair values that are equal to their carrying values. Both Companies carry their investments in equity securities at cost.

The condensed Income Statements of the two Companies for the year ending December 31, 2007, are as follows:

Condensed Income Statements
For The Year Ending December 31, 2007

	Noar	Soar
Revenues	$1,250,000	$960,000
Expenses	1,110,000	840,000
Net Income	$ 140,000	$120,000

During 2007, the sales of Soar Company include an amount of $125,000 which represents sales to Noar Company. Of these sales, merchandise which contains a gross profit of $18,000 remains in the December 31, 2007 Inventories of Noar Company.

Also during 2007, the Soar Company purchases $85,000 in merchandise from the Noar Company. At the end of 2007, $25,000 of this merchandise remains in the ending inventories of the Soar Company. Included in this amount is a gross profit of $12,000.

During 2007, the Noar Company declares and pays dividends of $80,000 while the Soar Company declares and pays dividends of $60,000. There were no other transactions between the two Companies in any of the years that are under consideration.

It was determined that there was a goodwill impairment loss for 2007 of $20,000 related to the Noar Company's investment in the Soar Company.

The condensed Balance Sheets of the two Companies as at December 31, 2007 are as follows:

Condensed Balance Sheets
As At December 31, 2007

	Noar	Soar
Investments	$3,800,000	$ 900,000
Other Net Identifiable Assets	4,540,000	3,410,000
Total Assets	$8,340,000	$4,310,000
No Par Common Stock	$5,000,000	$3,000,000
Retained Earnings	3,340,000	1,310,000
Total Shareholders' Equity	$8,340,000	$4,310,000

Required:

A. Prepare a consolidated Balance Sheet as at December 31, 2004.

B. Prepare a consolidated Income Statement and a consolidated Statement Of Retained Earnings for the year ending December 31, 2007, and a consolidated Balance Sheet as at December 31, 2007.

December 31, 2004 Consolidated Balance Sheet

7-61. Before preparing this Balance Sheet, an analysis of the two investments must be made:

	Noar In Soar	Soar In Noar
Investment Cost	$3,800,000	$900,000
Shareholders' Equity:		
85 Percent Of $4,000,000	(3,400,000)	
10 Percent Of $8,000,000		(800,000)
Differential	$ 400,000	$100,000

7-62. The $400,000 differential which arises on Noar's Investment In Soar will be allocated to Goodwill. The other differential will be, in effect, part of the amount that is deducted from the consolidated shareholders' equity as a reflection of the Soar Company's $900,000 investment in the common stock of Noar Company. Given these calculations, the required Balance Sheet is as follows:

Noar Company And Subsidiary
Consolidated Balance Sheet
As At December 31, 2004

Net Identifiable Assets ($8,000,000 + $4,000,000 - $3,800,000 - $900,000)		$7,300,000
Goodwill		400,000
Total Assets		$7,700,000
Non-Controlling Interest [(15%)($4,000,000)]		$ 600,000
Shareholders' Equity		
Common Stock	$5,000,000	
Retained Earnings	3,000,000	
Shares In Noar Held By Subsidiary	(900,000)	7,100,000
Total Equities		$7,700,000

2007 Consolidated Income Statement

7-63. Before proceeding to the consolidated Income Statement, it will be necessary to solve the following income equations of the two Companies. The Net Income of both Companies must be adjusted for unrealized inventory profits and intercompany dividends received. In addition, the $20,000 goodwill impairment loss reduces the Noar income equation.

Noar = $140,000 - $12,000 - [(85%)($60,000)] - $20,000 + [(85%)(Soar)]
Soar = $120,000 - $18,000 - [(10%)($80,000)] + [(10%)(Noar)]

7-64. Solving these equations gives:

Noar = $149,617
Soar = $108,962

7-65. Given these solutions, the required Income Statement is as follows:

Noar Company And Subsidiary
Consolidated Income Statement
For The Year Ending December 31, 2007

Revenues [$1,250,000 + $960,000 - $125,000 - $85,000 - (10%)($80,000) - (85%)($60,000)]	$1,941,000
Expenses ($1,110,000 + $840,000 - $125,000 - $85,000 + $12,000 + $18,000 + $20,000)	(1,790,000)
Non-Controlling Interest [(15%)($108,962)]	(16,344)
Consolidated Net Income	$ 134,656

2007 Consolidated Statement Of Retained Earnings

7-66. In order to prepare this statement, we need to solve the following equations related to the January 1, 2007 Retained Earnings balance:

Noar = $3,280,000 - $3,000,000 + [(85%)(Soar)]
Soar = $1,250,000 - $1,000,000 + [(10%)(Noar)]

7-67. Solving for these equations gives:

Noar = $538,251
Soar = $303,825

7-68. The required consolidated Statement Of Retained Earnings is as follows:

Noar Company And Subsidiary
Consolidated Statement Of Retained Earnings
For The Year Ending December 31, 2007

Opening Balance [$3,000,000 + (90%)($538,251)]	$3,484,426
Consolidated Net Income	134,656
Dividends [(90%)($80,000)]	(72,000)
Closing Balance	$3,547,082

December 31, 2007 Consolidated Balance Sheet

7-69. Using the information from the other financial statements, the consolidated Balance Sheet can be prepared as follows:

Noar Company And Subsidiary
Consolidated Balance Sheet
As At December 31, 2007

Net Identifiable Assets ($4,540,000 + $3,410,000 - $12,000 - $18,000)		$7,920,000
Goodwill ($400,000 - $20,000)		380,000
Total Assets		$8,300,000
Non-Controlling Interest [$600,000 + (15%)($303,825) + $16,344 - (15%)($60,000)]		$ 652,918
Shareholders' Equity:		
No Par Common Stock	$5,000,000	
Retained Earnings (From Statement)	3,547,082	
Shares In Noar Held By Subsidiary	(900,000)	7,647,082
Total Equities		$8,300,000

7-70. The only item in the preceding Balance Sheet which requires further explanation is the Non-Controlling Interest. We have computed this balance by first calculating the January 1, 2007 Non-Controlling Interest [$600,000 + (15%)($303,825)], adding the Non-Controlling Interest in 2007 income of $16,344 and subtracting $9,000 in dividends paid to non-controlling shareholders. There are, of course, more direct ways of calculating both this year end balance and the year end balance in Retained Earnings. We would suggest that you attempt the direct calculations of the end of year balances as a test of your understanding of this subject.

Intercompany Bondholdings

The Basic Problem

7-71. We have previously encountered intercompany liabilities. However, in the previous cases the intercompany balance was carried at the same value on the books of both the debtor and creditor company. These situations were further simplified by the fact that this carrying value was the maturity value of the intercompany liability. As a result of these facts, the amount of intercompany interest expense was equal to the amount of intercompany interest revenue and both amounts were equal to the amount of cash that was paid.

7-72. This meant that when we eliminated the intercompany expense and revenue there was no change in the combined income, the non-controlling shareholders' interest in income or consolidated net income. In a similar fashion, the elimination of the intercompany asset and liability served only to reduce the total consolidated assets and liabilities and had no effect on either the Non-Controlling Interest in the consolidated Balance Sheet or the Non-Controlling Interest in the consolidated Income Statement.

7-73. Marketable debt securities differ from other types of liabilities that we have encountered in our work on consolidations in two ways. First, this type of debt will generally be issued at a premium or discount from the amount that will be payable when it matures. The second difference is that, subsequent to its issuance, it will be traded at various prices which may be above or below its original issue price. These differences introduce complicating factors into the elimination of intercompany assets and liabilities and any related interest expense and interest revenue. These complications can be described as follows:

> **Single Entity Records** The fact that the bonds may be carried at a value other than their maturity value means that you must have some understanding of the procedures required to amortize a bond premium or discount and their effect on the amount of interest expense or interest revenue for the period under consideration. While this situation is not unique to consolidations, it does seem to be a point that causes difficulties for many students.
>
> **Consolidated Records** The fact that the bonds trade at prices other than those at which they were issued means that the parent (subsidiary) may purchase the subsidiary (parent) bonds at a price which is different from their carrying value on the books of the issuer. In this situation, the consolidated entity is purchasing the bonds from investors who are outside of the consolidated entity and, if the purchasing price differs from the carrying value of the liability, the consolidated entity will experience a gain or a loss on the retirement of the bonds.
>
> In addition, if the bonds are not cancelled, the amount of intercompany interest revenue will not be equal to the amount of intercompany interest expense. This means that the intercompany bondholding will have an influence on the non-controlling interest in income and on consolidated Net Income for as long as the bonds continue to pay interest.

7-74. Intercompany holdings of long-term marketable debt securities will be illustrated with a comprehensive three period example. In order to illustrate the income effects in subsequent periods, the example will be followed to the maturity date of the relevant bond issue.

Comprehensive Example

7-75. The basic data for Plug's acquisition of 80 percent of Slug's outstanding shares, and for the intercompany purchase of bonds is as follows:

> On December 31, 2003, the Plug Company purchases 80 percent of the outstanding voting shares of the Slug Company for cash in the amount of $3,200,000. On this date, the Slug Company's Balance Sheet disclosed No Par Common Stock in the amount of $1,500,000 and Retained Earnings of $2,500,000. All of the identifiable assets and liabilities of the Slug Company had carrying values that were equal to their fair values on that date.
>
> On December 31, 2004, the Slug Company issues Bonds Payable with a par value of $1,000,000. The bonds have a 10 percent coupon rate, mature on December 31, 2009 and pay interest annually on December 31. They are sold at a price of 105 for total cash proceeds of $1,050,000. The Slug Company accounts for the interest on these bonds by the straight line method.
>
> On December 31, 2007, the Plug Company purchases the entire $1,000,000 par value of this bond issue. The bonds are purchased in the open market at a price of 96 for a total purchase consideration of $960,000. The Plug Company accounts for the interest on these bonds by the straight line method.

Note On Straight Line Method If these Companies were subject to the requirements of Section 3855, "Financial Instruments - Recognition And Measurement", these bonds would likely be classified as held to maturity and accounted for by the amortized cost method. Under the recommendations of Section 3855, the straight line method of amortization can no longer be used. However, in order to focus on the complications involved in dealing with bonds in the context of preparing consolidated financial statements, we will continue to use this less complex method of amortization.

Except for the intercompany bondholdings and the related Interest Expense and Interest Revenue, there are no intercompany transactions in any of the years under consideration in this example. Further, no dividends were declared or paid by either Company during the years 2007, 2008, or 2009.

Single Entity Information

7-76. We will eventually deal with the preparation of consolidated financial statements for the years 2007 through 2009. However, in view of the difficulties that most students have with accounting for bond discount or premium amortization, we feel that it is useful to examine the entries that would be made in the single entity records of the two Companies before proceeding to the consolidation aspects of the problem.

7-77. In the years 2005 through 2009, the Slug Company would make the following annual entry to record Interest Expense:

Interest Expense	$90,000	
Bonds Payable - Premium	10,000	
Cash		$100,000

[To record the coupon interest of 10 percent on $1,000,000 and to amortize the premium of $10,000 ($50,000 ÷ 5)]

7-78. In the years 2008 and 2009, subsequent to the intercompany purchase of the bonds, the Plug Company would make the following entry to record Interest Revenue:

Cash	$100,000	
Bond Investment	20,000	
Interest Revenue		$120,000

[To record the coupon interest of 10 percent on $1,000,000 and to accumulate discount of $20,000 ($40,000 ÷ 2)]

7-79. For the years under consideration, the end of period balance sheet values for the bonds on the two Companies' books are as follows:

Date	Plug	Slug
December 31, 2007	$ 960,000	$1,020,000
December 31, 2008	980,000	1,010,000
December 31, 2009	1,000,000	1,000,000

2007 Data

7-80. The December 31, 2007 condensed Balance Sheets and the condensed Income Statements for the year ending December 31, 2007, for the Plug Company and its subsidiary, the Slug Company, are as follows:

Income Statements
For The Year Ending December 31, 2007

	Plug	Slug
Sales Revenue	$3,500,000	$1,200,000
Expenses Other Than Interest	$3,100,000	$ 900,000
Interest Expense	Nil	90,000
Total Expenses	$3,100,000	$ 990,000
Net Income	$ 400,000	$ 210,000

Balance Sheets
As At December 31, 2007

	Plug	Slug
Other Net Assets	$14,500,000	$6,000,000
Investment In Slug's Stock	3,200,000	N/A
Investment In Slug's Bonds	960,000	N/A
Total Assets	$18,660,000	$6,000,000
Bonds Payable - Par	Nil	$1,000,000
Bonds Payable - Premium	Nil	20,000
No Par Common Stock	$10,000,000	1,500,000
Retained Earnings	8,660,000	3,480,000
Total Equities	$18,660,000	$6,000,000

Required: Prepare a consolidated Balance Sheet as at December 31, 2007 and consolidated Statements Of Income and Retained Earnings for the year ending December 31, 2007.

Step A - Investment Elimination

7-81. In this example, the investment cost of $3,200,000 was exactly equal to the investor's proportionate share of the subsidiary's book value at the date of acquisition. Further, the problem also states that there are no fair value changes as at the acquisition date. As a consequence, there is no need to do an analysis of the investment account and the relatively simple investment elimination entry is as follows:

No Par Common Stock	$1,500,000	
Retained Earnings	2,500,000	
Non-Controlling Interest [(20%)($1,500,000 + $2,500,000)]		$ 800,000
Investment In Slug's Stock		3,200,000

7-82. The Non-Controlling Interest is 20 percent of the at acquisition book value of the Shareholders' Equity of Slug of $4,000,000 ($1,500,000 + $2,500,000).

Step B - Adjustments And Eliminations

7-83. In the absence of fair value changes or goodwill, there is no need to deal with the problem of write-offs of these amounts in subsequent accounting periods. Further, the example indicates that other than intercompany bondholdings and the related Interest Expense and Interest Revenue, there are no other intercompany transactions or dividends. As a consequence, the only adjustment or elimination to be dealt with here relates to intercompany bondholdings.

7-84. Before proceeding to the 2007 entry for dealing with these bonds, we will consider the general approach to be used in situations where there are intercompany holdings of long-term marketable debt securities.

General Procedures For Intercompany Bondholdings

7-85. The general procedures for dealing with intercompany holdings of long-term marketable debt securities involve three basic steps. These three steps can be described in the following manner:

> **Step One** The first Step in analyzing an intercompany purchase of bonds is to determine the total gain or loss resulting from the purchase. This is accomplished by subtracting the purchase price (asset value) of the bonds from the carrying value on the books of the issuing company (liability value) as at the date of the purchase.
>
> **Step Two** If there is a Non-Controlling Interest in the subsidiary company, the total gain or loss which was determined in Step One must be allocated to the holding company and the issuing company. While the *CICA Handbook* does not offer recommendations in this area, the general Canadian practice is to allocate on the basis of the relationship between the carrying values on the books of the two companies and the par or maturity value of the bonds. This somewhat arbitrary solution to the problem is called the "par value method".
>
> **Step Three** In the real world, bonds would often be cancelled subsequent to an intercompany purchase and no adjustments or eliminations would be required in periods subsequent to their purchase. However, this may not be the case. If not, Interest Expense and Interest Revenue will have to be eliminated in subsequent accounting periods. Since the amount of expense and revenue will not usually be equal, this elimination will have a net effect on income. This income effect will, over the remaining life of the bonds, reverse the consolidated gain or loss that was recorded in the year of the intercompany purchase. Therefore, you will have to determine and allocate the annual reversal of the gain or loss that will be reflected in the consolidated Income Statements in the years subsequent to the intercompany transaction.

Step One

7-86. As previously indicated, the intercompany gain or loss will be determined by subtracting the purchase price of the bonds from their carrying value on the books of the issuer. Using the December 31, 2007 values that were presented in the single entity information, the calculation would be as follows:

December 31, 2007 Liability	$1,020,000
December 31, 2007 Asset	960,000
Gain On Bond Retirement	$ 60,000

7-87. The economic logic of the preceding calculation is fairly obvious. The fact that we manage to retire a liability with a book value of $1,020,000 with a cash payment of $960,000 has resulted in a gain of $60,000. Correspondingly, in situations where the asset value used is greater than the liability retired, the preceding calculation will result in a negative number and this will reflect the fact that a loss on the bond retirement has occurred.

Step Two

7-88. In situations where the parent owns less than 100 percent of the outstanding shares of the subsidiary, the total gain or loss must be allocated between the purchasing company and the issuing company. This is necessary in order to appropriately split the effects of the gain or loss between the Non-Controlling Interest in income and consolidated Net Income.

7-89. In our opinion, all of the possible solutions to this allocation problem are arbitrary in nature. It would be possible to allocate 100 percent of the gain or loss to either the purchasing company or the issuing company. However, as the actions of both of these companies are required in order for the gain or loss to occur, it is impossible to provide a logical defense for choosing one of these methods over the other.

7-90. Given this situation, the method that is used most widely is something of a compromise between 100 percent allocation to either the holder or the issuer of the bonds. It is referred to as the par value method as it allocates the gain or loss on the assumption that the bonds were retired by the issuer of the bonds paying an amount equal to par value to the holder of the bonds. The resulting allocation process can be described from the point of view of each of the two companies as follows:

> **Bondholder** From the point of view of the bondholder, the bonds are an asset. As a consequence, if we assume that the bonds have been retired at par value, this company will have a loss on bonds that are carried at a premium over par value and a gain on bonds that are carried at a discount.
>
> **Bond Issuer** From the point of view of the bond issuer, the bonds are a liability. As a consequence, if we assume that the bonds have been retired at par value, this company will experience a gain on bonds that are carried at a premium and a loss on bonds that are carried at a discount.

7-91. In the illustration that is under consideration, the allocation would be as follows:

Bondholder

Par Value Received	$1,000,000
Book Value Eliminated	960,000
Share Of Total Gain	$ 40,000

Bond Issuer

Book Value Eliminated	$1,020,000
Par Value Given	1,000,000
Share of Total Gain	$ 20,000

Notes On The Step Two Allocation

7-92. The following points should be made with respect to the preceding allocation of the gain or loss:

A. The analysis is in terms of the holder and issuer, not the parent and subsidiary. Either company could be the holder or the issuer in a particular situation.

B. You will note that the Step Two allocations of $40,000 and $20,000 are equal to the total gain of $60,000 that was calculated in Step One. A less obvious fact is that even if there was no total gain or loss resulting from the Step One calculation, an allocation may still be required in Step B when the par value method is being used. For example, if the Plug Company had purchased the bonds for their carrying value on the books of Slug Company of $1,020,000, there would have been no net gain or loss on the retirement. However, if we apply the par value method of allocation we must charge a loss of $20,000 to the Plug Company as holder of the bonds and credit a gain to the Slug Company of $20,000 as the issuer of the liability.

C. As a final note, we remind you that the *CICA Handbook* is silent as to how this allocation process should be handled. This would appear to permit a variety of procedures in this area.

Step Three

7-93. The elimination of the intercompany asset and liability for consolidation purposes will, of course, result in subsequent eliminations of intercompany interest expense and revenue (assuming the bonds are not cancelled after the intercompany purchase). The elimination of the intercompany asset and liability results in a gain or loss in those situations in which the premium or discount reflected in the intercompany purchase price is not the same as the premium or discount on the books of the issuer at the time of the intercompany purchase.

7-94. This difference in premium or discount will also be reflected in the elimination of the intercompany Interest Expense and Interest Revenue. More specifically, there will be a difference in the amount of the expense and revenue that is eliminated in subsequent periods and the effect of this difference will be such that it will just exactly reverse the initial gain or loss on retirement of the bonds. The following calculations pertain to the example that is under consideration (the amounts can be found in the single entity information):

Annual Expense Elimination	$ 90,000
Annual Revenue Elimination	(120,000)
Annual Reduction In Income	($ 30,000)

7-95. Note that as a result of eliminating the above amounts, the combined income of the consolidated entity will be decreased by $30,000 per year for the two year period 2008 through 2009 and that this will exactly offset the $60,000 gain that was recognized for consolidation purposes in 2007. Apportionment of this $30,000 will be based on the gain allocation that was calculated in 2007. This would be as follows:

Plug's Annual Share Of Gain = $40,000 ÷ 2 = $20,000
Slug's Annual Share Of Gain = $20,000 ÷ 2 = $10,000

7-96. As you would expect, these amounts are equal to the premium and discount amortization in the single entity records of the two companies.

Step B - Bond Elimination Entry

7-97. With the preceding analysis of the intercompany bondholdings completed, we can now return to Step B of our general consolidation procedures. For 2007, the only entry that is required here is to eliminate the intercompany asset/liability position and to recognize the resulting gain. The entry is as follows:

Bonds Payable - Par	$1,000,000	
Bonds Payable - Premium	20,000	
Gain On Bond Retirement		$ 60,000
Investment In Slug's Bonds		960,000

7-98. Since the purchase occurred on December 31, 2007, there were no intercompany interest payments and, consequently, no elimination entries for Interest Expense or Interest Revenue.

Step C - Retained Earnings Distribution Schedule

7-99. The usual Step C schedule would allocate the Retained Earnings of the Slug Company since acquisition:

Book Value - January 1, 2007 ($3,480,000 - $210,000)	$3,270,000
Balance At Acquisition	(2,500,000)
Balance Since Acquisition	$ 770,000
Upstream Gain On Bonds - January 1, 2007	Nil
Adjusted Balance Since Acquisition	$ 770,000
Non-Controlling Interest In Retained Earnings Since Acquisition [(20%)($770,000)]	(154,000)
To Consolidated Retained Earnings	$ 616,000

7-100. The January 1, 2007 balance in the Retained Earnings of the Slug Company is the $3,480,000 balance from the December 31, 2007 Balance Sheet, less the $210,000 Net Income from the 2007 Income Statement.

Step C - Allocation Entry

7-101. The journal entry to implement the allocation determined in the preceding Paragraph is as follows:

Retained Earnings - Slug	$770,000	
Non-Controlling Interest		$154,000
Consolidated Retained Earnings		616,000

7-102. This entry provides the basis for the determination of the January 1, 2007 consolidated Retained Earnings balance of $8,876,000. It is Plug's January 1, 2007 balance of $8,260,000 (December 31, 2007 Balance Sheet amount of $8,660,000, less 2007 Net Income of $400,000) plus the preceding allocation of $616,000.

Non-Controlling Interest

7-103. The only difficult figure to compute for the 2007 consolidated Income Statement is the Non-Controlling Interest. It would be based on the reported income of the Slug Company, adjusted for the subsidiary's share of the gain on the intercompany purchase of bonds. This calculation is as follows:

Reported Income Of Slug	$210,000
Slug's Share Of Total Gain	20,000
Adjusted Income	$230,000
Non-Controlling Percent	20%
Non-Controlling Interest	$ 46,000

2007 Consolidated Income Statement

7-104. Given the preceding calculation of the Non-Controlling Interest, the 2007 consolidated Income Statement can be prepared as follows:

Plug Company And Subsidiary
Consolidated Income Statement
Year Ending December 31, 2007

Sales Revenue ($3,500,000 + $1,200,000)	$4,700,000
Interest Revenue	Nil
Gain On Bond Retirement	60,000
Total Revenues	$4,760,000
Expenses Other Than Interest ($3,100,000 + $900,000)	$4,000,000
Interest Expense	90,000
Total Expenses	$4,090,000
Combined Income	$ 670,000
Non-Controlling Interest	46,000
Consolidated Net Income	$ 624,000

2007 Consolidated Statement Of Retained Earnings

7-105. The consolidated Statement Of Retained Earnings for the year ending December 31, 2007, would be as follows:

Plug Company And Subsidiary
Consolidated Statement Of Retained Earnings
For The Year Ending December 31, 2007

January 1, 2007 Balance (See Step C Allocation Entry)	$8,876,000
Consolidated Net Income	624,000
December 31, 2007 Balance	$9,500,000

December 31, 2007 Consolidated Balance Sheet

7-106. The Non-Controlling Interest disclosed on the consolidated Balance Sheet is calculated by taking 20 percent of Slug's Shareholders' Equity ($4,980,000) adjusted for the subsidiary's $20,000 share of the gain on the intercompany bond transaction. That is, [(20%)($4,980,000 + $20,000)] is equal to the Non-Controlling Interest of $1,000,000.

7-107. The consolidated Balance Sheet for the first year of this problem would be prepared as follows:

Plug Company And Subsidiary
Consolidated Balance Sheet
As At December 31, 2007

Other Net Assets ($14,500,000 + $6,000,000)	$20,500,000
Investment In Slug's Stock ($3,200,000 - $3,200,000)	Nil
Investment In Slug's Bonds ($960,000 - $960,000)	Nil
Total Assets	$20,500,000
Bonds Payable - Par ($1,000,000 - $1,000,000)	Nil
Bonds Payable - Premium ($20,000 - $20,000)	Nil
Non-Controlling Interest (Paragraph 7-106)	$ 1,000,000
No Par Common Stock (Plug's Only)	10,000,000
Retained Earnings (Paragraph 7-105)	9,500,000
Total Equities	$20,500,000

2008 Data

7-108. The December 31, 2008 Balance Sheets and the Income Statements for the year ending December 31, 2008, for the Plug Company and its subsidiary, the Slug Company, are as follows:

Income Statements
For The Year Ending December 31, 2008

	Plug	Slug
Sales Revenue	$4,000,000	$1,500,000
Interest Revenue	120,000	Nil
Total Revenues	$4,120,000	$1,500,000
Expenses Other Than Interest	$3,700,000	$1,100,000
Interest Expense	Nil	90,000
Total Expenses	$3,700,000	$1,190,000
Net Income	$ 420,000	$ 310,000

Balance Sheets
As At December 31, 2008

	Plug	Slug
Other Net Assets	$14,900,000	$6,300,000
Investment In Slug's Stock	3,200,000	N/A
Investment In Slug's Bonds	980,000	N/A
Total Assets	$19,080,000	$6,300,000
Bonds Payable - Par	Nil	$1,000,000
Bonds Payable - Premium	Nil	10,000
No Par Common Stock	$10,000,000	1,500,000
Retained Earnings	9,080,000	3,790,000
Total Equities	$19,080,000	$6,300,000

Required: Prepare a consolidated Balance Sheet as at December 31, 2008 and consolidated Statements Of Income and Retained Earnings for the year ending December 31, 2008.

Step A - Investment Elimination

7-109. The following 2008 entry for the elimination of the investment account is identical to the 2007 entry.

No Par Common Stock	$1,500,000	
Retained Earnings	2,500,000	
Non-Controlling Interest		$ 800,000
Investment In Slug's Stock		3,200,000

Step B - Adjustments And Eliminations

7-110. The only Step B entry that is required is the entry to deal with the intercompany bondholding and the related Interest Expense and Interest Revenue. This entry would be as follows:

Bonds Payable - Par	$1,000,000	
Bonds Payable - Premium	10,000	
Interest Revenue	120,000	
Interest Expense		$ 90,000
Retained Earnings - Plug		40,000
Retained Earnings - Slug		20,000
Investment In Slug's Bonds		980,000

7-111. The only part of this entry that requires additional explanation is the credits to the Retained Earnings balances of the two Companies. These credits reflect the respective shares of the two Companies in the gain on the intercompany purchase of bonds. These amounts were recognized for consolidation purposes in 2007, but were not entered in the single entity records of either Company. As a consequence, an adjustment is required at this point. Note that the amount of the adjustment is the January 1, 2008 balance of the gain. During 2008, the Interest Expense/Interest Revenue elimination will reverse one-half of these amounts, leaving adjustments of $20,000 and $10,000 at the end of 2008.

Step C - Retained Earnings Distribution Schedule

7-112. The usual Step C schedule would be used to allocate the Retained Earnings of the Slug Company since acquisition:

Book Value - January 1, 2008	$3,480,000
Balance At Acquisition	(2,500,000)
Balance Since Acquisition	$ 980,000
Upstream Gain On Bonds - January 1, 2008	20,000
Modified Balance Since Acquisition	$1,000,000
Non-Controlling Interest In Retained Earnings Since Acquisition [(20%)($1,000,000)]	(200,000)
To Consolidated Retained Earnings	$ 800,000

Step C - Allocation Entry

7-113. The journal entry to implement the allocation determined in the preceding Paragraph is as follows:

Retained Earnings - Slug	$1,000,000	
Non-Controlling Interest		$200,000
Consolidated Retained Earnings		800,000

7-114. This entry provides the basis for the determination of the January 1, 2008 consolidated Retained Earnings balance. As expected, it is equal to the December 31, 2007 balance previously calculated. Alternatively, it can be calculated as follows:

Plug's January 1, 2008 Balance	$8,660,000
Plug's Gain On Bonds As At January 1, 2008	40,000
Preceding Step C Allocation	800,000
Consolidated Retained Earnings Balance - January 1, 2008	$9,500,000

Non-Controlling Interest In Income

7-115. The only difficult figure to compute for the 2008 consolidated Income Statement is the Non-Controlling Interest. It would be based on the reported income of the Slug Company, adjusted for the subsidiary's share of the reversal of the gain on the intercompany purchase of bonds. This calculation is as follows:

Reported Income Of Slug	$310,000
Slug's Share Of Gain Reversal	(10,000)
Adjusted Income	$300,000
Non-Controlling Percent	20%
Non-Controlling Interest	$ 60,000

2008 Consolidated Income Statement

7-116. Given the preceding calculation of the Non-Controlling Interest, the 2008 consolidated Income Statement can be prepared as follows:

Plug Company And Subsidiary
Consolidated Income Statement
For The Year Ending December 31, 2008

Sales Revenue ($4,000,000 + $1,500,000)	$5,500,000
Interest Revenue ($120,000 - $120,000)	Nil
Total Revenues	$5,500,000
Expenses Other Than Interest ($3,700,000 + $1,100,000)	$4,800,000
Interest Expense ($90,000 - $90,000)	Nil
Total Expenses	$4,800,000
Combined Income	$ 700,000
Non-Controlling Interest (Paragraph 7-115)	60,000
Consolidated Net Income	$ 640,000

2008 Consolidated Statement Of Retained Earnings

7-117. The 2008 consolidated Statement Of Retained Earnings would be as follows:

Plug Company And Subsidiary
Consolidated Statement Of Retained Earnings
For The Year Ending December 31, 2008

January 1, 2008 Balance (Paragraph 7-114)	$ 9,500,000
Consolidated Net Income (Paragraph 7-116)	640,000
December 31, 2008 Balance	$10,140,000

December 31, 2008 Consolidated Balance Sheet

7-118. The Non-Controlling Interest of $1,060,000 is calculated by taking 20 percent of Slug's net book value adjusted for the subsidiary's remaining $10,000 share of the gain on the intercompany bond transaction [(20%)($1,500,000 + $3,790,000 + $10,000)].

7-119. The consolidated Balance Sheet at the end of 2008 is as follows:

Plug Company And Subsidiary
Consolidated Balance Sheet
As At December 31, 2008

Other Net Assets ($14,900,000 + $6,300,000)	$21,200,000
Investment In Slug's Stock ($3,200,000 - $3,200,000)	Nil
Investment In Slug's Bonds ($980,000 - $980,000)	Nil
Total Assets	$21,200,000
Bonds Payable - Par ($1,000,000 - $1,000,000)	Nil
Bonds Payable - Premium ($10,000 - $10,000)	Nil
Non-Controlling Interest (Paragraph 7-118)	$ 1,060,000
No Par Common Stock (Plug's Only)	10,000,000
Retained Earnings (Paragraph 7-117)	10,140,000
Total Equities	$21,200,000

2009 Data

7-120. The December 31, 2009 Balance Sheets and the 2009 Income Statements for the Plug Company and its subsidiary, the Slug Company, are as follows:

Income Statements
For The Year Ending December 31, 2009

	Plug	Slug
Sales Revenue	$3,000,000	$1,000,000
Interest Revenue	120,000	Nil
Total Revenues	$3,120,000	$1,000,000
Expenses Other Than Interest	$2,600,000	$ 600,000
Interest Expense	Nil	90,000
Total Expenses	$2,600,000	$ 690,000
Net Income	$ 520,000	$ 310,000

Balance Sheets
As At December 31, 2009

	Plug	Slug
Other Net Assets	$15,400,000	$6,600,000
Investment In Slug's Stock	3,200,000	N/A
Investment In Slug's Bonds	1,000,000	N/A
Total Assets	19,600,000	$6,600,000
Bonds Payable - Par	Nil	$1,000,000
Bonds Payable - Premium	Nil	Nil
No Par Common Stock	$10,000,000	1,500,000
Retained Earnings	9,600,000	4,100,000
Total Equities	$19,600,000	$6,600,000

Required: Prepare a consolidated Balance Sheet as at December 31, 2009 and consolidated Statements Of Income and Retained Earnings for the year ending December 31, 2009.

Step A - Investment Elimination

7-121. The following 2009 entry for the elimination of the investment account is identical to the entries for 2007 and 2008.

No Par Common Stock	$1,500,000	
Retained Earnings	2,500,000	
Non-Controlling Interest		$ 800,000
Investment In Slug's Stock		3,200,000

Step B - Adjustments And Eliminations

7-122. Here again, the only Step B entry that is required is the one to deal with the intercompany bondholding and related Interest Expense and Interest Revenue. This entry would be as follows:

Bond Payable - Par	$1,000,000	
Interest Revenue	120,000	
Interest Expense		$ 90,000
Retained Earnings - Plug		20,000
Retained Earnings - Slug		10,000
Investment In Slug's Bonds		1,000,000

7-123. Most of the preceding journal entry is fairly obvious. The one possible difficulty would be with the credits to the opening Retained Earnings balances of the two Companies. These credits reflect the respective shares of the two Companies in the gain on the intercompany purchase of bonds, less one year's reversal of this gain through the elimination of Interest Revenue in excess of Interest Expense. By the end of 2009, the entire amount of the gain will be reversed and this will coincide with the fact that the bonds mature at this time.

Step C - Retained Earnings Distribution Schedule

7-124. The usual Step C schedule would be used to allocate the Retained Earnings of the Slug Company since the date of acquisition:

Book Value - January 1, 2009	$3,790,000
Balance At Acquisition	(2,500,000)
Balance Since Acquisition	$1,290,000
Upstream Gain On Bonds - January 1, 2009	10,000
Modified Balance Since Acquisition	$1,300,000
Non-Controlling Interest In Retained Earnings Since Acquisition [(20%)($1,300,000)]	(260,000)
To Consolidated Retained Earnings	$1,040,000

Step C - Allocation Entry

7-125. The journal entry to implement the allocation determined in the preceding Paragraph is as follows:

Retained Earnings - Slug	$1,300,000	
Non-Controlling Interest		$ 260,000
Consolidated Retained Earnings		1,040,000

7-126. This entry provides the basis for the determination of the January 1, 2009 consolidated Retained Earnings balance. It can be calculated as follows:

Plug's January 1, 2009 Balance	$ 9,080,000
Plug's Gain On Bonds As At January 1, 2009	20,000
Preceding Step C Allocation	1,040,000
Consolidated Retained Earnings Balance - January 1, 2009	$10,140,000

Non-Controlling Interest In Income

7-127. The only difficult figure to compute for the 2009 consolidated Income Statement is the Non-Controlling Interest. It would be based on the reported income of the Slug Company, adjusted for the subsidiary's share of the reversal of the gain on the purchase of bonds. This calculation is as follows:

Reported Income Of Slug	$310,000
Slug's Share Of Gain Reversal	(10,000)
Adjusted Income	$300,000
Non-Controlling Percent	20%
Non-Controlling Interest	$ 60,000

2009 Consolidated Income Statement

7-128. Given the preceding calculation of the Non-Controlling Interest, the 2009 consolidated Income Statement can be prepared as follows:

Plug Company And Subsidiary
Consolidated Income Statement
For The Year Ending December 31, 2009

Sales Revenue ($3,000,000 + $1,000,000)	$4,000,000
Interest Revenue ($120,000 - $120,000)	Nil
Total Revenues	$4,000,000
Expenses Other Than Interest ($2,600,000 + $600,000)	$3,200,000
Interest Expense ($90,000 - $90,000)	Nil
Total Expenses	$3,200,000
Combined Income	$ 800,000
Non-Controlling Interest (Paragraph 7-127)	60,000
Consolidated Net Income	$ 740,000

2009 Consolidated Statement Of Retained Earnings

7-129. The consolidated Statement Of Retained Earnings for the year ending December 31, 2009 would be as follows:

Plug Company And Subsidiary
Consolidated Statement Of Retained Earnings
For The Year Ending December 31, 2009

January 1, 2009 Balance (Paragraph 7-126)	$10,140,000
Consolidated Net Income (Paragraph 7-128)	740,000
December 31, 2009 Balance	$10,880,000

December 31, 2009 Consolidated Balance Sheet

7-130. The Non-Controlling Interest at this point is simply 20 percent of the book value of the Shareholders' Equity of Slug Company. That is, 20 percent of $5,600,000 is equal to the Non-Controlling Interest of $1,120,000.

7-131. The consolidated Balance Sheet at the end of 2009 would be prepared as follows:

Plug Company And Subsidiary
Consolidated Balance Sheet
As At December 31, 2009

Other Net Assets ($15,400,000 + $6,600,000)	$22,000,000
Investment In Slug's Stock ($3,200,000 - $3,200,000)	Nil
Investment In Slug's Bonds ($980,000 - $980,000)	Nil
Total Assets	$22,000,000
Bonds Payable - Par ($1,000,000 - $1,000,000)	Nil
Bonds Payable - Premium	Nil
Non-Controlling Interest (Paragraph 7-130)	$ 1,120,000
No Par Common Stock (Plug's Only)	10,000,000
Retained Earnings (Paragraph 7-129)	10,880,000
Total Equities	$22,000,000

A Final Note

7-132. The gain that was included in the computation of consolidated Net Income for 2007 has been reversed by the process of eliminating a larger amount of Interest Revenue than Interest Expense in 2008 and 2009. This means that the accounts now stand as they would have if the intercompany purchase of bonds had never taken place. We can see this by noting that the preceding consolidated Retained Earnings figure can be calculated without reference to the bonds. The calculation is as follows:

Plug Company's Balance		$ 9,600,000
Slug's Balance	$4,100,000	
Balance At Acquisition	(2,500,000)	
Balance Since Acquisition	$1,600,000	
Controlling Interest	80%	1,280,000
Consolidated Balance		$10,880,000

7-133. A further confirmation of this point is that the Non-Controlling Interest in the Balance Sheet is based on the carrying values of the subsidiary's net assets. In other words, the consolidated balances are at the levels they would be at if the intercompany purchase of bonds had never occurred. You should understand the reason for this before leaving the material on intercompany bondholdings.

Subsidiary Preferred Stock

Classification Of Preferred Stock

7-134. Because of their hybrid nature, preferred shares have always presented accountants with some difficulties in terms of determining the appropriate disclosure in the financial statements. While these securities may have some of the characteristics that we associate with debt securities (a specified rate of income, a claim in liquidation that is prior to the common shareholder), they also have attributes that we normally associate with common stock (no maturity date, no legal claim to income if dividends are not declared).

7-135. The problem is made more difficult by the fact that not all preferred shares have the same characteristics. For example, there are issues of preferred stock that have all of the characteristics of the corporation's common shares except for the fact that they do not have voting rights. It would seem fairly clear that this type of preferred stock should be classified as an equity item in the Balance Sheet.

7-136. In contrast, there are issues of preferred stock that not only have a fixed rate of dividends but, in addition, have a guaranteed redemption value. This type of preferred stock is clearly more akin to debt than to equity. This view is reflected in Section 3863, "Financial Instruments - Presentation", which requires that preferred shares involving a "contractual obligation on one party to the financial instrument (the issuer) either to deliver cash or another financial asset to the other party (the holder) or to exchange another financial instrument with the holder under conditions that are potentially unfavourable to the issuer", be classified as liabilities.

7-137. Until the introduction of Section 3860 (the predecessor to Section 3861) into the *CICA Handbook*, the common Canadian practice was to deal with all preferred shares as though they were a part of total shareholders' equity. Except in situations where the *CICA Handbook* requires classification as a liability, this practice continues.

7-138. A further exception to this disclosure exists when a subsidiary has preferred shares outstanding. In consolidated financial statements, the Canadian practice is to disclose the equity of the subsidiary's preferred shareholders in the net assets of the subsidiary company as a part of the Non-Controlling Interest. The basis for this practice is found in the following *Handbook* suggestion:

> **Paragraph 1600.68** Non-Controlling Interest is shown as a separate item on the balance sheet outside of shareholders' equity and may be composed of more than one class of equity interest.

7-139. You may recall from our previous discussions of the Non-Controlling Interest, that Paragraph 1600.69 of the *CICA Handbook* requires that the Non-Controlling Interest in the Balance Sheet be disclosed separately from shareholders' equity. In our opinion, this is not consistent with the treatment of other preferred stock balances.

Issues Raised By Consolidation

Non-Controlling Interest

7-140. The presence of preferred stock in the capital structure of a subsidiary, even in those cases where there are no intercompany holdings of the shares, complicates the computation of the Non-Controlling Interest and consolidated Retained Earnings.

7-141. The degree of complexity that these shares add to the problem of preparing consolidated financial statements is dependent on the nature of the income provision that has been written into the preferred share agreement. If the dividend claim is non-cumulative, the claim of the preferred shareholders against the total shareholders' equity of the subsidiary will not extend beyond the capital that they have contributed. However, if the dividend claim is cumulative and the subsidiary has missed paying the specified dividend in one or more previous periods, these preferred dividend arrearages will constitute a claim against the unappropriated Retained Earnings of the subsidiary.

7-142 Even more complicated is the situation in which the preferred shareholders have a right to participate in the income beyond the rate that is specified in the preferred share agreement. In this situation, the preferred shareholders will have an interest in their proportionate share of all of the Retained Earnings of the subsidiary.

Differentials

7-143. Further problems can be created when there are parent company purchases of preferred shares. If the shares have been purchased at a price that is equal to their claim on the carrying values of the net assets of the subsidiary, there is no problem as an equal amount of assets and equities will be eliminated and this, of course, will have no effect on anything other than total assets and equities.

7-144. However, if there is a discrepancy between the amount paid for the stock and its claim against the carrying values of the subsidiary's net assets, the elimination of the share balance and the related investment account will leave a differential to be allocated.

7-145. For example, if subsidiary preferred shares with a book value of $1,000,000 were acquired by the parent company at a cost of $1,200,000, the entry to eliminate the resulting intercompany balances would be as follows:

Preferred Shares	$1,000,000	
Differential	200,000	
Investment In Preferred Shares		$1,200,000

7-146. If common shares were involved, the Recommendations of the *CICA Handbook* would require that this differential be allocated to fair value changes and goodwill. However, preferred shares generally have a fixed claim in liquidation and, as a consequence, cannot be viewed as having a residual interest in the net assets of the corporation. Given this, we do not believe that differentials arising on the elimination of intercompany preferred shareholdings should be treated in the same manner as differentials on common shares.

7-147 While the *CICA Handbook* does not provide specific guidance on this issue, we are of the opinion that, when a parent company acquires outstanding subsidiary preferred shares, the transaction constitutes a retirement of these shares. From the point of view of the consolidated entity, the shares are no longer outstanding.

7-148. This corresponds to the treatment of intercompany holdings of bonds. As was noted earlier in this Chapter, intercompany acquisitions of bonds are treated as retirements, resulting in a gain or loss to be recorded in the consolidated financial statements. Note, however, the retirement of preferred shares would be a capital transaction and, as a consequence, the differential that arises on elimination of the intercompany balances would not be treated as a gain or loss.

7-149. If we view an acquisition by a parent company of outstanding subsidiary preferred shares as a retirement of these shares, any differential arising on the elimination of intercompany balances would be subject to the rules in *CICA Handbook* Section 3240, "Share Capital". Under these rules, a debit differential would normally be charged to Retained Earnings, while a credit differential would be credited to Contributed Capital. In the example in Paragraph 7-145, the $200,000 debit would be to Retained Earnings.

Examples - Basic Data

7-150. The problems associated with subsidiary preferred stock will be illustrated in three examples. The first Example is a simple one involving a subsidiary with an issue of non-cumulative preferred shares. There is a parent company purchase of these shares at a price that is equal to their carrying value on the books of the subsidiary.

7-151. Example Two is similar to Example One. However, in addition to the parent company purchase of these shares at a price that is equal to their claims against the carrying values of the subsidiary's net assets, we have added a complicating factor in that the preferred shares have a cumulative dividend provision.

7-152. Example Three is the most complex version of the problem. The parent company purchase of preferred shares remains in the Example. However, the preferred shares will be assumed to have a provision that provides their holders with full participation in the earnings of the subsidiary.

7-153. The same basic data will be used for all of the Examples to be presented. The parent company will be designated the Peel Company while the subsidiary will be the Seal Company. The basic information on the shareholders' equity, income and dividends of the two Companies is as follows:

	Peel	Seal
No Par Common Stock	$1,800,000	$600,000
Preferred Stock - 8 Percent, Par $50	Nil	300,000
Total Contributed Capital	$1,800,000	$900,000
Retained Earnings - January 1, 2007	$1,200,000	$300,000
2007 Net Income	150,000	60,000
2007 Dividends	Nil	Nil
Retained Earnings - December 31, 2007	$1,350,000	$360,000
2008 Net Income	150,000	60,000
2008 Dividends	Nil	Nil
Retained Earnings - December 31, 2008	$1,500,000	$420,000

The subsidiary has not paid dividends on the preferred shares in 2007 or 2008 and this, in turn, has prevented the payment of dividends on the common shares. As a result, the Net Income of the Peel Company does not contain investment income in either 2007 or 2008. This is due to the assumption that the Peel Company carries its investment in the Seal Company by the cost method.

During 2009, the Peel Company earns a Net Income of $120,000 before the recognition of any investment income from its subsidiary and the Seal Company has a Net Income of $150,000.

Example One - Non-Cumulative Case

7-154. In this first Example, assume that the Preferred Stock of the Seal Company is non-cumulative and non-participating. The data is as follows:

On January 1, 2007, the Peel Company purchases 40 percent of the Seal Company's 8 percent Preferred Stock for $120,000 in cash, and 60 percent of the Seal Company's Common Stock for $540,000 (60 percent of the $900,000 carrying value of Seal's Common Shareholders' Equity on that date) in cash. The purchases are made at book value and, at this time, the net identifiable assets of the Seal Company have fair values that are equal to their carrying values.

During 2009, the Peel Company does not pay any dividends while the Seal Company pays Common Stock dividends of $36,000 and Preferred Stock dividends of $24,000. The Balance Sheets of the two Companies on December 31, 2009 are as follows:

	Peel	Seal
Investment In Seal's Preferred Stock	$ 120,000	N/A
Investment In Seal's Common Stock	540,000	N/A
Other Net Assets	2,791,200	$1,410,000
Total Assets	$3,451,200	$1,410,000
Preferred Stock - 8%, Par $50	Nil	$ 300,000
No Par Common Stock	$1,800,000	600,000
Retained Earnings	1,651,200	510,000
Total Equities	$3,451,200	$1,410,000

The Retained Earnings balance of the Peel Company consists of the December 31, 2008 balance of $1,500,000, plus 2009 Net Income exclusive of investment income of $120,000, plus dividends received on Preferred Stock of $9,600 (40 percent of $24,000), plus dividends received on Common Stock of $21,600 (60 percent of $36,000).

Required: Calculate the 2009 consolidated Net Income. In addition, prepare a consolidated Statement Of Retained Earnings for the year ending December 31, 2009, and a consolidated Balance Sheet as at December 31, 2009 for the Peel Company and its subsidiary.

Step A - Investment Elimination

7-155. As both the common and preferred stock investments are made at prices that are equal to book values and no fair value changes are present on the acquisition date, no investment analysis schedule is necessary. Going directly to the investment elimination entry, where the investment in both the common and preferred stock will be eliminated, it is as follows:

Preferred Stock - 8 Percent, Par $50	$300,000	
No Par Common Stock	600,000	
Retained Earnings (At Acquisition)	300,000	
Investment In Seal's Preferred Stock		$120,000
Investment In Seal's Common Stock		540,000
Non-Controlling Interest ($360,000 + $180,000)		540,000

7-156. As usual, we have eliminated 100 percent of the investment accounts and 100 percent of the subsidiary's shareholders' equity as at the acquisition date. The only difference here is that the credit to the Non-Controlling Interest is made up of a common stock interest (40 percent of $900,000, or $360,000) and a Preferred Stock interest (60 percent of $300,000, or $180,000).

Step B - Adjustments And Eliminations

7-157. The only adjustment or elimination that is required here is the entry to eliminate the intercompany dividends. Other than the fact that two types of dividends are involved, it is the same entry that we have used for intercompany dividend eliminations in the past and is as follows:

Dividend Revenue ($21,600 + $9,600)	$31,200	
Non-Controlling Interest ($14,400 + $14,400)	28,800	
Preferred Dividends Declared		$24,000
Common Dividends Declared		36,000

Step C - Retained Earnings Distribution

7-158. The Retained Earnings of the Seal Company since acquisition to the beginning of 2009 is equal to $120,000 ($420,000 - $300,000) and since there are no adjustments or eliminations to be made against this amount, it will simply be split between non-controlling and controlling interests on the basis of their share of the Seal Company's common shares. That is, the Non-Controlling Interest will get 40 percent while the controlling interest is allocated 60 percent. The entry is as follows:

Opening Retained Earnings - Seal	$120,000	
Non-Controlling Interest		$48,000
Consolidated Retained Earnings		72,000

7-159. This entry reflects the fact that the non-participating Preferred Stock has no claim against the Seal Company's Retained Earnings in this Example.

Consolidated Net Income

7-160. The consolidated Net Income for 2009 of the Peel Company and its subsidiary can be calculated as follows:

Peel's Reported Net Income	$151,200
Less: Intercompany Dividends ($21,600 + $9,600)	31,200
Peel's Income Exclusive Of Dividends	$120,000
Equity Pickup:	
Common Stock [(60%)($150,000 - $24,000)]	75,600
Preferred Stock [(40%)($24,000)]	9,600
Consolidated Net Income	$205,200

Note that the common stock interest is based on the earnings of the common stockholders and not Net Income. That is, the preferred dividend claim must be subtracted from Net Income in order to arrive at the interest of the common stockholders. The fact that the preferred shares are non-cumulative means that, if the preferred dividends had not been declared, the claim of the preferred shareholders could have been ignored. In that case, the equity pickup would have been $90,000 (60 percent of $150,000).

Consolidated Statement Of Retained Earnings

7-161. As given in the Basic Data for the examples, on January 1, 2009, the Retained Earnings of the Peel Company amounts to $1,500,000. If we add the allocation of $72,000 from the Step C distribution entry, we have the opening consolidated Retained Earnings of $1,572,000. Given this, the consolidated Statement Of Retained Earnings for 2009 of the Peel Company and its subsidiary can be prepared as follows:

Peel Company And Subsidiary
Consolidated Statement Of Retained Earnings
For The Year Ending December 31, 2009

Balance - January 1, 2009	$1,572,000
Consolidated Net Income	205,200
Balance - December 31, 2009	$1,777,200

7-162. You may wish to verify the ending balance in consolidated Retained Earnings using a definitional calculation.

Non-Controlling Interest

7-163. The Non-Controlling Interest in the consolidated Balance Sheet can be calculated as follows:

Preferred Stock Interest [(60%)($300,000)]	$180,000
Common Stock Interest:	
Contributed Capital [(40%)($600,000)]	240,000
Retained Earnings [(40%)($510,000)]	204,000
Total Non-Controlling Interest	$624,000

Consolidated Balance Sheet

7-164. The consolidated Balance Sheet as at December 31, 2009, for the Peel Company and its subsidiary would be prepared as follows:

Peel Company And Subsidiary
Consolidated Balance Sheet
As At December 31, 2009

Investment In Seal's Preferred Stock ($120,000 - $120,000)	Nil
Investment In Seal's Common Stock ($540,000 - $540,000)	Nil
Other Net Assets ($2,791,200 + $1,410,000)	$4,201,200
Total Assets	$4,201,200
Preferred Stock - 8 Percent, Par $50 ($300,000 - $300,000)	Nil
Non-Controlling Interest (Paragraph 7-163)	$ 624,000
No Par Common Stock (Peel's Only)	1,800,000
Retained Earnings (Paragraph 7-161)	1,777,200
Total Equities	$4,201,200

Example Two - Cumulative Case

7-165. This example is based on the same basic data that was used in Example One. The major difference here is that we will assume that the subsidiary preferred shares have a cumulative dividend provision. However, we retain the assumption that these shares do not participate in earnings beyond their specified dividend rate. The data is as follows:

On January 1, 2007, the Peel Company purchases 40 percent of the Seal Company's 8 percent Preferred Stock for $120,000 in cash, and 60 percent of the Seal Company's Common Stock for $540,000 (60 percent of the $900,000 carrying value of Seal's Common Shareholders' Equity on that date) in cash. The purchases are made at book value and, at this time, the net identifiable assets of the Seal Company have fair values that are equal to their carrying values. On this investment date, there are no dividend arrearages on the shares of Preferred Stock.

During 2009, the Seal Company will pay Common Stock dividends of $36,000. However, because we are now dealing with cumulative Preferred Stock, the Seal Company must make up all dividend arrearages before the $36,000 dividend can be paid on the Common Stock. Since the Basic Data for the examples (paragraph 7-153) states that the Seal Company paid no preferred dividends in 2007 and 2008, the 2009 dividends on Preferred Stock will have to total $72,000. This is the annual dividend of $24,000 for a period of three years. The Balance Sheets for the two Companies on December 31, 2009 are as follows:

	Peel	Seal
Investment In Seal's Preferred Stock	$ 120,000	N/A
Investment In Seal's Common Stock	540,000	N/A
Other Net Assets	2,810,400	$1,362,000
Total Assets	$3,470,400	$1,362,000
Preferred Stock - 8%, Par $50	Nil	$ 300,000
No Par Common Stock	$1,800,000	600,000
Retained Earnings	1,670,400	462,000
Total Equities	$3,470,400	$1,362,000

The Retained Earnings balance of the Peel Company consists of the December 31, 2008 balance of $1,500,000, plus 2009 Net Income exclusive of investment income of $120,000, plus dividends received on Preferred Stock of $28,800 (40 percent of $72,000), plus dividends received on Common Stock of $21,600 (60 percent of $36,000).

Required: Calculate the 2009 consolidated Net Income. In addition, prepare a consolidated Statement Of Retained Earnings for the year ending December 31, 2009, and a consolidated Balance Sheet as at December 31, 2009 for the Peel Company and its subsidiary.

Step A - Investment Elimination

7-166. The investment elimination entry in this Example would be identical to that required in Example One. This is as follows:

Preferred Stock - 8 Percent, $50 Par	$300,000	
No Par Common Stock	600,000	
Retained Earnings	300,000	
Investment In Seal's Preferred Stock		$120,000
Investment In Seal's Common Stock		540,000
Non-Controlling Interest		540,000

Step B - Adjustments And Eliminations

7-167. As in Example One, the only adjustment that is required is to eliminate the intercompany dividends. It is as follows:

Dividend Revenue ($21,600 + $28,800)	$50,400	
Non-Controlling Interest ($14,400 + $43,200)	57,600	
Preferred Dividends Declared		$72,000
Common Dividends Declared		36,000

Step C - Retained Earnings Distribution

7-168. The Retained Earnings of the Seal Company since acquisition to the beginning of 2009 equals $120,000. However, in this Example Two, there are $48,000 (2 years at $24,000) in preferred dividend arrearages that have a prior claim on this balance. As a result of this fact, the preferred claim is $28,800 (60 percent of $48,000) while the non-controlling common shareholders have a $28,800 claim which is 40 percent of the balance of $72,000 ($120,000 - $48,000). Correspondingly, the allocation to consolidated Retained Earnings would be $19,200 (40 percent of $48,000) plus $43,200 (60 percent of $72,000) for a total of $62,400. The entry would be as follows:

Opening Retained Earnings - Seal	$120,000	
Non-Controlling Interest ($28,800 + $28,800)		$57,600
Consolidated Retained Earnings		62,400

Consolidated Net Income

7-169. The consolidated Net Income for 2009 of the Peel Company and its subsidiary can be calculated as follows:

Peel's Reported Net Income ($120,000 + $28,800 + $21,600)	$170,400
Intercompany Dividends ($21,600 + $28,800)	(50,400)
Peel's Income Exclusive Of Subsidiary Dividends	$120,000
Equity Pickups:	
Common Stock [(60%)($150,000 - $24,000)]	75,600
Preferred Stock [(40%)($24,000)]	9,600
Consolidated Net Income	$205,200

7-170. Note that this is the same consolidated Net Income that we arrived at in Example One. This means that the dividend arrearages and their payment during the current year have had no effect on the current year's consolidated Net Income.

Consolidated Statement Of Retained Earnings

7-171. As given in the Basic Data, on January 1, 2009, the Retained Earnings of the Peel Company equals $1,500,000. If we add the allocation of $62,400 from the Step C distribution entry, we have opening consolidated Retained Earnings of $1,562,400. Given this, the consolidated Statement Of Retained Earnings for 2009 of the Peel Company and its subsidiary would be prepared as follows:

Peel Company And Subsidiary
Consolidated Statement Of Retained Earnings
For The Year Ending December 31, 2009

Balance - January 1, 2009	$1,562,400
Consolidated Net Income	205,200
Balance - December 31, 2009	$1,767,600

Non-Controlling Interest

7-172. The Non-Controlling Interest in the consolidated Balance Sheet can be calculated as follows:

Preferred Stock Interest [(60%)($300,000)]	$180,000
Common Stock Interest:	
Contributed Capital [(40%)($600,000)]	240,000
Retained Earnings [(40%)($462,000)]	184,800
Non-Controlling Interest	$604,800

Consolidated Balance Sheet

7-173. The consolidated Balance Sheet as at December 31, 2009 of the Peel Company and its subsidiary is as follows:

Peel Company And Subsidiary
Consolidated Balance Sheet As At December 31, 2009

Investment In Seal's Preferred Stock ($120,000 - $120,000)	Nil
Investment In Seal's Common Stock ($540,000 - $540,000)	Nil
Other Net Assets ($2,810,400 + $1,362,000)	$4,172,400
Total Assets	$4,172,400

Preferred Stock - 8 Percent, $50 Par ($300,000 - $300,000)	Nil
Non-Controlling Interest (Paragraph 7-172)	$ 604,800
No Par Common Stock (Peel's Only)	1,800,000
Retained Earnings (Paragraph 7-171)	1,767,600
Total Equities	$4,172,400

Example Three - Participating Case

7-174. This final Example will continue to use the same basic data that was provided in Examples One and Two. The difference here will be that, in addition to being cumulative, we will assume that the subsidiary's preferred shares are participating.

7-175. Participation agreements can be based on percentages of par value or on the basis of the number of shares in the various classes under consideration. Since the Seal Company has No Par Common Stock, we will assume that the $600,000 in No Par Common Stock consists of 12,000 shares and that the participation is on a per share basis.

7-176. In effect, this means that after each of the 6,000 Seal Company preferred shares have received a dividend of $4 (8 percent of $50), the Seal Company common shares must also receive $4 per share before any further preferred dividends can be paid. After each class of shares have received this $4 per share, any additional dividends must be paid in equal per share amounts to both classes of equity interest. The data for this version of the example is as follows:

> On January 1, 2007, the Peel Company purchases 60 percent of the Seal Company Common Stock for $480,000 and 40 percent of the Seal Company Preferred Stock for $160,000. In each case the investment cost is equal to the book value of the equity investment acquired (See following Investment Analysis). On this investment date, all of the net identifiable assets of the Seal Company have fair values that are equal to their carrying values.
>
> The total dividends paid by the Seal Company during 2009 amount to $234,000. This amount can be analyzed as follows:

	Common (12,000 Shares)	Preferred (6,000 Shares)
2007 Arrearages At $4	$ 48,000	$24,000
2008 Arrearages At $4	48,000	24,000
2009 Regular At $4	48,000	24,000
2009 Extra At $1	12,000	6,000
Total Dividends	$156,000	$78,000

> The Balance Sheets of the two Companies as at December 31, 2009 are as follows:

	Peel	Seal
Investment In Seal's Preferred Stock	$ 160,000	Nil
Investment In Seal's Common Stock	480,000	Nil
Other Net Assets	2,904,800	$1,236,000
Total Assets	$3,544,800	$1,236,000
Preferred Stock - 8%, Par $50	Nil	$ 300,000
No Par Common Stock	$1,800,000	600,000
Retained Earnings	1,744,800	336,000
Total Equities	$3,544,800	$1,236,000

The Retained Earnings balance of the Peel Company consists of the December 31, 2008 balance of $1,500,000, plus 2009 Net Income exclusive of investment income of $120,000, plus dividends received on Preferred Stock of $31,200 (40 percent of $78,000), plus dividends received on Common Stock of $93,600 (60 percent of $156,000).

Required: Calculate the 2009 consolidated Net Income. In addition, prepare a consolidated Statement Of Retained Earnings for the year ending December 31, 2009, and a consolidated Balance Sheet as at December 31, 2009 for the Peel Company and its subsidiary.

Investment Analysis

7-177. The fact that the subsidiary's preferred shares are participating means that these shareholders have a claim on subsidiary Retained Earnings. More specifically, since there are 6,000 preferred shares outstanding and 12,000 common shares outstanding, the Seal Company Retained Earnings balance must be divided between the two classes of equity on a one-third (6,000 ÷ 18,000) to two-thirds (12,000 ÷ 18,000) basis. This means that the January 1, 2007 book value that would be associated with the Seal Company Common Stock would be the $600,000 of No Par Common Stock, plus two-thirds of the $300,000 in Retained Earnings, a total of $800,000.

7-178. The corresponding figure for the book value of the Seal Company Preferred Stock would be the $300,000 of Par $50 Preferred Stock, plus one-third of the $300,000 in Retained Earnings, a total of $400,000. This means that both of the investments that were made by the Peel Company on this date were made at book value. This can be seen as follows:

Common Stock Cost = $480,000 = [(60%)($800,000)]
Preferred Stock Cost = $160,000 = [(40%)($400,000)]

7-179. A similar computation will provide the Non-Controlling Interest as at the acquisition date. These calculations are as follows:

Common Stock Non-Controlling Interest = $320,000 = [(40%)($800,000)]
Preferred Stock Non-Controlling Interest = $240,000 = [(60%)($400,000)]

7-180. This gives a total Non-Controlling Interest of $560,000.

Step A - Investment Elimination

7-181. Based on the preceding analysis, the investment elimination entry would be as follows:

Preferred Stock - 8 Percent, $50 Par	$300,000	
No Par Common Stock	600,000	
Retained Earnings	300,000	
Investment In Seal's Preferred Stock		$160,000
Investment In Seal's Common Stock		480,000
Non-Controlling Interest		560,000

Step B - Adjustments And Eliminations

7-182. Here again, the only adjustment that is required is for the elimination of intercompany dividends. It is as follows:

Dividend Revenue ($93,600 + $31,200)	$124,800	
Non-Controlling Interest ($62,400 + $46,800)	109,200	
Preferred Dividends Declared		$ 78,000
Common Dividends Declared		156,000

Step C - Retained Earnings Distribution

7-183. The Retained Earnings of the Seal Company since acquisition to the beginning of 2009 equals $120,000. Of this amount, one-third or $40,000 is a part of the preferred stock equity while the balance or $80,000 belongs to the common shareholders. This means the preferred claim will be $24,000 [(60%)(1/3)($120,000)] while the non-controlling common claim will be $32,000 [(40%)(2/3)($120,000)].

7-184. In a similar fashion, the controlling claim is $16,000 [(40%)(1/3)($120,000)] on the preferred holding and $48,000 [(60%)(2/3)($120,000)] on the common holding. Note that no attention need be given to the two years of dividend arrearages that are present at January 1, 2009. This results from the fact that, whenever a preferred dividend arrearage is paid, an equivalent per share amount must be paid to the common shareholders. This establishes the common shareholders' claim to a two-thirds share of all of Seal's Retained Earnings. The journal entry to distribute the interests that we have just calculated is as follows:

Opening Retained Earnings - Seal	$120,000	
Non-Controlling Interest ($24,000 + $32,000)		$56,000
Consolidated Retained Earnings ($16,000 + $48,000)		64,000

Consolidated Net Income

7-185. The consolidated Net Income for 2009 of the Peel Company and its subsidiary can be calculated as follows:

Peel's Reported Net Income ($120,000 + $93,600 + $31,200)	$244,800
Intercompany Dividends	(124,800)
Peel's Income Exclusive Of Dividends	$120,000
Equity Pickups:	
Common Stock [(60%)(2/3)($150,000)]	60,000
Preferred Stock [(40%)(1/3)($150,000)]	20,000
Consolidated Net Income	$200,000

7-186. Note that with participating preferred stock, both equity pickups are based on Net Income rather than having the equity pickup of the common stock being based on this figure less preferred dividends.

Consolidated Statement Of Retained Earnings

7-187. As given in the Basic Data, on January 1, 2009, the Retained Earnings balance of the Peel Company is $1,500,000. If we add the allocation of $64,000 from the Step C distribution entry, we have the opening consolidated Retained Earnings balance of $1,564,000. Given this, the consolidated Statement Of Retained Earnings for 2009 of the Peel Company and its subsidiary can be prepared as follows:

Peel Company And Subsidiary
Consolidated Statement Of Retained Earnings
For The Year Ending December 31, 2009

Balance - January 1, 2009	$1,564,000
Consolidated Net Income	200,000
Balance - December 31, 2009	$1,764,000

Non-Controlling Interest

7-188. The Non-Controlling Interest calculation is complicated by the fact that when preferred shares are participating, they have a claim on the Retained Earnings in much the same manner as do the common shareholders. This claim is reflected in the following calculation of the Non-Controlling Interest:

Preferred Stock Interest:	
Contributed Capital [(60%)($300,000)]	$180,000
Retained Earnings [(60%)(1/3)($336,000)]	67,200
Common Stock Interest:	
Contributed Capital [(40%)($600,000)]	240,000
Retained Earnings [(40%)(2/3)($336,000)]	89,600
Total Non-Controlling Interest	$576,800

Consolidated Balance Sheet

7-189. The consolidated Balance Sheet as at December 31, 2009 of the Peel Company and its subsidiary is as follows:

Peel Company And Subsidiary
Consolidated Balance Sheet
As At December 31, 2009

Investment In Seal's Preferred Stock ($160,000 - $160,000)	Nil
Investment In Seal's Common Stock ($480,000 - $480,000)	Nil
Other Net Assets ($2,904,800 + $1,236,000)	$4,140,800
Total Assets	$4,140,800
Preferred Stock - 8 Percent, $50 Par ($300,000 - $300,000)	Nil
Non-Controlling Interest (Paragraph 7-188)	$ 576,800
No Par Common Stock (Peel's Only)	1,800,000
Retained Earnings (Paragraph 7-187)	1,764,000
Total Equities	$4,140,800

7-190. This completes our most complex Example of the consolidation procedures that are required in dealing with subsidiary issues of preferred stock.

Transactions Involving Subsidiary Shares

Types Of Transactions

7-191. Subsequent to the acquisition of a subsidiary that is to be consolidated, certain transactions involving the shareholders' equity of that subsidiary may affect the proportional equity positions of the parent and Non-Controlling Interests. Possible shareholders' equity transactions include the following:

- The purchase of additional subsidiary shares from an outside interest by the parent company.
- The purchase of additional subsidiary shares from an outside interest by the subsidiary company.
- The sale of a portion of the subsidiary shares to an outside interest by the parent company.
- The issue by the subsidiary company of additional shares to an outside interest.

7-192. The first two types of transactions do not involve anything that is really new and, therefore, can be dealt with in a brief manner. The latter two items, however, involve new procedures and will be illustrated in detail.

Parent Purchase Of Additional Subsidiary Shares

7-193. The purchase of additional subsidiary shares by the parent from an interest outside of the consolidated entity is really no different from the earlier purchase of shares which made the investee a subsidiary. It follows that the accounting treatment would be the same. This is reflected in the following *CICA Handbook* suggestion:

Paragraph 1600.39 When a parent company acquires additional shares in a subsidiary, that transaction will be accounted for in accordance with the guidelines provided in paragraphs 1600.07 - 1600.24.

7-194. Paragraphs 1600.07 - .24 deal with consolidation at the date of acquisition and require that amounts paid for subsidiary common shares be allocated to the fair values of the subsidiary's identifiable assets and to goodwill.

Subsidiary Purchase Of Its Own Shares

7-195. The acquisition by a subsidiary of some of its own outstanding shares has an economic effect that is similar to the purchase of additional shares by the parent company. The recommended accounting procedures are based on this view of the economic substance of the event. As found in Paragraph 1600.48, they are as follows:

Paragraph 1600.48 When a subsidiary acquires its own shares for cancellation from outside interests, the proportionate interest of the parent company after the transaction is increased. Since the transaction is similar in effect to the situation where the parent company acquires an additional interest in a subsidiary it may be accounted for in the same manner as a step-by-step acquisition.

7-196. The procedures for dealing step-by-step acquisitions were covered in Chapters 5 and Chapter 6.

Comprehensive Example For Complex Transactions

7-197. As indicated previously, both the sale of a portion of the subsidiary shares by the parent company and the issuance of additional shares by the subsidiary are sufficiently different and complex that they warrant detailed illustration. In order to do this in an adequate manner, a fairly comprehensive consolidation problem is required. We will illustrate both of these types of shareholders' equity transactions using the same basic example. The example, before the addition of any subsidiary shareholders' equity transactions is as follows:

Example On January 1, 2007, the Pure Company purchases 70 percent of the outstanding shares of the Sure Company for $2,100,000 in cash. At the time of this acquisition, the Sure Company had No Par Common Stock outstanding in the amount of $1,500,000 and Retained Earnings of $1,000,000. Also on that date, all of the identifiable assets and liabilities of the Sure Company had carrying values that were equal to their fair values except for a patent which had a fair value that was $300,000 greater than its carrying value. The remaining economic life of this patent is six years and it is being amortized by the straight line method.

It was determined that there was a goodwill impairment loss for 2008 of $14,000 related to the Pure Company's investment in the Sure Company.

On December 31, 2009, the adjusted but unclosed condensed trial balances of the two Companies are as follows:

	Pure	Sure
Investment In Sure (Cost)	$2,100,000	N/A
Other Net Identifiable Assets	6,500,000	$3,200,000
Total Expenses	1,300,000	600,000
Total Debits	$9,900,000	$3,800,000
No Par Common Stock	$4,000,000	$1,500,000
Retained Earnings (January 1)	4,100,000	1,500,000
Total Revenues	1,800,000	800,000
Total Credits	$9,900,000	$3,800,000

Required: Prepare a consolidated Balance Sheet as at December 31, 2009 and consolidated Statements Of Income And Retained Earnings for the year ending December 31, 2009.

Procedures

7-198. The preceding problem is a very simple one of a variety that we have encountered on several previous occasions. As a result, the journal entries will be presented without explanations, only for your convenience in understanding the basic data for the problem.

Step A - Investment Elimination Entry

7-199. The required investment elimination entry would be as follows:

No Par Common Stock	$1,500,000	
Retained Earnings	1,000,000	
Other Net Assets (Patent) [(70%)($300,000)]	210,000	
Goodwill [$2,100,000 - (70%)($1,500,000 + $1,000,000 + $300,000)]	140,000	
Non-Controlling Interest [(30%)($1,500,000 + $1,000,000)		$ 750,000
Investment In Sure		2,100,000

Step B - Adjustments

7-200. The only entry that is required here is for the amortization of the fair value change on the Patent and the goodwill impairment loss in the previous year. The entry is as follows:

Retained Earnings [($35,000)(2 years) + $14,000]	$84,000	
Total Expenses	35,000	
Other Net Identifiable Assets [(3)($35,000)]		$105,000
Goodwill		14,000

Step C - Retained Earnings Distribution

7-201. The balance in Sure's Retained Earnings is $416,000 ($1,500,000 - $1,000,000 - $84,000). The entry to allocate this balance would be as follows:

Retained Earnings	$416,000	
Non-Controlling Interest [(30%)($500,000)]		$150,000
Consolidated Retained Earnings [(70%)($500,000) - $84,000]		266,000

7-202. As usual, this entry establishes the opening balance for consolidated Retained Earnings. It would be the Pure Company's balance of $4,100,000 plus the preceding credit of $266,000 for a total of $4,366,000. This figure will be used in the preparation of the consolidated Statement Of Retained Earnings.

Consolidated Income Statement

7-203. The consolidated Income Statement would be prepared as follows:

Pure Company And Subsidiary
Consolidated Income Statement
For The Year Ending December 31, 2009

Total Revenues ($1,800,000 + $800,000)	$2,600,000
Total Expenses ($1,300,000 + $600,000 + $35,000)	1,935,000
Combined Income	$ 665,000
Non-Controlling Interest (30 Percent Of $200,000)	60,000
Consolidated Net Income	$ 605,000

Consolidated Statement Of Retained Earnings

7-204. The consolidated Statement Of Retained Earnings would be prepared as follows:

Pure Company And Subsidiary
Consolidated Statement Of Retained Earnings
For The Year Ending December 31, 2009

Balance - January 1, 2009 ($4,100,000 + $266,000)	$4,366,000
Consolidated Net Income	605,000
Balance - December 31, 2009	$4,971,000

Consolidated Balance Sheet

7-205. The consolidated Balance Sheet for the Pure Company and its subsidiary would be prepared as follows:

Pure Company And Subsidiary
Consolidated Balance Sheet
As At December 31, 2009

Investment In Sure ($2,100,000 - $2,100,000)	Nil
Other Net Identifiable Assets ($6,500,000 + $3,200,000 + $210,000 - $105,000)	$9,805,000
Goodwill ($140,000 - $14,000)	126,000
Total Assets	$9,931,000
Non-Controlling Interest (30 percent of $3,200,000)	$ 960,000
No Par Common Stock (Pure's Only)	4,000,000
Retained Earnings (Paragraph 7-204)	4,971,000
Total Equities	$9,931,000

Example One - Parent Sells Subsidiary Shares

7-206. In this first Example based on the preceding data, assume that prior to the preparation of consolidated financial statements on December 31, 2009, the Pure Company sells 10 percent of the shares of the Sure Company (this would be one-seventh of its 70 percent holding of Sure Company shares) for $600,000 in cash. In this situation, the following Recommendation is applicable:

> **Paragraph 1600.45** *When the parent company sells part of its holdings in a subsidiary to interests outside the consolidated group, any difference between the parent's underlying equity in the shares sold and the sale proceeds should enter into the determination of consolidated net income.* (April, 1975)

7-207. In the present situation, the application of this requirement will result in a gain on the transaction of $247,000. This is the excess of the sale price of $600,000 over the Pure Company's $353,000 underlying equity in the shares sold. This underlying equity can be calculated as follows:

Investment Cost	$2,100,000
Equity Pickup [(70%)($1,700,000 - $1,000,000)]	490,000
Patent Amortization (3 Years At $35,000)	(105,000)
Goodwill Impairment Loss	(14,000)
Total Underlying Equity	$2,471,000
Fraction Sold	1/7
Underlying Equity Sold	$ 353,000

7-208. This calculation will provide the basis for a new set of 2009 consolidated financial statements for the Pure Company and its subsidiary the Sure Company.

Consolidated Income Statement

7-209. The main difference in this new consolidated Income Statement would be the gain resulting from the Pure Company's sale of Sure shares. The Income Statement of the Pure Company and its subsidiary would be as follows:

Pure Company And Subsidiary
Consolidated Income Statement
For The Year Ending December 31, 2009

Total Revenues ($1,800,000 + $800,000 + $247,000)	$2,847,000
Total Expenses ($1,300,000 + $600,000 + $35,000)	1,935,000
Combined Income	$ 912,000
Non-Controlling Interest (30 Percent Of $200,000)	60,000
Consolidated Net Income	$ 852,000

7-210. Note that, because the sale of shares took place at the end of the year, the Non-Controlling Interest for the year remains at 30 percent for the 2009 year. In the December 31, 2009 consolidated Balance Sheet and in the consolidated Income Statements of future years, it will be at 40 percent.

Consolidated Statement Of Retained Earnings

7-211. The consolidated Statement Of Retained Earnings of the Pure Company and its subsidiary would be prepared as follows:

Pure Company And Subsidiary
Consolidated Statement Of Retained Earnings
For The Year Ending December 31, 2009

Balance - January 1, 2009 (Paragraph 7-202)	$4,366,000
Consolidated Net Income	852,000
Balance - December 31, 2009	$5,218,000

Consolidated Balance Sheet

7-212. The consolidated Balance Sheet of the Pure Company and its subsidiary would be prepared as follows:

Pure Company And Subsidiary
Consolidated Balance Sheet
As At December 31, 2009

Investment In Sure ($2,100,000 - $300,000 - $1,800,000)	Nil
Other Net Identifiable Assets ($6,500,000 + $3,200,000 + $210,000 - $105,000 + $585,000)	$10,390,000
Goodwill ($140,000 - $14,000 - $18,000)	108,000
Total Assets	$10,498,000
Non-Controlling Interest (40 Percent Of $3,200,000)	$ 1,280,000
No Par Common Stock (Pure's Only)	4,000,000
Retained Earnings (Paragraph 7-211)	5,218,000
Total Equities	$10,498,000

7-213. Several of the figures in the preceding statement require additional explanation. First, the $585,000 increase in the Other Net Assets reflects two things. The first is the added $600,000 in cash which resulted from the sale of the Sure Company shares.

7-214. The other component of the $585,000 relates to the fair value change on the patents. At the time of acquisition, we recognized 70 percent of the $300,000 total, or $210,000. This balance has been amortized for three years, leaving a balance of $105,000. Since the Pure Company has sold one-seventh of its holding in the Sure Company, one-seventh of the remaining fair value change must be removed from the accounts. This reduces Other Net Assets by $15,000 [($105,000)(1/7)], resulting in the net increase of $585,000 ($600,000 - $15,000).

7-215. The Investment in Sure account has been reduced by one-seventh of the cost of the investment and will be carried at $1,800,000 on the single entity records of Pure. The $18,000 reduction in the Goodwill account is one-seventh of the impaired balance of $126,000 ($140,000 - $14,000). Since Pure is disposing of one-seventh of its holding in Sure, a similar proportion of the Goodwill must be removed from the accounts.

7-216. Other changes in this consolidated Balance Sheet for Example One have been previously explained.

Example Two - Subsidiary Sells Subsidiary Shares

7-217. Assume that the Sure Company's shareholders' equity has consisted of 100,000 shares with no par value and that the Pure Company's 70 percent holding amounts to 70,000 of these shares. In this version of the Example, assume that the Sure Company issues to outside interests, an additional 16,667 of its common shares in return for $1,000,000 in cash.

7-218. Subsequent to this sale of shares, the Pure Company's 70,000 shares now represent a holding of approximately 60 percent (70,000 ÷ 116,667). In other words, the Pure Company's economic position is the same as it was in the previous Example in which it sold a portion of its holding of Sure Company shares.

7-219. In this situation, the *CICA Handbook* requires the following:

> **Paragraph 1600.47** *When a subsidiary company issues shares to interests outside the consolidated group, the effect of the change in the parent's interest as a result of the share issue should enter into the determination of consolidated net income.* (April, 1975)

7-220. The implementation of this provision will require the determination of the gain or loss resulting from the issue of shares. In this Example Two, we encounter the same gain as in Example One. The Pure Company's 60 percent share of the proceeds from the sale is $600,000 [(60%)($1,000,000)] and the underlying equity sold is again $353,000 or one-seventh of Pure's total underlying equity of $2,471,000 (paragraph 7-207). This gives a gain of $247,000 to be included in the consolidated Income Statement. With this information in hand, we can now proceed to the preparation of consolidated financial statements for this Example.

Consolidated Income Statement And Statement Of Retained Earnings

7-221. The consolidated Income Statement and the consolidated Statement Of Retained Earnings for the year ending December 31, 2009, would be the same in this Example as in Example One and will not be repeated here.

Consolidated Balance Sheet

7-222. The consolidated Balance Sheet would be prepared as follows:

Pure Company And Subsidiary
Consolidated Balance Sheet
As At December 31, 2009

Investment In Sure ($2,100,000 - $2,100,000)	Nil
Other Net Identifiable Assets ($6,500,000 + $3,200,000 + $210,000 - $105,000 + $985,000)	$10,790,000
Goodwill ($140,000 - $14,000 - $18,000)	108,000
Total Assets	$10,898,000
Non-Controlling Interest (40 percent of $4,200,000)	$ 1,680,000
No Par Common Stock (Pure's Only)	4,000,000
Retained Earnings (Paragraph 7-211)	5,218,000
Total Equities	$10,898,000

7-223. Most of the figures here are the same as in Example One. The only real difference is the fact that $1,000,000 in cash came into the consolidated entity in this Example, while only $600,000 was received in Example One. This $400,000 difference is reflected in a larger Other Net Identifiable Assets and by an additional $400,000 in the Non-Controlling Interest.

Consolidation With Investment At Equity

Basic Data

7-224. In order to illustrate the consolidation procedures that must be used when the investment in a subsidiary is carried by the equity method, we will use the same basic example that was introduced in Chapter 5 and expanded in Chapter 6. This example involved the Pleigh and Sleigh Companies and the basic data is as follows:

> On January 1, 2005, the Pleigh Company purchases 80 percent of the outstanding voting shares of the Sleigh Company for $3,200,000 in cash. On that date the Sleigh Company had No Par Common Stock of $2,000,000 and Retained Earnings of $1,500,000. On December 31, 2009, the adjusted trial balances of the Pleigh Company and its subsidiary, the Sleigh Company are as follows:

	Pleigh	Sleigh
Cash	$ 500,000	$ 300,00
Current Receivables	800,000	400,000
Inventories	2,500,000	1,700,000
Long-Term Note Receivable	200,000	Nil
Investment In Sleigh - At Equity	3,661,000	N/A
Land	1,500,000	1,000,000
Plant And Equipment (Net)	4,500,000	1,900,000
Cost Of Goods Sold	2,800,000	1,500,000
Amortization Expense	200,000	100,000
Other Expenses	364,000	616,000
Interest Expense	240,000	84,000
Dividends Declared	350,000	100,000
Total Debits	$17,615,000	$7,700,000

	Pleigh	Sleigh
Current Liabilities	$ 500,000	$ 200,000
Long-Term Liabilities	2,000,000	700,000
No Par Common Stock	8,000,000	2,000,000
Retained Earnings (January 1)	2,910,600	2,300,000
Sales	4,000,000	2,500,000
Interest Revenue	24,000	Nil
Investment Income	180,400	Nil
Total Credits	$17,615,000	$7,700,000

	Pleigh	Sleigh
January 1, 2009 Retained Earnings	$ 2,550,000	$ 2,300,000
2009 Net Income	500,000	200,000
Dividends Declared	(350,000)	(100,000)
December 31, 2009 Retained Earnings	$ 2,700,000	$2,400,000

Other Information:

1. At the date of Pleigh Company's acquisition of the Sleigh Company's shares, all of the identifiable assets and liabilities of the Sleigh Company had fair values that were equal to their carrying values except:

   - Inventories which had fair values that were $100,000 more than their carrying values,
   - Land with a fair value that was $150,000 less than its carrying value, and
   - Plant And Equipment which had a fair value that was $250,000 greater than its carrying value.

   The Plant And Equipment had a remaining useful life on the acquisition date of 20 years while the Inventories that were present on the acquisition date were sold during the year ending December 31, 2005. The Land is still on the books of the Sleigh Company on December 31, 2009. Both companies use the straight line method to calculate amortization.

2. In each of the years since Pleigh acquired control over Sleigh, the goodwill arising on this business combination transaction has been tested for impairment. No impairment was found in any of the years since acquisition.

3. Sleigh Company's Sales include sales of $300,000 to Pleigh Company. The December 31, 2009 Inventories of the Pleigh Company contain $100,000 of this merchandise purchased from Sleigh Company during 2009. In addition, the January 1, 2009 Inventories of the Pleigh Company contained $70,000 in merchandise purchased from Sleigh Company during 2008. All intercompany sales are priced to provide the selling company a gross margin on sales price of 40 percent.

4. On December 31, 2009, the Pleigh Company is holding Sleigh Company's long-term note payable in the amount of $200,000. Interest at 12 percent is payable on July 1 of each year. Pleigh Company has been holding this note since July 1, 2007.

5. During 2007, the Pleigh Company sold Land to the Sleigh Company for $100,000 in cash. The Land had a carrying value on the books of the Pleigh Company of $75,000.

6. During 2008, the Sleigh Company sold Land to the Pleigh Company for $150,000. This Land had a carrying value on the books of the Sleigh Company of $110,000.

7. On December 31, 2007, the Sleigh Company sold Equipment to the Pleigh Company for $600,000. The Equipment had originally cost the Sleigh Company $800,000 and, at the

time of the intercompany sale, had accumulated amortization of $350,000. On this date, it was estimated that the remaining useful life of the Equipment was three years with no net salvage value.

Required Prepare a consolidated Income Statement and a consolidated Statement Of Retained Earnings for the year ending December 31, 2009 and a consolidated Balance Sheet as at December 31, 2009 for the Pleigh Company and its subsidiary, the Sleigh Company.

Equity Method Data

Differences From Cost Method

7-225. As compared to the cost method version of this problem, the use of the equity method changed three items in the trial balance of the Pleigh Company. These are the Investment In Sleigh, Investment Income, and the Retained Earnings of Pleigh. The following schedules explain these changes.

Investment In Sleigh

7-226. The Investment In Sleigh account was increased to reflect the Pleigh Company's interest in the unremitted earnings of the Sleigh Company since it was acquired. However, this equity pickup has to be adjusted for fair value write-offs and both upstream and downstream unrealized intercompany profits. The relevant calculation would be as follows:

Investment Cost		$3,200,000
Sleigh's Closing Retained Earnings	$2,400,000	
Balance At Acquisition	(1,500,000)	
Balance Since Acquisition	$ 900,000	
Unrealized Upstream Profits:		
Land	(40,000)	
Closing Inventories	(40,000)	
Equipment Sale [($150,000 - (2)($50,000)]	(50,000)	
Adjusted Balance Since Acquisition	$ 770,000	
Non-Controlling Interest [(20%)($770,000)]	(154,000)	$616,000
Other Step B Adjustments:		
Fair Value Change On Inventories		(80,000)
Amortization Of Fair Value Change On Plant And Equipment [(5)($10,000)]		(50,000)
Downstream Profit On Land		(25,000)
Investment In Sleigh		$3,661,000

Retained Earnings Of Pleigh

7-227. Note that Pleigh's opening Retained Earnings balance of $2,910,600 is the same figure that we arrived at for consolidated Retained Earnings as at January 1, 2009 in the cost method version of this problem. As was noted in Chapter 5, this is not an accidental result. Rather, it is a result that will always occur in the application of the equity method as it is described in Section 3051 of the *CICA Handbook*. When the equity method is applied, both investor Net Income and investor Retained Earnings must be equal to the consolidated figures that would have resulted from preparing consolidated financial statements with the investee included.

7-228. The opening Retained Earnings balance of $2,910,600 can be verified with the following calculation:

Pleigh's Opening Retained Earnings Balance From Cost Method Version Of The Problem (See Chapter 6)		$2,550,000
Equity Pickup:		
Retained Earnings - January 1, 2009	$2,300,000	
Retained Earnings At Acquisition	(1,500,000)	
Balance Since Acquisition	$ 800,000	
Unrealized Upstream Profits:		
Land	(40,000)	
Opening Inventories	(28,000)	
Equipment - Beginning Of The Year	(100,000)	
Adjusted Balance Since Acquisition	$ 632,000	
Non-Controlling Interest [(20%)($632,000)]	(126,400)	505,600
Other Step B Adjustments:		
Fair Value Change On Inventories		(80,000)
Amortization Of Fair Value Change On Plant And Equipment [(4)($10,000)]		(40,000)
Downstream Profit On Land		(25,000)
Opening Retained Earnings Of Pleigh		$2,910,600

Investment Income

7-229. The balance in this account can be calculated as follows:

Sleigh's Reported Net Income	$200,000
Opening Inventory Profits	28,000
Closing Inventory Profits	(40,000)
Realization Of Equipment Profit	50,000
Sleigh's Adjusted Net Income	$238,000
Controlling Percent	80%
Controlling Interest	$190,400
Amortization Of Fair Value Change On Plant	(10,000)
Investment Income	$180,400

Procedural Approach

7-230. Except for the fact that the investment is carried by the equity method, this problem is identical to the one previously presented in Chapter 6. However, we will find that this change results in considerable alterations in the specific procedures that are required. We will still be using the basic three Step procedure that was developed in the previous Chapters. However, there will be a number of differences in its detailed application. These differences will be explained as we move through these Steps.

Step A Procedures

Investment Analysis

7-231. The investment analysis schedule is complicated by the fact that the $3,661,000 balance in the Investment In Sleigh account reflects the Retained Earnings of Sleigh from acquisition to January 1, 2009, and the 2009 Investment Income in excess of intercompany dividends of $100,400 [$180,400 - (80%)($100,000)].

7-232. Further, both the equity pickup and the Investment Income have been adjusted for fair value write-offs and both upstream and downstream unrealized profits. As a consequence, both the analysis of the Investment In Sleigh and the investment elimination entry will have to reflect all of these factors.

7-233. Since 100 percent of any downstream unrealized profits are being charged against the investor's proportionate share of other financial data, our usual two column fractional and 100 percent investment analysis schedule cannot be used. The following single column analysis will provide the information that is required:

Investment At Equity		$3,661,000
Book Value - January 1, 2009 [(80%)($4,300,000)]		(3,440,000)
Differential		$ 221,000
Fair Value Change:		
On Inventories		Nil
On Land [(80%)($150,000)]		120,000
On Plant [(80%)($250,000) - $40,000]		(160,000)
Investment Income In Excess Of Dividends		(100,400)
Unrealized Upstream Profits:		
Land	$ 40,000	
Opening Inventories	28,000	
Equipment [(2)($50,000)]	100,000	
Unrealized Upstream Profits	$168,000	
Controlling Interest Share	80%	134,400
Downstream Profit On Land [(100%)($25,000)]		25,000
Goodwill		$ 240,000

7-234. The unrealized intercompany profits are added in this schedule since they are like fair value decreases on assets and require a credit in the investment elimination entry.

Investment Elimination

7-235. An additional complication in making the investment elimination entry in this situation is that the Non-Controlling Interest will be affected by the presence of unrealized upstream profits. More specifically, the entry will eliminate 100 percent of these profits and the credit to the Non-Controlling Interest will be based on 20 percent of the $4,300,000 book value less the $168,000 in unrealized upstream profits. The resulting 20 percent of $4,132,000 would be equal to $826,400. The entry is as follows:

No Par Common Stock	$2,000,000	
Retained Earnings	2,300,000	
Plant And Equipment (Net)	160,000	
Goodwill	240,000	
Investment Income	100,400	
Investment In Sleigh		$3,661,000
Non-Controlling Interest		826,400
Land ($120,000 + $40,000 + $25,000)		185,000
Inventories		28,000
Plant And Equipment (Net)		100,000

7-236. In this type of situation, the investment elimination entry accomplishes a great deal. It removes all of the shareholders' equity of the subsidiary, eliminates the entire Investment In Sleigh account, establishes the adjusted beginning of the year balances for all of the fair value changes and goodwill, eliminates all of the beginning of the year unrealized intercompany profits, establishes the adjusted Non-Controlling Interest as at the beginning of the current year, and reduces the Investment Income account to the amount of intercompany dividends for the period.

Step B(1) - Intercompany Assets And Liabilities

7-237. The eliminations required by the presence of intercompany assets and liabilities are not affected by the use of the equity method. As a consequence, the entries will be the same as those used in the cost method version of the problem. The entries would be as follows:

Long-Term Liabilities	$200,000	
Long-Term Note Receivable		$200,000
Current Liabilities	$ 12,000	
Current Receivables		$ 12,000

Step B(2) - Fair Value Write-Offs

7-238. This elimination relates to the amortization and realization of fair value changes. Because the equity method records these adjustments in investment income and the investment account, in Step A we recorded the fair value change and goodwill balances net of amortization for the period from January 1, 2005 to January 1, 2009. However, as this is an "open trial balance" version of the problem, we will have to record any additional write offs for 2009 in order to correctly state the consolidated expenses.

Inventories

7-239. The Inventories that were present on January 1, 2005 were sold during that year. The related fair value change was fully reflected in the Investment Income and Investment In Sleigh account during that year. No further adjustment would be required at this point.

Plant And Equipment

7-240. An adjustment for one year's amortization on the fair value change will be required here. The amount is $10,000 and it would be recorded as follows:

Amortization Expense	$10,000	
Plant And Equipment (Net)		$10,000

7-241. This entry would leave the net Plant And Equipment adjustment at the appropriate year end figure of $150,000 (the $160,000 adjustment in Step A, less $10,000 here).

Step B(3) - Goodwill Impairment

7-242. The Other Information in our comprehensive problem notes that, while goodwill has been tested for impairment in each year since the acquisition of Pleigh Company occurred, no impairment has been found. As a consequence, no Step B-3 entry is required in this problem.

Step B(4) - Intercompany Expenses And Revenues

7-243. The eliminations required by the presence of intercompany expenses and revenues are not affected by the use of the equity method. The entries would be as follows:

Sales	$300,000	
Cost Of Goods Sold		$300,000
Interest Revenue	$ 24,000	
Interest Expense		$ 24,000

Step B(5) - Intercompany Dividends

7-244. This elimination is required by the presence of intercompany dividends. Under the equity method, the Investment Income that was recorded by the Pleigh Company included both dividends and an appropriate share of the unremitted 2009 earnings of the Sleigh Company. In Step A we eliminated Pleigh's share of the unremitted earnings of Sleigh against the Investment In Sleigh account. This left a balance of $80,000 ($156,400 - $76,400) in the Investment Income account. This $80,000 balance, which reflects the intercompany dividends received from the Sleigh Company, will now be eliminated using an entry similar to that which was required in the cost method version of the problem. The entry, which also removes the entire balance in the Dividends Declared account and reduces the Non-Controlling Interest in the consolidated Balance Sheet, is as follows:

Investment Income	$80,000	
Non-Controlling Interest (Balance Sheet)	20,000	
Dividends Declared		$100,000

Step B(6) - Unrealized Intercompany Profits

7-245. Our final Step B adjustments and eliminations relate to the treatment of unrealized intercompany profits. When the equity method is being used to carry the investment account in an open trial balance problem, the elimination of the investment balance will require the removal of the intercompany profits that were present as at the beginning of the current year. We saw this procedure demonstrated in our Step A elimination entry. At this stage, we must adjust the current year's expenses and revenues for any changes in the amount of such unrealized intercompany profits that have taken place during the current accounting period.

Unrealized Land Profits

7-246. You will recall that this problem contains a downstream profit on the sale of land of $25,000 and an upstream profit on a similar sale in the amount of $40,000. These amounts were eliminated from the Land account in Step A. Since there has been no change in the amount of these profits that is unrealized as at the end of 2009, there is no need to make any further entries with respect to these unrealized profits.

Unrealized Opening Inventory Profits

7-247. In Step A we credited Inventories for $28,000 in Sleigh Company profits that were in the January 1, 2009 Inventories of the Pleigh Company. Under normal circumstances these Inventories would be sold by December 31, 2009 and any profits of the Sleigh Company that were included in the sale would now be considered realized. In view of this, the following entry would be appropriate:

Inventories	$28,000	
Cost Of Goods Sold		$28,000

7-248. This journal entry serves to reverse the credit to Inventories that was made in Step A and to lower the consolidated Cost Of Goods Sold. This reflects the fact that unrealized profits were present in the beginning inventory that was included in the computation of this figure. The decrease in consolidated Cost Of Goods Sold increases consolidated Net Income by the opening upstream inventory profit which was realized during the current year.

Unrealized Closing Inventory Profits

7-249. At the end of 2009, $40,000 of the profits of Sleigh Company are still in the ending Inventories of the Pleigh Company. No adjustment was made for this fact in our Step A entry. As a consequence, it is necessary to make the following entry at this point:

Cost Of Goods Sold	$40,000	
Inventories		$40,000

7-250. This entry serves to reduce the Inventory figure for inclusion in the consolidated Balance Sheet and add a corresponding amount to the consolidated Cost Of Goods Sold. The increase in consolidated Cost Of Goods Sold decreases consolidated Net Income by the closing unrealized upstream profit.

Unrealized Profit On Equipment Sale

7-251. On December 31, 2007, the Sleigh Company sold equipment to the Pleigh Company and recognized a profit on the sale of $150,000. Since the asset had a remaining useful life at this time of three years, the profit is being realized through reduced amortization expense at the rate of $50,000 per year. Since $50,000 would have been realized in 2008, the remaining unrealized balance on January 1, 2009 would have been $100,000. This fact was reflected in Step A when we credited the Plant And Equipment account for $100,000.

7-252. During the year 2009, an additional $50,000 of the intercompany profit becomes realized so that at the end of 2009, only $50,000 of the profit on the sale of equipment remains unrealized. This fact requires the following entry to be made:

Plant And Equipment (Net)	$50,000	
Amortization Expense		$50,000

7-253. This entry serves to reduce the Step A credit to Plant And Equipment to the desired $50,000 and to make an appropriate $50,000 reduction in the amount that will be included in amortization expense in the consolidated Income Statement.

Step C - Distribution Of The Subsidiary Retained Earnings

7-254. When the Investment In Sleigh account is carried by the equity method, the Retained Earnings of the subsidiary since the date of acquisition are picked up in Investment Income, the Investment In Sleigh account and the Retained Earnings of the Pleigh Company. This was noted in the Step A investment elimination when we removed the entire balance in Sleigh's Retained Earnings account. With the elimination of the entire Retained Earnings balance against the investment account, no balance remains to be distributed in this step. Therefore, Step C procedures drop out. This would be the case whenever the investment account is carried by the equity method.

Preparation Of Consolidated Financial Statements

7-255. We have now completed all of the procedures necessary for the preparation of consolidated financial statements. As before, we will take the balances from the original trial balance, add and subtract the adjustments that have been made in our procedures, and arrive at the figures to be included in the consolidated financial statements. As the computations are not altered by the use of the equity method, the schedular verifications of consolidated Net Income and the closing consolidated Retained Earnings will be omitted in this version of the problem.

Consolidated Income Statement

Non-Controlling Interest

7-256. The calculation of the Non-Controlling Interest is the same as in the cost method version of the problem. It was as follows:

Sleigh Company's Reported Income	$200,000
Realized Gain On Equipment	50,000
Profits In Opening Inventories	28,000
Profits In Closing Inventories	(40,000)
Adjusted Subsidiary Income	$238,000
Non-Controlling Percent	20%
Non-Controlling Interest	$ 47,600

Statement Disclosure

7-257. The consolidated Income Statement of the Pleigh Company and its subsidiary would be prepared as follows:

Pleigh Company And Subsidiary
Consolidated Income Statement
Year Ending December 31, 2009

Sales ($4,000,000 + $2,500,000 - $300,000)	$6,200,000
Interest Revenue ($24,000 - $24,000)	Nil
Investment Income ($236,400 - $156,400 - $80,000)	Nil
Total Revenues	$6,200,000
Cost Of Goods Sold ($2,800,000 + $1,500,000 - $300,000 + $40,000 - $28,000)	$4,012,000
Amortization Expense ($200,000 + $100,000 + $10,000 - $50,000)	260,000
Interest Expense ($240,000 + $84,000 - $24,000)	300,000
Other Expenses ($364,000 + $616,000)	980,000
Total Expenses	$5,552,000
Combined Income	$ 724,000
Non-Controlling Interest (Paragraph 7-256)	47,600
Consolidated Net Income	$ 600,400

Consolidated Statement Of Retained Earnings

Statement Disclosure

7-258. Using the Net Income data, we can now prepare a consolidated Statement Of Retained Earnings. The January 1, 2009 consolidated Retained Earnings is simply the balance from the trial balance of the Pleigh Company. Adjustments, such as those required when the cost method is used, are not needed here. The consolidated Statement of Retained Earnings is as follows:

Pleigh Company And Subsidiary
Consolidated Statement Of Retained Earnings
Year Ending December 31, 2009

Balance - January 1, 2009	$2,910,600
Net Income	600,400
Dividends Declared (Pleigh's Only)	(350,000)
Balance - December 31, 2009	$3,161,000

Consolidated Balance Sheet

Non-Controlling Interest

7-259. In preparing the consolidated Balance Sheet, the only figure that does not flow directly from the journal entries is the Non-Controlling Interest. As was the case when the Investment In Sleigh was carried by the cost method, a direct calculation of the Non-Controlling Interest can be made by taking 20 percent of the subsidiary's net assets adjusted for end of the year upstream unrealized profits. This would be [(20%)($4,400,000 - $40,000 - $40,000 - $50,000)] and would equal $854,000.

7-260. Alternatively, we can arrive at this same figure through the various steps in the procedures. Step A allocated $826,400 to the Non-Controlling Interest. In Step B this was reduced because of the dividends of $20,000 to the non-controlling shareholders. If we take this net amount of $806,400 and add the Non-Controlling Interest disclosed in the consolidated Income Statement of $47,600, we get the Non-Controlling Interest for the consolidated Balance Sheet of $854,000.

Statement Disclosure

7-261. Given the preceding analysis, the consolidated Balance Sheet would be prepared as follows:

Pleigh Company And Subsidiary
Consolidated Balance Sheet
As At December 31, 2009

Cash ($500,000 + $300,000)	$ 800,000
Current Receivables ($800,000 + $400,000 - $12,000)	1,188,000
Inventories ($2,500,000 + $1,700,000 - $40,000)	4,160,000
Long-Term Note Receivable ($200,000 - $200,000)	Nil
Investment In Sleigh ($3,661,000 - $3,661,000)	Nil
Land ($1,500,000 + $1,000,000 - $185,000)	2,315,000
Plant And Equipment ($4,500,000 + $1,900,000 + $160,000 - $10,000 - $100,000 + $50,000)	6,500,000
Goodwill	240,000
Total Assets	$15,203,000
Current Liabilities ($500,000 + $200,000 - $12,000)	$ 688,000
Long-Term Liabilities ($2,000,000 + $700,000 - $200,000)	2,500,000
Non-Controlling Interest (Paragraph 7-259)	854,000
No Par Common Stock (Pleigh's Balance)	8,000,000
Retained Earnings (Paragraph 7-258)	3,161,000
Total Equities	$15,203,000

Problems For Self Study

(The solutions for these problems can be found in the separate Study Guide.)

Self Study Problem Seven - 1

On December 31, 2007, the Above Company acquired 70 percent of the outstanding voting shares of the Center Company for cash of $4,000,000. On this date, the Center Company had No Par Common Stock of $3,000,000 and Retained Earnings of $2,000,000. All of the Center Company's identifiable assets and liabilities had fair values that were equal to their carrying values, except Plant And Equipment which had a fair value that was $300,000 greater than its carrying value and had a remaining useful life of 20 years.

On December 31, 2008, the Center Company acquired 60 percent of the outstanding voting shares of the Below Company for cash of $2,000,000. On this date, the Below Company had No Par Common Stock of $2,000,000 and Retained Earnings of $1,000,000. All of the Below Company's identifiable assets and liabilities had fair values that were equal to their carrying values, except Plant And Equipment which had a fair value that was $500,000 less than its carrying value and had a remaining useful life of 20 years.

Both the Above and Center Companies carry their investments at cost. All Companies use the straight line method for all amortization calculations. All Companies have a December 31 fiscal year end.

On December 31, 2009, the condensed Balance Sheets and the 2009 Net Income of the Above, Center and Below Companies are as follows:

Condensed Balance Sheets
As At December 31, 2009

	Above	Center	Below
Net Monetary Assets	$1,500,000	$ 900,000	$ 700,000
Investments	4,000,000	2,000,000	Nil
Non-Monetary Assets	3,500,000	2,500,000	2,500,000
Total Assets	$9,000,000	$5,400,000	$3,200,000
No Par Common Stock	$6,000,000	$3,000,000	$2,000,000
Retained Earnings	3,000,000	2,400,000	1,200,000
Total Shareholders' Equity	$9,000,000	$5,400,000	$3,200,000
2009 Net Income	$400,000	$250,000	$200,000

Other Information:

1. No dividends were declared or paid by the Above, Center or Below Companies during the year ending December 31, 2009.

2. The December 31, 2009 Inventories of the Center Company contain merchandise purchased from the Below Company on which the Below Company had recorded a gross profit of $20,000.

3. The December 31, 2009 Inventories of the Above Company contain merchandise purchased from the Center Company on which the Center Company had recorded a gross profit of $30,000.

4. All of the Companies comply with the *CICA Handbook*'s requirement for annual tests for impairment of goodwill. No impairment was found in any of the years under consideration.

Required: For the Above Company and its subsidiaries, the Center and Below Companies:

A. Calculate consolidated Net Income for the year ending December 31, 2009.

B. Prepare a consolidated Balance Sheet as at December 31, 2009.

Self Study Problem Seven - 2

On December 31, 2006, the condensed Balance Sheets of the Push Company and the Shove Company were as follows:

Condensed Balance Sheets
As At December 31, 2006
(Prior To Share Acquisitions)

	Push	Shove
Net Assets	$10,000,000	$4,000,000
No Par Common Stock	$ 5,000,000	$3,000,000
Retained Earnings	5,000,000	1,000,000
Total Shareholders' Equity	$10,000,000	$4,000,000

On this date, the Push Company purchases 80 percent of the outstanding voting shares of the Shove Company for $3,400,000 and the Shove Company purchases 10 percent of the outstanding voting shares of the Push Company for $1,100,000. At this time, all of the identifiable assets and liabilities of both companies have fair values that are equal to their carrying values.

Both companies carry their investments at cost.

During 2007, the condensed Income Statements of the two companies are as follows:

Condensed Income Statement
For The Year Ending December 31, 2007

	Push	Shove
Revenues	$2,000,000	$800,000
Expenses	1,500,000	600,000
Net Income	$ 500,000	$200,000

During 2007, the only intercompany transactions were sales of merchandise. The Shove Company's sales to Push totalled $100,000, while the Push Company's sales to Shove were in the amount of $300,000. On December 31, 2007, the Inventories of the Push Company contain merchandise purchased from the Shove Company on which a gross profit of $10,000 had been recognized at the time of sale. Also on this date, the Inventories of the Shove Company contain merchandise purchased from the Push Company on which a gross profit of $75,000 had been recognized.

Both of the companies comply with the *CICA Handbook's* requirement for annual tests for impairment of goodwill. No impairment was found in any of the years under consideration.

The condensed Balance Sheets of the two companies as at December 31, 2007 are as follows:

Condensed Balance Sheet
As At December 31, 2007

	Push	Shove
Investments	$ 3,400,000	$1,100,000
Other Net Assets	7,100,000	3,100,000
Total Assets	$10,500,000	$4,200,000
No Par Common Stock	$ 5,000,000	$3,000,000
Retained Earnings	5,500,000	1,200,000
Total Shareholders' Equity	$10,500,000	$4,200,000

Required Prepare a consolidated Balance Sheet as at December 31, 2006, a consolidated Income Statement for the year ending December 31, 2007 and a consolidated Balance Sheet as at December 31, 2007 for the Push Company and its subsidiary, the Shove Company.

Self Study Problem Seven - 3

On January 1, 2004, the Pastar Company acquired 80 percent of the outstanding voting shares of the Slone Company for $1,800,000 in cash. On that date, the identifiable assets and liabilities of the Slone Company had fair values that were equal to their carrying values and the carrying value of Slone's Shareholders' Equity totalled $2,250,000. Subsequent to the business combination there are no intercompany transactions other than dividend payments and the following bond purchases and sales.

- On April 1, 1994, the Pastar Company issued 12 percent coupon bonds with a par value of $1,125,000 which were sold at 105 percent. They mature on April 1, 2014 and pay interest annually on April 1. On April 1, 2006, the Slone Company purchased $700,000 par value of the Pastar Company bonds in the open market at an average price of 101.5 percent.
- On January 1, 2008, the Slone Company issued at 98 percent, 5 percent coupon bonds with a par value of $3,000,000. They mature on January 1, 2013 and pay interest annually on December 31. On January 1, 2009, the Pastar Company purchased $1,200,000 par value of the Slone Company bonds in the open market at an average price of 102 percent.

The Pastar Company accounts for its investment in the Slone Company by the cost method. Both Companies use the straight line method to amortize bond discount or premium. Neither Company has issued any Common Stock since January 1, 2004.

Selected account balances from the Income and Retained Earnings Statements for the year ending December 31, 2009 and the Balance Sheets as at December 31, 2009 of Pastar and Slone are as follows:

	Pastar	Slone
Interest Revenue	$ 197,000	$ 104,000
Interest Expense	201,000	626,000
Net Income	673,000	89,000
Dividends Declared	85,000	13,000
Investments in Bonds	1,435,000	825,000
No Par Common Stock	5,000,000	1,500,000
Closing Retained Earnings	7,712,000	2,351,000

Required: Calculate the balances that would be shown on the consolidated financial statements of the Pastar Company and its subsidiary the Slone Company for the year ending December 31, 2009 for the following accounts:

A. Interest Revenue,
B. Interest Expense,
C. Non-Controlling Interest On The Consolidated Income Statement,
D. Consolidated Net Income,
E. Investments In Bonds,
F. Non-Controlling Interest On The Consolidated Balance Sheet, and
G. Closing Consolidated Retained Earnings.

Self Study Problem Seven - 4

On December 31, 2007, the Pointer and Setter Companies had the following condensed Balance Sheets:

Condensed Balance Sheets
As At December 31, 2007

	Pointer	Setter
Net Identifiable Assets	$1,400,000	$960,000
Preferred Stock - Par $100	Nil	$300,000
Common Stock - No Par	$1,130,000	540,000
Retained Earnings	270,000	120,000
Total Equities	$1,400,000	$960,000

At this time, all of the identifiable assets of the Setter Company have fair values that are equal to their carrying values. Setter Company has 4,500 common shares outstanding.

The annual dividend on the Setter Company's Preferred Stock is 9 percent of par value.

Required: The following are three independent Cases, each involving an acquisition of the Setter Company's common and preferred shares on December 31, 2007. For each Case, prepare a consolidated Balance Sheet as at December 31, 2007.

A. Assume that the Preferred Stock is cumulative and non-participating, and that dividends are not in arrears. The Pointer Company pays $175,000 for 50 percent of the Preferred Stock of the Setter Company and $610,000 for 90 percent of the Company's Common Stock.

B. Assume that the Preferred Stock is cumulative, non-participating, and that dividends are two years in arrears. The Pointer Company pays $140,000 for 40 percent of the Preferred Stock of the Setter Company and $550,000 for 80 percent of the Company's Common Stock.

C. Assume that the Preferred Stock is cumulative, fully participating on a per share basis, and that dividends are not in arrears. The Pointer Company pays $225,000 for 60 percent of the Preferred Stock of the Setter Company and $600,000 for 90 percent of the Company's Common Stock.

Self Study Problem Seven - 5

On January 1, 2007, the Winter Company purchased 180,000 of the 200,000 issued and outstanding voting shares of the Spring Company for $1,150,000 in cash. On this date, the Spring Company had No Par Common Stock of $860,000 and Retained Earnings of $425,000. All of the identifiable assets and liabilities of the Spring Company had fair values that were equal to their carrying values except for a fleet of delivery vans which had a fair value that was $53,250 less than its carrying value. These vans had a remaining useful life of 4 years with no net salvage value on this date. Both Companies use the straight line method for amortization calculations.

The condensed Income Statements for the year ending December 31, 2007, and the condensed Balance Sheets as at December 31, 2007, prior to the new issue of stock by the Spring Company, are as follows:

Condensed Income Statements
Year Ending December 31, 2007

	Winter	Spring
Total Revenues	$1,520,000	$432,000
Total Expenses	903,000	271,000
Net Income	$ 617,000	$161,000

Condensed Balance Sheets
As At December 31, 2007
(Prior To Spring's Stock Issue)

	Winter	Spring
Investment In Spring	$1,150,000	N/A
Net Other Identifiable Assets	5,478,000	$1,515,000
Total Assets	$6,628,000	$1,515,000
Liabilities	$ 215,000	$ 69,000
No Par Common Stock	1,800,000	860,000
Retained Earnings	4,613,000	586,000
Total Equities	$6,628,000	$1,515,000

The Winter Company accounts for its investment in the Spring Company by the cost method. There were no intercompany transactions and neither Company declared any dividends during the year ending December 31, 2007.

On December 31, 2007, the Spring Company issues an additional 22,222 of its authorized No Par Common Shares to investors in return for $150,000 in cash. There is no change in the Winter Company's holding of 180,000 of the Spring Company's outstanding shares. On December 31, 2007, all of the identifiable assets and liabilities of the Spring Company have fair values that are equal to their carrying values except for the fleet of delivery vans which has a fair value that is $46,500 less than its carrying value.

There was no impairment of Goodwill during the year ending December 31, 2007.

Required Prepare the consolidated Income Statement for the year ending December 31, 2007, and the consolidated Balance Sheet as at December 31, 2007, for the Winter Company and its subsidiary, the Spring Company.

Self Study Problem Seven - 6

On January 1, 2007, the Prime Company acquired 60 percent of the outstanding voting shares of the Sublime Company for $3 million in cash. On this date, the Sublime Company had No Par Common Stock of $3 million and Retained Earnings of $2 million.

All of Sublime's identifiable assets and liabilities had fair values that were equal to their carrying values except for the Accounts Receivable which had a total net realizable value that was $100,000 less than their carrying value, and a piece of equipment with a fair value that was $400,000 less than its carrying value. The remaining useful life of the equipment was 3 years.

Both Companies use the straight line method to calculate amortization. Prime carries its investment in Sublime by the equity method.

On December 31, 2009, the Balance Sheets of the Prime Company and its subsidiary, the Sublime Company, are as follows:

Balance Sheets
As At December 31, 2009

	Prime	Sublime
Cash and Current Receivables	$ 2,003,000	$ 1,000,000
Inventories	3,200,000	2,000,000
Investment in Sublime (At Equity)	5,497,000	N/A
Long-Term Receivables	800,000	1,500,000
Plant and Equipment (Net)	17,000,000	8,000,000
Land	5,000,000	Nil
Total Assets	$33,500,000	$12,500,000
Current Liabilities	$ 2,503,000	$ 1,200,000
Dividends Payable	Nil	300,000
Long-Term Liabilities	8,500,000	2,000,000
No Par Common Stock	6,000,000	3,000,000
Retained Earnings	16,497,000	6,000,000
Total Equities	$33,500,000	$12,500,000

Other Information:

1. During 2009, Prime sold $700,000 of merchandise to Sublime and 60 percent of these sales remain in the December 31, 2009 Inventories of Sublime. Sublime has not paid for any of the purchases from Prime that it has not resold. The December 31, 2008 Inventories of Sublime contained $280,000 of purchases from Prime. Prime's sales are priced to provide it with a 40 percent gross margin on cost.

2. During 2009, Prime bought and paid for $600,000 of merchandise purchased from Sublime of which 75 percent has been resold by December 31, 2009. The December 31, 2008 Inventories of Prime contained no purchases from Sublime. Sublime's sales are priced to provide it with a 25 percent gross margin on cost.

3. On July 1, 2007, the Sublime Company sold a machine it had built for a cost of $200,000 to the Prime Company for $150,000. The machine had an estimated useful life on July 1, 2007 of 5 years.

4. The Sublime Company purchased Land for $1.6 million from Prime on November 1, 2007. The land was originally purchased by Prime for $1 million. The purchase price is to be paid in four equal installments of $400,000 on January 1 of each year subsequent to

the sale. On October 1, 2009, Sublime sold the parcel of land to a party outside the consolidated entity for $2.5 million. This sale will not affect the terms of payment set up on the sale of land from Prime to Sublime in 2007.

5. On January 1, 2009, Prime sold a machine with a 3 year life to Sublime for proceeds of $100,000 which included a gain of $60,000.

6. During 2009, Prime earned Net Income of $2,500,000 and paid dividends of $500,000. Sublime earned Net Income of $600,000 in 2009 and has declared dividends of $300,000 which will be payable on January 15, 2010.

7. The annual goodwill impairment tests found that, prior to 2008, Sublime's goodwill had a fair value that exceeded its carrying value each year. In 2008, due to very poor operating income, Sublime's goodwill had a fair value that was $40,000 lower than its carrying value. In 2009, after a change in management, the fair value of Sublime's goodwill increased by $55,000.

Required:

A. Verify the Investment in Sublime account as it is shown on Prime's Balance Sheet as at December 31, 2009.

B. Prepare a consolidated Balance Sheet for the Prime Company and its subsidiary, the Sublime Company, as at December 31, 2009.

Assignment Problems

(The solutions for these problems are only available in the solutions manual that has been provided to your instructor.)

Assignment Problem Seven - 1

On December 31, 2005, the Plateau Company acquired 60 percent of the outstanding voting shares of the Valley Company for cash in the amount of $3,000,000. On this date the Valley Company had No Par Common Stock of $3,500,000 and Retained Earnings of $1,500,000. All of the Valley Company's identifiable assets and liabilities had fair values that were equal to their carrying values.

On December 31, 2007, all of the identifiable assets and liabilities of the Valley Company had carrying values that were equal to their fair values. Between December 31, 2005 and December 31, 2007, the Valley Company earned $800,000 and declared dividends of $300,000.

On December 31, 2007, the Crest Company acquired 90 percent of the outstanding voting shares of the Plateau Company for cash in the amount of $9,000,000. On this date the Plateau Company had No Par Common Stock of $5,000,000 and Retained Earnings of $3,000,000. Also on this date, all of the Plateau Company's identifiable assets and liabilities had fair values that were equal to their carrying values except the Investment In Valley and Long-Term Liabilities which had a fair value that was $500,000 less than their carrying value and a remaining term to maturity of eight years.

No dividends were declared or paid by the Crest, Plateau, or Valley Companies during the year ending December 31, 2009.

On December 31, 2009, the condensed Balance Sheets and the 2009 Net Income of the Crest, Plateau, and Valley Companies are as follows:

Condensed Balance Sheets
As At December 31, 2009

	Crest	Plateau	Valley
Net Current Assets	$ 2,000,000	$ 1,000,000	$ 500,000
Investments	9,000,000	3,000,000	Nil
Non-Current Assets	16,000,000	8,000,000	6,500,000
Total Assets	$27,000,000	$12,000,000	$7,000,000
Long-Term Liabilities	$ 1,000,000	$ 1,000,000	$1,000,000
No Par Common Stock	10,000,000	5,000,000	3,500,000
Retained Earnings	16,000,000	6,000,000	2,500,000
Total Equities	$27,000,000	$12,000,000	$7,000,000
2009 Net Income	$ 1,000,000	$ 2,000,000	$ 400,000

Other Information:

1. Both the Crest Company and the Plateau Company carry their investments using the cost method.

2. All companies use the straight line method for calculating amortization. All companies have a December 31 fiscal year end.

3. No Goodwill impairment was found in any of the years under consideration.

4. The December 31, 2009 Inventories of the Plateau Company contain merchandise purchased from the Valley Company on which the Valley Company had recognized a gross profit of $30,000. There were no purchases from the Valley Company in the December 31, 2008 Inventories of the Plateau Company.

5. The December 31, 2009 Inventories of the Crest Company contain merchandise purchased from the Plateau Company on which the Plateau Company had recorded a profit of $100,000. The December 31, 2008 Inventories of the Crest Company contain merchandise purchased from the Plateau Company on which the Plateau Company had recorded a profit of $500,000.

6. On December 15, 2009, the Crest Company sold a parcel of land to the Valley Company for $66,000. The land had been purchased by the Crest Company in 2006 for $94,000.

Required: For the Crest Company and its subsidiaries:

A. Compute consolidated Net Income for the year ending December 31, 2009.

B. Prepare a consolidated Statement Of Retained Earnings for the year ending December 31, 2009.

C. Prepare a consolidated Balance Sheet as at December 31, 2009.

Assignment Problem Seven - 2

On December 31, 2005, the condensed Balance Sheets of the Pine Company and the Maple Company are as follows:

Condensed Balance Sheets
As At December 31, 2005
(Prior to Share Acquisitions)

	Pine	Maple
Net Assets	$5,000,000	$2,000,000
No Par Common Stock	$1,000,000	$ 400,000
Retained Earnings	4,000,000	1,600,000
Total Shareholders' Equity	$5,000,000	$2,000,000

On this date, the Pine Company purchases 80 percent of the outstanding voting shares of the Maple Company for $1,850,000 in cash and the Maple Company purchases 5 percent of the outstanding voting shares of the Pine Company for $280,000 in cash. On the acquisition date, all of the identifiable assets and liabilities of both Companies have fair values that are equal to their carrying values.

Both Companies carry their investments at cost.

The condensed Income Statements of the two Companies for the year ending December, 31, 2007 are as follows:

Condensed Income Statements
Year Ending December 31, 2007

	Pine	Maple
Revenues	$1,000,000	$500,000
Expenses	600,000	350,000
Net Income	$ 400,000	$150,000

During 2007, the sales of Maple include $80,000 of merchandise that is purchased by Pine. Of these sales, merchandise which contains a gross profit of $30,000 to Maple remains in the December 31, 2007 inventories of Pine. The Maple Company also purchases merchandise from the Pine Company for $100,000 during 2007 and carries in its December 31, 2007 inventories, merchandise containing a gross profit of $25,000 to the Pine Company. There were no intercompany sales prior to 2007.

During 2006, Pine had Net Income of $200,000, while Maple had Net Income of $50,000. No dividends were paid by either Company during 2006 or 2007.

No Goodwill impairment was found in any of the years under consideration.

The condensed Balance Sheets of the two Companies as at December 31, 2007 are as follows:

Condensed Balance Sheets
As At December 31, 2007

	Pine	Maple
Investments	$1,850,000	$ 280,000
Other Net Assets	3,750,000	1,920,000
Total Assets	$5,600,000	$2,200,000
No Par Common Stock	$1,000,000	$ 400,000
Retained Earnings	4,600,000	1,800,000
Total Shareholders' Equity	$5,600,000	$2,200,000

Required: Prepare a consolidated Balance Sheet as at December 31, 2005, a consolidated Income Statement for the year ending December 31, 2007 and a consolidated Balance Sheet as at December 31, 2007 for the Pine Company and its subsidiary, the Maple Company. Your answer should be in accordance with the requirements of the *CICA Handbook*.

Assignment Problem Seven - 3

On January 1, 2008, the Pelt Company purchases 80 percent of the outstanding voting shares of the Smelt Company for cash of $800,000. At this time, Smelt had Common Stock of $410,000 and Retained Earnings of $240,000. Pelt's 80 percent share of this total equals $520,000 [(80%)($410,000 + $240,000). The $280,000 ($800,000 - $520,000) excess of the investment cost over the carrying value of the Smelt Company's net identifiable assets is allocated as follows:

Land	$ 40,000
Equipment (Expected useful life of 7 years with no net salvage value)	140,000
Goodwill	100,000
Total	$280,000

Both Companies use the straight line method to calculate amortization. They both close their books on December 31 of each year. The Pelt Company's Investment In Smelt Company is accounted for by the cost method.

During 2008, the Pelt Company reported earnings of $320,000 and declared dividends of $40,000. During this same period, the Smelt Company earned $120,000 and declared dividends of $20,000. On January 1, 2009, the Pelt Company had Retained Earnings of $2,400,000 and the Smelt Company had Retained Earnings of $340,000.

During the year ending December 31, 2009, the Pelt Company reported earnings of $160,000 and again declared dividends of $40,000. Smelt Company had a loss of $60,000 in 2009, but still declared a dividend of $20,000 for this period.

During 2008, the Smelt Company had purchases from the Pelt Company of $160,000. This merchandise had cost the Pelt Company $120,000. On December 31, 2008, 25 percent of these goods were still in Smelt's inventory. The Pelt Company had purchases from the Smelt Company of $240,000, for which the cost to the Smelt Company was $180,000. On December 31, 2008, one-third of these goods remained in the inventories of the Pelt Company. One year later, in 2009, the downstream unrealized gain in Smelt's closing inventory was only $8,000, while the upstream unrealized gain in Pelt's closing inventory had increased by $4,000.

The December 31, 2009 trial balance of the Smelt Company included 6 percent coupon bonds ($400,000 par value) at a carrying value of $416,000. These bonds will mature on December 31, 2013. As the premium is being amortized at the rate of $4,000 per year, the carrying value on January 1, 2009 was $420,000. On January 1, 2009, the Pelt Company purchased 60 percent of the Smelt Company bonds at a price of $224,000.

During both 2008 and 2009, the Pelt Company charged the Smelt Company an annual management fee of $21,000. This fee is included in the Operating Expenses of the Smelt Company and in the Miscellaneous Revenues of the Pelt Company.

Goodwill was tested for impairment in both 2008 and 2009. No impairment was found in either year.

Required: For the Pelt Company and its subsidiary, the Smelt Company:

A. Calculate the consolidated Net Income for the year ending December 31, 2009.

B. Calculate consolidated Retained Earnings as at December 31, 2009.

Assignment Problem Seven - 4

Keiser Ltd. owns 72 percent of the outstanding Common Stock of Doppler Inc. These shares were purchased when Doppler Inc. had a Retained Earnings balance of $1,265,000. At the time of this acquisition, there were no dividend arrearages on the outstanding cumulative Preferred Stock.

On December 31 of the current year, the Shareholder's Equity of Doppler Inc., subsequent to the payment of any dividends that are paid during the year, is as follows:

Common Stock (520,000 Shares Issued And Outstanding)	$5,720,000
Preferred Stock (130,000 Shares Issued And Outstanding)*	1,300,000
Retained Earnings	2,742,000
Total	$9,762,000

*The dividend provision on the Preferred Stock is cumulative and calls for an annual dividend of $0.75 per share. The dividend is payable on December 29 of each year.

Both Companies have a December 31 year end. Doppler Inc. has not issued any new Preferred Stock or Common Stock since Keiser Ltd. acquired its 72 percent interest in its Common Stock. Keiser Ltd. does not own any of the Preferred Stock of Doppler Inc.

Required: Provide the information or journal entries specified in each of the following five independent Cases.

Case A On December 31 of the current year, Keiser Ltd. acquires 21,000 of Doppler Inc.'s outstanding Preferred Stock at a cost of $9.50. There are no dividend arrearages on the Preferred Stock. Provide the journal entry that would be required to eliminate this Investment In Preferred Stock in the preparation of consolidated financial statements for the current year.

Case B On December 31 of the current year, dividends are one year in arrears on Doppler Inc.'s outstanding Preferred Stock. At this time, Keiser Ltd. acquires 65,000 of the Doppler Inc. Preferred Stock at a price of $11 per share. Provide the journal entry that would be required to eliminate this Investment In Preferred Stock in the preparation of consolidated financial statements for the current year.

Case C On December 31 of the current year, there are no dividend arrearages on Doppler Inc.'s Preferred Stock. At this time, the Inventories of Keiser Ltd. contain merchandise purchased from Doppler Inc. on which Doppler Inc. recognized a gross profit of $35,000. Calculate:

(1) the Non-Controlling Interest that would be shown in the consolidated Balance Sheet for Keiser Ltd. and its subsidiary as of December 31 of the current year; and

(2) Keiser Ltd.'s equity in Doppler Inc.'s Retained Earnings that would be included in the December 31 consolidated Retained Earnings balance.

Case D On December 31 of the current year, there are two years of dividend arrearages on the Doppler Inc. Preferred Stock. At this time, there are no unrealized intercompany profits. Calculate:

(1) the Non-Controlling Interest that would be shown in the consolidated Balance Sheet for Keiser Ltd. and its subsidiary as of December 31 of the current year, and

(2) Keiser Ltd.'s equity in Doppler Inc.'s Retained Earnings that would be included in the December 31 consolidated Retained Earnings balance.

Case E On December 31 of the current year, there are no dividend arrearages on Doppler Inc.'s Preferred Stock. At this time, there are no unrealized intercompany profits. The Doppler Inc. Preferred Stock has a participation provision and, under this provision, after both the Common Stock and the Preferred Stock have received a dividend of $0.75 per share, any further dividends must be paid in equal amounts on both classes of shares. On December 29 of the current year, both the Common Stock and the Preferred Stock received a dividend of $0.75 per share. Calculate:

(1) the Non-Controlling Interest that would be shown in the consolidated Balance Sheet for Keiser Ltd. and its subsidiary as of December 31 of the current year, and

(2) Keiser Ltd.'s equity in Doppler Inc.'s Retained Earnings that would be included in the December 31 consolidated Retained Earnings balance.

Assignment Problem Seven - 5

On December 31, 2007, the Pick Company purchased 80 percent of the 100,000 issued and outstanding voting shares of the Shovel Company for $1,900,000 in cash. On this date, all of the identifiable assets and liabilities of the Shovel Company had fair values that were equal to their carrying values except for Equipment which had a fair value that was $250,000 greater than its carrying value. This Equipment had a remaining useful life of 10 years at the time of this business combination. Both Companies use the straight line method for amortization computations. The Pick Company carries its Investment In Shovel using the cost method.

The condensed Balance Sheets of the two Companies, immediately after the transaction described in the preceding paragraph and the condensed open trial balances of the two Companies on December 31,2008, were as follows:

Condensed Balance Sheet
As At December 31, 2007

	Pick	Shovel
Investment In Shovel	$1,900,000	N/A
Net Other Identifiable Assets	5,100,000	$2,000,000
Total Assets	$7,000,000	$2,000,000
No Par Common Stock	$4,000,000	$1,000,000
Retained Earnings	3,000,000	1,000,000
Total Shareholders' Equity	$7,000,000	$2,000,000

Condensed Trial Balance
As At December 31, 2008

	Pick	Shovel
Investment In Shovel	$ 1,900,000	N/A
Net Other Identifiable Assets	5,900,000	$2,300,000
Total Expenses	3,200,000	700,000
Total Debits	$11,000,000	$3,000,000
No Par Common Stock	$ 4,000,000	$1,000,000
Retained Earnings - January 1	3,000,000	1,000,000
Total Revenues	4,000,000	1,000,000
Total Credits	$11,000,000	$3,000,000

There were no intercompany transactions and neither Company declared any dividends during the year ending December 31, 2008.

On December 31, 2008, all of the identifiable assets and liabilities of the Shovel Company have fair values that are equal to their carrying values except for the Equipment which now has a fair value that is $300,000 greater than its carrying value.

The test for impairment of goodwill in October, 2008, determined that the Goodwill arising from the purchase of Shovel shares had suffered a $10,000 impairment loss.

Required: For each of the following independent Cases, prepare a consolidated Income Statement for the year ending December 31, 2008 and a consolidated Balance Sheet as at December 31, 2008 for the Pick Company and its subsidiary, the Shovel Company.

Case One Assume that there are no changes in the Shareholders' Equity of the Shovel Company during the year ending December 31, 2008, or the percentage of Shovel Company shares that are held by the Pick Company on December 31, 2008.

Case Two Assume that there are no changes in the Shareholders' Equity of the Shovel Company during the year ending December 31, 2008, but that on December 31, 2008, the Pick Company purchases an additional 10,000 of the outstanding Shovel Company shares for $280,000.

Case Three Assume that there are no changes in the Shareholders' Equity of the Shovel Company during the year ending December 31, 2008, but that on December 31, 2008, the Pick Company sells 20,000 of its Shovel Company shares for $600,000 in cash.

Case Four Assume that on December 31, 2008, the Shovel Company issues an additional 25,000 of its authorized No Par Common Shares to investors in return for $750,000 in cash. There is no change in the Pick Company's holding of 80,000 of the Shovel Company's outstanding shares.

Assignment Problem Seven - 6

On January 1, 2002, the Poof Company purchased 40,000 common shares of the Spoof Company for $125 a share. On that date, Spoof had Common Stock - No Par of $3,500,000 and Retained Earnings of $1,500,000. At this time, Spoof had 50,000 common shares outstanding. Spoof has not issued or retired any common shares since that time.

When acquired, all of the identifiable assets and liabilities of Spoof had fair values that were equal to their carrying values with the following exceptions:

1. Inventories with fair values that were $200,000 greater than their carrying values.
2. Land in Loof County with a fair value that was $150,000 greater than its carrying value.
3. Plant and Equipment with a fair value that was $600,000 less than its carrying value and a remaining useful life of 16 years.

On January 1, 2006, Spoof sold a machine originally purchased for $1,100,000 on December 31, 2003, to Poof for $1,400,000. Spoof had been amortizing the asset over its estimated life of 22 years.

On September 1, 2010, Spoof sold its land in Loof County to Poof for a gain of $1,000,000. This was the same parcel of land that had a fair value that was $150,000 greater than its carrying value on January 1, 2002.

Both Companies use the straight line method for amortization calculations.

Other data for the year ending December 31, 2010 is as follows:

Income Statements
For The Year Ending December 31, 2010

	Poof	Spoof
Sales	$11,600,000	$3,000,000
Gain on Land Sale	Nil	1,000,000
Investment Income	436,000	Nil
Total Revenues	$12,036,000	$4,000,000
Cost of Goods Sold	$ 8,000,000	$1,500,000
Other Expenses	1,000,000	500,000
Total Expenses	$ 9,000,000	$2,000,000
Net Income	$ 3,036,000	$2,000,000

Balance Sheets
As At December 31, 2010

	Poof	Spoof
Cash and Current Receivables	$ 900,000	$ 300,000
Inventories	4,600,000	2,400,000
Investment in Spoof (At Equity)	7,560,000	N/A
Plant and Equipment (Net)	13,000,000	6,800,000
Land	6,000,000	2,500,000
Total Assets	$32,060,000	$12,000,000
Current Liabilities	$ 900,000	$ 400,000
Long-Term Liabilities	6,600,000	1,100,000
Common Stock - No Par	10,000,000	3,500,000
Retained Earnings	14,560,000	7,000,000
Total Equities	$32,060,000	$12,000,000

	Poof	Spoof
Dividends Declared and Paid	$1,000,000	$ 500,000
Intercompany Inventory Sales	2,000,000	1,000,000
Intercompany Purchases in:		
January 1, 2010 Inventories	200,000	450,000
December 31, 2010 Inventories	600,000	1,200,000

Poof Company's Investment in Spoof is carried by the equity method. Intercompany sales of inventory are priced to provide a gross profit margin on sales price of 33-1/3 percent for the Poof Company and 50 percent for the Spoof Company. Inventories of both Companies turn over within one year. Neither Company has a liability outstanding related to the intercompany inventory sales on December 31, 2010.

In each of the years since Poof acquired control over Spoof, the goodwill arising on this business combination transaction has been tested for impairment. In 2003, a Goodwill Impairment Loss of $270,000 was recognized. No impairment was found in any of the other years since acquisition.

Required: Using the preceding information, provide the following:

A. A verification of the balance in the Investment in Spoof account of $7,560,000.

B. A verification of the Investment Income of $436,000 which was recorded by the Poof Company in applying the equity method of accounting.

C. A calculation of what the December 31, 2010 balance of the Retained Earnings of the Poof Company would have been if the Investment in Spoof had been carried using the cost method since acquisition.

D. A consolidated Income Statement for the Poof Company and its subsidiary, the Spoof Company for the year ending December 31, 2010.

E. A consolidated Statement of Retained Earnings for the Poof Company and its subsidiary the Spoof Company for the year ending December 31, 2010.

F. A consolidated Balance Sheet for the Poof Company and its subsidiary the Spoof Company as at December 31, 2010.

Required: Using the preceding information, provide the following:

A. A verification of the balance in the investment in Spoot account of $[illegible].

B. A verification of the investment income of $[illegible] which was recorded by the Poot Company in applying the equity method of accounting.

C. A calculation of what the December 31, 2010 balance of the Retained Earnings of the Poot Company would have been if the investment in Spoot had been carried using the cost method since acquisition.

D. A consolidated Income Statement for the Poot Company and its subsidiary, the Spoot Company for the year ending December 31, 2010.

E. A consolidated Statement of Retained Earnings for the Poot Company and its subsidiary, the Spoot Company for the year ending December 31, 2010.

F. A consolidated Balance Sheet for the Poot Company and its subsidiary, the Spoot Company as at December 31, 2010.

Interests In Joint Ventures

Introduction

Coverage

8-1. Investments in joint ventures are characterized by the fact that, while the investor participates in the management of the investee, control is shared with one or more other investors. As will be discussed subsequently, such arrangements can be implemented in a variety of legal forms, including both corporate and partnership structures.

8-2. Standards for these arrangements could have been covered in Section 3051, "Investments". However, there are sufficient differences between joint venture arrangements and other types of investments that the AcSB concluded that a separate *CICA Handbook* Section was required. Briefly described, these differences are as follows:

> **Accounting Methods** Under current Canadian standards, joint ventures must be accounted for using proportionate consolidation. This method is not used for any other type of investment.
>
> **Non-Cash Capital Contributions** Because joint venture investors are not at arm's length with the investee, special rules are required for non-cash contributions of capital.
>
> **Intercompany Transactions** Because the presence of a joint management agreement introduces an element of objectivity to transfer prices on intercompany transactions, the profits resulting from such transactions are not fully eliminated in the same manner as was the case with transactions between a parent and a subsidiary.

8-3. These differences will be given detailed consideration in the material that follows.

Purpose And Scope Of Section 3055

8-4. Section 3055 deals with accounting for interests in joint ventures in the general purpose financial statements of profit oriented enterprises. It covers the reporting of joint venture assets, liabilities, revenues and expenses in the financial statements of venturers, regardless of the legal structure under which the joint venture activity takes place. However, the Section does not deal with the accounting to be used by the joint venture itself.

8-5. Joint venture accounting is only applicable in the economic circumstances outlined in Section 3055. There may be situations which fall within these circumstances that are not referred to as joint ventures. Section 3055 would be applicable in these situations, regardless of the term used by the venturer to identify the interest. In contrast, there may be situations that are referred to as joint venture arrangements that do not fall within the circumstances outlined in Section 3055. Section 3055 would not be applicable in these situations.

8-6. Accounting for interests in joint ventures that are not included in the consolidated financial statements of the venturer is dealt with in Sections 3051 or 3855 (see Chapter 2). Accounting for interests in joint ventures in the financial statements of not-for-profit enterprises is covered in Section 4450 (see Chapter 11).

Joint Ventures Defined

General Rules

8-7. A considerable amount of difficulty has been experienced in establishing a clear cut definition of what constitutes a joint venture. This reflects the fact that it is often difficult to distinguish this type of investment from other investment situations where the investor has the ability to exercise significant influence. The basic *Handbook* definition of a joint venture is as follows:

> **Paragraph 3055.03(c)** A **joint venture** is an economic activity resulting from a contractual arrangement whereby two or more venturers jointly control the economic activity.

8-8. This definition contains a number of terms that require further clarification. This clarification is provided in two additional Section 3055 definitions:

> **Paragraph 3055.03(b)** **Joint control** of an economic activity is the contractually agreed sharing of the continuing power to determine its strategic operating, investing and financing policies.

> **Paragraph 3055.03(e)** A **venturer** is a party to a joint venture, has joint control over that joint venture, has the right and ability to obtain future economic benefits from the resources of the joint venture and is exposed to the related risks.

8-9. With respect to the meaning of control, it can be assumed that the definition of control that is provided in Section 1590 is equally applicable in this context.

> **Paragraph 1590.03(b)** **Control** of an enterprise is the continuing power to determine its strategic operating, investing and financing policies without the co-operation of others.

8-10. From the preceding definitions it can be concluded that the most important distinguishing feature of a joint venture is that its economic activity is subject to joint control by two or more venturers. Such joint control would preclude any one of the venturers from having unilateral control over the venture's economic activity.

8-11. If the control agreement that is in place allows any one of the investors to exercise unilateral control, none of the investors will be able to classify their interest as a joint venture. The investor with unilateral control would classify its investment as a subsidiary, while the other investors would classify their interest as either a significantly influenced investee, a held-for-trading investee, or an available-for-sale investee.

8-12. There may be investors with an economic interest in a joint venture who do not participate under the agreement for joint control. This does not preclude the investors who do participate under the control agreement from classifying their investment as a joint venture. However, investors who do not participate under the agreement would not be able to use this classification and would have to classify their investment as either a significantly influenced investee, a held-for-trading investee, or an available-for-sale investee, as appropriate.

8-13. From the point of view of an individual interest in a joint venture, the venturer must have the right and ability to obtain future economic benefits from the resources of the joint venture and must be exposed to the risks related to the use of these resources. If the interest does not involve such risk and reward sharing, it should be viewed as a loan rather than as an equity interest in a joint venture. Long-term loan arrangements are normally classified as held-to-maturity investments.

8-14. The control agreement may take a variety of different forms. It may involve a contract between the various venturers or, alternatively, the agreement may be incorporated in the articles of incorporation or by-laws of the joint venture. The arrangement will normally be in writing and cover such matters as the activities, duration, policies and procedures of the joint venture, the allocation of ownership, the decision making process, the capital contributions by the venturers and the sharing by the venturers of the output, revenue, expenses or results of the joint venture.

8-15. The joint venture definitions do not prevent one of the venturers from acting as the manager for the enterprise. As long as this manager is acting within policies that have been agreed on under the terms of the contractual agreement for the venture, the enterprise can be viewed as a joint venture arrangement. However, if the manager has the continuing power to determine the strategic operating, investing, and financing policies of the enterprise, without review by the other equity interests, then the manager is in control of the venture and should classify the investment as a subsidiary.

Forms Of Organization

8-16. Section 3055 provides a discussion of the various forms and structures that can be used to carry out joint venture operations. Three basic forms are identified and they can be described as follows:

1. **Jointly Controlled Operations** This form involves the use of the assets and other resources of the individual venturers, rather than the establishment of a corporation, partnership or other enterprise, or a financial structure that is separate from the venturers themselves. Characteristics of this form would include:

   - Each venturer uses its own property, plant and equipment, and carries its own inventories for purposes of the joint venture activities.
   - Assets remain under the individual ownership and control of each venturer.
   - Each venturer incurs its own expenses and liabilities and raises its own financing.
   - The arrangement will provide for the sharing of revenues and of common expenses among the various venturers.

   An example of this form might involve several venturers combining their efforts to manufacture a product. In this situation, different parts of the manufacturing operation might be carried out by each of the venturers using their own assets and other resources. While each venturer would incur their own costs, they would receive a share of the revenues from the product, as per the terms of the joint venture agreement.

2. **Jointly Controlled Assets** In this situation, the joint venture involves the joint control and possible joint ownership by the venturers, of one or more assets contributed to or acquired for the use of the joint venture. Each venturer will take a share of the output from the assets and each will be responsible for a share of the expenses incurred. As was the case with jointly controlled operations, this type of joint venture does not involve the establishment of a corporation, partnership, or other enterprise, or a financial structure that is separate from the venturers themselves.

   Examples of this form of operation could involve the joint control of a rental property or the joint development of a natural resource property.

3. **Jointly Controlled Enterprise** This form of joint venture involves establishing a separate corporation or partnership in which each venturer has an investment interest. The separately established entity would operate much like other investment entities, except for the fact that it would be subject to the joint control of the various

venturers. Characteristics of this form would include:

- While each venturer contributes cash or other resources to the joint venture, the venture itself will own the assets, assume the liabilities, receive the revenues, and incur the expenses of the joint venture operations.
- The venture may enter into contracts in its own name and raise financing for the purposes of joint venture activity.
- In most cases, each venturer will share in the income of the jointly controlled enterprise. In a minority of cases, the venturers will share in the output of the enterprise, rather than the income.

Examples of this form would include any situation where two or more venturers transfer relevant assets into a separate corporation or partnership.

Classification Example

8-17. The following simple example illustrates the classification of joint ventures in the context of other types of investments in equities. Note that, in terms of form of organization, the example involves a jointly controlled enterprise.

Example A new company, the Venture Company, is formed and all of the shares are acquired by four investor Companies. These Companies and their proportionate ownership interests are as follows:

- Company A holds 60 percent of the shares.
- Company B holds 20 percent of the shares.
- Company C holds 15 percent of the shares.
- Company D holds 5 percent of the shares.

The four investor Companies sign an agreement that stipulates that Company A and Company D will not participate in the affairs or operations of the business. The agreement further specifies that in all areas essential to the operation of the business, decisions will be made by, and require the consent of, both Company B and Company C. The classification of the investment in the Venture Company by each of the investor Companies would be as follows:

Company A While Company A holds a majority of the voting shares in the Venture Company, the joint venture agreement prevents the Company from exercising the control that we normally associate with majority ownership. Further, it does not appear that Company A will have any real influence on the affairs of Venture Company. As a consequence, Company A would classify its investment in Venture Company as either held for trading or available for sale. As covered in Chapter 2, the investment could be accounted for using the cost method or a fair value method with changes in fair value allocated to Net Income or Other Comprehensive Income.

Companies B and **C** There is a contractual agreement in place under which two or more venturers control the enterprise. Further, under this agreement, B and C have joint control. Given their participation under the agreement and the fact that no single investor has unilateral control, Companies B and C would classify their investments in Venture Company as joint venture investments.

Company D This investor, because of its exclusion from any share of joint control, would classify the investment as held for trading or available for sale.

Accounting Methods

Joint Venture Recommendations

8-18. In terms of the other types of investments that were discussed in Chapter 2, joint venture arrangements appear to be most similar to investments in significantly influenced companies. While venturers in joint venture agreements cannot have unilateral control, they would always have influence in that, in order to classify an investment as a joint venture, they must participate in the management agreement.

8-19. This would suggest that joint ventures be accounted for by the equity method, the method that is used with other investments where the investor has influence but not control. However, in some situations there is a serious problem with the use of the equity method for joint ventures.

8-20. There are Canadian companies whose total economic activity consists of investments in a variety of joint venture arrangements. If such investor companies use the equity method, their financial statements would consist of a Balance Sheet in which there is only a single asset (Investments In Joint Ventures) and an Income Statement made up of a single revenue (Investment Income).

8-21. In situations such as this, the equity method would not constitute effective disclosure. As a consequence of this problem, Section 3055 requires the use of proportionate consolidation:

> **Paragraph 3055.17** *Interests in joint ventures should be recognized in the financial statements of the venturer using the proportionate consolidation method.* (January, 1995)

8-22. In making this recommendation, the AcSB argues that it is essential that each venturer reflect the substance and underlying economic reality of its interest, without regard to the structures or forms under which the joint venture activities take place. By providing financial statement users with the most appropriate information about the resources, obligations and operations of a venturer that conducts business through one or more joint ventures, the AcSB has indicated that it believes the proportionate consolidation method achieves this essential objective.

8-23. We are inclined to agree with this conclusion in situations where the majority of an enterprise's economic activity consists of investments in joint ventures. However, we do not feel that the use of proportionate consolidation is appropriate for all joint ventures.

8-24. This method includes a portion of investee assets, liabilities, expenses, and revenues that are not under the control of the investor company. This is not consistent with the general reasoning that supports the preparation of consolidated financial statements. Further, it puts Canada out of line with most other countries, as well as the relevant international accounting standard. For example, International Accounting Standard No. 31, "Financial Reporting Of Interests In Joint Ventures", encourages the use of proportionate consolidation, but permits the use of the equity method.

Proportionate Consolidation In Alternative Legal Forms

Joint Venture As A Separate Enterprise

8-25. Most of our discussion of proportionate consolidation will be based on situations where the legal form of the joint venture is an investment in a separate incorporated enterprise. The application of proportionate consolidation in this type of situation results in the venturer recognizing:

1. in its **Balance Sheet**, its share of the assets and its share of the liabilities of the jointly controlled enterprise; and
2. in its **Income Statement**, its share of the revenue and its share of the expenses of the jointly controlled enterprise.

8-26. While this separate enterprise arrangement is, for most of us, the most familiar type of joint venture arrangement, other forms and structures exist. These alternative forms are given brief attention in the material which follows.

Other Forms

8-27. Joint venture activities may be undertaken without establishing a separate enterprise through arrangements involving jointly controlled operations (see Paragraph 8-16). When this is the case, the *Handbook* indicates that using the proportionate consolidation method results in the venturer recognizing:

1. in its **Balance Sheet**, the assets that it controls and the liabilities that it incurs; and
2. in its **Income Statement**, its share of the revenue of the joint venture and its share of the expenses incurred by the joint venture.

8-28. A further alternative involves carrying on joint venture activities through arrangements involving only jointly controlled assets. In this situation, the *Handbook* indicates that use of the proportionate consolidation method results in the venturer recognizing:

1. in its **Balance Sheet**, its share of the jointly controlled assets and its share of any liabilities incurred jointly with the other venturers in relation to the joint venture; and
2. in its **Income Statement**, any revenue from the sale or use of its share of the output of the joint venture, and its share of any expenses incurred by the joint venture.

8-29. While recognizing the existence of alternative approaches to organizing joint venture activities, the more complex examples of joint venture procedures that are presented later in this Chapter will be based on situations in which the joint venture activities are carried out through a separate enterprise.

Cessation Of Joint Control

8-30. In situations where a separate enterprise has been established to carry out joint venture activities, proportionate consolidation will be required as long as the joint venture agreement is in effect. However, if joint control ceases to exist, other methods will have to be used.

8-31. If joint control has been lost because one investor has acquired unilateral control over the enterprise, the investor that has gained unilateral control will become subject to the recommendations of Section 1590, "Subsidiaries". In general, this will result in this investor using full consolidation procedures.

8-32. An individual investor may cease to participate in joint control for a variety of reasons. This could happen through one of the other investors acquiring unilateral control or, alternatively, through a change in the joint venture agreement such that the particular investor no longer participates in the control mechanism. For investors in this position, the requirements of either Section 3051, "Investments", or Section 3855, "Financial Instruments - Recognition And Measurement", becomes applicable. This would result in the application of the various methods that were discussed in Chapter 2.

8-33. A further possibility here is that joint venture operations would be discontinued. In this situation, the provisions of Section 3475, "Disposals Of Long-Lived Assets And Discontinued Operations" would be applicable.

Differential Reporting

8-34. Section 1300, "Differential Reporting" exempts qualifying enterprises from a group of specified *Handbook* recommendations. The following differential reporting option is provided in Section 3055 with respect to accounting for joint ventures:

> **Paragraph 3055.47** *An enterprise that qualifies under "Differential Reporting", Section 1300, may elect to use either the equity method or the cost method to account for its interests in joint ventures that would otherwise be accounted for using the proportionate consolidation method in accordance with paragraph 3055.17. All interests in joint ventures should be accounted for using the same method.* (January, 2002)

8-35. For those enterprises that choose to exercise this option, there are several additional recommendations. The first applies to situations where there has been a non-temporary decline in the value of the investment:

Paragraph 3055.48 *A loss in value of an interest in a joint venture not proportionately consolidated that is other than a temporary decline should be accounted for in accordance with the requirements of "Investments", Paragraphs 3051.18-.22.* (October, 2006)

8-36. You will recall that, in these situations, Section 3051 requires a write-down of the investment, with the amount of the write-down included in the determination of Net Income. This loss cannot be treated as an Extraordinary Item and the write down cannot be reversed if there is a subsequent recovery in the value of the investment.

8-37. Two other recommendations require additional disclosures when the differential reporting option is used:

Paragraph 3055.49 *Interests in joint ventures not proportionately consolidated should be presented separately in the balance sheet. Income or loss from those interests should be presented separately in the income statement.* (January, 2002)

Paragraph 3055.50 *An enterprise that has applied one of the alternative methods permitted by paragraph 3055.47 should disclose the basis used to account for interests in joint ventures.* (January, 2002)

Exercise Eight-1

Subject: Classification Of Investments

Mason Enterprises Inc. is a new corporation. It is owned by four corporations and their interests can be described as follows:

Company 1 This Company owns 40 percent of the outstanding voting shares, but does not participate in the management of the joint venture.

Company 2 This Company owns 25 percent of the outstanding voting shares and shares management control with Company 3.

Company 3 This Company owns 25 percent of the outstanding voting shares and shares management control with Company 2.

Company 4 This Company owns 10 percent of the outstanding voting shares, but does not participate in the management of the joint venture.

Indicate how Companies 1 through 4 would classify and account for their investment in Mason Enterprises Inc.

End of Exercise. Solution available in Study Guide.

Non-Cash Capital Contributions

The Problem

8-38. In making an investment in the shares or debt securities of an investee company, the consideration used by the investor company could be cash, shares or debt of the investor company, or non-monetary assets owned by the investor company. A problem arises in the case of non-monetary contributions in that, in most cases, the carrying value of the asset will be different than its fair value at the time of the transfer.

Example Vestor Inc. acquires a 25 percent equity interest in Vestee Ltd. by transferring Land with a carrying value of $500,000. The fair value of the land at the time of the transfer is $1,700,000.

8-39. The obvious question here is whether Vestor should record its capital contribution at the $500,000 carrying value of the Land or, alternatively, record the transaction at the $1,700,000 fair value of the Land.

8-40. We have not considered this issue in our discussion of other types of investments. Provided that Vestee Ltd. is not a joint venture and the parties to the transaction are dealing at arm's length, Vestor would record the transfer of Land at $1,700,000, resulting in the recognition of a $1,200,000 gain.

8-41. In contrast, the AcSB has concluded that special rules are required when an investor transfers a non-monetary asset to a joint venture in return for an equity interest in that venture. There are likely two reasons for this difference:

- Capital contributions of non-monetary assets are more common in the case of joint ventures than they are in the case of other types of investments.
- Even when the joint venturers are not related parties, the fact that they must construct a workable joint venture agreement introduces the possibility of non-arm's length behaviour.

Relevant Handbook Sections

Section 3055 - Interests In Joint Ventures

8-42. The basic rules for dealing with transfers of non-cash assets to joint ventures are in Section 3055. However, all or part of such transfers may be non-monetary in nature, thereby making Section 3831, "Non-Monetary Transactions", relevant.

8-43. A further problem arises because it is not uncommon for investors in a particular joint venture arrangement to be related parties. In this situation, Section 3840, "Related Party Transactions", provides guidance for dealing with non-monetary transactions between related parties.

8-44. In addition, Sections 3062, "Goodwill and Other Intangible Assets" and 3063, "Impairment Of Long-Lived Assets", also contain recommendations that may have influence on accounting for non-monetary capital contributions to joint ventures.

8-45. Given the applicability of these Sections, we will briefly examine their relevant provisions before looking at the more specific recommendations of Section 3055.

Section 3831 - Non-Monetary Transactions

8-46. The general recommendation on the treatment of non-monetary transactions in Section 3831 is as follows:

> **Paragraph 3831.06** *An entity should measure an asset exchanged or transferred in a non-monetary transaction at the more reliably measurable of the fair value of the asset given up and the fair value of the asset received, unless:*
>
> *(a) the transaction lacks commercial substance;*
> *(b) the transaction is an exchange of a product or property held for sale in the ordinary course of business for a product or property to be sold in the same line of business to facilitate sales to customers other than the parties to the exchange;*
> *(c) neither the fair value of the asset received nor the fair value of the asset given up is reliably measurable; or*
> *(d) the transaction is a non-monetary non-reciprocal transfer to owners to which paragraph 3831.14 applies.* (January, 2006)

8-47. In applying this recommendation in situations where a non-monetary asset is exchanged for an equity interest in a joint venture, the key issue is whether this exchange has "commercial substance". Fortunately, Section 3055 provides specific guidance on this issue:

> **Paragraph 3055.32** When the venturers are not related parties prior to the transfer to a joint venture of non-monetary assets, other than product or property held for sale in the ordinary course of business to facilitate sales to customers, the change in

control of the assets generally constitutes a change in the risk of the cash flows the venturers expect to receive. Accordingly, the transfer has commercial substance (see "Non-Monetary Transactions", Section 3831) and is measured at fair value provided the fair value is reliably measurable. When the venturers are related parties, the contribution is accounted for as a non-monetary transaction in accordance with "Related Party Transactions", Section 3840.

8-48. This guidance suggest that, in most cases, non-monetary capital contributions should be recorded at fair value, provided that this amount can be reliably measured. We will find, however, that the Section 3831 recommendation is modified by the more specific recommendations contained in Section 3055.

CD-ROM Note If you have an interest in this subject, we would refer you to our *Guide to Canadian Financial Reporting* which is included on the CD-ROM that accompanies this text. Chapter 52 contains detailed coverage of Section 3831, "Non-Monetary Transactions".

Section 3840 - Related Party Transactions

8-49. You will have noted that the last sentence of Paragraph 3055.32 indicates that, if the venturers are related parties, the recommendations of Section 3840 come into play. The general rule for related party transactions in Section 3840 is as follows:

Paragraph 3840.08 *A related party transaction should be measured at the carrying amount, except as specified in paragraphs 3840.18 and 3840.29.* (October, 1995)

8-50. Without going into detail, the exception found in Paragraph 3840.18 is not applicable here. However, the exception in Paragraph 3840.29 is relevant:

Paragraph 3840.29 *When a monetary related party transaction or a non-monetary related party transaction that has commercial substance is not in the normal course of operations, it should be measured at the exchange amount when:*

(a) the change in the ownership interests in the item transferred or the benefit of a service provided is substantive; and
(b) the exchange amount is supported by independent evidence. (January, 2006)

8-51. Note that "exchange amount" is not the same as fair value. It is defined in Section 3840 as follows:

Paragraph 3840.03(b) Exchange amount is the amount of consideration paid or received as established and agreed to by related parties.

8-52. With respect to the meaning of a "substantive" change in ownership, Section 3840 provides the following guidance:

Paragraph 3840.34 A change in the equity ownership interests in an item transferred, or the benefit of a service provided, is presumed to be substantive when a transaction results in unrelated parties having acquired or given up at least 20 percent of the total equity ownership interests in the item or service benefits, unless persuasive evidence exists to the contrary.

Paragraph 3840.35 A change of less than 20 percent of the total equity ownership interests in the item transferred, or benefit of a service provided, may be substantive when the degree of influence of the parties over the item transferred or service benefits provided has substantively changed. For example, when a joint venturer transfers an item to a joint venture, a related co-venturer may not have acquired at least 20 percent of the total ownership interests in the item after the transfer. However, if the item becomes jointly controlled by the various joint venturers as opposed to being controlled by one joint venturer, the rights and obligations to the item have substantially changed.

8-53. Putting this together means that, if the venturers are related parties, non-monetary capital contributions will be recorded at either carrying value or exchange value. If it is recorded at carrying value, the following recommendation is applicable:

> **Paragraph 3840.09** *When a related party transaction is measured at carrying amount, any difference between the carrying amounts of items exchanged, together with any tax amounts related to the items transferred, should be included as a charge or credit to equity.* (October, 1995)

8-54. Alternatively, when it is recorded at the exchange value, the treatment is different:

> **Paragraph 3840.42** *When a related party transaction is measured at the exchange amount, any gain or loss resulting from the transaction should be included in income for the period, unless another Handbook Section requires alternative treatment.* (October, 1995)

> **CD-ROM Note** If you have an interest in this subject, we would refer you to our *Guide to Canadian Financial Reporting* which is included on the CD-ROM that accompanies this text. Chapter 53 contains detailed coverage of Section 3840, "Related Party Transactions".

Exercise Eight-2

Subject: Non-Monetary Capital Contributions With Related Parties

Martin Inc. and Hague Ltd. form a joint venture. Martin and Hague are related parties as defined in Section 3840. As its capital contribution Martin Inc. transfers Land to the joint venture. The Land has a carrying value of $450,000 and a fair value of $625,000. The agreed upon exchange value is $575,000 in cash.

Provide the entries required on the books of Martin assuming the transaction is recorded (1) at carrying value, and (2) at the exchange amount.

End of Exercise. Solution available in Study Guide.

Section 3062 - Goodwill And Other Intangible Assets And Section 3063 - Impairment Of Long-Lived Assets

8-55. Section 3840 requires that transfers of non-monetary assets in return for an interest in similar assets be recorded at the carrying value of the assets transferred if the venturers are related parties. This clearly prohibits a venturer from recognizing his share of any gain on assets transferred to a joint venture in return for an equity interest in that venture. In turn, it would seem to suggest that losses would be similarly prohibited on such transfers. However, the loss situation is also influenced by the requirements of Section 3062, "Goodwill and Other Intangible Assets", and Section 3063, "Impairment of Long-Lived Assets". Consider the following example:

> **Example** Company X and Company Y, two unrelated companies, form a joint venture. Company Y's capital contribution consists of equipment with a fair market value of $500,000 and a carrying value of $350,000. Company X's capital contribution consists of an asset with a fair market value of $500,000 and a carrying value of $900,000. Each venturer receives a 50 percent equity interest in the joint venture.

8-56. Company X, in dealing with an arm's length party, has agreed to accept an equity interest that is worth $500,000 in return for an asset with a carrying value of $900,000. This is clear and objective evidence that the asset is worth less than its carrying value. Both Section 3062 and Section 3063 contain recommendations requiring the write-down of intangible or long-lived assets in such situations:

Paragraph 3062.18 *An intangible asset that is subject to amortization should be tested for impairment in accordance with the write-down provisions of "Impairment of Long-Lived Assets", Section 3063.* (January, 2002)

Paragraph 3062.19 *An intangible asset that is not subject to amortization should be tested for impairment annually, or more frequently if events or changes in circumstances indicate that the asset might be impaired. The impairment test should consist of a comparison of the fair value of the intangible asset with its carrying amount. When the carrying amount of the intangible asset exceeds its fair value, an impairment loss should be recognized in an amount equal to the excess.* (January, 2002)

Paragraph 3063.04 *An impairment loss should be recognized when the carrying amount of a long-lived asset is not recoverable and exceeds its fair value.* (April, 2003)

Paragraph 3063.06 *An impairment loss should be measured as the amount by which the carrying amount of a long-lived asset exceeds its fair value. If an impairment loss is recognized, the adjusted carrying amount becomes the new cost basis. For a depreciable long-lived asset, the new cost basis should be amortized in accordance with "Property, Plant And Equipment", Section 3061. An impairment loss should not be reversed if the fair value subsequently increases.* (April, 2003)

8-57. If an asset is transferred to a joint venture in return for an equity interest that has a lesser value, this would generally constitute evidence of a decline in the fair value of that asset. This would usually required the application of the impairment recommendations that we have cited, resulting in a write-down of the asset to its fair value. This would mean that, at the time of the transfer, the carrying value of the asset would be equal to its fair value.

CD-ROM Note If you have an interest in these subjects, we would refer you to our *Guide to Canadian Financial Reporting* which is included on the CD-ROM that accompanies this text. Chapters 30 and 31 contain detailed coverage of Section 3062 and Section 3063.

Losses On Non-Monetary Capital Contributions

8-58. At this point we have reviewed the several *CICA Handbook* Sections which may impact on the procedures to be used in accounting for non-monetary capital contributions. We will now turn our attention to the specific provisions of Section 3055. With respect to the provisions which relate to losses, we will use the following simple example:

Example A venturer has land with a current fair market value of $400,000 and an original cost of $500,000. The venturer intends to transfer this land to a joint venture in which he will have a 25 percent equity interest.

8-59. We would expect that, in most situations, the value established by the terms of the transfer to the joint venture would provide a strong indication that there has been a non-temporary decline in value. Given this, it is likely that, under the provisions of Section 3063, the land would be written down to its fair value of $400,000 prior to the transfer to the joint venture, resulting in the recognition of a loss of $100,000.

8-60. If the transfer terms are not sufficient evidence of a non-temporary decline in the value of the land, and the land is transferred to the joint venture in return for cash equal to its fair value of $400,000, Section 3831, "Non-Monetary Transactions", would not be applicable as cash would be involved. As a consequence, there would be no constraint on the venturer's ability to recognize losses or gains.

8-61. The situation becomes more complex if the land is not written down to its fair value prior to the transfer and is exchanged for an equity interest in the venture, rather than for cash or other monetary assets. This situation is covered in Section 3055 as follows:

Paragraph 3055.26 *When a venturer transfers assets to a joint venture and receives in exchange an interest in the joint venture, any loss that occurs should be charged to income at the time of the transfer to the extent of the interests of the other non-related* *venturers. When such a transaction provides evidence of a decline that is other than temporary in the carrying amount of the relevant assets, the venturer should recognize this decline by writing down that portion of the assets retained through its interest in the joint venture.* (January, 1995)

8-62. Returning to the example in Paragraph 8-58, Paragraph 3055.26 would require that at least $75,000 of the total loss of $100,000 ($400,000 - $500,000) be taken into income at the time of transfer. With the venturer in our example having a 25 percent equity interest in the joint venture, the $75,000 would represent the 75 percent interest of the other non-related venturers.

Exercise Eight-3

Subject: Losses On Non-Monetary Capital Contributions

As its capital contribution to a joint venture, Gravel Ltd. contributes capital assets with a fair value of $480,000 and a carrying value of $840,000. In return, Gravel receives a 25 percent interest in the joint venture and $380,000 in cash. The capital assets are not written down to fair value prior to the transfer.

Provide the journal entry to record Gravel Ltd.'s investment in the joint venture assuming the transfer:

- is not sufficient evidence of a non-temporary decline in the value of the assets,
- is sufficient evidence of a non-temporary decline in the value of the assets.

End of Exercise. Solution available in Study Guide.

Gains On Non-Monetary Capital Contributions

General Rules

8-63. With respect to the recognition of gains, the general recommendation is as follows:

Paragraph 3055.27 *When a venturer transfers assets to a joint venture and receives in exchange an interest in the joint venture, any gain that occurs should be recognized in the financial statements of the venturer only to the extent of the interests of the other non-related venturers, and accounted for in accordance with paragraphs 3055.28 and 3055.29.* (January, 1995)

8-64. Note carefully the difference between this recommendation on gains and the Paragraph 3055.26 recommendation on losses (Paragraph 8-61). The Paragraph 3055.26 recommendation requires that losses be taken into income, not just recognized in the financial statements. The Paragraph 3055.27 recommendation on gains refers only to recognition in the financial statements.

8-65. When we examine Paragraphs 3055.28 and 3055.29, we will find that, in some situations, none of the recognized gain will be taken into income at the time the asset is transferred to the joint venture. This would be accomplished by setting up a Deferred Gain account in the joint venturer's proportionately consolidated Balance Sheet.

8-66. While it is possible that no gain will be taken into income at the time the asset is transferred to the joint venture, the portion of the gain that must be recognized as a result of the recommendation in Paragraph 3055.26 will eventually be included in income. To the extent that this gain is not taken into income at the transfer date, it will be taken into income in some later accounting period. The timing of this income inclusion is governed by the following two recommendations:

Paragraph 3055.28 *When the contributing venturer receives cash or other assets that do not represent a claim on the assets of the joint venture, only that portion of the gain that relates to the amount of cash received or the fair value of the other assets received should be taken to income at the time of the transfer.* (January, 1995)

Paragraph 3055.29 *Any remaining portion of the gain that does not meet the conditions in paragraph 3055.28 should be deferred and amortized to income in a rational and systematic manner over the life of the contributed assets. If the contributed assets are non-depreciable, the deferred gain should be taken to income on a basis appropriate to the expected revenue or service to be obtained from their use by the joint venture. If the contributed assets are disposed of by the joint venture, any unamortized portion of the deferred gain should be taken to income.* (January, 1995)

8-67. In situations where the contributing venturer receives only an equity interest in the joint venture, Paragraph 3055.27 would require that the interest in the gain of the other joint venturers be recognized at the time the asset is transferred by the contributing venturer. However, Paragraph 3055.28 would prevent any portion of this recognized gain from being included in the contributing venturer's income at the time of transfer. The recognized portion of the gain would have to be included in income in subsequent periods as per the recommendation in Paragraph 3055.29.

Exercise Eight-4

Subject: Gains On Non-Monetary Capital Contributions (Case One)

As its capital contribution to a joint venture, Lorty Ltd. contributes capital assets with a fair value of $325,000 in return for a 25 percent equity interest in the new enterprise. The assets have a carrying value on the books of Lorty of $264,000.

Provide the journal entry to record Lorty Ltd.'s investment in the joint venture.

End of Exercise. Solution available in Study Guide.

Amounts To Be Included In Income

8-68. If the contributing venturer receives cash or other assets in addition to an equity interest, all or part of the recognized gain can be included in the contributing venturer's income at the time of transfer. Note, however, in applying Paragraph 3055.28, the amount of cash or other assets received must be reduced to the extent that they have been financed by the borrowing of the joint venture. This requirement is reflected in the following recommendation:

Paragraph 3055.30 *For purposes of paragraph 3055.28, in determining the portion of the gain that should be taken to income, the amount of cash received or the fair value of the other assets received should be reduced by the contributing venturer's proportionate interest in cash or other assets derived from, or financed by, borrowings of the joint venture and by any obligation assumed by the contributing venturer that would in substance reverse or negate the original receipt of cash or other assets.* (January, 1995)

8-69. The process of calculating the gain to be taken into income under Paragraph 3055.28 is described as follows:

Paragraph 3055.34 When the contributing venturer concurrently receives in exchange cash or other assets that do not represent in any way an investment in, or a claim on, the assets of the joint venture, and when the venturer has no commitments to reinvest such consideration received in the joint venture, the portion of the gain that would be taken to income referred to in paragraph 3055.28 would be the difference between:

(a) the fair value of the consideration received, i.e., the amount of cash received or the fair value of the other assets received less the portion of cash or other assets represented by the contributing venturer's proportionate interest in cash or other assets derived from, or financed by, borrowings of the joint venture and less any obligation assumed by the contributing venturer that in substance would reverse or negate the original receipt of cash or other assets; and

(b) the net carrying value of the assets considered to be partly sold, i.e., that portion of the aggregate carrying value of those assets determined by applying the ratio of the fair value of the consideration received over the fair value of the assets transferred.

8-70. After we have recognized the portion of the total gain specified in Paragraph 3055.27 and taken all or part of this gain into income as required by Paragraph 3055.28, we may be left with a Deferred Gain. This Deferred Gain will be taken into income in accordance with Paragraph 3055.29.

8-71. For depreciable assets, this will be in a rational and systematic manner over their remaining life. For non-depreciable assets, Paragraph 3055.29 requires that the Deferred Gain be taken into income on a basis appropriate to the expected revenues that the asset will produce. Paragraph 3055.29 also requires that, if the transferred asset is sold by the joint venture, any portion of the Deferred Gain that has not been taken into income in previous periods, should be taken into income when the sale occurs.

Example One - No Bank Financing

8-72. As an example of the application of Section 3055 recommendations in situations where the contributing venturer receives cash or other assets that do not represent an equity interest in the venture, consider the following arrangement from the point of view of Alpha Company:

> **Example** Alpha Company and Beta Company, two unrelated companies, form a joint venture. Alpha contributes a manufacturing plant with an estimated fair value of $700 and a carrying value of $300. Alpha receives cash of $100 from the joint venture and a 40 percent interest in the joint venture. Alpha is not obligated to reinvest the cash or make further contributions. Beta contributes cash of $900 to the joint venture in return for a 60 percent interest in the joint venture.

8-73. Applying Paragraph 3055.27, Alpha is able to recognize Beta's 60 percent share of the total gain. The maximum gain that can be recognized and the portion of this total gain that is taken into income at the time of the transfer would be calculated as follows:

Fair Value At Transfer	$700
Carrying Value At Transfer	(300)
Total Gain	$400
Alpha's Share (40 Percent)	(160)
Gain That Can Be Recognized (60%)	$240
Consideration Received (All Unencumbered)	$100
Carrying Value Of Assets Considered To Be Partly Sold [($100 ÷ $700)($300)]	(43)
Gain To Be Taken Into Income At Time Of Transfer	$ 57

8-74. Notice that, in this case, no bank financing was involved and, as a consequence, the proceeds of disposition are unencumbered and equal to the full amount of the cash received.

8-75. Alpha's initial investment in the joint venture, before the application of proportionate consolidation procedures, would be as follows:

Carrying Value Of Plant	$300
Gain That Can Be Recognized (60%)	240
Value Of Capital Contribution	$540
Equity Returned (Consideration Received)	(100)
Initial Investment	$440

Exercise Eight-5

Subject: Gains On Non-Monetary Capital Contributions (Case Two)

Barco Inc. has entered into a joint venture agreement with two other corporations. As its capital contribution, the Company contributes capital assets with a fair value of $426,000 and a carrying value of $310,000. In return, Barco receives a 20 percent equity interest in the joint venture and $176,000 in cash. The other two corporations each contribute cash in return for a 40 percent interest in the joint venture.

Provide the journal entry to record Barco Inc.'s investment in the joint venture.

End of Exercise. Solution available in Study Guide.

Example Two - Bank Financing

8-76. In the previous example, all of the cash received by Alpha came from the funds invested by Beta. In this second example, we will assume the joint venture requires bank financing in order to make the payment to Alpha:

Example Alpha Company and Beta Company, two unrelated corporations, form a joint venture. Alpha contributes a manufacturing plant with an estimated fair value of $1,000 and a carrying value of $250. Alpha receives cash of $800 and a 40 percent interest in the joint venture. Alpha is not obligated to reinvest the cash or make further contributions. Beta contributes cash of $300 to the joint venture in return for a 60 percent interest in the joint venture. The joint venture borrows $650 from a bank.

8-77. Paragraph 3055.27 requires that Alpha give recognition to Beta's 60 percent share of the gain. The maximum gain that can be recognized and the portion of this total gain that is taken into income at the time of the transfer would be calculated as follows:

Fair Value At Transfer	$1,000
Carrying Value At Transfer	(250)
Total Gain	$ 750
Alpha's Share (40 Percent)	(300)
Gain That Can Be Recognized (60%)	$ 450

Consideration Received	$ 800
Share Of Cash Borrowed [(40%)($800 - $300)]	(200)
Net Proceeds	$ 600
Carrying Value Of Assets Considered To Be Partly Sold [($600 ÷ $1,000)($250)]	(150)
Gain To Be Taken Into Income At Time Of Transfer	$ 450

8-78. Note that in the calculation of the net proceeds, recognition is given to the fact that only $300 of the $800 in cash received by Alpha came from Beta. The remaining $500 came from the proceeds of the bank loan and Alpha is responsible for 40 percent of this amount. This serves to illustrate the application of Paragraph 3055.30 (Paragraph 8-68).

8-79. Also note that the gain to be taken into income is the same amount as the total gain to be recognized. This results from the fact that the $600 Net Proceeds is equal to 60 percent of the fair value of the asset transferred, the same percentage as Beta's share of the joint venture. Given this situation, there is no further gain to be taken into income in subsequent periods.

8-80. The carrying value for Alpha's initial investment in the joint venture, before the application of proportionate consolidation procedures, would be calculated as follows:

Carrying Value Of Plant	$250
Gain That Can Be Recognized (60%)	450
Value Of Capital Contribution	$700
Equity Returned (Consideration Received)	(800)
Initial Investment (Liability)	($100)

8-81. Based on the fact that the amount received by Alpha from the joint venture ($800) exceeds the value of its contribution as measured under Section 3055 ($700), the interest in the joint venture is a liability rather than an asset.

Exercise Eight-6

Subject: Gains On Non-Monetary Capital Contributions (Case Three)

Tortly Ltd. has entered into a joint venture agreement with two other corporations. Tortly contributes assets with a fair value of $723,000 and a carrying value of $487,000. In return, Tortly receives a one-third interest in the joint venture and $123,000 in cash. Each of the other venturers contribute $50,000 in cash and capital assets with a fair market value of $550,000. The joint venture arranges a bank loan for $350,000 in order to finance its cash requirements.

Provide the journal entry to record Tortly Ltd.'s investment in the joint venture.

End of Exercise. Solution available in Study Guide.

Transactions Between A Venturer And A Joint Venture

Background

8-82. Section 3055 of the *CICA Handbook* requires that interests in joint ventures be accounted for by the proportionate consolidation method. This would suggest that joint venture accounting requires the usual full consolidation adjustments for fair value write-offs and upstream and downstream unrealized intercompany profits.

8-83. However, the fact that joint ventures are defined in a manner that creates a special relationship between its venturers has led the AcSB to make a different recommendation for dealing with profits arising on the intercompany transactions between a joint venture and its venturers.

8-84. To illustrate this difference, we will use an example in which an investee sells merchandise with a cost of $80,000 to one of its investor companies for $100,000, recording a profit of $20,000 which has not been realized through a subsequent resale by the investor company. Consider the differences in how this situation will be dealt with if the investee is a subsidiary, a significantly influenced company accounted for by the equity method or, alternatively, a joint venture accounted for by proportionate consolidation:

Subsidiary If the investee is a subsidiary, consolidation procedures would require that both the intercompany expense and revenue of $100,000 and the unrealized intercompany profit of $20,000 be eliminated. This conclusion results from the view that the parent and subsidiary are components of a single accounting entity and, as a consequence, a real sales transaction did not occur.

Significantly Influenced Company - Equity Method Under the equity method, the investor and investee are accounted for as separate entities and a real transaction did take place. As a consequence, there would be no elimination of the $100,000 intercompany expense and revenue. However, the presence of significant influence makes this a non-arm's length transaction, raising questions about the reliability of any profit figures that are reported. Given this, the *Handbook* recommendations require the elimination of 100 percent of any unrealized intercompany profits in the application of the equity method. This is accomplished by a reduction in the Investment Income account, rather than through adjustments of specific expenses and revenues.

Joint Ventures - Proportionate Consolidation As any investor who classifies an investment as a joint venture must participate in its management, venturers clearly have influence over the joint venture. As a consequence, transactions between venturers and the joint venture appear to be on a non-arm's length basis. However, there is a difference from the situation where the equity method is appropriate because the investor has significant influence over the investee.

In joint ventures, all of the venturers participate under the management agreement and are likely to pay careful attention to transactions that take place between the joint venture and other venturers. In fact, it would be unusual to find a joint venture agreement that does not specify the terms and conditions under which intercompany transactions can take place. Given this, it is reasonable to view transactions between a joint venture and its venturers as being arm's length in the sense that they are controlled by the relationship established in the joint venture arrangement or by an informal agreement among the joint venturers.

However, there is a problem. To the extent that the venturer has an equity interest in the joint venture, the intercompany transaction is, in effect, a transaction between the venturer and itself as represented by its interest in the joint venture. As a consequence, recognition of the particular venturer's share of the profit or loss does not appear to be appropriate.

The preceding discussion would suggest that, in the application of proportionate consolidation in joint venture situations, only the individual venturer's share of intercompany expenses, revenues, and unrealized profits would be eliminated. As will be discussed in the following material, this is the position taken in Section 3055 of the *CICA Handbook*.

Section 3055 Recommendations

Downstream Transactions

8-85. When there is a sale in the normal course of business operations from the venturer to the joint venture, commonly referred to as a downstream sale, Section 3055 makes the following recommendation:

> **Paragraph 3055.36** *When a venturer sells assets to a joint venture in the normal course of operations and a gain or loss occurs, the venturer should recognize the gain or loss in income to the extent of the interests of the other non-related venturers. When such a transaction provides evidence of a reduction in the net realizable value, or a decline in the value, of the relevant assets, the venturer should recognize the full amount of any loss in income.* (January, 1995)

8-86. To illustrate this provision, consider the following:

> **Example** On January 1, 2007, a group of joint venturers form Jointly Ltd.(JL) with a total investment of $1,000 in cash. One of the investors, Nordwell Inc. (NI), has received a 30 percent interest in return for $300 in cash. NI is a holding Company formed for this investment transaction and, on this date, the Company has no other assets or liabilities. The Balance Sheets of the two Companies on January 1, 2007 would be as follows:

Balance Sheets
As At January 1, 2007

	Nordwell	Jointly
Cash	Nil	$1,000
Investment In JL	$300	N/A
Total Assets	$300	$1,000
Common Stock (Total Equities)	$300	$1,000

During the year ending December 31, 2007, NI purchases merchandise on credit for $100 and sells it to JL for $160 in cash. The merchandise has not been resold at year end. Neither Company had other transactions during the year ending December 31, 2007. The Balance Sheets for the two Companies as at December 31, 2007 and the Income Statements for the year ending December 31, 2007 are as follows:

Balance Sheets
As At December 31, 2007

	Nordwell	Jointly
Cash	$160	$ 840
Inventory	Nil	160
Investment In JL	300	N/A
Total Assets	$460	$1,000
Accounts Payable	$100	Nil
Common Stock	300	$1,000
Retained Earnings	60	Nil
Total Equities	$460	$1,000

Income Statements
Year Ending December 31, 2007

	Nordwell	Jointly
Sales	$160	Nil
Cost Of Sales	100	Nil
Net Income	$ 60	Nil

8-87. The first step in the consolidation procedures would be to eliminate NI's Investment In JL, JL's Common Stock and, because we are using proportionate consolidation, the 70 percent interest of the other joint venturers in Jointly's assets. The entry would be as follows:

Common Stock (JL)	$1,000	
Cash [(70%)($840)]		$588
Inventory [(70%)($160)]		112
Investment In JL		300

8-88. As JL had no Income Statement items, there is no need for an entry to eliminate the interest of the other joint venturers in expenses or revenues. This means that the only other elimination entry is the one required to deal with the downstream sale. As NI can recognize this transaction to the extent of the interests of the other joint venturers, only NI's share of the Sales, Cost Of Sales, and unrealized profit in the closing Inventory will have to be eliminated. The required entry is as follows:

Sales [(30%)($160)]	$48	
Inventory [(30%)($160 - $100)]		$18
Cost Of Sales [(30%)($100)]		30

8-89. Given the preceding eliminations, the proportionate consolidation Balance Sheet and Income Statement can be prepared as follows:

Nordwell Inc.
Proportionate Consolidation Balance Sheet
(Downstream Profits)
As At December 31, 2007

Cash ($160 + $840 - $588)	$412
Inventory (Nil + $160 - $112 - $18)	30
Investment In JL ($300 - $300)	Nil
Total Assets	$442
Accounts Payable	$100
Common Stock	300
Retained Earnings ($60 - $18)	42
Total Equities	$442

Nordwell Inc.
Proportionate Consolidation Income Statement
(Downstream Profits)
Year Ending December 31, 2007

Sales ($160 - $48)	$112
Cost Of Sales ($100 - $30)	70
Net Income	$ 42

8-90. Note that, if full consolidation procedures had been applied, the entire intercompany transaction would have been eliminated and there would have been no content in the consolidated Income Statement for the year ending December 31, 2007.

8-91. As a final point on downstream transactions, note that the Paragraph 3055.36 recommendation (Paragraph 8-85) contemplates the possibility of recognizing 100 percent of a loss when the transaction provides evidence of a reduction in net realizable value. This is consistent with the Paragraph 3055.26 recommendation on capital contributions to joint ventures, (Paragraph 8-61) which also permits full recognition of a loss under these circumstances.

Exercise Eight-7

Subject: Downstream Intercompany Profits

Note Exercise Eight-8 is another version of this Exercise.

On January 1, 2007, a group of joint venturers form Combo Inc. (CI) with a total investment of $465,000 in cash. One of the investors, Bonder Ltd. (BL), has received a 25 percent interest in return for $116,250 in cash. BL is a holding Company formed for this investment transaction and, on this date, the Company has no other assets or liabilities. The Balance Sheets of the Companies on January 1, 2007 would be as follows:

Balance Sheets
As At January 1, 2007

	Bonder	Combo
Cash	Nil	$465,000
Investment In Combo	$116,250	N/A
Total Assets	$116,250	$465,000
Common Stock (Total Equities)	$116,250	$465,000

During the year ending December 31, 2007, BL purchases merchandise on credit for $56,000 and sells it to CI for $84,000 in cash. None of the merchandise has been resold at year end. Neither Company had any other transactions during the year ending December 31, 2007. The Balance Sheets for the two Companies as at December 31, 2007 and the Income Statements for the year ending December 31, 2007 are as follows:

Balance Sheets
As At December 31, 2007

	Bonder	Combo
Cash	$ 84,000	$381,000
Inventory	Nil	84,000
Investment In Combo	116,250	N/A
Total Assets	$200,250	$465,000
Accounts Payable	$ 56,000	Nil
Common Stock	116,250	$465,000
Retained Earnings	28,000	Nil
Total Equities	$200,250	$465,000

Income Statements
Year Ending December 31, 2007

	Bonder	Combo
Sales	$84,000	Nil
Cost Of Sales	56,000	Nil
Net Income	$28,000	Nil

For Bonder Ltd. and its investee, Combo Inc., prepare a proportionate consolidation Balance Sheet as at December 31, 2007, and a proportionate consolidation Income Statement for the year ending December 31, 2007.

End of Exercise. Solution available in Study Guide.

Upstream Transactions

8-92. When there is a sale from the joint venture to one of the venturers, commonly referred to as an upstream sale, the following recommendation applies:

> **Paragraph 3055.37** *When a venturer purchases assets from a joint venture in the normal course of operations, the venturer should not recognize its share of the profit or loss of the joint venture on the transaction until the assets are sold to a third party. However, when the transaction provides evidence of a reduction in the net realizable*

value, or a decline in the value of the relevant assets, the venturer should recognize its share of the loss in income immediately. (January, 1995)

8-93. In order to illustrate this provision, we will use the same basic example that was presented in Paragraph 8-86, modified to include an upstream rather than a downstream transaction. The example is as follows:

Example On January 1, 2007, a group of joint venturers form Jointly Ltd.(JL) with a total investment of $1,000 in cash. One of the investors, Nordwell Inc. (NI), has received a 30 percent interest in return for $300 in cash. NI is a holding Company formed for this investment transaction and, on this date, its only other asset or liability is cash of $220. The Balance Sheets of the two Companies on January 1, 2007 would be as follows:

Balance Sheets
As At January 1, 2007

	Nordwell	Jointly
Cash	$220	$1,000
Investment In JL	300	N/A
Total Assets	$520	$1,000
Common Stock (Total Equities)	$520	$1,000

During the year ending December 31, 2007, JL purchases merchandise for $150 in cash and sells it to NI for $220 in cash. The merchandise has not been resold at year end. Neither Company had other transactions during the year ending December 31, 2007. The Balance Sheets for the two Companies as at December 31, 2007 and the Income Statements for the year ending December 31, 2007 are as follows:

Balance Sheets
As At December 31, 2007

	Nordwell	Jointly
Cash	Nil	$1,070
Inventory	$220	Nil
Investment In JL	300	N/A
Total Assets	$520	$1,070
Common Stock	$520	$1,000
Retained Earnings	Nil	70
Total Equities	$520	$1,070

Income Statements
Year Ending December 31, 2002

	Nordwell	Jointly
Sales	Nil	$220
Cost Of Sales	Nil	150
Net Income	Nil	$ 70

8-94. A first entry is required to eliminate NI's Investment in JL, JL's Common Stock, and the other venturers' 70 percent interest in the assets, liabilities, expenses, and revenues of JL:

Common Stock (JL)	$1,000	
Sales [(70%)($220)]	154	
Cost Of Sales [(70%)($150)]		$105
Cash [(70%)($1,070)]		749
Investment In JL		300

8-95. If there had been an opening balance in JL's Retained Earnings, the preceding entry would have also eliminated that balance.

8-96. A second entry is required to eliminate NI's share of the intercompany Sales, Cost Of Sales, and the unrealized profit in the closing Inventory:

Sales [(30%)($220)]	$66	
Inventory [(30%)($220 - $150)]		$21
Cost Of Sales [(30%)($150)]		45

8-97. Using the preceding journal entries, the proportionate consolidation Balance Sheet and Income Statement can be prepared as follows:

Nordwell Inc.
Proportionate Consolidation Balance Sheet
(Upstream Profits)
As At December 31, 2007

Cash (Nil + $1,070 - $749)	$321
Inventory ($220 + Nil - $21)	199
Investment In JL ($300 - $300)	Nil
Total Assets	$520
Common Stock	$520
Retained Earnings	Nil
Total Equities	$520

Nordwell Inc.
Proportionate Consolidation Income Statement
(Upstream Profits)
Year Ending December 31, 2007

Sales (Nil + $220 - $154 - $66)	Nil
Cost Of Sales (Nil + $150 - $105 - $45)	Nil
Net Income	Nil

8-98. With respect to the proportionate consolidation Income Statement, we have not included any disclosure of the intercompany transaction. This reflects the fact that, while we can recognize the other venturers' share of the intercompany profit, it is not disclosed in the proportionate consolidation Income Statement.

8-99. Note that, in this example, the preceding consolidated Income Statement is the same as that which would result from the application of full consolidation procedures. That is, 100 percent of JL's expenses and revenues have been eliminated. There is, however, a different reason for the elimination of the other venturers' share of these expenses and revenues. In the preceding statement, these amounts were eliminated because we are using proportionate consolidation procedures. In full consolidation, these amounts would be eliminated because they were intercompany and the transactions which they reflect did not occur from a consolidated point of view.

Exercise Eight-8

Subject: Upstream Intercompany Profits (A different version of Exercise Eight-7)

On January 1, 2007, a group of joint venturers form Combo Inc. (CI) with a total investment of $465,000 in cash. One of the investors, Bonder Ltd. (BL), has received a 25 percent interest in return for $116,250 in cash. BL is a holding Company formed for this investment transaction and, on this date, the Company has no other assets or liabilities. The Balance Sheets of the two Companies on January 1, 2007 would be as follows:

Balance Sheets
As At January 1, 2007

	Bonder	Combo
Cash	Nil	$465,000
Investment In Combo	$116,250	N/A
Total Assets	$116,250	$465,000
Common Stock (Total Equities)	$116,250	$465,000

During the year ending December 31, 2007, CI purchases merchandise for $32,000 in cash and sells it to BL on account for $48,000. None of the merchandise has been resold at year end. Neither Company had any other transactions during the year ending December 31, 2007. The Balance Sheets for the two Companies as at December 31, 2007 and the Income Statements for the year ending December 31, 2007 are as follows:

Balance Sheets
As At December 31, 2007

	Bonder	Combo
Cash	Nil	$433,000
Accounts Receivable	Nil	48,000
Inventory	$ 48,000	Nil
Investment In Combo	116,250	N/A
Total Assets	$164,250	$481,000
Accounts Payable	$ 48,000	Nil
Common Stock	116,250	$465,000
Retained Earnings	Nil	16,000
Total Equities	$164,250	$481,000

Income Statements
Year Ending December 31, 2007

	Bonder	Combo
Sales	Nil	$48,000
Cost Of Sales	Nil	32,000
Net Income	Nil	$16,000

For Bonder Ltd. and its investee, Combo Inc., prepare a proportionate consolidation Balance Sheet as at December 31, 2007, and a proportionate consolidation Income Statement for the year ending December 31, 2007.

End of Exercise. Solution available in Study Guide.

Upstream And Downstream Transactions Compared

8-100. With both upstream and downstream intercompany profits, the venturer is allowed to recognize in its consolidated financial statements, the share of such profits that belongs to the other non-affiliated venturers . However, because proportionate consolidation is being used, the resulting disclosure is somewhat confusing.

8-101. In the consolidated Balance Sheet for the downstream profits example (Paragraph 8-89), none of the $60 intercompany profit is included in the Inventory balance. The $30 balance in this account is simply NI's 30 percent share of the $100 original cost of the Inventory. This does not mean, however, that we have not recognized the other venturers' 70 percent share of the profit. This is clear from the proportionate consolidation Income Statement which shows a profit equal to $42 (70 percent of $60). The reason that this $42 does not show up in the Inventory figure is that the Inventory belongs to JL and this means that proportionate consolidation procedures have removed 70 percent of all of JL's accounts. The $42 has been removed here, not because it is intercompany, but because proportionate consolidation procedures remove all values that belong to the other joint venturers.

8-102. The Inventory figure in the proportionate consolidation Balance Sheet in the upstream profits example in Paragraph 8-97 includes the 70 percent share of the $70 intercompany profit that belongs to the other joint venturers {$199 = [$150 cost to JL + (70%)($70)]}. The reason that the profit is included in the consolidated Inventory figure in this case is that the Inventory is on the books of NI. This means that it will not be eliminated by proportionate consolidation procedures.

8-103. However, the $49 profit is not included in the proportionate consolidation Income Statement. This reflects the fact that, in upstream transactions, the Sales and Cost Of Sales figures are from the books of JL. This means that 70 percent of these figures are eliminated through proportionate consolidation procedures, thereby eliminating in the proportionate consolidation Income Statement, the $49 profit that is included in the proportionate consolidation Balance Sheet. The investor, NI, had Sales and Cost Of Sales of nil and the joint venture's only sale was to NI. The fact that the total profit on this sale was unrealized results in a proportionate consolidation Income Statement where the Sales and the Cost Of Sales are also nil.

Comprehensive Example

Basic Data

8-104. The following comprehensive example will serve to illustrate the application of proportionate consolidation procedures:

> On January 1, 2007, Laroo Ltd. (LL) and Rotan Inc. (RI) establish a new corporation which will market products that both companies produce. LL has no affiliation with RI other than their common ownership of the new corporation. The new corporation is called Cooperative Enterprises Inc. (CEI).
>
> LL's capital contribution consists of a Building with a carrying value of $1,500,000 and a fair value of $2,000,000. The building is situated on leased land. The lease payments are at current fair market value and the lease is transferred to CEI at the time of its incorporation. On January 1, 2007, the remaining term of the lease is 20 years and this is also the remaining economic life of the building. In return for the building, LL receives 60 percent of CEI's voting shares and $200,000 in cash. LL records a gain of $500,000 on the transfer of the building.
>
> RI's capital contribution consists of $1,200,000 in cash. In return, RI receives 40 percent of CEI's voting shares.
>
> LL and RI sign an agreement which provides for joint control over CEI. All significant operating and financing decisions must be approved by both of the investor companies.

For the year ending December 31, 2007, the single entity Balance Sheets and Income Statements for LL and CEI are as follows:

Balance Sheets
As At December 31, 2007

	LL	CEI
Cash And Receivables	$ 1,500,000	$ 300,000
Inventories	4,800,000	1,500,000
Investment In CEI (At Cost)	1,800,000	N/A
Land	1,100,000	Nil
Building	3,500,000	2,000,000
Accumulated Amortization	(1,200,000)	(100,000)
Total Assets	$11,500,000	$3,700,000
Liabilities	$ 2,200,000	$ 200,000
Common Stock - No Par	5,000,000	3,000,000
Retained Earnings	4,300,000	500,000
Total Equities	$11,500,000	$3,700,000

Income Statements
For The Year Ending December 31, 2007

	LL	CEI
Sales	$ 4,200,000	$ 2,800,000
Gain On Sale Of Building	500,000	Nil
Cost Of Goods Sold	(2,500,000)	(1,500,000)
Amortization Expense	(700,000)	(100,000)
Other Expenses	(400,000)	(700,000)
Net Income	$ 1,100,000	$ 500,000

Other Information:

1. During the year ending December 31, 2007, CEI sells merchandise to LL for $420,000. This merchandise had cost CEI $350,000 and none of it has been resold by LL.

2. During the year ending December 31, 2007, LL sells merchandise to CEI for $860,000. This merchandise had cost LL $740,000 and one-half of it has been resold by CEI.

3. Neither LL nor CEI declare or pay dividends during the year ending December 31, 2007.

Required: Using proportionate consolidation procedures, prepare a consolidated Balance Sheet as at December 31, 2007 and a consolidated Income Statement for the year ending December 31, 2007, for LL and its investee CEI.

Investment Elimination

8-105. The journal entry to eliminate the Investment In CEI, CEI's Common Stock - No Par, CEI's Retained Earnings (At Acquisition), and the other venturer's (RI's) 40 percent share of the individual assets, liabilities, expenses, and revenues of CEI would be as follows:

Common Stock - No Par (CEI's)	$3,000,000	
Retained Earnings (At Acquisition)	Nil	
Accumulated Amortization (40%)	40,000	
Liabilities (40%)	80,000	
Sales (40%)	1,120,000	
Cash And Receivables (40%)		$ 120,000
Inventories (40%)		600,000
Building (40%)		800,000
Cost Of Goods Sold (40%)		600,000
Amortization Expense (40%)		40,000
Other Expenses (40%)		280,000
Investment In CEI		1,800,000

8-106. Note that, at this point, we are left with 60 percent of the carrying values of CEI's assets, liabilities, expenses, and revenues. Because we are using proportionate consolidation, there is no non-controlling interest to reflect RI's interest in the assets, liabilities, expenses, and revenues of CEI.

Analysis Of Gain On Capital Contribution

8-107. In transferring the Building to CEI, LL recognized a gain of $500,000 ($2,000,000 - $1,500,000). Under the provisions of Section 3055, this gain can only be recognized to the extent of the interest of the other non-affiliated venturer. This provides the following analysis:

Total Gain	$500,000
LL's Share (60 Percent)	(300,000)
Gain That Can Be Recognized (40%)	$200,000

8-108. To the extent that LL received cash or assets other than an equity interest in NVI, this gain can be taken into income at the time of transfer. The calculation of the amount to be taken into income at the time of transfer is as follows:

Consideration Received	$200,000
Carrying Value Of Asset Considered To Be Partly Sold:	
[($200,000 ÷ $2,000,000)($1,500,000)]	(150,000)
Gain To Be Taken Into Income At Time Of Transfer	$ 50,000

8-109. The remaining $150,000 ($200,000 - $50,000) of the gain that can be recognized, will be taken into income over the 20 year life of the Building. This will be at a rate of $7,500 per year.

8-110. As the $300,000 unrecognized gain will have to be removed from the consolidated carrying value of the Building, the consolidated Amortization Expense will have to be decreased annually by $15,000 ($300,000 ÷ 20 Years).

Gain Adjustment - Building

8-111. An entry is required to deal with the total gain recognized by LL on the transfer of the Building. The entry will leave the $50,000 of the gain that can be taken into income at transfer in the Gain On Sale Of Building account. The $300,000 of the gain that cannot be recognized will be removed from the Building account, while the $150,000 portion of the gain that will be recognized over the life of the Building will be allocated to a Deferred Gain account. The required entry is as follows:

Gain On Sale Of Building ($500,000 - $50,000)	$450,000	
Building (Unrecognized Portion)		$300,000
Deferred Gain ($200,000 - $50,000)		150,000

8-112. This entry, when combined with the earlier elimination of RI's 40 percent share of the Building, leaves a balance of $900,000 ($2,000,000 - $800,000 - $300,000). As would be expected, this is equal to LL's 60 percent share of the original $1,500,000 carrying value for the Building.

Deferred Gain Amortization And Amortization Adjustment

8-113. As one year has passed since the Building was transferred to CEI, one-twentieth of the Deferred Gain has been realized and can be taken into income. The appropriate entry is as follows:

Deferred Gain	$7,500	
Gain On Sale Of Building		$7,500

8-114. As CEI has recorded amortization on the $2,000,000 fair value of the Building, this must be adjusted to reflect the removal of the $300,000 unrecognized gain from this asset. This will require an annual adjustment of $15,000 ($300,000 ÷ 20 Years) as follows:

Accumulated Amortization	$15,000	
Amortization Expense		$15,000

8-115. This entry, when combined with the earlier elimination of RI's 40 percent share of the Building, leaves Accumulated Amortization and Amortization Expense at $45,000. As was the case with the Building account, this is equal to amortization at 5 percent on LL's $900,000 [(60%)($1,500,000)] share of the original carrying value of the building.

Intercompany Expenses And Revenues

8-116. There are intercompany expenses and revenues arising from both upstream ($420,000) and downstream ($860,000) sales of merchandise. In the case of joint ventures, intercompany sales and any related intercompany profit can be recognized to the extent of the share of the other non-affiliated venturers (Paragraphs 3055.36 and 3055.37).

8-117. With respect to downstream transactions, this means that we must eliminate the selling venturer's share of the sale and any unrealized profit resulting from the transaction. The remainder of the downstream sale and the related profit will remain in the proportionate consolidation results.

8-118. When an upstream transaction is involved, all of the sale and unrealized profit must be eliminated. While we can recognize the other non-related venturer's share of the profit in the consolidated Balance Sheet (it is included in an asset on the books of the venturer and not subject to proportionate consolidation procedures), the sale and profit belong to the other non-related venturer and will be removed by the proportionate consolidation procedures.

8-119. RI's 40 percent share of the upstream sale was eliminated in our first journal entry. This means that we will only need to eliminate $768,000 [(60%)($420,000) + (60%)($860,000)] of these sales. The required entry is as follows:

Sales	$768,000	
Cost Of Goods Sold		$768,000

Unrealized Inventory Profits

8-120. As some of the merchandise has not been resold, there are also unrealized intercompany profits to be eliminated. The upstream amount is $70,000 [(100%)($420,000 - $350,000)] and the downstream amount is $60,000 [(50%)($860,000 - $740,000)]. As was the case with upstream intercompany sales, we have already eliminated RI's 40 percent share of all of CEI's profits and, as a consequence, we only need to eliminate $42,000 [(60%)($70,000)] of the unrealized upstream profit of $70,000. With respect to the downstream profit, we will need to eliminate 60 percent of this total, an amount of $36,000 [(60%)(50%)($860,000 - $740,000)]. The entry to eliminate this total of $78,000 is as follows:

Cost Of Goods Sold - Upstream [$70,000 - (40%)($70,000)]	$42,000	
Cost Of Goods Sold - Downstream [(60%)($60,000)]	36,000	
Inventories		$78,000

8-121. Given these entries, the required consolidated Balance Sheet can be prepared as follows:

LL And Investee CEI
Consolidated Balance Sheet (Proportionate Basis)
As At December 31, 2007

Cash And Receivables ($1,500,000 + $300,000 - $120,000)	$ 1,680,000
Inventories ($4,800,000 + $1,500,000 - $600,000 - $78,000)	5,622,000
Investment In CEI ($1,800,000 - $1,800,000)	Nil
Land (LL's Only)	1,100,000
Building ($3,500,000 + $2,000,000 - $800,000 - $300,000)	4,400,000
Accumulated Amortization ($1,200,000 + $100,000 - $40,000 - $15,000)	(1,245,000)
Total Assets	$11,557,000
Liabilities ($2,200,000 + $200,000 - $80,000)	$ 2,320,000
Deferred Gain ($150,000 - $7,500)	142,500
Common Stock - No Par (LL's Only)	5,000,000
Retained Earnings (See Note)	4,094,500
Total Equities	$11,557,000

Note The balance in consolidated Retained Earnings can be verified with the following calculation:

LL's Balance - December 31, 2007	$4,300,000
Unrecognized Gain On Building Transfer	(300,000)
Deferred Gain On Building Transfer	(150,000)
Gain Realized During 2007	7,500
Amortization Adjustment	15,000
LL's Share Of Downstream Inventory Profit [(60%)($60,000)]	(36,000)
LL's Adjusted Balance	$3,836,500
Equity Pickup [(60%)($500,000 - $70,000)]	258,000
Consolidated Retained Earnings	$4,094,500

8-122. The required consolidated Income Statement would be prepared as follows:

LL And Investee CEI
Consolidated Income Statement (Proportionate Basis)
Year Ending December 31, 2007

Sales ($4,200,000 + $2,800,000 - $1,120,000 - $768,000)	$5,112,000
Gain On Sale Of Building ($500,000 - $450,000 + $7,500)	57,500
Cost Of Goods Sold ($2,500,000 + $1,500,000 - $600,000 - $768,000 + $78,000)	(2,710,000)
Amortization Expense ($700,000 + $100,000 - $40,000 - $15,000)	(745,000)
Other Expenses ($400,000 + $700,000 - $280,000)	(820,000)
Consolidated Net Income	$ 894,500

8-123. The consolidated Net Income figure can be verified with the following calculation:

LL's 2007 Net Income	$1,100,000
Unrecognized Gain On Building Transfer	(300,000)
Deferred Gain On Building Transfer	(150,000)
Gain Realized During 2007	7,500
Amortization Adjustment	15,000
LL's Share Of Downstream Inventory Profit [(60%)($60,000)]	(36,000)
LL's Adjusted Balance	$ 636,500
Equity Pickup [(60%)($500,000 - $70,000)]	258,000
Consolidated Net Income	$ 894,500

8-124. Note that the preceding adjustments to LL's Net Income are the same as the adjustments in the verification of consolidated Retained Earnings. This is because it is the first year of operations of CEI.

Disclosure

8-125. In order to give investors a better understanding of the extent to which the venturer's activities are carried out in the form of joint ventures, separate disclosure of the venturer's share of assets, liabilities, revenues, expenses, net income, and cash flows of the joint venture are required. This is reflected in the following recommendation:

> **Paragraph 3055.41** *A venturer should disclose the total amounts and the major components of each of the following related to its interests in joint ventures:*
>
> *(a) current assets and long-term assets;*
> *(b) current liabilities and long-term liabilities;*
> *(c) revenues, expenses and net income;*
> *(d) cash flows resulting from operating activities;*
> *(e) cash flows resulting from financing activities; and*
> *(f) cash flows resulting from investing activities.* (January, 1995)

8-126. This information would normally be presented on a combined basis for all of the venturer's joint venture activities. In those situations where substantially all of the activities of a venturer are carried out through joint ventures, a statement that this is the case would be sufficient disclosure.

8-127. Joint venture arrangements involve contingencies and commitments, even to the extent of an individual venturer becoming responsible for other venturers' shares of joint venture obligations. The need for disclosure in this type of situation is reflected in the following recommendation:

> **Paragraph 3055.42** *A venturer should disclose its share of any contingencies and commitments of joint ventures and those contingencies that exist when the venturer is contingently liable for the liabilities of the other venturers of the joint ventures.* (January, 1995)

8-128. Paragraph 3055.44 indicates that it is generally desirable to disclose a listing and description of significant interests in joint ventures, including the names and the proportion of ownership interest held in particular ventures. Other disclosure requirements may arise for joint ventures as the result of the application of other *CICA Handbook* Sections. For example, some of the recommendations of Section 3840, "Related Party Transactions" would often be applicable to joint ventures.

Joint Ventures In Canadian Practice

Statistics From Financial Reporting In Canada

8-129. Of the 200 companies surveyed for the 2006 edition of *Financial Reporting in Canada*, 61 companies indicated in their 2005 annual reports that they participated in one or more joint venture arrangements. Of the 61 companies, 59 accounted for these arrangements using proportionate consolidation, while the remaining 2 companies did not disclose the method used.

8-130. With respect to other types of disclosure, the following additional statistics are included for the 200 companies surveyed:

- 43 companies provided separate disclosure of the current and non-current assets of their joint ventures;
- 36 companies provided separate disclosure of the current and long-term liabilities of their joint ventures;
- 39 companies provided disclosure of revenues, expenses, and Net Income; and
- 42 companies disclosed the operating, financing, and investing cash flows of their joint venture arrangements.

Example From Practice

8-131. The following example is from the annual report of Transalta Corporation for the reporting period ending December 31, 2005. This example illustrates disclosure of joint ventures in a separate note to the financial statements. Included is a brief description of joint venture operations. Also disclosed is the percentage ownership in the individual joint venture investments.

Notes To Financial Statements

(Tabular Dollar Amounts In Millions Of Canadian Dollars)

Note 1 Summary Of Significant Accounting Policies (in part)

A. Consolidation (in part)

The consolidated financial statements include the accounts of TransAlta Corporation (TransAlta or the corporation), all subsidiaries and the proportionate share of the accounts of joint ventures and jointly controlled corporations.

Note 19 Joint Ventures

Joint ventures at December 31, 2005 included the following:

Joint venture	Ownership interest	Description
Sheerness joint venture	50%	Coal-fired plant in Alberta, of which TA Cogen has a 50 per cent interest, and is operated by Canadian Utilities
Meridian joint venture	50%	Cogeneration plant in Alberta, of which TA Cogen has a 50 per cent interest, and is operated by Husky Energy
Fort Saskatchewan joint venture	60%	Cogeneration plant in Alberta, of which TA Cogen has a 60 per cent interest, and is operated by TransAlta
McBride Lake joint venture	50%	Wind generation facilities in Alberta, operated by TransAlta
Goldfields Power joint venture	50%	Gas-fired plant in Australia, operated by TransAlta
CE Generation LLC	50%	Geothermal and gas plants in the United States, operated by CE Gen affiliates
Genesee 3	50%	Coal-fired plant in Alberta, operated by EPCOR Utilities Inc.

Summarized information on the results of operations, financial position and cash flows relating to the corporation's pro-rata interests in its jointly controlled corporations was as follows:

	2005	2004	2003
Results of operations			
Revenues	$ 619.9	$ 505.2	$ 539.0
Expenses	(481.1)	(424.3)	(429.3)
Non-controlling interests	(43.7)	(37.1)	(25.9)
Proportionate share of net earnings	$ 95.1	$ 43.8	$ 83.8
Cash flows			
Cash flow from operations	$ 111.5	$ 153.2	$ 498.7
Cash flow used in investing activities	(10.3)	(21.6)	(1,603.4)
Cash flow used in financing activities	(76.3)	(129.1)	1,131.5
Proportionate share of decrease in cash and cash equivalents	$ 24.9	$ 2.5	$ 26.8
Financial position			
Current assets	$ 162.5	$ 112.7	$ 125.9
Long-term assets	1,895.4	2,033.7	2,214.4
Current liabilities	(118.0)	(110.9)	(135.1)
Long-term liabilities	(552.7)	(635.6)	(806.2)
Non-controlling interests	(396.1)	(416.3)	(164.5)
Proportionate share of net assets	$ 991.1	$ 983.6	$ 1,234.5

CD-ROM Note If you are interested in more statistics and examples of disclosure of joint ventures, the CICA's *Financial Reporting in Canada* is available on the CD-ROM which is included with this text.

International Convergence

Standards

8-132. As indicated in this Chapter, the Canadian rules for accounting for joint ventures arrangements are found in *CICA Handbook* Section 3055, "Interests In Joint Ventures". The corresponding international standard is IAS No. 31, *Interests In Joint Ventures*.

Current Differences In Standards

Coverage

8-133. The rules in Section 3055 apply to all joint venture interests and do not vary with the legal form that is used. In contrast, IAS No. 31 has separate rules for jointly controlled operations, jointly controlled assets, and jointly controlled entities (i.e., a joint venture which is organized as a separate corporation or partnership).

8-134. Section 3055 does not have exceptions from its scope for particular types of enterprises. In contrast, IAS No. 31 excludes from its scope jointly controlled entities that are held by:

- venture capital organizations; or
- mutual funds, unit trusts, and similar entities including investment-linked insurance funds.

8-135. These exemptions are only applicable provided the interests in joint venture entities are classified as held for trading and accounted for at fair value.

Method Of Accounting

8-136. As we have noted, Section 3055 requires the use of proportionate consolidation to account for interests in joint ventures in the financial statements of profit oriented enterprises. There are no exceptions provided in the Section.

8-137. IAS No. 31 differs in that it allows the use of either proportionate consolidation or the equity method for interests in joint controlled entities. Other rules are applicable to jointly controlled assets and jointly controlled operations. In addition, exemptions are provided for some jointly controlled entities as described in Paragraph 8-137.

8-138. While the current IAS No. 31 is flexible with respect to the method to be used for interests in jointly controlled entities, this is not likely to continue. An Exposure Draft for a revised IAS No. 31 is expected during the first half of 2007. In order to reconcile IFRSs with U.S. standards, this Exposure Draft will almost certainly remove the proportionate consolidation option for joint venture entities. U.S. standards currently require the use of the equity method for interests in joint ventures and do not permit the use of proportionate consolidation.

Intercompany Transactions

8-139. As discussed in this Chapter, Section 3055 has fairly detailed rules for dealing with both non-monetary capital contributions to a joint venture, and for intercompany transactions between the venturer and venture that are in the normal course of operations.

8-140. The rules in IAS No. 31 are more general and do not distinguish between capital contributions and transactions in the normal course of business operations. The relevant paragraphs of IAS No. 31 are as follows:

> **Paragraph 48** When a venturer contributes or sells assets to a joint venture, recognition of any portion of a gain or loss from the transaction shall reflect the substance of the transaction. While the assets are retained by the joint venture, and provided the venturer has transferred the significant risks and rewards of ownership, the venturer shall recognise only that portion of the gain or loss that is attributable to the interests of the other venturers. The venturer shall recognise the full amount of any loss when the contribution or sale provides evidence of a reduction in the net realisable value of current assets or an impairment loss.
>
> **Paragraph 49** When a venturer purchases assets from a joint venture, the venturer shall not recognise its share of the profits of the joint venture from the transaction until it resells the assets to an independent party. A venturer shall recognise its share of the losses resulting from these transactions in the same way as profits except that losses shall be recognised immediately when they represent a reduction in the net realisable value of current assets or an impairment loss.

8-141. These recommendations are similar to those in the Canadian standards in that they required 100 percent recognition of losses. This applies to both upstream and downstream transactions.

8-142. With respect to downstream transfers with gains, both sets of standards provide for recognition of only the other venturers' share of such gains. However, the Canadian standard differs on capital contributions in that the amount that will be taken into income is limited by the amount of unrestricted cash received by the venturer in return for its contribution.

8-143. With respect to upstream transactions with gains, both sets of standards require elimination of the venturer's share of such gains. Stated alternatively, the venturer can only recognize the other venturers' share of upstream intercompany gains.

Additional Readings

8-144. In writing the material in the text, we have incorporated all of the relevant *CICA Handbook* recommendations, as well as material from other sources that we felt to be of importance.

8-145. While this approach meets the needs of the great majority of our readers, some of you may wish to pursue this subject in greater depth. To facilitate this, you will find a fairly comprehensive list of additional readings at the end of each relevant Chapter in our *Guide To Canadian Financial Reporting*.

> **CD-ROM Note** Our *Guide To Canadian Financial Reporting* is available on the CD-ROM which is included with this text.

Problems For Self Study

(The solutions for these problems can be found in the separate Study Guide.)

Self Study Problem Eight - 1

Each of the following independent Cases involves three companies which deal with each other at arm's length. They are Acres Ltd. (AL), Barrus Ltd. (BL), and Caron Ltd. (CL). In all cases presented, the three Companies are forming a joint venture called Collusive Ventures Ltd. (CVL) and the joint venture agreement gives them the following equity interests in this new enterprise:

Venturer	AL	BL	CL
Equity Interest In CVL	25 Percent	35 Percent	40 Percent

We will be concerned with accounting for the capital contribution being made by AL and, as a consequence, the capital contributions of BL and CL will be the same in all Cases. They are as follows:

BL This venturer contributes cash of $600,000 and other assets with a fair value of $450,000. This investment of $1,050,000 is equal to 35 percent of $3,000,000.

CL This venturer contributes cash of $400,000 and other assets with a fair value of $800,000. This investment of $1,200,000 is equal to 40 percent of $3,000,000.

Case One In return for its 25 percent equity interest in CVL, AL contributes non-monetary assets with a fair value of $750,000 and a carrying value on AL's books of $1,000,000. AL receives no other assets from CVL and CVL does not assume any additional debt at the time of its incorporation.

Case Two In return for its 25 percent equity interest in CVL, AL contributes non-monetary assets with a fair value of $1,100,000 and a carrying value on AL's books of $600,000. In addition to its 25 percent equity interest, AL receives $350,000 in cash. CVL does not assume any additional debt at the time of its incorporation.

Case Three In return for its 25 percent equity interest in CVL, AL contributes cash of $350,000 and non-monetary assets with a fair value of $400,000. The carrying value of these non-monetary assets on the books of AL is $250,000. AL receives no other assets from CVL and CVL does not assume any additional debt at the time of its incorporation.

Case Four In return for its 25 percent equity interest in CVL, AL contributes non-monetary assets with a fair value of $1,400,000 and a carrying value on AL's books of $1,100,000. In addition to its 25 percent equity interest, AL receives $650,000 in cash. At the time of incorporation, CVL borrows $1,000,000. The three venturers are responsible for this debt in proportion to their equity interests in CVL.

Case Five In return for its 25 percent equity interest in CVL, AL contributes non-monetary assets with a fair value of $2,500,000 and a carrying value on AL's books of $2,000,000. In addition to its 25 percent equity interest, AL receives $1,750,000 in cash. At the time of incorporation, CVL borrows $1,000,000. The three venturers are responsible for this debt in proportion to their equity interests in CVL.

Required: Following the Recommendations of Section 3055 of the *CICA Handbook*, determine the amount of the gain or loss that would be recognized in the financial statements, as well as the amount that would be included in the determination of Net Income, by AL at the time it makes its capital contribution to CVL.

Self Study Problem Eight - 2

On April 1, 2007, Sentinel Resources Ltd. and the Molar Oil Company jointly purchase Numa Inc. The enterprise will be operated as a joint venture and fits the joint venture definition contained in Section 3055 of the *CICA Handbook*. The main objective of Numa Inc. will be to develop oil fields in northern Alberta.

Sentinel Resources contributes $450,000 in cash for 45 percent of Numa Inc.'s outstanding voting shares while Molar Oil purchases the remaining 55 percent for $550,000. Other than the joint venture agreement, there is no affiliation of any sort between the two investor companies.

On April 1, 2007, after the purchase of Numa Inc., the condensed Balance Sheets of the three companies and the fair values of the identifiable non-current assets are as follows:

Condensed Balance Sheets
As At April 1, 2007

	Sentinel	Molar	Numa
Net Current Assets	$1,050,000	$ 950,000	$100,000
Investment in Numa	450,000	550,000	N/A
Other Non-Current Assets	5,300,000	7,600,000	840,000
Total Assets	$6,800,000	$9,100,000	$940,000
Common Stock - No Par	$4,000,000	$5,000,000	$940,000
Retained Earnings	2,800,000	4,100,000	Nil
Total Equities	$6,800,000	$9,100,000	$940,000
Non-Current Assets - Fair Values	$5,700,000	$9,800,000	$900,000

The fair values of the net current assets are equal to their carrying values. In each of the three companies, the difference between the fair values and carrying values of the non-current assets arises from Land.

For the year ending March 31, 2008, the condensed Income Statements, before the recognition of any investment income, and the dividends declared of the three Companies are as follows:

Condensed Income Statements
For The Year Ending March 31, 2008

	Sentinel	Molar	Numa
Revenues	$7,800,000	$9,600,000	$660,000
Expenses and Losses	(6,400,000)	(8,500,000)	(480,000)
Net Income	$1,400,000	$1,100,000	$180,000
Dividends Declared	$ 300,000	$ 500,000	$ 40,000

Also during the year ending March 31, 2008, the following transactions occurred between Numa Inc. and its investor companies:

1. On March 1, 2008, Molar Oil purchased crude oil from Numa Inc. for $390,000. The cost allocated to the oil by Numa Inc. is $314,000. All of this oil is being stored by Molar Oil and it will be sold in April, 2008.

2. On March 31, 2008, Sentinel Resources purchased Equipment from Numa Inc. for $95,000. The Equipment had been carried on the books of Numa Inc. at a net book value of $175,000. The resulting $80,000 loss is included in the Expenses And Losses of Numa.

Required: Using the Recommendations of Section 3055 of the *CICA Handbook*:

A. Prepare the condensed proportionate consolidation Balance Sheet of Sentinel Resources as at April 1, 2007, after the acquisition of 45 percent of Numa Inc.

B. Prepare the condensed proportionate consolidation Income Statement of Sentinel Resources Ltd. for the year ending March 31, 2008.

C. Prepare the condensed proportionate consolidation Income Statement of Molar Oil Company for the year ending March 31, 2008.

Self Study Problem Eight - 3

On January 1, 2007, the Daunton Company, Etna Company, and Lerner Company establish DEL Ltd. The three Companies sign an agreement which specifies that in all areas essential to the operation of DEL Ltd., decisions must be made by, and require the consent of, each of the three Companies. Other than this agreement, there is no affiliation of any sort between the three investor Companies. The new company is organized to do pharmaceutical research. The Daunton Company and the Etna Company each hold 40 percent of DEL Ltd's outstanding voting shares while the Lerner Company holds the remaining 20 percent.

During the year ending December 31, 2007, DEL Ltd. had Net Income of $475,000 and declared dividends of $75,000. On November 1, 2007, the Daunton Company purchased excess laboratory chemicals from DEL Ltd. for $16,000. They had been purchased by DEL Ltd. for $52,000 and had a limited shelf life. On December 31, 2007, the Etna Company purchased a patented process from DEL Ltd. for $183,000. The cost allocated to this process by DEL Ltd. was $100,000.

On December 31, 2007, the Joffry Company, which has no affiliation with the original investors, purchases all of the outstanding voting shares of DEL Ltd. held by the Daunton Company and the Etna Company. On that date, the condensed Balance Sheets of the Joffry Company and DEL Ltd. and the fair values of DEL Ltd.'s assets and liabilities are as follows:

Balance Sheets
As At December 31, 2007

	Joffry Book Value	DEL Ltd. Book Value	DEL Ltd. Fair Value
Current Assets	$ 780,000	$ 300,000	$320,000
Non-Current Assets	1,500,000	700,000	$650,000
Investment In DEL (At Cost)	720,000	N/A	
Total Assets	$3,000,000	$1,000,000	
Liabilities	$ 500,000	$ 200,000	$160,000
Common Stock (No Par)	1,000,000	400,000	
Retained Earnings	1,500,000	400,000	
Total Equities	$3,000,000	$1,000,000	

Required:

A. Assume that the Joffry Company signs an agreement which specifies that in all areas essential to the operation of DEL Ltd., decisions must be made by, and require the consent of, both the Lerner Company and the Joffry Company. Prepare the Balance Sheet for the Joffry Company as at December 31, 2007 assuming the Joffry Company uses proportionate consolidation to account for its investment in DEL Ltd.

B. Assume that there is no agreement that provides for participation in the affairs or operations of DEL Ltd. by the Lerner Company. Prepare the consolidated Balance Sheet for the Joffry Company and its subsidiary, DEL Ltd., as at December 31, 2007.

C. Provide the journal entries related to the Etna Company's income and dividends from its investment in DEL Ltd. for the year ending December 31, 2007, prior to the sale of DEL Ltd. Etna Company uses the equity method to account for its investment in DEL Ltd. in its single entity records. Your solution should include a detailed calculation of investment income.

Self Study Problem Eight - 4

On January 1, 2007, Barton Ltd. (BL) and Systems Inc. (SI) establish a new corporation which will market products that both Companies produce. BL has no affiliation with SI other than their common ownership of the new corporation. The new corporation will be called New Venture Inc. (NVI). BL and SI signed an agreement which provides for joint control over NVI. All significant operating and financing decisions must be approved by both of the investor Companies.

BL's capital contribution consists of a Building with a carrying value of $400,000 and a fair value of $1,200,000. The Building is situated on leased land. The lease payments are at current fair market value and the lease is transferred to NVI at the time of its incorporation. On January 1, 2007, the remaining term of the lease is 10 years and this is also the remaining economic life of the Building. In return for the building, BL receives 45 percent of NVI's voting shares and $300,000 in cash. BL records a gain of $800,000 on the transfer of the Building.

SI's capital contribution consists of $1,100,000 in cash. In return, SI receives 55 percent of NVI's voting shares.

For the year ending December 31, 2007, the single entity Income Statements and Balance Sheets for BL and NVI are as follows:

Income Statements
For The Year Ending December 31, 2007

	BL	NVI
Sales	$3,500,000	$2,300,000
Gain On Sale Of Building	800,000	Nil
Total Revenues	$4,300,000	$2,300,000
Cost Of Goods Sold	$2,200,000	$1,490,000
Amortization Expense	220,000	120,000
Other Expenses	340,000	150,000
Total Expenses	$2,760,000	$1,760,000
Net Income	$1,540,000	$ 540,000

Balance Sheets
As At December 31, 2007

	BL	NVI
Cash And Receivables	$1,600,000	$ 420,000
Inventories	3,420,000	1,160,000
Investment In NVI (At Cost)	900,000	N/A
Land	620,000	Nil
Building	2,120,000	1,200,000
Accumulated Amortization	(630,000)	(120,000)
Total Assets	$8,030,000	$2,660,000
Liabilities	$ 470,000	$ 120,000
Common Stock - No Par	4,800,000	2,000,000
Retained Earnings	2,760,000	540,000
Total Equities	$8,030,000	$2,660,000

Other Information:

1. During the year ending December 31, 2007, NVI sells merchandise to BL for $250,000. This merchandise had cost NVI $200,000 and none of it has been resold by BL.
2. During the year ending December 31, 2007, BL sells merchandise to NVI for $940,000. This merchandise had cost BL $860,000 and one-half of it has been resold by NVI.
3. Neither BL nor NVI declare or pay dividends during the year ending December 31, 2007.

Required: Using proportionate consolidation procedures, prepare a consolidated Balance Sheet as at December 31, 2007 and a consolidated Income Statement for the year ending December 31, 2007, for BL and its investee, NVI.

Assignment Problems

(The solutions for these problems are only available in the solutions manual that has been provided to your instructor.)

Assignment Problem Eight - 1

Both of the following Cases involve two companies which deal with each other at arm's length. The two companies are Boom Boom Ltd. (BBL) and Yum Yum Inc. (YYI). Boom Boom Ltd. is involved in processing popcorn products, while Yum Yum Inc. manufactures luxury ice cream products. They have decided to form a new company, Paradise Ventures Ltd. (PVL), in order to do research on the use of popcorn in ice cream products. The new company will be subject to a management agreement which gives BBL and YYI joint control of the investing, financing, and operating activities of the company.

The two Cases which follow describe the capital contributions made by BBL and YYI in the organization of PVL. They are independent of each other.

Case One BBL contributes cash of $1,500,000, one item of manufacturing equipment with a fair value of $560,000 and a carrying value of $450,000, and a second item of manufacturing equipment with a fair value of $740,000 and a carrying value of $860,000. The transfer of the second item of equipment to PVL is considered to be evidence of a non-temporary decline in the value of the equipment. In return for these capital contributions, BBL receives a 56 percent equity interest in PVL. YYI contributes $2,200,000 in cash in return for a 44 percent equity interest in PVL.

Case Two BBL contributes a manufacturing plant with a fair value of $1,840,000 and a carrying value of $1,320,000. In return for this plant, BBL receives cash of $1,000,000 and a 42 percent equity interest in PVL. BBL is not obligated to reinvest the cash. YYI contributes $600,000 in cash and other assets with a fair value of $560,000 and a carrying value of $423,000. In return for this capital contribution, YYI receives a 58 percent equity interest in PVL. PVL borrows $2,300,000 from the Royal Bank.

Required: For both of the preceding independent Cases, assume that in BBL's single entity financial statements, the Investment In PVL will be accounted for by the equity method and that, in determining the gain or loss on the transfer of the manufacturing plant to PVL, BBL will follow the Recommendations contained in Section 3055 of the *CICA Handbook*.

For each Case:

A. Determine the total gain or loss to be recognized by BBL on its transfer of the manufacturing plant and equipment to PVL. In addition, indicate the amount of this gain or loss that can be taken into income at the time of transfer.

B. Determine the value to be recorded in BBL's single entity financial statements as the initial Investment In PVL.

C. Provide the journal entry that would be used by BBL to record the investment transaction.

Assignment Problem Eight - 2

High Venture Ltd. (HVL, hereafter) is a research and development company with 1,000,000 outstanding voting shares that are held by three sponsoring corporations. When the Company was formed on January 1, 2007, Alpha Company invested $1,500,000 in cash in return for 300,000 of the HVL shares and Beta Company paid $2,000,000 in cash for 400,000 HVL shares.

Chi Company provided an office building and the land on which it is situated in return for the remaining 300,000 HVL shares. The land was carried on Chi's books at $450,000, while the building was carried at a net book value of $650,000 and has a remaining useful life of ten years. At the time of the transfer, the fair value of the land was $500,000 and the fair value of the building was $1,000,000. Chi recognizes a gain of $400,000 on the transfer of this property to HVL.

Other Information:

1. During the year ending December 31, 2007, HVL reports a Net Income of $250,000. Included in this figure is a gain of $30,000 resulting from the December 31, 2007 sale of unused equipment to Alpha Company. HVL does not declare any dividends during this year.

2. For the year ending December 31, 2007, and without including any investment income related to HVL, Alpha reports a Net Income of $350,000, Beta reports a Net Income of $675,000, and Chi reports a Net Income of $852,000. Alpha's Net Income includes a $20,000 gain resulting from the sale of merchandise to HVL. This merchandise is still in the December 31, 2007 inventories of HVL. Beta's 2007 Net Income includes a $60,000 gain on the sale of land to HVL at the end of 2007.

3. The joint venture agreement which governs the activities of HVL gives joint control of the operation to Alpha and Chi and prohibits Beta from exercising any influence over the affairs of HVL. It is anticipated that the joint venture will operate with the three investors for a minimum of five years. Other than the joint venture agreement, there is no affiliation of any sort between the three investor Companies. The joint venture agreement covers the terms of all intercompany transactions.

Required:

A. Indicate how each of the three investor Companies should classify their investment in HVL. Explain your conclusions.

B. Indicate the accounting method that should be used by each of the three investor Companies for dealing with their investment in HVL. Explain your conclusions.

C. For Alpha and Chi, calculate 2007 Net Income, including their appropriate share of the earnings of HVL.

Assignment Problem Eight - 3

On January 1, 2007, Saytor Ltd. acquires 35 percent of the outstanding common shares of Saytee Inc. at a cost of $3,066,000. On this date, the Shareholders' Equity of Saytee Inc. was as follows:

Common Stock - No Par	$4,500,000
Retained Earnings	3,700,000
Total Shareholders' Equity	$8,200,000

At this time, all of the identifiable assets and liabilities of Saytee Inc. have fair values that are equal to their carrying values. This means that the $196,000 excess of the purchase price ($3,066,000) over Saytor's 35 percent share of Saytee's book value ($2,870,000) will be allocated to Goodwill. There was no impariment of this Goodwill balance during the year ending December 31, 2007.

The remaining 65 percent of the shares of Saytee are owned by Paytor Ltd. Saytor has no affiliation with Paytor other than their common ownership of Saytee. Saytor and Paytor sign an agreement which provides for joint control over Saytee. All significant operating and financing decisions must be approved by both of the investor companies.

During the year ending December 31, 2007, Saytee Inc. has Net Income of $462,000 and declares and pays dividends of $250,000. For 2007, Saytee does not report any results of discontinued operations, extraordinary items or capital transactions. Other than Saytee's Dividends Declared, there are no transactions between the two Companies during the year. Saytor Ltd. carries its Investment In Saytee using the equity method. Both Companies have a December 31 year end.

The Balance Sheets for the two companies as at December 31, 2007 and the Income Statements for the year ending December 31, 2007, are as follows:

Saytor And Saytee Companies
Balance Sheets
As At December 31, 2007

	Saytor Ltd.	Saytee Inc.
Cash	$ 420,000	$ 270,000
Accounts Receivable	1,340,000	896,000
Inventories	2,370,000	3,560,000
Investment In Saytee (Note)	3,140,200	N/A
Plant And Equipment (Net)	3,170,000	5,708,000
Total Assets	$10,440,200	$10,434,000
Current Liabilities	$ 872,000	$ 462,000
Long-Term Liabilities	2,100,000	1,560,000
Common Stock - No Par	3,700,000	4,500,000
Retained Earnings	3,768,200	3,912,000
Total Equities	$10,440,200	$10,434,000

Note The equity value for the Investment In Saytee would be calculated as follows:

Cost On January 1, 2007	$3,066,000
Equity Pickup For 2007 [35%)($462,000 - $250,000)]	74,200
Investment At Equity	$3,140,200

Saytor And Saytee Companies
Income Statements
Year Ending December 31, 2007

	Saytor Ltd.	Saytee Inc.
Sales	$12,572,300	$8,623,000
Investment Income [(35%)($462,000)]	161,700	Nil
Total Revenues	$12,734,000	$8,623,000
Cost Of Sales	$ 7,926,000	$5,824,000
Amortization Expense	3,116,000	1,326,000
Other Expenses	1,132,000	1,011,000
Total Expenses	$12,174,000	$8,161,000
Net Income	$ 560,000	$ 462,000

Required: Using proportionate consolidation procedures, prepare the consolidated Balance Sheet as at December 31, 2007 and the consolidated Income Statement for the year ending December 31, 2007 for Saytor Ltd. and its investee, Saytee Inc. Your solution should comply with the Recommendations of Section 3055 of the *CICA Handbook*.

Assignment Problem Eight - 4

On January 1, 2007, Sparkling Ltd. (SL) and Raindrop Inc. (RI) formed a new corporation to market water fountains to be sold to local shopping malls. This new corporation will be called Fountain Venture Inc. (FVI). SL and RI have no affiliation with each other except for their joint ownership in FVI. SL and RI signed an agreement which provides for joint control over FVI. All significant operating and financing decisions must be approved by both of the investor companies.

SL's capital contribution is a warehouse with a carrying value of $600,000 and a fair value of $2,000,000. The building is located on leased land, with lease payments that are at current market values. On January 1, 2007, there are 10 years remaining on the lease. This is also the remaining economic life of the building. The lease is transferred to FVI at the time of incorporation. SL receives 48 percent of FVI's voting shares and $500,000 in cash. A gain of $1,400,000 is recorded by SL on the transfer of the building.

RI's capital contribution is $1,625,000 in cash. In return, RI receives 52 percent of FVI's voting shares.

For the year ending December 31, 2007, the single entity Income Statements and Balance Sheets for SL and FVI are as follows:

Income Statements
For The Year Ending December 31, 2007

	SL	FVI
Sales	$5,600,000	$3,600,000
Gain On Sale Of Building	1,400,000	Nil
Total Revenues	$7,000,000	$3,600,000
Cost Of Goods Sold	3,500,000	2,380,000
Amortization Expense	340,000	200,000
Other Expenses	540,000	230,000
Total Expenses	$4,380,000	$2,810,000
Net Income	$2,620,000	$ 790,000

Balance Sheets
As At December 31, 2007

	SL	FVI
Cash And Receivables	$ 2,600,000	$ 670,000
Inventories	5,480,000	1,850,000
Investment in FVI (At Cost)	1,500,000	N/A
Land	990,000	Nil
Building	3,400,000	2,000,000
Accumulated Amortization	(1,010,000)	(200,000)
Total Assets	$12,960,000	$ 4,320,000
Liabilities	$ 850,000	$ 405,000
Common Stock - No Par	7,680,000	3,125,000
Retained Earnings	4,430,000	790,000
Total Equities	$12,960,000	$ 4,320,000

Other Information:

1. During the year ending December 31, 2007, FVI sells merchandise to SL for $400,000. This merchandise had cost FVI $300,000 and 50 percent of it has been resold by SL.

2. During the year ending December 31, 2007, SL sells merchandise to FVI for $1,500,000. This merchandise had cost $1,380,000 and none of it has been resold by FVI.

3. Neither SL nor FVI declare or pay dividends during the year ending December 31, 2007.

Required: Using proportionate consolidation procedures, prepare a consolidated Balance Sheet as at December 31, 2007 and a consolidated Income Statement for the year ending December 31, 2007, for SL and its investee, FVI.

Translation of Foreign Currency Transactions

Introduction To Foreign Currency Translation

The Need For Translation

9-1. Virtually every Canadian business has some involvement with foreign currency translation. Even small enterprises will find themselves occasionally ordering some product from a U.S. supplier and, in most cases, this product will have to be paid for in U.S. dollars. In order to incorporate the cost of this product into Canadian dollar financial statements, the amount must be converted from U.S. currency into Canadian dollars.

9-2. For large, publicly traded companies, such enterprises will not only be engaged in purchase and sale transactions, in many cases they will often go to foreign capital markets in order to obtain needed financing. This financing will usually be obtained and repaid in a currency other than the Canadian dollar, again creating a need to convert the foreign currency into the domestic currency in order to prepare the required Canadian dollar financial statements.

9-3. Further, these larger enterprises often operate in one or more foreign countries. As these operations are usually carried out through a separate legal entity such as a subsidiary, it becomes necessary to translate complete financial statements of this separate entity in order for them to be included in the Canadian dollar financial statements of the parent company.

9-4. While a great variety of business events result in a need to translate foreign currency, they can be categorized into two broad groups:

Foreign Currency Transactions Business enterprises may find themselves engaged in foreign currency transactions. Such transactions would include:

- Buying or selling goods or services with the prices denominated in a foreign currency.
- Borrowing or lending money with the amounts that are payable or receivable denominated in a foreign currency.
- Acquiring assets, including available-for-sale, held-for trading, or held-to-maturity investments, that must be paid for in a foreign currency.
- Entering into foreign currency based derivatives in order to hedge foreign currency balances or anticipated transactions.

In these situations, foreign currency translation is required in order to convert individual assets, liabilities, expenses or revenues into Canadian dollars so that they can be included as an integral part of the financial statements of the domestic enterprise.

Foreign Currency Financial Statements A second situation which requires that domestic enterprises deal with the translation of foreign currencies arises when a Canadian investor company has subsidiaries, significantly influenced companies, or joint ventures that carry on their operations in a foreign country. Generally, the financial statements of these investees will be expressed in the currency of the country in which they operate. Thus, in order to either apply consolidation procedures or the equity method of accounting, the statements of these investees will have to first be translated into Canadian dollars.

Note, however, that there is no need to translate the financial statements of investees that are classified as available for sale, held for trading, or held to maturity. Such investments are carried at amortized cost or fair value, amounts that can be directly translated without translating the financial statements of the investee.

9-5. This Chapter deals with conceptual and procedural issues associated with foreign currency transactions. We will find that the issues associated with translating purchase, sale, and capital transactions are fairly easy to deal with. However, accounting for hedging relationships can be extremely complex.

9-6. In Chapter 10, we complete our coverage of foreign currency translation by dealing with the translation of foreign currency financial statements. This material is made more complex by the fact that it requires a fairly complete understanding of all aspects of GAAP in order to deal with the full sets of financial statements that must be translated.

Foreign Exchange Rate Terminology

9-7. A foreign exchange rate is essentially a ratio of the values of two currencies. As such, they can be expressed in terms of either currency. For example, the statement that the U.S. dollar is worth $1.15 Canadian is the equivalent of stating that the Canadian dollar is worth $0.869 U.S. ($1 ÷ $1.15). While we will usually express rates in terms of the currency's value in Canadian dollars (e.g., US$1 = C$1.15), you should be able to deal with either format and, in addition, be able to convert one format to the other.

9-8. Exchange rates are generally market determined and, because of this, they are constantly changing. A rate quoted on May 1 may be different on May 2. Indeed, for large transactions, the rate at 8:00 a.m. on May 1 may be different at 9:00 a.m. on May 1. Such day-to-day fluctuations reflect the volume of transactions in world-wide markets involving the two currencies that are reflected in a particular exchange rate.

9-9. There are also long-term trends in exchange rates. While there are many factors involved in such trends, the most important is relative rates of inflation. If a country has a very high rate of inflation relative to another country, there will almost certainly be a decline in the value of the currency of the country with the high rate of inflation relative to the currency of the country with little or no inflation.

9-10 The fact that exchange rates change over time means that the accountant has to choose the rate that is appropriate for the translation of each item in the financial statements. While average rates may be used to simplify the translation when a large volume of transactions is involved, the basic choice is whether to translate using the spot rate at the Balance Sheet date or, alternatively, using what is referred to as the historic rate. These rates can be described as follows:

Spot Or Current Exchange Rate The term spot rate is used to refer to the exchange rate at a particular point in time. In accounting literature, the most relevant spot rate is the one that prevails at the Balance Sheet date and, in this context, it is generally referred to as the current rate. For the purposes of translating a December 31, 2007 Balance Sheet, the December 31, 2007 exchange rate would be used as the current exchange rate. Note that, when comparative statements are presented, there would be a different current exchange rate for each Balance Sheet date.

Historic Exchange Rate This term is used to refer to the exchange rate that prevailed at the time a particular Balance Sheet item was acquired (asset) or incurred (liability). If an item of equipment was acquired on January 1, 2007, the historic rate would be the exchange rate that prevailed on that date, without regard to the date of the Balance Sheet in which the item of equipment is included.

9-11. In textbook examples, we generally assume that there is a single exchange rate at any point in time. In the real world, this is clearly not the case. As anyone who has exchanged currencies for travel outside of Canada is aware, financial institutions have different rates for buying a currency vs. selling the same currency. For example, as of today's date, it would cost $116.27 Canadian dollars to buy $100 U.S. dollars. However, if we wished to sell $100 U.S. dollars, we would receive only $115.73.

9-12. As illustrated in the preceding paragraph, at any given point in time, there will be at least two rates for a particular currency — the rate for selling the currency and the rate for buying the currency. These rates are sometimes referred to as the bid and ask rates. In addition, these rates will vary between financial institutions, as well as with the size of the transaction (e.g., better rates are usually available on larger transactions). Further, in less developed countries or countries where the government controls currency exchange, there may be a wide variety of rates depending on the type of transaction involved (e.g., a better rate for export proceeds, as opposed to import costs).

9-13. We will not illustrate the problem of multiple exchange rates in the material which follows. However, you should be aware that our references to a single exchange rate on a particular date are, in fact, a simplification of real world conditions.

Methods of Translation

Alternative Methods

9-14. At various points in time, four different translation methods have been used in Canadian practice. These methods differ in terms of which accounts are translated at current rates and which accounts are translated at historic rates. Briefly described, these methods are as follows:

- **Current/Non-Current Method** Under this method, current assets and liabilities are translated at current exchange rates, while non-current assets and liabilities are translated at historic exchange rates.
- **Monetary/Non-Monetary Method** Under this method, monetary assets and liabilities are translated at current exchange rates, while non-monetary assets and liabilities are translated at historic exchange rates.
- **Temporal Method** Under this method, assets and liabilities that are measured at current values are translated at current rates, while assets and liabilities that are measured at historic values are translated at historic rates.
- **Current Rate Method** Under this method, all assets and liabilities are translated at current rates.

9-15. Until the 1980's, the current/non-current method was the required method in both Canada and the United States. However, it is now recognized to be an inappropriate approach to translation and is no longer used in any jurisdiction. The monetary/non-monetary method is also flawed and, at this point in time, there is no knowledgeable support for, or usage of, this method. However, it is sufficiently similar to the temporal method that some confusion exists as to its applicability. As a consequence, we will provide a brief section that clarifies the difference between these two methods.

9-16. This leaves the temporal method and the current rate method. Depending on the application, both of these methods are conceptually sound and specified as appropriate in *CICA Handbook* Recommendations. However, this Chapter is directed at the translation of foreign currency transactions. For this purpose, the temporal method is the only acceptable method and, reflecting this fact, we will focus our attention on the application of this method.

9-17. The use of the current rate method is limited to situations involving self-sustaining foreign operations. As this material is covered in Chapter 10, we will defer our discussion of the conceptual basis for, and the application of, the current rate method until that Chapter.

Temporal Method

Conceptual Definition

9-18. Before considering the *CICA Handbook* definition of the temporal method, we will give consideration to the concepts underlying this approach. The basic feature of the temporal method is that the exchange rate used for the translation of a particular item is based on the manner in which the item is valued. More specifically with respect to Balance Sheet items:

- Items valued at current values are translated using current exchange rates.
- Items valued at historic values are translated using historic exchange rates.

9-19. Consider the following example:

Example As at December 31, 2007, the records of Trader Inc. indicate the following balances resulting from foreign currency transactions denominated in euros (€):

Accounts Receivable	€ 500,000
Inventories (At Replacement Cost)	€ 600,000
Equipment - Cost	€1,000,000

Assume that on December 31, 2007, the exchange rate between the Canadian dollar and the euro is €1 = $1.55. Both the Inventories and Equipment were purchased on June 30, 2007 when the exchange rate was €1 = $1.50.

Analysis Using the temporal method, the translated value of these balances would be as follows:

Accounts Receivable [(€500,000)($1.55)]	$ 775,000
Inventories [(€600,000)($1.55)]	$ 930,000
Equipment - Cost [(€1,000,000)($1.50)]	$1,500,000

Note that, because they are carried at a current value (replacement cost), the inventories are translated using the current rate at the Balance Sheet date. Because equipment is carried at historical cost under GAAP, it is translated at the historic exchange rate of €1 = $1.50, resulting in a value of $1,500,000. Regardless of future movements in the value of the euro, the cost of this equipment will remain unchanged at $1,500,000.

CICA Handbook Definition

9-20. The definition of the temporal method that is found in the *CICA Handbook* is as follows:

Paragraph 1651.03(c)(i) The **temporal method** is a method of translation that translates assets, liabilities, revenues and expenses in a manner that retains their bases of measurement in terms of the Canadian dollar (i.e., it uses the Canadian dollar as the unit of measure). In particular:

- monetary items are translated at the exchange rate in effect at the balance sheet date;
- non-monetary items are translated at historical exchange rates, unless such items are carried at market, in which case they are translated at the exchange rate in effect at the balance sheet date;

- revenue and expense items are translated at the exchange rate in effect on the dates they occur;
- depreciation or amortization of assets translated at historical exchange rates is translated at the same exchange rates as the assets to which it relates.

9-21. This definition of the temporal method is supported by the following definition of monetary items.

> **1651.03(b)** Monetary items are money and claims to money the value of which, in terms of the monetary unit, whether foreign or domestic, is fixed by contract or otherwise. Future income tax liabilities and assets are classified as monetary items.

9-22. While we prefer the more conceptual approach to defining the temporal method, there is no conflict between that approach and the *Handbook* approach. This *Handbook* approach requires that all monetary items and all non-monetary items carried at market be translated at current rates. As all monetary items are, by definition, carried at current market values, this is the equivalent of the more conceptually based statement that all items carried at current values be translated at current rates.

9-23. An unfortunate result of the *Handbook* approach to defining the temporal method is that many individuals, particularly accounting students, miss the point about translating non-monetary items at current rates when they are carried at market. As noted previously, they confuse the temporal approach with the monetary/non-monetary approach.

9-24. With the focus of this Chapter being on foreign currency transactions, we will not extend our discussion of the temporal method to cover expenses and revenues. However, we would note that a literal application of the temporal method rules to transactions such as purchases would require the translation of each item acquired at the rate which prevailed on the transaction date. When a large volume of such transactions is involved, the following guidance is appropriate:

> **Paragraph 1651.45 Use Of Averages Or Other Methods Of Approximation** Literal application of this Section might require a degree of detail in record keeping and computations that would be burdensome as well as unnecessary to produce reasonable approximations of the results. Accordingly, it is acceptable to use averages or other methods of approximation. For example, translation of the numerous revenues, expenses, gains and losses at the exchange rates at the dates such items are recognized is generally impractical, and an appropriately weighted average exchange rate for the period would normally be used to translate such items.

9-25. In many cases, it will be acceptable to use a simple average based on dividing the sum of the beginning of the period and end of the period exchange rates by two. However, the use of this unweighted calculation is based on two assumptions. First, the purchases or sales of the item being translated must have occurred uniformly over the averaging period, and second, the change in the exchange rate must have occurred uniformly over the averaging period. If either of these assumptions is not appropriate, then some type of weighted average must be used.

CICA Handbook Recommendations And Guidance

Method Of Translation

9-26. With respect to the method of translation for foreign currency transactions and the related financial statement items, the *CICA Handbook* uses three separate recommendations. The first specifies that the current rate must be used at the transaction date:

> **Paragraph 1651.14** *At the transaction date, each asset, liability, revenue or expense arising from a foreign currency transaction of the reporting enterprise should be translated into Canadian dollars by the use of the exchange rate in effect at that date.* [October, 2006]

9-27. While some of the balances that result from these foreign currency transactions will continue to be translated at the historic rate that applied on the transaction date, others will be translated at the current rates applicable to each Balance Sheet date:

> **Paragraph 1651.16** *At each balance sheet date, monetary items denominated in a foreign currency should be adjusted to reflect the exchange rate in effect at the balance sheet date.* (July, 1983)

> **Paragraph 1651.18** *At each balance sheet date, for non-monetary assets of the reporting enterprise that are carried at market, the Canadian dollar equivalent should be determined by applying the exchange rate in effect at the balance sheet date to the foreign currency market price.* (July, 1983)

9-28. As you have likely recognized, the combined effect of these three recommendations is to require the use of the temporal method for the translation of all foreign currency transactions.

9-29. With respect to Paragraph 1651.18, we would note that its application is becoming increasingly common. At an earlier point in time, the only non-monetary item that was commonly carried at its current value was inventories. However, requirements to use current fair values have been increasingly common in *CICA Handbook* recommendations (e.g., investments classified as held for trading or available for sale). This has resulted in additional applications of this recommendation.

Guidance On Identifying Monetary And Non-Monetary Items

9-30. While the *CICA Handbook* provides a definition of monetary items (see paragraph 9-21), it recognizes that the application of this definition can be difficult. To assist with this process, Section 1651 provides the following list of items that are non-monetary and carried at cost:

- Investments in equity instruments carried at cost
- Inventories carried at cost
- Prepaid items
- Property, plant and equipment and accumulated depreciation
- Patents, trademarks, licenses and formulas
- Goodwill
- Other intangible assets (including deferred charges)
- Deferred income
- Share capital (see Paragraph 9-31)
- Revenue and expenses related to non-monetary items, including:
    - Cost of goods sold
    - Depreciation and amortization (including amortization of deferred income)

9-31. With respect to the nature of share capital, preferred shares present a problem in that they may be either monetary or non-monetary, depending on the terms of the issue. Because of this, Section 1651 provides additional guidance as follows:

> **Paragraph 1651.47** Preference shares of a foreign operation held by the reporting enterprise are translated in the same manner as common shares (i.e., at historical rates) unless redemption is either required or imminent, in which case the current rate is used. ...

9-32. While it is not really necessary, the Section also provides specific guidance on future income tax balances:

> **Paragraph 1651.52** Future income tax liabilities and assets are monetary items and, as such, are translated at the current rate.

Exercise Nine-1

Subject: Application Of The Temporal Method

The temporal method is being used to translate the Balance Sheet items listed. For each item, indicate whether it would be translated at the current exchange rate at the Balance Sheet date or, alternatively, at the appropriate historic exchange rate.

1. Accounts Receivable.
2. Inventories (At Cost).
3. Inventories (At Net Realizable Value).
4. Prepaid Rent.
5. Long-Term Notes Receivable.
6. Land.
7. Goodwill.
8. Tax Payable.
9. Estimated Liability For Warranties.
10. Bonds Payable.
11. Future Income Tax Liability.
12. Preferred Shares.

End of Exercise. Solution available in Study Guide.

Exchange Gains And Losses

Nature Of Exchange Gains And Losses

9-33. Both of the translation methods that are in current use translate some Balance Sheet Items at current exchange rates. Under the temporal method, those items that are carried at current values are translated at current exchange rates. In contrast, under the current rate method, all assets and liabilities are translated at current exchange rates.

9-34. As exchange rates are constantly changing, the process of translating an item at current rates means that, even in cases where there is no change in the underlying foreign currency value, there will be changes in the translated balance. In the context of accounting for foreign currency transactions, these changes in value are generally referred to as exchange gains or losses.

9-35. As an example, assume that during the current calendar year, a Canadian enterprise had a liability of 1,000,000 British pounds (£). If the exchange rate increases from £1 = $2.25 on January 1 to £1 = $2.30 on December 31, the translated balances would be as follows:

December 31 Liability (£1,000,000 @ $2.30)	$2,300,000
January 1 Liability (£1,000,000 @ $2.25)	(2,250,000)
Increase In Canadian Dollar Value Of Liability	$ 50,000

9-36. As a liability is involved, this $50,000 increase in the translated balance from $2,250,000 to $2,300,000 is an exchange loss. If the £1,000,000 balance had been an asset, such as a receivable, the increase in value would have been an exchange gain. Correspondingly, when the translation process decreases a liability it creates an exchange gain and when the process decreases an asset, the result is an exchange loss.

9-37. Whether an exchange rate movement will result in a gain or a loss will depend on both the direction of the exchange rate change and whether the rate is being applied to an asset or a liability. The various possibilities are outlined in the following table:

Balance Subject To Translation	Direction Of Exchange Rate Movement (See Note)	Effect On Income
Asset	Increase	Gain
Asset	Decrease	Loss
Liability	Increase	Loss
Liability	Decrease	Gain

Note An example of an increase in the exchange rate would be a change from FC1 = $2 to FC1 = $3.

Required Treatment - Foreign Currency Transactions

Inclusion In Net Income

9-38. We have noted that exchange gains and losses result from translating items at current rates. It follows that, when the temporal method is used, exchange gains and losses will arise on monetary items and non-monetary items that are carried at market. This is reflected in the following recommendation which specifies the appropriate treatment of the gains and losses that are related to foreign currency transactions:

> **Paragraph 1651.20** *An exchange gain or loss of the reporting enterprise that arises on translation or settlement of a foreign currency-denominated monetary item or a non-monetary item carried at market should be included in the determination of net income for the current period.* (January, 2002)

Timing

9-39. This recommendation is clear, both with respect to the presentation of exchange gains and losses on foreign currency transactions (they must be included in Net Income), and with respect to their timing (for the current period).

9-40. We mention the timing issue because, until 2002, the *CICA Handbook* permitted the deferral and amortization of these balances when they were related to long-term monetary items. This resulted in the creation of some very suspect Balance Sheet accounts, usually titled "Deferred Exchange Gain" or "Deferred Exchange Loss".

9-41. Fortunately, the AcSB has removed this provision. It was clear accounts such as Deferred Exchange Gain or Deferred Exchange Loss did not meet the definition of an asset or liability. Given this, their inclusion in the Balance Sheet could not be justified. As the deferral of exchange gains and losses depended on using such accounts, the conclusion that they could not be included in a Balance Sheet meant that there was no longer any possibility of putting off the inclusion of these items in Net Income.

Exception For Available-For-Sale Investments

9-42. While this is not referred to in Section 1651, there is an exception to this general treatment for foreign currency transactions involving investments that have been classified as available for sale.

9-43. You will recall from Chapter 2 that available-for-sale investments are carried at fair value. This means that, if they are denominated in a foreign currency, they would be translated using current rates. This would result in the recognition of exchange gains and losses that would, under the general recommendation in Paragraph 1651.20, have to be included in the determination of Net Income.

9-44. The problem with this is that the changes in the fair value of available-for-sale investments are not included in Net Income. Rather, these changes are recognized as an item of Other Comprehensive Income. Given this, Section 3855, "Financial Instruments - Measurement And Recognition", makes the following recommendation:

> **Paragraph 3855.78** An entity applies "Foreign Currency Translation", Section 1651, to financial assets and financial liabilities that are monetary items in accordance with Section 1651 and denominated in a foreign currency. In accordance with Section 1651, any foreign exchange gains and losses on monetary assets and monetary liabilities are recognized in net income. An exception is a monetary item that is designated as a hedging instrument in either a cash flow hedge or a hedge of a net investment in a self-sustaining foreign operation (see "Hedges", Section 3865). A further exception is that the entire change in the fair value of a monetary available-for-sale financial asset, including foreign exchange gains and losses, is recognized directly in other comprehensive income. This is the same as for available-for-sale financial assets that are not monetary items in accordance with Section 1651 (for example, equity instruments). When there is a hedging relationship between a non-derivative monetary asset and a non-derivative monetary liability, changes in the foreign currency component of those financial instruments are recognized in net income.

9-45. This recommendation covers several issues:

- It reinforces the Paragraph 1651.20 recommendation that exchange gains and losses on financial assets and financial liabilities that are monetary items be included in income.
- It notes an exception to this treatment for monetary items that are designated as hedging instruments in either a cash flow hedge or a hedge of a net investment in a self-sustaining foreign operation. We will deal with this exception in our discussion of hedge accounting, later in this Chapter.
- It requires that the entire gain or loss on available-for-sale investments, including both changes in fair value and exchange gains and losses, be recorded as an item of Other Comprehensive Income. This is the issue that we are considering here.
- It notes that when there is a hedging relationship between a non-derivative monetary asset and a non-derivative monetary liability, changes in the foreign currency component of those financial instruments are recognized in net income. This follows from the recommendation in Paragraph 1651.20 and requires no further elaboration.

Required Treatment - Foreign Currency Financial Statements

9-46. While we will not be dealing with this subject until Chapter 10, you should be aware that, for those foreign operations that are classified as self-sustaining, there is a different treatment of exchange gains and losses. Instead of including these items in the determination of current Net Income, they are recognized as an item of Other Comprehensive Income.

9-47. The reasons for this difference will be fully explored in Chapter 10. However, we note the difference at this point as it will influence our discussion of hedging at a later point in this Chapter. More specifically, there is a particular form of hedge accounting that is required to deal with hedges of this type of foreign operation.

Disclosure

9-48. With respect to foreign currency transactions, the only disclosure requirement relates to information about the amount of any exchange gain or loss that is included in Net Income:

> **Paragraph 1651.37** *The amount of exchange gain or loss included in net income should be disclosed (see paragraphs 1651.20, 1651.24 and 1651.31). An entity may exclude from this amount those exchange gains or losses arising on financial instruments classified as held for trading in accordance with "Financial Instruments — Recognition And Measurement", Section 3855. An entity may also exclude from this*

amount exchange gains or losses on available-for-sale financial assets and cash flow hedges (see "Hedges", Section 3865) *included in any gains or losses removed from accumulated other comprehensive income and included in net income for the period.* (October, 2006)

9-49. This same disclosure requirement is also found in Section 1520, "Income Statement":

Paragraph 1520.03 *In arriving at the income or loss before discontinued operations and extraordinary items, the income statement should distinguish at least the following items: ...*

*(l) The amount of exchange gain or loss included in net income (*see "Foreign Currency Translation", Section 1651*). An entity may exclude from this amount those exchange gains or losses arising on financial instruments classified as held for trading in accordance with "Financial Instruments — Recognition And Measurement", Section 3855. An entity may also exclude from this amount exchange gains or losses on available-for-sale financial assets and cash flow hedges (*see "Hedges", Section 3865*) included in any gains or losses removed from accumulated other comprehensive income and included in net income for the period.* (October, 2006)

9-50. We would note here that, with respect to available-for-sale and held-for-trading investments, Section 3861 requires disclosure of changes in their fair value that occur during the year. When the investments are denominated in a foreign currency, the change in fair value will consist of a gain or loss on the underlying foreign currency value, combined with an exchange gain or loss. The normal practice is not to segregate these two components of the fair value change.

Specific Types Of Transactions

Foreign Currency Purchases And Sales

Conceptual Alternatives

9-51. When a Canadian company buys (sells) goods or services in a foreign country, the transaction will usually give rise to a foreign currency denominated payable (receivable). If the balance remains unpaid (uncollected) at the Balance Sheet date, it will be translated at the current rate of exchange, resulting in an exchange gain or loss that must be recognized.

9-52. Conceptually there are two possible treatments of these gains and losses:

One Transaction Perspective Under this view, when a Canadian company purchases or sells merchandise, the transaction is incomplete until the amount of Canadian dollars required to settle the related payable or receivable is determined. This means that any adjustment of the foreign currency receivable or payable that is required between the transaction date and the settlement date is viewed as part of the cost of the merchandise purchased or the sales price of the merchandise sold.

Two Transaction Perspective Under this alternative view, the purchase or sale of merchandise is viewed as a separate and distinct transaction from the ultimate settlement of the related receivable or payable balance. This means that the merchandise cost or sales price is firmly established as at the date of the transaction and any subsequent adjustment of the resulting receivable or payable is viewed as an exchange gain or loss resulting from the decision to carry exposed foreign currency balances.

9-53. An example will serve to illustrate these alternatives:

Example On December 12, 2007, a Canadian company purchase Inventory in Switzerland for 100,000 Swiss Francs (SF, hereafter). At this time SF1 = $0.94. When the company closes its books on December 31, 2007, the Inventory is still on hand and the Accounts Payable has not been paid. On this later date SF1 = $0.96.

Analysis When the Accounts Payable is translated, there will be an exchange loss of $2,000 [(SF100,000)($0.96 - $0.94)]. Under the one transaction perspective, the $2,000 would be allocated to the cost of the Inventory and would be excluded from Net Income until the Inventory is sold. Under the alternative two transaction perspective, the $2,000 loss would be deducted in the determination of Net Income for the year ending December 31, 2007.

9-54. As you have probably concluded, the one transaction perspective is not consistent with the Section 1651 recommendations on foreign currency transactions. This is specifically noted as follows:

Paragraph 1651.13 Once foreign currency purchases and sales, or inventories, fixed assets and other non-monetary items obtained through foreign currency transactions, have been translated and recorded, any subsequent changes in the exchange rate will not affect those recorded amounts.

Example

9-55. Applying the recommendations of Section 1651 to the example presented in Paragraph 9-53, the following journal entries would be required:

December 12, 2007

Inventory [(SF100,000)($0.94)]	$94,000	
Accounts Payable		$94,000

December 31, 2007

Exchange Loss [(SF100,000)($0.96 - $0.94)]	$2,000	
Accounts Payable		$2,000

9-56. If there are further changes in the exchange rate prior to the settlement of the Swiss Franc payable, an additional exchange gain or loss will be recorded. However, without regard to future movements of exchange rates, the amount charged to Cost Of Goods Sold for the Inventory will remain at $94,000.

Exercise Nine-2

Subject: Purchase Of Inventories In A Foreign Country

At the beginning of 2007, Impar Ltd. has no inventories that were purchased in a foreign currency. On October 1, 2007, the Company purchases inventories on account in Argentina at a cost of 560,000 Argentine Pesos (AP, hereafter). At this time the spot exchange rate was AP1.00 = $0.35.

On November 15, 2007, AP400,000 of these goods were sold for $225,000 in cash. Also on this date, the Company paid AP450,000 of the accounts payable. The spot exchange rate on this date was AP1.00 = $0.36.

At the Company's December 31 year end, the exchange rate is AP1.00 = $0.38. Impar Ltd. carries all of its inventories at cost.

Applying the recommendations of Section 1651, provide dated journal entries to record this information. In addition, calculate the balance for Inventories and Accounts Payable that would be disclosed in Impar Ltd.'s December 31, 2007 financial statements.

End of Exercise. Solution available in Study Guide.

Foreign Currency Capital Transactions

9-57. In addition to purchases and sales of goods and services, Canadian companies often issue securities in foreign capital markets. To the extent that equity securities are issued, the foreign currency amount received will be translated at the spot exchange rate on the date of issue and, in future periods, they will continue to be recorded at that rate. This creates a fairly simple situation in which no exchange gains or losses will arise.

9-58. In contrast, when debt securities are issued in foreign capital markets, the result is monetary balances which must be translated at the current exchange rate applicable to each Balance Sheet date. Once again, a simple example will serve to illustrate the required procedures.

Example - Capital Transactions On December 31, 2007, a Canadian company with a December 31 year end borrows 1,000,000 Foreign Currency units (FC, hereafter). To simplify the calculations, we will assume that this liability does not require the payment of interest. The liability will mature on December 31, 2012, five years after it was issued. Exchange rates and the translated value of the liability at December 31 for the years 2007 through 2012 are as follows:

Date	Spot Rate	Liability In Dollars
December 31, 2007	FC1 = $2.00	$2,000,000
December 31, 2008	FC1 = $2.50	$2,500,000
December 31, 2009	FC1 = $2.50	$2,500,000
December 31, 2010	FC1 = $1.80	$1,800,000
December 31, 2011	FC1 = $1.80	$1,800,000
December 31, 2012	FC1 = $2.25	$2,250,000

Analysis The journal entries required to record the preceding information would be as follows:

December 31, 2007 Issuance Of Debt

Cash [(FC1,000,000)($2.00)]	$2,000,000	
Long-Term Liability		$2,000,000

December 31, 2008 Adjustment

Exchange Loss [(FC1,000,000)($2.50 - $2.00)]	$500,000	
Long-Term Liability		$500,000

December 31, 2009 Adjustment

None required.

December 31, 2010 Adjustment

Long-Term Liability [(FC1,000,000)($2.50 - $1.80)]	$700,000	
Exchange Gain		$700,000

December 31, 2011 Adjustment

None required.

December 31, 2012 Adjustment

Exchange Loss [(FC1,000,000)($2.25 - $1.80)]	$450,000	
Long-Term Liability		$450,000

December 31, 2012 Payment Of Liability

Long-Term Liability [(FC1,000,000)($2.25)]	$2,250,000	
Cash		$2,250,000

Exercise Nine-3

Subject: Foreign Currency Debt

On January 1, 2007, Candor Inc. borrows 585,000 euros (€) from a French bank. Interest at 8 percent per annum is to be paid on December 31 of each year during the three year term of the loan. The principal amount must be repaid on December 31, 2009. Assume that at the time of the borrowing, the exchange rate is €1 = $1.55. It remains at this level until January 1, 2008, at which time it increases evenly throughout the year to €1 = $1.60 on December 31, 2008. It remains at this level until December 31, 2009, when it decreases to €1 = $1.57.

Provide the dated journal entries required to account for this loan during the three year period January 1, 2007 through December 31, 2009.

End of Exercise. Solution available in Study Guide.

Non-Strategic Investments

Introduction

9-59. In Chapter 2, we categorized investments in equity securities as either strategic (subsidiaries, joint ventures, and significantly influenced companies) or non-strategic (held for trading or available for sale). In the case of strategic investments in foreign jurisdictions, including those accounted for by the equity method, it is necessary to translate the complete set of investee financial statements for inclusion in the financial statements of the investor enterprise. The procedures for implementing this process will be covered in Chapter 10.

9-60. In this section we will be concerned with non-strategic investments that have been acquired in foreign jurisdictions. Such investments are usually paid for in foreign currency and, in general, will continue to be traded in markets that use a foreign currency. This means that, in addition to translating the cost of such investments, there may be an ongoing need to translate fair value amounts that are measured in a foreign currency.

9-61. In this section we will give separate attention to held-for-trading investments and available-for-sale investments. While they were not covered in Chapter 2 because they are not usually investments in equity securities, we will consider held-to-maturity investments here.

Held-To-Maturity Investments

9-62. The definition of held-to-maturity investments requires that they have fixed or determinable payments and a fixed maturity amount. This means that they would be classified as monetary and, if they were acquired through payment of a foreign currency, translated at the current rate at each Balance Sheet date.

Example On June 30, 2007, Investok Inc. acquires £500,000 in long-term debt of a British company. At this time £1 = $2.25. On December 31, 2007, when Investok closes its books, the exchange rate is £1 = $2.20.

Analysis The journal entries required to record this information would be as follows:

June 30, 2007

Investment In Bonds [(£500,000)($2.25)]	$1,125,000	
Cash		$1,125,000

December 31, 2007

Exchange Loss [(£500,000)($2.25 - $2.20)]	$25,000	
Investment In Bonds		$25,000

9-63. The $25,000 Exchange Loss would have to be included in the determination of the 2007 Net Income. It would be included in the disclosure of the exchange gains and losses included in income for the year (Paragraph 1651.37).

Available-For-Sale Investments Carried At Cost

9-64. In general, available-for-sale investments are carried at fair value. However, if they are "investments in equity instruments that do not have a quoted market price in an active market", Paragraph 3855.66(c) requires that they be carried at cost.

Example On June 30, 2007, Investok Inc. acquires £500,000 in equity securities of a British company. The investment is classified as available for sale and the shares do not have a quoted market price. At this time £1 = $2.25. On December 31, 2007, when Investok closes its books, the exchange rate is £1 = $2.20.

Analysis The journal entries required to record this information would be as follows:

June 30, 2007

Investment In Shares [(£500,000)($2.25)]	$1,125,000	
Cash		$1,125,000

December 31, 2007

No Entry Required

9-65. This holding of equity securities is a non-monetary asset carried at cost. This means that it would continue to be carried at its cost of £500,000, translated at the historic rate of $2.25. Given this, no entry would be required on December 31, 2007.

Held-For-Trading Investments

9-66. You will recall from Chapter 2 that held-for-trading investments are carried at their fair value. If they are debt securities they would be considered monetary assets. Alternatively, if they are equity securities, they would be non-monetary assets carried at current values. In either case, if they were measured in a foreign currency, they would have to be translated at current exchange rates applicable to each Balance Sheet date.

9-67. The changes in fair value on investments classified as held-for-trading must be included in the determination of Net Income for the period. When the fair values are measured in a foreign currency, the exchange gains or losses resulting from translation at current exchange rates must also be included in the determination of Net Income.

Example On June 30, 2007, Investok Inc. acquires £500,000 in equity securities of a British company. At this time £1 = $2.25. The investment is classified as held for trading. On December 31, 2007, when Investok closes its books, the market value of the securities has fallen to £480,000 and the exchange rate is £1 = $2.20.

Analysis The journal entries required to record this information would be as follows:

June 30, 2007

Investment In Shares [(£500,000)($2.25)]	$1,125,000	
Cash		$1,125,000

December 31, 2007

Fair Value Loss [(£500,000 - £480,000)($2.20)]	$44,000	
Exchange Loss [(£500,000)($2.25 - $2.20)]	25,000	
Investment In Shares [(£480,000)($2.20) - $1,125,000]		$69,000

9-68. The total loss on the shares results from a combination of the £20,000 decline in the fair value of the investments and the $0.05 decline in the exchange rate for the pound. We have presented these two items separately. Since Paragraph 1651.37 (see our Paragraph 9-48) allows this type of exchange loss to be excluded from separate disclosure of the amount of exchange gain or loss included in income, it is likely that the fair value and exchange losses will be presented as a combined amount of $69,000.

Exercise Nine-4

Subject: Held-For-Trading Investments (See also Exercise Nine-5)

On April 1, 2007, Hardin Ltd. acquires 10,000 shares of a Brazilian company for 300,000 Reals (R, hereafter). At this time R1 = $0.55. Hardin classifies the investment as held for trading. On October 1, 2007, the Brazilian company declares and pays a dividend of R1 per share. The exchange rate at this time is R1 = $0.56.

When Hardin closes its books on December 31, 2007, the fair value of the shares has declined to R250,000 and the exchange rate is R1 = $0.58.

On April 30, 2008, the shares are sold for R280,000. At this time the exchange rate is R1 = $0.60.

Provide the dated journal entries required to record this information.

End of Exercise. Solution available in Study Guide.

Available-For-Sale Investments Carried At Fair Value

9-69. As discussed in Chapter 2, available-for-sale investments are generally carried at fair value, the same measurement basis that is used for held-for-trading investments. As was the case with held-for-trading investments, if their value is measured in a foreign currency, this value must be translated using the current exchange rate applicable to each Balance Sheet date.

9-70. There is, however, an important difference between the treatment of fair value gains and losses on held-for-trading investments and the treatment of fair value gains and losses on available-for-sale investments. When an investment is classified as held for trading, these gains and losses are included in the determination of Net Income. In contrast, when an investment is classified as available for sale, these amounts are treated as an item of Other Comprehensive Income.

9-71. This difference in the treatment of fair value gains and losses suggests that a similar difference in the treatment of exchange gains and losses may be appropriate. In our general discussion of exchange gains and losses on foreign currency transactions we noted that, while these amounts were normally included in the determination of Net Income, there was an exception in the case of investments classified as available for sale (see our Paragraphs 9-42 through 9-45). *CICA Handbook* Paragraph 3855.78 requires that exchange gains and losses on this classification of investments be treated in the same manner as fair value changes on these investments. That is, they should be treated as items of Other Comprehensive Income.

Example On June 30, 2007, Investok Inc. acquires £500,000 in equity securities of a British company. At this time £1 = $2.25. The investment is classified as available for sale and the shares are traded in an active market. On December 31, 2007, when Investok closes its books, the market value of the securities has fallen to £480,000 and the exchange rate is £1 = $2.20.

Analysis The journal entries required to record this information would be as follows:

June 30, 2007

Investment In Shares [(£500,000)($2.25)]	$1,125,000	
Cash		$1,125,000

December 31, 2007

Other Comprehensive Income - Fair Value Loss [(£500,000 - £480,000)($2.20)]	$44,000	
Other Comprehensive Income - Exchange Loss [(£500,000)($2.25 - $2.20)]	25,000	
Investment In Shares [(£480,000)($2.20) - $1,125,000]		$69,000

9-72. When the investment is sold, all of the amounts included in Other Comprehensive Income must be reclassified as components of Net Income. If this investment was sold on January 1, 2008 for $1,056,000 [(£480,000)($2.20)], the total debit to Net Income and the total credit to Other Comprehensive Income would be $69,000 ($44,000 + $25,000). The debit to Net Income of $69,000 reflects the total decrease in the translated value of the investment ($1,056,000 - $1,125,000).

Exercise Nine-5

Subject: Available-For-Sale Investments (See also Exercise Nine-4)

On April 1, 2007, Hardin Ltd. acquires 10,000 shares of a Brazilian company for 300,000 Reals (R, hereafter). At this time R1 = $0.55. Hardin classifies the investment as available for sale. On October 1, 2007, the Brazilian company declares and pays a dividend of R1 per share. The exchange rate at this time is R1 = $0.56.

When Hardin closes its books on December 31, 2007, the fair value of the shares has declined to R250,000 and the exchange rate is R1 = $0.58.

On April 30, 2008, the shares are sold for R280,000. At this time the exchange rate is R1 = $0.60.

Provide the dated journal entries required to record this information.

End of Exercise. Solution available in Study Guide.

Hedging Foreign Currency Risk

A Word Of Caution

9-73. Hedging has become a very pervasive activity as enterprises struggle to deal with various types of risk in today's complex economic environment. In many cases it does not require any special accounting treatment beyond that specified in various *CICA Handbook* sections dealing with other issues.

9-74. However, in certain types of situations, it is necessary to use special procedures to ensure that financial statements properly reflect the economic substance of the transactions and events that are taking place. This group of special procedures is referred to as hedge accounting and has been codified in a new *CICA Handbook* Section 3865, "Hedges".

9-75. A complete presentation of hedging procedures, including those specified in Section 3865, would extend far beyond the scope of this text. For example, a book on this subject published by PriceWaterhouseCoopers runs to nearly 600 pages and is not totally comprehensive in its coverage.

9-76. Our goal here is to give you a general familiarity with this subject. We will only deal with hedges related to foreign currency translation. Further, we will only cover a limited number of situations. Finally, we will not provide significant coverage of the techniques required to determine hedge effectiveness. This is an introduction to the subject of hedging. As such, it will not serve as a guide for practitioners who deal with this subject at an advanced level.

Hedging Relationships

9-77. While Section 3865 does not provide a formal definition of hedging, it describes it as follows:

> **Paragraph 3865.02** Hedging is an activity designed to modify an entity's exposure to one or more risks by creating an offset between changes in the fair value of, or the cash flows attributable to, the hedged item and the hedging item (or changes resulting from a particular risk exposure relating to those items).

9-78. Implicit in this definition is the idea of a hedging relationship:

> **Paragraph 3865.07(b)** A **hedging relationship** is a relationship established by an entity's management between a hedged item and a hedging item that satisfies all of the conditions in this Section.

9-79. This is a fairly parochial definition in that hedging relationships exist that are not initiated by management and that do not meet the conditions of Section 3865. As defined here, a hedging relationship is a concept created for accounting purposes. Management identifies, for accounting purposes, a relationship to which it wants to apply hedge accounting.

Hedged Items

General Definition

9-80. Section 3865 defines a "hedged item" as follows:

> **Paragraph 3865.07(c)** A **hedged item** is all or a specified portion of a recognized asset, a recognized liability, an anticipated transaction, or a net investment in a self-sustaining foreign operation, or a group of similar recognized assets, recognized liabilities or anticipated transactions, having an identified risk exposure that an entity has taken steps to modify.

9-81. As is often the case with *CICA Handbook* definitions, several other defined terms are used as part of the description of hedged items. The first of these is "anticipated transaction" which is defined as follows:

> **Paragraph 3865.07(h)** An **anticipated transaction** is any transaction expected to occur in the future that has not yet given rise to a recognized asset or liability.

9-82. Anticipated transactions fall into one of two categories as defined in Section 3865:

> **Paragraph 3865.07(i)** A **firm commitment** is an anticipated transaction that is an agreement with an unrelated party, binding on both parties and usually legally enforceable, with the following characteristics:
>
> (i) The agreement specifies all significant terms, including the quantity to be exchanged, the fixed price, and the timing of the transaction. The fixed price may be expressed as a specified amount of the currency in which an entity measures the items in its financial statements or of another currency. It may also be expressed as a specified interest rate or specified effective yield.
>
> (ii) The agreement includes a disincentive for non-performance that is sufficiently large to make performance probable.
>
> **Paragraph 3865.07(j)** A **forecasted transaction** is an anticipated transaction for which there is no firm commitment.

9-83. As we shall see when we get into the details of accounting for hedging relationships, designating an anticipated transaction as a hedged item is especially problematical. This is because such transactions are not, in general, recognized in the financial statements.

9-84. We would also note that the conditions which define a "firm commitment" are very restrictive. Most anticipated transactions will not qualify for this classification and will have to be considered forecasted transactions.

Foreign Currency Applications

9-85. For purposes of this Chapter, dealing only with hedging relationships that are related to foreign currency risk, our consideration of hedged items will be limited to three items:

- Foreign currency denominated monetary assets and monetary liabilities.
- Anticipated transactions that are denominated in a foreign currency.
- An investment in a self-sustaining foreign operation.

Hedging Items

General Definition

9-86. Section 3865 defines hedging items as follows:

> **Paragraph 3065.07(d)** A **hedging item** is all or a specified percentage of a derivative, or all or a specified percentage of a group of derivatives offsetting a risk exposure identified in the hedged item. All or a specified percentage of:
>
> (i) a non-derivative financial asset;
> (ii) a non-derivative financial liability; or
> (iii) a group of non-derivative financial assets or non-derivative financial liabilities, provided that all non-derivative items in a group are similar;
>
> may be designated as a hedging item only for a hedge of a foreign currency risk exposure.

9-87. This definition indicates that, except in the case of hedging items related to foreign currency risk, hedging items must be derivatives. In the case of foreign currency risk, hedging items can be either derivatives or non-derivative financial assets and financial liabilities. Under this definition, non-financial assets and liabilities cannot be used as hedging items.

Foreign Currency Applications

9-88. A simple example will serve to indicate the types of items that can be used as hedging items related to foreign currency risk:

> **Example** On February 1, 2007, a Canadian company purchases merchandise in Germany for 500,000 Euros (€). The merchandise must be paid for in Euros on May 1, 2007. On February 1, 2007, the exchange rate is €1 = $1.55, resulting in a Canadian dollar liability of $775,000. The company wishes to ensure that exchange rate movements during the period February 1, 2007 to May 1, 2007 do not result in exchange gains or losses on this liability. This could be accomplished in one of several ways:
>
> - **Purchase Of Euros** The company could simply purchase €500,000 in currency on February 1, 2007 and hold this amount until it was needed to extinguish the liability. This simple solution would not be commonly used because the foreign currency does not provide any rate of return over the period in which it is held.
> - **Purchase Of Financial Assets** It will generally be more appropriate for the Canadian company to hedge its position through the purchase of a financial asset denominated in euros. For example, if they were to make short term investments in debt securities which were receivable in euros, this would hedge the €500,000 liability and, at the same time, provide some rate of return on the assets held.
> - **Purchase Of Non-Financial Assets** It would be possible for the company to hedge its €500,000 liability by purchasing a non-financial asset denominated in euros. Such assets as German land, inventories, or equipment could serve in this role. However, the acquisition and disposition of such assets would generally be less convenient than the other alternatives and, in addition, the fact that such assets do not have a fixed euro value could make them ineffective as a hedge.
>
>   In addition, if a non-financial asset was used, it would not satisfy Section 3865's definition of a hedging item. Because of this, hedge accounting could not be

used.

- **Entering A Forward Or Futures Exchange Contract** Perhaps the most convenient and commonly used solution to the problem of hedging the €500,000 liability would be to enter a forward or futures exchange contract to receive €500,000 on May 1, 2007. Under this approach, the hedging goal is accomplished, and no significant investment of funds is required.

9-89. In this Chapter, we will focus on the use of forward exchange contracts as hedging items. However, before specifically dealing with this type of arrangement, it is useful to describe the basic features of derivatives and the accounting procedures that are used for these financial instruments.

Derivatives

Basic Features

9-90. As indicated in the preceding section, various forms of derivatives are the primary type of hedging item. Derivatives can take many diverse forms and their terms can become very complex. Given this, a complete discussion of these financial instruments goes well beyond the scope of this Chapter. However, an understanding of the basic features of these arrangements is essential to an understanding of the material in this Chapter. To ensure that you have this fundamental understanding, we will provide a brief overview of the basic features of derivatives.

9-91. Section 3855, "Financial Instruments — Recognition And Measurement", defines derivatives as follows:

> **Paragraph 3855.19(e)** A **derivative** is a financial instrument or other contract within the scope of this Section with all three of the following characteristics:
>
> (i) its value changes in response to the change in a specified interest rate, financial instrument price, commodity price, foreign exchange rate, index of prices or rates, a credit rating or credit index, or other variable (sometimes called the "underlying"), provided in the case of a non-financial variable that the variable is not specific to a party to the contract;
>
> (ii) it requires no initial net investment or an initial net investment that is smaller than would be required for other types of contracts that would be expected to have a similar response to changes in market factors; and
>
> (iii) it is settled at a future date.

9-92. In somewhat simplified terms, derivatives belong to one of two general families:

Forward And Futures Contracts These arrangements involve a contractual agreement that requires performance from both parties at some future date. A typical example would be a forward exchange contract to exchange Canadian dollars for U.K. pounds. On the settlement date, one party to the contract must deliver Canadian dollars in return for U.K. pounds, while the other party must deliver U.K. pounds in return for Canadian dollars. Such a contract meets the Section 3855 definition of a derivative in that:

- its value changes in response to changes in a specified underlying;
- it requires no initial net investment; and
- it is settled at a future date.

Options Unlike forward and futures contracts, only one party to the arrangement is required to perform. These arrangements give the holder a right to buy or sell some specified asset at a specified price for a specified period of time. For example, assume Sarah Leung pays $120 to acquire a put option on 100 shares of Canac Ltd. at a price of $50 per share for a period of one year. This option gives Sarah the right to sell 100 Canac shares at a price of $50 per share to the writer of the option. Sarah may or may not own the shares at the time she acquires the put.

If the price of the Canac shares is $45 at the option expiry date, Sarah will exercise the option and receive $50 per share. If she owns the shares at this time, she will deliver the shares she owns. If she does not own the shares at this time, she will acquire them at $45 and receive $50 when they are transferred to the writer of the option.

Alternatively, if the price of the Canac shares is $55 at the option expiry date, Sarah can simply let the option expire. The option arrangement does not require her to deliver shares.

This option contract would meet the conditions specified in the Section 3855 definition of a derivative in that:

- its value changes in response to changes in a specified underlying;
- it requires an initial net investment that is smaller than would be required for other types of contracts that would be expected to have a similar response to changes in market factors; and
- it is settled at a future date.

9-93. While forward and futures contracts require that both parties perform, they differ in the manner in which they are entered into:

Forward Contracts Forward contracts are usually customized relationships between parties. These parties reach an agreement that specifies the exact amount of items to be exchanged, as well as the specific date on which the exchange will take place. In general, no consideration is required from the parties that are entering into these contracts. Financial performance is often guaranteed by a letter of credit.

Futures Contracts Futures contracts are exchange traded instruments that have standardized quantities (e.g., silver futures contracts are in multiples of 25,000 troy ounces) and standard delivery dates. Buyers and sellers of futures contracts are required to post a security deposit and to collateralize price movements. These margin accounts protect market participants from credit risk. Gains and losses on the futures contracts are exchanged between the contractual parties on a daily basis through their brokers. This feature is called "mark-to-market".

9-94. The principal advantage of forward contracts is that you can arrange hedges that fit your specific needs. If, for example, you have a €839,500 payable that is due on July 13 of the current year, you can negotiate a forward exchange contract to take delivery of €839,500 on that date. Alternatively, if euro futures contracts were in denominations of €100,000, with settlement on the first day of each month, going this route would require either an inadequate hedging position of €800,000, or an excessive position of €900,000. In addition, you would have to take delivery prior to the July 13 settlement date in order to be able to make the required payment.

9-95. A further advantage of forward contracts is that they do not require an exchange of cash before the settlement date. In contrast, a futures contract would involve receipts or disbursements of cash prior to the time the hedged transaction is realized. This creates a cash flow risk that, in some corporations, could create severe difficulties.

Accounting For Derivatives

9-96. The accounting procedures applicable to derivatives are found in *CICA Handbook* Section 3855, "Financial Instruments - Recognition And Measurement". In that Section, the definition of available-for-sale financial assets specifically excludes derivatives. Further, while derivatives may have fixed or determinable payments, Section 3855 specifically defines derivatives as held-for-trading financial instruments.

9-97. The basic accounting procedures that are applicable to held-for-trading financial assets can be described as follows:

Initial Recognition These assets must be initially recognized at their fair value. In the case of derivatives, this initial value will often be nil.

Subsequent Measurement After initial recognition, held-for-trading financial assets must be measured at their fair value at each Balance Sheet date.

Gains And Losses The gains and losses that result from recognizing the changing fair values for held-for-trading financial assets must be included in the Net Income of the period in which the change occurs.

9-98. As will be discussed at a later point, there may be a different treatment of gains and losses if hedge accounting is applicable. More specifically, we will find that, under certain circumstances, the gains and losses will be treated as an item of Other Comprehensive Income, rather than being included in the determination of Net Income.

Forward Exchange Contracts

Initial Recognition

9-99. As we have indicated, a forward exchange contract is an agreement between parties to exchange specified currencies at a specified exchange rate at a specified future point in time.

Example On January 1, 2007, Sandor Inc., a Canadian public company, enters into a forward exchange contract to take delivery of £100,000 on December 31, 2007 at a rate of £1 = $2.30. On January 1, 2007, the exchange rate is £1 = $2.26.

9-100. As evidenced by the fact that Sandor did not have to provide any consideration to acquire this contract, on January 1, 2007, it has a fair value of nil. This means that no journal entry is required on Sandor's books at the time of entering the contract. It would not be appropriate, under any circumstances, to record a receivable or payable in the amount of the settlement value of the contract.

9-101. You will note that, at the contract date, the forward rate of $2.30 is higher than the spot rate of $2.26, resulting in a premium payment of $4,000 [(£100,000)($2.30 - $2.26)]. The amount of this premium largely reflects interest differences between the two countries whose currencies are being exchanged.

Subsequent Measurement - No Intervening Balance Sheet Date

9-102. At the settlement date of December 31, 2007, the fair value of the contract will be equal to the face value of the contract, multiplied by the difference between the rate that is specified in the contract and the spot rate at the settlement date. For example, if the $2.26 spot rate on January 1, 2007 did not change during the year, the December 31, 2007 fair value of the contract would be a liability of $4,000 [(£100,000)($2.30 - $2.26)]. The entry required to settle the contract would be as follows:

Cash [(£100,000)($2.26)]	$226,000	
Loss On Contract	4,000	
Cash [(£100,000)($2.30)]		$230,000

In practical terms the contract could usually be settled net and this would be reflected in a credit to Cash for the net amount of $4,000.

9-103. If the spot rate changed during the year, the fair value will be more or less than $4,000. For example, assume that on December 31, 2007, the spot rate is £1 = $2.33. The entry to record the settlement of the contract would be as follows:

Cash [(£100,000)($2.33)]	$233,000	
Cash [(£100,000)($2.30)]		$230,000
Gain On Contract		3,000

Subsequent Measurement - Intervening Balance Sheet Date

9-104. In the preceding examples, we have assumed that no Balance Sheet date has occurred during the term of the contract. If this were not the case, we would have to determine and recognize the fair value of the forward contract at that date.

9-105. To illustrate this problem, we will use the example presented in Paragraph 9-99, modified by the assumption that Sandor Inc. has a year end on June 30, 2007 and the exchange rate changes over the term of the contract. On June 30, 2007, relevant exchange rates for that date and December 31, 2007 are as follows:

	June 30, 2007	December 31, 2007
Spot Rate	$2.28	$2.33
Six Month Forward Rate	$2.31	N/A

9-106. The most commonly used approach to determining the fair value of the contract on June 30 would be to take the difference between the $2.31 six month forward rate and the $2.30 rate that is in the contract. This amount of $1,000 [(£100,000)($2.31 - $2.30)] must be discounted to reflect the time value of money. Using an assumed rate of one-half percent per month, the discounted value of the asset would be $971 [($1,000)(.97052)]. Using this value, the required journal entry on June 30, 2007 would be as follows:

June 30, 2007

Forward Contract	$971	
Gain On Contract		$971

9-107. The required entry on the settlement date would be as follows:

December 31, 2007

Cash [(£100,000)($2.33)]	$233,000	
Cash [(£100,000)($2.30)]		$230,000
Forward Contract		971
Gain On Contract [(£100,000)($2.33 - $2.30) - $971]		2,029

As this is the settlement date, the fair value of the forward contract is $3,000 [(£100,000)($2.33 - $2.30)]. This gives a total gain of $3,000 ($3,000 - Nil) and, as we have previously recognized a gain of $971, the remaining gain is $2,029.

Exercise Nine-6

Subject: Forward Exchange Contracts

On November 1, 2007, Lockland Ltd. enters a forward exchange contract to take delivery of €250,000 on April 1, 2008 at a rate of €1 = $1.55. The spot rate of exchange on this date is €1 = $1.53. The Company closes its books and prepares financial statements on December 31 of each year. Exchange rates for the euro on relevant dates are as follows:

	December 31, 2007	April 1, 2008
Spot Rate	$1.54	$1.58
Three Month Forward Rate	1.56	N/A

The present value of $1 to be received after three months, discounted at one-half of one percent per month is $.98515.

Provide the dated journal entries that would be required to record this information.

End of Exercise. Solution available in Study Guide.

Hedge Accounting

Objective

9-108. The goal of entering a hedging relationship is to modify an enterprise's exposure to some type of risk. In many cases, the economic effect of the relationship will be reflected in the financial statements of the enterprise under the normal application of GAAP. However, this is not always the case.

> **Example** A Canadian corporation anticipates buying machinery in France for €1,000,000. While this transaction will not take place for six months, the corporation enters a forward exchange contract to take delivery of €1,000,000 at the time they expect to pay for the machinery.

9-109. Under the normal application of GAAP, the anticipated transaction will not be recognized in the financial statements. However, the forward contract must be recognized at fair value, with changes in this value included in Net Income. This is the case, despite the fact that any gains or losses on the anticipated transaction cannot be recognized. It can be argued that this application of GAAP does not reflect the economic substance of the hedging relationship.

9-110. Hedge accounting is a set of procedures designed to deal with this problem. If a hedging relationship qualifies for hedge accounting, Section 3865 creates exceptions that can be used when the normal application of GAAP does not produce results that reflect the economic substance of the underlying events.

Hedge Accounting Is Optional

9-111. We have stressed that hedging and hedges can exist and not be designated as part of a hedging relationship for accounting purposes. Accordingly, they would be accounted for without the use of hedge accounting. We would also like to emphasize that hedge accounting is never required. Its use is always at the option of management.

9-112. There are a number of reasons that management may choose not to use hedge accounting:

> **Lack Of Need** In many situations, normal GAAP will properly reflect the economic substance of a hedging relationship, without the use of special procedures. As we will see, this is the case when forward exchange contracts are used to hedge foreign currency financial assets and liabilities. In such situations, there is no need to use hedge accounting.
>
> **Failure To Meet Hedge Accounting Conditions** The conditions for using hedge accounting are fairly stringent. Some hedging relationships may not be able to meet these conditions.
>
> **Management Choice** As noted, the use of hedge accounting is optional. Section 3865 does not require its use under any circumstances. Management may decide that its use is not appropriate in particular circumstances or, given the difficulties that can be involved in qualifying for hedge accounting, that qualification is not worth the effort.

Qualifying For Hedge Accounting

9-113. In order for a hedge to qualify for hedge accounting, it must be designated as part of a hedging relationship and carefully documented at the inception of the relationship. If this is not done, hedge accounting cannot be used, even if in economic terms such a relationship exists.

9-114. In addition to designating and documenting a hedging relationship, Section 3865 also requires an ongoing evaluation of the effectiveness of the hedging relationship. Both at the inception of the hedging relationship and throughout its term, there must be an assessment of this issue. While this is not always the case, the procedures that must be applied in this assessment can be very complex. In our opinion, they go beyond the scope of this text.

9-115. Given this, when an example of hedge accounting is presented, we are going to assume that effectiveness is present on an ongoing basis. You should be aware that this assumption removes a significant practical problem. While effectiveness is often easy to demonstrate at the settlement date, ongoing effectiveness may be difficult to obtain. Practitioners cannot afford to ignore this problem.

Types Of Hedge Accounting

9-116. Section 3865 defines two different forms of hedge accounting. In simplified terms, they can be described as follows:

Fair Value Hedge Accounting Under this approach, gains and losses on the hedging item must be included in Net Income. Gains and losses on the hedged item that are attributable to the hedged risk must also be included in Net Income. Fair value hedge accounting can be used when the hedge is a hedge of the exposure to changes in the fair value of:

- a recognized asset or liability;
- an unrecognized firm commitment; or
- an identified portion of such an asset, liability, or firm commitment.

Cash Flow Hedge Accounting Under this approach, gains and losses on the hedging item are treated as items of Other Comprehensive Income, rather than as items to be included in the determination of Net Income. Cash flow hedge accounting can be used when the hedge is a hedge of the exposure to variability in cash flows associated with:

- a recognized asset or liability;
- a forecasted transaction; or
- the foreign currency risk in an unrecognized firm commitment.

9-117. While we will not deal with this issue in this text, when cash flow hedge accounting is used there may be an ineffective component of any gain or loss that arises on the hedging instrument. This ineffective component will be recognized on the same basis as would have been the case if the hedging instrument was not a part of a hedging relationship. For a derivative hedging instrument and for most non-derivative hedging instruments, this means inclusion in Net Income, rather than in Comprehensive Income.

9-118. While these abbreviated descriptions would not be sufficient if we were providing comprehensive coverage of hedge accounting, they are sufficient to deal with the limited number of foreign currency hedging situations that will be covered in this Chapter.

Hedges Of Exposed Monetary Balances

Treatment Without Hedging

9-119. A very common form of foreign currency risk involves monetary balances resulting from purchase or sale transactions.

Example On November 1, 2007, Torcan Ltd. a Canadian company with a December 31 year end, purchases merchandise in Switzerland for 1,000,000 Swiss Francs (SF, hereafter). Assume that, at this time, the exchange rate is SF1 = $0.90 and, as a consequence, both the merchandise and the resulting payable would be recorded at $900,000. On December 31, 2007, the exchange rate is SF1 = $0.92. The merchandise is paid for on February 1, 2008 when the exchange rate is SF1 = $0.95.

9-120. If, in this situation, no hedge of the exposed Swiss Franc liability was provided, Torcan would have to accrue a loss of $20,000 [(SF1,000,000)($0.92 - $0.90)] on December 31, 2007. As it would require $950,000 to pay the SF1,000,000 on February 1, 2008, a further exchange loss of $30,000 [(SF1,000,000)($0.95 - $0.92)] would have to be recorded on this settlement date. The required journal entries would be as follows:

November 1, 2007

Merchandise [(SF1,000,000)($0.90)]	$900,000	
Accounts Payable		$900,000

December 31, 2007

Exchange Loss [(SF1,000,000)($0.92 - $0.90)]	$20,000	
Accounts Payable		$20,000

February 1, 2008

Exchange Loss [(SF1,000,000)($0.95 - $0.92)]	$30,000	
Accounts Payable		$30,000
Accounts Payable ($900,000+ $20,000 + $30,000)	$950,000	
Cash [(SF1,000,000)($0.95)]		$950,000

Hedging With A Monetary Asset

No Hedge Accounting

9-121. Should the company not wish to be exposed to foreign exchange risk, a simple solution would be to acquire a Swiss Franc denominated asset. If we assume that on November 1, 2007 Torcan Ltd. acquires a SF1,000,000 term deposit to hedge its exposure, ignoring the interest that would accrue on the term deposit, the journal entries would be as follows:

November 1, 2007

Merchandise [(SF1,000,000)($0.90)]	$900,000	
Accounts Payable		$900,000
Term Deposit [(SF1,000,000)($0.90)]	$900,000	
Cash		$900,000

December 31, 2007

Exchange Loss [(SF1,000,000)($0.92 - $0.90)]	$20,000	
Accounts Payable		$20,000
Term Deposit [(SF1,000,000)($0.92 - $0.90)]	$20,000	
Exchange Gain		$20,000

February 1, 2008

Exchange Loss [(SF1,000,000)($0.95 - $0.92)]	$30,000	
Accounts Payable		$30,000
Term Deposit [(SF1,000,000)($0.95 - $0.92)]	$30,000	
Exchange Gain		$30,000
Accounts Payable ($900,000+ $20,000 + $30,000)	$950,000	
Cash [(SF1,000,000)($0.95)]		$950,000
Cash [(SF1,000,000)($0.95)]	$950,000	
Term Deposit ($900,000+ $20,000 + $30,000)		$950,000

9-122. Note that, in the preceding journal entries, we have simply applied the normal foreign currency translation rules as presented in Section 1651. We have made no use of the special hedge accounting rules from Section 3865. Despite this, the financial statements will reflect the objective of this hedging relationship — the losses on the hedged item have been exactly offset by the gains on the hedging item. Clearly, there is no obvious need to use hedge accounting procedures in this type of situation.

Exercise Nine-7

Subject: Hedge Of Monetary Liability With A Monetary Asset

On June 30, 2007, Numa Ltd. purchases merchandise in the U.S. for US$275,000. The merchandise must be paid for on January 1, 2008. Also on June 30, 2007, the Company purchases a U.S. dollar certificate of deposit with a maturity value of US$275,000. The certificate matures on January 1, 2008. On June 30, 2007, the exchange rate is US$1 = $1.15. It remains at this level until December 31, 2007, at which point the rate changes to US$1 = $1.20. Numa closes its books on December 31 of each year. The rate is unchanged at US$1 = $1.20 on January 1, 2008.

Provide the dated journal entries that would be required to record the described transactions. Ignore any entries that would be related to interest on the certificate.

End of Exercise. Solution available in Study Guide.

Applicability Of Hedge Accounting

9-123. As noted, in situations involving hedges of monetary assets and liabilities, the objectives of hedging can be achieved without the use of hedge accounting. If fair value hedge accounting was applied, the results would be exactly the same as those presented in the preceding section.

9-124. If cash flow hedge accounting was applied here, the losses on the Accounts Payable would still go into Net Income. However, the gains on the term deposit would go to Other Comprehensive Income. Given the asymmetrical nature of this result, this would be an unlikely application of hedge accounting. However, it could occur if cash flow hedge accounting had been used for the hedge of an anticipated purchase and the term of the hedging item extended beyond the transaction date. At the transaction date, the hedged item could become a monetary item. It is possible that the hedging enterprise would not bother to change their method of accounting.

Hedging With A Forward Exchange Contract

9-125. The normal GAAP for derivatives require that they be carried at fair value. This means that, when they are used as a hedging item, there is no real need to apply hedge accounting. The results would be largely identical, whether no hedge accounting was applied or fair value hedge accounting was applied.

9-126. To illustrate the procedures required in this situation, we will continue with the example first presented in Paragraph 9-119. It will be extended to include the use of a forward exchange contract as the hedging item.

Example On November 1, 2007, Torcan Ltd. a Canadian company with a December 31 year end, purchases merchandise in Switzerland for 1,000,000 Swiss Francs (SF, hereafter). Assume that, at this time, the exchange rate is SF1 = $0.90 and, as a consequence, both the merchandise and the resulting payable would be recorded at $900,000. The merchandise is to be paid for on February 1, 2008.

On November 1, 2007, Torcan also enters a contract to take delivery of SF1,000,000 on February 1, 2008 at a rate of SF1 = $0.92. Relevant rates for the Swiss Franc on December 31, 2007 and February 1, 2008 are as follows:

	December 31, 2007	**February 1, 2008**
Spot Rate	$0.92	$0.95
One Month Forward Rate	$0.93	N/A

9-127. The entries required to record this information are as follows:

November 1, 2007

Merchandise [(SF1,000,000)($0.90)]	$900,000	
Accounts Payable		$900,000

As its fair value is nil at this time, no entry would be required to record the forward exchange contract.

December 31, 2007

Exchange Loss [(SF1,000,000)($0.92 - $0.90)]	$20,000	
Accounts Payable		$20,000
Forward Contract (No Hedge Accounting)	$9,950	
Exchange Gain		$9,950

The undiscounted value of the forward contract is $10,000 [(SF1,000,000)($0.93 - $0.92)]. Using an assumed rate of one-half of one percent per month, the present value of this amount would be $9,950 [($10,000)(.99502)]. It is an asset as it provides the right to acquire Swiss francs at a rate that is less than the current one month forward rate.

As hedge accounting is not being used, this gain on the derivative would have to be given separate disclosure. This is the required treatment under Section 3855. If a hedging relationship had been designated and fair value hedge accounting used, the gains and losses could be netted.

February 1, 2008

Exchange Loss [(SF1,000,000)($0.95 - $0.92)]	$30,000	
Accounts Payable		$30,000
Forward Contract	$20,050	
Exchange Gain [(SF1,000,000)($0.95 - $0.92) - $9,950]		$20,050

As this is the settlement date, the fair value of the forward contract is an asset of $30,000 [(SF1,000,000)($0.95 - $0.92)]. As we have previously recognized a gain of $9,950, the remaining exchange gain is $20,050 ($30,000 - $9,950). In other words, since the rate on February 1, 2008 is greater than the forward rate on December 31, 2007, the value of the forward exchange contract has increased by $20,050 ($30,000 - $9,950) over this period and the asset must be written up.

Accounts Payable ($900,000+ $20,000 + $30,000)	$950,000	
Cash [(SF1,000,000)($0.95)]		$950,000
Cash [(SF1,000,000)($0.95)]	$950,000	
Forward Contract ($9,950 + $20,050)		$ 30,000
Cash [(SF1,000,000)($0.92)]		920,000

9-128. Note the numbers that are involved here with care. We have recognized an exchange loss on the Accounts Payable of $50,000 ($20,000 + $30,000). This has not been fully offset by the total gain on the forward contract of $30,000 ($9,950 + $20,050). The $20,000 difference results from the $0.02 difference between the spot and contract rates at the date that Torcan entered into the contract and reflects the premium rate that was paid to enter the forward exchange contract [(SF1,000,000)($0.92 - $0.90) = $20,000].

9-129. This net outcome would have been the same, without regard to the movement of the rate for Swiss Francs. While the forward contract has terms that are identical to the exposed liability, the gain (loss) on the hedging item will differ from the loss (gain) on the Accounts Payable by $20,000.

Exercise Nine-8

Subject: Hedge Of Monetary Liability With A Forward Exchange Contract (See Exercise Nine-9 for a different version of this Exercise)

On November 15, 2007, Sellor Inc. buys merchandise from an Australian firm for $625,000 Australian dollars (A$, hereafter). At this time, the exchange rate is A$1 = $0.94. The merchandise is to be received and paid for on March 1, 2008.

On November 15, 2007, Sellor Inc. also enters into a forward contract to take delivery of A$625,000 on March 1, 2008, at a rate of A$1 = $0.96. The Company has a December 31 year end. Sellor does not designate a hedging relationship between this contract and the exposed monetary position.

Relevant exchange rate data is as follows:

	December 31, 2007	March 1, 2008
Spot Rate	$0.95	$0.99
Two Month Forward Rate	$0.97	N/A

The present value of $1 to be received after two months at a rate of one-half of one percent per month is $0.99007.

Provide the dated journal entries required to record this information.

End of Exercise. Solution available in Study Guide.

Hedges Of Anticipated Transactions

Applicability Of Hedge Accounting

9-130. Anticipated transactions fall into two categories — firm commitments and forecasted transactions. If either category involves a foreign currency transaction, there will be foreign currency risk. However, as a firm commitment will specify the price at which the transaction will take place, it does not involve risk associated with the foreign currency price that will be paid. In contrast, a forecasted transaction will usually not have a specified price and, as a consequence, will have both foreign currency and price risk.

9-131. With respect to the foreign currency risk in an unrecognized firm commitment, the enterprise can use either fair value hedge accounting or cash flow hedge accounting. If the anticipated transaction cannot satisfy the fairly stringent conditions required for classification as a firm commitment, it will be classified as a forecasted transaction. In this case, only cash flow hedge accounting can be used.

9-132. As we have noted previously, the problem with hedging anticipated transactions is that such transactions are not recognized in the financial statements. This means that, in the absence of hedge accounting, the gains and losses on the hedging item will have to be taken into Net Income without any offsetting gain or loss on the hedged item. In this situation, some form of hedge accounting can be very helpful.

9-133. While fair value hedge accounting could be used here, it is not the common solution. One reason for this is that most anticipated transactions do not meet the stringent conditions required for the transaction to be classified as a firm commitment. The other reason is that fair value hedge accounting continues to include gains and losses on the hedging item in Net Income.

9-134. In contrast, cash flow hedge accounting solves the recognition mismatch by treating gains and losses on the hedged item as Other Comprehensive Income. They remain in this category until the anticipated transaction takes place, at which point they are reclassified, either to an asset value or to Net Income.

9-135. As it is the most commonly used solution in this situation, we will only illustrate the used of cash flow hedge accounting in this Chapter.

Hedge Of An Anticipated Transaction

No Hedge Accounting

9-136. In order to illustrate the issues that are involved in this situation, consider the following example:

> **Example** On October 1, 2007, Ardin Ltd. commits to purchasing merchandise in Germany at a cost of €500,000. At this time the spot rate for euros is €1 = $1.57. The merchandise is to be delivered and paid for on May 1, 2008.
>
> On October 1, 2007, Ardin also acquires a term deposit with a maturity value of €500,000 (ignore the interest that would accrue on this asset).
>
> On December 31, 2007, when Ardin closes its books, the exchange rate has decreased to €1 = $1.55. On May 1, 2008, the rate is €1 = $1.52.

9-137. If Ardin does not document and monitor the effectiveness of this hedging relationship, hedge accounting cannot be used. Assuming this to be the case, and normal GAAP procedures are used, the required journal entries would be as follows:

October 1, 2007

Term Deposit [(€500,000)($1.57)]	$785,000	
Cash		$785,000

December 31, 2007

Exchange Loss [(€500,000)($1.55 - $1.57)]	$10,000	
Term Deposit		$10,000

May 1, 2008

Exchange Loss [(€500,000)($1.55 - $1.52)]	$15,000	
Term Deposit		$15,000
Cash [(€500,000)($1.52)]	$760,000	
Term Deposit ($785,000 - $10,000 - $15,000)		$760,000
Merchandise [(€500,000)($1.52)]	$760,000	
Cash		$760,000

9-138. Despite the fact that the reduced value of the term deposit was mirrored by the reduced cost of the merchandise, losses must be recorded on December 31, 2007 and May 1, 2008. Cash flow hedge accounting can serve to alter this result.

Cash Flow Hedge Accounting Applied

9-139. Returning to the example in Paragraph 9-136, assume that Ardin implements the procedures that are required to use cash flow hedge accounting. That is, they have documented the hedging relationship, they have tested for effectiveness at each Balance Sheet date and, they have concluded that there is no ineffectiveness that needs to be included in income. Given this, the required journal entries would be as follows:

October 1, 2007

Term Deposit [(€500,000)($1.57)]	$785,000	
Cash		$785,000

December 31, 2007

Other Comprehensive Income - Exchange Loss On Cash Flow Hedge [(€500,000)($1.55 - $1.57)]	$10,000	
Term Deposit		$10,000

This amount will be closed to Accumulated Other Comprehensive Income in the December 31, 2007 Balance Sheet.

May 1, 2008

Other Comprehensive Income - Exchange Loss On Cash Flow Hedge [(€500,000)($1.55 - $1.52)]	$15,000	
Term Deposit		$15,000
Cash [(€500,000)($1.52)]	$760,000	
Term Deposit ($785,000 - $10,000 - $15,000)		$760,000
Merchandise [(€500,000)($1.52)]	$760,000	
Cash		$760,000

9-140. At this point, the hedging relationship no longer exists and the amounts that have been charged to Other Comprehensive Income must be reclassified. Paragraph 3865.56 allows this reclassification to be treated either as an adjustment of the cost of the asset acquired in the anticipated transaction or, alternatively, as a direct charge to income in the period that the acquired asset will affect Net Income. Using the former approach, the required entries would be as follows:

Merchandise	$25,000	
Other Comprehensive Income - Reclassification Adjustment ($10,000 + $15,000)		$25,000

9-141. In effect, the exchange losses on the term deposit will become an increase in the cost of goods sold in the period in which the merchandise is sold.

9-142. The alternative treatment would leave the $25,000 in Accumulated Other Comprehensive Income until such time as the merchandise is sold. If we assume that this merchandise is sold January 1, 2009 for $1,000,000, the required entries would be as follows:

January 1, 2009

Cash	$1,000,000	
Sales		$1,000,000
Cost Of Goods Sold	$760,000	
Merchandise		$760,000
Cost Of Goods Sold	$25,000	
Other Comprehensive Income - Reclassification Adjustment		$25,000

9-143. While this alternative treatment is permitted in Canada, it is not required. However, this is the treatment required under U.S. GAAP and is likely to be used by Canadian companies that sell their securities in U.S. markets.

Exercise Nine-9

Subject: Hedge Of An Anticipated Transaction With A Forward Exchange Contract (See Exercise Nine-8 for a different version of this Exercise)

On November 15, 2007, Sellor Inc. anticipates buying merchandise from an Australian firm for $625,000 Australian dollars (A$, hereafter). At this time, the exchange rate is A$1 = $0.94. The merchandise is to be received and paid for on March 1, 2008.

On November 15, 2007, Sellor Inc. also enters into a forward contract to take delivery of A$625,000 on March 1, 2008, at a rate of A$1 = $0.96. The Company has a December 31 year end.

This contract is designated as a hedge of the anticipated purchase of merchandise. Given this, Sellor will use cash flow hedge accounting. Assume that Sellor has tested for effectiveness and found no ineffectiveness that must be included in Net Income.

Relevant exchange rate data is as follows:

	December 31, 2007	**March 1, 2008**
Spot Rate	$0.95	$0.99
Two Month Forward Rate	$0.97	N/A

The present value of $1 to be received after two months at a rate of one-half of one percent per month is $0.99007.

Provide the dated journal entries required to record this information.

End of Exercise. Solution available in Study Guide.

Hedge Of Net Investments In Self-Sustaining Foreign Operations

Application Of Hedge Accounting

9-144. While we will not deal with translating the financial statements of foreign operations until Chapter 10, it is relevant here that, when a foreign operation is classified as self-sustaining, exchange gains and losses are not included in the determination of Net Income. Rather, they are treated as items of Other Comprehensive Income.

9-145. If an enterprise decides to hedge their net investment in this type of foreign operation, there is a problem similar to that encountered with anticipated transactions. Under normal GAAP, any gains and losses on the hedging item will have to be included in the determination of Net Income. This creates a mismatch in that gains and losses on the hedged item will be disclosed elsewhere.

9-146. To deal with this situation, Section 3865 allows the use of hedge accounting, described as follows:

> **Paragraph 3865.58** *A hedge of a net investment in a self-sustaining foreign operation, including a hedge of a monetary item that is accounted for as part of the net investment (see "Foreign Currency Translation", Section 1651), should be accounted for as follows:*
>
> *(a) the portion of the gain or loss on the hedging item that is determined to be an effective hedge (see paragraphs 3865.08 -.45) should be recognized in other comprehensive income (see "Comprehensive Income", Section 1530); and*
>
> *(b) the ineffective portion of the gain or loss on the hedging item should be recognized in net income.*
>
> *The gain or loss on the hedging item relating to the effective portion of the hedge that has been recognized in other comprehensive income should be recognized in net income in the same period during which corresponding exchange gains or losses arising from the translation of the financial statements of the self-sustaining foreign operation are recognized in net income.* (October, 2006)

9-147. In effect, this provision allows the use of cash flow hedge accounting in these circumstances.

Example

9-148. A simple example will serve to illustrate the preceding guidance on hedges of a net investment in a self-sustaining foreign operation.

Example On January 1, 2007, a Canadian company establishes a new subsidiary in France with an investment of €1,000,000. Assume that at this time €1 = $1.55. The subsidiary immediately borrows €700,000 and invests €1,700,000 in a tract of land near Paris. The foreign operation is classified as self-sustaining and there is a possibility that the subsidiary will be sold in December, 2007.

Because of concerns about movements in the euro for the year, on January 1, 2007, the company hedges its €1,000,000 net investment by entering a forward contract to deliver €1,000,000 at €1 = $1.57 on January 1, 2008.

During the year ending December 31, 2007, the subsidiary has no revenues or expenses. At December 31, 2007, €1 = $1.60. At this time, the fair value of the forward exchange contract is determined to be a liability of $30,000.

Analysis For the year ending December 31, 2007, there is a $50,000 [(€1,000,000)($1.60 - $1.55)] exchange gain on the net investment in the self-sustaining foreign operation. This $50,000 will be recorded as an item of Other Comprehensive Income. In addition there will be a loss on the forward contract of $30,000 [(€1,000,000)($1.60 - $1.57)]. This amount will also be recorded as an item of Other Comprehensive Income, partially offsetting the gain on the net investment.

Reduction In Net Investment

9-149. If there is a reduction in the net investment in a self-sustaining foreign operation, Section 1651, "Foreign Currency Translation" provides the following guidance:

Paragraph 1651.31 *An appropriate portion of the exchange gains and losses accumulated in the separate component of accumulated other comprehensive income should be included in the determination of net income when there is a reduction in the net investment.* (October, 2006)

9-150. Going with this is the just cited Paragraph 3865.58 requirement that amounts related to the hedging item should be included in Net Income when the gains or losses on the net investment are included in income. If, for example, the investment in our example were sold at the beginning of 2008, both the $50,000 gain on the net investment and the $30,000 loss on the forward contract would be reclassified from Comprehensive Income to Net Income. For an operating company, the timing of this reclassification to Net Income is a complex issue that goes beyond the scope of this text.

Discontinuance Of Hedge Accounting

9-151. Section 3865 provides guidance on when hedge accounting should be discontinued:

Paragraph 3865.61 *An entity should discontinue hedge accounting when a hedging relationship ceases to satisfy the conditions for hedge accounting. Those conditions cease to be satisfied when:*

(a) the hedging item ceases to exist as a result of its maturity, expiry, sale, termination, cancellation or exercise, unless it is replaced by another hedging item as part of the entity's documented hedging strategy;

(b) the hedged item ceases to exist as a result of its maturity, expiry, sale, termination, cancellation or exercise;

(c) the hedged item is an anticipated transaction and it is probable that the anticipated transaction will not occur by the end of the originally specified and documented time period or within an additional two-month period thereafter (in

rare cases, this period may be extended when extenuating circumstances related to the nature of the anticipated transaction and outside the control or influence of the reporting unit exist);

(d) *the entity terminates its designation of the hedging relationship (see paragraph 3865.28); or*

(e) *the hedging relationship ceases to be effective.* (October, 2006)

9-152. It also provides guidance on the accounting procedures to be used in these circumstances:

a) When a hedging item ceases to exist as a result of its maturity, expiry, sale, termination, cancellation or exercise and is not replaced as part of the entity's documented hedging strategy, any gains, losses, revenues or expenses associated with the hedging item that had previously been recognized in other comprehensive income as a result of applying hedge accounting are carried forward to be recognized in net income in accordance with paragraph 3865.55, 3865.56 or 3865.57.

(b) When a hedged item ceases to exist as a result of its maturity, expiry, sale, termination, cancellation or exercise, any gains, losses, revenues or expenses associated with the hedging item that had previously been recognized in other comprehensive income as a result of applying hedge accounting are recognized in the reporting period's net income along with the corresponding gains, losses, revenues or expenses recognized on the hedged item.

(c) When hedge accounting is discontinued for a cash flow hedge of an anticipated transaction, any gains, losses, revenues or expenses associated with the hedging item continue to be reported in other comprehensive income. When it is probable that the anticipated transaction will not occur within the period determined in accordance with paragraph 3865.61(c), any gains, losses, revenues or expenses associated with the hedging item that had previously been recognized in other comprehensive income as a result of applying hedge accounting are recognized in the reporting period's net income. An anticipated transaction that is no longer probable may still be expected to occur.

(d) When an entity terminates its designation of a hedging relationship or a hedging relationship ceases to be effective, hedge accounting is not applied to gains, losses, revenues or expenses arising subsequently. However, the hedge accounting applied to the hedging relationship in prior periods is not reversed. Any gains, losses, revenues or expenses previously recognized in other comprehensive income as a result of applying hedge accounting continue to be carried forward to be recognized in net income in accordance with paragraph 3865.55, 3865.56 or 3865.57.

Exercise Nine-10

Subject: Discontinuance Of Hedge Accounting

On September 30, 2007, Argent Inc. makes a plans to purchase Argentinian merchandise with a total cost of 260,000 Pesos (P). The merchandise will be delivered on January 15, 2008, and must be paid for on March 1, 2008.

On September 30, 2007, Argent also acquires an Argentinian short-term money market instrument for P260,000. This instrument is designated as a hedge of the forecasted purchase and, because a forecasted transaction is involved, Argent will use cash flow hedge accounting. Assume that no ineffectiveness exists in the hedging relationship.

Argent has a December 31 year end.

On January 4, 2008, Argent decides that it does not need the Argentinian merchandise and cancels the purchase order. Reflecting this decision, the money market instrument is sold on this date for P260,000.

Assume that the relevant exchange rates are as follows:

September 30, 2007	P1 = $0.37
December 31, 2007	P1 = $0.35
January 4, 2008	P1 = $0.34

Provide the dated journal entries required to record the described transactions. In addition, describe how the accounting treatment would differ if Argent had decided to discontinue its hedge on January 4, 2008, but still planned to take delivery of the merchandise on January 15, 2008.

End of Exercise. Solution available in Study Guide.

International Convergence

9-153. The Canadian rules for foreign currency translation are found in *CICA Handbook* Section 1651, "Foreign Currency Translation". The corresponding international standard is IAS No. 21, *The Effects Of Changes In Foreign Exchange Rates*. Differences between these standards will be discussed in the International Convergence section of Chapter 10.

9-154. With respect to hedging relationships, the relevant Canadian standard is *CICA Handbook* Section 3865, "Hedges". The corresponding international standard is IAS No. 39, *Financial Instruments: Recognition And Measurement*. In its *Implementation Plan For Incorporating IFRSs Into Canadian GAAP*, the AcSB has indicated that Section 3865 and IAS No. 39 are converged with one exception. IAS No. 39 permits fair value hedge accounting for a portfolio hedge of interest rate risk. This difference has no impact on the material in this Chapter.

Foreign Currency Translation In Canadian Practice

9-155. Statistics on, and examples of, Canadian practice with respect to foreign currency translation will be found in Chapter 10.

Additional Readings

9-156. In writing the material in the text, we have incorporated all of the relevant *CICA Handbook* recommendations, as well as material from other sources that we felt to be of importance.

9-157. While this approach meets the needs of the great majority of our readers, some of you may wish to pursue this

subject in greater depth. To facilitate this, you will find a fairly comprehensive list of additional readings at the end of each relevant Chapter in our *Guide To Canadian Financial Reporting*.

CD-ROM Note Our *Guide To Canadian Financial Reporting* is available on the CD-ROM which is included with this text.

Problems For Self Study

(The solutions for these problems can be found in the separate Study Guide.)

Self Study Problem Nine - 1

On December 31, 2007, the Jordanian government loans the Canadian Company, Petroteach, 5 million Jordan dinars (D, hereafter) interest-free. This money is to be used to establish a training center for skilled workers in the oil industry. The loan matures on December 31, 2011.

Assume that the relevant exchange rates for the next four years are as follows:

December 31, 2007	D1 = $1.60
December 31, 2008	D1 = $1.90
December 31, 2009	D1 = $1.80
December 31, 2010	D1 = $1.80
December 31, 2011	D1 = $1.50

The Petroteach Company closes its books on December 31 of each year and accounts for foreign currency transactions using the recommendations contained in Section 1651 of the *CICA Handbook.*

Required: Prepare the journal entries that would be required to account for the loan on December 31 of each year to maturity. In addition, calculate the total exchange gain or loss that resulted from having this loan outstanding and paying it off.

Self Study Problem Nine - 2

Candor Ltd. is a Canadian company with a December 31 year end. On July 1, 2007, Candor Ltd. acquires 5,000 shares of a French corporation at a cost of €75 per share. The total cost of the investment is €375,000.

On November 1, 2007, the French company declares and pays a dividend of €1 per share.

When Candor closes its books on December 31, 2007, the fair value of the shares has increased to €78 per share.

On May 1, 2008, all of the shares are sold for €80 per share.

July 1, 2007	€1 = $1.55
November 1, 2007	€1 = $1.54
December 31, 2007	€1 = $1.52
May 1, 2008	€1 = $1.50

Required:

A. Provide dated journal entries to record the preceding information assuming that Candor classifies its investment as held for trading.

B. Provide dated journal entries to record the preceding information assuming that Candor classifies its investment as available for sale.

Self Study Problem Nine - 3

On December 1, 2007, the Canadian Switzcan Company enters into a forward exchange contract to purchase 2,000,000 Swiss francs (SF, hereafter) on March 31, 2008 at a rate of SF1 = $0.90. Assume that the spot rates of exchange on dates relevant to this contract are as follows:

December 1, 2007	SF1 = $0.86
December 31, 2007	SF1 = $0.88
March 31, 2008	SF1 = $0.91

The three month forward rate on December 31, 2007 is SF1 = $0.92. The present value of $1 to be received after three months, discounted at a rate of one-half of one percent per month is $0.98515.

The Switzcan Company closes its books on December 31.

Required: In the following independent Cases, provide the journal entries that would be required on December 1, 2007, December 31, 2007 and March 31, 2008 to account for the forward exchange contract and any other transactions that are included in the individual Cases.

A. On December 1, 2007, Switzcan Company makes a commitment to its Swiss supplier to purchase merchandise on March 31, 2008. The cost of the merchandise is SF2,000,000, it will be delivered on March 31, 2008, and the invoice is payable on the delivery date. Management designates and documents a hedging relationship between the commitment and the forward contract. During the term of this relationship, they test for effectiveness and find no ineffectiveness that must be included in Net Income.

B. On December 1, 2007, Switzcan purchases merchandise from its Swiss supplier at a cost of SF2,000,000. The invoice must be paid on March 31, 2008. There is no designation or documentation of a hedging relationship.

C. On December 1, 2007, Switzcan decides to speculate in foreign currency via a forward exchange contract.

Self Study Problem Nine - 4

On November 1, 2007, the Riskless Company, a Canadian based trading company, sells merchandise to a New Zealand distributor for 5 million New Zealand dollars (NZ$, hereafter). The invoice is to be paid in New Zealand dollars by the New Zealand distributor on March 1, 2008.

To protect itself from foreign currency risk, Riskless enters into a forward exchange contract to deliver New Zealand dollars at a rate of NZ$1 = $0.81. Riskless does not designate or document a hedging relationship between the receivable and the forward exchange contract.

Also on November 1, 2007, the Riskless Company makes a commitment to purchase equipment from a New Zealand manufacturer for NZ$20 million. The equipment is to be delivered on May 1, 2008 and the entire purchase price must be paid on that date in New Zealand dollars.

To protect itself from foreign currency risk on this forecasted transaction, Riskless enters into a forward exchange contract to take delivery of New Zealand dollars on May 1, 2008 at a rate of NZ$1 = $0.83. Management designates and documents a hedging relationship between the commitment and the forward contract. During the term of this relationship, they test for effectiveness and find no ineffectiveness that must be included in Net Income. Given this, they will use cash flow hedge accounting.

The equipment is delivered and paid for on May 1, 2008.

Relevant exchange rates are as follows:

Date	Spot Rate For New Zealand Dollars
November 1, 2007	NZ$1 = $0.82
December 31, 2007	NZ$1 = $0.84
March 1, 2008	NZ$1 = $0.86
May 1, 2008	NZ$1 = $0.88

On December 31, 2007, the two month forward rate for delivering New Zealand dollars is NZ1 =$0.85. Also on this date, the four month forward rate for taking delivery of New Zealand dollars is NZ$1 = $0.87. The present value of $1 to be received in two months, discounted at a rate of one-half of one percent per month is $0.99007. The present value of $1 to be received in four months, discounted at a rate of one-half of one percent per month is $0.98025.

Riskless closes its books on December 31 of each year.

Required:

A. Provide the journal entries required to record the preceding information with respect to the sale, the resulting receivable, and the forward exchange contract to deliver New Zealand dollars. Your answer should include any adjusting entries that are required on December 31, 2007.

B. Provide the journal entries required to record the commitment, the forward exchange contract to take delivery of New Zealand dollars, the delivery of the equipment, and the payment of the invoice. Your answer should include any adjusting entries that are required on December 31, 2007.

Assignment Problems

(The solutions for these problems are only available in the solutions manual that has been provided to your instructor.)

Assignment Problem Nine - 1

The following Balance Sheet items may be recorded in a foreign currency:

1. Cash
2. Inventories (At Replacement Cost)
3. Prepaid Insurance
4. Long-Term Receivables
5. Equipment
6. Patents
7. Future Income Tax Assets
8. Taxes Payable
9. Warranty Obligations
10. Convertible Bonds

Required: Assume that all of these balances relate to foreign currency transactions and will be translated using the temporal method. For each of these balances, indicate whether it will be translated using the current exchange rate at the Balance Sheet date or, alternatively, the relevant historic rate.

Assignment Problem Nine - 2

The Svedberg Company, a Canadian company, begins operations on January 1, 2007. Its only business is the importation of educational chemistry sets from Sweden. The chemistry sets are paid for in Swedish krona (Kr, hereafter). Purchases during the first five years of operation are as follows:

Year	Quantity	Unit Price	Total Price
2007	5,000	Kr 500	Kr 2,500,000
2008	10,000	525	5,250,000
2009	12,000	540	6,480,000
2010	2,000	550	1,100,000
2011	Nil	530	-0- Nil

The Svedberg Company sells the sets in Canada for $200 per set. All of the sets are paid for and sold in the year following purchase. Inventories are accounted for under the first-in, first-out inventory flow assumption.

The Svedberg Company closes its books on December 31 of each of year.

Exchange rate data for the period under consideration was as follows:

January 1, 2007 to December 30, 2008	Kr1 = $.16
December 31, 2008 to December 30, 2009	Kr1 = $.19
December 31, 2009 to December 31, 2011	Kr1 = $.18

Required: Prepare the condensed Income Statements for years 2008 through 2011 that reflect information provided.

Assignment Problem Nine - 3

On December 31, 2007, the Ferber Company, a Canadian company, borrows 3,000,000 Malaysia ringgitt (R, hereafter) from the Malaysian government to finance the construction of a factory. This liability does not require the payment of interest. It will mature in four years on December 31, 2011.

The Ferber Company has a December 31 year end and exchange rates at Balance Sheet dates are as follows:

December 31, 2007	R1 = $0.40
December 31, 2008	R1 = $0.50
December 31, 2009	R1 = $0.30
December 31, 2010	R1 = $0.30
December 31, 2011	R1 = $0.42

The Ferber Company accounts for foreign currency transactions using the recommendations contained in Section 1651 of the *CICA Handbook*.

Required: Prepare the journal entries that would be required to account for the loan on December 31 of each year to maturity. In addition, calculate the total exchange gain or loss that resulted from having this loan outstanding and paying it off.

Assignment Problem Nine - 4

Foret Inc. is a Canadian company with a December 31 year end. On April 1, 2007, Foret Inc. acquires 20,000 shares of a Norwegian corporation at a cost of 50 Norwegian Kroner (NK, hereafter) per share. The total cost of the investment is NK1,000,000.

On October 15, 2007, the Norwegian company declares and pays a dividend of NK0.75 per share.

When Foret closes its books on December 31, 2007, the fair value of the shares has decreased to NK48 per share.

On September 1, 2008, all of the shares are sold for NK47 per share.

Relevant spot exchange rates for the Nowegian Kroner are as follows:

April 1, 2007	NK1 = $0.18
October 15, 2007	NK1 = $0.19
December 31, 2007	NK1 = $0.17
September 1, 2008	NK1 = $0.20

Required:

A. Provide dated journal entries to record the preceding information assuming that Foret Inc. classifies its investment as held for trading.

B. Provide dated journal entries to record the preceding information assuming that Foret Inc. classifies its investment as available for sale.

Assignment Problem Nine - 5

On December 1, 2007, the Hedgor Company, a Canadian based trading company, buys merchandise from a Hong Kong distributor for 2,000,000 Hong Kong dollars (HK$, hereafter). The merchandise is delivered on December 1, 2007. The invoice will be paid in Hong Kong dollars on April 1, 2008.

In order to protect itself from foreign exchange risk, Hedgor enters a forward exchange contract to buy HK$2,000,000 on April 1, 2008 at a rate of HK$1 = $0.17. The Company does not document a hedging relationship between the Accounts Payable and the forward exchange contract.

Also on December 1, 2007, the Hedgor Company receives a commitment from a North Korean customer to purchase merchandise for 500,000 North Korean won (W, hereafter). This merchandise is to be delivered on April 1, 2008 and the entire purchase price must be paid on this date. The Hedgor Company, contrary to its normal sales policies, agrees to accept payment in North Korean won.

In order to protect itself against changes in the exchange rate for the North Korean won, the company enters a forward exchange contract to deliver W500,000 at a rate of W1 = $0.53. The Company designates and documents a hedging relationship between the commitment and the forward contract.

During the term of this relationship, they test the relationship for effectiveness and find no ineffectiveness that must be included in Net Income. Given this, they will use cash flow hedge accounting.

The Hedgor Company closes its books on December 31 of each year.

Relevant data on exchange rates is as follows:

Date	Spot Rate For Hong Kong dollars	North Korean won
December 1, 2007	$.150	$0.51
December 31, 2007	$.165	$0.52
April 1, 2008	$.175	$0.54

In addition to the preceding spot rates, on December 31, 2007, the three month forward rate for receiving Hong Kong dollars is HK$1 = $0.18 while the three month forward rate for delivering North Korean won is W1 = $0.55.

The present value of $1 to be received after three months, discounted at a rate of one-half of one percent per month is $0.98515.

Required:

A. Provide the dated journal entries required to record the preceding information with respect to the purchase of merchandise in Hong Kong, the resulting payable, and the forward exchange contract to take delivery of the Hong Kong dollars. Your answer should include any adjusting entries that are required on December 31, 2007.

B. Provide the dated journal entries required to record the preceding information with respect to the commitment from the North Korean customer, the contract to deliver North Korean wons, the sale of the merchandise, and the collection of the resulting receivable. Your answer should include any adjusting entries that are required on December 31, 2007.

Assignment Problem Nine - 6

Required

In each of the following independent Cases, provide the journal entries required to record the foreign currency transactions described. All of the enterprises involved in these transactions have a December 31 year end. The present value of $1, discounted at a rate of 1 percent per month, for relevant periods is as follows:

One Month	$0.99010
Two Months	$0.98030
12 Months	$0.88745
24 Months	$0.78757

Case One

On November 15, 2007, Martin Ltd. sells merchandise in South Africa for 250,000 South African rands (R, hereafter). On this date, the spot rate for the rand was R1 = $0.15. Payment for this merchandise is expected on March 1, 2008 and, in order to hedge their position, on November 15, 2007 Martin Ltd. enters a forward exchange contract to deliver R250,000 on March 1, 2008 at a rate of R1 = $0.175. Martin does not designate a hedging relationship between the Accounts Receivable and the forward exchange contract. Additional exchange rates are as follows:

Spot Rate - December 31, 2007	R1 = $0.16
Two Month Forward Rate - December 31, 2007	R1 = $0.17
Spot Rate - March 1, 2008	R1 = $0.18

Case Two

On June 30, 2007, Wilson Inc. makes a commitment to buy Swiss merchandise at a cost of 125,000 Swiss francs (SF, hereafter). On this date, the spot rate for Swiss francs is SF1 = $.98. The merchandise is to be delivered and paid for on January 1, 2008. The Company decides to hedge this commitment by entering a forward exchange contract to take delivery of SF125,000 at a rate of SF1 = $1.01 on December 1, 2007. On this date, the exchange rate is SF1 = $.99.

The Company takes delivery of the Swiss francs on December 1, 2007 and purchases a SF125,000 Swiss term deposit that matures on January 1, 2008. This term deposit earns interest of SF1,000 during the the period December 1, 2007 through December 31, 2007. SF125,000 of the proceeds from the maturing term deposit are used to pay for the merchandise on January 1, 2008. The remaining SF1,000 is converted to Canadian dollars on January 1, 2008. The spot exchange rate on both December 31, 2007 and January 1, 2008 is SF1 = $.99.

Wilson Inc. does not use hedge accounting to deal with any of these transactions.

Case Three

On October 1, 2007, Lalonde Ltd. purchases merchandise in Sweden for 800,000 Swedish krona (K, hereafter). Payment for this merchandise is to be made on February 1, 2008. On October 1, 2007, the spot rate for the krona is K1 = $0.190. Also on October 1, 2007, Lalonde enters a forward exchange contract to take delivery of K2,000,000 at a rate of K1 = $0.180 on February 1, 2008.

The spot exchange rate on December 31, 2007 is K1 = $0.170. The one month forward rate on this date is $0.160. The payable for the merchandise and the forward exchange contract are settled on February 1, 2008. On this date, the spot rate for the Krona is K1 = $0.185.

Lalonde does not designate a hedging relationship between the Accounts Payable and the forward exchange contract.

Case Four

On January 1, 2007, Fin Min Ltd. is granted a £1,000,000, interest free loan from one of its British suppliers. The exchange rate at this time is £1 = $2.16. The loan matures on December 31, 2009 and, in order to hedge this obligation, Fin Min enters into a forward exchange contract to take delivery of £1,000,000 on December 31, 2009 at £1 = $2.17. Fin Min does not document a hedging relationship between the liability and the forward contract.

Relevant exchange rates are as follows:

Date	Spot Rate	Forward Rate To December 31, 2009
December 31, 2007	£1 = $2.18	£1 = $2.19
December 31, 2008	£1 = $2.15	£1 = $2.17
December 31, 2009	£1 = $2.30	N/A

The loan is repaid as scheduled on December 31, 2009.

Translation Of Foreign Currency Financial Statements

Introduction

Basic Issues

10-1. In the previous Chapter 9, we provided fairly comprehensive coverage of the concepts and procedures associated with the translation of balances resulting from transactions denominated in a foreign currency. In presenting this material, we had to deal with two basic issues:

- Selecting the appropriate method of translation.
- Determining the appropriate treatment of exchange gains and losses (i.e., adjustments arising on the translation of items at current rates of exchange on each Balance Sheet date).

10-2. With respect to the method of translation, we concluded that items resulting from foreign currency denominated transactions should be translated using the temporal method. As documented in Chapter 9, this view is reflected in the recommendations of Section 1651 of the *CICA Handbook*.

10-3. There are really two aspects related to the treatment of exchange gains and losses. The first issue is whether these items should be included in the determination of Net Income. With respect to the gains and losses arising on the translation of foreign currency transactions, we noted that Section 1651 concludes that these items should be included in that determination.

10-4. Once it has been decided that these items should be included in Net Income, a second issue arises with respect to when this should occur. Until 2002, the *CICA Handbook* required that translation gains and losses on long-term monetary items be deferred and amortized over the life of that item. However, this is no longer the case. Section 1651 now requires that all exchange gains and losses arising from the translation of foreign currency transactions be included in income in the period in which they are measured in the Balance Sheet. It is no longer possible to defer any portion of these gains and losses.

Modified Conclusions

10-5. The translation of foreign currency financial statements is a more complex process than the translation of foreign currency transactions. This complexity, along with additional conceptual issues that arise with certain types of foreign operations, leads to the need to modify our conclusions with respect to the two basic issues described in Paragraph 10-1.

10-6. However, this is not always the case. With investments that are designated "integrated foreign operations", the conclusions that we use for foreign currency transactions are applicable. However, there is another type of foreign operation, designated "self-sustaining foreign operations" in Canada, where standard setters throughout the world have concluded that a different method of translation, as well as a different treatment of exchange gains and losses, is required.

10-7. In addition to the two basic issues that were introduced in Chapter 9, a new issue arises when we translate a full set of financial statements. In translating the various amounts resulting from foreign currency transactions, the items were created within the context of preparing financial statements in Canada using Canadian generally accepted accounting principles (GAAP).

10-8. The situation is different here. In many cases the financial statements of the foreign investee will be prepared using the GAAP that prevails in the jurisdiction in which the operation is located. To one degree or another, there will be differences from Canadian GAAP. The question then becomes whether the foreign currency financial statements should be converted to Canadian GAAP prior to translation or, alternatively, translated as they were prepared in the foreign country without reconciliation with Canadian GAAP.

Approach

10-9. Our approach to this material will be organized as follows:

Accounting Principles As the issue arises with all types of foreign operations, we will deal first with the question of whether foreign currency financial statements should be converted to Canadian GAAP prior to their translation.

Classification Of Foreign Operations As our conclusions on other issues will be influenced by the type of foreign operation, the next section will consider the basis for classifying foreign operations as either integrated or self-sustaining. We will also give some attention to classification based on the functional currency, an alternative approach that is used in both international and U.S. accounting standards.

The Temporal Method Re-Visited We will find that the temporal method is required for translating the financial statements of integrated foreign operations. While the temporal method was covered in Chapter 9, its application to financial statements requires further clarification and this will be provided in this section.

The Current Rate Method For the translation of the financial statements of self-sustaining foreign operations, the current rate method of translation is required. In this section we will discuss the reasons for using a different translation method for this type of foreign operation, as well as the procedures required for the implementation of this method.

Exchange Gains And Losses For reasons that will be explained in this section, exchange gains and losses accruing to self-sustaining foreign operations are not included in Net Income. Rather they are allocated to a separate component of the investor company's shareholders' equity titled Accumulated Other Comprehensive Income.

10-10. Following these sections dealing with the conceptual and procedural issues related to the translation of foreign currency financial statements, we will present a fairly comprehensive example that illustrates the application of these techniques to both integrated and self-sustaining foreign operations.

Accounting Principles

The Issue

10-11. The issue here relates to the idea that GAAP are developed in response to the economic conditions which prevail in the environment where such principles are applied. This is often described as the major justification for the differences between the GAAP that exist in various countries of the world. A simple example of this idea might involve a country in which social customs are such that individuals do not take their debt obligations very seriously and frequently default on smaller amounts. In such a country, it is likely that revenue recognition would be based on cash collections rather than using accrual accounting for revenues as GAAP.

10-12. To the extent that there is validity in the view that locally developed GAAP reflect economic conditions in particular environments, it would follow that the performance of an investee operating in a foreign economic environment could best be measured using the GAAP that have been developed in that environment. In such situations, the foreign currency financial statements of the investee will usually be prepared using the GAAP which prevail in the foreign country. If, as the preceding line of reasoning suggests, the application of these foreign principles results in the most meaningful measure of the performance of the investee, it would suggest that these principles should not be altered before or during the translation process.

10-13. The problem, however, with retaining foreign GAAP in the translated statements of foreign investees is that, under either the equity method or consolidation, the foreign investee's statements are incorporated into the Canadian dollar statements of the investor company. This, of course, would mean that the resulting statements would not be based on the consistent application of a single set of generally accepted accounting principles.

CICA Conclusion

10-14. The AcSB's conclusion is based on the importance of consistency:

> **Paragraph 1651.04** Financial statements of foreign operations are adjusted, if necessary, to conform with accounting principles generally accepted in Canada when incorporating them in the financial statements of the reporting enterprise.

10-15. Note that this view is applicable, without regard to the type of foreign operation whose financial statements are being translated. Also note that, as more of Canada's trading partners move to using international standards, this will be a less important issue.

Exercise Ten-1

Subject: Alternative Accounting Principles

Foree Ltd. is a wholly owned subsidiary of Faror Inc., a Canadian public company. Foree is located in a country that permits the cash basis of revenue recognition. Using this basis, the Company reports revenues of 926,000 foreign currency units (FC). While not recorded in the Balance Sheet, at the beginning of the current year, Foree has Accounts Receivable of FC48,000, while at the end of the year, there is an Accounts Receivable balance of FC22,000. Throughout the year, the exchange rate is FC1 = $0.40.

Determine the Canadian dollar revenues that would be included in the consolidated financial statements of Faror Inc. as a result of its investment in Foree Ltd.

End of Exercise. Solution available in Study Guide.

Classification Of Foreign Operations

Current Canadian Approach

10-16. The *CICA Handbook* defines and classifies foreign operations as follows:

> **Paragraph 1651.03(a)** A **foreign operation** is a subsidiary, division, branch, joint venture or similar type of entity that undertakes and/or records its economic activities in a currency other than the reporting currency of the reporting enterprise. Foreign operations are divided into two categories:
>
> (i) **Integrated foreign operation** — A foreign operation that is financially or operationally interdependent with the reporting enterprise such that the exposure to exchange rate changes is similar to the exposure that would exist had the transactions and activities of the foreign operation been undertaken by the reporting enterprise.
>
> (ii) **Self-sustaining foreign operation** — A foreign operation that is financially and operationally independent of the reporting enterprise such that the exposure to exchange rate changes is limited to the reporting enterprise's net investment in the foreign operation.
>
> In some cases, a foreign entity may contain several distinct operations, some of which are integrated and some of which are self-sustaining.

10-17. In simple terms, an integrated foreign operation would take part in transactions with the Canadian investor company involving sales of goods or services from the foreign country to Canadian purchasers, purchases in Canada of merchandise or other goods to be used in the foreign country, or financing in Canadian capital markets. As there will be actual exchanges of Canadian dollars for the relevant foreign currency, there is real economic exposure to exchange rate risk.

10-18. In similar fashion, a straightforward example of a self-sustaining foreign operation would involve a foreign operation that has all of its transactions in the foreign economy. Sales are made locally, required purchases are made in the foreign country, and financing is obtained through local financial institutions or capital markets. In such situations, there would be no actual exchanges of the foreign currency for Canadian dollars and no real exposure to exchange rate risk.

10-19. Real world situations will rarely be this straightforward and, as a consequence, professional judgment will commonly be required in making this classification decision. This fact, along with a list of factors to be considered, is presented in the *CICA Handbook* as follows:

> **Paragraph 1651.10** Whether a foreign operation is classified as integrated or self-sustaining is dependent on the exposure of the reporting enterprise to exchange rate changes as determined by the economic facts and circumstances. Professional judgment is required in evaluating the economic factors which determine the exposure of a reporting enterprise to exchange rate changes. In making this determination, matters which would be taken into consideration include whether:
>
> (a) there are any factors which would indicate that the cash flows of the reporting enterprise are insulated from or are directly affected by the day-to-day activities of the foreign operation;
>
> (b) sales prices for the foreign operation's products or services are determined more by local competition and local government regulations or more by world-wide competition and international prices and whether such sales prices are primarily responsive on a short-term basis to changes in exchange rates or are immune to such changes;
>
> (c) the sales market for the foreign operation's products and services is primarily outside the reporting enterprise's country or within it;

(d) labor, materials and other costs of the foreign operation's products or services are primarily local costs or whether the foreign operation depends on products and services obtained primarily from the country of the reporting enterprise;

(e) the day-to-day activities of the foreign operation are financed primarily from its own operations and local borrowings or primarily by the reporting enterprise or borrowings from the country of the reporting enterprise;

(f) there is very little interrelationship between the day-to-day activities of the foreign operation and those of the reporting enterprise or whether intercompany transactions with the reporting enterprise form a dominant part of the foreign operation's activities.

10-20. It is the distinction between integrated foreign operations and self-sustaining foreign operations that provides the basis used in Section 1651 for establishing both the appropriate method of translation and the treatment to be given to exchange gains and losses.

Functional Currency Approach - IAS No. 21

Defined And Described

10-21. In general, this book focuses on Canadian accounting standards as presented in the *CICA Handbook*. However, international standards have a different approach to determining the accounting procedures to be used for translating foreign currency financial statements. Given the AcSB's plan to integrate international standards into Canadian GAAP, it is important that you have some familiarity with this approach.

10-22. The IASB approach, which is also used in the U.S., does not classify foreign operations as integrated or self-sustaining. Rather their rules for translating foreign currency financial statements are based on the concept of a functional currency. IAS No. 21, *The Effects Of Changes In Foreign Exchange Rates,* provides the following definition of functional currency:

> **Functional Currency** is the currency of the primary economic environment in which the entity operates.

10-23. This Standard elaborates on this concept as follows:

> **Paragraph 9** The primary economic environment in which an entity operates is normally the one in which it primarily generates and expends cash. An entity considers the following factors in determining its functional currency:
>
> (a) the currency:
> (i) that mainly influences sales prices for goods and services (this will often be the currency in which sales prices for its goods and services are denominated and settled); and
> (ii) of the country whose competitive forces and regulations mainly determine the sales prices of its goods and services.
>
> (b) the currency that mainly influences labour, material and other costs of providing goods or services (this will often be the currency in which such costs are denominated and settled).
>
> **Paragraph 10** The following factors may also provide evidence of an entity's functional currency:
>
> (a) the currency in which funds from financing activities (ie issuing debt and equity instruments) are generated.
> (b) the currency in which receipts from operating activities are usually retained.
>
> **Paragraph 11** The following additional factors are considered in determining the functional currency of a foreign operation, and whether its functional currency is the same as that of the reporting entity (the reporting entity, in this context, being the entity that has the foreign operation as its subsidiary, branch, associate or joint venture):

(a) whether the activities of the foreign operation are carried out as an extension of the reporting entity, rather than being carried out with a significant degree of autonomy. An example of the former is when the foreign operation only sells goods imported from the reporting entity and remits the proceeds to it. An example of the latter is when the operation accumulates cash and other monetary items, incurs expenses, generates income and arranges borrowings, all substantially in its local currency.

(b) whether transactions with the reporting entity are a high or a low proportion of the foreign operation's activities.

(c) whether cash flows from the activities of the foreign operation directly affect the cash flows of the reporting entity and are readily available for remittance to it.

(d) whether cash flows from the activities of the foreign operation are sufficient to service existing and normally expected debt obligations without funds being made available by the reporting entity.

Paragraph 12 When the above indicators are mixed and the functional currency is not obvious, management uses its judgement to determine the functional currency that most faithfully represents the economic effects of the underlying transactions, events and conditions. As part of this approach, management gives priority to the primary indicators in paragraph 9 before considering the indicators in paragraphs 10 and 11, which are designed to provide additional supporting evidence to determine an entity's functional currency.

Paragraph 13 An entity's functional currency reflects the underlying transactions, events and conditions that are relevant to it. Accordingly, once determined, the functional currency is not changed unless there is a change in those underlying transactions, events and conditions.

Application

10-24. Using this concept, IAS No. 21 classifies foreign operations into two categories:

- Foreign operations for which the functional currency is the reporting currency (e.g., a company which reports in Canadian dollars and has a foreign subsidiary for which the functional currency is the Canadian dollar).
- Foreign operations for which the functional currency is different from the reporting currency (e.g., a company which reports in Canadian dollars and has a German subsidiary for which the functional currency is the euro).

10-25. In general, this approach will produce results that will not be different than the current Canadian classification approach. More specifically:

- Those foreign operations of Canadian enterprises that are using the Canadian dollar as their functional currency are the same foreign operations that would be classified as integrated under the current Canadian classification system.
- Those foreign operations of Canadian enterprises that are using a foreign currency as their functional currency are the same enterprises that would be classified as self-sustaining under the current Canadian classification system.

Exercise Ten-2

Subject: Classification Of Foreign Operations And Functional Currency

A Canadian public company has four subsidiaries, each of which is located in a different country. They can be described as follows:

- The **German Subsidiary** is a merchandising firm with 100 percent of both its buying activity and its selling activity within Germany.
- The **Brazilian Subsidiary** manufactures a subassembly that is shipped to a

Canadian plant for inclusion in a product that is sold to customers located in Canada or in different parts of the world.

- The **Swiss Subsidiary** maintains its records in Swiss francs. The subsidiary's vendors and customers are located in France.
- The **U.S. Subsidiary** has its head office located in the United States and keeps its records in United States dollars. The subsidiary manufactures a product in Mexico, with all production being sold and shipped directly to Japan. Financing has been largely provided by borrowing in the United Kingdom.

For each subsidiary, indicate (1) whether it would be classified as an integrated or self-sustaining foreign operation and (2) its functional currency.

End of Exercise. Solution available in Study Guide.

Methods Of Translation

Integrated Foreign Operations

CICA Conclusion

10-26. The *Handbook* notes that for foreign operations, the ultimate objective of translation is to express financial statements of the foreign operation in Canadian dollars in the manner that best reflects the reporting enterprise's exposure to exchange rate changes as determined by the economic facts and circumstances.

10-27. Applying this concept to integrated foreign operations, the AcSB reaches the following conclusion:

> **Paragraph 1651.07** For integrated foreign operations, the reporting enterprise's exposure to exchange rate changes is similar to the exposure that would exist had the transactions and activities of the foreign operation been undertaken by the reporting enterprise. Therefore, the financial statements of the foreign operation are expressed in a manner that is consistent with the measurement of domestic transactions and operations. The translation method that best achieves this objective is the temporal method, because it uses the Canadian dollar as the unit of measure.

10-28. Following this general statement that the temporal method is the appropriate one for translating the financial statements of integrated foreign operations, the following more detailed guidance on the application of this method is provided:

> **Paragraph 1651.22** *Financial statements of an integrated foreign operation should be translated as follows:*
>
> *(a) Monetary items should be translated into the reporting currency at the rate of exchange in effect at the balance sheet date* (a.k.a., current rate).
>
> *(b) Non-monetary items should be translated at historical exchange rates, unless such items are carried at market, in which case they should be translated at the rate of exchange in effect at the balance sheet date.*
>
> *(c) Revenue and expense items should be translated in a manner that produces substantially the same reporting currency amounts that would have resulted had the underlying transactions been translated on the dates they occurred.*
>
> *(d) Depreciation or amortization of assets translated at historical exchange rates should be translated at the same exchange rates as the assets to which they relate.* (July, 1983)

Temporal Method Redux

10-29. While the temporal method was covered in some detail in Chapter 9, the discussion was solely in terms of foreign currency transactions. As we are now dealing with foreign currency financial statements, some additional issues require attention.

10-30. To begin, Paragraph 1651.07 states that the temporal method is the best method because "it uses the Canadian dollar as the unit of measure". This point can best be understood by noting that, in our current accounting model, most non-monetary assets are measured at historical cost. This means that, if you are using the Canadian dollar as your unit of measure, the Canadian dollar value for assets carried at historical cost should not change from period to period.

10-31. The temporal method accomplishes this by translating any balances that are carried at historical values in the foreign currency at the historic exchange rate that is applicable to their time of acquisition.

> **Example** If we acquired land in Germany for 500,000 euros (€), at a time when €1 = $1.40, the land would be initially translated to $700,000 [(€500,000)($1.40)]. Applying the temporal method of translation in future years, the €500,000 balance will continue to be translated at the historic rate of $1.40. This means that the land value will remain at $700,000, a result that reflects the application of historical cost accounting using the Canadian dollar as the unit of measure.

10-32. The other new issue in applying the temporal method is the translation of Income Statement items. The general rule from Paragraph 1651.29 is that revenue and expense items should be translated in a manner that produces substantially the same Canadian dollar amounts that would have resulted had the underlying transactions been translated on the dates they occurred.

10-33. A literal application of this recommendation would, in many cases, result in the need to translate millions of individual transactions, a process that would have costs that could not be justified in the terms of the benefits received. As was noted in Chapter 9, this is not necessary as noted in the following *Handbook* guidance:

> **Paragraph 1651.45** Literal application of this Section might require a degree of detail in record keeping and computations that would be burdensome as well as unnecessary to produce reasonable approximations of the results. Accordingly, it is acceptable to use averages or other methods of approximation. For example, translation of the numerous revenues, expenses, gains and losses at the exchange rates at the dates such items are recognized is generally impractical, and an appropriately weighted average exchange rate for the period would normally be used to translate such items.

10-34. This means that many of the expenses and revenues found in the Income Statement of an integrated foreign operation can be translated at an unweighted average exchange rate for the year. However, this is only appropriate when the following assumptions can be made:

- The item in question occurred uniformly over the period. For example, sales could be translated using the average rate, only if monthly or weekly sales were roughly the same throughout the reporting period.
- The change in the exchange rate occurred uniformly over the year. If, for example, the rate remained unchanged during the first 10 months of the year, followed by an increase of 15 percent in the last two months of the year, use of a simple average for the year would not be appropriate.

10-35. If these assumptions are not appropriate, than translation will require either the translation of individual items or the use of some type of weighted average.

10-36. It should also be noted that the use of an average would not be appropriate for a large transaction that occurred at a particular point in time. For example, dividends would normally be translated using the rate applicable on the declaration date. Note that it is the declaration date, not the payment date, that is relevant for translation purposes. This reflects the fact that this is the point in time when the liability is recognized.

10-37. A final point relates to expenses, gains, or losses that involve items that are translated at historical costs. Examples of this type of item would be as follows:

- **Amortization Expense** This expense would generally reflect the write-off of assets that are carried at historical costs. Given this, this expense would have to be translated at the same historical rate used to translate the assets that are subject to amortization.
- **Cost Of Sales** This expense reflects an outflow of non-monetary items and, given this, translation of the expense would generally require separate translation of the opening inventory (at historical rates), purchases (at the average for the year, provided the purchases occurred uniformly over the year), less the closing inventory (at historical rates).
- **Gains And Losses On Dispositions Of Capital Assets** In general, these gains and losses cannot be translated using a single rate. Rather, the proceeds will be calculated at the current rate of exchange on the transaction date, while the cost of the asset given up will be translated at the historical rate applicable to its acquisition.

Exercise Ten-3

Subject: Temporal Method Income Statement (See also Exercise Ten-4)

Temp Company is a wholly owned French subsidiary of a Canadian public company. It maintains its records in euros. The exchange rate for the current year increased uniformly over the year from €1 = $1.50 on January 1 to €1 = $1.60 on December 31. The Income Statement of this Company for the current year is as follows:

Temp Company
Income Statement
For The Current Year Ending December 31

Sales	€920,000
Gain On Sale Of Land	50,000
Total Revenues	€970,000
Expenses:	
Cost Of Sales	€470,000
Amortization Expense	132,000
Other Expenses	220,000
Total Expenses	€822,000
Net Income	€148,000

Other Information:

1. Sales, purchases, and Other Expenses occurred uniformly throughout the year.
2. All of the Company's non-monetary assets, except inventories, were acquired when €1 = $1.50.
3. The opening inventories of €50,000 were acquired when €1 = $1.53, while the closing inventories of €70,000 were acquired when the rate was €1 = $1.57.
4. The Gain On Sale Of Land resulted from a disposition of land with a cost of €80,000. The sale occurred on December 31 of the current year.

Prepare a translated Income Statement for the current year assuming that the Temp Company is classified as an integrated foreign operation.

End of Exercise. Solution available In Study Guide.

Self-Sustaining Foreign Operations

CICA Conclusions

10-38. We have noted that, with respect to both the translation of foreign currency transactions and the translation of the financial statements of integrated foreign operations, the *CICA Handbook* requires the use of the temporal method of translation.

10-39. We have also discussed the reasons for these conclusions, noting that a basic feature of the temporal method of translation is that it maintains the Canadian dollar as the unit of measure. This feature is best explained by the fact that the temporal method leaves the Canadian dollar value of items that are recorded at historical cost unchanged from period to period. If a €100,000 of Land is translated into $140,000 at its acquisition, it will remain at this $140,000 value for as long as it is held by the enterprise.

10-40. A different conclusion is reached with respect to self-sustaining foreign operations. This conclusion is found in the following recommendation:

> **Paragraph 1651.26** *Financial statements of a self-sustaining foreign operation should be translated as follows:*
>
> *(a) Assets and liabilities should be translated into the reporting currency at the exchange rate in effect at the balance sheet date.*
>
> *(b) Revenue and expense items (including depreciation and amortization) should be translated into the reporting currency at the exchange rate in effect on the dates on which such items are recognized in income during the period.*
>
> ...

10-41. The basis for this conclusion is described in the *Handbook's* discussion of the objectives of foreign currency translation:

> **Paragraph 1651.08** For self-sustaining foreign operations, the reporting enterprise's exposure to exchange rate changes is limited to its net investment in the foreign operation. Therefore, measuring such operations as if they had carried out their activities in Canadian dollars is considered to be less relevant than measuring the overall effect of changes in the exchange rate on the net investment in such operations. The financial statements of the foreign operation are expressed in Canadian dollars in a manner that does not change the financial results and relationships of the foreign operation. The translation method that best achieves this objective is the current rate method, because it uses the currency of the foreign operation as the unit of measure.

10-42. After giving attention to the required procedures under the current rate method, we will provide a more detailed discussion of the conceptual basis for using the current rate method for self-sustaining foreign operations.

Application Of The Current Rate Method

10-43. In its definitions section, Section 1651 defines the current rate method as follows:

> **Paragraph 1651.03(c)(ii)** The **current rate method** is a method of translation that translates assets, liabilities, revenues and expenses in a manner that retains their bases of measurement in terms of the foreign currency (i.e., it uses the foreign currency as the unit of measure). In particular:
>
> - assets and liabilities are translated at the exchange rate in effect at the balance sheet date;
> - revenue and expense items (including depreciation and amortization) are translated at the exchange rate in effect on the dates on which such items are recognized in income during the period.

10-44. The implementation of this definition in the Balance Sheet is very straightforward. As indicated in the definition, all of the assets and liabilities will be translated at the current exchange rate applicable to each Balance Sheet presented. The only problem in the application of the current rate method in the Balance Sheet is related to determining the various components of shareholders' equity.

10-45. As all of the assets and liabilities are translated at current rates, the total Shareholders' Equity balance must also reflect the current rate. However, we will find in the next section that, for self-sustaining foreign operations, exchange gains and losses are not included in income. Rather, they are allocated to the Balance Sheet as a separate component of Shareholders' Equity titled Accumulated Other Comprehensive Income (for companies that have not adopted Section 1530, "Comprehensive Income", this will be titled something like "Cumulative Translation Adjustment" or "Foreign Currency Translation Adjustments"). This means that the translated Shareholders' Equity will be made up of three components which can be described as follows:

> **Accumulated Other Comprehensive Income** This account will contain the net exchange gain or loss that has resulted from the translation of assets and liabilities since the acquisition of the foreign operation. This amount can be either positive (a net gain) or negative (a net loss) with respect to the total shareholders' equity balance.
>
> **Retained Earnings** This balance will reflect the cumulative translated income of the foreign operation, exclusive of exchange gains and losses and reduced by dividends declared.
>
> **Common Shares** As all of the exchange gains and losses have been allocated to Accumulated Other Comprehensive Income, the contributed capital account, Common Shares, will have to be translated at the historic exchange rate applicable to its issue date. This seeming anomaly is the only approach that will produce a total Shareholders' Equity that equals the difference between assets and liabilities when these balances are translated at current rates. It is likely that you will have a better grasp of this point after you have worked through the comprehensive example that is presented later in this Chapter.

10-46. With respect to Income Statement accounts, the definition of the current rate method refers to the use of the exchange rate in effect on each transaction date. As was the case with the temporal method, the use of some type of average will be appropriate for dealing with large volumes of a particular type of transaction. However, this is again conditional on taking into consideration the factors listed in Paragraph 10-34. These factors reflect the need to make assumptions about how the transactions occur over the period, as well as how the change in the exchange rate takes place over the period.

10-47. Also similar to the temporal method, the use of an average rate would not be appropriate for translating large items that occur on a particular date. The most common example of this that you will encounter in the problem material is a dividend declaration. For a significant transaction such as this, the rate on the declaration date should be used.

10-48. The major difference between the temporal method and the current rate method with respect to translating Income Statement items is with those expenses that involve items translated at historic rates under the temporal method. The two most common examples of this would be Amortization Expense and Cost Of Sales when inventories are carried at cost. Under the temporal method, these expenses have to be translated using the historic rates that applied when the items were acquired. In contrast, under the current rate method, these items will usually be translated using an average rate.

10-49. A further example of an Income Statement item involving historic rates under the temporal method would be gains and losses on the disposition of capital assets. You will recall that, under the temporal method the proceeds of disposition are translated at the current rate on the transaction date, while the cost of the asset is translated at the applicable historic rate. In contrast, under the current rate method, both the proceeds and the cost would be translated at the current rate on the transaction date.

Exercise Ten-4

Subject: Current Rate Method Income Statement (See also Exercise Ten-3)

Temp Company is a wholly owned French subsidiary of a Canadian public company. It maintains its records in euros. The exchange rate for the current year increased uniformly over the year from €1 = $1.50 on January 1 to €1 = $1.60 on December 31. The Income Statement of this Company for the current year is as follows:

Temp Company
Income Statement
For The Current Year Ending December 31

Sales	€920,000
Gain On Sale Of Land	50,000
Total Revenues	€970,000
Expenses:	
Cost Of Sales	€470,000
Amortization Expense	132,000
Other Expenses	220,000
Total Expenses	€822,000
Net Income	€148,000

Other Information:

1. Sales, purchases, and Other Expenses occurred uniformly throughout the year.
2. All of the Company's non-monetary assets, except inventories, were acquired when €1 = $1.50.
3. The opening inventories of €50,000 were acquired when €1 = $1.53, while the closing inventories of €70,000 were acquired when the rate was €1 = $1.57.
4. The Gain On Sale Of Land resulted from a disposition of land with a cost of €80,000. The sale occurred on December 31 of the current year.

Prepare a translated Income Statement for the current year assuming that the Temp Company is classified as a self-sustaining foreign operation.

End of Exercise. Solution available in Study Guide.

Why Self-Sustaining Companies Use The Current Rate Method

10-50. To this point, we have presented the recommendation requiring the use of the current rate method for self-sustaining foreign operations and discussed the implementation of this method. We have not, however, explained the basis for using a different method of translation for this type of operation.

10-51. For all purposes other than the translation of the financial statements of self-sustaining foreign operations, GAAP requires the use of the temporal method. It is a logical method that maintains the Canadian dollar as the unit of measure and there are, in fact, some analysts who believe it should be the method used in all foreign currency translation situations.

10-52. There is, however, a problem with the use of the temporal method in the translation of foreign currency financial statements. Because this method translates some assets and liabilities at current exchange rates and other assets and liabilities at historic exchange rates, the temporal method consistently alters - some would say distorts - economic relationships that were present in the foreign currency financial statements. A simple example will clarify this point:

Example On January 1, 2007, a Canadian Company establishes a subsidiary in France by investing 3,000,000 euros (€) at a time when the exchange rate was €1 = $1.50. On this same date, the subsidiary borrows an additional €3,000,000 and invests the entire €6,000,000 in Land. The resulting foreign currency Balance Sheet as at January 1, 2007 would be as follows:

Balance Sheet
As At January 1, 2007 (€)

Land	€6,000,000
Liabilities	€3,000,000
Shareholders' Equity	3,000,000
Total Equities	€6,000,000

Using either the temporal or the current rate method of translation, the translated Balance Sheet on this date would be as follows:

Balance Sheet
As At January 1, 2007 ($)

Land (At $1.50)	$9,000,000
Liabilities (At $1.50)	$4,500,000
Shareholders' Equity (At $1.50)	4,500,000
Total Equities	$9,000,000

During the year ending December 31, 2007, the subsidiary has no additional transactions subsequent to the borrowing and the purchase of land. As there is no economic activity during this year, the December 31 euro Balance Sheet would be the same as the January 1 Balance Sheet. However, if we assume that the exchange rate goes to €1 = $1.60, the translated Balance Sheet will vary, depending on whether the temporal or the current rate method is used. The two alternative Balance Sheets are as follows:

Balance Sheet
As At December 31, 2007 ($)

	Temporal	Current Rate
Land (At $1.50 And $1.60)	$9,000,000	$9,600,000
Liabilities (At $1.60)	$4,800,000	$4,800,000
Shareholders' Equity (As A Residual)	4,200,000	4,800,000
Total Equities	$9,000,000	$9,600,000

10-53. A significant economic relationship that is often considered by financial statement users is the percentage of debt to total equities. In the untranslated Balance Sheet, this relationship is 50 percent (€3,000,000 ÷ €6,000,000). When the current rate method is used, this 50 percent relationship is maintained ($4,800,000 ÷ $9,600,000).

10-54. In contrast, when the temporal method is used, this relationship is increased to 53.3 percent ($4,800,000 ÷ $9,000,000). The fact that this method retains the historic rate for the translation of the Land and, at the same time, uses the current rate to translate the monetary Liabilities, results in a Balance Sheet that makes the subsidiary appear to be a more heavily leveraged, and thereby riskier, enterprise.

10-55. This result is considered appropriate when there is real exposure to exchange rate risk, as could be the case with an integrated foreign operation. If the euro debt will have to be paid from revenues generated by sales in Canada that are paid for in Canadian dollars, the increased value of the debt relative to the translated value of the land is a real concern.

10-56. However, if we are dealing with a self-sustaining foreign operation, with revenues generated in euros, expenses are paid for in euros, and financing obtained in euros, there is no real foreign exchange risk. This would suggest that the current rate method, which uses the euro as the unit of measure, does a better job of measuring the performance of the foreign operation.

10-57. This is the basis for requiring the use of the current rate method for self-sustaining foreign operations. As such investees are, by definition, carrying on their operations in the relevant foreign currency, it is appropriate that the foreign currency be used as the unit of measure. By using this method, all of the economic relationships (e.g., debt to equity or gross margin on sales) remain unchanged by the translation process. If the operation has a 10 percent rate of return on assets in the foreign currency financial statements, that 10 percent rate of return will be maintained through the translation process.

Self-Sustaining Foreign Operations In Highly Inflationary Economies

10-58. In general, Paragraph 1651.26 requires that the current rate method be used to translate the financial statements of self-sustaining foreign operations. There is an exception to this, however, when the self-sustaining foreign operation is in a highly inflationary economy. This is covered in the last component of that recommendation as follows: (repeated in its entirety here for your convenience):

> **Paragraph 1651.26** *Financial statements of a self-sustaining foreign operation should be translated as follows:*
>
> *(a) Assets and liabilities should be translated into the reporting currency at the exchange rate in effect at the balance sheet date.*
>
> *(b) Revenue and expense items (including depreciation and amortization) should be translated into the reporting currency at the exchange rate in effect on the dates on which such items are recognized in income during the period.*
>
> *When the economic environment of the foreign operation is highly inflationary relative to that of the reporting enterprise, financial statements should be translated in the manner indicated in paragraph 1651.22.* (July, 1983) [**Byrd/Chen Note**: Paragraph 1651.22 describes the temporal method.]

10-59. The problem here is that the current rate method of translation that is generally required by Paragraph 1651.26, uses the foreign currency as the unit of measure. If that currency is rapidly losing value because of a high rate of inflation, it may not be an appropriate unit of measure. As an illustration of this problem, consider the following example:

> **Example** A self-sustaining foreign operation acquires Land for 500,000 Foreign Currency Units (FC, hereafter) at a time when FC1 = $1.00. During the following year, the local economy experiences a 1000 percent inflation. As would be expected, the exchange rate falls to FC1 = $0.10.

10-60. When the land was acquired, its translated value would have been $500,000 [(FC500,000)($1.00)]. If we continue to use the current rate method of translation, after one year, the translated value would have fallen to $50,000 [(FC500,000)($0.10)]. This approach would have introduced a degree of instability into the translated figures that was found unacceptable by the AcSB.

10-61. As a consequence, they require the use of the temporal method for self-sustaining foreign operations when they operate in an economic environment that is highly inflationary. Stated alternatively, when a foreign currency is subject to high rates of inflation, it is not an appropriate unit of measure and, as a consequence, the Canadian dollar should be used as the unit of measure.

10-62. We will find in the Section of this Chapter that deals with exchange gains and losses that, in general, self-sustaining operations do not include exchange gains and losses in Net Income. However, as is the case with the method of translation, when the self-sustaining foreign operation is in a highly inflationary economic environment, the rules change. Self-sustaining foreign operations located in such economies must include their exchange gains and losses in Net Income.

10-63. While the *CICA Handbook* offers no guidance on what constitutes a highly inflationary economic environment, in the U.S., Statement Of Financial Accounting Standards No. 52, "Foreign Currency Translation", suggests a guideline of 100 percent or more over a three year period. In the absence of *Handbook* guidance, it is likely that this guideline is being used in Canada.

Exchange Gains And Losses

Integrated Foreign Operations

CICA Handbook Requirements

10-64. In Chapter 9, we noted that exchange gains and losses arising on foreign currency transactions should be included in income as per the following recommendation:

> **Paragraph 1651.20** *An exchange gain or loss of the reporting enterprise that arises on translation or settlement of a foreign currency-denominated monetary item or a non-monetary item carried at market should be included in the determination of net income for the current period.* (January, 2002)

10-65. As was the case with the choice of translation methods, the exchange gains and losses of integrated foreign operations will be dealt with in the same manner as the translation gains and losses that arise on the translation of foreign currency transactions. This requirement is reflected in the following recommendation:

> **Paragraph 1651.24** *Exchange gains and losses arising on the translation of financial statements of an integrated foreign operation should be accounted for in accordance with paragraph 1651.20.* (July, 1983)

10-66. This recommendation reflects the fact that, because of their nature, integrated foreign operations will be involved in actual exchanges of currencies. Given this, the requirement that exchange gains and losses be included in Net Income is appropriate.

Self-Sustaining Foreign Operations

CICA Handbook Requirements

10-67. The *CICA Handbook* requires the following treatment of exchange gains and losses arising on the translation of the financial statements of a self-sustaining foreign operation:

> **Paragraph 1651.29** *Exchange gains and losses arising from the translation of the financial statements of a self-sustaining foreign operation should be recognized in a separate component of other comprehensive income, except when the economic environment of the foreign operation is highly inflationary relative to that of the reporting enterprise, in which case such exchange gains and losses should be treated in accordance with paragraph 1651.20.* (October, 2006)

10-68. Instead of including exchange gains and losses in Net Income as we did in the case of integrated foreign operations, self-sustaining foreign operations must present them as items of Other Comprehensive Income in the financial statement where this information is presented.

10-69. At the end of each accounting period, the item of Other Comprehensive Income will be closed to a separate Shareholders' Equity account, typically titled Accumulated Other Comprehensive Income. Section 1651 has a separate disclosure requirement for this balance:

Paragraph 1651.32 *Disclosure should be made of the significant elements that give rise to changes in the exchange gains and losses accumulated in the separate component of accumulated other comprehensive income during the period.* (July, 1983)

Why Exchange Gains And Losses Go To Comprehensive Income

10-70. As was the case with the selection of a translation method, the exchange gains and losses resulting from the translation of the financial statements of self-sustaining foreign operations are treated differently from other exchange gains and losses. Instead of being included in Net Income, they are excluded from that total and presented as a component of Other Comprehensive Income. A simple example can be used to why this approach is used.

> **Example** A French subsidiary of a Canadian company borrows €1,000,000 when the exchange rate is €1 = $1.40. This results in a translated value of $1,400,000. If the exchange rate goes to €1 = $1.50, the new translated value will be $1,500,000.

10-71. If this French subsidiary was an integrated foreign operation selling its product in Canada, it would have to use its Canadian dollar revenues to purchase the €1,000,000 required to repay the loan. In this case, there is clearly an out-of-pocket loss of $100,000. In contrast, if this was a self-sustaining foreign operation selling its product in France, the euro revenues could be used to repay the loan. This means that there would be no exchange of currencies and, more importantly, no real economic loss.

10-72. As, in general, self-sustaining foreign operations tend to operate largely in the foreign currency of the country in which they reside, exchanges of currency do not occur, resulting in the conclusion that such companies do not suffer real economic losses as the result of movements in exchange rates. This provides the basis for allocating these amounts to Comprehensive Income, without inclusion in Net Income.

Exception For Highly Inflationary Environments

10-73. As was the case when selecting a method of translation, the *CICA Handbook* makes an exception for self-sustaining foreign operations that are located in highly inflationary economic environments. The gains and losses of operations located in such environments must be included in Net Income, rather than being presented as an item of Other Comprehensive Income.

Reduction In Net Investment

10-74. When there is a partial or complete reduction in an enterprise's net investment in a self-sustaining foreign operation, a proportionate part of the relevant Accumulated Other Comprehensive Income balance must also be removed. When this occurs, the *Handbook* provides the following recommendation:

> **Paragraph 1651.31** *An appropriate portion of the exchange gains and losses accumulated in the separate component of accumulated other comprehensive income should be included in the determination of net income when there is a reduction in the net investment.* (October, 2006)

10-75. Examples of this type of situation would include:

- dilution or sale of part or all of the reporting enterprise's interest in the foreign operation; and
- reduction in the equity of the foreign operation as a result of capital transactions (for example, dividend distributions, capital restructuring).

10-76. This recommendation, in effect, calls for a reclassification of the accumulated exchange gains and losses from an item of Other Comprehensive Income to a determinant of Net Income. If the related Accumulated Other Comprehensive Income component has a credit balance (net exchange gain), it will be added in the determination of Net Income and deducted as a reclassification item in the determination of Comprehensive Income. Alternatively, if the Accumulated Other Comprehensive Income component has a debit balance (net exchange loss), it will be deducted in the determination of Net Income and added as a reclassification item in the determination of Comprehensive Income.

Calculation Of Exchange Gains And Losses

10-77. As was noted in Chapter 9, whenever an item is translated at current exchange rates, exchange gains and losses can arise on that item. For integrated foreign operations using the temporal method, exchange gains and losses only arise on items carried at current values. This would include all monetary items and a limited number of non-monetary items that may be carried at current value. For self-sustaining foreign operations using the current rate method, exchange gains and losses can arise on all of the items in the financial statements, without regard to how they are valued in the foreign currency financial statements.

10-78. Calculating exchange gains and losses on foreign currency transactions is a fairly simple process. If you buy something on account for £1,000 when £1 = $2.30, and you pay the account when £1 = $2.35, you have an exchange loss of $50 [(£1,000)($2.35 - $2.30)].

10-79. The situation is more complex when calculating the exchange gain or loss resulting from the translation of foreign currency financial statements. With respect to the temporal method, you need to prepare a schedule of changes in the items valued at current value (largely monetary items), translating the opening balance and the changes at the exchange rate applicable to the opening Balance Sheet and each transaction date. This gives a computed figure for the closing balance that is then compared with the actual balance translated at the closing Balance Sheet date rate. The difference is the exchange gain or loss for the period. For integrated foreign operations using the temporal method, this amount will be charged or credited to Net Income.

10-80. The process is much the same when the current rate method is used. The difference is that the schedule will be based on all changes in net assets, not just those that are carried at current values in the foreign currency financial statements.

10-81. These descriptions, however, are not very useful without being supported with numerical examples. Unfortunately, it is not possible to illustrate these procedures outside the context of a comprehensive example. Given this, we will defer further discussion of these calculations until after we have presented a comprehensive example of the translation of foreign currency financial statements.

Foreign Currency Financial Statements - Example

Basic Data

10-82. This comprehensive example involves a foreign subsidiary which will be consolidated. We will use this example to illustrate the translation process for both integrated and self-sustaining foreign operations. We will also extend the example to illustrate consolidation procedures for a foreign subsidiary. The consolidated statements will be based on the assumption that the subsidiary is a self-sustaining foreign operation. The example is as follows:

> On December 31, 2007, the Port Company acquires 100 percent of the outstanding voting shares of the Ship Company for 42.2 million Canadian dollars ($, hereafter). Port Company is a Canadian corporation and Ship Company is a trading company located in Switzerland. On the acquisition date, Ship Company had Common Stock of 20 million Swiss francs (SF, hereafter) and Retained Earnings of SF32 million.
>
> During 2010, neither Company disclosed comprehensive income items on their single entity books. The December 31, 2009 and December 31, 2010 Balance Sheets for the two Companies, as well as their Statements Of Net And Comprehensive Income for the year ending December 31, 2010 are as follows:

Balance Sheets
As At December 31, 2009
(000s Omitted)

	Port ($)	Ship (SF)
Cash	2,000	2,000
Accounts Receivable	7,600	8,000
Inventories	30,000	40,000
Investment In Ship (At Cost)	42,200	N/A
Plant And Equipment (Net)	132,000	60,000
Total Assets	213,800	110,000
Current Liabilities	43,800	6,000
Long-Term Liabilities	30,000	40,000
No Par Common Stock	60,000	20,000
Retained Earnings	80,000	44,000
Total Equities	213,800	110,000

Balance Sheets
As At December 31, 2010
(000s Omitted)

	Port ($)	Ship (SF)
Cash	6,800	2,000
Accounts Receivable	18,800	14,000
Inventories	56,000	54,000
Investment In Ship (At Cost)	42,200	N/A
Plant And Equipment (Net)	120,000	50,000
Total Assets	243,800	120,000
Current Liabilities	49,800	4,000
Long-Term Liabilities	30,000	40,000
No Par Common Stock	60,000	20,000
Retained Earnings	104,000	56,000
Total Equities	243,800	120,000

Statements Of Net And Comprehensive Income
For Year Ending December 31, 2010
(000s Omitted)

	Port ($)	Ship (SF)
Sales	390,000	150,000
Cost Of Goods Sold	340,000	120,000
Amortization Expense	12,000	10,000
Other Expenses	14,000	8,000
Total Expenses	366,000	138,000
Net Income And Comprehensive Income	24,000	12,000

Other Information:

1. On December 31, 2007, the carrying values of all identifiable assets and liabilities of the Ship Company are equal to their fair values.

2. Port Company carries its Investment In Ship at cost. There is no goodwill impairment loss in any year since acquisition.
3. Neither the Port Company nor the Ship Company declare or pay dividends during 2010.
4. Ship Company has had no additions to its Plant And Equipment account since December 31, 2007.
5. Exchange rates for the Swiss franc are as follows:

December 31, 2007	SF1 = $0.80
December 31, 2009	SF1 = $0.90
December 31, 2010	SF1 = $1.00
Average For 2010	SF1 = $0.95

6. The December 31, 2009 Inventories of the Ship Company are acquired when SF1 = $.88 and the December 31, 2010 Inventories are acquired when SF1 = $.99. Both Companies account for their Inventories using a FIFO assumption.
7. The 2010 Sales of Ship Company contain SF40 million that are made to Port Company. These goods are resold by Port Company during 2010. As at December 31, 2010, the Port Company owes the Ship Company $1,000,000 and the Ship Company owes the Port Company SF2,000,000. These loans do not bear interest and they are to be repaid in 2011. There are no intercompany loans outstanding as at December 31, 2009.
8. Sales, Purchases, Other Expenses and intercompany sales and purchases take place evenly throughout the year, making the use of average exchange rates appropriate. Both Companies use the straight-line method for computing all amortization charges.
9. For purposes of preparing the translated Balance Sheet in the self-sustaining version of the example, assume that the correct December 31, 2009 balance in the Accumulated Other Comprehensive Income account is a credit of $6,800,000. Given the information provided, this figure cannot be independently calculated.

Integrated Foreign Operation

10-83. If we assume that the Ship Company is an integrated foreign operation, the translated comparative Balance Sheets as at December 31, 2009 and December 31, 2010 and the Statement Of Net And Comprehensive Income for the year ending December 31, 2010 would be as follows:

Ship Company (Integrated Foreign Operation)
Translated Balance Sheet
As At December 31, 2009
(000s Omitted)

	Untranslated	Rate	Translated
Cash	SF 2,000	$0.90	$ 1,800
Accounts Receivable	8,000	$0.90	7,200
Inventories	40,000	$0.88	35,200
Plant And Equipment (Net)	60,000	$0.80	48,000
Total Assets	SF110,000		$92,200
Current Liabilities	SF 6,000	$0.90	$ 5,400
Long-Term Liabilities	40,000	$0.90	36,000
No Par Common Stock	20,000	$0.80	16,000
Retained Earnings	44,000	Note 1	34,800
Total Equities	SF110,000		$92,200

Ship Company (Integrated Foreign Operation)
Translated Balance Sheet
As At December 31, 2010
(000s Omitted)

	Untranslated	Rate	Translated
Cash	SF 2,000	$1.00	$ 2,000
Accounts Receivable	14,000	$1.00	14,000
Inventories	54,000	$0.99	53,460
Plant And Equipment (Net)	50,000	$0.80	40,000
Total Assets	SF120,000		$109,460
Current Liabilities	SF 4,000	$1.00	$ 4,000
Long-Term Liabilities	40,000	$1.00	40,000
No Par Common Stock	20,000	$0.80	16,000
Retained Earnings	56,000	Note 1	49,460
Total Equities	SF120,000		$109,460

Note 1 The December 31, 2009 Retained Earnings is simply the figure that balances assets and equities. Given the information in the problem, it cannot be determined independently. The December 31, 2010 figure of $49,460,000 can be calculated as the opening balance of $34,800,000, plus the Net Income of $14,660,000 (see following Statement Of Net And Comprehensive Income)

Ship Company (Integrated Foreign Operation)
Translated Statement Of Net And Comprehensive Income
For The Year Ending December 31, 2010
(000s Omitted)

	Untranslated	Rate	Translated
Sales	SF150,000	$0.95	$142,500
Opening Inventory	SF 40,000	$0.88	$ 35,200
Purchases	134,000	$0.95	127,300
Closing Inventory	(54,000)	$0.99	(53,460)
Amortization Expense	10,000	$0.80	8,000
Other Expenses	8,000	$0.95	7,600
Exchange Loss (Note 2)	N/A	N/A	3,200
Total Expenses	SF138,000		$127,840
Net And Comprehensive Income	SF 12,000		$ 14,660

Note 2 As we have noted, exchange gains and losses occur on items that are translated at current rates. When the temporal method is used, these items would be monetary items and non-monetary items that are carried at current values (in this example, this would involve only monetary items so we will refer simply to monetary items, rather than the more complete description which includes non-monetary items carried at current values). While the loss for the year could be calculated on each monetary balance and the transactions that alter that balance, this is not a practical solution.

The usual approach is to prepare a schedule of changes in monetary items and translate the changes in this schedule using an appropriately weighted average rate. This will give the closing foreign currency balance that would be present if there were no foreign exchange gain or loss for the period.

This computed closing balance is then compared with the actual closing balance to determine the amount of the gain or loss that has actually occurred during the period. In this example, the net monetary balance on December 31, 2009 is a liability of SF36,000,000 (SF2,000,000 + SF8,000,000 - SF6,000,000 - SF40,000,000). The required schedule is as follows:

Schedule Of Change In Net Monetary Balance
(000s Omitted)

	Untranslated	Rate	Translated
Opening Net Monetary Liability	(SF 36,000)	$0.90	($ 32,400)
Sales	150,000	$0.95	142,500
Purchases	(134,000)	$0.95	(127,300)
Other Expenses	(8,000)	$0.95	(7,600)
Computed Closing Net Monetary Liability			($ 24,800)
Less: Actual Closing Net Monetary Liability	(SF 28,000)	$1.00	(28,000)
Exchange (Gain) Loss - Net Income			$ 3,200

Note that the SF28,000,000 in the untranslated column can be verified by checking the net monetary liability balance in the December 31, 2010 Balance Sheet (SF2,000,000 + SF14,000,000 - SF4,000,000 - SF40,000,000 = SF28,000,000).

Note that, in this schedule, the inventory item is Purchases, not Cost Of Goods Sold. This reflects the fact that it is the acquisition of an inventory item that reduces the monetary balance by increasing Accounts Payable.

A further point to note here is that the construction of this schedule is such that if it ends in a positive number, a loss is involved. Correspondingly, a negative number will indicate a gain. The only way to restructure this schedule so that a positive number would be a gain, is to treat liabilities as a positive number, an approach which is even less intuitive than the preceding.

In terms of understanding the basis for this schedule, you can think of the closing balance of $24,800,000 as the liability balance that you would have had if all of the items had been converted to Canadian dollars at the beginning of the year and the revenues and expenses converted to Canadian dollars as received or paid. As this did not happen and the company continued to hold or owe Swiss francs, their value in Canadian dollars changes, resulting in an actual closing balance that differs from the computed balance.

For example, at the beginning of the year, the opening net monetary liability balance could have been paid with $32,400,000 [(SF36,000,000)($0.90)] Canadian dollars. Since it was not, at the end of the year its translated amount has increased to $36,000,000 [(SF36,000,000)($1.00)], resulting in a loss on this item of $3,600,000. A similar analysis can be made for each of the other items.

Self-Sustaining Foreign Operation

10-84. If we assume that the Ship Company is a self-sustaining foreign operation, the Balance Sheets as at December 31, 2009 and December 31, 2010 and the Income Statement for the year ending December 31, 2010, are as follows:

Ship Company (Self-Sustaining Foreign Operation)
Translated Balance Sheet
As At December 31, 2009
(000s Omitted)

	Untranslated	Rate	Translated
Cash	SF 2,000	$0.90	$ 1,800
Accounts Receivable	8,000	$0.90	7,200
Inventories	40,000	$0.90	36,000
Plant And Equipment (Net)	60,000	$0.90	54,000
Total Assets	SF110,000		$99,000
Current Liabilities	SF 6,000	$0.90	$ 5,400
Long-Term Liabilities	40,000	$0.90	36,000
No Par Common Stock	20,000	$0.80	16,000
Accumulated Other Comprehensive Income	N/A	Note 1	6,800
Retained Earnings	44,000	Note 1	34,800
Total Equities	SF110,000		$99,000

Ship Company (Self-Sustaining Foreign Operation)
Translated Balance Sheet
As At December 31, 2010
(000s Omitted)

	Untranslated	Rate	Translated
Cash	SF 2,000	$1.00	$ 2,000
Accounts Receivable	14,000	$1.00	14,000
Inventories	54,000	$1.00	54,000
Plant And Equipment (Net)	50,000	$1.00	50,000
Total Assets	SF120,000		$120,000
Current Liabilities	SF 4,000	$1.00	$ 4,000
Long-Term Liabilities	40,000	$1.00	40,000
No Par Common Stock	20,000	$0.80	16,000
Accumulated Other Comprehensive Income	N/A	Note 1	13,800
Retained Earnings	56,000	Note 1	46,200
Total Equities	SF120,000		$120,000

Note 1 With respect to the balances in the December 31, 2009 Shareholders' Equity, the Accumulated Other Comprehensive Income balance was given as it could not be calculated on the basis of the information in the example. With this figure given, the Retained Earnings is simply the figure that balances the assets and equities. As was the case with the Accumulated Other Comprehensive Income amount, this opening Retained Earnings figure cannot be calculated independently on the basis of the information in the example.

With respect to the December 31, 2010 figures, the $13,800,000 Accumulated Other Comprehensive Income balance can be calculated by taking the opening balance of $6,800,000 and adding the $7,000,000 exchange gain for the year (see Note 2). Similarly, the ending Retained Earnings balance of $46,200,000 can be calculated by taking the opening balance of $34,800,000 and adding the Net Income for the year of $11,400,000 (see following Statement Of Net And Comprehensive Income).

Ship Company (Self-Sustaining Foreign Operation)
Translated Statement Of Net And Comprehensive Income
For The Year Ending December 31, 2010
(000s Omitted)

	Untranslated	Rate	Translated
Sales	SF150,000	$0.95	$142,500
Cost Of Goods Sold	SF120,000	$0.95	$114,000
Amortization Expense	10,000	$0.95	9,500
Other Expenses	8,000	$0.95	7,600
Total Expenses	SF138,000		$131,100
Net Income	SF 12,000		$ 11,400
Comprehensive Income Item:			
Exchange Gain On Translation Of Financial Statements Of Self-Sustaining Foreign Operation	N/A	Note 2	7,000
Comprehensive Income			$ 18,400

Note 2 In contrast to the situation when the temporal method is used, the current rate method will translate all of the assets and liabilities at current rates. This means that there will be translation adjustments on all of these balances. Given this, the calculation of the exchange gain or loss for the period will be based on changes in all of the net assets. Starting with the opening net assets of SF64,000,000 (SF110,000,000 - SF6,000,000 - SF40,000,000), the required schedule is as follows:

Schedule Of Change In Net Assets
(000s Omitted)

	Untranslated	Rate	Translated
Opening Net Assets	SF 64,000	$0.90	$ 57,600
Sales	150,000	$0.95	142,500
Cost Of Goods Sold	(120,000)	$0.95	(114,000)
Amortization Expense	(10,000)	$0.95	(9,500)
Other Expenses	(8,000)	$0.95	(7,600)
Computed Closing Net Assets			$ 69,000
Less: Actual Closing Net Assets	SF 76,000	$1.00	76,000
Exchange (Gain) Loss - Other Comprehensive Income			($ 7,000)

As was the case with the similar schedule in the integrated foreign operation example, the final balance of SF76,000,000 can be verified in the December 31, 2010 Balance Sheet (SF120,000,000 - SF4,000,000 - SF40,000,000 = SF76,000,000). Here again, we suggest that it is useful to do this verification in order to ensure that one or more items have not been left out of the schedule.

Note that in this schedule, the inventory item is Cost Of Goods Sold, not Purchases. This reflects the fact that for self-sustaining foreign operations, calculations are based on the change in net assets, not the change in monetary items.

In this example, all of the changes in net assets occur uniformly over the year and, as a consequence, average exchange rates can be used. Given this, the computed closing balance could be calculated by translating the change in the net assets of SF12,000,000 (SF76,000,000 - SF64,000,000) by the average rate of $0.95. When this $11,400,000 [(SF12,000,000)($0.95)] is added to the translated opening balance of $57,600,000, it gives the computed closing balance of $69,000,000. You should note, however, that this only works when all of the changes in net assets occur uniformly over the year. If one or more of the changes does not satisfy this criteria, for example, a dividend declared at the year end, it will have to be translated at an exchange rate other than the simple average for the year. When this is the case, the more detailed schedular calculation is required.

Consolidated Financial Statements

10-85. We are now in a position to prepare consolidated financial statements for the Port Company and its subsidiary, the Ship Company. While consolidated statements could be prepared for either type of foreign operation, we will limit our presentation to the consolidated statements under the assumption Ship Company is a self-sustaining foreign operation.

10-86. The first step in the process of preparing consolidated financial statements would be to analyze the investment account. This can be done as follows:

Investment Cost	$42,200,000
Translated Book Value At Acquisition [(SF52,000,000)($0.80)]	(41,600,000)
Excess Of Cost Over Book Value	$ 600,000

10-87. Since there are no fair value changes present on the acquisition date (Item 1 of Other Information), the entire $600,000 would be allocated to goodwill. As indicated in Item 2 of Other Information, there has been no impairment of this Goodwill in any year since acquisition.

10-88. Given this investment analysis, the consolidated Balance Sheet, as at December 31, 2009, would be prepared as follows:

Port Company And Subsidiary
Consolidated Balance Sheet
As At December 31, 2009
(000s Omitted)

Cash ($2,000 + $1,800)	$ 3,800
Accounts And Other Receivables ($7,600 + $7,200)	14,800
Inventories ($30,000 + $36,000)	66,000
Investment in Ship ($42,200 - $42,200)	Nil
Plant And Equipment ($132,000 + $54,000)	186,000
Goodwill	600
Total Assets	$271,200
Current Liabilities ($43,800 + $5,400)	$ 49,200
Long-Term Liabilities ($30,000 + $36,000)	66,000
Common Stock - No Par (Port Company's)	60,000
Accumulated Other Comprehensive Income (Note 1)	6,800
Retained Earnings (Note 1)	89,200
Total Equities	$271,200

Note 1 The $6,800,000 balance for Accumulated Other Comprehensive Income was given in the example. The $89,200,000 Retained Earnings balance is simply the figure that will balance the total of assets with the total of equities. The information in the problem is not sufficient for an independent calculation of this balance.

10-89. The consolidated Balance Sheet, as at December 31, 2010, would be as follows:

Port Company And Subsidiary
Consolidated Balance Sheet
As At December 31, 2010
(000s Omitted)

Cash ($6,800 + $2,000)	$ 8,800
Accounts And Other Receivables [$18,800 + $14,000 - $1,000 - (SF2,000)($1.00)]	29,800
Inventories ($56,000 + $54,000)	110,000
Investment in Ship ($42,200 - $42,200)	Nil
Plant And Equipment (Net) ($120,000 + $50,000)	170,000
Goodwill	600
Total Assets	$319,200

Current Liabilities [$49,800 + $4,000 - $1,000 - (SF2,000)($1.00)]	$ 50,800
Long-Term Liabilities ($30,000 + $40,000)	70,000
Common Stock - No Par (Port Company's)	60,000
Accumulated Other Comprehensive Income (Note 2)	13,800
Retained Earnings (Note 2)	124,600
Total Equities	$319,200

Note 2 With respect to the December 31, 2010 figures, the $13,800,000 Accumulated Other Comprehensive Income balance can be calculated by taking the opening balance of $6,800,000 and adding the $7,000,000 exchange gain for the year (see following consolidated Statement Of Net And Comprehensive Income). Similarly, the ending Retained Earnings balance of $124,600,000 can be calculated by taking the opening balance of $89,200,000 and adding the Net Income for the year of $35,400,000 (see following consolidated Statement Of Net And Comprehensive Income).

10-90. The consolidated Statement Of Net And Comprehensive Income for the year ending December 31, 2010 would be prepared as follows:

Port Company And Subsidiary
Consolidated Statement Of Net And Comprehensive Income
Year Ending December 31, 2010
(000s Omitted)

Sales [$390,000 + $142,500 - (SF40,000)($0.95)]	$494,500
Cost Of Goods Sold [$340,000 + $114,000 - (SF40,000)($0.95)]	$416,000
Amortization Expense ($12,000 + $9,500)	21,500
Other Expenses ($14,000 + $7,600)	21,600
Total Expenses	$459,100
Net Income	$ 35,400
Comprehensive Income Item:	
Exchange Gain On Translation Of Financial Statements Of Self-Sustaining Foreign Operation	7,000
Comprehensive Income	$ 42,400

Changes In Classification Of Foreign Operations

10-91. There may be situations in which a foreign operation that was classified as integrated must be reclassified as self-sustaining. Alternatively, a foreign operation that was once considered self-sustaining could have its activities changed in a way that results in it being reclassified as an integrated foreign operation. In addition, the economic environment in which a self-sustaining entity is operating could become highly inflationary, resulting in a need to change the applicable accounting procedures.

10-92. When there is a need for reclassification, Section 1651 makes the following recommendation:

> **Paragraph 1651.36** *When there are significant changes in the economic facts and circumstances that require the translation method applied to a particular foreign operation to be changed, the change in method should be accounted for prospectively. Disclosure should be made of the reasons for the change in the translation method.* (July, 1983)

10-93. When the change is from self-sustaining to integrated (or the economic environment of a self-sustaining foreign operation becomes highly inflationary), the method of translation would be changed from the current rate method to the temporal method and exchange gains and losses would begin to be included in Net Income.

10-94. With respect to gains and losses in the Accumulated Other Comprehensive Income balance, prospective treatment would require that they continue to be carried forward in that account. The use of prospective treatment would also mean that the translated amounts for items carried at historical cost at the end of the period prior to the reclassification would become the historical basis for those items in subsequent periods.

10-95. When the reclassification is from integrated to self-sustaining (or the economic environment of a self-sustaining foreign operation ceases to be highly inflationary), the current rate method would be adopted at the beginning of the period in which the reclassification occurs. At the time of the change, the items that are carried at historical rates will have to be restated to current rates. The resulting exchange gains and losses would be allocated to Accumulated Other Comprehensive Income.

10-96. In periods subsequent to the reclassification, exchange gains and losses would be presented as an item of Other Comprehensive Income, rather than as a determinant of Net Income.

Disclosure And Financial Statement Presentation

10-97. The disclosure requirements of Section 1651 of the *CICA Handbook* are not extensive. We have already noted the only specific recommendations found in this Section. These are Paragraph 1651.32's requirement for disclosure of significant elements that give rise to changes in the exchange gain and loss component in Accumulated Other Comprehensive Income, and Paragraph 1651.36's requirement that disclosure be made of the reasons for any change in translation methods used for foreign operations. One other disclosure recommendation is included in the Section 1651:

> **Paragraph 1651.37** *The amount of exchange gain or loss included in net income should be disclosed (see paragraphs 1651.20, 1651.24 and 1651.31). An entity may exclude from this amount those exchange gains or losses arising on financial instruments classified as held for trading in accordance with "Financial Instruments — Recognition And Measurement", Section 3855. An entity may also exclude from this amount exchange gains or losses on available-for-sale financial assets and cash flow hedges (see "Hedges", Section 3865) included in any gains or losses removed from accumulated other comprehensive income and included in net income for the period.* (October, 2006)

10-98. A near identical disclosure requirement is found in Section 1520, "Income Statement":

> **Paragraph 1520.03** *In arriving at the income or loss before discontinued operations and extraordinary items, the income statement should distinguish at least the following items: ...*
>
> *(l) The amount of exchange gain or loss included in net income (*see "Foreign Currency Translation", Section 1651*). An entity may exclude from this amount those exchange gains or losses arising on financial instruments classified as held for trading in accordance with "Financial Instruments — Recognition And Measurement", Section 3855. An entity may also exclude from this amount exchange gains or losses on available-for-sale financial assets and cash flow hedges (*see "Hedges", Section 3865*) included in any gains or losses removed from accumulated other comprehensive income and included in net income for the period.* (October, 2006)

Translation Of An Investment Accounted For By The Equity Method

10-99. When an investee is accounted for by the equity method, the investment income that is recorded by the investor company is based on the reported income of the investee, subject to the usual consolidation adjustments. In the case of a foreign investee, the statements will have to be translated prior to the application of the equity method. In such situations, the *CICA Handbook* notes the following:

> **Paragraph 1651.38** The financial statements of a foreign investee accounted for by the equity method (see "Investments", Section 3051) are first translated into Canadian dollars in accordance with this Section; then the equity method is applied.

10-100. As the equity method could be applicable to either an integrated or a self-sustaining foreign operation, either the temporal or the current rate method may be applicable.

Other Issues

Transactions And Operations Of Foreign Operations Which Are Denominated In Another Currency

10-101. If a foreign operation of a Canadian company has its own foreign currency transactions or foreign currency operations, it will be necessary to translate these amounts and statements into the currency of the Canadian company's foreign operation using the recommendations of Section 1651. This could involve using either the temporal or the current rate method, depending on the nature of the items and, in the case of a foreign operation with a foreign operation of its own, the classification of this second tier investment. Once this has been accomplished, the Canadian company's foreign operation can be translated into Canadian dollars using either the temporal or current rate method as is appropriate.

Intercompany Balances

Integrated Foreign Operations

10-102. It is not uncommon for intercompany asset and liability balances to arise between a domestic investor company and its foreign investees. In such cases, translation of the foreign currency balance will usually result in exchange gains and losses and this raises the question of what is the appropriate treatment of these balances. With respect to balances related to integrated foreign operations, the *CICA Handbook* suggests:

Paragraph 1651.41 With respect to integrated foreign operations, exchange gains and losses relating to intercompany balances recorded by the reporting enterprise or the foreign operation will be treated in the same manner as those relating to other foreign currency receivables or payables in accordance with paragraph 1651.20.

Self-Sustaining Foreign Operations

10-103. The situation is more complex when a self-sustaining foreign operation is involved. In this case, the *CICA Handbook* distinguishes between ordinary intercompany balances (e.g., those arising on intercompany sales of merchandise) and intercompany balances that form part of the net investment (e.g., a holding of the foreign investee's redeemable preferred shares). Based on this distinction, the following guidance is provided:

Paragraph 1651.42 With respect to self-sustaining foreign operations, exchange gains and losses on intercompany account balances that are not included as part of the net investment are treated in the same manner as those relating to normal foreign currency trade balances in accordance with the appropriate requirements of this Section. Exchange gains and losses on intercompany account balances that form part of the net investment are recognized in the separate component of other comprehensive income in accordance with paragraph 1651.29.

Elimination Of Intercompany Profits

10-104. The issue here is related to the elimination of intercompany profits resulting from transactions between a reporting entity and a foreign investee. Specifically, it must be decided whether to make the elimination using the exchange rate that prevailed at the date of the transaction or, alternatively, using the rate that prevails at the balance sheet date. For integrated foreign operations the answer is clearly the use of the transaction date rate. Somewhat surprisingly, the AcSB concludes that this is also the most appropriate rate for self-sustaining foreign operations. Note that this will require that the transaction date rate also be used for any subsequent realization of unrealized profits that have been previously eliminated.

Differences In Financial Statement Dates

10-105. A foreign investee can have a different fiscal year end than that of the domestic investor. When this happens, Paragraph 1651.44 provides the following guidance:

Paragraph 1651.44 When the date of the financial statements of the foreign operation differs from that of the reporting enterprise, those assets and liabilities which are translated at the current rate would normally be translated at the rate in effect at the balance sheet date of the foreign operation, not at the rate in effect at the balance sheet date of the reporting enterprise. When there is a major change in exchange rates between the balance sheet dates of the foreign operation and the reporting enterprise, the effect of the change would be disclosed.

Non-Controlling Interest

10-106. In preparing consolidated financial statements, one or more foreign subsidiaries may have a non-controlling interest. In this situation, the *CICA Handbook* indicates the following:

Paragraph 1651.46 The non-controlling interest reported in an enterprise's consolidated financial statements is based on the financial statements of the foreign operation in which there is a non-controlling interest after they have been translated in accordance with this Section. In particular, the non-controlling interest reported includes the non-controlling interest's proportionate share of exchange gains and losses.

Preference Shares

10-107. With respect to the treatment of preference shares in translation, the *CICA Handbook* states the following:

> **Paragraph 1651.47** Preference shares of a foreign operation held by the reporting enterprise are translated in the same manner as common shares (i.e., at historical rates) unless redemption is either required or imminent, in which case the current rate is used. Preference shares held by non-controlling shareholders in an integrated foreign operation are also translated at historical rates unless redemption is either required or imminent, in which case the current rate would be used. Preference shares held by non-controlling shareholders in a self-sustaining foreign operation are translated at the current rate. (When the economic environment of a self-sustaining foreign operation is highly inflationary, the preference shares of the foreign operation are translated in the same manner as preference shares of integrated foreign operations.)

Application Of Lower Of Cost And Market

10-108. The exchange rate used to translate assets of an integrated foreign operation is dependent on the basis of their valuation in the foreign currency financial statements. If they are valued at cost, historical rates will be applicable while if they are valued at market or some other measure of current value, current exchange rates will be used.

10-109. This would be relevant in the application of lower of cost and market to the problem of inventory valuation. As a result, the translation process may result in the need to write down translated values even when there has been no write-down in the foreign currency statements.

> **Example** A German subsidiary has inventories purchased for 1,000,000 euros (€) when the exchange rate was €1 = $1.55. At the Balance Sheet date, these inventories have a market value of €1,050,000.
>
> **Analysis** There is clearly no need to write down the euro value as the market exceeds the cost. However, if we assume that the Balance Sheet date exchange rate has fallen to €1 = $1.40, the translated market value would be $1,470,000 [(€1,050,000)($1.40)]. As this would be lower than the translated cost of $1,550,000 [(€1,000,000)($1.55)], the translated market figure would be used.

10-110. It is also possible for the opposite situation to occur. That is, it may be necessary in the translated financial statements to reverse a write-down that has occurred in the foreign currency statements. In addition, Section 1651 notes that once an asset has been written down to market in the translated financial statements, that dollar amount would continue to be the carrying amount in the translated financial statements until the asset is sold or a further write-down is required.

Future Income Tax Assets And Liabilities

10-111. Section 3465, "Income Taxes" adopts the future income tax asset/liability approach. As the resulting tax allocation balances are monetary assets and liabilities, they are translated at current exchange rates. This would be the case for balances on the books of either integrated or self-sustaining foreign operations. This view is reflected in Paragraph 1651.52 as follows:

> **Paragraph 1651.52** Future income tax liabilities and assets are monetary items and, as such, are translated at the current rate.

Cash Flow Statement

10-112. There are a number of problems that arise in the translation of the Cash Flow Statement of a self-sustaining foreign operation. Paragraph 1651.53 of the *CICA Handbook* offers guidance on the following points:

(a) Cash from operations would be translated at the exchange rate at which the respective items are translated for income statement purposes.

(b) Other items would be translated at exchange rates in effect when the related transactions took place.

(c) The effect of subsequent exchange rate changes on the cash flows during the period and on cash and cash equivalents at the commencement of the period would be disclosed, so that cash and cash equivalents at the end of the period are translated at the exchange rate in effect on that date.

International Convergence

Standards

10-113. The Canadian rules for translating the financial statements of foreign operations are found in *CICA Handbook* Section 1651, "Foreign Currency Translation". The corresponding international standard is IAS No. 21, *The Effects Of Changes In Foreign Exchange Rates*.

10-114. While Section 1651 gives a limited amount of attention to foreign operations that are operating in hyperinflationary economies, this appears to be a much more important subject from the point of the IASB. They have a separate IAS No. 29, *Financial Reporting In Hyperinflationary Economies*, which provides much more detailed guidance on this subject.

AcSB Strategic Plan

10-115. The work plan of the IASB does not contain any mention of further work on the translation of the financial statements of foreign operations. In addition, the AcSB has indicated that it does not anticipate any further work in this area prior to the changeover date. Their plan appears to be to leave Section 1651 in place until the 2011 changeover date, at which time IAS No. 21 and IAS No. 29 will be converged into Canadian GAAP.

Differences

10-116. With respect to the translation of the financial statements of foreign operations, the differences between Section 1651 and the corresponding international standards can be described as follows:

Classification Of Foreign Operations Section 1651 classifies foreign operations as either integrated or self-sustaining. While the results are likely to be similar, IAS No. 21 classifies foreign operations on the basis of their functional currency. The appropriate accounting is then determined based on whether the functional currency is the reporting currency of the investor or, alternatively, the reporting currency of the foreign operation.

Non-Monetary Items Carried At Fair Value Section 1651 requires these balances to be translated using the rate applicable to the Balance Sheet date. In contrast, IAS No. 21 requires the use of the rate applicable to the date when the fair value was measured.

Hyperinflationary Economies Section 1651 requires the application of the temporal method to translate the financial statements of foreign operations that are located in hyperinflationary economies. In contrast, IAS No. 29 requires that the financial statements of such foreign operations be restated to remove the effects of price level change. In addition, IAS No. 29 provides considerable guidance with respect to the implementation of this restatement.

Foreign Currency Translation In Canadian Practice

Statistics From Financial Reporting In Canada

10-117. Section 1651 leaves few alternatives in its application. Integrated foreign operations and foreign currency transactions must be translated using the temporal method and self-sustaining foreign operations must be translated using the current rate method. Given this lack of alternatives in the translation of foreign currency statements and transactions, the 2006 edition of *Financial Reporting in Canada* does not present a significant amount of data in this area.

10-118. Foreign currency translation is a common element in the financial statements of public companies. Long-term debt can be expressed in a foreign currency, financial instruments often involve forward exchange contracts and other means of hedging foreign currency positions, and segmented information commonly involves information about geographic segments where results are originally expressed in a foreign currency. As an indication of its importance, in 2005, 180 of the 200 companies surveyed in the 2006 edition of *Financial Reporting in Canada*, discussed foreign currency translation in their Statement of Accounting Policies.

10-119. Of the 200 survey companies, 102 companies disclosed exchange gains or losses in their 2005 annual reports. With regards to the location of this disclosure, 69 companies provided disclosure on the face of the Income Statement, while 30 companies provided disclosure in the notes. The remaining 3 companies disclosed the information in their statement of accounting policies.

10-120. With respect to self-sustaining foreign operations, the now superseded Section 1650 required that exchange gains and losses be deferred and included in a separate section of Shareholders' Equity. A total of 125 companies disclosed such a section in their 2005 financial statements, of which 49 designated the balance as a "cumulative translation adjustment" and 37 referred to it as a "foreign currency translation adjustment". The remaining companies used a wide variety of other terminology.

10-121. Paragraph 1651.39 requires that disclosure be made of significant elements that gave rise to changes in this Shareholders' Equity balance. Such disclosure was made by only 21 of the 125 companies that disclosed this type of balance.

Example From Practice

10-122. Disclosure related to foreign currency translation can be found in the statement of accounting policies or, alternatively, in a note to the financial statements. Our example is from the annual report of Corus Entertainment Inc. for the year ending August 31, 2005 and illustrates both of these forms of disclosure. This example provides note disclosure of foreign currency gains and losses and disclosure of the foreign currency translation adjustment account which is referenced from the Shareholders' Equity section of the Balance Sheet.

Balance Sheet Disclosure (in part)
Consolidated Balance Sheets (in part)

AS AT AUGUST 31 [in thousands of Canadian dollars]	2005	2004
Shareholders' equity		
Share capital [note 14]	885,911	884,053
Contributed surplus [note 14]	3,558	1,287
Retained earnings (deficit)	50,802	(17,122)
Cumulative translation adjustment [note 20]	(10,009)	(7,038)
Total shareholders' equity	930,262	861,180

Notes to Financial Statements

(in thousands of Canadian dollars except share information)

2. Significant Accounting Policies (in part)

Foreign currency translation

The assets and liabilities of the Company's self-sustaining operations having a functional currency that is not in Canadian dollars are translated into Canadian dollars using the exchange rate in effect at the consolidated balance sheet date, and revenues and expenses are translated at the average rate during the year. Exchange gains or losses on translation of the Company's net equity investment in these operations are deferred as a separate component of shareholders' equity.

For integrated foreign operations monetary items are translated into Canadian dollars at exchange rates in effect at the consolidated balance sheet date and non-monetary items are translated at rates of exchange in effect when the assets were acquired or obligations incurred. Revenues and expenses are translated at rates in effect at the time of the transaction. Foreign exchange gains and losses are included in net income (loss) for the year.

Long-term debt denominated in U.S. dollars is translated into Canadian dollars at the year-end rate of exchange. Exchange gains or losses on translating long-term debt that qualifies for hedge accounting are offset against the corresponding exchange gains or losses arising on the cross-currency agreements.

Other exchange gains and losses are included in net income (loss) for the year.

20. Foreign Exchange Gains and Losses

The Company has reflected certain gains and losses in its consolidated statements of income (loss) and retained earnings (deficit) as a result of exposure to foreign currency exchange rate fluctuations. A portion of these gains and losses relate to operating activities while others are of a financing nature. Foreign exchange gains and losses are reflected in the consolidated financial statements as follows:

	2005	2004	2003
Consolidated statements of income (loss) and retained earnings (deficit)			
Direct cost of sales, general and administrative expenses	(825)	(1,222)	(772)
Other income, net	(3,338)	(2,245)	(6,638)
Total foreign exchange gain	(4,163)	(3,467)	(7,410)

An analysis of the cumulative translation adjustment shown separately in shareholders' equity is as follows:

Balance, August 31, 2003	(5,089)
Effect of exchange rate fluctuation on translation of net assets of self-sustaining foreign operations	(1,949)
Balance, August 31, 2004	(7,038)
Effect of exchange rate fluctuation on translation of net assets of self-sustaining foreign operations	(3,418)
Other	447
Balance, August 31, 2005	(10,009)

CD-ROM Note If you are interested in more statistics and examples of disclosure of foreign currency translation, the CICA's *Financial Reporting in Canada* is available on the CD-ROM which is included with this text.

Additional Readings

10-123. In writing the material in the text, we have incorporated all of the relevant *CICA Handbook* recommendations, as well as material from other sources that we felt to be of importance. This includes some, but not all, of the material from international accounting standards.

10-124. While this approach meets the needs of the great majority of our readers, some of you may wish to pursue this subject in greater depth. To facilitate this, you will find a fairly comprehensive list of additional readings at the end of each relevant Chapter in our *Guide To Canadian Financial Reporting*.

CD-ROM Note Our *Guide To Canadian Financial Reporting* is available on the CD-ROM which is included with this text.

Problems For Self Study

(The solutions for these problems can be found in the separate Study Guide.)

Self Study Problem Ten - 1

The Ambivalent Company is a Mexican subsidiary of a Canadian parent company and its accounts are included in the Canadian dollar consolidated financial statements of the parent company. On December 31, 2007, the following selected balances were included in the foreign currency Balance Sheet of the Ambivalent Company (all amounts are expressed in Mexican pesos which are designated P hereafter):

	Debits	**Credits**
Cash	P 500,000	
Long-Term Receivables	1,500,000	
Inventories	2,000,000	
Plant And Equipment	5,000,000	
Accounts Payable		P 700,000
Long-Term Liabilities		1,200,000
Accumulated Amortization On Plant And Equipment		2,500,000

The Long-Term Receivables and Plant And Equipment were acquired several years ago when P1 = $0.20. The Long-Term Liabilities were also issued at this time.

The Inventories were acquired for P2,100,000 when P1 = $0.10. However, they are carried at their net realizable value as measured at December 31, 2007. The exchange rate on December 31, 2007 is P1 = $0.11.

Required: Translate the preceding account balances using:

A. the temporal approach.
B. the current rate approach.

Self Study Problem Ten - 2

Investco Ltd. is a Canadian real estate and property developer which decided to hold a parcel of land in downtown St. Michael's, Barbados, for speculative purposes. The land, costing 12,000,000 Barbadian dollars (B$, hereafter) was financed by a five-year bond (B$9,000,000), which is repayable in Barbadian dollars, and an initial equity injection by Investco of B$3,000,000. These transactions took place on January 1, 2007, at which time a Barbadian subsidiary company was created to hold the investment.

Investco plans to sell the land at the end of five years and use the Barbadian dollar proceeds to pay off the bond. In the interim, rent is being collected from another company which is using the land as a parking lot. Rental revenue is collected and interest and other expenses are paid at the end of each month. The 2007 year end draft financial statements of the Barbadian subsidiary company are as follows:

Income Statement
For The Year Ended December 31, 2007

Rental Revenue	B$1,000,000
Interest Expense	(990,000)
Other Expenses	(10,000)
Net Income	Nil

Balance Sheet
As At December 31, 2007

Cash	Nil
Land	B$12,000,000
Total Assets	B$12,000,000
Bond (Due December 31, 2011)	B$ 9,000,000
Common Stock	3,000,000
Total Equities	B$12,000,000

Assume the exchange rates were as follows:

January 1, 2007	B$1 = C$0.60
December 31, 2007	B$1 = C$0.70
Average, 2007	B$1 = C$0.64

Required:

A. Prepare the translated 2007 financial statements (including a Statement of Comprehensive Income, if required), following Canadian generally accepted accounting principles and assuming:

   i) the Barbadian subsidiary is an integrated foreign operation.
   ii) the Barbadian subsidiary is a self-sustaining foreign operation.

B. Which translation method better reflects Investco's economic exposure to exchange rate movements? Explain.

C. Which translation method would Investco be required to use? Explain.

(SMA Adapted)

Self Study Problem Ten - 3

Sentex Limited of Montreal, Quebec, has an 80 percent owned subsidiary, Cellular Company Inc., which operates in Erewhon, a small country located in Central America. Cellular was formed on January 1, 2007 by Sentex and Erewhon Development Inc. which is located in Erewhon. Advantages to Sentex of locating in Erewhon are: easy access to raw materials, low operating costs, government incentives, and the fact that the plastics market of Erewhon is not well developed. All management, including the Chief Operating Officer, Mr. V. Globe, has been appointed by Sentex. Top management of Cellular is paid directly by Sentex.

Cellular makes plastic coatings from petrochemical feedstock purchased from Mexico. The process is automated but still uses significant amounts of native Erewhonese labour. The government of Erewhon has determined that this type of development is good for the country, and has underwritten 22,000 cuzos (local currency of Erewhon) of staff training expenses in 2007 by reducing the taxes payable by Cellular. This employment assistance is not expected to continue in the future.

Approximately 75 percent of total sales by Cellular are made to Sentex, which uses the plastic coatings in its Montreal operations. These coatings are generally of a heavy grade and require special set-up by Cellular. The Sentex orders are handled directly by Mr. Globe and his assistant, Mr. A. Oppong, and the price is set on the basis of variable costs of manufacture, plus freight and a 30 percent markup, less applicable export tax incentives. The export tax incentive received by Cellular has been about 1,000 cuzos per order. Plastic coatings are also sold to both commercial and wholesale outlets in Erewhon, with commercial users constituting 20 percent of the total sales revenue of Cellular.

Cellular has agreed with the Erewhon government not to pay any dividends out of profits for two years. After that, it is anticipated that the majority of profits will be remitted by Cellular to Sentex and its other major stockholder, Erewhon Development Inc. The opening balance sheet of Cellular Company Inc. at January 1, 2007, was as follows:

Cellular Company Inc.
Balance Sheet As At January 1, 2007 (in cuzos)

Cash	30,000
Fixed Assets	350,000
Total Assets	380,000
Long-Term Debt	180,000
Common Stock	200,000
Total Equities	380,000

All debt financing was provided by Sentex. The debt was incurred on January 1, 2007, in cuzos, and is secured by the assets of Cellular.

For the year ending December 31, 2007, Cellular's Income Statement is as follows:

Cellular Company Inc.
Income Statement For the Year Ended December 31, 2007
(in cuzos)

Sales		600,000
Cost Of Goods Sold		(400,000)
Gross Margin		200,000
Selling And Administrative Expenses	(70,000)	
Interest	(20,000)	(90,000)
Net Income Before Taxes		110,000
Local Taxes	(33,000)	
Less Allowance For:		
Export Incentive	6,500	
Training Costs	22,000	(4,500)
Net Income After Taxes		105,500

Cellular's Balance Sheet as at December 31, 2007 is as follows:

Cellular Company Inc.
Balance Sheet As At December 31, 2007
(in cuzos)

Cash	25,000
Note Receivable	100,000
Accounts Receivable	65,000
Inventories (At Cost)	90,000
Total Current Assets	280,000
Fixed Assets	
(At Cost Less Accumulated Amortization Of $120,000)	230,000
Land (For Future Development)	10,000
Total Assets	520,000

Accounts Payable	30,000
Taxes Payable	4,500
Total Current Liabilities	34,500
Long-Term Liabilities:	
10 Percent Bonds Payable Due January 1, 2014	180,000
Total Liabilities	214,500
Common Stock	200,000
Retained Earnings	105,500
Total Equities	520,000

Other Information:

1. Raw material and labour costs were incurred uniformly throughout the year.
2. Sales were made uniformly throughout the year.
3. The Fixed Assets were acquired on January 1, 2007, and are amortized using the sum-of-the-years'-digits method over four years.
4. The Note Receivable is a 90-day non-interest-bearing note received from a customer in exchange for merchandise sold in October, 2007.
5. Land was purchased on December 31, 2007, for 10,000 cuzos.
6. The following exchange rates were in effect for the 2007 year:

Rate at January 1, 2007	1 cuzo = $2.00 Canadian
Average rate for the year 2007	1 cuzo = $1.82 Canadian
Rate at December 31, 2007	1 cuzo = $1.65 Canadian

7. Cost Of Goods Sold and Inventories include amortization of 98,000 cuzos and 22,000 cuzos, respectively. The calculation of Cost Of Goods Sold, in cuzos, is as follows:

Material Purchases	300,000
Labour	70,000
Total Purchases	370,000
Amortization	120,000
Total Goods Available	490,000
Closing Inventory	(90,000)
Cost Of Goods Sold	400,000

Required Sentex is in the process of preparing consolidated financial statements for the year ended December 31, 2007.

A. Which method of translation should Sentex use, according to Canadian generally accepted accounting principles? Justify your selection using the information from the question.

B. Calculate the exchange gain or loss on the accounts of Cellular Company Inc.

C. Prepare the translated Balance Sheet as at December 31, 2007 and the translated Income Statement for the year ending December 31, 2007 for Cellular Company Inc.

(SMA Adapted)

Self Study Problem Ten - 4

Royce Ltd. is a British company with all of its facilities located in Manchester, England. The Company was founded on December 31, 2003. However, on December 31, 2004, all of its outstanding shares were acquired by Beaver Inc., a publicly traded Canadian company. You have been assigned the task of translating Royce's financial statements from U.K. pounds (£) into Canadian dollars for inclusion in the consolidated financial statements of Beaver Inc.

Royce Ltd.'s Balance Sheets as at December 31, 2007 and December 31, 2008, as well as its Statement Of Income And Change In Retained Earnings for the year ending December 31, 2008, are as follows:

Royce Ltd.
Balance Sheets
As At December 31

	2008	2007
Cash	£ 212,000	£ 187,000
Accounts Receivable	350,000	327,000
Inventories	1,856,000	1,528,000
Plant And Equipment (Net)	4,900,000	5,320,000
Land	600,000	800,000
Total Assets	£7,918,000	£8,162,000
Current Liabilities	£ 87,000	£ 143,000
Long-Term Liabilities	700,000	1,000,000
Common Stock - No Par	5,600,000	5,600,000
Retained Earnings	1,531,000	1,419,000
Total Equities	£7,918,000	£8,162,000

Royce Ltd.
Statement Of Income And Change In Retained Earnings
Year Ending December 31, 2008

Sales	£6,611,000
Gain On Sale Of Land	125,000
Total Revenues	£6,736,000
Cost Of Goods Sold	£4,672,000
Amortization Expense	420,000
Selling And Administrative Expenses	1,230,000
Interest Expense	84,000
Loss On Debt Retirement	50,000
Total Expenses	£6,456,000
Net Income	£ 280,000
Less: Dividends On Common Shares	(168,000)
Increase In Retained Earnings	£ 112,000

Other Information:

1. All £5,600,000 of Royce's Common Stock - No Par was issued when the Company was founded on December 31, 2003. With respect to the proceeds, £800,000 was used to acquire the Land which is shown in the December 31, 2007 Balance Sheet. Of the remaining proceeds, £4,400,000 was used to acquire Plant And Equipment with an estimated useful life of 20 years. This Plant And Equipment is being depreciated on a straight line basis.

2. One -quarter of the Land which was acquired when Royce was founded was sold on July 1, 2008. The proceeds of disposition were £325,000, resulting in a reported gain on the sale of £125,000.
3. Royce still owns all of the Plant And Equipment that was acquired when the Company was founded. In addition, a further £2,000,000 of Plant And Equipment was acquired on January 1, 2007. This more recently acquired Plant And Equipment was estimated to have a useful life of 10 years at the time of its acquisition and is being depreciated by the straight line method over this period.
4. The acquisition of Plant And Equipment described in Item 3 was financed with £1,000,000 of internally generated funds along with £1,000,000 of debt financing. The stated rate of interest on the debt is 12 percent per annum, with payments required on July 1 and January 1 of each year. The debt was issued on January 1, 2007 at its maturity value and is scheduled to mature on December 31, 2016. However, on January 1, 2008, 30 percent of this debt was retired through a payment of £350,000 in cash, resulting in a loss of £50,000.
5. The December 31, 2007 Inventories were acquired on October 1, 2007 and the December 31, 2008 Inventories were acquired on July 1, 2008. The 2008 Sales and purchases occurred uniformly over the year. The cost of Inventories is determined on a FIFO basis.
6. Because of the nature of Royce's business, a majority of the 2008 Selling And Administrative Expenses were incurred in the second half of the year. Specifically, it is estimated that two-thirds of these expenses were in the second half of 2008, with only one-third being incurred in the first half of the year.
7. The 2008 dividends were declared on October 1, 2008 and paid on December 31, 2008.
8. Selected spot rates for the U.K. Pound are as follows:

December 31, 2003	£1 = $2.20
December 31, 2004	£1 = $2.18
January 1, 2007	£1 = $2.15
October 1, 2007	£1 = $2.11
December 31, 2007	£1 = $2.08
July 1, 2008	£1 = $2.04
October 1, 2008	£1 = $2.02
December 31, 2008	£1 = $2.00

During 2008, the exchange rate moved uniformly downward throughout the year.

Required:

A. Assume that Beaver Inc. has classified Royce Ltd. as an integrated foreign operation. To assist in the preparation of Beaver Inc.'s consolidated financial statements, prepare, in Canadian dollars:

i. a Balance Sheet as at December 31, 2007,
ii. a calculation of the exchange gain or loss on the accounts of Royce Ltd. for the year ending December 31, 2008,
iii. a Statement of Income and Change in Retained Earnings for the year ending December 31, 2008, and
iii. a Balance Sheet as at December 31, 2008.

B. Assume that Beaver Inc. has classified Royce Ltd. as a self sustaining foreign operation. You have been provided with the information that the correct December 31, 2007 balance in the Accumulated Other Comprehensive Income account is a credit of $772,000. To assist in the preparation of Beaver Inc.'s consolidated financial statements, prepare in Canadian dollars:

i. a Balance Sheet as at December 31, 2007,
ii. a calculation of the exchange gain or loss on the accounts of Royce Ltd. for the year ending December 31, 2008,
iii. a Statement of Net And Comprehensive Income for the year ending December 31, 2008,
iv. a Statement of Changes in Shareholders' Equity for the year ending December 31, 2008, and
v. a Balance Sheet as at December 31, 2008.

Self Study Problem Ten - 5

The comparative Balance Sheets and the 2008 Income Statement of the Brazal Company, in New Cozos (NC, hereafter) are as follows:

Brazal Company
Comparative Balance Sheets
As At December 31

	2008	2007
Cash And Current Receivables	NC11,000,000	NC 6,500,000
Long-Term Receivable	5,000,000	5,000,000
Inventories	8,000,000	9,500,000
Plant And Equipment	23,000,000	17,000,000
Accumulated Amortization	(5,000,000)	(4,000,000)
Land	6,000,000	3,000,000
Total Assets	NC48,000,000	NC37,000,000
Current Liabilities	NC 3,000,000	NC 5,000,000
Long-Term Liabilities	10,000,000	Nil
No Par Common Stock	20,000,000	18,000,000
Retained Earnings	15,000,000	14,000,000
Total Equities	NC48,000,000	NC37,000,000

Brazal Company
Income Statement
For The Year Ending December 31, 2008

Sales	NC50,000,000
Interest Revenue	1,000,000
Total Revenues	NC51,000,000
Cost Of Goods Sold	NC30,000,000
Tax Expense	10,000,000
Amortization Expense	2,000,000
Other Expenses	5,000,000
Total Expenses	NC47,000,000
Income Before Extraordinary Items	NC 4,000,000
Extraordinary Loss	(2,000,000)
Net Income	NC 2,000,000

Other Information:

1. The Brazal Company was formed as the wholly owned subsidiary of a Canadian public company. On the date of incorporation, January 1, 2001, No Par Common Stock was

issued for NC18 million and the proceeds were used to purchase Plant And Equipment for NC17 million on the same day. There were no further purchases or disposals of Plant And Equipment from January 1, 2001 to December 31, 2007. The Brazal Company uses the straight line method to calculate Amortization Expense.

2. The Long-Term Receivable resulted from a sales transaction on January 1, 2007 and is receivable on December 31, 2011. Interest at a rate of 20 percent per year is paid on the principal and is recorded in Interest Revenue.
3. The December 31, 2007 Inventories were acquired on October 1, 2007. The Inventories in the December 31, 2008 Balance Sheet were acquired on October 1, 2008.
4. On January 1, 2008, Plant And Equipment with an original cost of NC4 million and a net book value of NC3 million was expropriated by the local government for cash of NC1 million. The loss arising from this transaction is considered extraordinary.
5. On January 1, 2008, Long-Term Liabilities with a maturity date of December 31, 2017 and an interest rate of 12 percent were issued for total proceeds of NC10 million. These funds were used to purchase NC10 million in equipment on April 1, 2008. The equipment has an estimated useful life of 10 years.
6. The Land on the books on December 31, 2007 was acquired on January 1, 2007. The 2008 purchase of Land for NC3 million occurred on July 1, 2008.
7. Sales, Interest Revenue, Purchases and Other Expenses occurred evenly throughout the year. This would make the use of average indexes appropriate.
8. The Tax Expense accrued evenly throughout the year and was paid in two equal installments of NC5 million on July 1, 2008 and NC5 million on December 31, 2008.
9. Assume the foreign exchange rate data for the New Cozo and the Canadian dollar is as follows:

January 1, 2001	NC1 = $.100
January 1, 2007	NC1 = $.060
October 1, 2007	NC1 = $.045
December 31, 2007	NC1 = $.040
Average for 2007	NC1 = $.050
April 1, 2008	NC1 = $.038
July 1, 2008	NC1 = $.035
October 1, 2008	NC1 = $.032
December 31, 2008	NC1 = $.030
Average for 2008	NC1 = $.035

10. Dividends of NC1 million were declared and paid on October 1, 2008.
11. The new issue of NC2 million in No Par Common Stock occurred on April 1, 2008.
12. The Inventory is accounted for on the First-In, First-Out cost flow assumption.

Required:

A. Assume that the Brazal Company is classified as an integrated foreign operation. Prepare, in Canadian dollars:
   i. a calculation of the exchange gain or loss on the accounts of Brazal Company for the year ending December 31, 2008,
   ii. a Statement of Income and Change in Retained Earnings for the year ending December 31, 2008,
   iii. a Balance Sheet as at December 31, 2007, and
   iv. a Balance Sheet as at December 31, 2008.

B. Assume that the Brazal Company is classified as a self-sustaining foreign operation. You have been provided with the information that the correct December 31, 2007 balance in the Accumulated Other Comprehensive Income account is a debit of $887,500.

Prepare, in Canadian dollars:

i. a Balance Sheet as at December 31, 2007,
ii. a calculation of the exchange gain or loss on the accounts of Brazal Company for the year ending December 31, 2008,
iii. a Statement of Net And Comprehensive Income for the year ending December 31, 2008,
iv. a Statement of Changes in Shareholders' Equity for the year ending December 31, 2008, and
v. a Balance Sheet as at December 31, 2008.

Assignment Problems

(The solutions for these problems are only available in the solutions manual that has been provided to your instructor.)

Assignment Problem Ten - 1

Telemark Inc., a Canadian manufacturer of cross-country ski equipment, has incorporated a wholly owned Norwegian operating subsidiary, Suomi Inc. All of the subsidiary's capital results from the issuance of a 25 year, 11 percent mortgage for 3,500,000 Norwegian krone (K, hereafter) on April 1, 2007.

Suomi Inc. uses the total proceeds to finance the purchase of an office building on that date. The first interest payment of K385,000 and the first principal repayment of K140,000 are payable on April 1, 2008.

The total cost of the real estate has been allocated 80 percent to the building and 20 percent to the land. The building has an estimated useful life of 25 years and no net salvage value.

Both Telemark Inc. and Suomi Inc. use the straight line method to calculate amortization expense. They both have a March 31 year end.

Assume the exchange rate for the Norwegian krone had the following values:

April 1, 2007	K1 = $0.19
March 31, 2008	K1 = $0.15

The exchange rate changed uniformly over the year ending March 31, 2008.

Required:

A. Suomi Inc. can be classified as an integrated foreign operation or a self-sustaining foreign operation by Telemark Inc. For both cases, calculate the effect of the building purchase and related mortgage on the consolidated financial statements of Telemark Inc. for the year ending March 31, 2008. Specifically, translate the Balance Sheet and Income Statement accounts of Suomi Inc. affected by the building purchase, mortgage, and any translation adjustments.

B. What is the principal determinant of whether a foreign operation is classified as integrated or self-sustaining? Provide one example of the factors that should be considered in the analysis. Using your calculations in Part A, briefly discuss which method would provide more favorable results for the shareholders of Telemark Inc. in the current year and in the future.

(SMA Adapted)

Assignment Problem Ten - 2

On December 31, 2006, the Maple Leaf Company, a Canadian company, buys $7,000,000 worth of euros (€, hereafter) at a rate of €1 = $1.40. The resulting €5,000,000 is used to establish a new German subsidiary company, the Rhine Company, on this same date.

Also on this date, the Rhine Company borrows, at an annual rate of 10 percent, an additional €5,000,000 in Germany. The debt must be repaid after ten years. The Rhine Company then invests the entire cash balance of €10,000,000 in a tract of land. The land is immediately leased for a period of ten years with the lessee agreeing to pay the Rhine Company €1,000,000 at the end of each year.

During the subsequent year, the only activities of the Rhine Company are the collection of the lease payment and the payment of the interest on the Long-Term Debt. To simplify the problem, all other expenses and revenues of the Company have been ignored.

The Rhine Company's Income Statement for the year ending December 31, 2007 and its Balance Sheet as at December 31, 2007 in euros are as follows:

Income Statement
Year Ending December 31, 2007

Lease Revenue	€1,000,000
Interest Expense	500,000
Net Income	€ 500,000

Balance Sheet
As At December 31, 2007

Cash	€ 500,000
Land	10,000,000
Total Assets	€10,500,000
Long-Term Debt	€ 5,000,000
Contributed Capital	5,000,000
Retained Earnings	500,000
Total Equities	€10,500,000

The exchange rate increased to €1 = $1.60 on January 1, 2007 and remained unchanged at that level until January 1, 2008.

Required: Prepare the Rhine Company's translated Statement of Net And Comprehensive Income for the year ending December 31, 2007 and the Company's translated Balance Sheet as at December 31, 2007 in Canadian dollars using the alternative methods described in the following three Cases.

Case One Assume that the temporal method is used for the translation of all assets and liabilities and that exchange adjustments are included in Net Income in the year in which the exchange rate change occurs.

Case Two Assume that the temporal method is used for the translation of all assets and liabilities and that exchange adjustments are treated as Other Comprehensive Income.

Case Three Assume that the current rate method is used for the translation of all assets and liabilities and that exchange adjustments are treated as Other Comprehensive Income.

Assignment Problem Ten - 3

The Israeli Company, Afula Inc., is a wholly owned subsidiary of the Canadian company, Goodnite Inc. Goodnite Inc. acquired its investment in the shares of Afula on January 1, 1994. The Statement Of Income And Change In Retained Earnings for Afula Inc. in Israeli New Shekels (S, hereafter) for the year ending December 31, 2007 is as follows:

Afula Company
Statement of Income and Change in Retained Earnings
Year Ending December 31, 2007

Sales Revenue	S4,500,000
Cost Of Goods Sold	S1,500,000
Amortization Expense	225,000
Interest Expense	150,000
Selling And Administrative Expense	375,000
Taxes (At 30 Percent)	675,000
Total Expenses	S2,925,000
Income Before Extraordinary Items	S1,575,000
Extraordinary Loss On Expropriation Of Land (Net Of S45,000 In Taxes Recovered)	(255,000)
Net Income	S1,320,000
Dividends Declared	(120,000)
Increase In Retained Earnings	S1,200,000

Other Information:

1. Sales occur evenly throughout the year.

2. The inventory on hand on January 1, 2007 was purchased on September 30, 2006 for S450,000. Purchases during 2007 of S1,800,000 occurred evenly over the first three quarters. The inventory on hand on December 31, 2007 was purchased on September 30, 2007. Inventory is accounted for on a first-in, first-out inventory flow assumption.

3. The Amortization Expense pertains to a building which was purchased on January 1, 1997.

4. The Interest Expense relates to the 10 percent, 20 year bonds which were issued for S1,500,000 on January 1, 2007.

5. The Selling And Administrative Expenses occurred evenly over the year.

6. Income Taxes on ordinary income accrued evenly over the year.

7. The Extraordinary Loss arises from the expropriation of a parcel of land which was purchased on January 1, 1997 for S750,000. This land was expropriated by the local government on December 31, 2007 for proceeds of S450,000.

8. The dividends of Afula Inc. were declared on September 30, 2007 and paid on December 31, 2007.

9. The net monetary assets of Afula Inc. on January 1, 2007, before the issuance of the S1,500,000 in bonds (see Part 4), totalled S2,250,000.

10. Changes in the exchange rate between the New Israeli Shekel and the Canadian dollar occurred uniformly over the year 2007. Assume the exchange rate was as follows:

January 1, 1997	S1 = $.20
September 30, 2006	S1 = $.24
January 1, 2007	S1 = $.25
March 31, 2007	S1 = $.27
June 30, 2007	S1 = $.29
September 30, 2007	S1 = $.31
December 31, 2007	S1 = $.33
Average For 2007	S1 = $.29

Required: Translate the Statement Of Income And Change In Retained Earnings of the Afula Company for use in the preparation of the 2007 consolidated financial statements of the Goodnite Company assuming:

A. the Afula Company is an integrated foreign operation.
B. the Afula Company is a self-sustaining foreign operation.

Note that a Statement of Comprehensive Income is not required.

Assignment Problem Ten - 4

On December 31, 2005, the Olaf Company, a Danish retail operation, was acquired by a Canadian company. On this acquisition date, the carrying values of all of the identifiable assets and liabilities of the Olaf Company equalled their fair values and the Canadian parent purchased 100 percent of the voting shares of Olaf at their book value. On December 31, 2005, the Olaf Company had the following account balances in krone (Kr, hereafter):

Retained Earnings	Kr 192,000
No Par Common Stock	Kr1,200,000
Land	Kr 600,000
Equipment	Kr 510,000
Accumulated Amortization - Equipment	Kr 70,000
Building	Kr2,100,000
Accumulated Amortization - Building	Kr 320,000

The adjusted Trial Balance of the Olaf Company for the year ending December 31, 2007 is as follows:

Cash	Kr 150,000
Accounts Receivable	255,000
Inventory	510,000
Equipment	690,000
Building	2,100,000
Land	600,000
Cost of Goods Sold	2,400,000
Amortization Expense	240,000
Other Expenses	960,000
Dividends Declared	600,000
Total Debits	Kr8,505,000
Accounts Payable	Kr 450,000
Long-Term Note Payable	900,000
No Par Common Stock	1,200,000
Retained Earnings	600,000
Sales	4,500,000
Accumulated Amortization	840,000
Allowance For Doubtful Accounts	15,000
Total Credits	Kr8,505,000

Other Information:

1. Sales and inventory Purchases occurred uniformly over the year. The Other Expenses include Kr6,000 of bad debts which were credited to the Allowance For Doubtful Accounts on December 31, 2007. Also on December 31, 2007, Kr9,000 in bad debts were written off against the Allowance For Doubtful Accounts. The remainder of the Other Expenses occurred uniformly over the year.

2. The exchange rate for the Danish krone and the Canadian dollar is as follows:

December 31, 2005	Kr1 = $0.1000
December 31, 2006	Kr1 = $0.1600
Average for the 2006 fourth quarter	Kr1 = $0.1525
December 31, 2007	Kr1 = $0.2000
Average for 2007	Kr1 = $0.1800
Average for the 2007 fourth quarter	Kr1 = $0.1950

3. The dividends were declared on January 1, 2007.

4. Year end Inventories are purchased uniformly over the last quarter of each year. On December 31, 2006 the Inventories totalled Kr750,000 and on December 31, 2007 they totalled Kr510,000.

5. On January 1, 2007, equipment was purchased for Kr180,000. It has an estimated useful life of six years with no anticipated net salvage value. The Olaf Company uses the straight line method to calculate Amortization Expense.

6. The December 31, 2007 Accumulated Amortization balance is allocated Kr240,000 to the Equipment and Kr600,000 to the Building.

7. The Long-Term Note Payable was issued on January 1, 2006 and is due on January 1, 2010.

8. The Olaf Company had current monetary assets of Kr230,000 and current monetary liabilities of Kr890,000 as at December 31, 2006.

Required: The Olaf Company is classified as an integrated foreign operation by its Canadian parent. Its financial statements are translated to be included in the consolidated financial statements of the Canadian parent. Prepare the following in Canadian dollars:

A. A calculation of the exchange gain or loss on the accounts of Olaf Company for 2007.

B. The translated Statement of Income and Change in Retained Earnings of the Olaf Company for the year ending December 31, 2007.

C. The translated Balance Sheet of the Olaf Company as at December 31, 2007.

You may find it useful to translate the adjusted trial balance as of December 31, 2007 prior to preparing the financial statements required.

Assignment Problem Ten - 5

The Statement of Income and Change in Retained Earnings and the comparative Balance Sheets for the year ending March 31, 2008, of the Bulgar Company, a Bulgarian company, in Bulgarian lev (L, hereafter) are as follows:

Bulgar Company
Statement Of Income And Change In Retained Earnings
For The Year Ending March 31, 2008

Sales	L67,263,750
Total Revenues	L67,263,750
Cost of Goods Sold	L45,000,000
Amortization Expense	2,700,000
Other Expenses	13,725,500
Taxes	1,650,000
Total Expenses	L63,075,500
Net Income	L 4,188,250
Dividends On Common Stock	(1,500,000)
Increase in Retained Earnings	L 2,688,250

Bulgar Company
Balance Sheets As At March 31

	2008	2007
Cash And Current Receivables	L 4,938,250	L 2,900,000
Inventories	3,450,000	3,750,000
Plant And Equipment	27,000,000	27,000,000
Accumulated Amortization	(7,200,000)	(4,500,000)
Land	7,500,000	4,500,000
Total Assets	L35,688,250	L33,650,000
Current Liabilities	L 1,150,000	L 1,800,000
Long-Term Liabilities	9,000,000	9,000,000
No Par Common Stock	22,500,000	22,500,000
Retained Earnings	3,038,250	350,000
Total Equities	L 35,688,250	L33,650,000

Other Information:

1. On April 1, 2005, the date of incorporation of the Bulgar Company, No Par Common Stock was issued for L22.5 million. The proceeds were used to purchase Plant And Equipment for L18,000,000 and Land for L4,500,000 on the same day. The Plant and Equipment had an estimated service life of ten years with no anticipated salvage value. The Bulgar Company uses the straight line method to calculate Amortization Expense.

2. On April 1, 2006, additional Plant and Equipment was purchased with the proceeds from a L9 million issue of bonds maturing on April 1, 2016. These additions also have a ten year estimated service life with no anticipated salvage value.

3. The March 31, 2007 Inventories were acquired on January 1, 2007. The Inventories in the March 31, 2008 Balance Sheet were acquired on January 1, 2008. The Bulgar Company uses the first-in, first-out inventory flow assumption.

4. Sales, Purchases and Other Expenses occurred evenly throughout the year. The taxes were paid quarterly in equal installments.

5. On October 1, 2007, Land was purchased for cash of L3 million.

6. The dividends on common stock were declared on January 1, 2008 updated and paid on February 1, 2008.

7. The exchange rate movements occurred evenly throughout the year. The average exchange rate for the year ending March 31, 2008 was L1 = $.84. Other foreign exchange rate data for the lev and the Canadian dollar was as follows:

April 1, 2005	L1 = $.75
April 1, 2006	L1 = $.78
January 1, 2007	L1 = $.78
March 31, 2007	L1 = $.82
July 1, 2007	L1 = $.85
October 1, 2007	L1 = $.84
January 1, 2008	L1 = $.83
March 31, 2008	L1 = $.85

Required:

A. Assume that the Bulgar Company is classified as an integrated foreign operation. Prepare, in Canadian dollars:

i. a calculation of the exchange gain or loss on the accounts of Bulgar Company the year ending March 31, 2008,
ii. a Statement of Income and Change in Retained Earnings for the year ending March 31, 2008,
iii. a Balance Sheet as at March 31, 2007, and
iv. a Balance Sheet as at March 31, 2008.

B. Assume that the Bulgar Company is classified as a self-sustaining foreign operation. You have been provided with the information that the correct March 31, 2007 balance in the Accumulated Other Comprehensive Income account is a credit of $1,797,000.

Prepare, in Canadian dollars:

i. a Balance Sheet as at March 31, 2007,
ii. a calculation of the exchange gain or loss on the accounts of Bulgar Company the year ending March 31, 2008,
iii. a Statement of Net And Comprehensive Income for the year ending March 31, 2008,
iv. a Statement of Changes in Shareholders' Equity for the year ending March 31, 2008, and
v. a Balance Sheet as at March 31, 2008.

Assignment Problem Ten - 6

Canco is a Canadian corporation that specializes in the selling of men's and women's pants. In an attempt to diversify its product line, it acquired 80 percent of the outstanding voting shares of the Forco Company on December 31, 2007 for $10 million in cash. Forco is a Kiev based company that is famous for a hand embroidered line of sweaters that it sells. Because of the extensive use of common distribution channels that will be possible after this business combination, Forco is classified as an integrated foreign operation.

Forco's accounting records are expressed in Ukrainian Hryvnias (H, hereafter). The comparative Balance Sheets of the two Companies as at December 31, 2007 and December 31, 2008 and the Income Statements of the two Companies for the year ending December 31, 2008 are as follows:

Balance Sheets
As At December 31, 2007
(000s Omitted)

	Canco	Forco
Cash	$ 1,000	H 8,000
Accounts Receivable	1,000	10,000
Inventories	3,000	7,000
Investment In Forco (Cost)	10,000	N/A
Plant And Equipment (Net)	5,000	6,000
Land	Nil	2,000
Total Assets	$20,000	H33,000
Current Liabilities	$ 1,000	H 3,000
Long-Term Liabilities	5,000	5,000
No Par Common Stock	5,000	15,000
Retained Earnings	9,000	10,000
Total Equities	$20,000	H33,000

Balance Sheets
As At December 31, 2008
(000s Omitted)

	Canco	Forco
Cash	$ 2,000	H 10,000
Accounts Receivable	3,100	11,200
Inventories	4,000	9,000
Investment In Forco (Cost)	10,000	N/A
Plant And Equipment (Net)	4,400	4,300
Land	Nil	3,000
Total Assets	$23,500	H37,500
Current Liabilities	$ 1,500	H 3,500
Long-Term Liabilities	5,000	5,000
No Par Common Stock	5,000	15,000
Retained Earnings	12,000	14,000
Total Equities	$23,500	H37,500

Canco And Forco Companies
Income Statements
For The Year Ending December 31, 2008
(000s Omitted)

	Canco	Forco
Sales	$35,000	H40,000
Cost Of Goods Sold	$28,000	H32,000
Amortization Expense	1,000	500
Selling And Administrative Expenses	1,600	1,500
Other Expenses And Losses	600	1,000
Tax Expense	800	1,000
Total Expenses	$32,000	H36,000
Net Income	$ 3,000	H 4,000

Other Information:

1. Assume that selected exchange rates between the Hryvnia and the Canadian dollar are as follows:

January 1, 2002	H1 = $.210
March 1, 2002	H1 = $.220
July 1, 2007	H1 = $.230
December 31, 2007	H1 = $.240
Average For 2007	H1 = $.230
May 1, 2008	H1 = $.250
July 1, 2008	H1 = $.255
September 1, 2008	H1 = $.260
December 31, 2008	H1 = $.270
Average For 2008	H1 = $.255

The exchange rate changed uniformly throughout the period under consideration.

2. At the time Canco acquired its interest in Forco, all of the identifiable assets and liabilities of Forco had carrying values that were equal to their fair values except for Equipment which had a fair value that was H1,500,000 greater than its carrying value. The remaining useful life of this Equipment on December 31, 2007 was twelve years. Forco's Plant And Equipment was acquired on March 1, 2002. Both Companies use straight line calculations for all amortization charges.
3. There was no impairment of the goodwill in any of the years under consideration.
4. Selling And Administration Expenses occurred uniformly over the second half of 2008. Sales, Purchases, Other Expenses, and Tax Expense took place evenly throughout the year.
5. The December 31, 2007 Inventories of Forco were purchased on July 1, 2007. The December 31, 2008 Inventories of Forco were purchased on September 1, 2008.
6. The Long-Term Liabilities of the Forco Company were issued on January 1, 2002 and mature on January 1, 2012. Forco's No Par Common Stock was also issued on January 1, 2002.
7. Neither of the two Companies declared or paid dividends during 2008.
8. Forco's Land consists of two parcels. One was acquired on July 1, 2007 for H2,000,000 and the second was purchased for H1,000,000 on September 1, 2008.
9. On May 1, 2008, Canco purchases Equipment from Forco at a price of $250,000. The Equipment has a carrying value of H1,200,000 on the books of Forco and a remaining useful life at the time of the sale of four years. This is not the Equipment on which there was a fair value change at the time Canco acquired Forco.
10. On May 1, 2008, Forco sold H5,000,000 in merchandise to Canco. Of this sale, Canco had H2,000,000 remaining in the December 31, 2008 Inventories. Sales are priced to provide a gross profit of 20 percent on the sales price. Both Companies account for Inventories on a First In, First Out basis.

Required:

A. Prepare translated Balance Sheets as at December 31, 2007 and December 31, 2008, and a translated 2008 Income Statement for the Forco Company.

B. Using the translated financial statements from Part A, prepare consolidated Balance Sheets as at December 31, 2007 and December 31, 2008, and a consolidated Income Statement for the year ending December 31, 2008, for the Canco Company and its subsidiary, the Forco Company. Ignore the effect of intercompany transactions on the consolidated Tax Expense.

Accounting For Not-For-Profit Organizations

Introduction

11-1. Until 1989, not-for-profit organizations were not subject to the Recommendations of the *CICA Handbook* and, as a consequence, they were in a position to use virtually any accounting principles that they wished. Not surprisingly, this led to a situation in which different not-for-profit organizations used a wide variety of procedures, resulting in financial statements that made meaningful interpretation by users extremely difficult.

11-2. This began to change in 1989. While recognizing that its Recommendations were not applicable in all areas of not-for-profit accounting, the *CICA Handbook* became applicable to these organizations in general. This change was accompanied by the addition of Section 4230, "Non-Profit Organizations - Specific Items", to the *Handbook*. This small Section provided limited guidance on such matters as pledges, donated materials and services, and restricted amounts, and was withdrawn in 1998.

11-3. Since 1989, the CICA's Accounting Standards Board and its Not-For-Profit Task Force have worked on developing accounting standards to deal with certain areas where these organizations have unique problems. This process reached fruition with the issuance of six *CICA Handbook* Sections in 1996 and one additional Section in 1997. These Sections are:

Section 4400 Financial Statement Presentation By Not-For-Profit Organizations

Section 4410 Contributions - Revenue Recognition

Section 4420 Contributions Receivable

Section 4430 Capital Assets Held By Not-For-Profit Organizations

Section 4440 Collections Held By Not-For-Profit Organizations

Section 4450 Reporting Controlled And Related Entities By Not-For-Profit Organizations

Section 4460 Disclosure Of Related Party Transactions By Not-For-Profit Organizations

11-4. It is likely that these Recommendations have led to improved financial reporting by not-for-profit organizations. While some not-for-profit organizations may choose not to comply with some or all of these Recommendations, the need to have credibility with the users of their financial statements, particularly those who contribute resources, certainly encourages full or partial compliance.

Not-For-Profit Organizations Defined

11-5. The definition of not-for-profit organizations does not include government entities. Recommendations applicable to federal, provincial, territorial, and local governments and to other government entities, such as funds, agencies, and corporations are found in the separate *CICA Public Sector Accounting Handbook* issued by the Public Sector Accounting Board (PSAB).

11-6. All seven of the relevant *CICA Handbook* Sections repeat the same definition of not-for-profit organizations. This definition is as follows:

> **Paragraph 4400.02(a) Not-for-profit organizations** are entities, normally without transferable ownership interests, organized and operated exclusively for social, educational, professional, religious, health, charitable or any other not-for-profit purpose. A not-for-profit organization's members, contributors and other resource providers do not, in such capacity, receive any financial return directly from the organization.

11-7. The preceding definition makes it clear that there are three characteristics associated with being a not-for-profit organization. These are:

1. Not-for-profit organizations normally do not have a transferable ownership interest.
2. Not-for-profit organizations are operated exclusively for social, educational, professional, religious, health, charitable, or other not-for-profit purposes.
3. The resource providers, be they members or contributors, do not stand to benefit because of their status as resource providers.

11-8. In many cases, the application of this definition is very straightforward. For organizations that have no activity other than raising funds and using these funds in achieving not-for-profit goals, there is little question as to their status as a not-for-profit organization. This would apply to such organizations as the Canadian Cancer Society or the United Way.

11-9. However, the classification of other organizations may be less clear cut. For example, while golf and country clubs are not usually organized to make a profit, use of the facilities generally requires the payment or contribution of a membership fee. This means that the members benefit because of their status as resource providers. Similar problems exist with condominium corporations and various types of agricultural co-operatives.

11-10. There are other problems related to organizations such as hospitals and universities, where a government organization is often the principal contributor. If such organizations are considered to be government agencies, then they are subject to the Recommendations of the Public Sector Accounting Board. Alternatively, if they are considered to be not-for-profit organizations, the *CICA Handbook* Recommendations are applicable.

GAAP For Not-For-Profit Organizations

General Approach

11-11. Unlike the situation with public sector organizations, where a separate *Public Sector Accounting Handbook* provides guidance, not-for-profit organizations are subject to the regular *CICA Handbook* provisions. This is reflected in the fact that Section 1100, "General Accepted Accounting Principles", does not contain a scope exemption for these organizations.

11-12. There is recognition, however, that some specialized recommendations were needed. For example, profit oriented organizations do not normally have to deal with contributions or pledges. As was noted in the introduction to this Chapter, these needs have been dealt with by adding seven specialized *CICA Handbook* Sections.

11-13. There is also an introduction to Section 4400 through 4460 that contains an Appendix that sets out the applicability of the various *CICA Handbook* Sections to not-for-profit organizations. As the great majority of *Handbook* Sections are designated as applicable, reproducing the entire Appendix would not be useful. However, we do feel that it is important that you have some awareness of the Sections having either limited applicability or no applicability. These Sections are as follows:

Section 1300	Differential Reporting
Section 1520	Income Statement
Section 1530	Comprehensive Income
Section 1540	Cash Flow Statements
Section 1581	Business Combinations*
Section 1590	Subsidiaries*
Section 1625	Comprehensive Revaluation Of Assets And Liabilities
Section 1701	Segment Disclosure
Section 1751	Interim Financial Statements
Section 1800	Unincorporated Businesses
Section 3055	Interests In Joint Ventures*
Section 3061	Property, Plant, And Equipment
Section 3062	Goodwill And Other Intangible Assets
Section 3063	Impairment Of Long-Lived Assets
Section 3240	Share Capital
Section 3251	Equity
Section 3260	Reserves
Section 3465	Income Taxes
Section 3500	Earnings Per Share
Section 3610	Capital Transactions
Section 3800	Accounting For Government Assistance
Section 3805	Investment Tax Credits
Section 3840	Related Party Transactions
Section 3841	Economic Dependence
Section 3870	Stock-Based Compensation And Other Stock-Based Payments
Section 4100	Pension Plans
Section 4210	Life Insurance Enterprises

* These Sections contain guidance that may be relevant to some not-for-profit organizations.

Overview Of Handbook Sections For Not-For-Profit Organizations

11-14. The material that is contained in the seven *Handbook* Sections presents a number of ideas. Some aspects of these ideas are confusing and, in addition, they are interrelated in a manner that cuts across the boundaries of the individual Sections. Before proceeding to a more detailed consideration of these Sections, we would like to give you a broad overview of their content and the manner in which we intend to present the material.

11-15. A basic issue that is covered in these new Sections is the use of fund accounting. While we will describe fund accounting concepts in more detail in the next section of this Chapter, we would note that this is a form of accounting in which the total entity is disaggregated into a group of components or funds. Though it has no applicability to profit-oriented enterprises, it has been, and continues to be, widely used by both government and not-for-profit organizations.

11-16. Section 4400 establishes that not-for-profit organizations can use fund accounting in any format that they wish. However, there is a constraint. Unless it is used in the form that the Section describes as the "restricted fund method", the organization will be limited in its approach to revenue recognition. This does not become clear until you read Section 4410 which deals specifically with revenue recognition. As a result, our detailed coverage of

Section 4410 will precede our in-depth coverage of Section 4400.

11-17. Section 4410 indicates that not-for-profit contributions must be recognized using either the "restricted fund method" or the "deferral method". The restricted fund method allows restricted contributions to be recognized when they are received, as opposed to being deferred until there is compliance with the restrictions, either through making expenditures or through the passage of time (restrictions may require certain types of expenditures or they may require that the funds be used in specified periods of time).

11-18. This restricted fund method, which provides for earlier recognition of restricted revenues, can only be used in the context of fund accounting. Further, it is only available when the approach to fund accounting is based on classifying funds in terms of their restrictions. It is not available with any other form of fund accounting.

11-19. The combined Recommendations of Sections 4400 and 4410 result in a situation in which a Canadian not-for-profit organization can use its choice of three different approaches to preparing its financial statements. These approaches can be described as follows:

Aggregated (Non-Fund) Accounting If the organization chooses not to use fund accounting, it will present its financial statements on an aggregate basis. If this approach is used, the deferral method of revenue recognition must be adopted.

Fund Accounting - Restricted Fund Basis If the organization uses fund accounting and classifies its funds in terms of externally imposed restrictions, it can use the restricted fund method of revenue recognition for contributions received.

Fund Accounting - Other Basis If the organization uses fund accounting and classifies its funds on any basis other than externally imposed restrictions (for example, funds classified by activity such as providing counseling or meals), it must use the deferral approach to revenue recognition for its contributions.

11-20. The preceding results of the combined reading of Sections 4400 and 4410 provides the basis of accounting for not-for-profit organizations in Canada. The other material in the seven Sections can be described as follows:

Section 4400 In addition to providing for the use of fund accounting, Section 4400 contains Recommendations on the form and content of the four financial statements that should be presented by not-for-profit organizations.

Section 4410 This Section provides detailed guidance on the restricted fund and deferral methods of revenue recognition. Guidance is also provided for not-for-profit revenues other than contributions (e.g., investment income).

Section 4420 This brief Section could have been incorporated into Section 4410. Its only content is a Recommendation with respect to the measurement of contributions receivable. Guidance is also provided on pledges and bequests.

Section 4430 This important Section deals with capital assets held by not-for-profit organizations. Prior to the issuance of Section 4430, most organizations did not recognize their capital assets in their Balance Sheets, charging purchased items to expense in the period acquired and, in many cases, not giving any recognition to contributed capital assets. Section 4430 changes this situation by requiring that both purchased and contributed assets be recorded in the Statement Of Financial Position of the organization. It also deals with related issues such as the amortization of capital assets after they have been recorded in the accounts.

Section 4440 This brief Section deals with collections (e.g., the Henry Moore works held by the Art Gallery Of Ontario). It serves to make this type of capital asset exempt from the Recommendations of Section 4430.

Section 4450 This Section deals with the reporting that is required for controlled, significantly influenced, or other related entities in the financial statements of not-for-profit organizations.

Section 4460 This Section deals with the disclosure standards for related party transactions in the financial statements of not-for-profit organizations. Measurement issues are not dealt with in this Section.

11-21. In our approach to this material, we will begin by providing a general description of the concepts and procedures that are involved in fund accounting. This will be followed by a detailed discussion of revenue recognition for not-for-profit organizations, including the appropriate procedures for dealing with contributions receivable. This will include consideration of how the type of fund accounting adopted will influence the revenue recognition method used. With this material in hand, we will then present the material contained in Section 4400 on financial statement presentation.

11-22. At this point an example will be presented to illustrate the three basic approaches that can be used by not-for-profit organizations in preparing their financial statements. In this first example we will not include capital assets. Following this example, we will discuss the material in Sections 4430 and 4440 dealing with the capital assets of not-for-profit organizations. After we have reviewed this material, our first example will be extended to include capital assets, providing a fairly comprehensive illustration of the various methods that can be used by not-for-profit organizations.

11-23. The remainder of the Chapter will consider the *Handbook* Sections on the reporting entity and related party transactions, as well as a brief description of encumbrance accounting procedures.

Fund Accounting

Basic Concepts

11-24. As we have noted, fund accounting is widely used by both government organizations and not-for-profit organizations. It involves dividing the reporting entity into a number of pieces that are referred to as funds. As defined by the National Council On Governmental Accounting (a U.S. organization), a fund is defined as follows:

> A fund is defined as a fiscal and accounting entity with a self balancing set of accounts recording cash and other financial resources, together with all related liabilities and residual equities or balances, and changes therein, which are segregated for the purpose of carrying on specific activities or attaining certain objectives in accordance with special regulations, restrictions, or limitations.

11-25. Some of the typical funds that would be used by a not-for-profit organization would be as follows:

- **Current (Or Operating) Fund - Unrestricted** Unrestricted contributions such as donations, bequests, grants and other income are reported in this fund, together with the day-to-day operating costs.

- **Current Fund - Restricted** Current restricted funds are expendable funds restricted by the contributors for special purpose expenditures of a current nature.

- **Endowment (Donor Designated) Fund** This fund contains assets donated to an organization with the stipulation by the donor that only the income earned can be used, either for the general purposes of the organization or for special purposes. The asset is, therefore, restricted and non-expendable. Gains and losses realized on endowment investments may be transferable to other funds, depending on the terms of the original gift.

- **Board Designated Fund** The difference between this fund and a donor designated endowment fund is that, in the latter case, the board does not have access to the principal. Resources allocated for a particular purpose by the board of directors can be used for another purpose if the board wishes to change its previous allocation.

- **Plant Or Capital Asset Fund** This grouping normally comprises long-term assets such as land, building, furniture and equipment.
- **Custodial Funds** These are funds held in trust for other organizations.

11-26. Once the appropriate group of funds has been established, the *CICA Handbook* defines fund accounting as follows:

> **Paragraph 4400.02(c) Fund accounting** comprises the collective accounting procedures resulting in a self-balancing set of accounts for each fund established by legal, contractual or voluntary actions of an organization. Elements of a fund can include assets, liabilities, net assets, revenues and expenses (and gains and losses, where appropriate). Fund accounting involves an accounting segregation, although not necessarily a physical segregation, of resources.

Example

11-27. An example can be used to illustrate the ideas associated with fund accounting:

> **Example** Community Sports Ltd. is established on December 31 of the current year to encourage hiking in the summer and skiing in the winter. On this date, it receives unrestricted contributions of $500,000. Its Board allocates these contributions as follows:

General Administration	$100,000
Hiking Promotion	250,000
Skiing Promotion	150,000
Total	$500,000

> There are no other transactions before the December 31 year end.

11-28. If we assume that fund accounting is not used, the Statement of Operations for the current year and the Statement of Financial Position as at the year end would be as follows:

Community Sports Ltd.
Statement of Operations For The Current Year

Revenues	$500,000
Expenses	Nil
Excess Of Revenues Over Expenses	$500,000

Community Sports Ltd.
Statement of Financial Position As At December 31

Cash	$500,000
Total Assets	$500,000
Unrestricted Net Assets	$500,000

11-29. If the organization decides to use fund accounting, it would probably have separate funds for hiking and skiing, as well as an operating fund. In applying fund accounting, Community Sports could either put together three separate sets of financial statements or, alternatively, present all of the funds in a multi column format. The latter approach is illustrated as follows:

Community Sports Ltd.
Statement Of Operations For The Current Year

	Operating Fund	Hiking Fund	Skiing Fund	Total
Revenues	$100,000	$250,000	$150,000	$500,000
Expenses	Nil	Nil	Nil	Nil
Excess Of Revenues Over Expenses	$100,000	$250,000	$150,000	$500,000

Community Sports Ltd.
Statement of Financial Position As At December 31

	Operating Fund	Hiking Fund	Skiing Fund	Total
Cash	$100,000	$250,000	$150,000	$500,000
Total Assets	$100,000	$250,000	$150,000	$500,000
Unrestricted Net Assets	$100,000	$250,000	$150,000	$500,000

11-30. While this example is far too simple to be generally useful, it does serve to illustrate the basic difference between fund accounting and the more familiar aggregated approach to financial reporting.

The Need For Fund Accounting

11-31. While fund accounting has been widely used in both government and not-for-profit organization accounting, there are those who question its usefulness. The two basic problems with fund accounting can be described as follows:

Fund Definition Individual organizations can define the funds that they will use in a totally arbitrary fashion. This means that similar organizations can be made to appear very different through the use of a different group of funds. Further, the use of arbitrarily defined funds can be used to obscure the overall performance of the organization.

Interfund Transfers Until Section 4400 was added to the *CICA Handbook*, there were no rules governing the reporting of interfund transfers. Such transfers could be made at the discretion of the organization and could be reported in a manner that suggested more activity than the organization was actually experiencing.

11-32. These problems lead some authorities to suggest that fund accounting be eliminated. However, this form of accounting has a long tradition of use. Further, fund accounting has many supporters in the not-for-profit accounting community.

11-33. These supporters point out that a unique feature of not-for-profit organizations is the fact many of the resources that they receive are subject to various types of restrictions on their use. They argue that fund accounting is a very effective way of disclosing and keeping track of these restrictions. This is probably the primary argument that influenced the Accounting Standards Board in their decision to allow continued use of fund accounting in the not-for-profit area.

CICA Recommendations

11-34. While recognizing that fund accounting has potential difficulties, Section 4400 of the *CICA Handbook* allows the use of this approach in preparing the financial statements of not-for-profit organizations. The Board has, however, made a number of Recommendations that will deal with some of the problems.

11-35. To deal with the potentially arbitrary nature of fund definitions, Section 4400 makes the following Recommendation:

> **Paragraph 4400.06** *An organization that uses fund accounting in its financial statements should provide a brief description of the purpose of each fund reported.* (April, 1997)

11-36. This requires that not-for-profit organizations provide some rationale for the particular array of funds they are using. It is also noted that each fund reported should be presented on a consistent basis from year to year. If there are changes, they will have to be reported as changes in accounting policies.

11-37. With respect to the form of presentation, Section 4400 notes that fund accounting statements can be presented either individually, or in a multi-column format. It is even acceptable to use different formats for different statements of the same organization. The only constraint is that each format used satisfies the Recommendations made in the Section.

11-38. With respect to the problem of reporting interfund transfers, Section 4400 Recommends the following:

> **Paragraph 4400.12** *Interfund transfers should be presented in the statement of changes in net assets.* (April, 1997)
>
> **Paragraph 4400.13** *The amount and purpose of interfund transfers during the reporting period should be disclosed.* (April, 1997)
>
> **Paragraph 4400.14** *The amounts, terms and conditions of interfund loans outstanding at the reporting date should be disclosed.* (April, 1997)

11-39. These Recommendations will prevent interfund transfers from being treated as revenues in the Statement Of Operations. In addition, it should discourage the use of interfund transfers to give a false impression of activity, in that it requires a statement as to the purpose of these transactions.

11-40. If the organization uses a multi-column approach to disclosure, interfund loans and advances would be presented in the individual funds, but eliminated from the totals column of the statement. If a single column format is used, the only disclosure of these amounts would be in the notes to the financial statements.

Revenue Recognition - Handbook Section 4410

The Matching Principle Revised

11-41. You are all familiar with the application of the matching principle in profit oriented accounting. The major goal of a profit oriented enterprise is to generate revenues and, hopefully, profits. Revenues are recognized when they are earned and the resulting consideration can be reasonably measured. While this usually occurs when goods are sold, there are variations on this such as the percentage of completion method of recognizing revenue.

11-42. The situation with contributions received by not-for-profit organizations is different. The goal of these organizations is to deliver services. This means that, instead of starting with recognizing revenues, not-for-profit organizations focus on the cost of delivering services. When these costs are determined, the appropriate revenues are matched against the costs of providing services. In other words, the matching process is reversed, as compared to the situation with a profit oriented enterprise.

11-43. Because of this reversal, the usual Section 3400 revenue recognition procedures are not applicable to contributions received by not-for-profit organizations. Given this situation, revenue recognition is one of the areas where not-for-profit organizations need their own accounting standards.

Recognition Alternatives For Not-For-Profit Organizations

11-44. The basic Recommendation on revenue recognition for not-for-profit organizations is as follows:

> **Paragraph 4410.10** *An organization should recognize contributions in accordance with either:*
>
> *(a) the deferral method; or*
>
> *(b) the restricted fund method.* (April, 1997)

11-45. This Recommendation is a bit flawed in that it refers to the recognition of "contributions" under these two methods. As we will find out when we examine the more detailed provisions of Section 4410, these two methods are also applied to revenues other than contributions (e.g., investment income).

11-46. The first of these methods is defined as follows:

> **Paragraph 4410.02(d)** Under the **deferral method** of accounting for contributions, restricted contributions related to expenses of future periods are deferred and recognized as revenue in the period in which the related expenses are incurred. Endowment contributions are reported as direct increases in net assets. All other contributions are reported as revenue of the current period. Organizations that use fund accounting in their financial statements without following the restricted fund method would account for contributions under the deferral method.

11-47. As implied by the name, this method requires that the recognition of revenues that are restricted with respect to their use be deferred until that use actually occurs. For example, if an organization receives contributions of $500,000 during 2007, with the use of the funds being restricted to expenses that will be incurred in 2008, these revenues will not be included in the 2007 Statement Of Operations. Rather, they will be deferred and recognized in the 2008 Statement Of Operations.

11-48. The alternative restricted fund method is defined as follows:

> **Paragraph 4410.02(e)** The **restricted fund method** of accounting for contributions is a specialized type of fund accounting which involves the reporting of details of financial statement elements by fund in such a way that the organization reports total general funds, one or more restricted funds, and an endowment fund, if applicable. Reporting of financial statement elements segregated on a basis other than that of use restrictions (e.g., by program or geographic location) does not constitute the restricted fund method.

11-49. This terminology is somewhat unfortunate in that it really refers to a method of applying fund accounting (i.e., funds established on the basis of restrictions), rather than to a method of revenue recognition. However, if this definition is read in conjunction with other provisions in Section 4410, it becomes clear that what is being referred to here is really the cash basis of revenue recognition. (If the not-for-profit organization records contributions receivable, these would also be included in the revenues of the period, an issue that will be discussed in a later section of this Chapter.)

11-50. Returning to our example from Paragraph 11-47, if the organization receives contributions in 2007 that are restricted to expenses that will be incurred in 2008, use of the restricted fund method would permit these contributions to be recognized as revenues in 2007.

11-51. What the definition of the restricted fund method really clarifies is that it can only be used in situations where the not-for-profit organization has the following grouping of funds :

- A general or operating fund.
- One or more restricted funds.
- One or more endowment funds, if applicable.

11-52. As the restricted fund method allows earlier recognition of revenues from contributions, it is likely that this requirement will encourage not-for-profit organizations to classify their funds in terms of externally imposed restrictions. This would seem appropriate in that the primary argument for the continued use of fund accounting is that it is an effective way of disclosing and keeping track of restrictions on the use of contributions.

11-53. This is a fairly subtle solution to the problem of fund classification. Organizations are permitted to use any array of funds that they choose. However, if the basis for selection is not restrictions on contributions, they will have to use the deferral method of revenue recognition for contributions. This has the effect of creating two forms of fund accounting:

1. Fund accounting with funds classified to disclose restrictions.
2. Fund accounting with funds classified on any other basis (the normal alternative would be to disclose programs).

11-54. When these two applications of fund accounting are added to the possibility of using aggregated or non-fund accounting, we then have three different approaches to preparing the financial statements of not-for-profit organizations. While these alternatives were described in our overview of the relevant *Handbook* Sections, their description is repeated here to reinforce our discussion of the revenue recognition alternatives presented:

Aggregated (Non-Fund) Accounting If the organization chooses not to use fund accounting, it will present its financial statements on an aggregate basis. If this approach is used, the deferral method of revenue recognition must be adopted.

Fund Accounting - Restricted Fund Basis If the organization uses fund accounting and classifies its funds in terms of externally imposed restrictions, it can use the restricted fund method of revenue recognition for contributions received.

Fund Accounting - Other Basis If the organization uses fund accounting and classifies its funds on any basis other than externally imposed restrictions (i.e., restrictions on the use of funds imposed by donors), it must use the deferral approach to revenue recognition for its contributions.

Revenues Of Not-For-Profit Organizations

Contributions

11-55. A unique feature of not-for-profit organizations is the fact that they receive a significant portion of the revenues in the form of contributions. Section 4410 defines the various types of contributions received by not-for-profit organizations as follows:

Paragraph 4410.02(b) A **contribution** is a non-reciprocal transfer to a not-for-profit organization of cash or other assets or a non-reciprocal settlement or cancellation of its liabilities. Government funding provided to a not-for-profit organization is considered to be a contribution.

There are three types of contributions identified for purposes of this Section:

(i) A **restricted contribution** is a contribution subject to externally imposed stipulations that specify the purpose for which the contributed asset is to be used. A contribution restricted for the purchase of a capital asset or a contribution of the capital asset itself is a type of restricted contribution.

(ii) An **endowment contribution** is a type of restricted contribution subject to externally imposed stipulations specifying that the resources contributed be maintained permanently, although the constituent assets may change from time to time.

(iii) An **unrestricted contribution** is a contribution that is neither a restricted contribution nor an endowment contribution.

11-56. As further elaboration of the preceding definitions, Section 4410 defines restrictions as follows:

Paragraph 4410.02(c) Restrictions are stipulations imposed that specify how resources must be used. External restrictions are imposed from outside the organization, usually by the contributor of the resources. Internal restrictions are imposed in a formal manner by the organization itself, usually by resolution of the board of directors. Restrictions on contributions may only be externally imposed. Net assets or fund balances may be internally or externally restricted. Internally restricted net assets or fund balances are often referred to as reserves or appropriations.

11-57. The important point to note here is that, for purposes of applying the revenue recognition rules of Section 4410, only externally imposed restrictions qualify for defining restricted contributions. While the concept of external restrictions can be fairly complex in practice, the basic idea is that a contribution is restricted if the contributor has some type of recourse if the funds are not used in the manner specified. The degree of formality that is associated with the restriction may vary from situation to situation.

Other Not-For-Profit Organization Revenues

11-58. Because of the diversity of not-for-profit organizations, different organizations receive different types of revenues. Not all of these require special attention in Section 4410. For example, a not-for-profit hospital may operate a tuck shop to sell various consumer products that its clients and their visitors require. This type of operation is analogous to other similar activities found in profit oriented operations (e.g., a hotel may have a similar operation). Revenues of this type would be subject to the usual revenue recognition rules that apply to profit oriented enterprises.

11-59. Many not-for-profit organizations also have investment income. While some of these revenues may be equivalent to the investment income received by profit oriented enterprises, there is the possibility that contributors of the income earning assets have attached restrictions to the income produced. Because of this possibility, Section 4410 provides Recommendations for dealing with the investment income of not-for-profit organizations.

Application Of The Deferral Method

11-60. As indicated in the definition of the deferral method, some types of not-for-profit organization revenues must be deferred and only recognized when the related expenses are incurred. In simple terms, this deferral procedure applies directly to amounts that are restricted, whereas, amounts of revenues that are not restricted can be recognized as received. Section 4410 does, however, provide fairly detailed guidance on the application of this method to various types of revenues. This guidance is as follows:

Unrestricted Contributions These contributions can be recognized in the period in which they are received or become receivable.

Restricted Contributions The basic idea here is that the recognition of restricted contributions must be deferred until the restriction is fulfilled. The actual implementation of this will depend on the type of restriction that is involved:

Expenses Of Current Period If the restriction is for current period expenses, the contributions should be recognized in the current period.

Expenses Of Future Periods In this case, the contributions should be recognized in the same period or periods in which the related expenses are made.

Purchase Of Capital Assets If the restriction is based on acquiring capital assets that will be amortized, the contributions should be recognized on the same basis that the amortization expense is recorded. Alternatively, if the contributions are restricted to the acquisition of non-amortizable assets, they should be recorded as direct increases in net assets, without being disclosed as a revenue in the Statement Of Operations.

Repayment Of Debt The recognition pattern here will depend on the purpose for which the debt was incurred:

- If the debt was for expenses of one or more periods, the repayment contributions should be recognized when the related expenses are recognized.
- If the debt was for the acquisition of non-amortizable capital assets, the repayment contributions should be added directly to net assets without being recorded as revenues in the Statement Of Operations.
- If the debt was for any other purpose, the repayment contributions should be recognized as revenue in the current period.

Endowment Contributions These contributions should be recorded as direct increases in net assets during the current period. They should not be included in the revenues disclosed in the Statement Of Operations.

Investment Income As was the case with contributions restricted to the repayment of debt, the treatment of investment income amounts is dependent on their nature:

- If the investment income is not subject to external restrictions, it should be recognized as a revenue during the current period.
- If the investment income must be added to the principal amount of resources held for endowment, the net investment income should be recorded as a direct increase or decrease in net assets, not as a revenue in the Statement Of Operations.
- If the investment income is subject to other types of restrictions, it should be allocated to income on the same basis as was used for restricted contributions (e.g., if it is restricted to purchases of amortizable capital assets, it should be recognized as a revenue on the same basis as the amortization expense is recorded).

Application Of The Restricted Fund Method

11-61. In contrast to the deferral method, the restricted fund method generally allows revenues to be recognized in the period in which they are received or become receivable. Here again, however, Section 4410 provides fairly detailed guidance for individual types of revenues:

Unrestricted Contributions These contributions can be recognized in the period in which they are received or become receivable. They should be disclosed in the general fund.

Restricted Contributions The treatment here will depend on whether a restricted fund is being used for the particular type of restriction that is involved. For example, if an organization receives contributions that are restricted to providing food for the homeless, the treatment of these contributions will depend on whether a separate restricted fund has been established for this type of activity.

Contributions With A Corresponding Restricted Fund In this case, the restricted contributions should be recognized as a revenue of the related fund in the period in which they are received or become receivable.

Contributions With No Corresponding Restricted Fund These contributions should be recognized on the same basis as they would be under the deferral method (e.g., if they are restricted to purchases of amortizable capital assets, they should be recognized as a revenue on the same basis as the amortization expense is recorded).

Endowment Contributions These contributions should be recognized as a revenue of the endowment fund in the period in which they are received or become receivable. Note the difference here from the treatment of these amounts under the deferral method. Under the deferral method, endowment contributions are not recorded as revenues, but as direct increases in the endowment fund assets.

Investment Income As was the case under the deferral method, the treatment of investment income amounts is dependent on their nature:

- If the investment income is not subject to external restrictions, it should be recognized as a revenue during the current period. It would be included in the general fund.
- If the investment income must be added to the principal amount of resources held for endowment, the net investment income should be recorded as a revenue in the Statement Of Operations of the endowment fund in the period in which it becomes received or receivable.
- If the investment income is subject to a restriction for which there is a corresponding restricted fund, it should be included as a revenue in the Statement Of Operations of that fund in the period in which it becomes received or receivable. If no corresponding restricted fund exists, it should be recognized on the same basis as under the deferral method.

Contributions Receivable (Section 4420)

11-62. Not-for-profit organizations often receive promises to make contributions at some future point in time, thereby creating potential assets in the form of contributions receivable. The problem here is that the underlying documentation for such receivables is highly variable. Such documentation ranges from a carefully prepared will that provides a very specific grant of assets to the not-for-profit organization, to a simple pledge card which may have been signed at the end of an emotional fund raiser fueled by large quantities of alcohol or other mind altering substances.

11-63. In the former case, recognition of the receivable and the related revenue presents no accounting problems. The latter case is more problematical in that it is certainly not legally enforceable and, depending on the circumstances, may or may not be collectible.

11-64. Section 1000, "Financial Statement Concepts", provides general criteria for the recognition of items in the financial statements. The Section points out that items should only be recognized if:

- they involve giving up or receiving economic benefits; and
- they have a reasonable basis for measurement.

11-65. It would be our opinion that this provides adequate guidance for dealing with the contributions that are receivable by not-for-profit organizations. They clearly involve receiving economic benefits and, while the question of having a reasonable basis of measurement is complicated by the lack of a legal claim for some receivables, the underlying concept is little different than that applicable to other receivables.

11-66. Despite this basic similarity, a separate Section 4420 was added to the *CICA Handbook* to deal with the contributions receivable of not-for-profit organizations. The basic Recommendation of this Section is as follows:

> **Paragraph 4420.03** *A contribution receivable should be recognized as an asset when it meets the following criteria:*
>
> *(a) the amount to be received can be reasonably estimated; and*
> *(b) ultimate collection is reasonably assured.* (April, 1997)

11-67. The Section points out that these rules are equally applicable to both pledges and bequests. In addition to this Recommendation with respect to recognition, the Section also makes a Recommendation with respect to the disclosure of contributions receivable:

> **Paragraph 4420.08** *When a not-for-profit organization has recognized outstanding pledges and bequests in its financial statements, the following should be disclosed:*
>
> *(a) the amount recognized as assets at the reporting date; and*
> *(b) the amount recognized as revenue in the period.* (April, 1997)

Non-Monetary Contributions

11-68. The great majority of contributions to not-for-profit organizations are in the form of cash or cash equivalents. However, many of these organizations also receive contributions in the form of non-monetary assets. Such contributions range from major works of art that are clearly of significant value, to garbage bags full of discarded clothing that may actually have a negative value in terms of their costs of disposal.

11-69. A similar problem arises with contributed services. Volunteer services can range from an experienced accountant preparing the financial statements of the not-for-profit organization to a local socialite who insists on being at every fund raiser, despite the fact that she manages to offend at least half of the potential contributors who she speaks with.

11-70. The *CICA Handbook* deals with both of these problems with the following Recommendation:

> **Paragraph 4410.16** *An organization may choose to recognize contributions of materials and services, but should do so only when a fair value can be reasonably estimated and when the materials and services are used in the normal course of the organization's operations and would otherwise have been purchased.* (April, 1997)

11-71. This Recommendation establishes two criteria for the recognition of non-monetary contributions:

- Their value must be subject to reasonable estimation. While this is not explicitly stated, it is likely that many items would not be recognized because the cost of estimation would likely exceed any benefits to be achieved through this process.
- Contributed goods and services would only be recognized if they would have otherwise been purchased. This is likely to eliminate the recognition of a significant portion of the voluntary services received.

Revenue Related Disclosure

Contributions

11-72. Section 4410 requires the following general disclosure related to contributions:

> **Paragraph 4410.21** *An organization should disclose:*
>
> *(a) the policy followed in accounting for endowment contributions; and*
> *(b) the policies followed in accounting for restricted contributions.* (April, 1997)
>
> **Paragraph 4410.22** *An organization should disclose its contributions by major source.* (April, 1997)
>
> **Paragraph 4410.23** *An organization should disclose the policy followed in accounting for contributed materials and services.* (April, 1997)
>
> **Paragraph 4410.24** *An organization should disclose the nature and amount of contributed materials and services recognized in the financial statements.* (April, 1997)

Deferral Method

11-73. Section 4410 makes the following Recommendations with respect to the disclosure of deferred contributions:

> **Paragraph 4410.52** *Deferred contributions balances should be presented in the statement of financial position outside net assets.* (April, 1997)
>
> **Paragraph 4410.53** *An organization should disclose the nature and amount of changes in deferred contributions balances for the period.* (April, 1997)

11-74. One additional Recommendation for the disclosure of net investment income by organizations using the deferral method is as follows:

Paragraph 4410.55 *An organization should disclose the following related to net investment income earned on resources held for endowment:*

(a) the amounts recognized in the statement of operations in the period;

(b) the amounts deferred in the period;

(c) the amounts recognized as direct increases or decreases in net assets in the period; and

(d) the total earned in the period. (April, 1997)

Restricted Fund Method

11-75. For organizations using the restricted fund method, the following Recommendations are applicable to deferred contributions:

Paragraph 4410.73 *When restricted contributions are recognized in the general fund in accordance with paragraph 4410.65, any deferred contributions balances should be presented in the statement of financial position outside net assets.* (April, 1997)

Paragraph 4410.74 *When restricted contributions are recognized in the general fund in accordance with paragraph 4410.65, the nature and amount of changes in deferred contributions balances for the period should be disclosed.* (April, 1997)

11-76. One additional disclosure Recommendation deals with the net investment income of organizations using the restricted fund method:

Paragraph 4410.76 *An organization should disclose the following related to net investment income earned on resources held for endowment:*

(a) the amounts recognized in the general fund in the period;

(b) the amounts recognized in each restricted fund in the period;

(c) the amounts recognized in the endowment fund in the period;

(d) any amounts deferred in the period; and

(e) the total earned in the period. (April, 1997)

Financial Statement Presentation Handbook Section 4400

Required Financial Statements

11-77. Section 1000 of the *CICA Handbook*, "Financial Statement Concepts", describes the financial statements normally included for both profit-oriented and not-for-profit organizations. For not-for-profit organizations, the list is reiterated in Section 4400:

Paragraph 4400.05 Financial statements for a not-for-profit organization normally include:

(a) a statement of financial position;
(b) a statement of operations;
(c) a statement of changes in net assets; and
(d) a statement of cash flows.

11-78. Section 4400 notes that other titles may be used for these statements. In addition, it may be desirable to combine statements. For example, many organizations will combine the Statement Of Operations with the Statement Of Changes In Net Assets.

11-79. Section 4400 also provides a general disclosure requirement with respect to the nature of not-for-profit organizations.

Paragraph 4400.04 *A clear and concise description of a not-for-profit organization's purpose, its intended community of service, its status under income tax legislation and its legal form should be included as an integral part of its financial statements.* (April, 1997)

11-80. The remaining Recommendations of Section 4400 relate to specific financial statements and will be considered in the context of those statements.

Statement Of Financial Position

General Recommendations

11-81. Without regard to whether or not fund accounting is used, a not-for-profit organization must provide all fund totals for each item presented in the Statement Of Financial Position. This is reflected in the following Recommendation:

Paragraph 4400.18 *For each financial statement item, the statement of financial position should present a total that includes all funds reported.* (April, 1997)

11-82. The preparation of this Statement should be based on the general *CICA Handbook* rules, including Section 1510 which provides Recommendations on segregating current assets and current liabilities. However, certain additional disclosure items are unique to not-for-profit organizations. These additional items are as follows:

Paragraph 4400.19 *The statement of financial position should present the following:*

(a) net assets invested in capital assets;
(b) net assets subject to restrictions requiring that they be maintained permanently as endowments;
(c) other restricted net assets;
(d) unrestricted net assets; and
(e) total net assets.

For items (b)-(d), each component of revenue, expense, gain and loss that is required by primary sources of GAAP (see "Generally Accepted Accounting Principles", Section 1100) to be recognized directly in the statement of changes in net assets should be separately identified, classified by nature. (October, 2006)

11-83. The total net asset figure, a figure analogous to owners' equity for a profit oriented enterprise, may also be referred to as "Fund Balances" or "Accumulated Surplus (Deficit)". Note that this balance does not include deferred contributions.

11-84. With respect to the "net assets invested in capital assets" balance, the amount disclosed should be reduced by related debt. [**Byrd/Chen Note:** This conclusion does not appear in any Recommendation. However, it is implicit in the use of the term net, and reinforced by the example in the Appendix to Section 4400.] When the deferral method is used, the balance does not include any amount of deferred restricted contributions received for the purchase of capital assets.

Disclosure Of External Restrictions

11-85. External restrictions are of significance because they limit the organization's financial flexibility. Given this, Section 4400 has additional disclosure Recommendations for these amounts. For organizations using the deferral method, the Recommendation is as follows:

Paragraph 4400.26 *The following should be disclosed:*

(a) the amounts of deferred contributions attributable to each major category of external restrictions with a description of the restrictions; and

(b) the amount of net assets subject to external restrictions requiring that they be maintained permanently as endowments. (April, 1997)

11-86. The corresponding Recommendation for organizations using the restricted fund method is as follows:

Paragraph 4400.28 *The following should be disclosed:*

(a) *the amount of net assets (fund balances) subject to external restrictions requiring that they be maintained permanently as endowments;*

(b) *the amounts of net assets (fund balances) attributable to each major category of other external restrictions with a description of the restrictions; and*

(c) *the amounts of deferred contributions attributable to each major category of external restrictions with a description of the restrictions.* (April, 1997)

Statement Of Operations

General Recommendations

11-87. The objective of this statement is to communicate information about changes in the organization's economic resources and obligations for the period. The information it contains can be used to evaluate the organization's performance during the period, including its continued ability to provide services. The statement can also be used to evaluate management.

11-88. Section 4400 does not contain specific Recommendations as to classification of expenses, recognizing that different organizations may classify by object (e.g., wage, rent, advertising), while others may classify by function or program (e.g., feeding the poor, providing shelter for the homeless). To the extent that the organization has items listed in Section 1520 of the *CICA Handbook*, the individual disclosure requirements of that Section would be applicable here.

11-89. Not-for-profit organizations have a tradition of reporting certain revenue items net of the related expenses. An example of this would be the net proceeds of particular fund raising events. In an effort to limit this type of disclosure, Section 4400 provides the following Recommendation:

Paragraph 4400.37 *Revenues and expenses should be disclosed at their gross amounts.* (April, 1997)

11-90. This disclosure could either be in the Statement Of Operations or, alternatively, in the notes to the financial statements. To the extent that the items relate to the organization's main, ongoing service delivery activities, disclosure in the Statement Of Operations is preferred.

Deferral Method

11-91. For those organizations using the deferral method, the following Recommendation is applicable:

Paragraph 4400.33 *The statement of operations should present*

(a) *for each financial statement item, a total that includes all funds reported; and*

(b) *total excess or deficiency of revenues and gains over expenses and losses for the period.* (April, 1997)

11-92. The first part of the Recommendation applies when some form of fund accounting is being used in conjunction with the deferral method. It ensures that information will be provided for the organization as a whole. The remainder of the Recommendation calls for the presentation of a not-for-profit organization's equivalent to a "bottom line".

Restricted Fund Method

11-93. Section 4400 contains the following Recommendation that is specific to those organizations using the restricted fund method:

Paragraph 4400.35 *The statement of operations should present the following for the period:*

(a) the total for each financial statement item recognized in the general fund;
(b) the total for each financial statement item recognized in the restricted funds, other than the endowment fund;
(c) the total for each financial statement item recognized in the endowment fund; and
(d) excess or deficiency of revenues and gains over expenses and losses for each of the general fund, restricted funds other than the endowment fund and the endowment fund. (April, 1997)

11-94. As was the case with the Recommendation for organizations using the deferral method, this Recommendation ensures that information is available for the total organization and that a "bottom line" is presented for the specified fund balances.

Statement Of Changes In Net Assets

11-95. This Statement is the not-for-profit equivalent of the Statement Of Changes In Shareholders' Equity for a profit oriented corporation. For a not-for-profit organization, it will disclose information about changes in the portions of net assets attributable to endowments, to capital assets, and to other external and internal restrictions. It provides information with respect to the organization's overall accumulation or depletion of assets. For those not-for-profit organizations that use fund accounting, this Statement may also be referred to as a Statement Of Changes In Fund Balances.

11-96. Disclosure items that are unique to not-for-profit organizations are specified in the following Recommendation:

Paragraph 4400.41 *The statement of changes in net assets should present changes in the following for the period:*

(a) net assets invested in capital assets;
(b) net assets subject to restrictions requiring that they be maintained permanently as endowments;
(c) other restricted net assets;
(d) unrestricted net assets; and
(e) total net assets. (April, 1997)

Statement Of Cash Flows

11-97. The general rules presented in Section 1540, "Cash Flow Statements" of the *CICA Handbook* are, for the most part, applicable here. In addition, Section 4400 adds two Recommendations that are specific to the Statement Of Cash Flows of not-for-profit organizations. They are as follows:

Paragraph 4400.46 *The statement of cash flows should report the total changes in cash and cash equivalents resulting from the activities of the organization during the period. The components of cash and cash equivalents should be disclosed.* (April, 1997)

Paragraph 4400.47 *The statement of cash flows should distinguish at least the following:*

(a) cash from operations: the components of cash from operations should be disclosed or the excess of revenues over expenses should be reconciled to cash flows from operations; and
(b) the components of cash flows resulting from financing and investing activities, not included in (a) above. (April, 1997)

11-98. Section 4400 notes that cash receipts from operations would include unrestricted contributions, restricted contributions that are to be used for operations, and other revenues arising from the organization's ordinary activities, such as fees for services, proceeds on the sale of goods and unrestricted investment income. Cash disbursements for operations would comprise expenditures made by the organization in carrying out its service delivery activities.

11-99. Components of cash flows from financing activities would include cash contributed that is restricted for the purpose of acquiring capital assets and cash contributed for endowment. Cash receipts and disbursements related to the assumption and repayment of debt would also be presented as components of cash flows from financing activities. Components of cash flows from investing activities would include the acquisition of capital assets, the purchase of investments, and the proceeds on disposal of major categories of assets, such as capital assets and investments.

11-100. Section 4400 notes that non-cash financing and investing transactions (e.g. contributions of capital assets) should be reported as a cash inflow combined with a cash outflow. We would note that Section 1540 would exclude this type of transaction from the Cash Flow Statement.

11-101. The Section also indicates that, in situations where a Cash Flow Statement would not provide additional useful information, no such Statement need be prepared. This might apply, for example, to an organization with relatively simple operations and few or no significant financing and investing activities.

Example 1 (No Capital Assets)

Basic Data

11-102. At this point, we would like to present an example that illustrates the three accounting approaches that can be used by a not-for-profit organization (i.e., aggregate accounting, restricted fund accounting, and other basis fund accounting). This example will illustrate a number of the Recommendations for revenue recognition and financial statement presentation.

11-103. It will not, however, include capital asset considerations. A second version of this example will be presented after we have discussed Sections 4430 (Capital Assets) and 4440 (Collections). This second example will be a continuation of this example with the addition of purchased and contributed capital assets. We will use the data of this example in three different cases in order to illustrate the alternatives that are available in not-for-profit accounting.

11-104. The basic data for this example is as follows:

Organization And Purpose On January 1, 2007, the Local Care Society (LCS) is organized as a not-for-profit organization. Its purpose is to serve the needs of its local community in two areas:

- The provision of meals for elderly individuals who are unable to leave their homes (meals activity).
- The provision of winter clothing for children who are living in poverty (clothing activity).

The organization will have a December 31 year end.

Endowment Contributions Initial funding is provided by a wealthy individual who makes an endowment contribution of $50,000. These funds are invested in debt securities. There are no restrictions on the income that is produced by these investments. During the year ending December 31, 2007, such income amounted to $4,000.

Unrestricted Contributions The organization solicits and receives unrestricted contributions which are then allocated to both the meals activity and the clothing activity by the organization's Board Of Directors. During the year ending December 31, 2007, $400,000 in contributions were received. At year end, an additional

$35,000 in contributions were receivable. The receivable is related to the meals activity. The Board believes that this is a reasonable estimate of the amount that will actually be collected. The $435,000 total was allocated $285,000 to the meals activity and $150,000 to the clothing activity.

Restricted Contributions The organization accepts additional contributions that are restricted to use in the clothing activity. These funds are segregated and a separate report is made to contributors on their usage. During the year ending December 31, 2007, restricted contributions of $125,000 were received. No contributions are receivable at year end.

Expenses During the year ending December 31, 2007, the organization incurred the following expenses:

	Meals Activity	Clothing Activity
Wages And Salaries	$ 20,000	$ 25,000
Cost Of Materials Provided	180,000	190,000
Transportation Costs	30,000	5,000
Other Expenses	15,000	20,000
Total	$245,000	$240,000

It is estimated that 40 percent ($96,000) of the expenses related to the clothing activity have been made from the restricted contributions.

On December 31, 2007, there were outstanding Accounts Payable related to the meals activity expenses of $30,000.

Case One - No Fund Accounting

11-105. In this Case, we will assume that LCS is not using fund accounting. This means that they will have to use the deferral method of revenue recognition. It also means that all of the entries required during the year will be recorded in a single journal. In reviewing these journal entries, we would remind you that, for a not-for-profit organization, the Balance Sheet account that is analogous to Shareholders' Equity for a corporation is titled Net Assets. The required entries would be as follows:

Endowment Contributions

Cash	$50,000	
Net Assets - Restricted For Endowment Purposes		$50,000

(Paragraph 4400.19 requires segregation of amounts that are restricted for endowment purposes)

Investment Of Endowment Contributions

Investments	$50,000	
Cash		$50,000

Investment Income

Cash	$4,000	
Revenue - Investment Income		$4,000

(As there are no restrictions on this Investment Income, it can be recognized in the current period.)

Unrestricted Contributions

Cash	$400,000	
Contributions Receivable	35,000	
Revenue - Unrestricted Contributions		$435,000

Restricted Contributions

Cash	$125,000	
Deferred Contributions		$125,000

(Under the deferral method, restricted contributions cannot be recognized until the related expenses are incurred. The Deferred Contributions account is a Balance Sheet account that must be disclosed outside the Net Asset balance.)

Expenses

Wages And Salaries ($20,000 + $25,000)	$ 45,000	
Cost Of Materials Provided ($180,000 + $190,000)	370,000	
Transportation Costs ($30,000 + $5,000)	35,000	
Other Expenses ($15,000 + $20,000)	35,000	
Cash ($245,000 + $240,000 - $30,000)		$455,000
Accounts Payable		30,000

Amortization Of Deferred Contributions

Deferred Contributions [(40%)($240,000)]	$96,000	
Revenue - Amortization Of Deferred Contributions		$96,000

[Contributions that are restricted to expenses for clothing can be recognized as revenue to the extent that such expenses have been incurred. In this case the amount is $96,000, leaving a Deferred Contributions balance of $29,000 ($125,000 - $96,000)].

Closing Entry

Revenue - Unrestricted Contributions	$435,000	
Revenue - Amortization Of Deferred Contributions	96,000	
Revenue - Investment Income	4,000	
Wages And Salaries		$ 45,000
Cost Of Materials Provided		370,000
Transportation Costs		35,000
Other Expenses		35,000
Net Assets - Unrestricted		50,000

(All of the expenses and revenues would be closed to the Net Assets - Unrestricted balance at the end of the fiscal year. The $50,000 is a balancing figure that is also calculated on the Statement of Operations and Fund Balances.)

11-106. Based on these journal entries required financial statements would be as follows:

LCS Organization (Case One)
Statement Of Operations And Fund Balances
Year Ending December 31, 2007

Revenues:	
Unrestricted Contributions	$435,000
Amortization Of Deferred Contributions	96,000
Investment Income	4,000
Total Revenues	$535,000
Expenses:	
Wages And Salaries	$ 45,000
Cost Of Materials Provided	370,000
Transportation Costs	35,000
Other Expenses	35,000
Total Expenses	$485,000
Excess Of Revenues Over Expenses	$ 50,000
Opening Unrestricted Net Assets	Nil
Closing Unrestricted Net Assets	$ 50,000

LCS Organization (Case One)
Statement Of Cash Flows
Year Ending December 31, 2007

Cash Flows From Operating Activities:	
Unrestricted Contributions	$400,000
Restricted Contributions	125,000
Investment Income	4,000
Expenses	(455,000)
Total	$ 74,000
Cash Flows From Financing And Investing:	
Endowment Contributions	50,000
Investment Of Endowment Contributions	(50,000)
Increase In Cash	$ 74,000
Opening Cash Balance	Nil
Closing Cash Balance	$ 74,000

LCS Organization (Case One)
Statement Of Financial Position
As At December 31, 2007

Cash (From Statement Of Cash Flows)	$ 74,000
Investments	50,000
Contributions Receivable	35,000
Total	$159,000
Accounts Payable	$ 30,000
Deferred Contributions	29,000
Net Assets:	
Restricted For Endowment Purposes	50,000
Unrestricted	50,000
Total	$159,000

Case Two - Restricted Fund Accounting

11-107. In this Case, we will assume that LCS establishes separate funds for endowment contributions, restricted clothing activity contributions, and a general fund. Given this, the organization will be able to use the restricted fund basis of revenue recognition. Reflecting this, separate journal entries will have to be made for each of the defined funds.

11-108. A further point here is that, when fund accounting is used, the Statement of Financial Position account that we referred to as Net Assets in Case One will be titled Fund Balances. Both of these titles refer to the not-for-profit organization equivalent of Shareholders' Equity for a corporation. While both are acceptable, the *Handbook* tends to use the term Fund Balances in those examples that involve any type of fund accounting.

11-109. The required journal entries are as follows (explanations that are unchanged from Case One will not be repeated here):

Endowment Fund Entries

Endowment Contributions

Cash	$50,000	
Fund Balances - Restricted For Endowment Purposes		$50,000

Investment Of Endowment Contributions

Investments	$50,000	
Cash		$50,000

General Fund Entries

Investment Income

Cash	$4,000	
Revenue - Investment Income		$4,000

(The entry is in the general fund as there are no restrictions on the use of this income)

Unrestricted Contributions

Cash	$400,000	
Contributions Receivable	35,000	
Revenue - Unrestricted Contributions		$435,000

Expenses

Wages And Salaries [$20,000 + (60%)$25,000)]	$ 35,000	
Cost Of Materials Provided [$180,000 + (60%)($190,000)]	294,000	
Transportation Costs [($30,000 + (60%)($5,000)]	33,000	
Other Expenses [$15,000 + (60%)($20,000)]	27,000	
Cash [$245,000 + (60%)($240,000) - $30,000)]		$359,000
Accounts Payable		30,000

Closing Entry - General Fund

Revenue - Unrestricted Contributions	$435,000	
Investment Income	4,000	
Wages And Salaries		$ 35,000
Cost Of Materials Provided		294,000
Transportation Costs		33,000
Other Expenses		27,000
Fund Balances - Unrestricted		50,000

(Note that this is the same $50,000 credit to the unrestricted fund balance (net assets) as was made in Case One)

Restricted Fund Entries

Restricted Contributions

Cash	$125,000	
Revenue - Restricted Contributions		$125,000

(Note that, as the restricted fund method of accounting is being used, all of the restricted contributions can be recorded as revenue, without regard to when the related expenses are incurred.)

Expenses

Wages And Salaries [(40%)($25,000)]	$ 10,000	
Cost Of Materials Provided [(40%)($190,000)]	76,000	
Transportation Costs [(40%)($5,000)]	2,000	
Other Expenses [(40%)($20,000)]	8,000	
Cash [(40%)($240,000)]		$96,000

Closing Entry - Restricted Fund

Revenue - Restricted Contributions	$125,000	
Wages And Salaries		$ 10,000
Cost Of Materials Provided		76,000
Transportation Costs		2,000
Other Expenses		8,000
Fund Balances - Restricted For Clothing		29,000

[Note that the $29,000 of restricted contributions that have not been spent is included in the Fund Balances. This is in contrast to the deferral method where this balance is shown as Deferred Contributions and not included in Fund Balances (Net Assets)].

11-110. Using the preceding journal entries, the required financial statements would be prepared as follows:

LCS Organization (Case Two)
Statement Of Operations And Fund Balances
Year Ending December 31, 2007

	General Fund	Restricted Fund	Endowment Fund
Revenues:			
Unrestricted Contributions	$435,000		
Restricted Contributions		$125,000	
Investment Income	4,000		
Endowment Contributions			$50,000
Total Revenues	$439,000	$125,000	$50,000
Expenses:			
Wages And Salaries	$ 35,000	$ 10,000	
Cost Of Materials Provided	294,000	76,000	
Transportation Costs	33,000	2,000	
Other Expenses	27,000	8,000	
Total Expenses	$389,000	$ 96,000	Nil
Excess Of Revenues Over Expenses	$ 50,000	$ 29,000	$50,000
Opening Fund Balances	Nil	Nil	Nil
Closing Fund Balances	$ 50,000	$ 29,000	$50,000

LCS Organization (Case Two)
Statement Of Cash Flows
Year Ending December 31, 2007

	General Fund	Restricted Fund	Endowment Fund
Cash Flows From Operating Activities:			
Unrestricted Contributions	$400,000		
Restricted Contributions		$125,000	
Investment Income	4,000		
Expenses	(359,000)	(96,000)	
Total	$ 45,000	$ 29,000	Nil
Cash Flows From Financing And Investing:			
Endowment Contributions			$50,000
Investments Acquired	Nil	Nil	(50,000)
Increase In Cash	$ 45,000	$ 29,000	Nil
Opening Cash Balance	Nil	Nil	Nil
Closing Cash Balance	$ 45,000	$ 29,000	Nil

LCS Organization (Case Two)
Statement Of Financial Position
As At December 31, 2007

	General Fund	Restricted Fund	Endowment Fund	Total
Cash (From Statement Of Cash Flows)	$ 45,000	$ 29,000		$ 74,000
Investments			$ 50,000	50,000
Contributions Receivable	35,000			35,000
Total	$ 80,000	$ 29,000	$ 50,000	$159,000
Accounts Payable	$ 30,000			$ 30,000
Fund Balances:				
Restricted For Clothing		$ 29,000		29,000
Restricted For Endowment			$ 50,000	50,000
Unrestricted	50,000			50,000
Total	$ 80,000	$ 29,000	$ 50,000	$159,000

11-111. As this example illustrates, when the restricted fund method is used, all-fund totals are not required for either the Statement Of Operations or the Statement Of Cash Flows. However, such totals are always required for the Statement Of Financial Position.

Case Three - Fund Accounting On Other Basis

11-112. This final version of our Case will also assume that LCS uses fund accounting. However, it will not qualify for the restricted fund method of revenue recognition as it classifies its funds by programs rather than by restrictions. They will use a general fund, a meals activity fund, and a clothing activity fund. Endowment funds will be accounted for through the general fund. As was the situation in Case Two, separate journal entries will have to be made for each of the defined funds. These entries are as follows:

General Fund Entries

Endowment Contributions

	Debit	Credit
Cash	$50,000	
Fund Balances - Restricted For Endowment Purposes		$50,000

(Despite the fact that there is no separate endowment fund, separate disclosure must be given to the portion of the Fund Balances amount that is restricted for endowment purposes.)

Investment Of Endowment Contributions

	Debit	Credit
Investments	$50,000	
Cash		$50,000

Investment Income

	Debit	Credit
Cash	$4,000	
Revenue - Investment Income		$4,000

(The entry is in the general fund as there are no restrictions on the use of this income)

Closing Entry - General Fund

	Debit	Credit
Revenue - Investment Income	$4,000	
Fund Balances - Unrestricted		$4,000

Meals Fund Entries

Unrestricted Contributions

Cash	$250,000	
Contributions Receivable	35,000	
Revenue - Unrestricted Contributions		$285,000

(While the Board has allocated this amount to meal activity, this is not an external restriction and, as a consequence, it can be recognized as a current revenue.)

Expenses

Wages And Salaries	$ 20,000	
Cost Of Materials Provided	180,000	
Transportation Costs	30,000	
Other Expenses	15,000	
Cash ($245,000 - $30,000)		$215,000
Accounts Payable		30,000

Closing Entry - Meal Fund

Revenue - Unrestricted Contributions	$285,000	
Wages And Salaries		$ 20,000
Cost Of Materials Provided		180,000
Transportation Costs		30,000
Other Expenses		15,000
Fund Balances - Unrestricted		40,000

Clothing Fund Entries

Unrestricted Contributions

Cash	$150,000	
Revenue - Unrestricted Contributions		$150,000

(While the Board has allocated this amount to clothing activity, this is not an external restriction and, as a consequence, it can be recognized as a current revenue.)

Restricted Contributions

Cash	$125,000	
Deferred Contributions		$125,000

(As the deferral method is being used, the recognition of these contributions as revenue must be deferred.)

Expenses

Wages And Salaries	$ 25,000	
Cost Of Materials Provided	190,000	
Transportation Costs	5,000	
Other Expenses	20,000	
Cash		$240,000

Amortization Of Deferred Contributions

Deferred Contributions [(40%)($240,000)]	$96,000	
Revenue - Amortization Of Deferred Contributions		$96,000

(As was the situation in Case One, Deferred Contributions can be recognized as revenues to the extent of related expenses.)

Closing Entry - Clothing Fund

Revenue - Unrestricted Contributions	$150,000	
Revenue - Amortization Of Deferred Contributions	96,000	
Wages And Salaries		$ 25,000
Cost Of Materials Provided		190,000
Transportation Costs		5,000
Other Expenses		20,000
Fund Balances - Unrestricted		6,000

{The $6,000 credit to Fund Balances - Unrestricted reflects the unused portion of the $150,000 of unrestricted contributions that was allocated to clothing [$150,000 - (60%)($240,000)]}

11-113. Using the preceding journal entries, the required financial statements can be prepared as follows:

LCS Organization (Case Three)
Statement Of Operations And Fund Balances
Year Ending December 31, 2007

	General Fund	Meals Activity Fund	Clothing Activity Fund	Total
Revenues:				
Unrestricted Contributions		$285,000	$150,000	$435,000
Restricted Contributions			96,000	96,000
Investment Income	$4,000			4,000
Total Revenues	$4,000	$285,000	$246,000	$535,000
Expenses:				
Wages And Salaries		$ 20,000	$ 25,000	$ 45,000
Cost Of Materials Provided		180,000	190,000	370,000
Transportation Costs		30,000	5,000	35,000
Other Expenses	Nil	15,000	20,000	35,000
Total Expenses	Nil	$245,000	$240,000	$485,000
Excess Of Revenues Over Expenses	$4,000	$ 40,000	$ 6,000	$ 50,000
Opening Fund Balances	Nil	Nil	Nil	Nil
Closing Fund Balances	$4,000	$ 40,000	$ 6,000	$ 50,000

LCS Organization (Case Three)
Statement Of Cash Flows
Year Ending December 31, 2007

	General Fund	Meals Activity Fund	Clothing Activity Fund	Total
Cash Flows From Operating Activities				
Unrestricted Contributions		$250,000	$150,000	$400,000
Restricted Contributions			125,000	125,000
Investment Income	$ 4,000			4,000
Expenses		(215,000)	(240,000)	(455,000)
Total	$ 4,000	$ 35,000	$ 35,000	$ 74,000
Cash Flows From Financing And Investing:				
Endowment Contributions	50,000			50,000
Investments Acquired	(50,000)	Nil	Nil	(50,000)
Increase In Cash	$ 4,000	$ 35,000	$ 35,000	$ 74,000
Opening Cash Balance	Nil	Nil	Nil	Nil
Closing Cash Balance	$ 4,000	$ 35,000	$ 35,000	$ 74,000

LCS Organization (Case Three)
Statement Of Financial Position
As At December 31, 2007

	General Fund	Meals Activity Fund	Clothing Activity Fund	Total
Cash (From Statement of Cash Flows)	$ 4,000	$35,000	$35,000	$ 74,000
Investments	50,000			50,000
Contributions Receivable		35,000		35,000
Total	$54,000	$70,000	$35,000	$159,000
Accounts Payable		$30,000		$ 30,000
Deferred Contributions			$29,000	29,000
Fund Balances:				
Restricted For Endowment	$50,000			50,000
Unrestricted	4,000	40,000	6,000	50,000
Total	$54,000	$70,000	$35,000	$159,000

Capital Assets Of Not-For-Profit Organizations Handbook Sections 4430 And 4440

Background To The Problem

11-114. For many years, the traditional practice of not-for-profit organizations was not to record capital assets in the financial statements. In general, such assets were charged to expense when acquired, leaving no balance to be subject to amortization in future periods.

11-115. However, with the addition of Section 4430 in 1996, "Capital Assets Held By Not-For-Profit Organizations", this practice has been significantly curtailed. The basic purposes of this Section was to align to the capital asset accounting practices of not-for-profit organizations with those specified for profit oriented enterprises in Section 3061, "Property, Plant, And Equipment". In fact, much of Section 4430 simply duplicates the content of Section 3061.

11-116. While the content of Section 4430 parallels that of Section 3061, there are two important exceptions to the general rules applicable to the capital assets of not-for-profit organizations. These exceptions are dealt with in the next Section.

Exceptions To Capital Assets Rule

Small Organizations

11-117. In general, Section 4430 requires that not-for-profit organizations record capital assets at their acquisition cost and, in the case of assets with a limited life, amortize this cost in a systematic manner over that life. Based on the argument that such procedures might have costs that exceed their benefits in the case of smaller organizations, the AcSB created an exemption for smaller not-for-profit organizations.

11-118. Section 4430 defines the organizations that are eligible for this exemption as follows:

> **Paragraph 4430.03** Organizations may limit the application of this Section to the Recommendation in paragraph 4430.40 if the average of annual revenues recognized in the statement of operations for the current and preceding period of the organization and any entities it controls is less than $500,000. When an organization reports some of its revenues net of related expenses, gross revenues would be used for

purposes of this calculation.

11-119. When this exemption is used by an organization, additional disclosure is required as follows:

Paragraph 4430.40 *Organizations meeting the criterion in paragraph 4430.03 and not following the other Recommendations of this Section should disclose the following:*

(a) the policy followed in accounting for capital assets;

(b) information about major categories of capital assets not recorded in the statement of financial position, including a description of the assets; and

(c) if capital assets are expensed when acquired, the amount expensed in the current period. (April, 1997)

Collections

11-120. Collections are defined in Section 4440 as follows:

Paragraph 4440.03(b) **Collections** are works of art, historical treasures or similar assets that are:

(i) held for public exhibition, education or research;

(ii) protected, cared for and preserved; and

(iii) subject to an organizational policy that requires any proceeds from their sale to be used to acquire other items to be added to the collection or for the direct care of the existing collection.

11-121. A typical example of a collection would be a group of paintings held by a not-for-profit art gallery. Such assets often present significant valuation problems. Perhaps, more importantly, they generally do not depreciate in value. If they do experience a change in value, it is more likely to be in an upward direction. Further, they are not a resource that can be used by the organization for any other purpose.

11-122. Given these considerations, it is not surprising that the Accounting Standards Board decided not to apply the requirements of Section 4430 to these assets. This is accomplished in a less than straightforward manner. Section 4430 does not simply say that these assets are exempt from its Recommendations. Rather, it provides the following definition of Capital Assets:

Paragraph 4430.05(b) **Capital assets**, comprising tangible properties, such as land, buildings and equipment, and intangible properties, are identifiable assets that meet all of the following criteria:

(i) are held for use in the provision of services, for administrative purposes, for production of goods or for the maintenance, repair, development or construction of other capital assets;

(ii) have been acquired, constructed or developed with the intention of being used on a continuing basis;

(iii) are not intended for sale in the ordinary course of operations; and

(iv) are not held as part of a collection.

11-123. By excluding collections from the definition of capital assets, the Accounting Standards Board has, in effect, exempted these assets from the Recommendations of Section 4430.

Recognition And Measurement

Initial Recognition

11-124. The basic Recommendation here is as follows:

> **Paragraph 4430.06** *A capital asset should be recorded on the statement of financial position at cost. For a contributed capital asset, cost is considered to be fair value at the date of contribution. In unusual circumstances when fair value cannot be reasonably determined, the capital asset should be recorded at nominal value.* (April, 1997)

11-125. This Recommendation requires that the capital assets of not-for-profit organizations be recorded at cost and, in addition, it specifies that the cost of a contributed capital asset is its fair value at the time of contribution.

11-126. Fair value, as defined in Paragraph 4430.05, is the amount of the consideration that would be agreed upon in an arm's length transaction between knowledgeable, willing parties who are under no compulsion to act. Use of nominal values is acceptable when fair value cannot be reasonably determined.

11-127. The Section makes a number of additional points with respect to capital assets:

- The cost should include all costs necessary to put the asset into use.
- If an asset is acquired by a not-for-profit organization, at a cost that is substantially below fair value, it should be recorded at fair value, with the difference reported as a contribution.
- The cost of a basket purchase should be allocated on the basis of the relative fair values of the assets acquired.
- The cost of self constructed or self developed assets should include direct costs of construction or development, along with any overhead costs directly attributable to the construction or development activity. In the case of self developed intangibles, future benefits may be so uncertain that recording the costs of development as an asset cannot be justified.
- A betterment should be capitalized. These are defined as service enhancements that increase capacity, lower operating costs, extend the useful life, or improve the quality of output of the asset.

11-128. Other than the possibility of recording a contribution as part of an asset acquisition transaction, all of these suggestions are consistent with the treatment given to the capital assets of profit oriented enterprises.

Amortization

11-129. With respect to amortization, Section 4430 contains the following Recommendation:

> **Paragraph 4430.16** *The cost, less any residual value, of a capital asset with a limited life should be amortized over its useful life in a rational and systematic manner appropriate to its nature and use by the organization. Amortization should be recognized as an expense in the organization's statement of operations.* (April, 1997)

11-130. This Recommendation serves to put the capital assets of not-for-profit organizations on virtually the same footing as those of profit oriented enterprises. The discussion in Section 4430 of this Recommendation is similar to that contained in Section 3061 on this subject, providing for the use of different amortization methods and encouraging the estimation of residual value in determining the amount to be written off.

11-131. Section 4430 points out that, along with land, works of art and historical treasures may have virtually unlimited lives. This would suggest that amortization would not be appropriate in these circumstances. We would remind you that, if the work of art is part of a collection (as defined in Section 4440), the Recommendations of Section 4430 are not applicable.

11-132. When fund accounting is used, the fund to which amortization will be charged is a matter of judgment. The common answers would be to charge these amounts to either the capital asset fund or the general fund.

11-133. As is the case with Section 3061, Section 4430 requires a periodic review of amortization:

> **Paragraph 4430.23** *The amortization method and the estimate of the useful life of a capital asset should be reviewed on a regular basis.* (April, 1997)

11-134. Events that might indicate a need for revision would include the following:

- a change in the extent the capital asset is used;
- a change in the manner in which the capital asset is used;
- removal of the capital asset from service for an extended period of time;
- physical damage;
- significant technological developments; and
- a change in the law or environment affecting the period of time over which the capital asset can be used.

Asset Retirement Obligations

11-135. Section 4430 contains a Recommendation on asset retirement obligations that is identical to the one found in Section 3061 on this subject:

> **Paragraph 4430.25** *Obligations associated with the retirement of property, plant and equipment are accounted for in accordance with "Asset Retirement Obligations", Section 3110.*

11-136. Given the nature of not-for-profit organizations, we would expect that the application of this Recommendation to this type of entity would be relatively rare.

Write Downs

11-137. Again following the pattern established in Section 3061, Section 4430 makes the following Recommendation in this area:

> **Paragraph 4430.28** *When a capital asset no longer has any long-term service potential to the organization, the excess of its net carrying amount over any residual value should be recognized as an expense in the statement of operations. A write down should not be reversed.* (April, 1997)

Disposals

11-138. The difference between the net proceeds of a disposal and the net carrying value of an asset is normally recorded as a gain or loss in the Statement Of Operations. If there are unamortized deferred contributions related to the capital asset disposed of, they would be recognized as revenue in the period of disposal, provided that all related restrictions have been complied with.

Presentation And Disclosure

All Capital Assets

11-139. For all capital assets of not-for-profit organizations, the following disclosure is required:

> **Paragraph 4430.31** *For each major category of capital assets there should be disclosure of:*
>
> *(a) cost;*
> *(b) accumulated amortization, including the amount of any write downs; and*
> *(c) the amortization method used, including the amortization period or rate.* (April, 1997)

Paragraph 4430.32 *The net carrying amounts of major categories of capital assets not being amortized should be disclosed.* (April, 1997)

Paragraph 4430.33 *The amount of amortization of capital assets recognized as an expense for the period should be disclosed.* (April, 1997)

Paragraph 4430.34 *The amount of any write downs of capital assets should be disclosed in the financial statements for the period in which the write downs are made.* (April, 1997)

Contributed Capital Assets

11-140. Further Recommendations are made with respect to contributed capital assets:

Paragraph 4430.37 *The nature and amount of contributed capital assets received in the period and recognized in the financial statements should be disclosed.* (April, 1997)

Paragraph 4430.38 *Information should be disclosed about contributed capital assets recognized at nominal value.* (April, 1997)

Example 2 (Includes Capital Assets)

Basic Data

11-141. This is an extension of the example that was presented in Paragraph 11-104. It involves the same Local Care Society (LCS) and extends their activities into the year ending December 31, 2008. It is made more complex by the addition of capital assets and their amortization. The basic data for LCS for the year ending December 31, 2008 is as follows:

Endowment Contributions There are no additional endowment contributions during the year ending December 31, 2008. The endowment investments have income of $3,000 during this period.

Unrestricted Contributions During the year ending December 31, 2008, $600,000 in unrestricted contributions were received. In addition, the $35,000 in contributions that were receivable at the end of 2007 are collected in full during 2008. At year end, there is an additional $40,000 in contributions that are receivable. The receivable is related to the meals activity. The Board believes that this is a reasonable estimate of the amount that will actually be collected. This $640,000 total was allocated $360,000 to the meals activity, $180,000 to the clothing activity, and $100,000 for the acquisition of a building to be used in the organization's operations.

Capital Assets On July 1, 2008, the organization acquires a building for a total cost of $100,000. Of this total, $20,000 represents the fair value of the land on which the building is situated and the remaining $80,000 reflects the fair value of the building. The estimated useful life of the building is 10 years and no significant residual value is anticipated. The organization uses straight line amortization, charging only one-half year's amortization in the year in which an asset is acquired.

Restricted Contributions The organization continues to accept additional contributions that are restricted to use in the clothing activity. During the year ending December 31, 2008, restricted contributions of $175,000 were received. No restricted contributions are receivable at year end.

Expenses During the year ending December 31, 2008, the organization incurred the following expenses:

	Meals Activity	Clothing Activity
Wages And Salaries	$ 25,000	$ 20,000
Cost Of Materials Provided	210,000	230,000
Transportation Costs	35,000	15,000
Other Expenses	15,000	25,000
Total	$285,000	$290,000

It is estimated that 50 percent of the expenses related to clothing activity have been made from restricted funds. On December 31, 2008, there were outstanding Accounts Payable related to the meals activity expenses of $25,000.

Case One - No Fund Accounting

11-142. In this Case, we will assume that LCS is not using fund accounting. This means that they will have to use the deferral method of revenue recognition. Based on this approach, the required journal entries are as follows:

Investment Income

Cash	$3,000	
Revenue - Investment Income		$3,000

Unrestricted Contributions

Cash	$35,000	
Contributions Receivable (Opening)		$35,000

Cash	$600,000	
Contributions Receivable (Closing)	40,000	
Revenue - Unrestricted Contributions		$640,000

Acquisition Of Capital Assets

Land	$20,000	
Building	80,000	
Cash		$100,000

Amortization Of Capital Assets

Amortization Expense [($80,000)(1/10)(1/2)]	$4,000	
Accumulated Amortization		$4,000

Restricted Contributions

Cash	$175,000	
Deferred Contributions		$175,000

(As the deferral method is being used, these contributions must be deferred until the related expenses are incurred.)

Expenses

Accounts Payable (Opening)	$30,000	
Cash		$30,000

Wages And Salaries ($25,000 + $20,000)	$ 45,000	
Cost Of Materials Provided ($210,000 + $230,000)	440,000	
Transportation Costs ($35,000 + $15,000)	50,000	
Other Expenses ($15,000 + $25,000)	40,000	
Cash ($285,000 + $290,000 - $25,000)		$550,000
Accounts Payable (Closing)		25,000

Amortization Of Deferred Contributions

Deferred Contributions [(50%)($290,000)]	$145,000	
Revenue - Amortization Of Deferred Contributions		$145,000

(Restricted contributions can be included in revenue to the extent of current expenses related to these contributions.)

Closing Entry

Revenue - Unrestricted Contributions	$640,000	
Revenue - Amortization Of Deferred Contributions	145,000	
Revenue - Investment Income	3,000	
Amortization Expense		$ 4,000
Wages And Salaries		45,000
Cost Of Materials Provided		440,000
Transportation Costs		50,000
Other Expenses		40,000
Net Assets - Invested In Capital Assets ($100,000 - $4,000)		96,000
Net Assets - Unrestricted ($209,000 - $96,000)		113,000

(Paragraph 4400.19 requires separate disclosure of the amount of the Net Asset balance that has been invested in capital assets. Note that the amount is disclosed net of accumulated amortization. All of the expenses and revenues would be closed to the Net Assets - Unrestricted balance at the end of the fiscal year. The $209,000 is a balancing figure that is also calculated on the Statement of Operations and Fund Balances.)

11-143. Using these journal entries, the required financial statements would be prepared as follows:

LCS Organization (Case One)
Statement Of Operations And Fund Balances
Year Ending December 31, 2008

Revenues:	
Unrestricted Contributions	$640,000
Amortization Of Deferred Contributions	145,000
Investment Income	3,000
Total Revenues	$788,000
Expenses:	
Wages And Salaries	$ 45,000
Cost Of Materials Provided	440,000
Transportation Costs	50,000
Amortization Expense [($80,000/10)(1/2)]	4,000
Other Expenses	40,000
Total Expenses	$579,000
Excess Of Revenues Over Expenses	$209,000
Invested In Capital Assets (Net)	(96,000)
Opening Unrestricted Net Assets	50,000
Closing Unrestricted Net Assets	$163,000

LCS Organization (Case One)
Statement Of Cash Flows
Year Ending December 31, 2008

Cash Flows From Operating Activities:	
Unrestricted Contributions ($600,000 + $35,000)	$635,000
Restricted Contributions	175,000
Investment Income	3,000
Expenses ($285,000 + $290,000 + $30,000 - $25,000)	(580,000)
Total	$233,000
Cash Flows From Financing And Investing:	
Capital Assets Acquired	(100,000)
Increase In Cash	$133,000
Opening Cash Balance	74,000
Closing Cash Balance	$207,000

LCS Organization (Case One)
Statement Of Financial Position
As At December 31, 2008

Cash (From Statement Of Cash Flows)		$207,000
Investments		50,000
Contributions Receivable		40,000
Capital Assets:		
Land		20,000
Building	$80,000	
Accumulated Amortization	(4,000)	76,000
Total Assets		$393,000
Accounts Payable		$ 25,000
Deferred Contributions*		59,000
Net Assets:		
Restricted For Endowment Purposes		50,000
Invested In Capital Assets		96,000
Unrestricted		163,000
Total Equities		$393,000

*Unamortized deferred contributions amount is calculated as follows:

Balance - December 31, 2007	$ 29,000
Additions	175,000
Expenses Incurred [(50%)($290,000)]	(145,000)
Balance - December 31, 2008	$ 59,000

Case Two - Restricted Fund Accounting

11-144. In this Case, we will assume that LCS establishes separate funds for endowment contributions, restricted clothing activity contributions, and a general fund. Capital assets will be accounted for in the general fund. Given this classification of funds, the organization will be able to use the restricted fund basis of revenue recognition. With the use of fund accounting, separate journal entries will have to be made for each of the defined funds.

Endowment Fund Entries

No entries are required in the endowment fund as, during 2008, no new contributions were received and no new investments were made.

General Fund Entries

Investment Income

	Debit	Credit
Cash	$3,000	
Revenue - Investment Income		$3,000

(The entry is in the general fund as there are no restrictions on the use of this income)

Unrestricted Contributions

	Debit	Credit
Cash	$35,000	
Contributions Receivable (Opening)		$35,000

	Debit	Credit
Cash	$600,000	
Contributions Receivable (Closing)	40,000	
Revenue - Unrestricted Contributions		$640,000

Acquisition Of Capital Assets

	Debit	Credit
Land	$20,000	
Building	80,000	
Cash		$100,000

Amortization Of Capital Assets

	Debit	Credit
Amortization Expense [($80,000)(1/10)(1/2)]	$4,000	
Accumulated Amortization		$4,000

Expenses

	Debit	Credit
Accounts Payable (Opening)	$30,000	
Cash		$30,000

	Debit	Credit
Wages And Salaries [$25,000 + (50%)$20,000)]	$ 35,000	
Cost Of Materials Provided [$210,000 + (50%)($230,000)]	325,000	
Transportation Costs [($35,000 + (50%)($15,000)]	42,500	
Other Expenses [$15,000 + (50%)($25,000)]	27,500	
Cash [$285,000 + (50%)($290,000) - $25,000)]		$405,000
Accounts Payable (Closing)		25,000

Closing Entry - General Fund

	Debit	Credit
Revenue - Unrestricted Contributions	$640,000	
Revenue - Investment Income	3,000	
Amortization Expense		$ 4,000
Wages And Salaries		35,000
Cost Of Materials Provided		325,000
Transportation Costs		42,500
Other Expenses		27,500
Fund Balances - Invested In Capital Assets		96,000
Fund Balances - Unrestricted ($209,000 - $96,000)		113,000

(As in Case One, the $209,000 increase in the general fund's balance must be allocated to both an unrestricted amount and to an amount invested in capital assets.)

Restricted Fund Entries

Restricted Contributions

Cash	$175,000	
Revenues - Restricted Contributions		$175,000

(As the restricted fund method is being used, all of these contributions can be included in the revenues of the current period.)

Expenses

Wages And Salaries [(50%)($20,000)]	$ 10,000	
Cost Of Materials Provided [(50%)($230,000)]	115,000	
Transportation Costs [(50%)($15,000)]	7,500	
Other Expenses [(50%)($25,000)]	12,500	
Cash [(50%)($290,000)]		$145,000

Closing Entry - Restricted Fund

Revenue - Restricted Contributions	$175,000	
Wages And Salaries		$ 10,000
Cost Of Materials Provided		115,000
Transportation Costs		7,500
Other Expenses		12,500
Fund Balance - Restricted For Clothing		30,000

11-145. Using the preceding journal entries, the required financial statements can be prepared as follows:

LCS Organization (Case Two)
Statement Of Operations And Fund Balances
Year Ending December 31, 2008

	General Fund	Restricted Fund	Endowment Fund
Revenues:			
Unrestricted Contributions	$640,000		
Restricted Contributions		$175,000	
Investment Income	3,000		
Total Revenues	$643,000	$175,000	Nil
Expenses:*			
Wages And Salaries	$ 35,000	$ 10,000	
Cost Of Materials Provided	325,000	115,000	
Transportation Costs	42,500	7,500	
Amortization Expense	4,000	-0-	
Other Expenses	27,500	12,500	
Total Expenses	$434,000	$145,000	Nil
Excess Of Revenues Over Expenses	$209,000	$ 30,000	Nil
Invested In Capital Assets (Net)	(96,000)		
Opening Fund Balances	50,000	29,000	$50,000
Closing Fund Balances	$163,000	$ 59,000	$50,000

*All of the meals activity expenses, plus 50 percent of the clothing activity expenses have been allocated to the general fund. The restricted fund has been allocated 50 percent of the clothing activity expenses.

LCS Organization (Case Two)
Statement Of Cash Flows
Year Ending December 31, 2008

	General Fund	Restricted Fund	Endowment Fund
Cash Flows From Operating Activities:			
Unrestricted Contributions	$635,000		
Restricted Contributions		$175,000	
Investment Income	3,000		
Expenses	(435,000)	(145,000)	
Total	$203,000	$ 30,000	Nil
Cash Flows From Financing And Investing:			
Capital Assets Acquired	(100,000)		
Increase In Cash	$103,000	$ 30,000	Nil
Opening Cash Balance	45,000	29,000	Nil
Closing Cash Balance	$148,000	$ 59,000	Nil

LCS Organization (Case Two)
Statement Of Financial Position
As At December 31, 2008

	General Fund	Restricted Fund	Endowment Fund	Total
Cash (From Statement Of Cash Flows)	$148,000	$59,000		$207,000
Investments			$50,000	50,000
Contributions Receivable	40,000			40,000
Capital Assets:				
Land	20,000			20,000
Building	80,000			80,000
Accumulated Amortization	(4,000)			(4,000)
Total	$284,000	$59,000	$50,000	$393,000
Accounts Payable	$ 25,000			$ 25,000
Fund Balances:				
Restricted For Clothing		$59,000		59,000
Restricted For Endowment			$50,000	50,000
Invested In Capital Assets (Net)	96,000			96,000
Unrestricted	163,000			163,000
Total	$284,000	$59,000	$50,000	$393,000

11-146. As was noted in our first example, when the restricted fund method is used, all-fund totals are required only in the Statement Of Financial Position.

Case Three - Fund Accounting On Other Basis

11-147. This final version of our Case will also assume that LCS uses fund accounting. However, it will not qualify for the restricted fund method of revenue recognition as it classifies its funds by programs rather than by restrictions. They will use a general fund, a meals activity fund, and a clothing activity fund. Endowment funds will be accounted for through the general fund.

General Fund Entries

Investment Income

Cash	$3,000	
Revenue - Investment Income		$3,000

(The entry is in the general fund as there are no restrictions on the use of this income)

Unrestricted Contributions

Cash	$100,000	
Revenue - Unrestricted Contributions		$100,000

(The remaining unrestricted contributions, including those that are still receivable, have been allocated to the meals and clothing funds.)

Acquisition Of Capital Assets

Land	$20,000	
Building	80,000	
Cash		$100,000

Amortization Of Capital Assets

Amortization Expense [($80,000)(1/10)(1/2)]	$4,000	
Accumulated Amortization		$4,000

Closing Entry - General Fund

Revenue - Unrestricted Contributions	$100,000	
Revenue - Investment Income	3,000	
Amortization Expense		$ 4,000
Fund Balances - Unrestricted		3,000
Fund Balances - Invested In Capital Assets		96,000

(The increase in the general fund balance from operations is $99,000 and $96,000 of this amount must be allocated to a separate account for investments in capital assets.)

Meals Fund Entries

Unrestricted Contributions

Cash	$35,000	
Contributions Receivable (Opening)		$35,000
Cash	$330,000	
Contributions Receivable (Closing)	30,000	
Revenue - Unrestricted Contributions		$360,000

Expenses

Accounts Payable (Opening)	$30,000	
Cash		$30,000
Wages And Salaries	$ 25,000	
Cost Of Materials Provided	210,000	
Transportation Costs	35,000	
Other Expenses	15,000	
Cash		$260,000
Accounts Payable (Closing)		25,000

Closing Entry - Meals Fund

Account	Debit	Credit
Revenue - Unrestricted Contributions	$360,000	
Wages And Salaries		$ 25,000
Cost Of Materials Provided		210,000
Transportation Costs		35,000
Other Expenses		15,000
Fund Balances - Unrestricted		75,000

Clothing Fund Entries

Unrestricted Contributions

Account	Debit	Credit
Cash	$180,000	
Revenue - Unrestricted Contributions		$180,000

Restricted Contributions

Account	Debit	Credit
Cash	$175,000	
Deferred Contributions		$175,000

(As the deferral method is being used, the recognition of these contributions as revenue must be deferred.)

Expenses

Account	Debit	Credit
Wages And Salaries	$ 20,000	
Cost Of Materials Provided	230,000	
Transportation Costs	15,000	
Other Expenses	25,000	
Cash		$290,000

Amortization Of Deferred Contributions

Account	Debit	Credit
Deferred Contributions	$145,000	
Revenue - Restricted Contributions		$145,000

(The deferred contributions can be recognized as revenue to the extent that they have been used in the current period to incur expenses.)

Closing Entry

Account	Debit	Credit
Revenue - Unrestricted Contributions	$180,000	
Revenue - Restricted Contributions	145,000	
Wages And Salaries		$ 20,000
Cost Of Materials Provided		230,000
Transportation Costs		15,000
Other Expenses		25,000
Fund Balance - Unrestricted		35,000

(The addition to the Fund Balance - Unrestricted reflects the $180,000 in unrestricted contributions, less the $145,000 [($290,000)(50%)] in expenses that were not paid for out of restricted contributions.)

11-148. Using the preceding journal entries, the required financial statements can be prepared as follows:

LCS Organization (Case Three)
Statement Of Operations And Fund Balances
Year Ending December 31, 2008

	General Fund	Meals Activity Fund	Clothing Activity Fund	Total
Revenues:				
Unrestricted Contributions	$100,000	$360,000	$180,000	$640,000
Restricted Contributions			145,000	145,000
Investment Income	3,000			3,000
Total Revenues	$103,000	$360,000	$325,000	$788,000
Expenses:				
Wages And Salaries		$ 25,000	$ 20,000	$ 45,000
Cost Of Materials Provided		210,000	230,000	440,000
Transportation Costs		35,000	15,000	50,000
Amortization Expense	$ 4,000			4,000
Other Expenses		15,000	25,000	40,000
Total Expenses	$ 4,000	$285,000	$290,000	$579,000
Excess Of Revenues Over Expenses	$ 99,000	$ 75,000	$ 35,000	$209,000
Invested In Capital Assets	(96,000)			(96,000)
Opening Unrestricted Fund Balances	4,000	40,000	6,000	50,000
Closing Unrestricted Fund Balances	$ 7,000	$115,000	$ 41,000	$163,000

LCS Organization (Case Three)
Statement Of Cash Flows
Year Ending December 31, 2008

	General Fund	Meals Activity Fund	Clothing Activity Fund	Total
Cash Flows From Operating Activities				
Unrestricted Contributions*	$100,000	$355,000	$180,000	$635,000
Restricted Contributions			175,000	175,000
Investment Income	3,000			3,000
Expenses*		(290,000)	(290,000)	(580,000)
Total	$103,000	$ 65,000	$ 65,000	$233,000
Cash Flows From Financing And Investing:				
Capital Assets Acquired	(100,000)			(100,000)
Increase In Cash	$ 3,000	$ 65,000	$ 65,000	$133,000
Opening Cash Balance	4,000	35,000	35,000	74,000
Closing Cash Balance	$ 7,000	$100,000	$100,000	$207,000

LCS Organization (Case Three)
Statement Of Financial Position
As At December 31, 2008

	General Fund	Meals Activity Fund	Clothing Activity Fund	Total
Cash (From Statement Of Cash Flows)	$ 7,000	$100,000	$100,000	$207,000
Investments	50,000			50,000
Contributions Receivable*		40,000		40,000
Capital Assets				
Land	20,000			20,000
Building	80,000			80,000
Accumulated Amortization	(4,000)			(4,000)
Total	$153,000	$140,000	$100,000	$393,000
Accounts Payable*		$ 25,000		$ 25,000
Deferred Contributions			$ 59,000	59,000
Fund Balances:				
Restricted For Endowment	$ 50,000			50,000
Invested In Capital Assets	96,000			96,000
Unrestricted	7,000	115,000	41,000	163,000
Total	$153,000	$140,000	$100,000	$393,000

*All of the receivables and payables have been allocated to the meals activity fund. The Unrestricted Contributions of $355,000 have been adjusted for the contributions receivable ($360,000 + $35,000 - $40,000). The expenses of $290,000 allocated to the meals activity fund have been adjusted for the Accounts Payable ($285,000 + $30,000 - $25,000).

11-149. Note that, when fund accounting is used with the deferral method, all-fund totals must be included for all of the financial statements. This is in contrast to fund accounting with the restricted fund method. In this latter case, all-fund totals are only required for the Statement Of Financial Position.

Reporting Controlled And Related Entities Handbook Section 4450

Background

11-150. The accounting Recommendations applicable to profit oriented enterprises provide detailed guidance on accounting for various types of related entities. Section 4450 is designed to provide similar guidance for the related entities of not-for-profit organizations.

11-151. While Section 4450 does not require the consolidation of all controlled affiliates, it specifies the disclosure that is required when consolidation is not used for these entities. It also deals with the presentation and disclosure that is required when a not-for-profit organization participates in joint venture arrangements, or has significant influence over another organization.

Related Entities Defined

11-152. Section 4450 begins by defining possible relationships between a not-for-profit organization and other related entities. These definitions are found in Paragraph 4450.02 as follows:

Control of an entity is the continuing power to determine its strategic operating, investing and financing policies without the co-operation of others.

Joint control of an economic activity is the contractually agreed sharing of the continuing power to determine its strategic operating, investing and financing policies.

A **joint venture** is an economic activity resulting from a contractual arrangement whereby two or more venturers jointly control the economic activity.

Significant influence over an entity is the ability to affect the strategic operating, investing and financing policies of the entity.

An **economic interest** in another not-for-profit organization exists if:

(i) the other organization holds resources that must be used to produce revenue or provide services for the reporting organization; or

(ii) the reporting organization is responsible for the liabilities of the other organization.

11-153. The definitions related to control, joint control, and significant influence are the same as those used by profit oriented enterprises and, as such, require no further explanation. However, the concept of "economic interest" is unique to the not-for-profit accounting area and, as a consequence, warrants further discussion.

11-154. While the preceding definition lays out the general rules for determining economic interest, Paragraph 4450.10 provides further guidance by listing possible indicators of such an interest:

(a) The other organization solicits funds in the name of and with the expressed or implied approval of the reporting organization, and substantially all of the funds solicited are intended by the contributor or are otherwise required to be transferred to the reporting organization or used at its discretion or direction;

(b) The reporting organization transfers significant resources to the other organization, whose resources are held for the benefit of the reporting organization;

(c) The other organization is required to perform significant functions on behalf of the reporting organization that are integral to the reporting organization's achieving its objectives; or

(d) The reporting organization guarantees significant liabilities of the other organization.

11-155. The Section also notes that economic interests can exist in varying degrees of significance. There are situations where the relationship is such that the reporting organization would not be able to function in its current form without the organization in which it has an economic interest. In such cases, the existence of the economic interest may be a strong indicator that control exists. In contrast, some economic interests are much more limited and exist without the reporting entity having control or even significant influence.

11-156. Factors to be considered in the determination of economic interest would include whether the other organization is required to transfer resources or perform functions for the reporting organization. Further, externally imposed restrictions on the other organization's assets could create an economic interest.

11-157. However, a funding relationship where the other organization is not obliged to provide resources to the reporting organization is usually not considered to be an economic interest. Similarly, a situation where another organization holds fund raising events from time to time for the benefit of the reporting organization does not automatically create an economic interest.

11-158. With these definitions in mind, we can now deal with Section 4450's specific Recommendations concerning entities that are related to a not-for-profit organization.

Controlled Not-For-Profit Organizations

Basic Recommendation

11-159. Section 4450 is permissive with respect to the accounting to be used by a not-for-profit organization in accounting for controlled not-for-profit organizations. It allows the reporting entity to choose between three different alternatives:

> **Paragraph 4450.14** *An organization should report each controlled not-for-profit organization in one of the following ways:*
>
> *(a) by consolidating the controlled organization in its financial statements;*
>
> *(b) by providing the disclosure set out in paragraph 4450.22; or*
>
> *(c) if the controlled organization is one of a large number of individually immaterial organizations, by providing the disclosure set out in paragraph 4450.26.* (April, 1997)

11-160. The first and probably best choice on this list is consolidation. If the controlling organization rejects this alternative for an individually material entity, it must provide the following disclosure for the not-for-profit organization that is controlled:

> **Paragraph 4450.22** *For each controlled not-for-profit organization or group of similar controlled organizations not consolidated in the reporting organization's financial statements, the following should be disclosed, unless the group of controlled organizations is comprised of a large number of individually immaterial organizations (see paragraph 4450.26):*
>
> *(a) total assets, liabilities and net assets at the reporting date;*
>
> *(b) revenues (including gains), expenses (including losses) and cash flows from operating, financing and investing activities reported in the period;*
>
> *(c) details of any restrictions, by major category, on the resources of the controlled organizations; and*
>
> *(d) significant differences in accounting policies from those followed by the reporting organization.* (April, 1997)

11-161. Note that there is no mention of using the equity method here. As the controlled entity is a not-for-profit organization, it is unlikely to have equity interests outstanding. In the absence of a measurable equity interest, the equity method cannot be used.

11-162. A final possibility for dealing with controlled not-for-profit organizations is as follows:

> **Paragraph 4450.26** *An organization may exclude a group of controlled organizations from both consolidation and the disclosure set out in paragraph 4450.22, provided that*
>
> *(a) the group of organizations is comprised of a large number of organizations that are individually immaterial; and*
>
> *(b) the reporting organization discloses the reasons why the controlled organizations have been neither consolidated nor included in the disclosure set out in paragraph 4450.22.* (April, 1997)

11-163. This, in effect, allows a not-for-profit organization to provide no disclosure of a group of controlled entities. Judgment would be required in applying this provision. However, it would be applicable in situations where the number of controlled entities is so large that the de facto exercise of control is not practically feasible.

Consolidated Financial Statements

11-164. The preparation of consolidated financial statements is covered in Section 1600 of the *CICA Handbook*. Most of the procedures listed there will be fully applicable to preparing these statements in the context of not-for-profit organizations. However, the fact that not-for-profit organizations usually do not have a transferable ownership interest may necessitate some modification of these procedures.

Other Considerations

11-165. The Section notes that control may or may not be accompanied by an economic interest. If such an interest is present, its nature and extent must be disclosed.

11-166. As an additional point, there is no requirement for consistency in the application of Paragraph 4450.14. A not-for-profit organization could choose to consolidate some controlled entities, while choosing only to provide additional disclosure for other similar controlled entities.

Controlled Profit Oriented Enterprises

11-167. Because profit oriented enterprises will have a transferable ownership interest, the equity method becomes a feasible alternative. For this type of controlled enterprise, the not-for-profit organization can choose between two alternatives:

> **Paragraph 4450.30** *An organization should report each controlled profit oriented enterprise in either of the following ways:*
>
> *(a) by consolidating the controlled enterprise in its financial statements; or*
> *(b) by accounting for its investment in the controlled enterprise using the equity method and providing the disclosure set out in paragraph 4450.32.* (April, 1997)

11-168. Without regard to the method chosen, disclosure is required as follows:

> **Paragraph 4450.31** *For a controlled profit oriented enterprise, regardless of whether it is consolidated or accounted for using the equity method, the following should be disclosed:*
>
> *(a) the policy followed in reporting the controlled enterprise; and*
> *(b) a description of the relationship with the controlled enterprise.* (April, 1997)

11-169. If the equity method is chosen, additional disclosure requirements are applicable:

> **Paragraph 4450.32** *For each controlled profit oriented enterprise or group of similar controlled enterprises accounted for using the equity method, the following should be disclosed:*
>
> *(a) total assets, liabilities and shareholders' equity at the reporting date; and*
> *(b) revenues (including gains), expenses (including losses), net income and cash flows from operating, financing and investing activities reported in the period.* (April, 1997)

Joint Ventures

11-170. A choice of two methods of accounting is available to not-for-profit organizations that participate in joint venture arrangements:

> **Paragraph 4450.36** *An organization should report each interest in a joint venture in either of the following ways:*
>
> *(a) by accounting for its interest using the proportionate consolidation method in accordance with* "Interests In Joint Ventures", *Section 3055; or*
> *(b) by accounting for its interest using the equity method and disclosing the information set out in paragraph 4450.38.* (April, 1997)

11-171. Whether the choice is proportionate consolidation or the use of the equity method, the following disclosure must be provided:

> **Paragraph 4450.37** *For an interest in a joint venture, regardless of whether it is reported using the proportionate consolidation or the equity method, the following should be disclosed:*
>
> *(a) the policy followed in reporting the interest; and*
> *(b) a description of the relationship with the joint venture.* (April, 1997)

11-172. As was the case with controlled profit oriented enterprises, additional disclosure is required when the equity method is used:

> **Paragraph 4450.38** *For each interest in a joint venture, or group of similar interests, accounted for using the equity method, the following should be disclosed:*
>
> *(a) the reporting organization's share of the joint venture's total assets, liabilities and net assets, or shareholders' equity, at the reporting date;*
>
> *(b) the reporting organization's share of the joint venture's revenues (including gains), expenses (including losses), and cash flows from operating, financing and investing activities reported in the period; and*
>
> *(c) significant differences in accounting policies from those followed by the reporting organization.* (April, 1997)

Significantly Influenced Not-For-Profit Organizations

11-173. The required presentation and disclosure for this type of related entity is as follows:

> **Paragraph 4450.40** *When the reporting organization has significant influence in another not-for-profit organization, the following should be disclosed:*
>
> *(a) a description of the relationship with the significantly influenced organization;*
> *(b) a clear and concise description of the significantly influenced organization's purpose, its intended community of service, its status under income tax legislation and its legal form; and*
> *(c) the nature and extent of any economic interest that the reporting organization has in the significantly influenced organization.* (April, 1997)

11-174. The fact that the equity method is not required here once again reflects the fact that most not-for-profit organizations do not have a transferable ownership interest.

Significantly Influenced Profit Oriented Enterprises

11-175. Reflecting the fact that profit oriented enterprises will have a transferable ownership interest, the Section 4450 Recommendation here requires the use of the equity method:

> **Paragraph 4450.43** *When the reporting organization has significant influence over a profit oriented enterprise, the investment should be accounted for using the equity method in accordance with* "Long-Term Investments", Section 3050. (April, 1997)

Disclosure Of Economic Interest

11-176. When a not-for-profit organization has an economic interest in a related entity, the following disclosure is required:

> **Paragraph 4450.45** *When an organization has an economic interest in another not-for-profit organization over which it does not have control or significant influence, the nature and extent of this interest should be disclosed.* (April, 1997)

Information At Different Dates

11-177. When the financial statements of the not-for-profit organization and the related entity are not based on the same fiscal period, the following disclosure is required:

Paragraph 4450.47 *When the fiscal periods of the reporting organization and the other entity do not substantially coincide, the financial information required to be disclosed in accordance with paragraph 4450.22, .32 or .38 should be as at the other entity's most recent reporting date and the following should be disclosed:*

(a) the reporting period covered by the financial information; and

(b) the details of any events or transactions in the intervening period that are significant to the reporting organization's financial position or results of operations. (April, 1997)

Disclosure Of Related Party Transactions By Not-For-Profit Organizations Handbook Section 4460

Purpose

11-178. This final *Handbook* Section on not-for-profit organizations is concerned with the disclosure of related party transactions. It is analogous to Section 3840 which deals with the related party transactions of profit oriented enterprises. As is the case with Section 3840, this Section does not apply to management compensation arrangements, expense allowances, or other payments to individuals in the normal course of operations.

Definitions

11-179. Section 4460 contains definitions for not-for-profit organizations, control, joint control, significant influence, and economic interest, that are identical to those found in Section 4450, "Reporting Controlled And Related Entities By Not-For-Profit Organizations". It also contains the same definition of fair value as is found in Section 4430, "Capital Assets Held By Not-For-Profit Organizations". These definitions will not be repeated here. Definitions in this Section that have not been previously presented are as follows:

Related parties exist when one party has the ability to exercise, directly or indirectly, control, joint control or significant influence over the other. Two or more parties are related when they are subject to common control, joint control or common significant influence. Two not-for-profit organizations are related parties if one has an economic interest in the other. Related parties also include management and immediate family members.

A **related party transaction** is a transfer of economic resources or obligations between related parties, or the provision of services by one party to a related party, regardless of whether any consideration is exchanged. The parties to the transaction are related prior to the transaction. When the relationship arises as a result of the transaction, the transaction is not one between related parties.

Identification Of Related Parties

11-180. The Section provides guidance with respect to the identification of related parties. It is expressed in terms of commonly encountered related parties:

Paragraph 4460.04 The most commonly encountered related parties of a reporting organization include the following:

(a) an entity that directly, or indirectly through one or more intermediaries, controls, or is controlled by, or is under common control with, the reporting organization;

(b) an individual who directly, or indirectly through one or more intermediaries, controls the reporting organization;

(c) an entity that, directly or indirectly, is significantly influenced by the reporting organization or has significant influence over the reporting organization or is under common significant influence with the reporting organization;

(d) the other organization when one organization has an economic interest in the other;
(e) management: any person(s) having authority and responsibility for planning, directing and controlling the activities of the reporting organization. (Management would include the directors, officers and other persons fulfilling a senior management function.)
(f) an individual that has either significant influence or joint control over the reporting organization;
(g) members of the immediate family of individuals described in paragraphs (b), (e) and (f). (Immediate family comprises an individual's spouse and those dependent on either the individual or the individual's spouse.);
(h) the other party, when a management contract or other management authority exists and the reporting organization is either the managing or managed party; and
(i) any party that is subject to joint control by the reporting organization (In this instance a party subject to joint control is related to each of the venturers that share that joint control. However, the venturers themselves are not related to one another solely by virtue of sharing of joint control.).

11-181. Those of you familiar with Section 3840 which provides Recommendations with respect to the related party transactions of profit oriented enterprises, will recognize that this list is very similar to the list that is found in that Section.

Disclosure

General Recommendation

11-182. Section 4460 makes the following Recommendation with respect to the disclosure of related party transactions:

Paragraph 4460.07 *An organization should disclose the following information about its transactions with related parties:*

(a) a description of the relationship between the transacting parties;
(b) a description of the transaction(s), including those for which no amount has been recorded;
(c) the recorded amount of the transactions classified by financial statement category;
(d) the measurement basis used for recognizing the transaction in the financial statements;
(e) amounts due to or from related parties and the terms and conditions relating thereto;
(f) contractual obligations with related parties, separate from other contractual obligations;
(g) contingencies involving related parties, separate from other contingencies. (April, 1997)

Description Of The Relationship

11-183. The Section encourages the use of accurate terminology when complying with Paragraph 4460.07(a). Terms such as controlled organization, significantly influenced organization, or organization under common control, are preferable to more general descriptions such as affiliate or associate. Disclosure here should include a description of the manner in which control or influence is exercised.

Description Of Transactions

11-184. A description of all transactions, including information about the nature of any items exchanged, is required by Paragraph 4460.07(b). As noted in that Paragraph, this would include transactions, for example an exchange of management services, for which no amounts are recorded in the accounting records.

Amounts And Measurement

11-185. As with Section 3840 for profit oriented enterprises, Section 4460 requires not-for-profit organizations to disclose the aggregate amount of related party transactions, along with the measurement basis used in recording them. This is particularly important here because, unlike Section 3840, Section 4460 does not include Recommendations with respect to how such related party transactions should be measured.

Other Disclosure Considerations

11-186. Section 4460 makes the following additional points with respect to the disclosure of the related party transactions of not-for-profit organizations:

- When there are amounts due to and from related parties, disclosure includes the relationship between the parties, as well as the nature of the transactions that created the balances.
- When transactions occur between two organizations both of which will be included in the consolidated financial statements, the transactions will be completely eliminated from the financial statements. This means that no disclosure of such transactions will be required. However, when the equity method is used to account for a related party, any profit or loss on the transaction will be eliminated, but the other components of the transaction will remain in the records of the related organizations. As a result, disclosure will be required in this type of situation.
- In disclosing a not-for-profit organization's contractual obligations and contingencies, Section 3280, "Contractual Obligations", and Section 3290, "Contingencies", would be applicable. Separate disclosure is required for the contractual obligations and contingencies of related parties.

Other Concepts

Budgetary Control

11-187. Budgets are of importance to all types of organizations, whether they are profit oriented, not-for-profit, or government organizations. Reflecting this situation is the fact that a variety of procedures exist to assist management track and control both expenses and revenues. With respect to profit oriented enterprises, these procedures are never reflected in the actual financial statements that are presented to users.

11-188. However, not-for-profit organizations sometimes record budgeted amounts in their accounting records. For example, an organization with budgeted revenues of $2,500,000 and budgeted expenses of $2,400,000, might make the following entry:

Budgeted Revenues	$2,500,000	
Budgeted Fund Balance		$ 100,000
Budgeted Expenses		2,400,000

11-189. This entry would establish a sort of fund that could be used to make ongoing comparisons between actual and budgeted figures. In most cases, these amounts would be closed out at the end of the year and would not be included in published financial statements. Given that these amounts do not form a component of the financial reporting process, we do not believe that they warrant further coverage in this text.

Encumbrance System

11-190. A set of procedures referred to as an encumbrance system is used by some not-for-profit organizations as a control mechanism. Normally, the acquisition of goods and services is not recorded in the accounts until the items are delivered or services received. Under an encumbrance system, and entry is made at the time a purchase order is issued.

Example On January 10, 2007, Ardvan issues a purchase order for merchandise that is expected to cost $1,850. On January 31, 2007, the goods are received along with an invoice for $1,923.

Analysis The journal entry that would be made at the time the purchase order is issued would be as follows:

Encumbrances	$1,850	
Estimated Commitments		$1,850

When the goods are delivered, they would be recorded with the usual entry, followed by a reversal of the encumbrance entry:

Merchandise	$1,923	
Accounts Payable		$1,923
Estimated Commitments	$1,850	
Encumbrances		$1,850

11-191. The basic idea behind these procedures is to provide control over expenses. It is believed that if the not-for-profit organization records its commitment, it is less likely to go over the amounts that it has budgeted for expenses.

11-192. A problem arises at the end of the period in that there will usually be outstanding commitments and these will be reflected in the encumbrance system accounts. However, these accounts reflect purchase commitments. Such commitments are executory contracts and should not be recorded in the financial statements (an exception to that is made for certain leasing arrangements under Section 3065 of the *CICA Handbook*).

11-193. As an encumbrance system balances internal matters that should not be part of the financial reporting process, we will give this subject no further attention in this material.

International Convergence

11-194. At this point in time, the IASB has not issued any IFRSs that deal with not-for-profit organizations. Further, there is nothing in their work plan that suggests that they anticipate doing any work in this area in the foreseeable future.

11-195. In its *Implementation Guide For Incorporating IFRSs Into Canadian GAAP*, the AcSB notes the absence of IFRSs dealing with not-for-profit issues. However, there is no indication of how they will deal with this matter. If changeover occurs at the scheduled date of 2011, the Sections of the *CICA Handbook* that are currently in use by not-for-profit organizations will disappear. When this occurs, Canadian not-for-profit organizations will have to use the IFRSs in place of the Sections of the *Handbook* that have been removed.

11-197. The question then becomes whether the AcSB will retain Sections 4400 through 4460 in order to provide guidance in the areas that are unique to the needs of not-for-profit organizations. It does not appear that a firm decision on this issue has been made at this time.

Additional Readings

11-198. In writing the material in the text, we have incorporated all of the relevant *CICA Handbook* recommendations, as well as material from other sources that we felt to be of importance. While this approach meets the needs of the great majority of our readers, some of you may wish to pursue this subject in greater depth. To facilitate this, you will find a fairly comprehensive list of additional readings at the end of each relevant Chapter in our *Guide To Canadian Financial Reporting*. EIC Abstracts related to not-for profit organizations are available in the Appendix to Chapter 62.

CD-ROM Note Our *Guide To Canadian Financial Reporting* is available on the CD-ROM which is included with this text.

Problems For Self Study

(The solutions for these problems can be found in the separate Study Guide.)

Self Study Problem Eleven - 1

Note Self Study Problem Eleven-2 is a different version of this problem.

On January 1, 2007, the Environmental Protection Society (EPS) is organized as a not-for-profit organization. Its purpose is to serve two needs in its province:

- Planting trees in urban areas.
- Cleaning up litter along various secondary roads.

The organization has a December 31 year end.

Other Information:

1. The initial funding for the organization is provided by a group of wealthy individuals who make an endowment contribution of $132,000. The funds are invested in debt securities. All of the income earned by these endowment funds is restricted to use in the Society's tree planting activities. During the year ending December 31, 2007, the income on the endowment investment totalled $6,450.

2. The organization solicits and receives unrestricted contributions from a large number of sources. Such contributions are allocated to both tree planting and to litter cleanup by the board of directors of the organization. During the year ending December 31, 2007, $582,000 of such contributions were received and, at the end of the year, an additional $127,000 in contributions were receivable. The Board believes that this is a reasonable estimate of the amount that will actually be collected. The $709,000 total was allocated $490,000 to tree planting and $219,000 to litter cleanup.

3. The organization accepts additional contributions that are restricted to use in the tree planting activities. These funds are segregated and a separate report is made to contributors on their usage. During the year ending December 31, 2007, restricted contributions of $146,000 were received and, at the end of the year, an additional $23,000 of restricted contributions were receivable.

4. The organization operates out of fully furnished office space that is rented for $2,500 per month. Three-quarters of the space is used for tree planting activities, with the remainder used for litter cleanup activities.

5. During the year ending December 31, 2007, the organization incurred the following expenses:

	Tree Planting Activities	Litter Cleanup Activities
Wages And Salaries	$328,000	$ 86,000
Cost Of Materials Provided	107,000	32,000
Rent	22,500	7,500
Other Expenses	72,500	36,500
Total	$530,000	$162,000

A total of 20 percent ($106,000) of the expenses related to tree planting activities were paid for out of the restricted contributions bank account. On December 31, 2007, there were outstanding Accounts Payable related to the litter cleanup activity expenses of $42,000.

6. EPS uses fund accounting with funds established for endowment contributions and restricted tree planting amounts, in addition to a general fund. Given this they use the restricted fund method of revenue recognition.

Required:

A. Prepare journal entries, including closing entries, to record the information in the problem.

B. Prepare a Statement Of Operations And Fund Balances and a Statement Of Cash Flows for the year ending December 31, 2007, and a Statement Of Financial Position as at December 31, 2007.

Self Study Problem Eleven - 2

Note Self Study Problem Eleven-1 is a different version of this problem.

On January 1, 2007, the Environmental Protection Society (EPS) is organized as a not-for-profit organization. Its purpose is to serve two needs in its province:

- Planting trees in urban areas.
- Cleaning up litter along various secondary roads.

The organization has a December 31 year end.

Other Information:

1. The initial funding for the organization is provided by a group of wealthy individuals who make an endowment contribution of $132,000. The funds are invested in debt securities. There are no restrictions on the use of the income resulting from this investment. During the year ending December 31, 2007, the income on the endowment investment totalled $6,450.

2. The organization solicits and receives unrestricted contributions from a large number of sources. Such contributions are allocated to both tree planting and to litter cleanup by the board of directors of the organization. During the year ending December 31, 2007, $582,000 of such contributions were received and, at the end of the year, an additional $127,000 in contributions were receivable. These receivables are allocated to the tree planting fund. The Board believes that this is a reasonable estimate of the amount that will actually be collected. The $709,000 total was allocated $490,000 to tree planting and $219,000 to litter cleanup.

3. The organization accepts additional contributions that are restricted to use in the tree planting activities. These funds are segregated and a separate report is made to contributors on their usage. During the year ending December 31, 2007, restricted contributions of $146,000 were received and, at the end of the year, an additional $23,000 of restricted contributions were receivable. These receivables were allocated to the tree planting fund.

4. The organization operates out of fully furnished office space that is rented for $2,500 per month. Three-quarters of the space is used for tree planting activities, with the remainder used for litter cleanup activities.

5. During the year ending December 31, 2007, the organization incurred the following expenses:

	Tree Planting Activities	Litter Cleanup Activities
Wages And Salaries	$328,000	$ 86,000
Cost Of Materials Provided	107,000	32,000
Rent	22,500	7,500
Other Expenses	72,500	36,500
Total	$530,000	$162,000

A total of 20 percent ($106,000) of the expenses related to tree planting activities were paid for out of the restricted contributions bank account. On December 31, 2007, there were outstanding Accounts Payable related to the litter cleanup activity expenses of $42,000.

6. EPS uses fund accounting with funds established for tree planting activities and litter cleanup activities, in addition to a general fund. Endowment contributions are accounted for in the general fund. Because of this, they use the deferral method of revenue recognition.

Required:

A. Prepare journal entries, including closing entries, to record the information in the problem.

B. Prepare a Statement Of Operations And Fund Balances and a Statement Of Cash Flows for the year ending December 31, 2007, and a Statement Of Financial Position as at December 31, 2007.

Self Study Problem Eleven - 3

The Good Samaritan Centre (GSC) was established on January 1, 2007 to provide food to the needy in the local community through a soup kitchen. The soup kitchen provides three meals a day. The GSC also opened a clothing cupboard on July 1, 2007 in the basement of the soup kitchen. GSC is run by a small number of permanent employees with the help of part-timers and a large group of dedicated volunteers.

Other Information:

1. Initial funding for the Centre was provided by the estate of Owen Moses in the amount of $800,000. These funds were used and allocated as follows:

   Unrestricted Contributions A total of $330,000 was allocated to unrestricted contribution.

   Capital Expenditures Of the unrestricted contributions, $220,000 was used to purchase an old restaurant, with $100,000 of this amount allocated to land. A further $20,000 was used to purchase a used van. The building will be amortized over 20 years on a straight line basis, while the van will be amortized using the declining balance method with a rate of 20 percent. The van has an expected residual value of $500. The organization will take one-half year's amortization in the year in which a capital asset is acquired.

   Endowment Contributions $100,000 of the total was designated an endowment contribution. The contributions were invested and, during the year ending December 31, 2007, investment income relating to these investments totaled $15,970. There are no restrictions on the use of income from this fund.

   Restricted Contributions $370,000 of the total was restricted for the clothing cupboard activities.

2. Daniel Smith, the executive director for the GSC, was very proactive in securing support from the local community and the United Way. Contributions for the year totaled $725,000, with $225,000 restricted for use in the clothing cupboard. Daniel was able to negotiate with a local radio station to have the advertising for the annual drive to stock the clothing cupboard donated rather than paying the $2,100 cost.

3. During the year ending December 31, 2007, the organization incurred the following expenses:

	Soup Kitchen	Clothing Cupboard
Wages And Salaries	$150,000	$ 30,000
Cost Of Materials	250,000	100,000
Transportation Costs	5,000	3,000
Other Expenses	4,200	26,000
Totals	$409,200	$159,000

All of the expenses of the clothing cupboard were paid for with restricted contributions.

4. The organization will use fund accounting with funds established for endowment contributions and restricted clothing cupboard contributions, as well as a general fund. Given this, they will use the restricted fund method of revenue recognition.

Required:

A. Prepare journal entries to record the information in the problem, including closing entries for each fund.

B. Prepare the Statement Of Operations And Fund Balances for the year ending December 31, 2007, a Cash Flow Statement for the year ending December 31, 2007, and the Statement Of Financial Position at December 31, 2007.

Self Study Problem Eleven - 4

Note This Self Study Problem is extended in Assignment Problem Eleven-1.

On January 1, 2007, the Winter Sports Society (WSS) is organized as a not-for-profit organization. Its purpose is to serve the needs of its local community in two areas:

- Encouraging children to learn ice skating outside of the arena environment.
- The provision of cross country ski equipment to needy senior citizens.

The organization will have a December 31 year end.

Other Information:

1. Initial funding is provided by a wealthy individual who makes an endowment contribution of $87,000. These funds are invested in debt securities. There are no restrictions on the income that is produced by these investments. During the year ending December 31, 2007, such income amounted to $4,370.

2. The organization solicits and receives unrestricted contributions. Such contributions are allocated to both skating promotion and ski equipment provision by the organization's board of directors. During the year ending December 31, 2007, $726,000 in contributions were received. At year end, an additional $56,000 in contributions were receivable.

The board believes that this is a reasonable estimate of the amount that will actually be collected. This total was allocated $410,000 to the skating activity and $372,000 to the skiing activity. All of the receivables are allocated to the skating activity.

3. The organization accepts additional contributions that are restricted to use in the provision of ski equipment to needy senior citizens. These funds are segregated and a separate report is made to contributors on their usage. During the year ending December 31, 2007, restricted contributions of $242,000 were received. No restricted contributions are receivable at year end. All of these restricted contributions are deposited in a separate bank account.

4. The organization operates out of a fully furnished office space that is rented for $2,000 per month. The use of the space is split equally between the skating and skiing activities of the organization.

5. During the year ending December 31, 2007, the organization incurred the following expenses:

	Skating Activity	Skiing Activity
Wages And Salaries	$173,000	$ 71,000
Cost Of Materials Provided	32,000	274,000
Transportation Costs	41,000	33,000
Rent	12,000	12,000
Other Expenses	27,000	31,000
Total	$285,000	$421,000

A total of 50 percent ($210,500) of the expenses related to the skiing activity have been paid for out of the restricted contributions bank account. On December 31, 2007, there were outstanding Accounts Payable related to the skating activity expenses of $30,000.

Required: Prepare a Statement Of Operations And Fund Balances for the year ending December 31, 2007, a Statement Of Cash Flows for the year ending December 31, 2007 and a Statement Of Financial Position as at December 31, 2007under each of the following assumptions:

A. WSS does not use fund accounting. They use the deferral method of revenue recognition.

B. WSS uses fund accounting, with funds established for endowment contributions and restricted skiing contributions, in addition to a general fund. They use the restricted fund method of revenue recognition.

C. WSS uses fund accounting, with funds established for skating activities and skiing activities, in addition to a general fund. Endowment contributions are dealt with through the general fund. They use the deferral method of revenue recognition.

Journal entries are not required.

Assignment Problems

(The solutions for these problems are only available in the solutions manual that has been provided to your instructor.)

Assignment Problem Eleven - 1

Note This is an extension of Self Study Problem Eleven-4. It involves the same Winter Sports Society (WSS) and extends their activities into the year ending December 31, 2008. This problem cannot be solved without referring to information in that version of the problem. This version includes capital assets and their amortization.

Additional Information:

1. There are no additional endowment contributions during the year ending December 31, 2008. The endowment fund investments have income of $4,820 during this period.

2. During the year ending December 31, 2008, $842,300 in unrestricted contributions were received. At year end, there is an additional $53,250 in contributions that are receivable. The board believes that this is a reasonable estimate of the amount that will actually be collected. This total was allocated $510,050 to the skating activity, $243,500 to the skiing activity, and $142,000 for the acquisition of a building to be used in the organization's operations. All of the receivables are allocated to the skating activity.

3. On July 1, 2008, the organization acquires a building for a total cost of $142,000. Of this total, $37,000 represents the fair value of the land on which the building is situated and the remaining $105,000 reflects the fair value of the building. The estimated useful life of the building is 20 years and no significant residual value is anticipated. The organization uses straight-line amortization, charging only one-half year's amortization in the year in which an asset is acquired.

4. The organization continues to accept additional contributions that are restricted to use in the skiing activity. As in the past, these funds are placed in a separate bank account. During the year ending December 31, 2008, restricted contributions of $317,600 were received. No contributions are receivable at year end.

5. During the year ending December 31, 2008, the organization incurred the following expenses:

	Skating Activity	Skiing Activity
Wages And Salaries	$345,600	$ 32,400
Cost Of Materials Provided	48,200	362,300
Transportation Costs	19,400	21,600
Rent	6,000	6,000
Other Expenses	23,300	45,900
Total	$442,500	$468,200

The records show that 56 percent of the expenses related to the skiing activity were made from restricted funds. On December 31, 2008, there were outstanding Accounts Payable related to the skating activities expenses of $32,430.

Required: Prepare a Statement Of Operations And Fund Balances for the year ending December 31, 2008, a Statement Of Cash Flows for the year ending December 31, 2008 and a Statement Of Financial Position as at December 31, 2008, under each of the following assumptions:

A. WSS does not use fund accounting and recognizes revenue on a deferral basis.

B. WSS uses fund accounting, with funds established for endowment contributions and restricted skiing contributions, in addition to a general fund. They use the restricted fund method of revenue recognition.

C. WSS uses fund accounting, with funds established for skating activities and skiing activities, in addition to a general fund. Endowment contributions are dealt with through the general fund. They use the deferral method of revenue recognition.

Journal entries are not required.

Assignment Problem Eleven - 2

The Osgoode Hospital was founded in 1982 in order to provide limited patient care services in the local community. It is a not-for-profit organization and was originally funded by donations of $8,400,000. These funds were used to acquire land and to construct and equip their current facility. Prior to 2007, all accounting was done through a single general fund.

In 2007, it instituted a new fund raising campaign to raise funds for replacing some of its aging equipment. As the funds raised in this campaign can only be used for this purpose, management has established a separate restricted fund. There are no restrictions on the use of any income produced by investments made in this fund. Osgoode will account for this Replacement Fund using the restricted fund method. However, they will continue to use the deferral method for the General Fund.

As of December 31, 2007, the Balance Sheets of the Hospital's two funds are as follows:

	General Fund	Replacement Fund
Cash	$ 65,000	$125,000
Accounts Receivable	105,000	
Allowance For Bad Debts	(18,000)	
Supplies Inventory	46,000	
Investments (At Cost)		325,000
Land	1,090,000	
Building	5,800,000	
Building - Accumulated Amortization	(1,550,000)	
Equipment	1,950,000	
Equipment - Accumulated Amortization	(588,000)	
Total Assets	**$6,900,000**	**$450,000**
Accounts Payable	$ 46,000	
Deferred Contributions - Building And Equipment	5,612,000	
Invested In Land	1,090,000	
Externally Restricted Fund Balance	N/A	$450,000
Unrestricted Fund Balance	152,000	
Total Liabilities And Fund Balance	**$6,900,000**	**$450,000**

Other Information:

1. During 2008, Osgoode billed the provincial government and its patients a total amount of $3,263,000. Of this amount, $2,247,000 was for room and board, with the balance being for professional services. All accounts are due within 30 days.

2. Collections of Accounts Receivable during 2008 totaled $2,984,000.

3. During 2008, $27,000 of Accounts Receivable had to be written off. At the end of the year, is is estimated that further write offs will be equal to 1 percent of annual billings.

4. Equipment costing $82,000 was acquired with cash from the Replacement Fund.

5. During 2008, Osgoode paid operating expenses of $3,216,000. They also paid $196,000 for supplies.

6. During 2008, an individual contributes $375,000 on condition that this full amount be invested in government bonds. While the income from these bonds can be used for any purpose, the principal cannot be used. Osgoode established an Endowment Fund for this contribution.

7. During 2008, the hospital received unrestricted contributions of $161,000. In addition, it received interest payments of $12,000 from the investments held in the endowment fund.

8. Accounts Payable balances are related to operating expenses and to supplies. The respective amounts at December 31, 2007 and December 31, 2008, are as follows:

	December 31 2007	December 31 2008
Operating Expenses	$32,000	$35,000
Inventory Of Supplies	14,000	18,000
Total	$46,000	$53,000

9. Supplies on hand on December 31, 2008 totaled $28,000.

10. Amortization on the building for 2008 was $65,000. For the equipment, the total amortization was $97,000, of which $12,000 related to equipment purchased by the Replacement Fund.

11. On December 31, 2008, accrued interest on the investments in the Replacement Fund was $17,000. There are no restrictions on the use of this income.

Required: Provide the journal entry that would be required to record each item of Other Information. In addition, indicate the fund in which each journal entry would be recorded.

Assignment Problem Eleven - 3

The Bookkeepers' Rehabilitation Fund is a registered Canadian charity, organized to provide rehabilitation for those Chartered Bookkeepers (CB's, hereafter) that have found so much stress in their daily work that they have been driven to various acts of depravity.

The fund maintains several residences where such individuals are provided with a comprehensive program of physical and mental therapy. The program is carefully designed to restore them to their former status as esteemed professionals. The work of the fund is supported by a combination of user fees, support from various community organizations, and an annual fund raising dinner.

The accounting system of this organization is based on three funds. These are an Operating Fund, a Capital Fund, and a Capital Asset Fund. As the name implies, all operating revenues and most operating expenses are recorded in the Operating Fund.

The Capital Fund is used to record major grants from government organizations. Also recorded here would be allocation of these grants to either the Capital Asset Fund or the Operating Fund, as well as income from investments made with Capital Fund resources.

The Capital Asset Fund is designed to record capital assets purchased from both the Capital Fund and the Operating Fund. Amortization of these assets is also recorded in this fund as a direct reduction of the Fund Balance

On January 1 of the current year, the Balance Sheets of the three Funds are as follows:

Operating Fund

Assets	
Cash	$290,000
Temporary Investments (At Cost)	605,000
Interest Receivable	28,000
Fees Receivable	47,000
Total	$970,000
Equities	
Accounts Payable	$205,000
Wages Payable	155,000
Unrestricted Balance	610,000
Total	$970,000

Capital Fund

Assets	
Cash	$ 28,000
Term Deposits	895,000
Total	$923,000
Equities	
Fund Balance	$923,000
Total	$923,000

Capital Asset Fund

Assets	
Furniture and Fixtures	$4,150,000
Buildings	3,110,000
Accumulated Amortization	(2,585,000)
Total	$4,675,000
Equities	
Fund Balance	$4,675,000
Total	$4,675,000

Other Information:

1. During the year, the Fund billed user fees totalling $3,395,000. Collections for the year were $3,102,000 while, at the end of the year, $172,000 in billed fees were judged to be uncollectible.

2. During the year, community organizations pledged total contributions of $11,215,000. At the end of the current year, $275,000 of this amount had not been received. There are no restrictions on the use of these contributions.

3. The annual fund raising dinner is scheduled for December 1. A separate Dinner Fund is established to account for this event and, on November 1, $875,000 was advanced from the Operating Fund to set up this special Fund. The event was a success, generating total revenues of $3,425,000 and incurring total costs of $1,015,000. All revenues had been collected at the event but there were $130,000 in costs which had not been paid. The Dinner Fund repaid the original $875,000 advanced from the Operating Fund and, in addition, disbursed $2,395,000 as a loan to the Operating Fund.

4. During the year, salaries and wages of $11,422,000 were paid. At the end of the current year, accrued salaries and wages amounted to $217,000.

5. During the year, invoices for goods and services were received in the amount of $4,427,000. Payments on Accounts Payable for the year were $4,425,000.

6. The Temporary Investments in the Operating Fund were sold during the year for $617,000. Also during the year, the Operating Fund collected interest of $63,000, including the $28,000 accrual in the January 1 Balance Sheet.

7. Under a special grants program, the Federal Government has agreed to provide $5,000,000 towards the acquisition of an existing building. The building is to be converted into a large new residence to accommodate the increasing numbers of CBs requiring the help of the Fund. The first $2,000,000 of this grant was received during the current year. The Bookkeepers' Rehabilitation Fund incurred costs of $205,000 in anticipation of acquiring the new building. A total of $15,000 of these costs were unpaid at year end. Of the remaining cash, $1,750,000 was invested in term deposits. Both the principal and interest of all term deposits were rolled over every thirty days, with the total balance rising to $2,765,000 on December 31 of the current year.

8. Amortization on the capital assets amounts to $890,000 for the year.

Required: For each of the four funds, including the temporary Dinner Fund:

A. Provide the journal entry that would be required to record each item of Other Information. Your solution should indicate the fund in which each journal entry would be recorded.

B. Provide a Statement Of Operations And Fund Balances and a Statement Of Financial Position. Note that there is no Statement Of Operations And Fund Balances for the Capital Asset Fund.

Assignment Problem Eleven - 4

On August 15, 2004, the European Exchange Club (EEC) was formed in an effort to create a united social group out of several separate regional clubs in the vicinity of the city of Decker, located in central Canada. The purpose of the group is to combine resources to meet the recreational, cultural, and social needs of its collective members. EEC was formed through the collaboration of the following clubs and their memberships:

	Members
The Canadian Russian Society	12,300
The Italian Clubs Of Canada	10,800
Portuguese Cultural Foundation	4,100
Association Of Greeks Of The World	2,700
The German Groups	1,100
Other	1,700
Total	32,700

It is now December 2007. EEC's executives have spent the past few years planning and preparing for its operation. The club's community centre is expected to be fully completed next year. The facilities of the club will include the following:

- a multi-purpose building to house banquets, meetings and arts activities
- hiking trails
- indoor/outdoor tennis facilities
- bicycle trails
- baseball diamonds
- an indoor/outdoor pool
- a soccer field

The multi-purpose building is 75 percent complete, and EEC's executives have stated that it is "approximately within budget." Estimated building costs were outlined in a 2004 feasibility study, as follows:

Construction Cost	$2,300,000
Site Preparation Costs	400,000
Furniture And Fixtures	550,000
Consulting Fees	120,000
Miscellaneous	80,000
Total	$3,450,000

The four acres of land on which the facility is built were provided by the provincial government by way of a five-year lease at $1 a year. The adjacent land of 60 acres was contributed to the club by The Italian Clubs Of Canada. Previously, this land had been leased to a farmer for $54,000 a year. The 64 acres will be used for the following projects, which will incur the additional costs listed below:

Hiking Trails	$ 595,000
Baseball Diamonds	30,000
Soccer Field	22,000
Bicycle Trails	95,000
Indoor/Outdoor Pool	700,000
Indoor/Outdoor Tennis Facilities	300,000
Total	$1,742,000

In addition to these development costs, the club faces annual operating costs of approximately $740,000, outlined in Exhibit I. John Mendez-Smith, the newly elected president of the club, has approached your firm, Young and Kerr Accountants, to prepare a report that provides recommendations on accounting. You took the notes appearing in Exhibit II at a meeting with the club's president and executive committee.

Required: Prepare the report.

(CICA Adapted)

Exhibit I
European Exchange Club
Yearly Budget

Operating Revenues	
Membership Fees	$ 91,000
Social Rentals	185,000
Meeting Rentals	50,000
Sport Rentals	23,000
Concessions	61,000
Fundraising Events	225,000
Total Operating Revenues	$635,000
Operating Costs	
Salaries	$363,000
Administrative Costs	39,000
Maintenance	126,000
Utilities	112,000
Educational Scholarships	100,000
Total Operating Costs	$740,000

Exhibit II
Notes Taken From Your Meeting With
Mr. Mendez-Smith And The Executive Committee

1. Under the lease agreement with the province, EEC is responsible for maintenance and all costs of improvements. The lease agreement provides for 20 renewal terms of five years' duration each. Renewal is based on the condition that EEC makes the club's services available to all present and future EEC member-clubs and their membership.

2. EEC has requested an operating grant from the provincial government. Its proposal requests the province to provide EEC with annual funds to cover 50 percent of "approved" operating costs incurred to provide services to all club members.

   The City of Decker wishes to construct an arena and a swimming pool and has opposed the proposed operating grant. The City has asked to be the first in line for available provincial funds.

   The committee members suspect that they will have to compromise on their proposal and are having problems determining the minimum annual funds required by the club from the province.

3. The Russian and Italian clubs have been arguing with other clubs over the equalization payments required from each club. Currently, each club makes payments to EEC based upon their proportionate membership. Payments for each calendar year are made on February 1 of the following year.

The Russian group performs the administrative functions of EEC and has charged, and will continue to charge, the club only 50% of the market value of these services.

4. The accounting function is a major concern of the member-club representatives. In particular, they have raised the following issues:
   a) Several fund raising events are organized by individual member clubs.
   b) Any donations to EEC are received through the member clubs.
   c) No accounting has been made of services donated to EEC by the members of the individual clubs.
   d) EEC has approached a bank to assist in future phases of the club's development. The bank has informed EEC that it is interested in asset values and EEC's ability to repay the loans.

Accounting For Partnerships

International Convergence

12-1. To date, the IASB has focused on the financial reporting needs of publicly accountable enterprises. The current content of the IFRSs does not provide exemptions for other types of enterprises such as unincorporated businesses, nor does it provide separate standards for such organizations.

12-2. It appears that this is going to change. In late 2006, the IASB issued an Exposure Draft, *International Reporting Standard For Small And Medium-Sized Entities*. The Exposure Draft defines these entities as non-publicly accountable entities that publish general purpose financial statements for external users. This is roughly the same group of organizations that qualify for using the differential reporting options that are provided in Section 1300 of the *CICA Handbook*. The Exposure Draft proposes a standard that provides a somewhat simplified application of the IFRSs.

12-3. Given this development,. it is unlikely that unincorporated businesses will have to comply with the generally applicable IFRSs when they are adopted into Canadian GAAP at the changeover date. We would expect that until the changeover date, unincorporated businesses will continue to be eligible for Section 1300's differential reporting options. When changeover occurs, it is likely that the IASB Exposure Draft's simplified standards will be available to unincorporated businesses.

Introduction To Unincorporated Businesses

Legal Environment

12-4. Because of the requirements of provincial securities regulators, companies whose securities are publicly traded must consistently follow the generally accepted accounting principles (GAAP) that are contained in the *CICA Handbook* or other authoritative sources. Failure to do so can lead to modifications to the audit report and, in extreme cases, a suspension of trading in the company's securities. Even if the corporation's securities are not publicly traded, compliance with *Handbook* Recommendations will generally be required by the federal or provincial corporations act under which the corporation was established.

12-5. The situation is different with respect to unincorporated businesses. As their ownership interests cannot be publicly traded, they are not subject to the requirements of provincial securities regulation. Further, the establishment of such businesses does not require the creation of an artificial legal entity and, as a consequence, they are not subject to rules such as those found in corporate enabling statutes. These facts mean that unincorporated businesses are not generally subject to the Recommendations of the *CICA Handbook*.

12-6. There is, however, often a constraint on the ability of such businesses to avoid *Handbook* Recommendations. When unincorporated businesses require financing, it is not uncommon for creditors to require audited financial statements. When this is the case, the issuance of an unqualified auditor's report will generally require compliance with GAAP. It should be noted, however, that Section 1300, "Differential Reporting", exempts non-publicly accountable enterprises from a number of *Handbook* requirements. Most unincorporated businesses would be considered non-publicly accountable enterprises and, as a consequence, can choose to be exempt from the specified requirements.

Handbook Requirements

12-7. For unincorporated enterprises, GAAP also includes a group of Recommendations that are specifically applicable to this type of business. This situation is described in Section 1800 as follows:

> **Paragraph 1800.01** Minimum standards of disclosure which apply to unincorporated businesses as well as incorporated businesses are dealt with elsewhere in this *Handbook*. Special problems arise, however, in statements of unincorporated businesses because such businesses, unlike limited companies, are not entities separate from their owners. Only these special problems are dealt with in this Section.

User Needs

12-8. Unincorporated businesses can be divided into two categories — proprietorships where there is a single owner, and partnerships where there are two or more owners. (While it is possible to argue that unincorporated joint ventures are a third category, we will view them as a type of partnership for accounting purposes.)

12-9. With respect to those situations where there is a single owner of the business, in the absence of a requirement for audited financial statements, these businesses can use any accounting procedures they wish, including doing no accounting at all except as required by taxation authorities. The objective of financial statements here is to meet the needs of the single owner, with no concern for other equity interests. When creditors advance funds to the business, they may require that their interest be protected by the preparation of audited financial statements, in which case the Recommendations of the *CICA Handbook*, including those contained in Section 1800, come into play. Given this situation, we do not believe that proprietorship accounting requires any discussion beyond that provided with respect to the Recommendations of Section 1800.

12-10. The situation is different with respect to partnerships. As more than one equity interest is involved, financial statements must provide a basis for fair allocation and distribution of partnership resources. This requirement applies not only with respect to income reporting, it applies in a variety of situations, including admittance of a new partner, retirement of an existing partner, and liquidation of the partnership. These problems are not dealt with in Section 1800 or elsewhere in the *Handbook*. As a consequence, this Chapter is largely devoted to the issues associated with accounting for partnerships.

12-11. Our coverage of partnership accounting will follow the discussion of the more general Recommendations that are contained in Section 1800.

Recommendations Of Section 1800

Disclosing The Entity

12-12. A basic problem with accounting for unincorporated businesses relates to the fact that for this type of business, whether it is a proprietorship or a partnership, there is no legal distinction between the business and its owners. However, given the assumption that financial statements should reflect the economic entity, accountants will generally prepare financial statements which reflect the distinction between the business and its owners. To avoid possible confusion that might result from using this approach, Section 1800 makes the following two Recommendations:

Paragraph 1800.04 *The financial statements of an unincorporated business should indicate clearly the name under which the business is conducted and, where practicable, the names of the owners.* (January, 1969)

Paragraph 1800.05 *It should also be made evident that the business is unincorporated and that the statements do not include all the assets, liabilities, revenues and expenses of the owners.*

Transactions With Owners

12-13. An additional problem arises with unincorporated businesses in that any salaries, interest, or other payments to the owners of the business are not really arm's length transactions. Because of this, Section 1800 requires separate disclosure of these amounts:

Paragraph 1800.07 *Any salaries, interest or similar items accruing to owners of an unincorporated business should be clearly indicated by showing such items separately either in the body of the income statement or in a note to the financial statements.*

12-14. In some situations, there are no payments by the unincorporated business to its owner or owners. To avoid any possible confusion in this area, Section 1800 makes the following Recommendation:

Paragraph 1800.08 *If no such charges are made in the accounts, this fact should be disclosed in the financial statements.*

12-15. While the issue is not discussed in Section 1800, there is a further issue with respect to the treatment of salary and interest payments to the owners of an unincorporated business. The issue here is whether such amounts should be disclosed as a distribution of the entity's net income (i.e., deducted after the determination of net income) or, alternatively, disclosed as a determinant of net income (i.e., deducted as an expense in the determination of the entity's net income). This issue will be discussed more completely in our material on partnership accounting.

Income Taxes

12-16. Under Canadian income tax legislation, proprietorships and partnerships are not taxable entities. This means that, while the owners will be taxed on the income of unincorporated businesses, the businesses are not directly liable for any taxes on their income. While it would be possible to include the personal taxes applicable to the income of the business in the financial statements of the business, the AcSB does not feel this to be appropriate and makes the following Recommendation:

Paragraph 1800.10 *No provision for income taxes should be made in the financial statements of businesses for which income is taxed directly to the owners.* (January, 1968)

12-17. Because of the somewhat unusual nature of this situation as compared to corporate financial statements, Section 1800 makes an additional Recommendation with respect to disclosure:

Paragraph 1800.11 A business that is not subject to tax because its income is taxed directly to its owners would disclose that fact. A public enterprise that is not subject to tax because its income is taxed directly to its owners would also disclose the net difference between the tax bases and the reported amounts of the enterprise's assets and liabilities. (See "Income Taxes", Disclosure, Section 3465.)

Statement Of Owner's Capital Accounts

12-18. Section 1000 of the *CICA Handbook* indicates that profit oriented enterprises would normally provide a Statement Of Retained Earnings. Section 1800 is more specific in this area in that it requires a Statement Of Owners' Capital Accounts. The Recommendation is as follows:

> **Paragraph 1800.12** *The financial statements of unincorporated businesses should include a statement setting out the details of the changes in the owners' equity during the period and this statement should set out separately contributions of capital, income or losses, and withdrawals.*

Introduction To Accounting For Partnerships

Partnerships Defined

12-19. In the case of the corporate form of organization, a separate legal entity is involved and this separate legal entity can be established under either the Canada Business Corporations Act or one of the provincial corporation acts. In contrast, partnerships do not constitute an entity which is legally separate from the owners of the business. Further, there is no national legislation in Canada that is analogous to the Uniform Partnership Act which prevails throughout the United States. As a consequence, we can discuss the legal aspects of partnerships in Canada only within the context of provincial legislation.

12-20. Fortunately, this does not present significant problems as differences between legislation in the various provinces do not have a significant impact on accounting procedures. In addition, a large part of the legislation is designed to cover situations where some aspects of the partner's rights and obligations have not been covered in the partnership agreement. As a consequence, the contents of the partnership agreement become the dominant consideration in the accounting area.

12-21. In simple terms, a partnership is an agreement between two or more entities to undertake some business enterprise. A somewhat more formal definition is found in the Ontario Partnerships Act as follows:

> **Partnership Defined** Partnership is the relation that subsists between persons carrying on a business in common with a view to profit, but the relation between the members of a company or association that is incorporated by or under the authority of any special or general Act in force in Ontario or elsewhere, or registered as a corporation under any such Act, is not a partnership within the meaning of this act.

12-22. This more specific definition excludes the possibility of having a partnership with corporate entities as partners and, in effect, restricts the legal meaning of the term to partnerships between individuals. This involves more in the way of legal form than it does substance as, clearly, corporations do form "partnerships" to undertake particular business ventures. However, as a result of this type of definition, in Canada we tend to refer to these corporate "partnerships" as joint ventures.

12-23. Most of the businesses which fall within the legal definition of partnerships are small relative to Canadian public corporations. In terms of the nature of their business activities, the majority would be involved in either merchandising activities or professional activities such as the provision of accounting, legal or medical services. One of the main reasons for the use of the partnership form by such professionals reflects the fact that, in some provinces, professionals such as accountants, lawyers, and doctors have restrictions on their ability to incorporate.

Partnership Agreements

12-24. As is implied in the preceding definition, all that is required to establish a partnership is an agreement between the parties that are involved. This agreement could be as simple as a "handshake deal" based purely on oral discussions. However, if significant resources are involved, this type of arrangement is likely to be very unsatisfactory.

12-25. Even between good friends with the best of intentions, disputes will invariably arise and can seriously disrupt the business activities of the enterprise. As a consequence, partnership agreements should be established in writing, preferably with professional advice, and be designed to cover as many of the possible areas of activity as feasible. A normal agreement would deal with at least the following:

- The names of the partners, the starting date and duration of the agreement, and the amount and type of assets to be contributed by the partners.
- The manner in which profits and losses are to be shared, including any provisions for salaries, interest on drawings, interest on loans from the partnership, and interest on loans to the partnership.
- The nature of the activities that the enterprise will undertake.
- The authority and responsibilities to be vested in each partner.
- The amount of insurance on the lives of the partners to be paid to the surviving partners as beneficiaries.
- The procedures to be used in liquidation, including provisions for dealing with the arbitration of disputes.

12-26. In the absence of a properly drawn up agreement, any one of these items could become the sources of a dispute and, if it cannot be resolved informally, litigation. A well thought out partnership agreement can prevent many potential conflicts.

Characteristics Of Partnerships

Approach

12-27. As with other forms of business organizations, the partnership form of organization can be associated with a specific group of characteristics. These characteristics are frequently presented as lists of advantages and disadvantages. However, in actual fact, the situation is somewhat more complex than that and, as a reflection of that fact, our discussion will be somewhat broader in nature. The basic characteristics of the partnership form of business organization are described in the following material.

Limited Life

12-28. We have previously noted that a partnership does not generally exist as a legal entity separate from the participating partners. As a consequence, the life of a partnership is terminated by the death or retirement of any of the partners. Further, from a strict legal point of view, even the admission of a partner creates a new partnership and terminates the legal life of the previous organization.

12-29. The continuing need to create new legal entities is expensive, can be the source of protracted disputes, and may lead to serious disruptions of the normal business activities of the organization. It would seem clear that, relative to the corporate form of organization, this characteristic must be viewed as a disadvantage of partnerships. Note, however, that a well constructed partnership agreement will have provisions for dealing with the addition of new partners and the withdrawal of existing partners.

Unlimited Liability

12-30. Also related to the absence of a separate legal existence for the partnership is the unlimited liability that confronts the participating partners. What this means is that if the partnership encounters serious financial difficulties, creditors can look not only to the assets of the business for satisfaction but, in addition, can lay claim to the personal assets of the partners.

12-31. Here again, this characteristic is generally cited as a disadvantage relative to the corporate form of organization as it significantly extends the liability of any potential partner, and, thereby, may reduce their interest in investing.

12-32. Note, however, that this is probably not an accurate analysis when partnership organizations are compared to similar sized corporations. For smaller or owner-managed corporations, creditors will generally require that shareholders provide a personal guarantee for repayment of any amounts extended. This means that, in effect, the shareholders of such corporations do not have unlimited liability.

12-33. There is a possible way of avoiding the problem of unlimited liability and this is by establishing a certain number of limited partners. This simply means that any partner that is so designated has his liability limited to some specified amount, generally the amount that has been invested. However, legislation on limited partnerships requires that every such organization have at least one general partner with unlimited liability.

Ease Of Formation

12-34. This issue is somewhat less clear cut. In general, it is fair to say that a partnership is somewhat easier to form than a corporation. Two people can simply make an informal agreement to undertake some business activity and a partnership is formed. In contrast, the process of incorporation involves complying with a number of legislative requirements and will generally involve legal expenses of at least $500 to $1,000.

12-35. However, small corporations are constructed along a fairly simple format, with the rights and obligations of the owners clearly established by the relevant enabling legislation. In contrast, partnerships often tend to evolve along more individualized patterns. In this type of situation, the construction of an appropriate and comprehensive partnership agreement may, in fact, be more complex than would be the formation of a corporation.

Mutual Agency

12-36. This simply means that each partner has the authority to act for the partnership and to enter into contracts which are binding with respect to all of the partners. Depending on the particular provincial legislation, this may be limited in cases where the partner has acted beyond the normal scope of business operations and without specific authority resulting from the partnership agreement.

12-37. When this characteristic is viewed in the context of the unlimited liability to which most partners are exposed, it would seem clear that it can be an undesirable feature of the partnership form of business organization. A bad decision on the part of one partner can have seriously adverse effects on the other participants in the partnership.

Co-Ownership Of Property And Profits

12-38. The individual partners have no claim to any of the specific assets of the business but, rather, acquire an interest in all of the assets. The property becomes jointly owned by all partners and each partner has an ownership interest in the profits of the partnership. The major difficulty with this arrangement is that when partners are admitted or retired, the amount of the new or retiring partner's interest must be established. This may prove to be a difficult and time consuming process.

Regulation

12-39. This issue is relatively clear cut. Compared to corporations, partnerships have the advantage of being less subject to regulation and supervision by all levels of government than would enterprises which are organized as corporations. This would be particularly true if the corporation were publicly traded and had to comply with the extensive reporting requirements to which such organizations are subjected.

Taxation

12-40. As a result of the lack of a separate legal identity for enterprises organized as partnerships, the *Income Tax Act* contains no definition of what constitutes a partnership.

12-41. However, the *Income Tax Act* requires that partnership income be calculated on the assumption that the partnership is a separate person resident in Canada and that its fiscal period is its taxation year. Each partner's share of the income from the partnership from any business or property and its capital gains (or losses) is treated as his income or gain. These amounts will be included in the partner's tax return, without regard to whether the amounts are actually distributed to the partner.

12-42. In considering taxation, there are a number of complex factors that must be taken into consideration. A discussion of the taxation of partnerships would not be appropriate in this material on financial reporting. However, we would note that tax considerations can be an important factor when evaluating the partnership form of organization.

Evaluation

12-43. A quick review of the preceding list of characteristics makes the position of the partnership form of organization clear. From a legal point of view, partnerships have very few differences from proprietorships. The choice between these two forms will be decided by the number of entities involved.

12-44. The choice between partnership and corporate forms, however, is more complex. For small businesses, limited life and unlimited liability may not be particularly influential, and the ease of formation and lack of regulation may push the owners in the direction of the partnership form. As we have noted previously, the tax issue could be extremely important and in actual fact, tax considerations may be the primary consideration in making the choice.

12-45. As we begin to consider larger enterprises, the issue generally becomes easier to resolve. If the capital requirements of an enterprise are such that a large investor group must be involved, the problems associated with limited life, unlimited liability, and mutual agency become virtually insurmountable. In this type of situation, the corporate form of organization becomes the only reasonable alternative.

Partnerships And The Accounting Entity

12-46. One of the fundamental assumptions of financial reporting is that accountants should concentrate on providing financial reports for definable business or economic entities. However, much of the accountant's activity takes place in an environment in which various types of legal entities are defined. Since these legal definitions will invariably have some influence on the information needs of financial statement users, the accountant's position is one which involves a potential conflict.

12-47. In many cases this conflict does not arise. For a simple corporation with no subsidiaries, the legal and economic entities will generally coincide and, as a result, the financial statements prepared to represent the economic entity will be the same as those that would be prepared to meet any of the requirements of the legal entity. However, this is not always the case.

12-48. The most important example of a conflict between the legal and economic entities is the situation where a parent company has one or more subsidiaries that can be considered a part of the same economic entity as the parent or investor company. In this case, the accountant deals with the conflict by preparing consolidated financial statements which concentrate on the economic entity rather than the separate legal entities that are represented by the parent and subsidiary companies.

12-49. A similar type of conflict arises in dealing with the financial statements of partnerships. From a legal point of view, the real entities involved in a partnership are the partners themselves. As we have noted, the law does not make a distinction between the status of a partner's personal home and a building in which there is a joint interest with other partners.

12-50. While the individual partners may wish to have personal financial statements prepared, in judging the performance or position of the partnership as a business entity, it is important to have financial statements which segregate the assets, liabilities, expenses, and revenues of the partnership from those of the partners. In order to accomplish this goal, the accountant must look through the legal form of the organization and prepare statements which reflect the economic substance of the business.

12-51. This is why we find that, in practice, most accountants are accustomed to viewing partnerships as separate entities with a continuity of life, accounting policies, and asset valuations. It should be noted, however, that the principles and procedures that are used in segregating this accounting entity from its conflicting legal environment are not nearly as developed and well established as those used in the similar process of preparing consolidated financial statements.

Partnership Owners' Equity Accounts

12-52. In accounting for a proprietorship, a single owner's equity account is generally adequate as there are no legal or equity apportionment issues which require the segregation of any part of this balance. In contrast, accounting for the owners' equity of a corporation requires, as a minimum, a strict segregation of contributed and earned capital in order to meet the usual legal requirement that dividends can only be paid from earned capital. The situation with partnership owners' equity is less clear cut.

12-53. From the point of view of general legislation on partnerships, there is no reason to segregate any portion of the owners' equity balance. However, the need to account for the individual equity balances of each partner and information requirements related to implementing the partnership agreement with respect to profit sharing, drawings, and loans, will generally lead to some partitioning of the owners' equity balance. While this may vary from partnership to partnership, the usual pattern will involve three separate types of accounts for each partner. These will normally be:

Loans If it is permitted under the partnership agreement, partners may sometimes borrow funds from the enterprise. In some situations, a partner may loan funds to the organization. In maintaining equitable relationships between the partners, it is important that this type of transaction be carefully segregated from either drawings against salaries or profits, or increases and decreases in invested capital. To facilitate this segregation, it is the usual practice to set up separate loan receivable and payable accounts for each partner who has an outstanding loan balance. These accounts would not be closed at the end of the period but, rather, would be carried until such time as the balance is paid.

Drawings In most situations, each partner will have a drawing account. This account will generally be used to account for two types of transactions. First, when a partner withdraws any amounts of salary to which he is entitled, it will be debited to this account. In addition, withdrawals that are made by the partner in anticipation of his annual share of profits would also be debited to this account. This account would not be used for withdrawals of partnership assets that could be viewed as permanent reductions in invested capital, nor would the account be used for loans. At the end of the accounting period, this account will generally be closed to the partner's capital account.

Capital Accounts This is the basic account to which each partner's original investment will be credited. In subsequent years it will be changed by:

- Additional investments of capital by the partner.
- Capital withdrawals by the partner.
- Allocations of partnership income or losses.
- Allocations resulting from the year end closing of the partner's drawing account.

12-54. The preceding describes a typical set of owners' equity accounts for a partnership. There are, of course, many possible variations. In addition, if the partnership agreement places any specific restrictions on any or all of the capital balances of the partners, additional accounts may be required to reflect these restrictions.

Partnership Formation

Proportionate Capital Contributions

12-55. The obvious starting point for any discussion of accounting for partnerships would be to consider the transactions required at the inception of the business. If the partnership is not formed from any predecessor organizations, it is simply a matter of recording the assets that have been contributed by the partners. For example, if X and Y form a partnership by each investing $100,000 in cash, the journal entry would be as follows:

Cash	$200,000	
X, Capital		$100,000
Y, Capital		100,000

12-56. The procedures are only slightly more complex when the assets are other than cash or when the partnership assumes one or more liabilities of a partner. The basic point here is that the assets and liabilities should be recorded at their fair values as measured at the formation date.

12-57. For example, if in the preceding situation X, instead of investing $100,000 in cash, gives the new enterprise a building with a fair value of $150,000 and the enterprise assumes X's mortgage on the building in the amount of $50,000, the entry would be as follows:

Cash	$100,000	
Building	150,000	
Mortgage Payable		$ 50,000
X, Capital		100,000
Y, Capital		100,000

Disproportionate Capital Contributions

12-58. In some situations, partners may be credited with capital balances that are not equal or proportionate to the fair values of the identifiable net assets they are contributing. This would generally reflect the fact that one or more partners is bringing some factor other than identifiable net assets into the business. This could involve special skills, a favorable reputation in the industry, or simply personal assets at a level that enhance the fund raising capacity of the partnership.

12-59. To illustrate, we can return to the example in Paragraph 12-55. Assume, however, that X is granted an interest equal to that of Y in both capital and income, but that X only contributes $80,000 in cash while Y continues to contribute $100,000. The most reasonable interpretation of this situation is that X has contributed, in addition to the $80,000 in cash, goodwill in the amount of $20,000. Under this interpretation, the appropriate entry would be:

Cash	$180,000	
Goodwill	20,000	
X, Capital		$100,000
Y, Capital		100,000

12-60. An alternative interpretation that is frequently used in practice would involve the assumption that Y is granting a bonus to X of $10,000. Under this assumption, no Goodwill would be recorded and both capital accounts would be recorded at $90,000. This effectively assumes that Y has paid $100,000 for a one-half interest in a business that is worth $180,000. We are of the opinion that this is not a reasonable interpretation of the economic substance of the transaction.

12-61. It is not uncommon for a partnership to be formed with one or more of the partners contributing an existing proprietorship. This type of transaction is somewhat more complex in that it would be necessary to determine the fair values of all of the identifiable assets and liabilities, as well as any existing goodwill, for any predecessor enterprise.

12-62. Despite these additional complications, the principles involved are no different than in those cases where the partners contribute only identifiable assets. All of the contributed identifiable assets and liabilities and any existing goodwill would be recorded as the new partnership's assets and, at the same time, the partners' capital accounts would be credited for the amounts contributed. If there was a disparity between the net assets contributed and the amount allocated to the various partners' capital accounts, it can be dealt with by the recognition of additional goodwill being contributed by one or more partners, or on the basis of bonus payments to one or more partners. As we have previously indicated, we believe that the former interpretation is the more reasonable of the two alternatives.

Exercise Twelve-1

Subject: Partnership Formation

Ellen Lee, Francis Holt, and Geraldine Page form a new partnership. Ellen contributes $825,000 in cash and Francis contributes investments with a fair value of $825,000. Geraldine contributes a business with a fair value of $825,000. Geraldine's business owned Inventories with a fair value of $50,000 and a building with a fair value of $700,000. The partners will share profits and losses equally. Provide the journal entry to record the formation of the partnership.

End of Exercise. Solution available in Study Guide.

Partnership Income

General Principles

12-63. The design of an appropriate and equitable system for the allocation of partnership income is one of the more important components of any properly designed partnership agreement. If the agreement fails to specify a plan for sharing the income of the enterprise, most provincial legislation calls for income to be shared equally. As in many cases, such equal sharing would not be considered an equitable arrangement, most partnership agreements devote considerable attention to the problem of income allocation.

12-64. The partnership income allocation problem is made complex by the fact that partners may contribute a variety of different services to the enterprise. In most cases, all partners will contribute some portion of the partnership capital, either in cash or in the form of some other types of assets. In addition, it would be normal for some or all of the partners to work in the enterprise on an ongoing basis.

12-65. Beyond this, one or more of the partners may possess very substantial personal financial resources which may enhance the ability of the enterprise to obtain a better credit rating, resulting in either more financing or financing at a more favorable rate. The investment of such a partner carries a higher level of risk since the partner could lose considerably more in the event the partnership experiences financial adversity or bankruptcy.

12-66. All of this means that, in order to provide a completely equitable income sharing arrangement, the partnership agreement should give consideration to amounts of capital contributed, the worth of services provided to the partnership by working partners, and any differential amounts of risk related to the amount of personal assets owned by the various partners.

Types Of Arrangements

12-67. In practice, consideration is not always given to all of these factors. While many variations are possible, four types of income sharing arrangements seem to be the most common. They are as follows:

Fixed Ratios The simplest type of arrangement would involve simply sharing on the basis of some agreed upon ratio, other than that established by relative capital contributions. The ratio will generally be the same for both profits and losses but may, in particular circumstances, differ depending on whether or not the business is successful.

Capital Contributions Under this approach, capital balances would be used as a basis for determining each partner's share of partnership profits or losses. When this approach is used, the partnership agreement must make clear which capital balance is to be used in establishing profit sharing ratios. It could be the balance originally invested, the beginning of the year balance, or the end of the year balance. However, the most reasonable approach would seem to be to use the average balance for the year. It would also be necessary to specify the effects of loans and/or drawings on the determination of the relevant capital balance.

Salaries With Ratios For Any Remainder Here salaries are established for the partners that work in the enterprise and any income or loss balance that remains is allocated on the basis of either fixed or capital contribution ratios. Here again, if fixed ratios are used, they will usually apply to both profits and losses.

Salaries And Interest With Ratios For Any Remainder In this type of plan, all factors are considered. Partners are given credit for services rendered in the form of salaries, for capital contributed in the form of interest, and for any other risk considerations in the ratios established for distributing any remaining balance of profit or loss. When this approach is used, the partnership agreement must clearly establish the priority of the various types of claims. If earnings are not adequate to cover all three allocations, it becomes important to know whether salary claims take precedence over interest claims, or whether interest claims stand ahead of allocations for the assumption of additional risk.

12-68. It is our opinion that the last approach described will provide the most useful information. There are, of course, difficulties associated with establishing reasonable salary levels in non-arm's length situations, as well as some question as to whether capital contributed at risk should be viewed as earning "interest".

12-69. However, this type of arrangement allows all of the components of a partner's relationship with the business to be given consideration. In addition, it gives a better indication of the performance of the enterprise itself. If, for example, the business is earning less than the fair value of the services rendered by the partners, then a failure to charge enterprise income with salaries will obscure the fact that, from an economic point of view, the business is losing money.

12-70. Profit sharing is the most likely source of disputes among the partners. As a consequence, it is important that the partnership agreement not only provide a method for sharing partnership income but that, in addition, the means of determining that income be established as well. The amount of detail required will vary from agreement to agreement. However, at a minimum, the accounting period and the source from which accounting procedures will be adopted should be included as a part of the agreement.

Allocation Procedures

Example

12-71. In order to illustrate the various types of profit sharing arrangements described in Paragraph 12-67, a simple example will be used:

Example The S and T Partnership has two partners, S and T. The data for the current calendar year is as follows:

	Partner S	Partner T
Original Investment	$40,000	$60,000
Capital Balance, January 1	55,000	65,000
Additional Investment, April 1	5,000	Nil
Drawings, June 30	4,000	6,000
Additional Investment, October 1	Nil	3,000

For the current year ending December 31, the S and T Partnership earned a Net Income of $15,000, before consideration of any salaries to the partners or interest on their capital contributions.

Fixed Ratios

12-72. This type of arrangement is sufficiently simple that it requires little discussion. If, for example, the agreement called for profits to be shared equally, S and T would be credited with $7,500 each. This amount, reduced by the balances in the Drawings accounts would be closed to the end of the period Capital accounts, leaving S with a balance of $63,500 ($55,000 + $5,000 - $4,000 + $7,500) and T with a balance of $69,500 ($65,000 - $6,000 + $3,000 + $7,500).

12-73. This type of profit sharing arrangement would, in most circumstances, be very easy to administer. However, it can be criticized for failing to give weight to the varying capital and service contributions that the two partners may be making to the enterprise.

Capital Contributions

12-74. As we have previously noted, when profit sharing is to be based on the relative capital contributions of the partners, there are various ways in which this approach can be applied. If it was based on original contributions, the income to be allocated to each partner could be calculated as follows:

S's Share = [($15,000)($40,000 ÷ $100,000)] = $6,000
T's Share = [($15,000)($60,000 ÷ $100,000)] = $9,000

12-75. Alternatively, if unweighted end of the year capital balances, without the inclusion of the year's income were used ($56,000 + $62,000), the relative income shares of the two partners would be calculated as follows:

S's Share = [($15,000)($56,000 ÷ $118,000)] = $7,119
T's Share = [($15,000)($62,000 ÷ $118,000)] = $7,881

12-76. The most equitable way of using capital contributions as a basis for profit sharing is to use the weighted average capital balance for the year. In using this approach, the partnership agreement would specify what amounts are to be included in the weighted average capital calculation. In this example, we will assume that drawings are treated as reductions of capital when they occur and that income for the year is not included in the calculation. On this basis, the weighted average capital balances would be calculated as follows:

Weighted Average Capital Balances
For The Year Ending December 31

	Amount	Weight	Weighted Amount
For Partner S:			
January 1, Balance	$55,000	12/12	$55,000
Added Investment - April 1	5,000	9/12	3,750
Drawings - June 30	(4,000)	6/12	(2,000)
Totals	$56,000		$56,750

	Amount	Weight	Weighted Amount
For Partner T:			
January 1, Balance	$65,000	12/12	$65,000
Added Investment - October 1	3,000	3/12	750
Drawings - June 30	(6,000)	6/12	(3,000)
Totals	$62,000		$62,750

12-77. Given the preceding calculations, the partners' respective shares of income could be calculated as follows:

S's Share = [($15,000)($56,750 ÷ $119,500)] = $7,123

T's Share = [($15,000)($62,750 ÷ $119,500)] = $7,877

Salaries With Ratios For Any Remainder

12-78. As we move to this somewhat more complex type of profit sharing arrangement, we will assume that both S and T work in the partnership and it is their belief that the fair value of their services would be $5,000 for S and $3,000 for T. The partnership agreement then specifies that any profit or loss after the deduction of these salaries should be split on the basis of 40 percent to S and 60 percent to T. On this basis, the profit for the year would be split as follows:

S's Share = [(40%)($15,000 - $5,000 - $3,000)] = $2,800

T's Share = [(60%)($15,000 - $5,000 - $3,000)] = $4,200

12-79. This means that the total distributions to the two partners would be as follows:

	Partner S	Partner T	Totals
Salaries	$5,000	$3,000	$ 8,000
Profit Shares	2,800	4,200	7,000
Totals	$7,800	$7,200	$15,000

12-80. In this type of arrangement, it is important for the partnership agreement to specify exactly what happens in the event income is less than the salaries. In this case, if income before the consideration of salaries had only been $5,000, the deduction of salaries would have created a $3,000 loss.

12-81. Normally, this loss would be split using the same 40 percent, 60 percent ratio and this would have resulted in a reduction in the capital accounts of the two partners. However, there is nothing to prevent the two partners from putting a clause into the partnership agreement which provides for salaries to be accrued only when partnership income is sufficient to provide for them.

Salaries And Interest With Ratios For Any Remainder

12-82. In this final case, we will assume that the partnership agreement calls for salaries of $5,000 for S and $3,000 for T, interest at 10 percent on the beginning of the year capital balances, and for the remaining profit or loss to be allocated on the basis of 40 percent to S and 60 percent to T. The balance to be distributed on the basis of these ratios can be calculated as follows:

Income Before Salaries Or Interest	$15,000
Salaries ($5,000 + $3,000)	(8,000)
Balance Before Interest	$ 7,000
Interest [(10%)($55,000 + $65,000)]	(12,000)
Balance To Be Distributed	($ 5,000)

12-83. On the basis of the 40:60 sharing plan in the partnership agreement, this loss would be distributed $2,000 to S and $3,000 to T and this would result in the following total distribution to the two partners:

	Partner S	Partner T	Totals
Salaries	$5,000	$3,000	$ 8,000
Interest	5,500	6,500	12,000
Loss	(2,000)	(3,000)	(5,000)
Totals	$8,500	$6,500	$15,000

12-84. As was the case when only salaries and fixed ratio sharing was involved, it is important for the partnership agreement to provide a clear indication of what happens when salaries and, in this case, interest on capital balances exceeds income. The normal procedure would be to give priority to salaries, followed by interest on capital contributions, with any remaining profit or loss distributed in agreed upon ratios. Again, however, there is nothing to prevent the partnership agreement from specifying some alternative type of arrangement.

Exercise Twelve-2

Subject: Partnership Distributions

The Banner Partnership has two partners, Mr. Ban and Ms. Nerr. Data for the current calendar year is as follows:

	Mr. Ban	Ms. Nerr
Original Investment	$250,000	$500,000
Capital Balance, January 1	350,000	500,000
Drawings During The Year	22,000	63,000

The partnership agreement calls for each partner to receive a salary equal to 20 percent of Net Income before consideration of salaries to partners or interest on capital contributions. Each partner is also entitled to a 10 percent return on the beginning of the year capital balance. Any profit or loss that remains after salaries and interest on capital will be shared equally by the two partners.

For the current year ending December 31, the Banner Partnership earned a Net Income of $78,000, before consideration of any salaries to the partners or interest on their capital contributions. Determine the distribution to the partners.

End of Exercise. Solution available in Study Guide.

Disclosure

12-85. In partnership accounting, the meaning of the term Net Income is not entirely clear. If the partnership agreement calls for the payment of salaries to the partners, and these amounts are fairly representative of the fair value of the services rendered by the partners, it would seem appropriate to deduct these amounts as operating expenses before arriving at a Net Income figure.

12-86. However, if the partnership agreement calls for some form of interest on invested capital, our conventional approach to the calculation of Net Income does not provide for deductions of amounts allocated to the ownership interest of the enterprise. If, however, loans by the partners to the partnership were involved, interest on such liability amounts might be included in the determination of Net Income.

12-87. Probably as a reflection of the fact that transactions between partners and the partnership are less than fully arm's length in nature, the conventional procedure is to disclose Net Income before any distributions to the partners. For example, if we assume that the $15,000 income figure from Paragraph 12-71 was based on Revenues of $40,000 and Expenses of $25,000, and that distributions were as calculated in Paragraph 12-83, the partnership Income Statement could be as follows:

S And T Partnership
Income Statement For The Current Year

Revenues	$40,000
Expenses	25,000
Net Income	$15,000

12-88. The actual distribution of this income would then be disclosed in a Statement Of Changes In Owners' Equity as follows:

S And T Partnership
Statement Of Changes In Owners' Equity For The Current Year

	Partner S	Partner T	Totals
Balance, January 1	$55,000	$65,000	$120,000
Additional Investment	5,000	3,000	8,000
Balance Before Income And Drawings	$60,000	$68,000	$128,000
Net Income	8,500	6,500	15,000
Drawings	(4,000)	(6,000)	(10,000)
Balance, December 31	$64,500	$68,500	$133,000

Changes In The Partnership Group

The Conceptual Problem

12-89. Under most provincial legislation in Canada, any change in the participating group of partners involves a dissolution of the existing partnership agreement and necessitates the preparation of a new one. In the absence of a specific alternative provision in the partnership agreement, this would include all of the following types of events:

- The admission of a new partner.
- The retirement or death of one of the existing partners.
- The transfer of an existing partnership interest to a new owner.

12-90. Since the partnership agreement forms the only legal basis for the existence of a partnership, a legal perspective would view the preceding events as involving the formation of a new business enterprise.

12-91. Under generally accepted accounting principles, all of the assets and liabilities transferred to a new business should be recorded at their fair values as at the date the business is formed. This would also include the recording of any goodwill that might be contributed by the investors or their predecessor business organizations. We observed this principle in the examples illustrating the formation of a completely new partnership (Paragraphs 12-55 through 12-62).

12-92. However, we are now faced with a more difficult question. Should the fact that any ownership change involves the formation of a new legal agreement lead us to the application of the asset and liability revaluation procedures that are generally required in the formation of a new business entity? The alternative would, of course, be to assume a continuity of existence similar to that of a corporation. Under this assumption, a change in the ownership interest has no real effect on the continuity of the accounting records and does not provide a basis for any revaluation of asset or liability balances.

12-93. While the legal answer is clear, it is not necessarily satisfactory. As we have noted previously, the primary concern of accountants is with economic substance rather than with legal form. As a result, the real question to be answered is, does a change in ownership interest of a partnership involve the creation of a new economic entity or, alternatively, does such a change involve only a change in legal form as represented by the new partnership agreement? In the Paragraphs which follow, this issue is considered in the context of the various types of transactions which can result in changes in the partnership group.

Alternative Solutions

Exchange Of Interests Outside The Partnership

12-94. In some situations, an exchange of interests takes place outside of the partnership entity. More specifically, there are situations in which an existing partner sells his interest to a new partner, with the consideration being exchanged directly between the individuals.

12-95. In this type of situation, no new assets enter the partnership books, the partnership is generally not directly involved in the negotiations related to the transaction, and the new partner will normally assume exactly the same rights and obligations that were associated with the previous partner. In fact, it is not uncommon for the partnership agreement to provide for the implementation of such transfers without a legal dissolution of the partnership.

12-96. Given these facts, it would be our view that treating this type of ownership change as the formation of a new business entity would rarely be an appropriate approach. It follows from this view that continuity of the partnership accounting records should be maintained and that no changes would be made in the carrying values of any of the assets or liabilities of the partnership.

Admission And Retirement Of Partners

12-97. The situation is less clear cut when a partnership admits a new partner or an existing partner leaves through death or retirement. It is our view that a single solution to the problem does not exist and, in the absence of clear cut guidelines for determining whether a new economic entity has been created, some amount of judgment will have to be applied.

12-98. For example, in a large public accounting firm with hundreds of partners, the admission and retirement of partners are events which occur with great frequency. Further, these admissions and retirements will generally not have any real influence on the continuity of the business activities in which the firm is engaged. In these circumstances, it would be extremely unreasonable to view the admission or retirement of a partner as the creation of a new economic entity and, as a consequence, no break in the continuity of the accounting records should occur.

12-99. Alternatively, assume that a partnership with two partners has been operating the same retail store for twenty years. When a new partner is brought in, he contributes cash in an amount equal to the fair value of the existing partnership net assets. The three partners intend to use this cash to open a new operation in a different line of business.

12-100. In this situation, a case can be made for the idea that a new business entity has been created and that this new entity is acquiring a group of identifiable assets, goodwill, and liabilities that should be recorded at new values measured as at the date of the admission of the new partner.

12-101. As another example of the formation of a new economic entity, assume that a partnership with three partners has been operating for many years. One partner leaves, taking with him one-third of the assets and clients of the partnership. The remaining partnership could be considered a new economic entity.

Lack Of Guidelines

12-102. Unfortunately, many situations are not as clear cut as those described in the preceding Paragraphs. Further complicating the problem at the present time, is the fact that there are no existing guidelines for the determination of whether the admission or retirement of a partner constitutes the formation of a new economic entity. As a consequence, we find alternative treatments being applied in practice.

12-103. When it is assumed that the admission or retirement of a partner does not involve the formation of a new business entity, the respective equity interests are allocated on the basis that the newly admitted or retiring partner is either paying a bonus to or receiving a bonus from the other partners in the organization. This approach will be illustrated in the material dealing with both admissions and retirements of partners.

12-104. In contrast, when it is assumed that the admission or retirement of a partner does involve the formation of a new business entity, identifiable assets will be revalued to their fair values and goodwill, if applicable, will be recorded.

12-105. There is also a compromise solution that is sometimes encountered. There appears to be a continuing reluctance on the part of some accountants to record goodwill in partnership admission and retirement transactions. This leads to procedures under which fair values are recorded for identifiable assets and liabilities, but any goodwill being acquired by the new business is ignored.

12-106. It would be our position that this compromise position is not appropriate. If the circumstances of the admission or retirement are such that the resulting partnership can be viewed as a new economic entity, then generally accepted accounting principles would require the recording of any goodwill acquired by this new entity. As a consequence, the examples in the material on the admissions and retirements of partners will illustrate only the complete procedures that we associate with the formation of a new entity.

Exchange Of Ownership Interests

12-107. The following is an example of an exchange in ownership interest outside of the partnership structure.

Example The Balance Sheet of the STU Partnership on December 31 of the current year is as follows:

STU Partnership
Balance Sheet As At December 31

Total Net Assets	$1,500,000
Partner S, Capital	$ 500,000
Partner T, Capital	500,000
Partner U, Capital	500,000
Total Capital	$1,500,000

The partnership agreement calls for all profits and losses to be shared on an equal basis. On this date, Partner U sells his interest to a new partner V for $600,000, who pays this amount of cash directly to Partner U.

12-108. You will recall our argument that, in this type of situation, there would rarely be justification for the revaluation of partnership assets (Paragraph 12-96). Given this view, the appropriate entry on the partnership books to record the transaction would be as follows:

Partner U, Capital	$500,000	
Partner V, Capital		$500,000

12-109. This would leave the December 31 Balance Sheet unchanged except for the new name which attaches to one of the capital accounts.

12-110. You should also note that the entry and the resulting Balance Sheet would not be affected by the amount paid by Partner V for Partner U's proportionate interest. As we have previously noted, it would be very rare for this type of transaction to result in the creation of a new economic entity. As a result, any business valuation information that is implicit in the transfer price of the partnership interest will generally not be used as a basis for any revaluation of assets or recognition of goodwill.

Admission Of New Partners

Basic Example

12-111. In view of the fact that additions to the partnership's assets are involved and because alternative assumptions as to the nature of the transaction have greater applicability in the case of partnership admissions, accounting for them requires greater elaboration than was the case with an exchange of partnership interests. To facilitate your understanding of the problems involved, a single basic example will be used to illustrate four cases of a partner admission.

Case 1:	Consideration Exceeds Book Value	- New Entity Assumption
Case 2:	Consideration Exceeds Book Value	- Continuity Assumption
Case 3:	Consideration Below Book Value	- New Entity Assumption
Case 4:	Consideration Below Book Value	- Continuity Assumption

Example The Balance Sheet of the AB Partnership as at December 31 of the current year is as follows:

AB Partnership
Balance Sheet As At December 31

Total Net Assets	$500,000
Partner A, Capital	$250,000
Partner B, Capital	250,000
Total Capital	$500,000

The partnership agreement calls for Partners A and B to share all profits and losses equally. In all of the examples which follow, they are admitting Partner C with a one-third interest in assets, profits and losses. This means that the three partners will each have equal shares after the admission of Partner C. On December 31, before the admission of Partner C, the fair values of the net assets of the AB Partnership are equal to $600,000, $100,000 more than their carrying value.

Admission Case One - Consideration Exceeds Book Value - New Entity

12-112. As a first example, assume that Partner C pays cash of $325,000 to the partnership in return for a one-third interest in assets, income, and losses, and that the admission of this partner can be viewed as the creation of a new economic entity.

12-113. The admission price implies a total value for the new partnership of $975,000 ($325,000 ÷ 1/3) and a value for the combined interest of Partners A and B of $650,000 [($975,000)(2/3)]. Since the total fair values of the net assets of the partnership only amount to $600,000, this would imply the existence of Goodwill in the amount of $50,000.

12-114. As in this Case we are going to assume that the admission of Partner C creates a new business entity, we will recognize both the $100,000 increase in the fair value of the Net Assets and the $50,000 in Goodwill:

Net Assets	$100,000	
Goodwill	50,000	
Partner A, Capital		$75,000
Partner B, Capital		75,000

12-115. After this adjustment, the entry to record the admission of Partner C would be as follows:

Cash (Net Assets)	$325,000	
Partner C, Capital		$325,000

12-116. The resulting Balance Sheet for the new partnership would be as follows:

ABC Partnership
Balance Sheet As At December 31

Net Identifiable Assets ($500,000 + $100,000 + $325,000)	$925,000
Goodwill	50,000
Total Assets	$975,000
Partner A, Capital ($250,000 + $75,000)	$325,000
Partner B, Capital ($250,000 + $75,000)	325,000
Partner C, Capital	325,000
Total Capital	$975,000

Admission Case Two - Consideration Exceeds Book Value - Continuity

12-117. In this Case, we will assume that Partner C makes the same $325,000 investment which we considered in Case One. However, the circumstances are such that the admission does not break the continuity of the existing business entity and, as a consequence, we would not view C's admission to the Partnership as a basis for revaluing assets.

12-118. Given this interpretation, after C's admission, the Net Assets will total $825,000 ($500,000 + $325,000) and each one-third interest will be valued at $275,000 [($825,000)(1/3)]. In effect, we are assuming that C is paying a bonus of $25,000 to each of the existing partners:

Cash	$325,000	
Partner A, Capital		$ 25,000
Partner B, Capital		25,000
Partner C, Capital		275,000

12-119. The resulting Balance Sheet would appear as follows:

ABC Partnership
Balance Sheet As At December 31

Total Net Assets ($500,000 + $325,000)	$825,000
Partner A, Capital ($250,000 + $25,000)	$275,000
Partner B, Capital ($250,000 + $25,000)	275,000
Partner C, Capital	275,000
Total Capital	$825,000

Admission Case Three - Consideration Below Book Value - New Entity

12-120. In this Case, we will assume that C is admitted to a one-third interest in the Partnership in return for cash of $200,000 and that the admission can be interpreted as resulting in the formation of a new business entity.

12-121. The fact that C acquired his interest for less than the book value of the other partners' interests could mean one of two things. First, this lower value could imply that the existing partnership has negative goodwill. However, this interpretation is not widely used in present practice. Rather, a second interpretation, that Partner C was allowed to invest less cash because he is bringing goodwill into the business, is used.

12-122. If there is a reasonable basis for this interpretation, then we believe that the assumption that a new business entity is being formed would still require the recording of the identifiable assets at their fair values. While this would often not be done in practice, the solution which follows adjusts these assets to their fair values. The adjusting entry would be as follows:

Net Assets	$100,000	
Partner A, Capital		$50,000
Partner B, Capital		50,000

12-123. With this adjustment completed, the interests of Partners A and B have been increased to $300,000. Assuming that Partner C's interest is also worth $300,000, the fact that he is admitted with a cash payment of only $200,000 implies that he is bringing goodwill with a value of $100,000 to the partnership. Based on this economic interpretation, the entry to record the admission of Partner C would be as follows:

Cash	$200,000	
Goodwill	100,000	
Partner C, Capital		$300,000

12-124. Note that, if we had not recorded the fair value changes on the partnership's net assets, Partner C would have only been credited with $50,000 in Goodwill and the capital accounts of the three partners would be at $250,000. However, based on the preceding entries, the Balance Sheet of the ABC Partnership would be prepared as follows:

ABC Partnership
Balance Sheet As At December 31

Net Identifiable Assets	
($500,000 + $100,000 + $200,000)	$800,000
Goodwill	100,000
Total Assets	$900,000
Partner A, Capital ($250,000 + $50,000)	$300,000
Partner B, Capital ($250,000 + $50,000)	300,000
Partner C, Capital	300,000
Total Capital	$900,000

Admission Case Four - Consideration Below Book Value - Continuity

12-125. In this Case, we will assume that C is admitted to the Partnership in return for a cash payment of $220,000 and that the admission does not constitute the formation of a new business entity.

12-126. Since the admission of C does not constitute a basis for the revaluation of assets, then we must assume that the existing partners are each granting C a bonus. The total assets will amount to $720,000 ($500,000 + $220,000) and C's one-third interest will amount to $240,000 ($720,000 ÷ 3). To be able to record this $240,000 amount for C, $20,000 must be transferred from the capital accounts of A and B ($10,000 each). Based on this analysis, the entry to record C's admission to the partnership would be as follows:

Cash	$220,000	
Partner A, Capital	10,000	
Partner B, Capital	10,000	
Partner C, Capital		$240,000

12-127. The resulting Balance Sheet for the ABC Partnership would be as follows:

ABC Partnership
Balance Sheet As At December 31

Total Net Assets ($500,000 + $220,000)	$720,000
Partner A, Capital ($250,000 - $10,000)	$240,000
Partner B, Capital ($250,000 - $10,000)	240,000
Partner C, Capital	240,000
Total Capital	$720,000

Exercise Twelve-3

Subject: Admission Of A New Partner (New Entity Assumption)

The Martin Partnership has two partners, Sam Martin and his sister Glenda Martin. The partnership agreement allocates 60 percent of profits and losses to Sam, with the remaining 40 percent going to Glenda. The partnership Balance Sheet as at December 31 of the current year is as follows:

Martin Partnership
Balance Sheet As At December 31

Total Net Assets (Fair Value = $1,150,000)	$1,000,000
Sam Martin, Capital	$ 600,000
Glenda Martin, Capital	400,000
Total	$1,000,000

On this date, the younger brother of the two partners, Fred Martin, is admitted to the partnership with a 20 percent interest in profits and losses. In return for this interest, Fred contributes $300,000 in cash to the partnership. The partners will account for the transaction on a new entity basis. Provide the journal entry required to admit Fred to the partnership, as well as the Balance Sheet that would be prepared after his admission.

Exercise Twelve-4

Subject: Admission Of A New Partner (Continuity Assumption)

The Martin Partnership has two partners, Sam Martin and his sister Glenda Martin. The partnership agreement allocates 60 percent of profits and losses to Sam, with the remaining 40 percent going to Glenda. The partnership Balance Sheet as at December 31 of the current year is as follows:

Martin Partnership
Balance Sheet As At December 31

Total Net Assets (Fair Value = $1,150,000)	$1,000,000
Sam Martin, Capital	$ 600,000
Glenda Martin, Capital	400,000
Total	$1,000,000

On this date, the younger brother of the two partners, Fred Martin, is admitted to the partnership with a 20 percent interest in profits and losses. In return for this interest, Fred contributes $300,000 in cash to the partnership. The partners will account for the transaction on a continuity basis. Provide the journal entry required to admit Fred to the partnership, as well as the Balance Sheet that would be prepared after his admission.

End of Exercises. Solutions available In Study Guide.

Retirement Of Existing Partners

Basic Example

12-128. As was the case in our consideration of the admission of new partners, we will use a single basic example for four different Cases illustrating the retirement of partners. The cases are the same as those used with the admission of partners and are as follows:

Case 1: Consideration Exceeds Book Value - New Entity Assumption
Case 2: Consideration Exceeds Book Value - Continuity Assumption
Case 3: Consideration Below Book Value - New Entity Assumption
Case 4: Consideration Below Book Value - Continuity Assumption

Example The Balance Sheet of the XYZ Partnership as at December 31 of the current year is as follows:

XYZ Partnership
Balance Sheet As At December 31

Total Net Assets	$600,000
Partner X, Capital	$200,000
Partner Y, Capital	200,000
Partner Z, Capital	200,000
Total Capital	$600,000

The partnership agreement calls for Partners X, Y, and Z to share all profits and losses equally. On December 31, it has been determined that the fair values of the identifiable Net Assets of the XYZ Partnership total $690,000. In the Cases which follow, Partner Z is being retired through a payment of partnership cash.

Retirement Case One - Consideration Exceeds Book Value - New Entity

12-129. In this first Case, we will assume that Partner Z is retired in return for a payment of $250,000 in partnership cash and the circumstances are such that the remaining partnership can be viewed as a new business entity.

12-130. The $250,000 payment to Partner Z for his one-third interest implies a total value for the business of $750,000. This is $150,000 in excess of the book values of these assets and, given the fact that it has been determined that the identifiable assets have a total fair value of $690,000, this $150,000 excess would be allocated $90,000 to the identifiable assets and $60,000 to Goodwill. The entry to accomplish this allocation is as follows:

Net Identifiable Assets	$90,000	
Goodwill	60,000	
Partner X, Capital		$50,000
Partner Y, Capital		50,000
Partner Z, Capital		50,000

12-131. Given the preceding adjustment, the entry to retire Partner Z would be as follows:

Partner Z, Capital ($200,000 + $50,000)	$250,000	
Cash (Net Identifiable Assets)		$250,000

12-132. The resulting Balance Sheet for the XY Partnership, after the retirement of Partner Z, would be as follows:

XY Partnership
Balance Sheet As At December 31

Net Identifiable Assets	
($600,000 + $90,000 - $250,000)	$440,000
Goodwill	60,000
Total Assets	$500,000
Partner X, Capital	$250,000
Partner Y, Capital	250,000
Total Capital	$500,000

Retirement Case Two - Consideration Exceeds Book Value - Continuity

12-133. In this Case, we will again assume that Partner Z is retired in return for partnership cash in the amount of $250,000. However, in this case the interpretation will be that this retirement did not result in a new business entity and a need to revalue assets. As the payment to Z is $50,000 in excess of the book value of his interest, we will have to assume that Partner X and Partner Y are each paying a bonus of $25,000 to Partner Z. The retirement entry which would reflect that assumption is as follows:

Partner X, Capital	$ 25,000	
Partner Y, Capital	25,000	
Partner Z, Capital	200,000	
Cash		$250,000

12-134. The resulting Balance Sheet for the XY Partnership would be as follows:

XY Partnership
Balance Sheet As At December 31

Total Net Assets ($600,000 - $250,000)	$350,000
Partner X, Capital ($200,000 - $25,000)	$175,000
Partner Y, Capital ($200,000 - $25,000)	175,000
Total Capital	$350,000

Retirement Case Three - Consideration Below Book Value - New Entity

12-135. We will assume in this situation that Partner Z is retired in return for a payment of $180,000 and that the retirement can be viewed as resulting in the formation of a new business entity.

12-136. The price paid to Partner Z for his one-third interest implies a total value for the enterprise of $540,000 [(3)($180,000)], a value that is $60,000 less than the $600,000 carrying value of the Net Assets and $150,000 less than their fair value of $690,000. This means that either the Partnership has negative goodwill in the amount of $150,000 ($690,000 - $540,000) or that there are factors in Partner Z's personal situation that make him willing to sacrifice a part of his equity in order to retire from the business.

12-137. If Partner Z has actually made a sacrifice in order to facilitate his retirement, the amount of this sacrifice could be measured by the $20,000 difference between his capital balance of $200,000 and the retirement price of $180,000, and it would be appropriate to credit this amount to the capital accounts of Partners X and Y. This would result in a solution identical to that which would be used if we assume partnership continuity and use the bonus method to retire Z. This solution is illustrated in Case Four (see Paragraph 12-141).

12-138. Alternatively, if we assume that the deficiency relates to negative goodwill, generally accepted accounting principles require such amounts to be charged to specific assets (see our discussion of this issue in Chapter 3). This means that we cannot adjust the Net Assets to their current fair values of $690,000. Rather, we will have to write them down to the $540,000 balance implied in the purchase price. The entry for this adjustment would be as follows:

Partner X, Capital	$20,000	
Partner Y, Capital	20,000	
Partner Z, Capital	20,000	
Net Assets		$60,000

12-139. After the preceding adjustment, the entry that would be required to retire Partner Z would be as follows:

Partner Z, Capital	$180,000	
Cash		$180,000

12-140. The resulting Balance Sheet for the XY Partnership would be as follows:

XY Partnership
Balance Sheet As At December 31

Total Net Assets ($600,000 - $60,000 - $180,000)	$360,000
Partner X, Capital ($200,000 - $20,000)	$180,000
Partner Y, Capital ($200,000 - $20,000)	180,000
Total Capital	$360,000

Retirement Case Four - Consideration Below Book Value - Continuity

12-141. We again assume in this Case that Partner Z is retired in return for a payment of $180,000, but that the transaction did not result in the formation of a new business entity. Since there is no basis for the revaluation of any of the Partnership assets, we will have to assume that Z is paying a bonus of $10,000 each to Partners X and Y. The journal entry to retire Partner Z under this assumption would be as follows:

Partner Z, Capital	$200,000	
Partner X, Capital		$ 10,000
Partner Y, Capital		10,000
Cash		180,000

12-142. The resulting Balance Sheet for the XY Partnership would be as follows:

XY Partnership
Balance Sheet As At December 31

Total Net Assets ($600,000 - $180,000)	$420,000
Partner X, Capital ($200,000 + $10,000)	$210,000
Partner Y, Capital ($200,000 + $10,000)	210,000
Total Capital	$420,000

Exercise Twelve-5

Subject: Retirement Of Existing Partner (New Entity Assumption)

The Roma Partnership has three partners, Tony Roma, his brother Ricky Roma, and his sister Bianca Roma. The partnership agreement allocates 40 percent of the profits and losses to Tony, with 30 percent going to Ricky and 30 percent going to Bianca.

Roma Partnership
Balance Sheet As At December 31

Total Net Assets (Fair Value = $1,375,000)	$1,200,000
Tony Roma, Capital	$ 480,000
Ricky Roma, Capital	360,000
Bianca Roma, Capital	360,000
Total	$1,200,000

For personal reasons, Bianca wishes to withdraw from the partnership. After some negotiation, her brothers have agreed that she will receive $450,000 of partnership cash in return for her 30 percent interest in profits and losses. The remaining partners believe that her retirement should be accounted for on a new entity basis. Provide the journal entry required to record Bianca's retirement, as well as the Balance Sheet that would be prepared after her withdrawal.

Exercise Twelve-6

Subject: Retirement Of Existing Partner (Continuity Assumption)

The Roma Partnership has three partners, Tony Roma, his brother Ricky Roma, and his sister Bianca Roma. The partnership agreement allocates 40 percent of the profits and losses to Tony, with 30 percent going to Ricky and 30 percent going to Bianca.

Roma Partnership
Balance Sheet As At December 31

Total Net Assets (Fair Value = $1,375,000)	$1,200,000
Tony Roma, Capital	$ 480,000
Ricky Roma, Capital	360,000
Bianca Roma, Capital	360,000
Total	$1,200,000

For personal reasons, Bianca wishes to withdraw from the partnership. After some negotiation, her brothers have agreed that she will receive $450,000 of partnership cash in return for her 30 percent interest in profits and losses. The remaining partners believe that her retirement should be accounted for on a continuity basis. Provide the journal entry required to record Bianca's retirement, as well as the Balance Sheet that would be prepared after her withdrawal.

End of Exercises. Solutions available In Study Guide.

Partnership Liquidation

General Procedures

Solvent Partnerships

12-143. In the context of partnership accounting, the term liquidation refers to situations in which the partners agree to terminate their operation of the enterprise, convert the assets to cash, pay off any outstanding liabilities, and distribute the remaining cash to the partners. In some cases, the business may be sold as a unit in a single transaction while, in other cases, the liquidation process may involve individual asset sales over some period of time.

12-144. Whether sold as a unit or disposed of on a piece by piece basis, the liquidation of the partnership assets will invariably involve gains and losses. While the partnership agreement might have a special provision dealing with gains and losses arising at the time of liquidation, such gains and losses would normally be allocated to the partners on the basis of their usual profit sharing ratios. These gains and losses will then be added or subtracted to the capital accounts of the partners and these capital account balances will serve as the basis for distributing any partnership cash that is left subsequent to the payment of partnership liabilities.

12-145. If the partnership experiences losses in the liquidation process, one or more partners may end up with a debit or negative balance in their capital account. If this happens, such partners are responsible for eliminating this balance by making additional capital contributions from their personal assets. If, in this process, the concerned partners become personally insolvent and cannot provide the assets necessary to eliminate their debit capital balances, then any remaining debit balance in their accounts will become additional partnership losses to be shared by the remaining partners.

Insolvent Partnerships

12-146. If the partnership experiences particularly severe losses in the process of liquidation, it may find itself in a situation in which its liabilities exceed its assets. In this case, the partnership is said to be insolvent and one or more of the capital accounts will have debit balances. In fact, it is possible that all of the capital accounts may have such balances. The only statement that can be made with certainty when the partnership is insolvent is that the sum of the debit capital balances exceeds the sum of any credit balances which may exist.

12-147. As is the case when debit balances develop in the capital accounts of a solvent partnership, the partners in this position must eliminate this debit balance by making additional capital contributions from their personal assets. If they become personally insolvent in the process of making these contributions, any remaining debits must be allocated to other partners, with the process continuing until all of the partners are insolvent or contributions from the partners' personal assets have been sufficient to satisfy all creditor claims.

12-148. In the following material, several Cases will be presented to illustrate the preceding general procedures. The Cases will cover situations in which there is a single distribution of cash to the partners as well as the somewhat more complex situations in which the cash distributions take the form of a number of installment payments over some period of time.

Single Step Liquidations

Basic Example

12-149. The following basic example will be used to illustrate three different Cases of single step liquidations:

Example The Balance Sheet of the JKL Partnership as at December 31 of the current year is as follows:

JKL Partnership
Balance Sheet As At December 31

Total Assets	$680,000
Liabilities	$250,000
Partner J, Capital	180,000
Partner K, Capital	130,000
Partner L, Capital	120,000
Total	$680,000

The partnership agreement calls for all profits and losses, including any which arise in the process of liquidation, to be shared equally between the three partners.

Liquidation Case One - All Capital Balances Sufficient To Absorb Share Of Liquidation Loss

12-150. In this first, relatively simple case, we will assume that the assets are sold for $590,000 in cash, resulting in a liquidation loss of $90,000 ($680,000 - $590,000). This would be allocated to the capital balances of the partners as follows:

	Partner J	Partner K	Partner L	Total
Balance Before Liquidation	$180,000	$130,000	$120,000	$430,000
Share Of Liquidation Loss	(30,000)	(30,000)	(30,000)	(90,000)
Adjusted Balance	$150,000	$100,000	$ 90,000	$340,000

12-151. The adjusted balance would be the amount of cash to be distributed to each partner. This means that of the total of $590,000, the creditors would receive $250,000 and the partners would receive the remaining $340,000 as per the schedule in the preceding Paragraph.

Liquidation Case Two - Some Capital Balances Not Sufficient To Absorb Share Of Liquidation Loss

12-152. In this somewhat more complex case, we will assume that the assets are sold for only $260,000 in cash, resulting in a liquidation loss in the amount of $420,000 ($680,000 - $260,000). This loss would be allocated to the capital balances of the partners as follows:

	Partner J	Partner K	Partner L	Total
Balance Before Liquidation	$180,000	$130,000	$120,000	$430,000
Share Of Liquidation Loss	(140,000)	(140,000)	(140,000)	(420,000)
Adjusted Balance	$ 40,000	($ 10,000)	($ 20,000)	$ 10,000

12-153. At this point, there are a number of possibilities. If Partners K and L are solvent, they will be called on to contribute additional investment funds in the amount of $10,000 and $20,000 respectively. This would give total cash of $290,000 which would be distributed on the basis of $250,000 to the creditors and $40,000 to Partner J.

12-154. However, things may not go quite so smoothly. Assume, for example, that Partner L has become personally insolvent and is unable to contribute additional funds. Because Partner L has not been able to absorb his full share of the liquidation loss, the additional $20,000 will have to be allocated equally to Partners J and K. This will leave Partner J with a balance of $30,000 and Partner K with a deficit of $20,000. Assuming Partner K to be solvent, he would then have to contribute an additional $20,000 to the partnership, providing a total amount to be distributed of $280,000. This would be distributed on the basis of $250,000 to the creditors and $30,000 to Partner J.

Liquidation Case Three - Partnership Insolvent

12-155. In this final example of a single step liquidation, we will assume that the assets are sold for only $230,000, resulting in a loss of $450,000. Further, as the cash balance of $230,000 is $20,000 smaller than the liabilities of the partnership, the enterprise is now said to be insolvent. As we have noted previously, this means that one or more of the partners will now have debit balances in their capital accounts. This is made evident in the following allocation schedule:

	Partner J	Partner K	Partner L	Total
Balance Before Liquidation	$180,000	$130,000	$120,000	$430,000
Liquidation Loss	(150,000)	(150,000)	(150,000)	(450,000)
Adjusted Balance	$ 30,000	($ 20,000)	($ 30,000)	($ 20,000)

12-156. If both Partner K and Partner L are solvent, this situation presents no real problem. These partners will contribute to the Partnership an additional $20,000 and $30,000, respectively. This will provide a total cash balance of $280,000, of which $250,000 will go to the creditors and $30,000 will be paid to Partner J.

12-157. Alternatively, if all three of the partners are insolvent, Partner J will not receive his $30,000 adjusted balance and a plan for distributing the $230,000 to the creditors will have to be established.

12-158. However, a more likely scenario lies between these two extremes. This is that some partners will be solvent while others will be insolvent. To illustrate this possibility, assume that Partner L is insolvent, while Partners J and K remain personally solvent. Partner L's debit balance of $30,000 will be split evenly between Partners J and K, leaving a $15,000 credit for Partner J and a $35,000 debit for Partner K. Partner K will then have to contribute an additional $35,000, giving a total cash balance for the Partnership of $265,000. Of this amount, $250,000 will be distributed to the creditors with the remaining $15,000 going to Partner J.

Exercise Twelve-7

Subject: Partnership Liquidation

The Balance Sheet of the Taylor Partnership as at December 31 of the current year is as follows:

Taylor Partnership
Balance Sheet As At December 31

Total Assets	$950,000
Liabilities	$360,000
James Taylor, Capital	230,000
Sarah Taylor, Capital	205,000
Carly Taylor, Capital	155,000
Total	$950,000

The partnership agreement calls for James Taylor to receive 50 percent of all profits and losses, with the other two partners sharing the remaining 50 percent on the basis of 25 percent each. The assets of the partnership are sold for $430,000. After paying the liabilities, the remaining $70,000 is distributed to the partners. Assuming that all partners have the necessary resources to make up for any deficiency in their capital accounts, how much of the $70,000 would each of the partners receive?

End of Exercise. Solution available In Study Guide.

Installment Liquidations

General Principles

12-159. In situations where the liquidation of the partnership assets takes place over a considerable period of time, it would be possible to delay any cash distributions to the partners until the entire liquidation process is complete. However, in most cases the partners will prefer to have partial distributions made as the liquidation progresses. If it is decided that such installment distributions are to be made, then it becomes necessary to calculate the amount of each installment that will be distributed to each partner.

12-160. Two factors complicate this calculation. First, until the liquidation is complete, the partnership does not know what the total amount of the gain or loss on liquidation will be. A second factor relates to the possibility that one or more partners may become insolvent and may not be able to make any payments that might be required to eliminate debit balances in their capital accounts.

12-161. The two problems are generally dealt with by making the following two assumptions at the time of each installment distribution:

1. After each distribution, assume that the remaining assets will be disposed of for nil proceeds, with no further distributions of cash to the partners as a result of their disposition.
2. Assume that any partner with a capital deficiency subsequent to a distribution will not be able to eliminate it through additional capital contributions to the partnership. This means that there will be no additional funds from this source available for distribution to the partners.

12-162. In making distributions based on these assumptions, it is likely that a point will be reached where the partners' remaining capital balances are in the same ratios as their profit sharing percentages. At this point, any further distributions can simply be based on the applicable profit sharing percentages.

12-163. A simple example will be used to illustrate the general principles that have been described.

Example On December 31 of the current year, the EFG Partnership has the following Balance Sheet:

EFG Partnership
Balance Sheet As At December 31

Total Assets	$900,000
Liabilities	$300,000
Partner E, Capital	300,000
Partner F, Capital	180,000
Partner G, Capital	120,000
Total	$900,000

The partnership agreement calls for the partners to share all profits and losses equally. Cash from the sale of assets becomes available in four installments during the year. The amounts of the installments are as follows:

First Installment	$330,000
Second Installment	150,000
Third Installment	120,000
Fourth Installment	60,000
Total	$660,000

At this point, all of the partnership assets have been sold and there will be no further distributions to the partners.

12-164. The total assets were $900,000 when the liquidation began and with proceeds of $660,000, this means that, overall, the partners will experience a $240,000 loss. If this were a single step liquidation, the amounts to be paid to the partners could be calculated as follows:

If Single Step Liquidation

	Partner E	Partner F	Partner G	Total
Balance Before Liquidation	$300,000	$180,000	$120,000	$600,000
Share Of Liquidation Loss	(80,000)	(80,000)	(80,000)	(240,000)
Adjusted Balance	$220,000	$100,000	$ 40,000	$360,000

12-165. The preceding calculation provides the goal for our installment distributions. The installments must be allocated in such a fashion that the total amounts distributed to each partner will be equal to the amounts calculated in the preceding Paragraph.

12-166. With respect to the first installment of $330,000, the first $300,000 will have to be paid to the partnership creditors. This leaves only $30,000 for the partners and, if we assume that they will receive no further distributions, their total loss would be $570,000 ($600,000 - $30,000). The loss would be allocated as follows:

First Installment = $330,000

	Partner E	Partner F	Partner G	Total
Balance Before Liquidation	$300,000	$180,000	$120,000	$600,000
Share Of Liquidation Loss	(190,000)	(190,000)	(190,000)	(570,000)
Adjusted Balance	$110,000	($ 10,000)	($ 70,000)	$ 30,000

12-167. As both Partner F and Partner G have negative balances, all of the $30,000 remaining cash would be paid to Partner E, leaving a balance in that partner's capital account of $270,000 ($300,000 - $30,000).

12-168. The sum of the first and second installments is $480,000. If this second installment were, in fact, the last payment to the partners, the total loss on the $900,000 in assets would be $420,000. Assuming that Partner G is not able to make up the capital deficiency which arises at this stage, the second installment would be distributed on the basis of the following schedule:

Second Installment = $150,000

	Partner E	Partner F	Partner G	Total
Balance After First Installment	$270,000	$180,000	$120,000	$570,000
Share Of Liquidation Loss	(140,000)	(140,000)	(140,000)	(420,000)
Preliminary Balance	$130,000	$ 40,000	($ 20,000)	$150,000
Distribution Of The Capital Deficiency Of Partner G	(10,000)	(10,000)	20,000	Nil
Adjusted Balance	$120,000	$ 30,000	Nil	$150,000

12-169. The second installment of $150,000 would be distributed $120,000 to Partner E and $30,000 to Partner F. This would leave the capital balance of Partner E at $150,000 ($270,000 - $120,000). Partner F's balance would also be at $150,000 ($180,000 - $30,000). However, both of these balances remain larger than that of Partner G and, as a consequence, it is not yet possible to distribute future installments on the basis of profit sharing ratios.

12-170. The third installment brings the total proceeds to $600,000. If this were viewed as the last installment, the total loss on the $900,000 in assets would be $300,000 and this would be distributed as per the following schedule:

Third Installment = $120,000

	Partner E	Partner F	Partner G	Total
Balance After Second Installment	$150,000	$150,000	$120,000	$420,000
Share Of Liquidation Loss	(100,000)	(100,000)	(100,000)	(300,000)
Adjusted Balance	$ 50,000	$ 50,000	$ 20,000	$120,000

12-171. Based on the preceding schedule, the third installment would be distributed $50,000 each to Partners E and F, and $20,000 to Partner G. Also of importance is the fact that at this point, the remaining balance in each of the Partner's capital accounts is $100,000.

12-172. Since these balances are equal and the profit and loss allocation is based on equal shares, we are now in a position where the Partners' shares of total capital are equal to their income shares. As noted in Paragraph 12-162, when this stage is reached, subsequent distributions of cash can be made on the basis of profit and loss sharing ratios. This means that the fourth installment of $60,000 will simply be distributed $20,000 to each partner.

12-173. We have now completed the allocation of all four installments. We noted in Paragraph 12-164 that, if the liquidation had taken place in a single step, Partner E would have received $220,000, Partner F, $100,000, and Partner G, $40,000. Since our goal was to achieve an identical result through the various installments, it is useful to verify that this has, in fact, happened. The following schedule provides this verification:

	Partner E	Partner F	Partner G	Total
First Installment	$ 30,000	Nil	Nil	$ 30,000
Second Installment	120,000	$ 30,000	Nil	150,000
Third Installment	50,000	50,000	$20,000	120,000
Fourth Installment	20,000	20,000	20,000	60,000
Total Distribution	$220,000	$100,000	$40,000	$360,000

12-174. This serves to verify that we have distributed the cash that became available in the installment liquidation steps in a manner that complied with the partnership agreement.

Installment Liquidation Distribution Schedules

12-175. The preceding section illustrated the calculations required to deal with a known schedule of cash distributions as they became available over a period of time. A somewhat different approach to this problem can be involved in administering liquidations. Rather than calculating the allocation of cash distributions as they occur, a schedule of distributions could be required in advance of any specified amounts becoming available. To illustrate the approach to be used in solving this type of problem, the following simple example will be used.

Example On December 31 of the current year, the PQR Partnership has the following Balance Sheet:

PQR Partnership
Balance Sheet As At December 31

Total Net Assets	$2,400,000
Partner P, Capital	$1,400,000
Partner Q, Capital	650,000
Partner R, Capital	350,000
Total	$2,400,000

The partnership agreement calls for all profits and losses, including any which arise in the process of liquidation, to be shared on the basis of 50 percent for P, 30 percent for Q, and 20 percent for R.

12-176. If the respective capital balances were in proportion to the profit sharing ratios, the solution to this problem would be very simple. Distributions would simply be made on the basis of the profit sharing percentages. However, in the preceding example, Partner P's capital balance is more than his 50 percent share of profits while the other partner's capital balances are below their share of profits. This makes it necessary to calculate the loss absorbing capacity of each partner's capital account. These calculations are as follows:

Partner P ($1,400,000 ÷ 50%) = $ 2,800,000

Partner Q ($650,000 ÷ 30%) = $ 2,166,667

Partner R ($350,000 ÷ 20%) = $ 1,750,000

12-177. What we have calculated here is the amount of loss that each partner, given his profit sharing percentage, could absorb without his capital account having a deficit balance. For example, if the loss was $2,800,000, P's share of this loss would be $1,400,000, an amount that would serve to exactly eliminate his capital balance of $1,400,000.

12-178. As Partner P is in a position to absorb his share of a $2,800,000 loss, all cash distributions would go to Partner P until this loss absorbing capacity is reduced to the next highest amount, the $2,166,667 capacity of Partner Q. This would mean that the first $316,667 [($2,800,000 - $2,166,667)(50%)] would go to Partner P, reducing his capital account to $1,083,333. At this point, new loss absorbing capacities could be calculated as follows:

Partner P ($1,083,333 ÷ 50%) = $2,166,667

Partner Q ($650,000 ÷ 30%) = $2,166,667

Partner R ($350,000 ÷ 20%) = $1,750,000

12-179. In order to equalize the loss absorbing capacities of all three partners, Partners P and Q will have to receive the next $333,333 in distributions [($2,166,667 - $1,750,000)(80%)] on the basis of a 50:30 ratio. This means that Partner P will receive $208,333 [(50/80)($333,333)] and be left with a balance of $875,000 ($1,083,333 - $208,333). Correspondingly, Partner Q will receive $125,000 [(30/80)($333,333)], and be left with a balance of $525,000 ($650,000 - $125,000).

12-180. Subsequent distributions of partnership assets can simply be based on the normal profit sharing ratios of each of the three partners. This is a reflection of the fact that, subsequent to the second distribution, the loss absorbing capacities of the three Partners are now equal as shown in the following calculations:

Partner P ($875,000 ÷ 50%) = $1,750,000

Partner Q ($525,000 ÷ 30%) = $1,750,000

Partner R ($350,000 ÷ 20%) = $1,750,000

12-181. It also means that the capital balances of the three partners are in proportion to their profit and loss sharing ratios. This can be seen in the following schedule:

	Partner P	Partner Q	Partner R	Total
Original Balance	$1,400,000	$650,000	$350,000	$2,400,000
First Distribution	(316,667)	Nil	Nil	(316,667)
Second Distribution	(208,333)	(125,000)	Nil	(333,333)
Remaining Balance	$ 875,000	$525,000	$350,000	$1,750,000

12-182. A quick verifying calculation will demonstrate that the capital balances of the three partners are now in the ratio 50:30:20, the same basis on which they share profits and losses.

Incorporation Of A Partnership

12-183. Under some circumstances, successful partnerships may give consideration to the advantages to be gained from incorporating. These advantages could include an improved tax situation, the ability to raise additional funds more efficiently, or the desire to remove personal assets from the risks associated with participating in a partnership.

12-184. In such situations, the accounting complications are not particularly significant. The fundamental decision that must be made is to decide whether or not the change in legal form constitutes the creation of a new business entity.

12-185. While there is room for the application of judgment in this situation, we are of the opinion that the incorporation of a partnership generally creates a new business entity. This will mean that there is a need to adjust all of the assets and liabilities that are being transferred to the corporation at their current fair values. It would also be appropriate to record any partnership goodwill that has been acquired by the newly formed corporation. However, because of valuation problems associated with this intangible asset, this will generally not occur in many practical situations.

12-186. The accounting records for the corporation could simply be a continuation of the old records of the partnership. In most cases, however, a new set of books will be opened. The appropriate entries would involve recording the newly acquired assets at their fair values and setting up a liability to the partners for the value of the net assets transferred. This liability would then be discharged by the issuance of shares of capital stock.

Problems For Self Study

(The solutions for these problems can be found in the separate Study Guide.)

Self Study Problem Twelve - 1

Jim Bond and Bob Ray organized the Bond And Ray Partnership on January 1 of the current year. The following entries were made in their capital accounts during the current year:

	Debit	Credit	Balance
Bond Capital:			
January 1		$20,000	$20,000
April 1		5,000	25,000
October 1		5,000	30,000
Ray Capital:			
January 1		40,000	40,000
March 1	$10,000		30,000
September 1	10,000		20,000
November 1		10,000	30,000

Partnership Net Income, computed without regard to salaries or interest, is $20,000 for the current year.

Required: Indicate the distribution of Net Income between the partners under the following independent profit-sharing conditions:

A. Interest at 4 percent is allowed on average capital investments, and the remainder is divided equally.

B. A salary of $9,000 is to be credited to Ray; 4 percent interest is allowed to each partner on his ending capital balance; residual profits or losses are divided 60 percent to Bond and 40 percent to Ray.

C. Salaries are allowed to Bond and Ray in amounts of $8,300 and $9,500, respectively, and residual profits or residual losses are divided in the ratio of average capital balances.

D. A bonus of 20 percent of partnership Net Income is credited to Bond, a salary of $5,000 is allowed to Ray, and residual profits or residual losses are shared equally. (The bonus and salary are regarded as "expenses" for purposes of calculating the amount of the bonus.)

Self Study Problem Twelve - 2

The partnership of George Brown and Terry Green was formed on February 28 of the current year. At that date the following assets, recorded at their fair values, were contributed:

	George Brown	Terry Green
Cash	$35,000	$ 25,000
Merchandise	N/A	45,000
Building	N/A	100,000
Furniture And Equipment	15,000	N/A

The building is subject to a mortgage loan of $30,000 which is to be assumed by the partnership. The partnership agreement provides that George and Terry share profits or losses equally.

Required:

A. What are the capital balances of the partners on February 28 of the current year?

B. If the partnership agreement states that the initial capital balances of the partners should be equal, and no recognition should be given to any intangible assets contributed, what are the partners' capital balances on February 28 of the current year?

C. Given the facts stated in requirement B, except that any contributed goodwill should be recognized in the accounts, what are the partners' capital balances on February 28 of the current year? How much goodwill should be recognized?

Self Study Problem Twelve - 3

Allison, Brook, And Carey are partners. Douglas is to be admitted to the partnership at the end of the current fiscal year. On this date, the profit sharing ratios and capital balances of the original partners are as follows:

Partner	Profit Sharing	Capital Balance
Allison	60%	$194,000
Brook	30%	$130,000
Carey	10%	$ 76,000

Required:

A. Assume that Douglas is admitted to the partnership by investing $80,000 for a 20 percent interest in capital and profits. What alternative methods could be used to record the admission of Douglas to the partnership? Provide the journal entries for each method.

B. Assume that Douglas purchases a 20 percent interest in the partnership ratably from the existing partners by paying $84,000 cash directly to the partners. What alternative methods could be used to record the admission of Douglas to the partnership? Provide the journal entries for each method.

Self Study Problem Twelve - 4

Several years ago, Tom, Dick, and Harry Jones formed a partnership to carry on their professional activities. The partnership agreement calls for profits and losses to be shared according to the following percentages:

Brother	Percent
Tom	20
Dick	30
Harry	50

At the end of the Partnership's current fiscal year, the condensed Balance Sheet of the Partnership was as follows:

The Jones Brothers Partnership
Condensed Balance Sheet

Total Identifiable Assets	$164,000
Liabilities	$ 45,000
Tom Jones, Capital	26,000
Dick Jones, Capital	41,000
Harry Jones, Capital	52,000
Total Equities	$164,000

The brothers estimate that the current fair values of the identifiable assets total $189,000.

Required: The brothers are considering a number of alternatives for expanding, contracting, or liquidating their partnership. Provide the information which is indicated for each of the four independent alternatives that are described in the following paragraphs:

A. Tom Jones is prepared to sell his interest in the Jones Brothers Partnership to his sister Shirley. He would give up his interest in return for $31,500 in cash to be paid directly to him. Provide the journal entry(ies) on the books of the Partnership to record this change in ownership interest.

B. The brothers are prepared to admit their sister Shirley into the Partnership with a 20 percent interest in profits and losses. She will be required to contribute $40,000 in cash to the Partnership in return for this interest. The partners believe that the admission of Shirley would be of sufficient importance to account for the transaction on a new entity basis. Provide the journal entry(ies) on the books of the Partnership to record the admission of Shirley Jones to the Partnership.

C. Dick Jones may wish to retire from the Partnership. If this retirement takes place, the brothers have agreed that Dick should receive a cash payment of $54,000 for his 30 percent interest in the Partnership. The partners do not believe that this retirement is a sufficient change in the business to warrant any revaluation of the Partnership assets. Provide the journal entry(ies) that would be required on the books of the Partnership to record the retirement of Dick Jones.

D. As all three of the brothers have developed separate business interests in recent years, they may decide to liquidate the Partnership. It is their belief that the identifiable assets of the partnership could be sold for their fair values which total $189,000. If the liquidation was carried out and the anticipated amount of cash received for the assets, provide the journal entry(ies) to record the transaction and the distribution of the resulting cash balance.

Self Study Problem Twelve - 5

Jones, Smith, and Doe are partners in a retailing business which has been operating for a number of years. Their profit sharing and capital balances on December 31 of the current year are as follows:

Partner	Profit Sharing	Capital Balance
Jones	30 Percent	$ 327,000
Smith	45 Percent	482,000
Doe	25 Percent	191,000

Required: The following Cases represent three different and completely independent transactions. In each Case, we will assume that the transaction took place on December 31 of the current year. You are to provide any journal entries that would be required to record the transaction that has been described.

Case 1 Breem is admitted to the partnership with a one-third interest in profits and capital. In return for this interest he makes a cash payment of $540,000 to the partnership. It is determined that the price paid by Breem reflects the fact that the Partnership has unrecorded Goodwill. This Goodwill is to be recorded as part of the admission transaction.

Case 2 Doe gives up his share of the partnership in return for a cash payment of $171,000. The remaining partners decide not to revalue assets to reflect the price that was paid to Doe in this transaction.

Case 3 It is decided that the partnership is to be liquidated. Because of the size of the business, the assets will be liquidated in several groups. After the sale of the first group of Partnership assets, some of the proceeds are used to pay off the creditors of the Partnership. After the payments to the creditors have been made, $100,000 in cash remains and this is distributed to the Partners as per the partnership agreement.

Self Study Problem Twelve - 6

The condensed Balance Sheet of the Portly, Brawn and Large partnership just prior to liquidation is as follows:

Portly, Brawn and Large Partnership
Condensed Balance Sheet

Total Assets	$1,032,000
Accounts Payable	$ 72,000
Portly, Loan	48,000
Portly, Capital	112,000
Brawn, Capital	320,000
Large, Capital	480,000
Total Equities	$1,032,000

Portly, Brawn, And Large share profits and losses in the ratio of 1: 4 : 5, respectively.

Required: Construct a systematic plan showing how cash should be distributed to the various equities as it becomes available during the liquidation process.

Assignment Problems

(The solutions for these problems are only available in the solutions manual that has been provided to your instructor.)

Assignment Problem Twelve - 1

Journalize the admission of Brown to the partnership of Black and Blue in each of the following independent Cases. The capital balances of Black and Blue are $20,000 and $20,000 and they share profits and losses equally.

A. Brown is admitted to a one-third interest in capital, profits, and losses with a contribution of $20,000.

B. Brown is admitted to a one-fourth interest in capital, profits, and losses with a contribution of $24,000. Total capital of the new partnership is to be $64,000.

C. Brown is admitted to a one-fifth interest in capital, profits, and losses upon contributing $6,000. Total capital of the new partnership is to be $50,000.

D. Brown is admitted to a one-fifth interest in capital, profits, and losses by the purchase of one-fifth of the interests of Black and Blue, paying $2,000 directly to Black and $2,000 directly to Blue. Total capital of the new partnership is to be $40,000.

E. Brown is admitted to a one-fifth interest in capital, profits, and losses by the purchase of one-fifth of the interests of Black and Blue, paying $9,000 directly to Black and $8,000 directly to Blue. Total capital of the new partnership is to be $55,000.

F. Brown is admitted to a one-third interest in capital, profits, and losses upon contributing $14,000, after which each partner is to have an equal capital equity in the new partnership.

G. Brown is admitted to a one-fifth interest in capital, profits, and losses upon contributing $14,000. Total capital of the new partnership is to be $70,000.

Assignment Problem Twelve - 2

A number of years ago, John, Joseph, Judas, and Jerry Goody formed a partnership to carry on their professional activities. The partnership agreement calls for profits and losses to be shared according to the following percentages:

Brother	Percent
John	18
Joseph	23
Judas	32
Jerry	27

At the end of the Partnership's current fiscal year, the condensed Balance Sheet of the Partnership was as follows:

The Goody Brothers Partnership
Condensed Balance Sheet

Total Identifiable Assets	$978,000
Liabilities	$114,000
John Goody, Capital	162,000
Joseph Goody, Capital	193,000
Judas Goody, Capital	268,000
Jerry Goody, Capital	241,000
Total Equities	$978,000

The brothers estimate that the current fair values of the identifiable assets total $1,200,000.

Required: The brothers are considering a number of alternatives for expanding, contracting, or liquidating their partnership. Provide the information which is indicated for each of the five independent alternatives that are described in the following paragraphs:

A. John Goody is prepared to sell his interest in the Goody Brothers Partnership to his sister Jill. He would give up his interest in return for $197,000 in cash to be paid directly to him by Jill. Provide the journal entry on the books of the Partnership to record this change in ownership interest.

B. Because of poor health, Judas Goody wishes to retire from the partnership and move to Rangoon. If the retirement takes place, the other Brothers are prepared to pay Judas $197,000 for his 32 percent interest in the Partnership. The partners do not believe that this retirement is a sufficient change in the business to warrant any revaluation of the Partnership assets. Provide the journal entry that would be required on the books of the Partnership to record the retirement of Judas Goody.

C. All of the brothers have developed separate business interests in recent years and, as a consequence, they are considering the liquidation of the partnership. It is their belief that the identifiable assets of the Partnership could be sold for their fair values which total $1,200,000. However, to realize this value the assets will have to be sold over an extended period of time. The brothers anticipate that the first sale of assets would bring in cash of $423,000. Provide the journal entry to record the distribution of this $423,000.

D. The brothers are planning to admit their sister Jill into the partnership with a 20 percent interest in profits and losses. She will be required to contribute $312,000 in cash to the Partnership in return for this interest. The partners believe that admission of Jill would be of sufficient importance to account for the transaction on a new entity basis. Provide the journal entry on the books of the Partnership to record the admission of Jill Goody to the Partnership.

E. In order to increase his interest in the partnership, Jerry Goody acquires two percentage points of the interests of each of his brothers. This total of six percentage points will bring his interest to 33 percent and, in order to acquire this additional interest, he pays an additional $96,000 into the partnership. The partners agree that this transaction is not important enough to justify any new basis of accounting for the Partnership's assets. Provide the journal entry to record the change in ownership interests.

Assignment Problem Twelve - 3

A number of years ago, Ellen, Eileen, Edna, and Edwina Lee formed a partnership to carry on their professional activities. The partnership agreement calls for profits and losses to be shared according to the following percentages:

Sister	Percent
Ellen	13
Eileen	8
Edna	42
Edwina	37

At the end of the Partnership's current fiscal year, the condensed Balance Sheet of the Partnership was as follows:

The Lee Sisters Partnership
Condensed Balance Sheet

Total Identifiable Assets	$4,118,000
Liabilities	$ 226,000
Ellen Lee, Capital	511,000
Ellen Lee, Drawing	(52,000)
Eileen Lee, Capital	342,000
Edna Lee, Capital	1,576,000
Edna Lee, Drawing	(108,000)
Edwina Lee, Capital	1,623,000
Total Equities	$4,118,000

The sisters estimate that the current fair values of the identifiable assets total $4,876,000.

Required: The sisters are considering a number of alternatives for expanding, contracting, or liquidating their partnership. Provide the information which is indicated for each of the five independent alternatives that are described in the following paragraphs:

A. Because of personal differences with the other sisters, Edna Lee would like to retire from the Partnership and move to another city. The other sisters have agreed to pay Edna $1,845,000 of Partnership funds and eliminate her $108,000 drawing in return for her 42 percent interest. They also feel that Edna's departure will improve the operations of the business and therefore it is an appropriate occasion to revalue the Partnership's identifiable assets. Provide the journal entry(ies) that would be required on the books of the Partnership to record the retirement of Edna Lee.

B. The youngest sister of the partners, Elvira Lee, would like to enter the partnership. Eileen Lee is prepared to give up her 8 percent interest if Elvira will pay her $423,000 in cash. Provide the journal entry(ies) on the books of the Partnership to record this change in ownership interest.

C. In order to increase her 8 percent interest in the Partnership, Eileen Lee acquires four percentage points of the interests of each of the other sisters. This brings her total interest in the Partnership to 20 percent and reduces the interests of the other sisters correspondingly. To acquire this additional interest, Eileen pays $642,000 in cash to the Partnership. The partners do not believe that this transaction is of sufficient importance to revalue the partnership assets. Provide the journal entry(ies) to record this transaction on the books of the Partnership.

D. It is the intention of the sisters to liquidate the partnership. In order to get satisfactory prices for the various partnership assets, they have decided to sell them in an orderly fashion over the next twelve months. They anticipate that the first sale of assets should bring in $1,250,000 in cash. Indicate the amounts that would be distributed to the partnership creditors and the four sisters if the first sale does bring in this estimated amount.

E. John Chong is to be admitted to the partnership with a 20 percent interest in profits and losses. He will be required to pay cash of $1,263,000 to the Partnership. The partners believe that this admission is of such significance that the transaction should be accounted for using the new entity approach. Provide the journal entry(ies) required to record this transaction on the books of the Partnership.

Assignment Problem Twelve - 4

Two years ago, Tammy, Jessica and Donna formed a partnership, FHR Enterprises, to carry on various fundraising and publicity activities. The partnership agreement calls for profits and losses to be shared according to the following ratios:

Partner	Ratio
Tammy	3/6
Jessica	2/6
Donna	1/6

At the end of FHR Enterprises' current fiscal year, its condensed Balance Sheet was as follows:

FHR Enterprises
Condensed Balance Sheet

Current Monetary Assets		$527,000
Furniture and Fixtures (Net)		130,000
Total Identifiable Assets		$657,000
Liabilities		$225,000
Tammy, Capital	$216,000	
Jessica, Capital	144,000	
Donna, Capital	72,000	432,000
Total Equities		$657,000

An independent appraisal estimates the current fair values of the furniture and fixtures total $118,000.

Required: Provide the information which is indicated for each of the independent alternatives that are described in the following paragraphs:

A. Donna retires from the Partnership to pursue a new career as an author. She receives a cash payment of $90,000 for her interest in FHR Enterprises. Tammy and Jessica plan to continue in partnership and maintain the original income sharing ratio. Provide the journal entry(ies) that would be required on the books of the Partnership to record the retirement of Donna assuming:

   i. Tammy and Jessica do not believe that this retirement is a sufficient change in the business to warrant any revaluation of the Partnership assets.

   ii. Tammy and Jessica believe that this retirement is a sufficient change that the remaining partnership can be viewed as a new business entity.

B. FHR Enterprises admits Ollie into the Partnership. Ollie is given a 25 percent interest in capital, and profits and losses. Tammy, Jessica and Donna will share the remaining 75 percent of the partnership earnings in the same original ratio existing prior to the admission of Ollie.

   i. FHR Enterprises agrees to admit Ollie into the Partnership for an investment of $120,000 in cash. Before Ollie is admitted, Tammy withdraws $15,000 cash from the partnership. The original partners do not believe that this admission is a sufficient change in the business to warrant any revaluation of the Partnership assets. Provide the journal entry(ies) on the books of the Partnership to record the cash withdrawal and the admission of Ollie to the Partnership.

   ii. FHR Enterprises admits Ollie into the Partnership for an investment of $150,000 in cash. The original partners believe that this admission is a sufficient change that the remaining partnership can be viewed as a new business entity. Provide the journal entry(ies) on the books of the Partnership to record the admission of Ollie to the Partnership.

Assignment Problem Twelve - 5

Joe Green and his brother Pete have operated as partners in a small greenhouse business for thirty years. They are nearing retirement age and Pete would like to sell his share of the business and move to Florida. Joe's son, Tom, has worked in the greenhouse operation since he was a child and has gradually taken on more responsibility, so that he is now acting as manager. He has $20,000 in savings and can borrow $30,000 more to invest in the partnership with his father. Tom would continue as manager and Joe would gradually reduce his involvement, acting as a consultant when required. Tom wants to build a new packing house and implement a hydroponic growing system, but requires more capital to do so.

The Green Partnership currently has a demand loan from the bank with an interest rate of 7 percent. Tom's brother, Robert, a successful doctor, is willing to invest $80,000, but is not sure whether he wants to be a partner in the business.

The partnership Balance Sheet as at December 31, 2007 is as follows:

Green Partnership
Balance Sheet
December 31, 2007

Cash	$ 10,000
Supplies	5,000
Equipment (Net)	30,000
Land And Buildings (Net)	60,000
Total Assets	$105,000
Accounts Payable	$ 5,000
Bank Loan	15,000
Joe, Capital	42,500
Pete, Capital	42,500
Total Equities	$105,000

An independent appraiser has estimated the following fair values at December 31, 2007:

Supplies	$ 4,000
Equipment	$ 46,000
Land And Buildings	$100,000

Required: The following Parts are independent of each other.

A. Assume that Pete and Joe dissolve their partnership and that Joe, Tom, and Robert form a partnership on January 1, 2008.

1. Prepare the new partnership Balance Sheet. Show all calculations and state your assumptions.
2. What items should be specified in the new partnership agreement?
3. Discuss how the income or loss for 2008 could be allocated to the new partners.
4. How would the Balance Sheet and income allocation change if Robert contributes financially, but is not admitted as a partner?

B. Assume that Pete gives up his share of the partnership for a cash payment of $60,000 on January 1, 2008. Joe decides not to revalue the assets to reflect the price that Pete was paid. Provide the journal entry to record Pete's retirement.

C. Assume that Pete gives up his share of the partnership for a cash payment of $70,000 on January 1, 2008. Joe decides to revalue the assets as he views the resulting enterprise as a new business entity. On that same date, Tom invests $50,000 for a 50 percent share in the partnership and Robert decides to lend the Green partnership $80,000 in the form of a Note Payable. Joe and Tom decide that Tom is bringing goodwill into the partnership.

1. Provide the journal entries to record the preceding transactions and prepare the Balance Sheet of the new partnership as at January 1, 2008.

2. On January 2, 2008, Joe contributes an additional $25,000 in capital to the partnership. Later that day, the partners are informed that their greenhouse is situated on a site that has been contaminated by radioactive waste. They decide to liquidate the partnership immediately and receive a total of $22,000 for the Supplies, Equipment, Land And Buildings of the partnership. Calculate the amount of cash that would be distributed to each partner on the liquidation of the partnership.

D. Assume that Pete gives up his share of the partnership on January 1, 2008 and on that date, both Tom and Robert purchase a one-third share in the partnership. During the year, Joe has drawings of $28,000 and Tom has drawings of $45,000. These withdrawals are equal to the salaries for Joe and Tom, respectively, as stated in the partnership agreement. The agreement also allows each partner a 10 percent interest on his ending capital balance, without inclusion of the year's income or any withdrawals. Any residual profits or losses are shared equally.

The income of the Green Partnership for the year ending December 31, 2008, computed without regard to salaries to the partners or interest on the capital contributions of the partners, was equal to $200,000. The ending capital balances, calculated before consideration of withdrawals or income of the year, are equal to $70,000 for Joe, $50,000 for Tom and $80,000 for Robert. Calculate the income share for each partner for the year.

(SMA Adapted)

Assignment Problem Twelve - 6

At the year end of the current fiscal year, the Balance Sheet of the Norton, Simon, Carly, and Jones Partnership is as follows:

Norton, Simon, Carly, and Jones Partnership
Condensed Balance Sheet

Monetary Assets	$ 573,000
Non-Monetary Assets	1,114,000
Total Assets	$1,687,000
Current Liabilities	$ 71,500
Long-Term Liabilities	26,500
Norton, Capital	173,000
Simon, Capital	337,000
Carly, Capital	692,000
Jones, Capital	387,000
Total Equities	$1,687,000

The Partnership agreement calls for profit and loss sharing on the following basis:

Norton	10 Percent
Simon	20 Percent
Carly	40 Percent
Jones	30 Percent

Because of irreconcilable differences between the partners, it has been decided that the Partnership will be liquidated as soon as possible. However, the partners are agreed that the assets should be disposed of in an orderly fashion, even if it requires some delay in their ultimate disposition. The cash proceeds of all sales will be distributed as they become available.

Required: Prepare a schedule for the distribution of the cash which will result from the sale of Partnership assets.

Assignment Problem Twelve - 7

You have been shortlisted for a position as financial consultant for a major Canadian consulting firm. As part of the recruitment procedure, you are asked to demonstrate your basic knowledge of partnerships. Specifically, you are presented with the following four independent partnership scenarios and are asked to write a brief note on each, identifying the relevant issues, concerns and implications of the related circumstances.

The situations are briefly summarized as follows:

1. Partnership A has run into financial difficulty. In discussing the problem, Bert and Ernie, two of the partners, conclude that unless additional financing can be found, the business should be sold or wound up. Oscar, the third partner, joins them and announces that their troubles are over as he has just signed an agreement with Sue, making her a full partner in exchange for an investment of $200,000. Neither Bert nor Ernie has ever met Sue.

2. Heather and Bernie have just formed Partnership B. Heather has considerable experience and has made a substantial investment in the business. Bernie, on the other hand, has less experience and has made a smaller investment. Bernie will be working full time in the partnership, while Heather, in the short run, will keep her job outside the partnership and assist Bernie only when needed.

3. Partnership C has run into financial difficulty, and one of the partners has just left town, leaving the other partners to pay off all the debts of the business.

4. Moe and Larry are the sole partners in Partnership D. The partnership has been profitable and has expanded rapidly. Moe is in favor of incorporating the business at this time, but Larry would like more information before making a decision.

Required: Prepare the required note for each situation.

(SMA adapted)

Assignment Problem Twelve - 8

Sally Hart, architect, has operated a sole proprietorship in Guelph since 2001. The practice has become quite successful, in no small part due to Sally's aggressive marketing and excellent reputation in the community.

However, it is now August 2008 and Sally has decided to form a partnership with a recent graduate, Mary Seoul. The new partnership is to take effect immediately after her existing fiscal year, August 31, 2008.

Sally has come to you for assistance in the financial accounting aspects of the new partnership. Specifically, she is interested in how the assets being brought into the partnership will be valued on the opening Balance Sheet.

According to the new partnership agreement, Sally will be contributing all assets and liabilities used in her existing practice to the new partnership. This includes the capital assets, working capital and long-term debt. The working capital consists of accounts receivable, supplies and trade accounts payable. There is an extensive amount of "work-in-progress" (WIP) on Sally's accounts that will also be transferred. In the past, Sally has not recorded WIP on her books of account. The capital assets consist of the single office building used in the practice, desks, chairs and drafting tables.

As Mary has no capital assets and no clients, it was agreed her contribution would be in the form of cash.

The agreement stipulates that they will each own 50% of the new partnership, as well as sharing equally in all billings made and expenses incurred, effective September 1, 2008.

Sally has informed you that, due to deflation, the property used as an office has a fair market value below its original cost. Its value is also below the existing mortgage. The mortgage is secured by the property as well as a personal guarantee from Sally.

Finally, Sally informed you that she is being sued by a disgruntled client. The lawsuit implicates Sally as the cause of structural damage in a home she designed in 2003. Sally is concerned since the amount of the lawsuit is in excess of her insurance coverage. While the outcome of the lawsuit is not known at this time, it is expected to be resolved within 12 months.

Required: Advise Sally on how each of the assets and liabilities transferred should be valued on the opening Balance Sheet of the new partnership. The bank holding the mortgage requires the financial statements to be prepared in accordance with generally accepted accounting principles.

(OICA Adapted)

Assignment Problem Twelve - 9

Length, Width and Hite (LWH) is a firm of architects, with one office in a large Canadian city. The firm has been in operation for over 20 years and, as of September 1, 2008, had 18 partners and a staff of 60. LWH owns a building in which it occupies three floors and it rents out the other three. The firm also has ownership interests of 10% to 50% in several properties. The ownership usually arose because the builders had difficulty paying architects' fees to LWH, and the firm accepted equity interests. Most of these properties have mortgages.

The firm's year end is December 31. Your employer, CA & Co., chartered accountants, has performed compilation engagements, for income tax purposes, for LWH for many years. The last compilation engagement was conducted at December 31, 2007 and you were in charge of the assignment.

On September 2, 2008, the managing partner of LWH, Mr. Lee, informed you that LWH has decided to wind up the practice as of November 30, 2008. Apparently, the partners had several disagreements, so they decided to dissolve the partnership. Mr. Lee and 5 other partners of LWH intend to form a new partnership, Vector and Company (VC), and the others will each choose between forming a new partnership or proceeding on their own. The staff will be divided among the new practices. The clients will choose the partner with whom they wish to remain associated.

Mr. Lee has asked CA & Co. to accept two special engagements:

1. The partners of LWH want to wind up the firm "equitably," and want assurance that each partner receives a "fair share" of the equity. Mr. Lee wants CA & Co. to identify the financial information to be used for the winding up of LWH and to explain why this information is necessary. Furthermore, he would like CA & Co. to indicate how it would substantiate the financial information.

   As part of the dissolution agreement, the partners of LWH agreed to have a report prepared describing the financial information other than financial statements that will be useful to the partners in their new practices. CA & Co. has been asked to prepare this report.

2. Mr. Lee requires CA & Co.'s assistance in selecting significant accounting policies for VC.

The engagement partner, Jim Spinney, has asked you to prepare a memo discussing the nature of the special engagements and work to be performed. The memo should address the issues raised and provide the information required by Mr. Lee. Relevant tax considerations should be identified in the memo.

You have made several inquiries, and have learned the following.

1. At November 30, 2008, LWH will have receivables outstanding and a material amount of work in progress. LWH currently has:
   a. Ownership of its building, which has a mortgage with a 12% interest rate, due in 2011.
   b. Several interests in properties, as stated previously.
   c. A copyright on a design for grocery stores, for which it is entitled to royalties over the next 12 to 15 years.
   d. Leases on computer equipment that expire over the period 2010 through 2011. The lease payments exceed current market rates. LWH is required to make monthly payments to the lessor.
   e. Office equipment and architectural materials and equipment.
   f. Artwork, a library, and miscellaneous assets. Most of the costs were expensed several years ago.
   g. Various pension obligations to a few non-partners who hold or have held administrative positions.

2. The building, property interests, copyright, artwork, library, and miscellaneous assets will be transferred to VC. Some computer leases, some equipment, and some pension obligations will not be transferred to VC but will accompany the non-VC partners. The non-VC partners will be occupying separate premises.

3. All vehicles and some equipment are leased from a company owned by the spouses of the three most senior partners of LWH. The leases extend to 2013 and were set at fair market value at the time that they were signed. However, the lease payments are now well above fair market value. All three partners are becoming partners of VC. The vehicles and equipment are to be assigned to VC, under the proposed terms of the wind-up of LWH.

4. VC will be using a different bank from the one that LWH uses. However, both banks use the same lending formula for maximum loans: 70% of current receivables and 40% of work in progress. LWH's bank has agreed to give the partnership three months after November 30, 2008, to pay the loan that will be outstanding on LWH's wind-up date. Both banks require personal guarantees from each partner. VC's new bank requires the financial statements of VC to be reviewed. Mr. Lee has asked CA & Co. to perform a review of VC as at December 31, 2008, its first fiscal year end.

5. LWH partners who have retired in the past are paid 20% of their equity per year for five years from the date of their retirement.

6. Partners receive interest at the prime rate on their outstanding loans to the LWH partnership. Only some partners have lent funds to LWH.

7. LWH charges each client at a standard cost per hour. This charge to work in progress includes labour, overhead, and a profit element. Generally, the labour cost for non-partners is about 40% of the standard costing rate. Most receivables are invoiced at 80% to 120% of the standard cost shown in the client work in progress account.

Required Prepare the memo to Jim Spinney.

(CICA Adapted)

INDEX

A

B

D

E

F

G

H

J

L

M

R

S

T

U

V

"AS IS" LICENSE AGREEMENT AND LIMITED WARRANTY

READ THIS LICENSE CAREFULLY BEFORE OPENING THE BOTH CD PACKAGES. BY OPENING THE PACKAGES, YOU ARE AGREEING TO THE TERMS AND CONDITIONS OF THIS LICENSE. IF YOU DO NOT AGREE, DO NOT OPEN THE PACKAGES. PROMPTLY RETURN THE UNOPENED PACKAGES AND ALL ACCOMPANYING ITEMS TO THE PLACE YOU OBTAINED THEM. THESE TERMS APPLY TO ALL LICENSED SOFTWARE ON THE DISKS EXCEPT THAT THE TERMS FOR USE OF ANY SHAREWARE OR FREEWARE ON THE DISKETTES ARE AS SET FORTH IN THE ELECTRONIC LICENSES LOCATED ON THE DISKS:

1. GRANT OF LICENSE and OWNERSHIP: The enclosed computer programs and any data ("Software") are licensed, not sold, to you by Pearson Education Canada Inc. ("We" or the "Company") in consideration of your adoption of the accompanying Company textbooks and/or other materials, and your agreement to these terms. You own only the disk(s) but we and/or our licensors own the Software itself. This license allows instructors and students enrolled in the course using the Company textbook that accompanies this Software (the "Course") to use and display the enclosed copies of the Software for academic use only, so long as you comply with the terms of this Agreement. You may make one copy for back up only. We reserve any rights not granted to you.

2. USE RESTRICTIONS: You may not sell or license copies of the Software or the Documentation to others. You may not transfer, distribute or make available the Software or the Documentation, except to instructors and students in your school who are users of the adopted Company textbook that accompanies this Software in connection with the course for which the textbook was adopted. You may not reverse engineer, disassemble, decompile, modify, adapt, translate or create derivative works based on the Software or the Documentation. You may be held legally responsible for any copying or copyright infringement that is caused by your failure to abide by the terms of these restrictions.

3. TERMINATION: This license is effective until terminated. This license will terminate automatically without notice from the Company if you fail to comply with any provisions or limitations of this license. Upon termination, you shall destroy the Documentation and all copies of the Software. All provisions of this Agreement as to limitation and disclaimer of warranties, limitation of liability, remedies or damages, and our ownership rights shall survive termination.

4. DISCLAIMER OF WARRANTY: THE COMPANY AND ITS LICENSORS MAKE NO WARRANTIES ABOUT THE SOFTWARE, WHICH IS PROVIDED "AS-IS." IF THE DISKS ARE DEFECTIVE IN MATERIALS OR WORKMANSHIP, YOUR ONLY REMEDY IS TO RETURN THEM TO THE COMPANY WITHIN 30 DAYS FOR REPLACEMENT UNLESS THE COMPANY DETERMINES IN GOOD FAITH THAT THE DISKS HAVE BEEN MISUSED OR IMPROPERLY INSTALLED, REPAIRED, ALTERED OR DAMAGED. THE COMPANY DISCLAIMS ALL WARRANTIES, EXPRESS OR IMPLIED, INCLUDING WITHOUT LIMITATION, THE IMPLIED WARRANTIES OF MERCHANTABILITY AND FITNESS FOR A PARTICULAR PURPOSE. THE COMPANY DOES NOT WARRANT, GUARANTEE OR MAKE ANY REPRESENTATION REGARDING THE ACCURACY, RELIABILITY, CURRENTNESS, USE, OR RESULTS OF USE, OF THE SOFTWARE.

5. LIMITATION OF REMEDIES AND DAMAGES: IN NO EVENT SHALL THE COMPANY OR ITS EMPLOYEES, AGENTS, LICENSORS OR CONTRACTORS BE LIABLE FOR ANY INCIDENTAL, INDIRECT, SPECIAL OR CONSEQUENTIAL DAMAGES ARISING OUT OF OR IN CONNECTION WITH THIS LICENSE OR THE SOFTWARE, INCLUDING, WITHOUT LIMITATION, LOSS OF USE, LOSS OF DATA, LOSS OF INCOME OR PROFIT, OR OTHER LOSSES SUSTAINED AS A RESULT OF INJURY TO ANY PERSON, OR LOSS OF OR DAMAGE TO PROPERTY, OR CLAIMS OF THIRD PARTIES, EVEN IF THE COMPANY OR AN AUTHORIZED REPRESENTATIVE OF THE COMPANY HAS BEEN ADVISED OF THE POSSIBILITY OF SUCH DAMAGES. SOME JURISDICTIONS DO NOT ALLOW THE LIMITATION OF DAMAGES IN CERTAIN CIRCUMSTANCES, SO THE ABOVE LIMITATIONS MAY NOT ALWAYS APPLY.

6. GENERAL: THIS AGREEMENT SHALL BE CONSTRUED AND INTERPRETED ACCORDING TO THE LAWS OF THE PROVINCE OF ONTARIO. This Agreement is the complete and exclusive statement of the agreement between you and the Company and supersedes all proposals, prior agreements, oral or written, and any other communications between you and the company or any of its representatives relating to the subject matter.

Should you have any questions concerning this agreement or if you wish to contact the Company for any reason, please contact in writing: Editorial Manager, Pearson Education Canada, 26 Prince Andrew Place, Don Mills, Ontario M3C 2T8.

Installation Instructions for the Student CD-ROM

NOTE: There are a significant number of hypertext links in the infobases to the *CICA Handbook.* To make these links work properly, you should install these infobases in the same folder as the *CICA Handbook* infobase (e.g., C:\Program files\VPL\NFO) at step 8, below.

Installing the Software and Infobases

1. Insert the CD-ROM in your CD drive. The CD should auto-start on your system. If the CD does not auto-start, select Run from your Start button; in the Run dialogue box, key in your CD-drive letter followed by **:\START.EXE** and press OK.
2. Click the **Folio Views / Infobases** button from the left menu, and then click **Install Folio Views Software**.
3. Follow the on-screen instructions until you reach the Setup Type screen.
4. At the Setup Type screen, select **Install (typical)**.
5. At the Choose Destination Location screen, accept the default location (C:\Program Files\VPL\) and press Next, or browse to select another location (be sure to create a directory); if choosing another location we recommend **:\CICA.** Press OK and then press Next to continue.
6. At the Setup Complete screen, press Finish.
7. If the Setup screen closes, repeat steps 1 and 2, then click **Install GCFR Infobase**. If the Setup screen is still open, click **Install GCFR Infobase**.
8. Click **Unzip**.
   (If you did not choose to install the Folio Views software to the default location, click **Browse...** and navigate to where you installed the software and select the **NFO** folder.)
9. Click OK, then Close to close the Winzip Self Extractor window.
10. If the Setup screen closes, repeat steps 1 and 2, then click **Install FRIC Infobase**. If the Setup screen is still open, click **Install FRIC Infobase**.
11. Click **Unzip**.
    (If you did not choose to install the Folio Views software to the default location, click **Browse...** and navigate to where you installed the software and select the **NFO** folder.
12. Click OK, then Close to close the Winzip Self Extractor window.
13. Click Exit on the bottom right corner of the Setup screen to exit.

Note: To open the infobases, navigate to Start > All Programs > Virtual Professional Library > Folio Views 4.5.

Please see the preceding page for the Pearson Education Canada license agreement. Do not open the CD-ROM package until you have read this license.